Citizen Clem

A Biography of Attlee

John Bew

riverrun

First published in Great Britain in 2016 by riverrun
An imprint of

Quercus Editions Limited
Carmelite House
50 Victoria Embankment
London EC4Y 0DZ

An Hachette UK company

A CIP catalogue record for this book is available
from the British Library

HB ISBN 978 1 78087 989 5
EBOOK ISBN 978 1 78429 973 6

10 9 8 7 6 5

Typeset by Jouve (UK), Milton Keynes

Printed and bound in Great Britain by Clays Ltd, St Ives plc

Citizen Clem

by John Bew

Castlereagh: The Biography of a Statesman

For Jo

Acknowledgements

For their assistance and encouragement in the course of writing this book I would like to thank Jon Riley and Josh Ireland at Quercus and Georgina Capel and Rachel Conway at Capel Associates. I am grateful to the staff at the various archives and libraries I visited. In particular, I would like to thank those at the John W. Kluge Center at the Library of Congress, where I spent a year in 2013–14; the National Archives at Kew; Toynbee Hall; the Bodleian Library, where the bulk of Attlee's papers are kept; and the Churchill Archives Centre in Cambridge. For further assistance with research and reference finding, I am grateful to Lynne Middleton, Gabriel Elefteriu and Andrew Ehrhardt. In different ways, Lord Radice, Jason Cowley, Mary Creagh, Jon Cruddas, Tristram Hunt, Jon Parry, Andrew Roberts and Brendan Simms provided words of encouragement and guidance at different stages of the project. A special thanks must go to Robert Crowcroft, who was extremely generous with his time and expertise. That the War Studies Department at King's College London has been a happy place to work is credit to my colleagues there. Michael Rainsborough, Mervyn Frost, Theo Farrell, Rudra Chaudhuri, and Thomas Rid have been particularly helpful. Close friends such as Martyn Frampton, Inigo Gurruchaga, Shiraz Maher, Dean Godson and Alexander Hitchens have provided support and relief. This book was partly written with those friends and family who read the last one (or at least pretended to) in mind, such as Ed and Jess Gerrard, Dan Hawthorne, Susan Ramsay, Ryan Evans, Magnus Ryan, Martin Newth, James Mythen, Matt Hughes, Matt Perl, James Nicholson, William Farmer, Philip McCreery, Richard Houston, Stephen Greenlees, Tristan Stubbs, Ted Wright, Jonathan Scherbel-Ball and Tosh Barnham. Maybe Tommy, Georgia, Esme, Mia and Zac might read it one day too. My mother and father both gave invaluable advice, and much else besides, from start to finish. The Attlee story is one that intersects with aspects of our family history: from a great-grandfather in Lancashire who was a railway worker and trade unionist and kept a first edition of Jack London's 1902 *People of the Abyss* on his shelf; to a great-uncle who was a navigator in the bombing campaign against Germany; and grandparents who married in India, having served there during the war, and then became the founding GPs at one of the first NHS practices established in Belfast. The book is dedicated to my wife, Jo, for keeping me fed, watered and sane. It is also dedicated to the memory of Stephen Hayward who, I hope, would have enjoyed it.

In our modern life the sense of unity is not realised, and all the pervading duties of citizenship are lost sight of in the wilderness of interests of both individuals and groups. Our extraordinarily complex life, our far too numerous activities, our strong assertion of individual liberty which we very imperfectly understand, and the assumed importance of our occupation as self-seekers and self-developers – all these things tend to drive the citizen idea into the background. Yet in theory and also in fact it is still the necessary and single basis of social duty and social morality.

E. J. Urwick, *A Philosophy of Social Progress*, 1912,
quoted by Clement Attlee in *The Social Worker*, 1920.

It has been said that one of the greatest dangers of civilisation today is that man's conquests in the realms of science have outstripped his moral progress. It is the greatest task which lies ahead of us all in the Labour and Socialist movement to see to it that the citizen's sense of obligation to the community keeps pace with the changes effected in the structure of society. We need to stress duties as well as rights.

Clement Attlee,
Speech to the 47th Annual Labour Party Conference
in Scarborough, 19 May 1948.

Contents

Prologue

The Elusive Attlee

Twenty years after the Labour Party's great election victory of 1945, Earl Attlee, its former leader, was asked about his emotions on becoming prime minister that July. 'Just to know that there were jobs to be done,' he replied. Undeterred by Attlee's typically abrupt response, his interviewer pressed again. The Labour Party had been formed in 1900, and only forty-five years later it had achieved one of the largest parliamentary majorities in British history, with a record 12 per cent swing in its favour. Attlee had been there through its early struggles, stump-speaking under dim street lights in the East End, a witness to its near annihilation in 1931, when it was reduced to just fifty-two seats, and a central figure in its slow recovery over the following decade. He had become Labour leader in 1935 against expectations and brought the party into the wartime coalition in 1940, siding with Winston Churchill at Britain's darkest hour. As the Second World War drew to an end, Attlee's party had won an overwhelming mandate to carry out the most radical manifesto ever presented to the British electorate by a major party. The interviewer made one last attempt to draw this most reticent man out of his shell. 'Have you ever felt in any way, Lord Attlee, as being . . . a man of destiny . . . this kind of emotion which Winston Churchill has written about so much?' The response was no more forthcoming. 'No. I had not much idea of destiny . . . you see, I didn't regard myself as a political hero.' As for Churchill, Britain's great wartime leader, thrown out of power by the British people in the flush of victory, his finest hour: 'I was sorry for the old boy.'[1]

It is not always easy to separate Attlee, the individual, from the achievements of his government of 1945 to 1951. This administration bestrides the twentieth century like the bridge between two worlds – before and after the mobilisation of the country for total war, which had strained every sinew of the state and the people in a way that transformed Britain. Many of the things it did in office still shape British politics today. The most iconic of these is the establishment of the National Health Service (NHS) in 1948, which still stands as a totem to the Attlee government, and has attained a near-mythic status in British political life. Just three weeks after the NHS came into being, Attlee announced the start of the London Olympics, in a broadcast to the nation on 28 July 1948. When the Olympics returned to the British capital in 2012, it was the NHS which was the centrepiece of Danny Boyle's opening ceremony – a sentimental paean to the best of Britishness. Yet it is all too easily forgotten that the NHS was just one pillar of a new comprehensive and universal system of insurance, welfare and family allowances to be enjoyed by all citizens, regardless of their means. Taken together, this implied nothing less than a new contract between the individual and the state: a British 'New Deal'. It was, as Attlee saw it, a great evolutionary leap in the ideal of citizenship which set Britain apart from so many nations. The prerequisite for this new social contract was the maintenance of almost full employment. In material terms alone, this was a revolutionary break from the 1930s, when, at the height of the Great Depression, unemployment had peaked at 3.5 million, with as many as 70 per cent out of work in some of the hardest-hit areas.

That this became known as the 'post-war consensus' did not fully convey the long and often bitter struggles that had preceded it: the emergence of the Labour movement at the end of the nineteenth century; the battle for trade union rights and social insurance; the sense of betrayal experienced by thousands of ex-servicemen after 1918 (of which Attlee was one); through to the General Strike of 1926 and the hunger marches of the mid-thirties. For Attlee, it was the most remarkable story that many of the things that he and his comrades had made the case for since the early 1900s – addressing tiny gatherings on street corners or at the gates of the east London docks – were finally embraced by the majority of the electorate, and significant portions of the Establishment. If this was a new consensus, it was to be welcomed. There followed many other changes from 1945 to 1951 which, taken together, amounted to a transformation of the basis of British political, economic and social life. Much of this was experimental. No government in Britain had ever placed more emphasis on economic planning. For better or worse, nationalisation of the Bank of England, the coal mines, electricity and railways shaped the landscape of the country for decades. The history of Britain in the second half of the twentieth century took place within a framework established by Attlee and his ministers. The effects were felt further afield too. Under Attlee, Britain played a leading role in the creation of the United Nations and the North Atlantic Treaty Organisation, and granted independence to India, Burma and Ceylon, while being accused of 'scuttling' elsewhere, in Palestine and Persia.

In many ways, we continue to live in a world of Attlee's creation. Yet if the NHS is still treated as sacrosanct, other things that his government was responsible for, such as the building of an independent nuclear deterrent, remain highly controversial. Attlee's legacy has been contested by many since: most obviously by Conservative critics of the 'post-war consensus' who decried the heavy financial cost of the new welfare regime, bemoaned the failure to modernise British industry, and condemned the unprecedented interference of the state in social and economic life;[2] but also by many of those on the left who were frustrated by what they perceived as Attlee's steady pragmatism, who questioned his bona fides as a 'true' socialist, and argued that he missed the opportunity for genuine revolution in favour of mild reform.

Even some of the eulogies for the Attlee government are pointedly selective in what they celebrate. Typical of such cherry-picking was *The Spirit of '45*, a 2013 documentary film by the socialist director, Ken Loach, based on footage from the election of that year, which focused on the creation of the NHS, the provision of social housing and the nationalisation of the mines, but barely touched on foreign affairs – failing to mention Ernest Bevin, the foreign secretary, or the $3 billion from America's Marshall Plan that enabled many of these changes.[3] If anything, Loach's story was of a revolution betrayed by the timid (moderates in Labour), or the venal (Thatcherites). Its hero was more Aneurin Bevan, the Minister of Health and Housing, than the prime minister himself. In fairness to Loach, Attlee's stiff and awkward demeanour, as captured on contemporary newsreel, did not lend itself easily to dramatisation, particularly when contrasted to Bevan's penchant for theatre and bombast. From the street lanterns in Limehouse to the flash bulbs of a White House press conference, he squirmed in the limelight.

It was once said of Attlee that he was like a cricket ball – the higher he rose, the more elusive he became.[4] In an oft-quoted phrase, Professor

Vernon Bogdanor once called Attlee 'the enigma' of twentieth-century British history. This book begins with the assertion that the enigma has yet to be cracked. In seeking out the real or 'unorthodox' Attlee, the first trap to avoid is that of viewing him solely through the prism of 1945. Another difficulty we face is that Attlee was so reticent about expounding his political principles, or speaking at any length about the value system and ethical precepts that underlay them. It is hard to think of another politician who reached such prominence and gave so little away. He could be opaque, verging on obtuse. As one journalist wrote of him in 1941, 'A gentleman does not explain how he feels on the pilgrimage to Damascus: an English gentleman least of all.'[5]

It is just as well, perhaps, that Attlee did not see himself as a political hero, or a man of destiny. For, in many ways, he has been granted his wish not to be lionised, placed on a pedestal, or subjected to the scrutiny that inevitably follows. Throughout his career, although he was a loyal party man, and received loyalty in return from those who valued such traits, he never inspired followers or sycophants. While he had some life-long political friendships, self-declared 'Attleeites' were rare. There was never a cult around him as there was around other political titans of the era, such as Bevan or Herbert Morrison in Labour, or Churchill or Anthony Eden in the Conservative Party. Nor has there been one invented for him since. The Labour Party of Harold Wilson defined itself by its association with modernity, the 'white heat of technology'. The Labour Party of Tony Blair was a conscious break from the Labour past, and was defiantly ahistorical. In the era of New Labour, Attlee seemed to fade further than ever from view. To some, this was a source of regret. In 2009, the Labour MP Frank Field wrote that the British political classes in general 'have too limited an appreciation of Attlee's values', adding that their failure to offer an 'Attlee-style leadership' had 'much impoverished public life in Britain, to the regret of many voters who are thereby denied a real choice at the ballot box'.[6]

It was somewhat to my surprise then that, in the course of writing this book, Attlee began to experience an unlikely return to fashion. In 2011, one of the most insightful explorations of Attlee's political thought was produced by the Labour MP Jon Cruddas in the Attlee Memorial Lecture of that year. Cruddas distinguished between the 'orthodox' Attlee and the 'unorthodox' Attlee. The orthodox version was a decent man but a dry and rather colourless functionary: a good chairman, reliable colleague and capable administrator. The unorthodox version was a more romantic figure: passionate, patriotic, ethical, and visionary.[7] Cruddas's assessment was superior to most of those in the academic domain, where the orthodox version of Attlee has been taken at face value. This book picks up the 'unorthodox' Attlee, though it offers a different interpretation of the component parts of the Attlee brain and – perhaps just as importantly – the Attlee heart.

One of the major themes of the book is that patriotism was the glue that bound together so much of what Attlee did. Yet, as Cruddas noted in his memorial lecture, such patriotism does not sit easily in a modern Labour Party stuck 'listlessly between poles of economic liberalism and remote cosmopolitanism'. Cruddas was one of a small number of Labour intellectuals associated with the Blue Labour movement, launched by the Labour peer and academic Maurice Glasman in 2010. For those associated with Blue Labour, Attlee presented something of a conundrum. On the one hand, Blue Labour's emphasis on 'family, faith and work with a commitment to the common good' seemed to chime with Attlee's own beliefs. On the other hand, Blue Labour expressed a desire to look back further than 1945 and to dive deeper into Labour's earlier radical traditions. To a certain extent, the great victory of 1945 was identified as the moment when Labour began to lose its ethical and patriotic core – drifting into managerialism, vapid liberalism and abstraction.[8] Thus, even while Cruddas expressed admiration for Attlee, he made clear his own preference for his radical pacifist predecessor as leader, George Lansbury.

For whatever reason, as the New Labour era passed, a reappraisal and a re-imagining of Attlee began to take shape. The notion that he might have some lessons for the modern left began to gain some traction. What was not clear was what these lessons might be. On a number of occasions during his ill-fated tenure as Labour Party leader from 2010 to 2015, Ed Miliband named Clement Attlee as the politician he most admired. Understandably, Miliband evoked Attlee with reference to his own prospects. First, he pointed out that Attlee had been underestimated but had belied the low expectations of him. Second, observed Miliband, Attlee had also presided over a radical government in an age of austerity (a feat which he hoped to replicate were he to win office).[9] This attempt to invoke the spirit of Attlee did not go unchallenged. When Miliband led in the polls at one point in the 2015 election campaign, the Conservative prime minister

David Cameron responded that Miliband's Labour was no longer the party of Attlee – one which had represented working people – but rather a 'bunch of hypocritical, holier-than-thou sneering socialists'.[10]

Over the years, there has certainly been some cross-fertilisation of the Attlee name. Attlee's son, Martin, who married the daughter of a Conservative MP, joined the Social Democratic Party in 1982. One of the founders of the SDP was Roy Jenkins, who knew Attlee from when he was a young boy and became his first biographer, in 1945.[11] The Attlee legacy has been sprinkled further still. Attlee's grandson, John, 3rd Earl Attlee, now sits on the Conservative benches in the House of Lords, and has suggested that his grandfather might have struggled to feel at home in the modern Labour Party. Attlee retains more cross-party appeal than nearly everyone in his party, even among those who were staunchly opposed to his ideals. As Margaret Thatcher set out to dismantle Attlee's post-war consensus, she made no secret of her admiration for his integrity and determination. 'Of Clement Attlee I was an admirer ... His was a genuinely radical and reforming government . . . No one could have questioned Labour's record in implementing socialism.'[12]

This leads to an important question: beyond the certain circumstantial similarities identified by Ed Miliband, what sort of mantle did Attlee bequeath to later generations? It is a question that became more important following the Labour Party's crushing defeat in 2015. As it searched for a new political formula, authenticity and purpose, the example of Attlee was turned to again. In truth, there are elements of both desperation and opportunism in this. The Labour Party is not replete with stories of success. Some of the focus on Attlee can be explained by a conscious attempt to create white noise around the memory of another electorally successful Labour leader, Tony Blair. Only one of the four candidates who fought for the leadership of the Labour Party following Miliband's resignation in May 2015 presented themselves as the heir to Blair, and they ended up at the bottom of the ballot. In a wilful disregard of recent history, the other candidates sought alternative lily pads of legitimacy. Specifically, a number of them sought to invoke the 'spirit of '45' and to elevate Attlee as the icon around which a divided party could unite. Somewhat implausibly, even the supporters of Jeremy Corbyn – the surprise candidate who emerged from the far left of the party to win the leadership – took to wearing T-shirts with the slogan 'What Would Clement Do?' emblazoned across the front. The present author is among those who viewed Corbyn as a distinct break from the political tradition in which Attlee stood.[13]

This question – 'What would Clement do?' – is easy to ask, but not so easy to answer. In reality, there was a convenient element of amnesia in this exhumation of Attlee for modern political purposes. The man never inspired such cultish devotion before. The Labour Party has always had an ambiguous relationship with its former leader, despite the great electoral and legislative successes over which he presided. In fact, he faced no fewer than four attempts to force him out of the leadership and almost incessant carping about his performance. In the course of researching this book – reading contemporary memoirs, diaries, and the press – one could not help but be struck by the volume and persistence of the criticisms of him, particularly by those on the left. They are given full weight here, for two reasons. First, it would be a whitewashing of the historical record to ignore the constant underestimation of Attlee. Second, the extent of the hostility shown towards him (particularly from within his party) should caution us against the disingenuous myth-making around him today.

This act of rediscovery is therefore undertaken at a time when discussions of Attlee's legacy are inevitably coloured by current events. As a number of his previous biographers have observed, it is hard not to relate Attlee to one's own preoccupations. One of the best recent books on Attlee is primarily a study of his leadership style and political skills, written by a Labour MP, Nicklaus Thomas-Symonds.[14] The first, Roy Jenkins's 1945 *Interim Biography* was written at close quarters, by a friend of the family. The most detailed account of Attlee's life remains Kenneth Harris's 1982 work, the 'official' version of his career, based on the close relationship which Harris, political correspondent of the *Observer*, built with him in his later years. Trevor Burridge began his 1986 account by recalling listening to Attlee's voice on the wireless as a young conscript in the RAF; and Francis Beckett, who gets closer than most to the soul of his subject, saw himself very much as a child of Attlee's Britain, born four days after VE day.[15] In what follows, I must acknowledge some debts: to each of these previous biographers; along with the great historians of the British left of the twentieth century such as Paul Addison, Peter Clarke, Ross McKibbin, Kenneth O. Morgan and Ben Pimlott; and the work of a new generation of scholars, among which Robert Crowcroft's *Attlee's War: World War II and the Making of a Labour Leader* stands out.[16]

When it comes to portraying the 'spirit of the times', Peter Hennessey has done more than anyone to bring to life the era of Attlee's government in his book *Never Again*. Yet he has also written eloquently about the potential pitfalls of writing the history of one's times. For a historian of a younger generation, the challenge is not merely to recount those events, to join historiographical debates, or to provide desiccated accounts of government policy, but to keep alive some sense of the spirit, ethos, mood and meaning of the past: what Hennessey calls 'the emotional factor' in history.[17] It should be made clear at the outset that the aim of this book is not to review and reinterpret all the decisions made by Attlee as a politician, to chart the 'road to '45', or to provide another critical assessment of his government's legislative programme. This has been done by others with great skill already, and there is no desire to undertake a dialogue with other historians on every policy detail.[18] Instead, the goal is to get deeper inside Attlee's brain and his heart, before the age of Attlee fades from view entirely: to unpack those contents and tell a larger story through them. This is to appreciate what Attlee himself called 'the importance of the human factor in society as against the mechanics'.[19]

Does any of this matter today? Those who go searching through the weeds of Attlee's government for practical lessons on how to run a government in the twenty-first century are engaging in a fruitless act of technocratic archaeology. Much of what Attlee achieved was tied to a twentieth-century project that had many successes, and some failures, to its name. If something is salvageable from his government's legislation, it is ethos rather than process. This unobtrusive progressive patriotism – built on a sense of rights and duties, a malleable civic code rather than a legal writ, with its emphasis on the 'common wealth' above individual self-fulfilment – bound together everything that Attlee did. It has been scuffed and worn down over the years. It may live on in Britain, in some unfashionable form, but it does not have an Attlee to give it coherence.

London, March 2016

Part One

Patriot, Citizen, Soldier, 1889–1918

Introduction: The Red Flag

The people's flag is deepest red,
It shrouded oft our martyred dead
And ere their limbs grew stiff and cold,
Their hearts' blood dyed its every fold.
So raise the scarlet standard high,
Beneath its shade we'll live and die,
Though cowards flinch and traitors sneer,
We'll keep the red flag flying here.

Jim Connell, 'The Red Flag', 1889

I *Kut-al-Amara, Mesopotamia, April 1916*

On the evening of 4 April 1916, Captain Clement Attlee of the Sixth Battalion of the South Lancashire Regiment weaved his way through a dusty and crumbling trench, repeating instructions, exchanging a few words with his men, and making sure their watches were in sync with his own. His two subalterns, John Lindley and Henry Lechler, had charge of the left and right flank of his company, respectively. In a trench ten yards behind was the other officer of the company, Captain Bayspoole, who was to lead the second line. They were due to charge over the top before dawn broke. As the sun set and the evening temperature cooled, Attlee described how the minutes passed slowly before the 'coming zero hour'.[1] Thoughts drifted back to home and family. He wondered what would happen if he lost his life. He was immensely close to his siblings but he would leave no legacy: no children, no books, no great achievements to his name, just another soldier lost in action. At Gallipoli, where he had been only a few months before, he had been deprived of many good friends and comrades. He kept a personal record of their names but he knew most of them would be forgotten before long.[2]

Captain Attlee was thirty-three years old, five foot nine inches and balding.[3] His khaki uniform hung loosely over his skinny, bird-like frame. He had dark eyes, sharp aquiline features, and a close-clipped moustache. His prominent cranium looked as if it had been pushed up through a thin thatch of mousy brown hair that had all but disappeared by early adulthood, save for a small, resilient tuft at the top. It was later said he bore more than a passing resemblance to the Russian revolutionary Vladimir Lenin, though in 1916 neither man was much known outside their own country. Captain Attlee was no revolutionary. On one level, in fact, he appeared the caricature of the English public schoolboy officer. Nor was he an admirer of Lenin. Yet the comparison was not entirely amiss. Despite his privileged background and upper middle-class accent, Captain Attlee had spent much of the previous decade as a socialist street-corner agitator in east London. In the officers' mess, he was regarded as something of a radical.

Despite the strong Mesopotamian sun, which had finally begun to bake the trenches after weeks of heavy rain, the temperature – peaking at 29°C at that time of year – dropped considerably as the evening set in, causing Attlee and his men to shudder. The Sixth Battalion were at Sunnaiyat, a small settlement on the outskirts of a garrison town called Kut-al-Amara, 100 miles southeast of Baghdad, 150 miles northwest of Basra, and about halfway up the River Tigris, the arterial route which connected the two ancient cities. The battle for the fortress of Kut had already proved to be one of the bloodiest, and ultimately most fruitless, British engagements of the First World War in the Middle East. Attlee and his men were poised to enter it.

The goals of the British campaign in Mesopotamia were to protect the Anglo-Persian oil installations in Abadan, capture the town of Basra and the coastal territory where the Tigris entered the Persian Gulf and, in the words of the South Lancashire Regiment's official history, 'impress the Arab inhabitants of the country, and other territories lying between the Ottoman Empire and India'.[4] Under General Charles Townshend, the

Anglo-Indian Army had initially had great success in pushing the Turks away from Basra and back up the Tigris. In September 1915, Townshend had taken Kut with relative ease and hoped to pursue the retreating Turks to Baghdad. The tide had turned, however, as the Turks were reinforced by 30,000 men from the north. Instead, they forced Townshend back to Kut once more, where they laid siege throughout the winter. Vastly outnumbered and starving, under flurries of snow and a barrage of artillery fire, Townshend and his men sent for help to try to break the siege.[5] The first relief force, under Lieutenant General Fenton Aylmer, had arrived at Kut in January 1916. On the outskirts of the town the fighting was so fierce that Aylmer quickly realised that further reinforcements were needed. News soon reached Port Said, where Attlee and his regiment were messed after their exploits in Gallipoli, that Kut was about to fall, and that the British faced a massacre unless help was sent immediately.

After leaving Port Said at the start of February 1916, Captain Attlee and the Sixth Battalion of the South Lancashires sailed down the Suez Canal, through the Red Sea, the Gulf of Aden, and the Arabian Sea and then, finally, entered the Persian Gulf. On 25 February 1916, they arrived at the mouth of Shatt-el-Arab, just south of Basra, where the Tigris and the Euphrates converged. Moving further upriver to the British garrison at Basra, the troops were given copies of the *Basrah Times*, a two-page newssheet which gave them news of the progress of the war on the Western Front, and of the recent bombing of Yarmouth and Lowestoft by German warplanes. On the second page of the *Basrah Times* were advertisements for English stores where soldiers' families could buy provisions to send to them, along with a guide to Mesopotamia – information on high tides and sunset and sunrise times, as well as weather forecasts. In April temperatures could rise as high as 36°C, though the previous weeks had seen torrential rains.[6]

At Basra, Attlee and his men stayed on board their steamship, the *Elephanta*, as the spring rains had so swamped the British camp as 'to make it like a morass'. The landscape was covered in date palms, silhouetted against the red sky as evening set in, with the noise of thousands of bullfrogs croaking through the night. After moving their supplies, they disembarked from their steamships and moved into two paddle boats for the shallower water of the Tigris. On both sides, a large lighter was attached to the boats, allowing them to carry about a hundred mules each. The troops – supplemented by an Indian cavalry regiment – occupied the upper deck, where they slept on the floor. The lower was taken up by engines, boilers, the cook's galley and the quarters of the Iraqi crew. The soldiers bought chickens from the marsh Arabs on the riverbank and ate tinned plum puddings that their families had sent them from Britain before their departure from Port Said. The joke was that the combination made for a passable version of Christmas dinner.

Snow had been melting in the north, which meant that the Tigris had risen to within a few inches of its banks. Attlee's subaltern, Captain Lindley, described it as 'a slow flowing river which twists and winds about the country like a huge snake'. They passed through villages of mat and mud huts, and saw children swimming and fishermen standing near the banks, using tridents to spear their catch. To Lindley, it was like a scene from a thousand years ago. As well as the din from millions of crickets, there were thousands of wild ducks, storks, flamingos and blue-and-white kingfishers in the river and on the shore. Casting their eyes beyond the banks, the men were struck by the fact that the land of biblical legend, said to be the Garden of Eden, was so barren. It was as if the curse of Adam and Eve had ruined the land for ever. They stopped at the town of Amarah, reassured by the sight of the Union Jack flying high, and entered a bazaar, 'a scene that was truly Eastern', with shopkeepers smoking bubbling hookahs and bargaining over goods. These included, among their Arabian wares, English tinned foods from Birmingham and Manchester – a reminder of the vast reach of the British Empire. The smell of tobacco, curry and spices filled the air under the low roof of the bazaar.[7]

More than at any other stage of the war, Captain Attlee longed for home. The previous year, when stationed in Greece, before taking part in the landings at Gallipoli, he had at least been comforted by the beautiful sights of the Aegean. After all, this was the setting of the *Odyssey* and the tragedies of Euripides, which he had read when studying classics at school. Dug into trenches on the beach at Gallipoli, he had dreamed of Oxford and the River Cherwell, where he had whiled away his university days. Even then, despite the flies and the sand, he had still been able to appreciate the colours and sharp outlines of the hills in the crystal-clear morning light. There were at least 'some alleviations to soften the feeling of separation'. Since then, as he moved 'from Europe to Asia and from Africa to Asia, the links with my previous life became fewer'. In Egypt, at Port Said, and then

Mesopotamia, the separation from home became more acute than ever. The smells and scents, 'the most potent of all memory producers, were utterly foreign, and the longing to see England again became more and more intense'. It was at this point that he first began to reflect on how he would be remembered, if at all, were he to die in this strange land, without a wife or a child.[8] He crafted a poem to reflect his mood, which he ended by adapting a biblical line, used in different ways by Percy Shelley and Rudyard Kipling, his two favourite poets:

> If this dawn usher in eternal night.
> If I should die before another day,
> I shall not leave a child behind to say
> 'My father fought and died in Freedom's fight.'
> Nor has the power been granted me to write
> Books that the minds of other men shall sway,
> Keeping my name in memory away
> To unborn generations a delight.
> I have not books or children; thought alone,
> Sprung from my words in others' minds like seeds
> Fall'n by the wayside on the road of life.
> What harvest shall be reaped where I have sown?[9]

Such morbid thoughts were unsurprising given the bleak news that came back from the front line. When they reached Wadi, a camp about fifty miles south of Kut, the Sixth Battalion learned that General Aylmer had made another attempt to break through to Townshend to relieve the siege, taking heavy casualties at Dujaila on 8 March. A new plan was devised to use the reinforcements in an attempt to break through the Turkish position on the northeast of the town. Captain Attlee was briefed and the operation was carefully planned and rehearsed with scale models on the dusty ground. The divisional commander was Lieutenant General Frederick Maude, whom Attlee found 'a first-rate leader' who 'explained everything to us very fully'.[10] On 16 March they left camp to begin their march, loading the mules with shovels, picks, water and ammunition. The desert air filled with Lancashire accents, cursing as the beasts kicked and bit at their masters. The rains of the early spring had given way to searing heat in the day, but it was cold and damp when the sun set. Packs of jackals circled the camp. They 'made the nights hideous with their yelpings and howls' and occasionally ventured into tents to see what they could scavenge.[11]

The pace slowed as they came closer to the Turkish forces at Kut, under the command of the experienced Prussian field marshal, Colmar Freiherr von der Goltz, who had surrounded Townshend in the fort. Adopting tactics more common on the Western Front, Attlee's men dug themselves into the northeast flank of the Turkish besiegers.[12] While the regiment was full of volunteers, some of the more experienced men described fighting in the desert as 'a sort of mixture between the Boer War and the modern styles of war-fare', with the added perils of machine guns and occasional visits by German dive-bombers.[13] They had got closer to the enemy than first expected – around 100 yards – and an artillery barrage had largely destroyed the barbed wire that protected the three lines of Turkish trenches.[14]

The attack started at 4.45 a.m. on 5 April, about forty minutes before the sun was due to rise.[15] In the middle of the line, Captain Attlee led the way, scrambling over the top with his weapon on his back, one hand for balance and the other clasping the red flag of the South Lancashire Regiment. To his right, Attlee could see, in the flashes of fire that lit up the landscape, that Lechler had gone over the parapet too early and shouted, in the din of artillery fire, for his subaltern to get down.[16] Meeting no resistance, the men charged onwards. The first line of trenches was taken by the Sixth King's Own (Royal Lancashire Regiment) and the second by the Sixth East Lancashire Regiment. Having passed through the first two lines, the British barrage continued so heavily that it was in danger of hitting Attlee's men. But they pushed on and reached the third trench, to signal back to the artillery that the enemy had fled, and stop firing accordingly. Unbeknown to the British, the Turks had evacuated their position during the night of 3 April, leaving behind only a few machine gunners, and an ironic message, in French, the language of international diplomacy, 'Goodbye until the next battle.'

Just as Captain Attlee was about to plant the red flag in the third trench, everything went blank. The next thing he knew, he was returning to consciousness, sitting, oddly, bolt upright. A shell had hit the trench, spraying shrapnel through the battalion. Attlee's corporal had seen him fly through the air at some considerable height, landing in a sitting position. As he came to, he heard the corporal ask him if he was in pain, looked down at his body and saw he was drenched in blood. There was a bullet in his left thigh and a large piece of shrapnel had torn a considerable hole in his right buttock, with cuts, bruises and burns across his frame. He could not move his leg but the pain had not yet set in.[17] As the shelling stopped, he was placed on a stretcher and carried back across the lines to the field hospital. There had been relatively few casualties in the attack, with only eighteen wounded.

On closer inspection, it appeared that one piece of shrapnel had entered the back of his thigh and gone right through him. A bullet which had also gone through the flesh was found in his equipment. The right buttock also received extensive superficial wounds and there was a small tear in his groin and damage to his knee joint which made it impossible to walk.[18] His injuries had been caused by friendly fire in the confusion provoked by the fact that the Turks had retreated a few hundred metres overnight. In truth, however, Captain Attlee was luckier than he knew; and not for the first time in the war. As he was evacuated from the battlefield, his men attacked again that very night in a costly manoeuvre. General Maude muscled through the next Turkish line but the division took 1,300 casualties in just a few hours.[19] In Port Said, news soon reached headquarters that the assault had failed, and Townshend had been forced to surrender.[20] The list of casualties came through to the men, eager to learn the fate of their friends. Captain Attlee was 'wounded', Captain Lindley 'lightly wounded', Bayspoole was missing and Lechler killed.[21] Of the four officers who had led the attack that morning, only two had survived. One, the public school boy with unusual political views, carried off the battlefield for the second of three times during the First World War, would become the future prime minister of Britain.

II

Two weeks later, as Captain Attlee began his recovery at the garrison in Basra, he picked up his pen and wrote to his older brother Tom, a pacifist who was facing prosecution for his stance as a conscientious objector back in England. He spoke of his sadness at the loss of so many good men, including Lechler, his subaltern, who had been 'knocked out' in the assault. He played down the extent of his injuries and was deeply conscious of his own good fortune, having missed the worst of the fighting, as had happened at Gallipoli in 1915, when sickness had kept him away from his battalion. He felt he had no right to be in anything but good spirits. In classic Attlee fashion, there was nothing to do but put on a brave face. 'By the way,' he joked to Tom, with whom he had joined the Independent Labour Party in 1908, 'it might be interesting to the comrades to know I was hit while carrying the red flag to victory.' As he had joked to his commanding officer, the colour was a fitting complement to his political persuasions.[22]

The red flag was both the emblem of international socialism and the anthem of the British Labour movement. The famous song of that name had been written by the Irish-born London socialist Jim Connell in 1889, on a train journey from Charing Cross to New Cross, during the London dock strike of that year. Connell was an early figurehead of the socialist movement and worked on the *Labour Leader*, the newspaper of Keir Hardie, the founder of the Independent Labour Party.[23] These were the stories and songs which any new recruit was reared on. When Clement Attlee joined the organisation in January 1908, he was told of the 'heroic struggles of the pioneers in the misty past' and the dock strike of 1889, which had taken place when he was only six years old.[24]

While Vladimir Lenin viewed the British Labour movement with contempt, he made an exception for Connell, awarding him the Order of the Red Banner in 1922, the highest honour in the Soviet Union. While 'The Red Flag' had become the song of the British Labour Party, it also had a radical association with communism. At the time of the first Labour government in 1924, when the 'Red threat' had been whipped up by the Conservative press, King George V expressed his concern about the singing of the song at Labour meetings. The Labour prime minister, Ramsay MacDonald, warned the king that his MPs might sing it in Parliament, while reassuring him that he hoped to end the practice soon, given its embarrassing connotations.

The tradition of singing 'The Red Flag' outlasted MacDonald and his betrayal of Labour in 1931. On 1 August 1945, as the House of Commons reassembled after the post-war election, the defeated opposition leader Winston Churchill was treated to a rendition of 'For He's a Jolly Good Fellow' by Conservative MPs as he entered the chamber. As soon as they were finished, George Griffiths, the Labour backbencher, cleared his throat and began to sing 'The Red Flag'. 'Through the ancient chamber rang the words of the left-wing inspirational hymn,' as a rather shocked American reporter from *Time* magazine described. The Labour backbenchers followed Griffiths' lead with relish, making sure the Conservative minority knew that Labour's moment had come. On the frontbench, the new Labour government looked somewhat uneasy, and shifted in their seats. Slowly, and with some reluctance, some of the ministers stood up, if only briefly, to mouth some words. None looked more awkward than Clement Attlee, the leader – and the man who had presided over its great triumph. Attlee had sung the 'The Red Flag' many times before; but, now that Labour was tasked with national responsibilities, he was not so comfortable with a display of such naked tribalism under the scrutiny of the public eye.[25]

When Attlee became leader of the Labour Party ten years earlier, in 1935, he seemed to be an unlikely figurehead in a decade dominated by more forceful and flamboyant personalities, at home and abroad. At a loss as to what to say about this rather unthreatening-looking socialist, it was the *Daily Mail* that first made the observation that he had a similar-shaped head to that of Lenin. In truth, the comparison was somewhat forced. The newspaper, which prided itself on attacking the dangerous radicals of the Labour Party ('the socialist party' as it insisted on calling it), found it hard to present Labour's newly appointed leader as some sort of closet revolutionary.[26] In purely physical terms, however, others – including George Orwell – believed there was something in the comparison with Lenin.[27]

In her 1941 book, *The Men Around Churchill*, the American journalist René Kraus also described Attlee as a 'lean Lenin in a non-revolutionary community'. He was 'English of the English', though without any of the bombast associated with John Bull – the caricature of a beer-drinking Englishman. He was painfully shy and modest and kept up his guard at all times, 'lest strange eyes pierce his shell'. But rather than the comparison with Lenin, Kraus was struck by something else. For an outsider, Attlee seemed to be the Englishman's ideal antidote to Oswald Mosley, Britain's most famous fascist, and the man whom he had replaced as Chancellor of the Duchy of Lancaster ten years before. Mosley was bold, self-confident, well built and handsome, with seal-like, sleek black hair. Yet while Mosley and his fascist movement flashed, glowed and faded, Attlee's steady stewardship of the Labour Party had been one of the reasons that Britain had not fallen into the extremism that had beset so many of its European neighbours.[28]Attlee's laconicism punctured the atmosphere that men like Mosley needed to thrive. His anti-egotism was a weapon that undermined the shrill, the pompous and the absolutist, from wherever they came on the political spectrum. 'I object to dictatorships, whether in blue shirts, green shirts, or any other kind of shirts, but I equally object when they are boiled shirts,' he once remarked, referring to the stiff-necked and self-righteous, whether they were liberals, conservatives, fascists or communists.[29]

After he led Labour to victory in 1945, Attlee was subject to more scrutiny than ever before. For American observers, who had grown used to Churchill during the war, the new prime minister seemed a particularly strange creature in the democratic age. Here was a man who saw no need for the science of public relations, nor showed much willingness to adapt to the requirements of mass media. The *Washington Post* compared him to Caspar Milquetoast, an American cartoon character famed for his safe choices and boring personality – always having the bland dish of milk and toast for every meal.[30] More favourably, he also earned comparisons with the level-headed midwesterner, Harry Truman, who never quite escaped the shadow of Franklin Roosevelt, but showed himself to be a leader of steely resolve. These two men's lives were to converge on some of the most pressing issues of the age, including the atomic bomb, the early cold war, and the Korean War.

As his close friend Jack Lawson wrote of him, Attlee was 'the least like a revolutionary character that one could imagine. Neither in appearance nor speech does he strike the imagination of crowds.'[31] Yet here was the paradox. Attlee presided over a government that was the most radical of the twentieth century. The longer his career went on, the more people understood the lofty purpose that underlay it. And so the sense that he had been underestimated began to take hold. A profile in the *Observer* in 1949 suggested that there was more to the Lenin comparison than one might assume. What he shared was a similar quality of private decision, 'that ability to follow his own analysis of events to its logical conclusion, unperturbed by the feelings of those around him', or by his own 'feelings, fears, or vanities'.[32] There was also something of the revolutionary in his incorruptibility. Dining with Attlee shortly after his election victory of 1945, Lord Gladwyn commented that he was 'a living exception to Lord Acton's dictum that all power corrupts'.[33] Over time, observers of Attlee came to a fuller appreciation of the force of character that buttressed it.

By 1953, after the end of Attlee's government, R. J. Cruikshank, the historian of the Victorian Liberal Party, described the Labour leader as 'a revolutionary buttoned up inside a cricket blazer'. His political trick was to appear as a classic Victorian, or Britain's family solicitor 'advising the old lady very sagely on her investments'. Cruikshank had heard many Conservatives say of him, 'Such a fine little chap – trustworthy – honest – patriotic.' The English were suspicious of showmanship and cleverness on the part of their leaders. It was almost as if they absolved him of the sins of socialism. He was the Englishman's ideal type, with his stiff upper lip reinforced by its neat moustache. Who else could have so successfully presided over the great social revolution that began in 1945 but Attlee, 'elected dictator of a turbulent and rebellious party'? Attlee's revolution was 'not only bloodless but almost painless'. The British people had been hypnotised by 'the most successful political dentist in history'.[34]

III

In 1979, a memorial statue of Attlee was unveiled in the House of Commons. Margaret Thatcher, who disapproved of almost everything Attlee's government did on the home front but always admired his integrity, sat smiling in the front row, a few empty seats away from James Callaghan, then Labour leader. That statue was seven feet eight inches high, and was placed on a specially-made stand, making it three inches taller than the statue of Churchill, which already stood in the Members' Lobby. This was deliberate. Attlee was given some extra inches to make up for the lack of mass in comparison to the Churchill statue. He weighed in at eleven cubic metric tonnes to Churchill's nineteen, and some thought this a little unfair.[35]

It was not Lenin or Truman to whom Attlee was most often compared but Winston Churchill. While Attlee may have suffered from comparisons with Churchill, he did not see it that way. In fact, he revelled in the association with a man whose greatness, and many flaws, he understood better than most. The connection went back to childhood. When he was a young boy, his mother had employed a governess, Miss Hutchinson, who had also once looked after Churchill. Attlee enjoyed a story about how one day a maid had entered the room and asked Miss Hutchinson if she had rung the bell, only for little Winston to say, 'I rang. Take away Miss Hutchinson, she is very cross.'³⁶ Born in 1874, Winston was nine years his senior. As a schoolboy, Attlee had celebrated victory in the Battle of Spion Kop, and the relief of Ladysmith in the Boer War, from where Churchill reported as a correspondent for the *Morning Post*.³⁷ He recalled, in his last year at school, and later at Oxford, hearing of this remarkable young man who had already seen five campaigns and had written books about them. He remembered hearing about Churchill's election to Parliament in 1900 for the constituency of Oldham when Attlee, then a Conservative, 'hailed him as a rising hope of our Party'.³⁸

In 1911, a few years after Attlee had converted to socialism – when he was making his name as a stump speaker and street activist for the Independent Labour Party – he saw Churchill in person for the very first time. As a social worker in the East End, he was a spectator at the Siege of Sidney Street that January when Churchill, as home secretary, deployed the army to accost a group of Latvian anarchists. Four years later, by a twist of fate, Attlee found his life in Churchill's hands. The campaign that he fought in Gallipoli in 1915 was the brainchild of Churchill, as First Lord of the Admiralty in the wartime coalition. While it had cost thousands of lives, and Churchill his job in the government, Attlee always believed that the strategic conception had been sound.³⁹ 'I was in some of Mr. Churchill's shows,' Attlee told a rally of Labour Party supporters in 1924. 'I was in Sidney Street as a spectator . . . I was in Gallipoli. I will give the devil his due and say that I think Mr. Churchill was right about Gallipoli.' ⁴⁰

It was in 1924 that Attlee came to know Churchill personally, when the latter returned to the House of Commons, having lost his seat two years before. He regarded Churchill as one of the worst Chancellors of the Exchequer in history, a position he held from 1924 to 1929. Yet even when they clashed on domestic issues, Attlee did not deny Churchill a 'certain idealism', though it was an idealism 'that was most unfortunate for the rank and file of the country'. What marked out Churchill as someone he admired? 'Courage, imagination, a great knowledge of things', even if 'he always wanted someone by him at a certain point to say "Now don't be a bloody fool." '⁴¹ It is often suggested that Churchill cut a somewhat forlorn figure for much of the 1930s, alienated from his party's leadership, thudding around on the backbenches. Churchill made much of this in his own writings, referring to these as his 'wilderness years'. Reading Attlee's letters from the era, one gets a very different picture. Almost every letter that Attlee sent to his brother about parliamentary life contained some reference to 'Winston'. Winston could appear hopelessly out of touch on issues such as India, for example, but he remained a point of reference – a titan, albeit a weary one, in Attlee's mind.

It was the Labour Party that put Churchill into Number 10 Downing Street in 1940 by refusing to serve under Neville Chamberlain. Without this, Churchill's anointing was far from inevitable, as Chamberlain retained the support of the majority of his own party. As Churchill's deputy in government, Attlee was often accused of unthinking loyalty to the prime minister. This was a view expressed by the chiefs of the general staff, who saw him as a 'yes man' to an unpredictable and sometimes reckless prime minister. The same allegation was also made by elements of the Labour Party, dissatisfied by what they saw as uncritical subservience to a Conservative-led regime. When Churchill made a special effort to keep Attlee close by his side in 1942 and 1943, it was not only because he understood the importance of keeping Labour in the coalition; it was also because Attlee backed him on the major arguments on strategy with the chiefs of staff. Indeed, he was more loyal than many of Churchill's Conservative colleagues, including apparatchiks such as Lord Beaverbrook. That this relationship survived the dark years of 1940–2 was of central importance to the successful prosecution of the war.

Attlee bested Churchill emphatically at the election of 1945, and, to the great surprise of the parliamentary sketch writers, in a number of the parliamentary debates that followed. Yet the Labour leader still expressed wonderment at having been at Churchill's side through these great events, or opposite him on the parliamentary benches, even when their relations turned to acrimony. 'What a career! What a man! We shall not see his like again.'[42] In later years, when both men were retired, Attlee would take pleasure from sitting with Churchill and listening to his booming voice, unperturbed by the fact that Winston refused to use his ear trumpet and therefore could not hear anyone else talk. 'I knew my Winston,' he would say, with some pride.[43]

To propose that Attlee was somehow greater than Churchill, then, would be to open this book with a claim that would have caused Attlee himself to guffaw. As Lord Bridges once wrote, he was 'free from any sense of personal self-importance or from any wish to be treated with exaggerated respect'.[44] Nonetheless, the gallons of ink spilled on Churchill – and the insatiable appetite for books about him – have created something of an imbalance in our understanding of twentieth-century Britain. This needs some correction. On the one hand, Attlee's life rightfully deserves a place alongside the Churchill legend, without in any way taking away from it. On the other hand, one could also argue that it is also more emblematic, and more representative, of Britain in his time. Indeed, it is difficult to think of another individual through whom one can better tell Britain's story from the high imperialism of Queen Victoria's Golden Jubilee of 1887, through two world wars, the Great Depression, the nuclear age and the cold war, and the transition from empire into commonwealth.

It was in a parliamentary debate with Attlee that Churchill declared that history would be kind to him, because he intended to write it. By contrast, Attlee's biography *As it Happened* was dry as dust, bordering on the diffident. 'It's a good title,' said Aneurin Bevan, one of his most persistent critics. 'Things happened to him. He never did anything.'[45] After reading the book, his long-time colleague Hugh Dalton commented that only a certain type of Englishman could have produced a work so self-effacing and unembellished, that made so little of his own role in the defining events of his time. The book reminded Dalton of a comment made by Sir John Dill, the Chief of the Imperial General Staff in 1941, when describing the Battle of Britain to an audience of Americans: 'No, our air force wasn't wholly inactive.'[46] Attlee was a great admirer of John Dill, as a typically British type of hero, so he would not have objected to the comparison.[47]

As with John Dill's description of the Battle of Britain, the Attlee story is much more dramatic than he himself ever conveyed. As he did not have the Churchillian gift of self-portrait, some of the storytelling has to be done for him. It is for that reason that the first act opens on the trenches of Mesopotamia as Britain's future prime minister stormed towards the enemy carrying the red flag of his regiment. This episode is chosen to illustrate a larger point. It is that Clement Attlee was more *heroic* than he is often given credit for. In using the word 'hero', it stresses not so much his personal bravery as his agency in shaping the course of modern British history. The intention is not to offer a value judgement on what constitutes greatness, but to invoke the spirit of Thomas Carlyle's 'great man' theory: an individual who can shape the course of history, rather than simply being carried along by events. One must be careful not to turn Attlee into something he was not: a swashbuckling man of the moment, with a sharp tongue to match his sword. But he was a man of his age, whose appreciation of the time in which he lived was superior to many others. He did not change the direction of British history through a single act, but he coaxed it in a certain direction, with more skill, and more idealism, than he has been given credit for.

IV

Attlee is not without admirers. For that reason, there is no need to rescue him from attempts to besmirch his reputation, or to engage in a historical rescue mission. In 2004, a survey of British academics listed him as the greatest prime minister of the twentieth century.[48] He has never been an unpopular figure, or inspired much hostility. Even those whom he criticised found it hard to resent him. As the historian A. J. P. Taylor put it, notwithstanding the fact that Attlee was rather unpleasant about him, 'Attlee grows on you.'[49] Nonetheless, he has been disparaged in subtler ways, which this book seeks to address. Some of the criticisms made by contemporaries – about failures in his leadership in the summer of 1947, for example – were justified, and are dealt with in the course of the text. Other attempts to disparage him require a firmer rebuttal because they point to deeper misconceptions. The first, as mentioned already, is the imputation Attlee was a mere passenger in the great events of his time.

Even when he became prime minister, Attlee was surrounded by larger personalities. Sitting on the frontbench with his ministers, he looked like he had been wedged, with some difficulty, between the thick-set frames of Ernie Bevin and Nye Bevan, the representatives of the right and left of the party, respectively. 'Churchill is an Everest surrounded by Snowdons,' commented the Independent trade unionist MP, William Brown, 'Attlee is a Snowdon surrounded by Mont Blancs.'[50] On either side of Bevin and Bevan were the tall, self-confident and bespectacled Stafford Cripps, undoubtedly Attlee's intellectual superior; and the cheeky cockney wit Herbert Morrison, with his cartoon quiff, at ease with himself and his party. The fifth member of the big five was Hugh Dalton, whom Attlee beat to a lectureship at the London School of Economics in 1912 but who regarded it as a matter of inevitability, and therefore of no particular urgency, that his superior talents would see him supersede Attlee. With the exception of Bevin, each of these men at some point coveted the leadership that Attlee held. None attained it – partly because they clashed with each other and partly because they underestimated its incumbent.

Attlee's critics could see that he was nimble, for sure. But mostly they thought he was lucky: lucky to be in the right place at the right time in 1931, as one of the few senior Labour MPs to keep his seat in the electoral catastrophe of that year; lucky to still be leader when Labour had the chance to join the wartime coalition in 1940; luckier still not to be deposed by his own party in 1945, at the same moment that his country decided to dispense with Churchill; and, most of all, lucky that his chief rivals, supposedly superior men such as Herbert Morrison and Ernie Bevin, cancelled each other out with their jealousies. Thus he was often compared to some sort of small animal. Hugh Dalton called him both a 'little mouse' and a 'poor little rabbit'. For Neville Chamberlain he was a 'cowardly cur', and for Lord Beaverbrook, he was a 'sparrow'.[51] For the wit and writer Malcolm Muggeridge (not, as commonly thought, Churchill) he was a 'sheep in sheep's clothing'.[52] Against expectations, Attlee's spry little frame proved more robust than those of many of his peers. In a reworking of the famous fable, the tortoise outlasted the hares.[53] This metaphor only gets us so far, however. Notwithstanding a certain admiration for his physical fortitude and mental equilibrium, it does little to counter the impression that he was a meek observer of events.

The second disparaging assumption about Attlee – more commonly found on the left – was that there were no hidden depths to him, no real intellectual substance, or serious political thought; and that he was merely an empty vessel who bore the imprint of his party, and regarded it as his job to find a compromise between the competing strains within it. The *New Statesman*'s review of Attlee's autobiography in 1954 offers a prime example of such sentiments. The 'average reader', it was suggested, would be forgiven for losing patience long before the end of this 'lamely written, clumsily constructed book, much of it as boring as the minutes of a municipal gas undertaking'. Mr Attlee was 'no Alcibiades or Churchill – not even a Pepys or a Trollope'. Yet, ventured the reviewer, there was no point in digging any deeper. The real Attlee could be found in the pages of *As it Happened*, 'so long as one doesn't make the mistake of looking for something bigger than reality'. In the *New Statesman's* assessment, Attlee held to a 'practical, progressive and mildly Socialist creed', which was, 'at the same time, parochial, incomplete and begging most of the great philosophical questions'. When one stripped away his undoubted integrity and capacity for hard work, there was very little left. Those searching for something else – ideas, passion or curiosity – would search in vain. 'In every chapter one finds an utter obliviousness and disregard of theories and values which are outside Mr. Attlee's range. Men and ideas are flattened down to the level at which he can comprehend them; and there is never a qualm expressed lest perhaps something is being missed.' Attlee's 'competent revolution' contributed 'almost nothing new or imaginative to the pool of ideas with which men seek to illuminate human nature and its environment'.[54]

Another favourite theme of Attlee's critics was to sneer at the sporting clichés and 'ethical homilies' to which he often reverted, as an indication of his intellectual shallowness. In 1967, just after his death, *The Economist* commented that Attlee 'stayed in his shell: what he made clear was it was a hard shell'. Yet, according to the obituary writer, there was no point trying to crack some hidden code: 'In parliament or in public he was nothing other than himself . . . middle class with no ambitions to be anything else . . . a thinking man with no pretensions to be an intellectual.'[55] The philosopher Isaiah Berlin could appreciate that he was a highly ethical prime minister but could not resist a swipe at his 'minor public school morality'.[56] Whenever asked for his verdict on Attlee, his health minister Nye Bevan – the hero of the British left – would also snort about his 'suburban middle class values'. He would then perform a party piece to make his point that the Labour leader had no intellectual depth, or reserves of passion. This was to reach to his shelves and begin to read the radical writer William Hazlitt's essay on William Pitt, written after the latter's death in 1806. Just like Pitt, Attlee had 'no strong feelings, no distinct perceptions . . . [Having] no insight into human nature, no sympathy with the passions of men, or apprehension of their real designs, he seemed perfectly insensible to the consequences of things, and would believe nothing until it actually happened.' On finishing the excerpt, Bevan would add his own flourish. 'Only the bovine English could have brought forth such a Mirabeau to guide the beginnings of their Revolution. Here was no Lenin leading the masses but rather Labour's Lord Liverpool, the Arch-Mediocrity . . .'[57]

One might say that the failure of imagination was less on the part of Attlee himself and more on that of his critics. Either way, the consequence is that Attlee remains *underappreciated*, rather than simply *underestimated*. So, while the first goal of the book is to re-inject something of the epic quality into the Attlee story, the second is to unpack Attlee's belief system, values and ethical code; and also to recapture the foundations of his political thought. This is not to claim that Attlee was some sort of undervalued theorist of socialist economics; indeed, on such matters, he was self-confessedly hopeless. Nor is the intention to make the case that Attlee was, contrary to his reputation, an intellectual. 'I was never an intellectual,' Attlee once remarked, adding pointedly, 'they would not have allowed me as such.'[58] In a telling phrase, his closest ally in government, Ernie Bevin, preferred to see it another way. Attlee was mercifully free of the 'university-complex' which afflicted many of the self-styled intellectuals on the left.[59] Attlee's political thought and belief system were far richer and more textured than has previously been assumed.

V

To begin to come to a truer understanding of Attlee is to rediscover a sense of the mental world in which he was made. In a 1934 biography of Oliver Cromwell – a book which Attlee greatly enjoyed – the writer John Buchan explained that a biographer, when approaching his subject, 'must search not only amongst the arcana of his age, its hidden forces and imponderable elements, but among the profundities of the human spirit'.[60] Attlee's written and verbal output itself was neither particularly enlivening nor revealing. To bridge the gap to his mind, this book offers a greater exploration of what Attlee *read*, to understand the intellectual and cultural setting in which he operated and the notions that conditioned his own political creed. We begin to see that Attlee had a much more vivid imagination and multi-layered political brain than is often presumed, and that the range was much greater than his critics ever understood.

In January 1954, Attlee wrote an essay in the *National and English Review* on 'The Pleasure of Books', in which he described looking over at the three thousand books he had acquired, covering two walls of his study, 'the accumulation of many years – old friends and newcomers'.[61] As his friend, the Durham MP Jack Lawson wrote of him when he was prime minister, 'In the midst of all his labours he keeps pace with the thought of the time. He misses no book which matters.' Throughout his career, through the different challenges of opposition and office, 'he could be seen in the library of the House of Commons, after a quick lunch, reading some new book . . . History, philosophy and economics and literature to engage his mind in spite of cabinet meetings, endless committees and speeches in the House and in the country.'[62]

In a revealing comment, Attlee once remarked that 'rank and file' novelists were a better indicator of the mood of a nation at any given time than the supposed classics or epoch-defining books.[63] To a certain extent, his own literary tastes reflected that sentiment. Alongside favourite 'classics' by Jane Austen and Anthony Trollope, he enjoyed detective novels, particularly those by Agatha Christie, and portraits of English society by Angela Thirkell, Howard Spring and John Galsworthy – adaptions of which were later made into films and television shows. Before that, his first love was poetry. Indeed, from his school days onwards, he would not only recite poetry to friends and family, but also compose his own verse. While Attlee's own efforts were often witty and sometimes poignant, he made no claim to be a master of the form. But his reading of poetry shaped his worldview. Indeed, one could go so far as to say that Rudyard Kipling, William Blake, Percy Shelley and John Milton provide a script for his political life. 'My mind is stored with poetry,' he once said, describing how he would set himself the task of recalling lines from the classics on long journeys or on long nights in the trenches during the Great War. 'It has always been a pleasure to me that places and times bring poetry to my mind.' He recalled the work of Horace and Euripides when stationed at Gallipoli in 1915. Sitting with a group of Danish resistance fighters in 1940, he recited John Milton's *Samson Agonistes* when, after enduring the Blitz, British bombers took off for Berlin. It was a 'winged expedition' executing 'errands on the wicked'.[64]

How to make sense of these fragments, and paint a larger picture from them? One book that particularly impressed Attlee was *The Road to Xanadu: A Study in the Ways of the Imagination* by the American academic John Livingston Lowes. In a study of two of the most famous poems of Samuel Taylor Coleridge, *The Rime of the Ancient Mariner* and *Kubla Khan*, Lowes used Coleridge's notebook to connect the books he read at any particular time with the images he conjured in his poetry. Attlee read this book in the long nights of the Blitz when he was forced to take shelter under the Treasury building in Whitehall and had no official papers with him. He thought it got closer than anything he had read to understanding Coleridge's vast imagination.[65] The following chapters borrow something of the approach that Livingston Lowes adopted in *The Road to Xanadu* and turn it back on Attlee himself. Accordingly, they are constructed around the poetry, prose and historical works that Attlee consumed at particular points in his life. Attlee kept no notebook; and his personal archives are notably sparse.[66] But a close inspection of his speeches and letters (particularly to his brother Tom), and the diaries and memoirs of those around him, reveal what he was reading at various points in his life. Each chapter begins with a segment of poetry, prose, history or song that was in Attlee's mind or on his lips at that time, or which set the mood around him. These are juxtaposed with a scene or a moment from his life at that point – so that the ideas, and the words in which they were expressed, are not detached from a sense of time and place. As Attlee said of Rudyard Kipling and William Morris, for example, it was important to understand them as creatures of context to reach a full appreciation of their work.

In a memorable phrase, Attlee once compared Churchill to 'one of those layer cakes. There was a layer of seventeenth century, a layer of eighteenth century, a layer of nineteenth century, and possibly even a layer of twentieth century. You were never sure which layer would be uppermost,' he wrote in 1963.[67] To an extent that has not been fully comprehended, Attlee was his own historical layer cake, albeit one with different layers and different ingredients. In later years, when discussing the great characters of history with Attlee, Mary Wilson, the wife of the future Labour prime minister, Harold, told him that her favourites were the 'romantic ones: Charles II, Prince Rupert of the Rhine, Byron . . .' Attlee's response was telling: 'Bad history, wrong people.'[68] Attlee's conception of good history, right people, revealed his preference for the Roundheads over the Cavaliers. He should be understood as the twentieth-century inheritor of a tradition born in the era of the English Civil War – that of the classical republicans: those who paid homage to the idea of the *commonweal*, their sense of obligations and liberties embodied by the symbols of the sword and the plough.[69] He believed that the democratic ethos in British politics pre-dated the establishment of a fully democratic system. He applauded Oliver Cromwell's statement that he would 'rather have a plain, russet-coated Captain, that knows what he fights for, and loves what he knows, than that you call a Gentleman and is nothing else'.[70] At one stage, he even proposed that a socialist state might make use of regional commissars – not on the Soviet model but in the mould of the army chaplains in Cromwell's army, who carried the 'root of the matter in them'.[71]

It would be a mistake, however, to present Attlee as a latter-day Cromwell, or even as an inheritor of the Cromwellian tradition.[72] Attlee admired the work of the Victorian writer Thomas Carlyle, particularly his critique of utilitarianism. But he did not share the extent of Carlyle's admiration for Cromwell. For Carlyle, Cromwell was the archetypal example of the 'great man' who could change the course of history, through word, will and deed. In the 1930s, it was Oswald Mosley who embraced the heroic ideal of the Carlylean Cromwell. Yet Attlee was one of the most effective antidotes to the neo-Cromwellians whose flame flickered in this treacherous decade. He preferred more nuanced historical accounts that emphasised the strategic and self-defeating errors that Cromwell made.[73] The degeneration of the English Revolution into dictatorship was something that bore heavily on his mind, particularly after 1933. Nor was there the slightest hint of anti-monarchism in his make-up. For Attlee, loyalty to the Crown was 'the most natural thing'.[74] This was genuine and strongly felt, reflected in his personal friendship with King George VI, whose death in 1952 shook him greatly.

Even though they sniped at him from the backbenches, Attlee retained a taste for a 'good type of puritanical Radical', such as the Methodist and Liberal MP Isaac Foot, whose son Michael Foot carried that tradition into the Labour Party.[75] He understood the crucial role that the nonconformist conscience had played for the early activists of the socialist movement – both in terms of creating a rallying cause and providing the spiritual impetus to action. Men like George Lansbury, whom he knew from the East End and whom he was to serve under as deputy leader in the Labour Party, derived their zeal from their faith in God.[76] While he did not share this faith, he was both deft and sincere when talking about the moral purpose of politics, both in foreign and domestic affairs. Some of his best speeches were given to religious audiences. He talked of 'spiritual warfare' and rejected both 'materialism' and 'pacifism' as a 'hedonistic dislike of taking responsibility', he declared in 1946. 'We are happy warriors. Let our trumpets give out no uncertain note.'[77]

That Attlee was comfortable speaking in such terms reflected the fact he was a child of the late Victorian age. Even the Conservative propagandist Colm Brogan described him in 1949 as one of the last of a dying breed: a 'classic Victorian moralist'.[78] Each of his previous biographers has stressed his Victorian heritage. What is less appreciated is that Attlee thought Victorian moralising went too far, at times. His ethical code was of a more tolerant variety. It is fair to say that he hated self-righteousness. This explains his undisguised contempt for William Gladstone, the leader of the late Victorian Liberal Party. According to Lord Longford, Attlee was 'not only the least selfish politician of the first rank . . . but the most ethical Prime Minister in the whole of British history'. The difference was that he lacked the 'Christian earnestness of Mr. Gladstone' and was 'happily without the latter's power of self-deception'.[79] A similar sentiment was reflected in Attlee's fondness for a comment made to him by the Tory MP Thomas Moore, which he often quoted. 'You know when I was young I was always talking about my conscience. But I thought it over and I came to the conclusion that what I called my conscience was just my own bloody conceit.'[80]

There were two foundation stones to Attlee's ethical and political code, which remained with him for the rest of his life and which provided the clue to his whole career. The first was an appreciation of citizenship – an interchange of rights and duties and responsibilities – as the glue that kept societies together. This is explained in the following chapters, which portray Attlee as a classic 'citizen soldier'. The second, intimately connected to the first, was patriotism. Patriotism, in the tradition of the russet-coated captain, was the striving for a constitutional and societal ideal. It meant fidelity not to caste or cohort, but to the idea that the *commonweal* was the first goal of government.[81] Above all, it was a sense of patriotism that underpinned Attlee's socialism. It should be made clear that this was a worldview that rejected uncritical chauvinistic jingoism or imperialism – ugly by-products of nationalism that encouraged racism or undercut the fellowship of man. Such was the horror of the First World War that he once dreamed of a 'world state' in which individual countries would pool their sovereignty. Nonetheless, he believed that love of country could be a noble and unifying thing.

Captain Clement Attlee, small in frame and thin in voice, shot in the buttocks as he carried the red flag over the top in 1916, may not be the greatest Briton of the twentieth century. This book argues that he has a good claim to be its first-ranked citizen.

2

'With apologies to Rudyard Kipling'

God of our fathers, known of old,
    Lord of our far-flung battle-line,
Beneath whose awful Hand we hold
    Dominion over palm and pine –
Lord God of Hosts, be with us yet,
Lest we forget – lest we forget!

The tumult and the shouting dies;
    The Captains and the Kings depart:
Still stands Thine ancient sacrifice,
    An humble and a contrite heart.
Lord God of Hosts, be with us yet,
Lest we forget – lest we forget!

Far-called, our navies melt away;
    On dune and headland sinks the fire:
Lo, all our pomp of yesterday
    Is one with Nineveh and Tyre!
Judge of the Nations, spare us yet,
Lest we forget – lest we forget!

If, drunk with sight of power, we loose
    Wild tongues that have not Thee in awe,
Such boastings as the Gentiles use,
    Or lesser breeds without the Law –

Lord God of Hosts, be with us yet,
Lest we forget – lest we forget!

For heathen heart that puts her trust
    In reeking tube and iron shard,
All valiant dust that builds on dust,
    And guarding, calls not Thee to guard,
For frantic boast and foolish word –
Thy mercy on Thy People, Lord!

Rudyard Kipling, 'Recessional', 1897

I *St Paul's Cathedral, London, 1897*

On Tuesday, 22 June 1897, Queen Victoria celebrated her Diamond Jubilee, marking sixty years on the throne. A procession of seventeen carriages carried the royal family, the heads of the armed services of the British Empire, and a train of foreign dignitaries from Buckingham Palace to St Paul's Cathedral. After a service of thanksgiving, the carriages trundled to Mansion House for lunch. The procession crossed London Bridge to the south bank of the River Thames, then back across Westminster Bridge and onto the Mall. Hundreds of thousands of Britons stood by the roadside, packing the pavements or cramming onto balconies in order to catch a sight of the monarch, waving flags and cheering. It was a spectacle that embodied the pinnacle of British power and imperial grandeur. London was the metropole and Victoria was queen of an empire that stretched across the globe. That night, bonfires and illuminations were lit across the capital and the rest of the country, and there were celebrations throughout Victoria's dominions in Australia, Canada, India, the Middle East and the West Indies.

Rudyard Kipling wrote two poems for the occasion. The first was the 'White Man's Burden', which became, for many, synonomous with Anglo-Saxon imperial pretence and racial superiority. Kipling decided not to use this one for the Jubilee and instead reworked it to apply to the American invasion of the Philippine Islands in 1899. The sentiments impressed

Theodore Roosevelt who became American president in 1901. Needing another poem for the Jubilee, Kipling penned 'Recessional'. Taking the form of a prayer, it was supposed to be a reminder to Britain that the ultimate judge would not be the grandeur of her empire but the grace of God. It combined celebration of empire with a growing wariness about the burden which it implied. The line on which the first four verses ended – 'Lest we forget – lest we forget!' – were to have profound echoes in British history, later used to commemorate those who died in the service of the British Empire in the First World War.

Among the hundreds of thousands of spectators who thronged the streets that day was the fourteen-year-old Clement Attlee. Over the course of his career, as the man who granted independence to India, Burma and Ceylon, no Briton was to do more to bring that empire to a close. In later years, he would reflect on the scene of the Diamond Jubilee. On that June day, Clement and his seventeen-year-old brother, Tom, had been taken to see the parade by their aunt.[1] They were members of a social class for whom these celebrations represented much more than a public holiday. Two weeks later, on Friday, 5 July, they were in the presence of Her Imperial Majesty again at Windsor Castle, where they sang 'Auld Lang Syne' and 'God Save the Queen'. Tom nearly fainted in the heat and the excitement, as the queen reviewed the Public School Volunteer Corps, of which the boys' school, Haileybury College, was a leading participant. For a family like the Attlees, Victoria's empire was not only a source of pride but a world of potential opportunity and adventure. The display was natural to young Clement. Loyalty was instilled in him from his earliest years. Indeed, one of his first memories was the Golden Jubilee of 1887, ten years before. When just four years old, he had taken great pride in helping plant the Union Jack on the porch of the family home, Westcott, at 18 Portinscale Road in the village of Putney.[2]

Clement Richard Attlee was born in that home on 3 January 1883, to Henry and Ellen Attlee. He was the seventh child and fourth son in a family of eight. The eldest were two boys, Bernard and Robert, both of whom had long left home by the time Clement came to adolescence. They were followed by the three girls – Mary, Dorothy, and Margaret (Mig), who acted as the glue between the older and younger boys. Of the three youngest, there was Thomas (born in 1880), then Clement (1883), and the youngest child Laurence (1884). These last three remained particularly close, as there was an eight-year gap between Thomas and Mig. Though he was not quite the youngest, Clement (or 'Clem') was certainly the smallest, and all his brothers outgrew him.[3] It was a happy childhood. Between brothers and sisters, and children and parents, there was immense and lasting affection. Clement was raised with great 'reverence for my seniors' in a 'happy and united' atmosphere, in a 'typical family of the professional middle class . . . of Victorian England'.[4]

The Attlee name was long established in Surrey: the family traced it back to the Domesday Book and believed that it may have derived from a John de la Leigh, who was granted a property in Effingham in Surrey after the Norman Conquest of 1066. An alternative version of family history suggested a connection to Sir Richard Attlee (a reputed friend of Robin Hood).[5] Either way, what was beyond doubt was that the Attlees had attained a small but significant fortune for themselves over previous generations, primarily through corn mills and brewing. Their social status was secure. The Attlee children's paternal grandfather, Richard Attlee, had been to Westminster School and Cambridge University.

Henry Attlee, Richard's ninth child, was born in Dorking in 1841 and sent to a London solicitor to train at the age of sixteen. He became a highly successful and respected barrister, and, by the time his youngest boys were born, a senior partner at his co-owned firm, Druces & Attlee. After his marriage to Ellen Bravery of Wandsworth, the daughter of Thomas Simons Watson, secretary of the Art Union of London, they bought what became the family home in Putney. The birthplace of Thomas Cromwell and Edward Gibbon, Putney was, by the late Victorian era, a commuter town with regular trains to Charing Cross, which left Henry Attlee with a short walk along the Strand to his offices in Middle Temple.

The family home was a large villa with two storeys. There was a terrace at the back of the house with a bank down to a lawn, with paths, shrubs and a kitchen garden with fruit bushes and trees. This led onto a tennis court. As well as three domestic servants, the family employed a full-time gardener, Mr Gee, a 'good-natured fellow with that inexhaustible patience which the unwearying chatter of childhood demands'. From the garden, they could hear the roar of the London traffic in the distance, as horses and carriages moved along the cobbled streets.[6] On summer days, the children would wait excitedly for their father to return from central London. On first appearance, Henry Attlee appeared rather austere, with a long white beard, top hat, and dress suit. All his children, however, remembered him as warm, convivial and affectionate. On those occasions when he had won a case in court, he was known to chase them through the garden and leap through the flowerbeds. Recalling such scenes, Laurence, the youngest, described the childhood as 'a story almost too good to be true'.[7]

Just half an hour's walk away was the home where their mother had been raised, The Gables, and where the Attlee children spent much of their childhood. It was there, in a Queen Anne house on the edge of Wandsworth Common, where their maternal grandfather, Thomas Simons Watson, lived. It was the Watson side of the family who gave the Attlee children their taste for the arts. More than a hundred years older than the Attlees' newly-built modern suburban villa, The Gables had something of a bohemian air. It was set back from the road, hidden behind iron railings, with wisteria on the redbrick walls and a pebble path leading to a large and unruly garden. In the smoking room, their grandfather and Uncle Alick would read *The Times*, while the children browsed the overflowing bookcases, explored the cluttered attic or played Kriegspiel, a board game which was something between chess and risk.[8]

The smog and grime of central London seemed far away from this affluent, suburban lifestyle. Both family homes were surrounded by an abundance of green spaces. With fresh air and almost constant exercise, Clement grew stronger. In spring the children would cycle through Richmond Park and Kingston, all the way to Hampton Court. At Easter, they would watch the Oxford and Cambridge Boat Race on the Thames (cheering for Oxford, which the boys were all to attend, albeit at different colleges). Summer holidays were spent playing tennis or cricket, or on family visits to the seaside at Sheringham, Norfolk. In 1898, as Clement reached his late teens, Henry Attlee also bought a Huguenot country house, Comarques, in Thorpe-le-Soken in Essex, which had 200 acres of land. This became a meeting place for the siblings and the extended family once they had left home.

The Attlees did not wear their wealth ostentatiously, and were conscious of their privilege. They all took with them into their adult life a sense of citizenship and service to a broader community and those less fortunate than themselves. As committed Anglicans there was a strong tradition of 'good works' in the family. Henry Attlee was on the council of

St Bartholomew's Hospital in London and his wife Ellen also involved herself in charitable activity through the church. Bible study was part of the morning routine. The eldest son, Bernard, became a clergyman. The eldest daughter, Mary, went to South Africa as a missionary.[9] Though he knew his scripture, and appreciated the humanising role it played in society – and in the Labour movement – Clement was never much of a believer himself. He appreciated the 'ethics' of Christianity, but eschewed the 'mumbo jumbo' around it. In this respect, he differed from his siblings, who all kept up their church attendance into later life. Restless and impatient, he could never sit still long enough through a church service to think any more deeply about religion. But in most other respects he inherited traits that were common to every Attlee child. From an early age, humility and tolerance were inculcated in them. This would serve Clement well in a long career in politics, where these traits were not always in abundance. Above all, as he put it in a telling phrase, 'We were not encouraged to have a good conceit of ourselves.'[10]

II

Politics had a place in the Attlee family home but was never a source of tribal identification. Most of the extended family, including Attlee's mother and the Watsons, were supporters of the Conservative Party. By contrast, Richard Attlee was a supporter of the Liberal Party of William Gladstone. At one stage, he appears to have considered running for Parliament but he was not particularly politically active. Henry Attlee's liberalism was relatively mainstream, though one of his friends was Joseph Sturge, the Radical MP for Birmingham; and another of his uncles once professed to have been a supporter of the Chartists. On the defining issue in British politics in the decade of Clement's birth – William Gladstone's decision to support Home Rule for Ireland, which had split the Liberal Party – Henry Attlee had sided with the party leader. Clement remembered hearing the issue discussed at length in the house. While Ellen preferred them to avoid political debates in the home, these were always good natured.[11] Richard Attlee would even set his children problem-solving political essays such as 'How to Govern Ireland?'[12]

Richard Attlee never tried to impose his Liberal convictions on his children, and most of them imbibed the Conservative instincts which were dominant in the extended family. Indeed, Clement appears to have been left, from an early age, with a disdain for the Liberal Party which he never shook. In particular, and here he differed from his father markedly, he developed a strong distaste for William Gladstone. For his supporters, Gladstone's advocacy of Home Rule for Ireland was a noble and foresighted act of statesmanship, which he had been willing to pursue even at the expense of destroying his party. For Attlee, Gladstone's behaviour – his willingness to impale his party on his own conscience – had been vainglorious, self-important and destructive. The more he read about Gladstone in later life, the more he disliked him. Attlee considered Gladstone's piety and religious faith to be symptoms of his vanity. After reading Philip Magnus's biography of Gladstone many years later, he concluded that he was a 'dreadful person' and hopeless leader. He seemed to have little idea of managing a Cabinet; and even less of dealing with Queen Victoria, who hated him. He had done little to alleviate the social conditions of the English working class, though, as a committed evangelical, he had expressed concern for the moral redemption of sex workers. 'Curious his complete blindness in relation to the social problem except prostitution,' Attlee was to write, pointedly.[13]

This distaste for Gladstone grew with age. Roy Jenkins, who wrote biographies of both men, thought that Attlee rather overdid this. 'Gladstone was not a dreadful person,' wrote Jenkins, even if he 'could be portentous and a little ridiculous, particularly when dealing with young women'. 'It was quite understandable that Attlee should take against this . . . but it was both a little narrow and carrying his laconic dismissiveness too far to build a general censure upon it.'[14] Whether or not Attlee was being unfair to Gladstone is secondary to the fact that he could not bear him. This irreverence and eye-rolling response to instances of moral posturing seem to have been ingrained in him from an early age. There was something in his character which meant that he had little tolerance for what he perceived to be faddism and the politics of martyrdom.

As the smallest and sickliest of the children – his younger brother, Laurence, soon outgrew him – Clement was home-schooled for longer than his siblings. Though the details are vague, family members believed that this was because a severe case of chickenpox left lingering doubts about his health.[15] That he was not socialised with peers from an early age may partly explain his shyness, a trait that he never lost, even after decades in the public eye. On the other hand, it is worth noting that Tom, his immediate senior, suffered even more from this. Moreover, the fact that Clement was the smallest of five brothers may also have contributed to the other side of his personality: a good-natured competitiveness and a desire to make his voice and his presence felt. In the family surroundings of Wescott or The Gables, he was one of the noisier siblings. His sister Mig recalled that he excelled at charades. Laurence and Tom also noted that he was a very good mimic, particularly when it came to politicians of the day.[16]

There were other advantages to home schooling. His mother was fluent in French and Italian, and her son became a competent linguist who managed to maintain both languages to a respectable level throughout his life. Later, as Labour leader, he once addressed a gathering of international socialists in Milan in a long speech, made without notes, in fluent Italian. The house had a well-stocked library, and the children were all familiar with the works of Walter Scott, Charles Dickens, Charlotte Brontë, Thomas Hardy and Jane Austen. Clement became a voracious reader, with a taste for adventure stories common to many boys of his age. A favourite was *The Arabian Nights*, also enjoyed by a young Churchill.[17] There was *Tom Brown's School Days* and *Boys' Own Paper*, as well as copies of *Punch* scattered around the house. In later years, when he was prime minister, he reread Rudyard Kipling's *Captains Courageous* – the story of a spoilt heir to a fortune forced to find hidden depths of character when he finds himself in a great storm at sea – and the adventure books of Robert Louis Stevenson, in particular 'The Merry Men'.[18] His friends described how he had a 'boyish zeal' for new designs of tanks and fighter planes, despite professing a general abhorrence of war.[19] Typically, his early heroes were swashbuckling men of action rather than of deep reflection and thought. Foremost among them was Giuseppe Garibaldi, the Italian general whose victories on the battlefield had united his country, and who died in 1882, the year before Attlee's birth.[20]

This appetite for adventure stood Attlee in good stead, and acted as a counterbalance to his shyness in unfamiliar company. He was certainly more outgoing than his elder brother Tom, whom he joined in 1892 at Northaw Place, a small prep school in Hertfordshire run by the Rev F. J. Hall, a friend of their father's. Tom, who was dreamy and melancholy, recalled how for many years to come his heart sank on seeing the ticket booth at King's Cross Station.[21] Clement's intrepidity meant he made friends more easily. It helped that he was marginally more athletic – or, at least, physically braver. He threw his little frame around the rugby pitch and was passionate about cricket, though he flitted around at the wicket like a butterfly and his bowling displayed neither force nor trickery.[22] Among his contemporaries was William Jowitt, who moved through the ranks of the legal profession, and eventually into the Labour Party, later serving as the Lord Chancellor in Attlee's government.

At Northaw, Clement read up to four books a week. Above all, however, he fell in love with poetry. As Tom, the more cerebral of the two, put it, poetry became their 'ruling passion'. The romantics – John Keats, Percy Shelley and William Blake – were Tom's favourites, all of whom were to make their mark on his younger brother too.[23] At first, it was the Poet Laureate Alfred Tennyson who reigned supreme in Clem's affections, and whose short memorable lines, and mythic tales, were suited to his tastes. 'How I recall the shock of his death in 1892,' he later wrote, on hearing of Tennyson's passing as a nine-year-old. Tennyson appeared as immortal as W. G. Grace, the great cricketer, or Queen Victoria. Other early favourites included Robert Browning and George Meredith. More than anyone, however, after the death of Tennyson, it was Rudyard Kipling who set the tone for his emergence into adulthood. Among the boys at school, Kipling was by far the most popular poet, a fact which, as Attlee put it, reflected 'the imperialism of the turn of the century'.[24]

III

Though his poem of that name had yet to be published, the idea of the 'White Man's Burden' which Kipling evoked would have been familiar to the Attlee boys as they entered their teenage years. In May 1896, at the age of thirteen, Clement moved on to Haileybury College in Hertfordshire, a larger school of 520 boys. Granted a royal charter in 1864, it had a long-standing connection with the East India Company, and one of its professed aims was to train its students to run the British Empire in India. The headmaster was Canon E. Lyttelton, who was later headmaster of Eton College.

It was sometimes said that Haileybury was 'more Etonian than Eton itself, though a bit cheaper'.[25]

Haileybury was a less intimate environment than Northaw, and required another process of firming up. With a shudder, Tom, who was bullied, recalled the windswept quad at the school (one of the largest of its kind), the draughty classrooms with ink-stained wooden desks and the dining hall with wood panelling engraved with the names of the first XV.[26] Clement watched, learned, and avoided the same traps. Indeed, unlike Tom, he imbibed the ethos. He became very fond of his school and was delighted to encounter Old Haileyburians throughout the rest of his life – usually in India, the army and the diplomatic service. He also embraced the military ethos of the school. He was a keen member of the Volunteer Rifle Corps, and would spend a week at the end of July at camp in Aldershot, drilling and practising his shooting.

As he reached adolescence in this basin of imperialist sentiment, Attlee became more interested in politics and more confident in his own convictions. One school report from his time at Haileybury described him as rather 'self-opinionated, so much so that he gives very scant consideration to the views of other people'. His younger brother Laurence confirmed the picture. 'He was really quite an argumentative boy, and most of all he liked to argue about politics. Not so much about politics, but the personalities. He could be very cutting about them, and very funny.'[27] Clement did not open himself up to any form of sentimentality. At school, having escaped the watchful eye of his mother, he grew further disenchanted with church attendance and religious observance and became, without ever uttering the word, an atheist.

Thus Haileybury encouraged a certain worldview, which chimed perfectly with the events of the Diamond Jubilee. While the certainties of the Victorian era were being steadily undercut, this was not immediately apparent to the boys at Haileybury. Tom's diaries recorded the main political events of the time and the things that the boys at Haileybury discussed. Only in hindsight could he piece together the fragments of a changing world. In 1898, a year after the Jubilee, William Gladstone, the great titan of late Victorian liberalism, died. The same year, the British government agreed a loan with the Chinese government for the development of Chinese railways, hoping to offset expanding Russian influence in the Far East; and the

Dreyfus affair unfolded in France, as the novelist Émile Zola protested against anti-Semitism and corruption in the French army. Germany also emerged as a power on the world stage. The boys at Haileybury celebrated British victories in Egypt, and did not perceive the threats that were emerging to the British Empire. They were almost unanimous in their fondness for Kipling's verses but did not yet detect the sense of foreboding contained therein.[28]

Clement later recalled being thrilled as a schoolboy by the sight of large portions of the classroom map coloured in pink, to mark them out as part of Victoria's dominions. 'It was an intoxicating vision for a small boy, for, as we understood it, all these people were ruled for their own good by strong silent men, civil servants and soldiers as portrayed by Kipling.'[29] In 1900, as he entered his final year at Haileybury, he was caught up in the jingoism and surge of patriotic feeling surrounding the Boer War. In February, British troops won famous victories at Pieter's Hill and Hart's Hill, as part of the Battle of Tugela Heights. The Boer forces withdrew and on 1 March, Lord Dundonald marched into Ladysmith, relieving the siege on the town. Alongside him walked Winston Churchill, a recently decommissioned soldier and now a war correspondent for the *Morning Post*. Attlee joined his fellow schoolboys in a protest against the headmaster, Edward Lyttelton, for his failure to grant a public holiday in celebration of the victory. They marched down to the neighbouring market town of Hertford and 'indulged in a patriotic celebration'. Clement was one of the seventy-two caned that evening. As an older boy, he was made an example of. He muttered resentfully that Lyttelton must have Boer sympathies.[30] The same night Tom enjoyed a boozy night in Oxford, and even mixed his fists with some local 'riff raff'. It was also during the war that Clement Attlee earned his first income – a shilling a day for acting as a superintendent at a fortnight-long summer camp of the Rifle Corps, who drilled in the hope, rather than expectation, that they would be called to war. Predictably, he won the prize for best-kept tent.[31]

IV

On the very same day that Pieter's Hill and Hart's Hill fell, 27 February 1900, a meeting was held at Memorial Hall in Farringdon in Clerkenwell, where the Labour Party was formed. Following a resolution from the

Scottish socialist Keir Hardie, the father of the movement, the assembled delegates agreed to support 'a distinct Labour group in Parliament, who shall have their own whips, and agree upon their policy, which must embrace a readiness to cooperate with any party which for the time being may be engaged in promoting legislation in the direct interests of labour.'[32]

The formation of the Labour Party made no mark at all on the world of young Clement Attlee. He presumed, in the words of Gilbert and Sullivan,

> That every boy and every gal
> That's born into the world alive
> Is either a little Liberal
> Or else a little Conservative![33]

Events in faraway places were of much greater interest to him than cloth-cap gatherings just ten miles from his family home. Haileybury had hardened what were essentially Conservative – and most decidedly imperialist – political convictions. He was aware that such a thing as socialism existed but did not think it worth much consideration. As for the plight of the poor in England, he showed no sign of empathy; quite the contrary. One of his earliest poems, which appeared in the Haileybury magazine in 1899, was a strongly worded attack on the London cabbies who were striking at the time. Before long, he predicted, these upstarts would be forced to beg for their fares.[34]

Clement followed Tom, once again, to Oxford in the autumn of 1901. His academic record was good, if not consistently first class, and he chose to study Modern History. Robert, the eldest, had been to Oriel, Bernard to Merton, and Tom was about to enter his final year at Corpus Christi. Clement was sent to University College, and the Haileybury mentality went with him. He roomed with two friends from school and also spent much time with his brothers. In addition to Tom, who had finally found his confidence, Bernard, who had entered the Church, had been given a parish at Wolvercote, on the outskirts of the city. The brothers relished the freedom at Oxford, which contrasted to their regimented existence at Haileybury. They were given a generous stipend by their father and embraced the university lifestyle – rowing, reading and socialising. 'Your time at Oxford was your own,' said Tom, 'and you did not waste a bit of it.' In welcome contrast to the windswept Haileybury quad, he recalled the small, opaque windows of the libraries, the smell of breakfast drifting across the quad and of dusty books in the Bodleian.[35]

Similar to Haileybury, the Oxford of 1901–4 gave little clue to the rapidly changing world outside. Only an occasional motor car would pass through. Though Attlee arrived the year that Queen Victoria passed away, the city was strangely cocooned from the certainties that died with her. 'The Victorian Age had only just ended and there was little apprehension of the troubles that lay ahead when the civilization enshrined in Oxford was to be assailed by the barbarians – Hitler and Stalin,' he later reflected.[36]

While Attlee was a capable student, his studies never gained his undivided attention. Some tutors suggested he could have achieved a first-class degree, but he found himself dreaming and reading around the history syllabus. A reference written for him by one of his Oxford tutors described him as a 'level-headed, industrious, dependable man with no brilliance of style . . . but with excellent sound judgement'.[37] 'Solid worker always capable of covering the necessary quote,' read another.[38] While he did not better the second-class degree that Tom also attained, Clement did later reflect that, if he had not had a life in politics, he would have liked to have been a don. The study of history was to become more important to him later in life. His sister Mary believed that his knowledge of the subject was 'of the greatest help to him, for not only has it provided him with a sound understanding of the causes of tendencies in modern society, but it is a subject which gives every intelligent student of it perspective and a sense of balance.'[39]

At Oxford, Attlee specialised in Italian and Renaissance history and confessed a liking for 'ruthless strongmen'. This was something that later experience, not least the rise of Benito Mussolini in Italy, saw him repudiate. For the moment, however, it reinforced his belief that Liberals were 'waffling unrealistic have-nots who did not understand the basic facts of life'.[40] It is ironic that Attlee became the first Oxford graduate to be elected as a Labour Party MP, because the university did little to spark any serious interest in politics. While there were a number of prominent Liberal intellectuals at the university, the overriding ethos was Conservative. Attlee, who later recalled one of his tutors for the Italian Renaissance turning up for a supervision in full hunting gear, abided by the status quo.[41] He saw no need to challenge the existing system. He never spoke at the Oxford Union, though he did engage in one debate in his college debating society, on the question of imperial protection. This idea, recently championed by Joseph Chamberlain, was to forge the British Empire into a self-sustaining economic unit, protected by high duties on goods imported from outside. This was a controversial break from Victorian liberal free-market orthodoxy. Attlee never much understood economics. It was a matter of instinct that saw him take the side of the protectionists against a fellow student, Basil Blackett, who was later to become a director of the Bank of England. He confessed that his Conservative stance on most issues was not based on deep reflection. When confronted with liberals or radicals, he found himself adopting 'a rather common poise of cynicism'.[42] It had not crossed his mind to question the order or structure of society. 'The capitalist system was as unquestioned as the social system. It was just there. It was not known under that name because one does not give a name to something of which one is unconscious.' When speaking to the Cambridge University Labour Club many years later, he put it this way: 'In my day we were extraordinarily backward. I was a very backward boy myself – we knew nothing about socialism.'[43] He remained, at this stage of life, a 'good old fashioned imperialist conservative'.[44]

As he reached adulthood, there was not much that was inquisitive or curious about this young man. While he was not unappreciative of the privilege to which he had been born, it seemed to have left him without much imagination about the world around him. As a follower rather than a seeker, the natural thing seemed to pursue the path in life expected of him. When he graduated in 1904, he followed his father's footsteps into the legal profession, without ever expressing much interest, or any great passion for the subject. His early adventurism seemed somewhat repressed. While he dreamed of doing 'impossibly brilliant things', he had little idea of what these might be.[45]

In the autumn of 1904 he entered the Lincoln's Inn chambers of Sir Philip Gregory, a leading conveyancer. Through his father's connections, he had already dined at Inner Temple and had every advantage to flourish in this world. He was shortlisted for a position at the Charity Commission but was regarded as too inexperienced, so he spent the next months in his father's office, as he studied for his Bar examinations. He also worked under Theobald Matthew, a famous Common Law barrister and celebrated wit. In Matthew's chambers, he came to know Lord Robert Cecil, the third son of the Conservative prime minister, the Marquis of Salisbury, and Malcolm Macnaghten, an austerely evangelical Ulster Protestant who became a High Court judge. Attlee observed these characters with affection and admiration but he exhibited no particular drive to join their ranks. He followed their political debates – arguments over Ireland continued after Gladstone's death – but this did not seem to trigger his passions any more. His shyness kept him out of their disputes. On Macnaghten's prompting, he confessed that he was 'quite impartial' on religious questions. After his pupillage, he moved to different chambers, but was coming to the conclusion that he was 'not really much interested in the law and had no ambition to succeed'.[46]

It could be said that Haileybury and Oxford had produced a well-qualified and privileged drifter, content with his lot in life but rather diffident in his approach to it. This was not helped, perhaps, by Henry Attlee's generosity to his children – providing them with every opportunity but perhaps too generous a stipend to instil the fear of failure. Clement was eventually called to the Bar by the Inner Temple in March 1906 and was well placed for a legal career. That year, however, he was to undergo a personal political revolution that took him on a very different path.

V

As the story begins to turn to Attlee's conversion to socialism after 1905, it would be easy to assume that he left this world of Rudyard Kipling and the Haileybury Rifle Corps behind. Yet one of the most important things to understand about Attlee's personal revolution was that it did not entail a rupture with the world in which he had been raised for the previous twenty-three years. It was not that he repudiated all that he had been shown and taught to date; it was that he came to reinterpret its meaning.

When Attlee gave the Chichele Lectures at Oxford in May 1960, sixty years after he had arrived there as an undergraduate, he cast his mind back to the Diamond Jubilee of 1897. He remembered seeing Victoria and the retinue of kings and queens behind her, followed by the contingent of troops, 'black men, brown men, yellow men, white men from all parts of the far flung empire, from every continent'. He recalled returning in the evening to Putney and seeing bonfires blazing across the heath. 'It was a memorable day. It marked the highest point of imperialism.'[47] For a four-teen-year-old boy, this was an exciting spectacle. It was only years later that he came to view the event as a 'turning point in world history'. The Diamond Jubilee had been a 'triumphant exhibition of materialism and colonialism'. But 'just about when those two movements had reached their peak, there began the process of falling away.'[48]

It was as he looked back at the Diamond Jubilee that Attlee also began to recognise the cautionary subtext in Kipling's 'Recessional'. 'Most of us boys at that time were imperialists with an immense pride in the achievements of our race. It was curious that the one warning note against our overweening pride should have been struck by the chief popularizer of imperialism, Rudyard Kipling, in his "Recessional".'[49] The poem was not an uncritical celebration of British superiority but a warning that empire begat great responsibility. Ultimately, one would 'reap what one had sown'.

It may well be that Attlee came to appreciate the deeper message embedded in Kipling's poem through his reading of the novelist and socialist, H. G. Wells, eighteen years his senior, whom he first heard speak in 1906. 'The prevailing force in my undergraduate days was not Socialism but Kiplingism,' Wells wrote in his 1911 novel The New Machiavelli, 'we were all, you must understand, very distinctly Imperialists also, and professed a vivid sense of the "White Man's Burden".' He 'coloured the very idiom of our conversation'. As Wells observed, Kipling had been 'so mercilessly and exhaustively mocked, criticized and torn to shreds' that this deeper message had been forgotten.[50] Writing to Tom in 1949, shortly after Indian independence, Attlee also bemoaned the 'modern denigration' of Kipling's work 'without appreciation of the period in which the subject lived'.[51] A few lone voices on the left understood that it was one thing to reject Kipling's imperialism, but quite another to fail to appreciate the power of his patriotism. Thus George Orwell also wrote that, for all Kipling's flaws, 'Recessional' survived the sniggers of those in 'pansy-left circles'.[52]

Closer to home was the influence of his father Henry. Clement never shared his father's Liberal convictions, and certainly not his admiration for William Gladstone. Yet his father's voice, and his obvious decency, made itself felt in different ways. Writing to Tom shortly after his Chichele lectures, he remembered how a frown had come across Henry Attlee's face when he had read the story of the Jameson Raid in The Times at the breakfast table.

This tragi-comical incident, over Christmas 1895, left an ugly legacy which was to be one of the causes of the Anglo-Boer War that began in 1899. The raid was the idea of Leander Starr Jameson, the Scottish-born colonial administrator and friend of Britain's most notorious imperialist in southern Africa, Cecil Rhodes. Jameson's plan was to spark an uprising of British expatriates in the Boer-controlled Transvaal Republic, by making an incursion using a band of mercenaries. The Transvaal Republic had won independence from the British in the 1850s but Jameson had his eyes on the gold reserves which had recently been discovered there.[53]

For the Attlee boys, the intrepid Jameson was a hero; for their Liberal father, his behaviour was to be condemned. For one, it was a naked and thinly disguised act of rapaciousness. For another, it was plainly illegal. What Attlee inherited from his father was the sense that the British Empire 'was an extension of Britain' herself. British behaviour in the south of Africa became even more controversial during the Second Boer War, from 1899 to 1902. Those who opposed the war, such as Henry Attlee, believed the good name of the country was being besmirched by the actions of a 'rather unsavoury cosmopolitan clique of financiers in Johannesburg', who were falsely claiming to act in the interests of the empire. How could the British criticise the actions of other colonial powers in the 'scramble for Africa' – such as Belgium, Germany and France – when it acted in ways that were just as ignoble?[54]

If Attlee saw the Diamond Jubilee as a turning point of history, he also came to view the Anglo-Boer War of 1899–1902 as the beginning of the end for the British Empire. The British 'revolt against imperialism' began with the acrimony and self-examination which that war prompted.[55] In his final year at Haileybury, Attlee had condemned his headmaster for being too pro-Boer. Over time, he came to appreciate that the unease of Edward Lyttellton was the same as that of his father. If the dubious premise on which it was fought was not enough, the conduct of the war itself further undermined faith in the empire. First there was a series of scandals about the conduct of British troops. This was a conflict in which Britain had introduced the first mass internment camps. Meanwhile, the physical condition of British troops caused some hand wringing too. Drawn from the working class, British soldiers had been sickly and malnourished compared to their Boer opponents. As H. G. Wells described, boasts about the superiority of British civilisation and the Anglo-Saxon race suddenly looked rather unfounded. 'To advance upon your enemy singing about his lack of cleanliness and method went out of fashion altogether! The dirty regressive Boer vanished from our scheme of illusion.'[56] Furthermore, the British were increasingly dependent upon troops from the colonies to maintain the empire in contested places. As Attlee noted, there was even a volunteer ambulance section from India in South Africa. In one of the great ironies of British imperial history, it was raised and commanded by India's future nationalist leader, Gandhi.[57]

Many years later, Attlee would discuss the events with South Africa's future prime minister, Jan Christiaan Smuts, who had fought on the Boer side. While he had not understood what his father and headmaster did at the time, he understood that a gangrene had begun to infect the British Empire just at the moment when it seemed at its most powerful. Jingoism and greed had seen the British abandon the restraint which they had previously placed upon their imperial endeavours. As Attlee understood it, the imperial project had got out of control. 'Successive British governments, not excepting that of Disraeli right down to that of Lord Salisbury, were opposed to territorial expansion in Africa,' he wrote, 'whether the urge came from idealists who wished to bring to an end the exploitation of the Africans by Arab slave traders or from Cape-to-Cairo imperialist dreamers like Rhodes.' Joseph Chamberlain, the exponent of imperial protection whom he had defended at Oxford, was, Attlee later argued, the 'first statesman of the imperialist school'. The Jameson Raid was the clearest example of the unintended consequences of this new departure.[58] In 1960, when Elizabeth Pakenham, the niece of Joseph Chamberlain, published her history of the Jameson Raid, Attlee criticised it as an attempt to absolve her uncle of blame.[59]

The empire project had gone severely awry; it had lost its moral compass, it seemed to be retarding rather than encouraging the spread of civilised values. Ultimately, following the Boer War, it was increasingly difficult for a people who claimed to be democrats to behave in this manner. Not only did this type of imperialism run 'counter to the doctrine of democracy and equality'; it was also hard to maintain a 'false idea of superiority' on these terms.[60] 'The phrase "the White Man's burden" and the word "Shahib" epitomised this attitude,' he later wrote, distinguishing between the true meaning of Kipling's verse and the lazy way in which it was used by others.[61]

Indira Gandhi, the future prime minister of India, later observed that Attlee embodied the 'non-imperial face' of Britain, 'a reassuring counterweight to the haughty men of the Raj in India. I came to appreciate the Understatement which characterises the best in Britain and of which Lord Attlee was a good example.'[62] Yet this should not blind us to the fact that Attlee's own relationship with the British Empire began with a firm emotional attachment to the imperial ideal.

To the end of his life, Attlee maintained that there were two sides to colonialism. He explained this idea in a little-known article he wrote for the *Spectator* in 1956, shortly after he had resigned the leadership of the Labour Party. The article was a review of two recent biographies. One was of Cecil Rhodes, the man who embodied Victorian high imperialism more than any other. The other was of Frederick Lugard, 1st Baron Lugard, a distinguished soldier and colonial administrator who had fought in Afghanistan, Sudan and Burma and served as governor in both Hong Kong (1907–12) and modern-day Nigeria (1914–19). Attlee contrasted Lugard, 'the practical idealist inspired by the spirit of service to the African', with Cecil Rhodes, 'the dreamer of Empire, consumed with a lust for power'.

In abjuring Rhodes's vision, Attlee did not want Britain to forget or disparage men such as Lugard, or reject every aspect of their imperial past. 'To many people of the present day, colonialism is the evil exploitation of the darker races in the interests of the white people,' he wrote. That this was so was, in Attlee's view, largely due to the activities of Rhodes and his associates in the late Victorian era. He did not deny Rhodes his own form of idealism – a belief in a *pax Britannica* in Africa, inspired by the precedent ancient Rome. Ultimately, however, his ideals were sullied by his greed, and the greed of his cronies, and he became 'more and more ruthless as power corrupted'. The blame could not be laid at the door of individuals only. They grew out of a national sickness in the England of the 1890s 'with its vulgarity and money worship'. Vested interests had encouraged his reckless adventurism. Middle-class investors – readers of *The Times* in places like Putney – had gambled on his success through the Chartered Company, 'that curious Victorian device whereby governments sought to evade responsibility while furthering capitalist enterprises and imperialist expansion on the cheap'.

Lugard's life spoke to something else: a more honourable tradition of

British engagement with the rest of the world. In the first half of the nineteenth century, these energies were channelled towards Britain's role in the abolition of the slave trade. Later, the humanitarian impulse was redirected to missionary work. Africa offered a spectacle of 'heathen lands afar where black darkness brooded'. Middle-class Britain, families like the Attlees, had been inspired by the courage and devotion of men such as David Livingstone, the Scottish explorer and evangelical. In Attlee's view, Lugard carried on this tradition in the secular sphere with his support for the principle of gradual transition to self-government. Thus, he was 'one of the inspirers of that conception of trusteeship by the whites for the less-developed peoples which is now the accepted doctrine of colonial policy'. Lugard was not without his own flaws, and had made sure that he was well remunerated in the course of his career. Nonetheless, for his efforts to suppress slavery and his work in ameliorating the conditions of natives, Attlee described him as 'a man of immense moral and physical strength, able to hold his own against every physical obstacle and equally tenacious when having to deal with persons of high position at home, above all (and here is the contrast to Rhodes) scrupulous as to means and uncorrupted by power'. As Attlee wrote in 1956, Lugard had a long-term vision, 'not only trusteeship in the future but African self-government now in process of realisation'.[63]

No Briton did more to oversee the transition of the British Empire into a British Commonwealth than Attlee. Ultimately, however, Attlee's approach to the British Empire was never intended as a repudiation of its whole history. Rather, he wanted to rid the British nation of the stain of events like the Jameson Raid, and the stigma of racism and self-aggrandisement. He hoped, above all, to salvage something honourable from the morass. When it came to India, that meant making good on the promise of self-government that the British had always held out for some distant future. The unwritten contract had to be fulfilled.

Attlee remained a patriot throughout his life. But by patriotism he meant something quite distinct from the raw imperial pride or unthinking nationalism that he had felt as a young man. He believed that it was possible to have 'intense loyalty to . . . [one's] immediate surroundings' while also being loyal to the 'larger conceptions and interests of the human race'.[64] Kipling's 'Recessional' made Attlee's heart beat with pride in 1897, but when he returned to the poem in adulthood, it also set in motion something in his brain. He was not the only man of this generation to follow this course. In *The New Machiavelli*, Wells wrote that Kipling's verse had a strange and abiding influence on his conversion to socialism. Kipling 'helped to broaden my geographical sense immensely, he provided phrases for just that desire for discipline and devotion and organised effort the Socialism of our time failed to express.'[65] Through the Diamond Jubilee procession of 1897 and the Haileybury Rifle Corps, Attlee had ingested something similar: a desire for discipline, devotion and order. This informed his critique of empire; but it was also to shape his conception of socialism. In fact, one of Attlee's first poems in which he outlined his socialism was to borrow the form of Kipling's 'Recessional' but adapt it to the condition of the poor. Mischievously, he gave it the subtitle: 'with apologies to Rudyard Kipling'.[66] You could take the boy out of Haileybury; but you could not take Haileybury out of the boy.

3

News from Nowhere

When the hope of realizing a communal condition of life for all men arose, quite late in the nineteenth century, the power of the middle classes, the then tyrants of society, was so enormous and crushing, that to almost all men, even those who had . . . such hopes, it seemed a dream . . . Looking back now, we can see that the great motivating power of the change was a longing for freedom and equality, akin if you please to the unreasonable passion of the lover; a sickness of the heart that rejected with loathing the aimless solitary life of the well-to-do educated man of that time.

Old Hammond, in William Morris, *News from Nowhere*, 1890.[1]

I *Hammersmith, London, 2102.*

A weak, sharp-boned and choleric man, William Gaunt, wakes up in his home in Hammersmith in west London. As far as Gaunt can recall, he had gone to bed on a cold and dark winter's night in 1889. He begins to piece together the events of the previous evening in his mind. He remembers attending a meeting of the Socialist League in the early evening, taking a busy commuter train across a grimy and noisy city, walking across an ugly suspension bridge over the River Thames – its dirty water shining in the moonlight – letting himself into his cramped little apartment, and collapsing into bed, wrapping himself in the covers to bring some warmth to his weary bones. The following morning, however, William Gaunt can't quite shake the feeling of slumber and discombobulation. In the course of a fitful night's sleep, he sees he has kicked his bed sheets off. His apartment, which had been cold and damp when he went to sleep, feels unusually warm for winter. After splashing his face with water, dressing and gathering his wits, he opens the door and is taken aback by the sight of a shining sun and blue skies. The trees are lush with leaves and flowers are in bloom, as if it is a summer's day. It soon begins to dawn on him that the city in which he lives has been transformed. In fact, it does not look much like a city at all. Greenery and vegetation have sprouted up where concrete once stood. The dirty River Thames which he had walked past the previous evening now seems clear and clean, with people swimming in it or fishing for salmon.

What Gaunt does not yet know is that this is the year 2102 and the world, as he knows it, no longer exists. He begins a voyage of discovery into the heart of twenty-second-century London along the Thames. On the banks of the river, near Chiswick, Gaunt meets a cheery young boatman named Dick. Still confused by what he sees, he poses as a traveller eager to see the city, and Dick offers to be his guide. They board the boat and begin their journey down a crystal-clear River Thames. There are many fewer buildings than Gaunt remembers. As they weave their way along the river, they pass under an ornate bridge, as beautiful as the famous Ponte Vecchio of Florence.

At Westminster, they moor the boat and walk to the British Museum, where they meet Dick's 105-year-old uncle, a historian called 'old Hammond'. Hammond begins to tell Gaunt the story of London over the past two hundred years. England has become a communist society. Hammond speaks about the revolution of 1952, which culminated in a great battle between the government and the people in Trafalgar Square. The old historian explains that there were once Liberal and Conservative Parties, who shared power between them, but under whose collective misgovernment the old system began to creak. At first, in the early decades of the twentieth century, the ruling classes tried to reform the system by offering welfare and insurance to the poor. There was some attempt to apply 'practical' and 'state socialism' by ameliorating the conditions of the workers. Ultimately, however, as old Hammond explains, these efforts failed because they only ameliorated existing conditions, rather than rejecting the existing economic and political system at its very foundations. This was a familiar Marxist script. Capitalism was doomed to fail. Thus revolution eventually came in the middle of the century.

As Gaunt travels through the city, from west to east, he sees that Kensington is now covered in woodlands, and that the Houses of Parliament have been turned into a vegetable market, with pigs grazing freely at the fringes. Piccadilly, once the home of department stores and luxury goods, has nothing but a few quaint shops in which no money is exchanged. Trafalgar Square, the site of a bloody revolution a century and a half before, is flanked by modest houses with lush common gardens and orchards on all sides. London looks almost like a Kentish village. There are no trains or motor cars and the air is fresh and clear. There is an easy social harmony and no crime, no currency, and no government. The people seek pleasure, not profit from their work. Post-revolutionary England is a socialist utopia, two centuries and a world away from the 'modern Babylon' in which Gaunt fell asleep in 1889.

This is a tale told in William Morris's *News from Nowhere*, which was published in serial form in the *Commonweal* journal from early 1890.[2] Morris – the poet, socialist and world-famous textile worker – was, at that time, head of the Socialist League in London. William Gaunt, prematurely aged and sickly, was based on Morris himself. At the end of *News from Nowhere*, Gaunt wakes up, but he refuses to believe he had simply had a dream. What he had seen was a vision of a utopia for which the true socialist must strive. He would not wait until the year 2102. Morris believed this was possible within two or three generations, and that the socialist revolution might even occur as early as 1952. A lecture on William Morris had done nothing to capture Clement Attlee's imagination at Haileybury.[3] By 1945–51, as Attlee led the first majority socialist government, he had the ideas of William Morris emblazoned upon his mind.

II

Just fifteen years after *News from Nowhere* was published, Attlee began a journey from west to east London, which bears some comparison with the one taken by William Gaunt in 2102. In 1905, at the age of twenty-two, he was in his first year in chambers though still living at home with his family in Putney. One foggy evening in October 1905, he was met by his younger brother Laurence, who was twenty years old and about to enter the second year of his studies at Oxford. The two young men set off from Putney station, changed trains at Fenchurch Street, and travelled on to Stepney Green station in east London.

Within just a few steps of the station, they entered a very different world from that in which they had been raised. Putney and Stepney were connected by the same dirty river. In one of his early poems, Attlee described travelling along the 'weary waters sad and brown . . . Threading the close packed reaches of the town' as they headed towards 'squalid tenements of ill renown'.[4] This was the dark heart of the 'Outcast London' of the East End – densely populated by dockworkers, casual labourers and notorious for unemployment, poverty, crime and disease.[5] As the *Observer* put it in 1944, Attlee 'went Left by going east'.[6]

That evening the two Attlee boys headed towards the Haileybury Club, an institution founded by their old school, where working-class boys between the ages of fourteen and eighteen met under the supervision of Haileyburians. The idea to visit was Laurence's, and they made the journey largely out of a sense of duty to their old school. This would have seemed perfectly natural to the Attlee family, who were all engaged in 'good works' and had some experience of the slums of east London. The eldest son, Bernard, had taken on a curacy in nearby Haggerston, which had an associated boys' club. In summer, the children were invited to stay in the Attlees' holiday home in Essex. Two of his aunts ran a voluntary school at which Dorothy and Mig volunteered, and Tom Attlee had also recently begun volunteering at a Christian boys' club in nearby Hoxton.

Now the two youngest siblings made their way along the same path. On their first visit, Laurence and Clem met Cecil Nussey, an old Haileyburian and also an aspiring barrister. They learned that the club was connected to the Territorial Army and volunteers were expected to become non-commissioned officers. The boys represented 'D' Company of the 1st Cadet Battalion of the Queen's Regiment. They took part in drilling and wore military uniforms, with the assumption that this would encourage them to take pride in their appearance. There was a gym and a parade yard, and rifles stored for them to learn how to clean and load. Outside the club, these young lads had neither time nor opportunity for education. They were employed as cheap casual labour, mostly without the trade union representation available to those in the established manufacturing occupations in other areas of the country.

Clement was much impressed by what he saw. Within a few weeks, he had become a regular visitor to the club. On 13 March 1906, he took a commission in the Territorial Army and became a second lieutenant in the 1st Cadet Battalion. He threw himself into the local area and got to know the families of the young lads he trained. He invited his sister Mary to visit to teach the local children to sing, and brought teaspoons and forks to teach the older boys how to look after their younger siblings by chopping up their food.[7] By the spring of 1906 he was there almost every evening in the week, as well as refereeing football matches on Saturdays.

There was nothing revolutionary about the sense of social conscience that he felt. He taught the boys a Haileyburian version of self-discipline, whether through drilling and parade, or sport. In many ways, he was acting in a manner expected of a patriotic old Haileyburian. Yet the experience of 'outcast London' jarred with him in other ways. Attlee remained a patriot but his understanding of what patriotism meant was changing. Stories of imperial greatness seemed hollow in this new environment. In the heart of Queen Victoria's great empire were malnourished and orphaned children, forced into casual labour if they were lucky, often forced to steal in order to survive. At one level, this was a matter of simple humanity. Some personal stories resonated with him greatly. Many years later, when introducing the National Insurance provisions of 1946, Attlee referred back to a conversation he had had with a young girl in his early days at the Haileybury establishment. As he made his way back to the station, she had asked him where he was going, and he had replied that he was 'going home for tea'. In reply, she had said that she was going home 'to see if there was any tea'.

Yet this instinctive sympathy should not be confused with pity, for which he had little patience. The other emotion that Attlee felt, and arguably more strongly, was admiration. He was deeply impressed, above all, by the sense of fellowship and solidarity that he encountered in the children at the club, and the families of the area that he came to know. He was struck by the generosity he saw within working-class communities, where families rallied in support of others in times of hardship or unemployment. The issue was not one of character. The people he encountered 'were not poor through their lack of fine qualities'. Contrary to what he had heard, the slums were 'not filled with the dregs of society'. Social work was not the same thing as charity. Condescension was to be avoided at all costs. Recalling his experience in later years, Attlee described how 'the rather noisy crowd of boys on bicycles with long quiffs of hair turned over the peaks of their caps, whom he had always regarded as bounders, become human beings to him, and he appreciates their high spirits, and overlooks what he would formerly have called vulgarity.' In turn, those who encountered Attlee recognised in him a quality that they did not often see in the middle and upper classes: 'He came to us as a shy little man. He became our friend because he had lived with us and got to know our problems and because he had no swank.' What made a gentleman to these young lads? 'I reckon a gentleman is a bloke wot's the same to everybody.'[8]

Attlee's private papers contain fond reminiscences of taking the recruits out on parade. They describe a typical scene as one squad is dismissed and another is called out to parade. Fifteen boys put belts on and take carbines from the racks in the drill hall. For forty minutes Attlee barks orders at them, while watching their interactions closely. Young Blois, a thin lad with a mop of brown hair says, 'When I'm grown up I want to join the artillery.' 'What is Bloisy?' his friend Joe Beard jests, 'a sponge?' Another two boys, Badger and Treweek, come along and ask when they will graduate from the recruits. 'You're coming on all right,' Attlee tells them, promising to give them rifle training the following week. 'Coo, that's the stuff,' they reply. Another group of boys are put through their paces in the gymnasium, while one lad plays the bugle in the background. A little fair-haired boy called Albert Spain asks to see Attlee privately about his sister Lou, who spends all her time dressing up and does not help their mother in keeping the home. 'It ain't right,' says Albert, 'she wants 'er bottom smacking.' Attlee asks Miss Elliot, another volunteer, to pay a visit to the family home to see if they need any help. Meanwhile, down in the office, an animated discussion is going on between the boys and the club manager Mr Nussey. 'Is God a Jew?' asks one. Before Nussey can answer, another interjects that 'His dad was,' to which a third notes that his mother was a Roman Catholic.[9]

There was something about this independence of spirit, banter and unfiltered honesty that captivated the young barrister. He once described Stepney as a 'noisy, rather rough, and drunken environment'.[10] Yet he did not see his involvement at the Haileybury Club as some sort of sombre duty to be carried out with a long face and a heavy heart. Writing about social work in later years, he mocked the way in which such efforts were

presented as 'drab, dusty and uninspiring, with a touch of the patronising . . . about them'. The classic Victorian picture of charity contained, in
the foreground, 'a number of people in sad coloured garments with a par-
son or two among them sitting round a deal table in an aroma of soap and
water or disinfectant, obviously engaged in doing their duty towards their
neighbours, who are represented in the background by a shabby and ill-at-
ease group of mothers and children'.[11] For Attlee, thrown into this chaotic
but friendly world, nothing could be further from the truth. In March
1907, eighteen months after his first visit, Attlee replaced Nussey as the
resident manager, and moved to the East End to live in the club permanently.[12] The annual salary was a basic £50, though his father continued to
support him with a large allowance. While they approved of his efforts,
they believed he would return to a full-time professional career in due
course. Indeed, in his first year as manager, Attlee continued to travel to
the Bar in search of briefs.

For much of 1907, then, Britain's future prime minister could be seen,
before 8 a.m., making his way to Stepney Green station for the short journey to Charing Cross. He cut an incongruous figure in the slums – a
Dickensian creature, strolling along with his top hat, tailcoat and cane.[13] At
a distance, he appeared the very image of the purposeless middle-class
gentleman that William Morris described in the pages of the socialist journal, *Commonweal*, suffering from 'a sickness of the heart that rejected with
loathing the aimless solitary life of the well-to-do educated man of that
time'.[14] In truth, however, he had found a sense of mission. In his 1945 biography, Roy Jenkins described Attlee's experience in the East End as his
'road to Damascus'.[15] Yet, a lesser-known profile of him from the time got
closer to the truth. There was 'no ukase, no burning of books, no apoca-
lypse'. Instead, he 'matured into socialism'.[16]

III

It would be wrong to think of Attlee as a pioneer in this world. The last
quarter of the nineteenth century had seen growing attention paid to the
material and mental state of the urban poor. The Haileybury Club itself
followed the model of previous 'settlements' in the East End and elsewhere,
whereby the middle and upper classes would embed themselves in

poverty-stricken areas in order to alleviate and study its causes. In 1883, the year that Attlee was born, arrangements were being put in place for the foundation of Toynbee Hall, one of the most famous of all the early settlements, and an institution that Attlee would come to know well. It was named after the Oxford historian and social reformer Arnold Toynbee, who died that year. As well as being a devout Christian, Toynbee had been inspired by the Oxford historian T. H. Green, from whom he took an understanding of the importance of citizenship – the recognition of duties as well as rights – in creating the basis of a good society. Green's doctrine of 'personal service' defined Toynbee's activities. Added to this were the ideas of the educationalist, Matthew Arnold, who saw education as the basis of character, and character as the basis of successful living. These notions of citizenship and duty to a broader community were to influence Attlee's own early thinking, but he was to take them in a different direction.[17]

That British elites began to turn their attention to the condition of the working classes in this way was not simply a matter of moral concern. The timing of Toynbee Hall's foundation in 1884 was revealing for other reasons too. The Third Reform Act, passed that same year, expanded the franchise wider than ever before to include a large portion of the working classes. In many other European states, democratisation had seen the rise of socialist parties, who presented themselves as the true representatives of the working class. With a global economic depression, this put pressure on the existing social and political status quo. The prospect of radicalism or unrest in London was a particular area of concern. The capital was the fastest-growing city in the world and its politics were given a further jolt in the direction of democracy by the creation of the London County Council in 1889 (something that was to provide the launch pad for Attlee's career).

There was an undeniably patrician element to such activities. The assumption behind Toynbee Hall was that new urban communities lacked the sort of social leadership that pre-industrial societies had. Another elite-led organisation established in London in 1884 was the Fabian Society. While the Fabian Society was to become associated with socialism, it initially arose out of the Fellowship of the New Life. The founding objective of the Fellowship of the New Life was the 'cultivation of a perfect character in each all'. It emphasised the importance of setting an example to society of 'clean living' and some of its members advocated pacifism, vegetarianism, abstinence and teetotalism as the best way to salvation for the poor.

Toynbee Hall was run by Canon Samuel Barnett, a Church of England curate, and his wife Henrietta. Their work in the settlement movement was pioneering in that it questioned the worth of 'do goodery' and 'indiscriminate charity'. As Canon Barnett explained to *Time* magazine in January 1885, the settlement movement grew extremely quickly, and was in danger of becoming a national obsession. He warned that 'they who watch the new movement are not without fear lest in hurry or in reaction the possible good may be lost.' Barnett identified two dangers in particular: 'isolated action' and 'officialism'. London was full of societies promoting thrift, cleanliness, abstinence and good living. But too often such activities fell victim to moralising and unwanted interference in people's lives. As Barnett put it: 'Talk there must be; but it would be well if they, who at meetings and over dinner tables discuss the lives of the poor, felt their words to be pledged to be redeemed by acts. A little more silence about schemes, a little more respect for the sacredness of the home, even when the home is without the protection of a front door or servant, would be a symptom of the self-restraint without which there is no progress.'[18] These were concerns that Attlee intuitively shared. They may partly explain his disdain for William Gladstone's rescue work among the 'fallen women' who worked as prostitutes on the street.

While many of those involved in the settlement movement were Christians, socialist ideas also began to spread among a minority of them. As William Morris wrote in 1889 in *Commonweal*, the journal of the Christian Social Union, 'the signs of the spread of Socialism among the English-speaking peoples are both abundant and striking.' While he was a leading figure in the socialist movement, Morris was disdainful of many of those from the bourgeoisie who affected socialist sympathies at West End dinner parties. By the end of the 1880s, it seemed that a certain tincture of socialism, albeit 'generally very watery', was an almost necessary ingredient in most novels which aim to be 'serious and life-like'.[19]

One such novel was *In Darkest London*, written by Margaret Harkness and published in 1889. Harkness was not unsympathetic to the work of those in the settlement movement. Nonetheless, she raised concerns about whether it was making any difference in the area. Of Toynbee Hall, she asked, for example, 'why one sees so little result from so much effort'.

The story was told from the perspective of Captain Lobe, an earnest young evangelical Christian man, working for the Salvation Army. Walking through the 'hellish ghettos' of London with an 'S' on his lapel, Lobe visits the sweatshops, workhouses, alleyways, pubs and brothels of a city creaking under the pressure of massive overcrowding and immigration. Whitechapel Road is 'the most cosmopolitan place in London', and Harkness describes how: 'A grinning Hottentot elbows his way through a crowd of long-eyed Jewesses. An Algerian merchant walks arm-in-arm with a native of Calcutta. A little Italian plays pitch-and-toss with a small Russian. A Polish Jew enjoys sauer-kraut with a German Gentile.' Ultimately this is too much for Lobe to compute. He is a man of faith rather than intellect, who suffers from a nagging realisation that his own efforts, valiant as they are, can only scratch the surface.[20]

In Harkness's view, the poor were fed up waiting for divine intervention. The area was ripe for new political ideas. Thus Lobe encounters a group of anarchists near Bow and stops to hear them speak. In some countries anarchists made their point with dynamite; in England, it seemed, they were 'amiable lunatics' who had little appetite for the fight. On another street corner at Aldgate, he and a friend come across a meeting of socialists talking about 'class oppression'.

In Darkest London provides a useful anatomy of the socialist scene in 1899, just a few years before Attlee's arrival into this world. First, there was the Social Democratic Federation led by Henry Hyndman, a follower of Karl Marx, who 'talks very big' but seemed to make little progress. The SDF had branches all over the country but no money and only a few hundred committed activists. Second was the Socialist League under William Morris, the 'grand old poet'. Morris was a man who called himself a 'stalwart Socialist' but who looked as if a 'breath would blow him into space'. Like William Gaunt, he had blue eyes and pink cheeks and looked 'like a David about to slay our present competitive system with a pebble and sling'. The third was the Fabian Society, under which umbrella the intellectuals huddled. In Harkness's view, they were 'well-meaning people, who listen to a lecture every fortnight, and when it is done tear the lecturer to bits and flap their little wings over his carcase'.

While these factions floundered and squabbled, Harkness was nonetheless convinced that a political transformation was on the horizon. Like William Morris, she acknowledged that the idea of socialism was 'in the air, it is touching everyone, and tingeing everything'. It was growing every day, 'both the sentiment *and* the economic theory'. Many who abhorred the name actually followed its precepts more closely than those who gloried in it. Alongside the three factions she described, she identified a fourth group which was beginning to emerge. This she described as 'an embryonic labour-party', which was spreading all over the United Kingdom, as the Chartist movement had in the 1830s and 1840s. With unerring accuracy, Harkness predicted that in just a few years time all the prominent socialists would go into this new party, 'leaving the scum to die a lingering death' in the Socialist League and the Social Democratic Federation.[21] Her words were prophetic, as the Labour Party was founded just a few months later.

One of the most powerful literary interventions on the question of poverty in the London slums was to come from an outsider. Published in 1903, *People of the Abyss* was a study of Whitechapel, written by the American writer Jack London, the bestselling author of *White Fang* and *The Call of the Wild*. London spent the summer of 1902 living among the poor of the area, staying in workhouses and sometimes sleeping on the streets of the 'unending slum' he saw before him.[22] Like Harkness, Jack London concluded that mere 'good works' were ultimately hopeless. 'These people who try to help! Their college settlements, missions, charities and what not, are failures,' he wrote. 'They have worked faithfully,' he was prepared to credit them, 'but beyond relieving an infinitesimal fraction of misery and collecting a certain amount of data which might otherwise have been more scientifically and less expensively collected, they have achieved nothing.' For this American observer, Britain was creating an underclass, a short and stunted people, 'a breed strikingly differentiated from their master's breed, a pavement folk, as it were, lacking stamina and strength.' The men were caricatures of what men should be and the women and children were pale and anaemic, 'with eyes ringed darkly, who stoop and slouch, and are early twisted out of all shapeliness and beauty'.

What made Jack London's interjection so powerful was the way in which he presented this crushing poverty as a national sickness – something that raised serious questions about the future of the British Empire. One scene that stuck in his mind was the coronation of King Edward VII on 9 August 1902, following the death of Queen Victoria. As middle-class families such as the Attlees cheered the procession along the Mall, most of the East Enders stayed clear of the West End and took the opportunity of a day off to get drunk. Only at the fringes of the celebrations did these two worlds meet, with truncheon-wielding police officers keeping the riff-raff back, or forcing the homeless to vacate the benches on which they slept.

Just as the Diamond Jubilee had been a cause for reflection on the future of the British Empire, the coronaton of Edward VII demonstrated the extent to which Britain was a divided nation. It seemed now that the boundary between matters of conscience and national survival was becoming blurred. Other nations, including the United States, were catching up with Britain in the industrial game. Whether in the factory or on the battlefield, the British citizens he came across were no match for those in the New World:

> Brutalised, degraded, and dull, the Ghetto folk will be unable to render efficient service to England in the world struggle for industrial supremacy which economists declare has already begun. Neither as workers nor as soldiers can they come up to the mark when England, in her need, calls upon them, her forgotten ones; and if England be flung out of the world's industrial orbit, they will perish like flies at the end of summer.[23]

What appeared as two parallel universes were, the outsider could see, inescapably intertwined.

Seen this way, the health of the working classes was now directly connected to the health of the empire. It was through this realisation that the issue of poverty began to impress itself upon patriots like Clement Attlee. During the early stages of the Anglo-Boer War, he had celebrated the victories on the battlefield. In the years between the Diamond Jubilee and the death of Queen Victoria, things had started to go sour. In the Boer War of 1899–1901, the poor physical condition of the working-class soldiers in the British Army had become not only a matter of national shame, but a question of national security. Now Parliament began to take notice more than ever before. The Committee on Physical Deterioration, set up in 1903, revealed that a significant portion of the army were malnourished, weak-boned, stunted and suffering from chronic health problems. In the same vein, Charles Booth's multi-volume *Inquiry into Life and Labour of the People in London* (1886–1903), showed that a third of the East End was below the poverty line, which he had devised as the minimum acceptable standard of living for body and soul. Joseph Rowntree's 1903 study of poverty in York confirmed that this was not just a problem confined to London or Lancashire.

It was at the boys' club at Haileybury that Attlee began his intellectual enquiry into the problem of poverty that confronted him in the East End. At 6 p.m., the club closed and the boys were asked to go out into the 'foggy muddy East London streets'. At this point, Attlee would return to the office for a cup of cocoa, often with Cecil Nussey, who still visited, or another volunteer. As the staff gradually melted away into the evening, heading back to their homes and their families, Attlee was left alone to read. In a note in his private papers, he recalled one such evening studying *Riches and Poverty*, a 1905 study by the Anglo-Italian statistician and economist Leo Chiozza Money.[24] This calculated that 89 per cent of private property was owned by less than a million people, while the remaining amount was distributed between almost forty million.[25] Attlee quickly came to the conclusion himself that the Poor Law system had failed its purpose miserably. Little had changed since the 1830s, when it distinguished between the 'deserving' and 'undeserving' poor, and forced its recipients to enter the cruel regime of the Victorian poor house. Social work could only go so far in alleviating this problem. As this was a national problem, it would need the attention of the state.

IV

It is a testament to the closeness of the Attlee family that Laurence had led his elder brother Clement to the Haileybury Club. Likewise, it was no surprise that Clement turned to his siblings again, as he tried to make sense of the world around him. The greatest influence upon him was his immediate senior Tom, whom he had followed to Northaw, Haileybury, and Oxford.

After his miserable years at Haileybury, Tom had found Oxford both liberating and exhilarating. In his last year at Corpus Christi he had begun to open his mind to new ideas. He established a reading and discussion group at Oxford, the Tenterden Club, which Clem would sometimes attend. It was as an aspiring architect that he developed a great fondness for the work of John Ruskin, the great Victorian art critic, writer and draughtsman. He began by reading Ruskin's *Lectures on Architecture and Painting* and his famous chapter on 'The Nature of Gothic' in *The Stones of Venice*. Ruskin, along with other 'Young England' writers such as Thomas Carlyle, despaired at the brutalising effects of the Industrial Revolution on the natural world, but also the stultifying effects of orthodox political economy. They believed that the cults of individualism and utilitarianism associated with a capitalist society diluted the higher qualities in mankind, such as fellowship and heroism.

Through his reading of Ruskin, Tom experienced 'an epiphany' and soon became a self-declared socialist. As he later explained of his conversion, 'arguments that linked Ugliness with the Condition of the People, and the system that was responsible for that condition, appealed with great force.' To this point, he had been a Conservative, like his other brothers. But while conservatism only seemed to promise the 'upholstery of a dingy servitude', socialism opened the door to 'sunlight and air'.[26]

It was through this door that Tom discovered the work of William Morris, who was Ruskin's great disciple. He soon became a devoted follower of the veteran socialist, who had died in 1896. He made a pilgrimage to Morris's home in the Cotswolds, Kelmscott Manor, just a few miles from Oxford. He read Morris's depiction of a socialist utopia in *News from Nowhere* with which this chapter started. He also read Morris's radical 1888 novel, *The Dream of John Ball*, a story about a leader of the Peasants' Revolt of 1381, famous for the line, 'When Adam delved and Eve span, who was then the gentleman?'

Tom had joined the Christian Social Union, founded in 1889 by Henry Scott Holland. While membership of the Union never reached beyond 6,000, its magazine *Commonwealth* had a wider influence. It was in *Commonwealth* that *News from Nowhere* had first been serialised. While Clem worked at the Haileybury Club, Tom volunteered in another boys' home in nearby Hoxton. It had been founded by F. D. Maurice, a professor of theology and one of the leading figures in the Christian Socialist movement. While Clem taught the boys how to clean a rifle, the Christian Socialists tended to lean towards pacificism. Nonetheless, Tom provided the texts through which his younger brother learned about the meaning of socialism. It was through the work of Ruskin and Morris, that he also 'entered the Socialist fold'.[27] He too 'began to understand their social gospel'.[28]

These influences remained with Attlee for the rest of his life. The language of Ruskin and Morris left a lasting imprint on his political lexicon. When Attlee spoke of 'commonwealth' and solidarity, of improving the lived environment through municipal reform in the 1920s, or the building of garden cities in the 1940s, he did so in a way that was directly influenced by their work. A number of the key figures in the twentieth-century Labour Party shared this heritage. When reading a Spanish history of the British Labour movement, he was amused and happy to see *News from Nowhere* appear as *Noticias de Ninguna*.[29] When he was prime minister many years later, Harold Laski, then Labour Party chairman, gave him a leather-bound volume which contained Ruskin's essay on Gothic architecture, and excerpts of Morris.[30] In Christmas 1949, he told Tom how he was reading a biography of Morris, given to him by Creech Jones, one of his Cabinet ministers.[31]

Yet this is not the whole story. While Ruskin and Morris formed the basis of Tom Attlee's socialism, they only get us so far in our understanding of Clem's worldview. The two men began in 2102, with William Gaunt's journey across London, as told in *News from Nowhere*. Starting from that point, however, they began to move in different directions. One reason for this was that Christian faith was not the answer for Clem. He understood the central importance of the Christian ethos to British socialism. He celebrated a creed that was 'inclusive rather than exclusive' and 'preached a socialism which owed far more to the Bible than Karl Marx ... a way of life rather than an economic dogma'.[32] But he believed that matters of conscience were just that and no more. Another difference was that there was a strongly aesthetic element to Tom's conversion to socialism. He devoted his life to architecture and the arts, and shared Morris's disgust at the way in which the Industrial Revolution had scarred the natural environment. Again, Clem could share some of these sentiments, but it was not something that he dwelt on for long. He was orientated to action rather than reflection. To that end, he sought alternative outlets for his energies.

In October 1907, with Tom at his side, he visited the headquarters of the Fabian Society in Clement's Inn, and became a member. From the outset, however, it was clear that Fabianism was not quite for him either. On the day he joined, he felt as if Edward Pease, the secretary, viewed him and Tom as if they were 'two beetles who had crept under the door'. He attended public Fabian meetings at Essex Hall, where great intellectuals would slug it out on the platform. There was Chiozza Money, reeling off statistics, and H. G. Wells with his 'little piping voice'. Looking up at George Bernard Shaw and Sidney Webb, he leaned over to Tom and asked, 'Do we have to grow a beard to join this show?' Part of him thought there was something remote and superior about these intellectuals. He found H. G. Wells 'unimpressive'.[33] In the case of George Bernard Shaw, he respected him as a playwright but not so much as a political thinker.[34] On his bookshelves, he kept the 'massive series' of works on poverty by Sidney Webb and his wife Beatrice Webb. These were 'much studied in earlier days' but he rarely turned to them again after 1918. He came to call the Fabian power couple the 'beauty and the beast'.[35] He followed Chiozza Money's career and noted his influence on Lloyd George and Winston Churchill.[36] Yet, although this was an extreme example of Fabian delinquency, Attlee watched with bemusement as Chiozza Money veered between various political parties and ended up as a sympathiser and apologist for Adolf Hitler and Benito Mussolini.[37]

There was something ponderous, pontifical and self-important about the intellectuals at the Fabian Society, which caused Attlee to look elsewhere. Just a few weeks later, Attlee tried a different tack, at the invitation of a fiery Welsh dockworker called Tommy Williams. It was in conversation with Williams that Attlee first declared himself, without much thought as to what this meant, to be a socialist. In response, Williams directed Attlee's attention to the Independent Labour Party (ILP), founded by the Scotsman Keir Hardie in 1885. Attlee immediately found Hardie's practical approach to achieving social reform, expressed in his book *From Serfdom to Socialism*, more appealing than utopianism or intellectualism.[38] Within a matter of months, this 'rather cynical young Tory had become a fervent socialist and a street-corner propagandist in the Independent Labour Party'. As Attlee was to put it many years later, this 'at least cured my shyness.'[39]

Tom, who grew one of the Fabian beards that his brother had mocked, joined the Wandsworth branch of the ILP, while Clem invested all his efforts in Stepney. He also joined the National Union of Clerks, in part so that he could get more knowledge of the workings of a trade union.[40] Along with the Fabians and the trade union movement, the ILP was one of the three main tributaries that flowed into the Labour Party. It had been created in 1900 as an umbrella group for socialist members in Parliament, and Hardie had become its first MP that year. The Labour Party was growing quickly in London and the Attlees came to know its leaders. One was Will Crooks, MP for Woolwich from 1903. Another was George Lansbury, originally from East Anglia, but an adopted son of the city – 'Lansbury of London', as Attlee called him – and another admirer of William Morris.[41]

Attlee came to know the pioneers of the Labour movement extremely well, and would later reminisce about these exciting times. He would stand with Crooks at the gates of the docks in Poplar and help collect money for Crooks's salary so he could afford to attend Parliament (before MPs were paid a working salary). In later years, Attlee often paid tribute to the 'humane' and deeply moral creed of the early leaders. What he admired about Crooks and Lansbury most, however, was their tolerance. Both were teetotallers, for example, but they appreciated the right of the working man to have a drink. They did not impose their own version of the good life on others. Crooks argued for a reduction in the number of pubs but did not want to ban them all. His message was informed by the mantra that 'an old woman can steer her old man past two but not past half a dozen.'[42] The same was the case with Lansbury, who opposed a ban on drinking in the Royal Parks during his time as Commissioner of Works in London. As he put it, he was animated by a 'desire always to chain down misery and set happiness free'. 'I love England,' he once said, 'and especially dear, ugly East London, more than I can say.'[43]

The Liberal Party landslide at the 1906 general election produced a government that paid more attention to the social question than any before it. The 'New Liberal' welfare reforms that followed were a source of encouragement to those in the social reform movement such as Attlee. At that time, the Labour Party's priority was not so much social reform but trade union rights. Those Labour MPs who did enter the Commons in 1906 gave their support to the Liberal government on the grounds that they promised to reverse the Taff Vale judgement of 1901, which had set the precedent that unions could be sued by employers for going on strike. Many were suspicious about the interference of the state in the life of the individual, and were particularly hostile to means testing on things such as the provision of school meals.[44] One of the Liberal government's innovations was to establish Care Committees, which were attached to local schools. These enlisted the help of volunteers to visit the homes of children who were deemed to be vulnerable, and speak to their parents or offer help. To these, both Tom and Clem pledged their support.

The broader Attlee family remained close, and the siblings would meet up regularly for meals, or to see exhibitions and sporting events. On 19 November 1908, they were bound closer together after the bearded frame of Henry Attlee was found slumped over his desk at work. He had died suddenly of a heart attack. Henry had left his family secure. Ellen and the children had a sizeable sum of £70,000 left to share between them. Though 'slumming it' in Stepney, Attlee continued to enjoy advantages that many others did not. In September 1907, he travelled to North America for the first time. He sailed to Boston and walked around Harvard University, before taking the train to New York and staying at the Murray Hill Hotel on 42nd Street in Manhattan. He walked around the Bowery and Wall Street and managed to get a fine view of the city and the skyscrapers from the newly completed Williamsburg Bridge. He then took a steamer up the Hudson through to Albany and Toronto, where he met his sister Mary and visited Niagara Falls.[45]

Following his father's death, he was also able to abandon his legal practice entirely and commit his activities full-time to the socialist cause in Stepney. 'I remember, on giving up practice at the bar, being congratulated by my friends in a poor district in much the same terms as would have been employed had I at last given up the drink,' he recalled.[46] All his intellectual energies were invested in the movement. In 1909 he secured the nomination as the ILP candidate in the Stepney borough election. Though he polled only sixty-nine votes, his political career had started. As the branch secretary, he was responsible for keeping levels of activism up. Despite his shyness, he would stand on street corners or outside the docks and try to recruit trade unionists to the cause.

From this local platform, Attlee began to acquaint himself with national politics. In April 1909 he and Tom attended the ILP Conference in Edinburgh. They met 'Uncle' Arthur Henderson, a key figure in the development of the party's national strategy, and other Labour stalwarts such as Mary Macarthur, a Labour pioneer born in Glasgow in 1880, who became General Secretary of the Women's Trade Union League – and whom he viewed with awe.[47]

Alongside Tom, he began to become more active in national campaigns. One such cause was the National Anti-Sweating League, which called for legislation to improve conditions in factories. On this he worked closely with J. J. Mallon, secretary of the National League to Establish a Minimum Wage and a future secretary of Toynbee Hall. He was particularly influenced by Margaret Bondfield, an undercover journalist, who posed as an assistant in a factory to expose the conditions of sweated labour. When Attlee was prime minister, Bondfield, who became the first female Cabinet minister as Minister of Labour in 1929–31, sent him her autobiography. As Attlee reflected nostalgically, it covered 'so much of our period'.[48]

The most important campaign that Attlee was involved in during these early years was the National Committee for the Breaking-up of the Poor Law. At the start of 1909, the Royal Commission on the Poor Law had split over how best to reform a system of welfare that was clearly out of date. The so-called *Majority Report*, agreed to by most members of the coalition, advocated important reforms to the existing system of the workhouses and put a burden of responsibility on local authorities. The *Minority Report*, supported by George Lansbury and Beatrice Webb, argued for a radical change in the concept of welfare. Responsibility for the poor must be assumed by central government, rather than palmed off on local authorities, they argued.

In the summer of 1909, Attlee was hired by the Webbs as a propagandist for the Minority cause. He was asked to organise lectures in order to make the group's findings known to the public, and win support for their proposals. 'What I think you need to make you a *first rate organiser*,' Beatrice Webb wrote to him, 'is rather more of the quality of "Push" and the habit of a rapid transaction of business.'[49] These words made their mark; they were repeated almost verbatim by Attlee in later years to describe his style when chairing Cabinet. 'She was a most persuasive talker,' he later recalled, 'and had the gift, invaluable in a propagandist, of implying that agreeing with her contentions was evidence of high intelligence in the hearer.'[50]

As for the *Minority Report*, Attlee believed that it was 'the seed from which later blossomed the welfare state'. More importantly, as 'one who enlisted under her banner', he later believed that the episode proved to the Webbs that they had put too much faith in persuading non-socialists of their views, and that the changes they desired would not come from the Liberal Party. And yet, the experience with the Webbs also underlined to Attlee the limits of the intellectualism inherent in the Fabian approach to politics. 'I do not think that she was really at ease with ordinary people,' he commented on Beatrice Webb, 'She was too much the intellectual and did not understand the thought processes of people with a different background from her own.' In particular, Attlee felt that she underestimated the extent to which 'a movement such as that of the British Labour Party is influenced by sentiment.'[51]

This emphasis on 'sentiment' was revealing. In essence, Attlee was describing the thing that drove him on in his early political career. Of course he understood the importance of knowledge and statistics, in the works of Chiozza Money, Charles Booth or the Webbs. Yet, equally, he confessed that he preferred more literary and 'less statistical' accounts of conditions in the slums. Two later favourites included Robert Tressell's famous 1914 novel *The Ragged-Trousered Philanthropists* and Patrick MacGill's *Children of the Dead End*, also published in the year that Britain went to war.[52]

By embedding himself in the East End, there was no danger of Attlee succumbing to Fabian aloofness. It was in his poetry that his raw sentimentalism was given full expression. 'Limehouse', written in 1912, spoke in emotive terms about the hunger, homeless children, infant mortality and broken homes which poverty created:

> In Limehouse, in Limehouse, before the break of day,
> I hear the feet of many men who go upon their way,
> Who wander through the City,
> The grey and cruel City,
> Through streets that have no pity
> The streets where men decay.

> In Limehouse, in Limehouse, by night as well as day,
> I hear the feet of children who go to work or play,
> Of children born of sorrow,
> The workers of tomorrow
> How shall they work tomorrow
> Who get no bread today?

> In Limehouse, in Limehouse, today and every day
> I see the weary mothers who sweat their souls away:
> Poor, tired mothers, trying

To hush the feeble crying
Of little babies dying
For want of bread today.

In Limehouse, in Limehouse, I'm dreaming of the day
When evil time shall perish and be driven clean away,
When father, child and mother
Shall live and love each other,
And brother help his brother
In happy work and play.[53]

In just a few years, Attlee had formed a great attachment to Limehouse, which remained with him for the rest of his life. At certain moments he felt it acutely: when stationed with his regiment in Lancashire in 1918; or when touring bombed-out homes as a member of the government during the Blitz. His fondness for the locale did not take away from the broader, national patriotism he had felt at the time of the Diamond Jubilee. Yet the conditions he saw caused him to examine the foundations of that feeling of national pride. To be uncritically proud of one's nation was not to truly love it. How could one celebrate the glory of the empire when, as Jack London had observed, Britain was losing a battle with poverty at the heart of the imperial metropole? It was in 1910, a decade after he had recited 'Recessional' that he wrote a parody called 'Stepney', which described the dispossessed and the poverty-stricken wandering the streets just a few miles to the east of Buckingham Palace.[54] In another poem, 'The English Flag', Kipling had asked 'And what should they know of England who only England know?' Having witnessed conditions in Stepney, Attlee now turned another Kipling verse on its head. 'What do they know of England who only the Empire know?'[55] The words were directed at his younger self.

V

Attlee's conversion to socialism had begun in 1906. Within a few years, however, it was in danger of giving way to frustration. When a vacancy emerged to be secretary at Toynbee Hall – the most famous of the east London missions – in August 1909, he was the obvious choice to fill the void.[56] It was a sign of his restlessness that he was only to hold the position until May 1910.

Toynbee's activities had evolved considerably since the 1880s. It provided office space for local civic institutions such as the Stepney Distress Committee. Industrial disputes between employers and workers' groups, such as the Tea Packers' Union, were mediated on its premises.[57] In 1903 Canon Barnett had sought to recruit a sub-warden in order to inject fresh thinking into the institution. He identified the 24-year-old William Beveridge, a recent graduate of Oxford, who was making his name writing about poverty and social provision for the *Morning Post*, and whose famous report of 1942 was to provide the basis for the Attlee government's welfare reforms. Beveridge was rather disheartened by what he saw at Toynbee in the early 1900s. He found the education committee, run by Oxford dons, 'appallingly learned' in its emphasis on subjects such as classical Greek, which had little interest for, or relevance to, the poor of east London. In Beveridge's view, the Christian emphasis on the improvement of character was misplaced. The problems of poverty and social dislocation had to be placed 'in a scientific way'. These were national problems, 'hindrances to the future of the state'.[58]

Asked to fill a similar role in 1909, it is no surprise that Attlee expressed similar concerns. Toynbee Hall was well intentioned in its activities, but he had come to the conclusion that the mission movement was going nowhere. He viewed the warden T. E. Harvey as 'a vague and amiable Liberal'.[59] As an ILP firebrand, he came to suspect that the trustees of Toynbee regarded him as a 'bit of a bolshie'.[60]

It was in 1910 – the year of two general elections, in February and December – that Attlee began to commit himself to national politics. After leaving Toynbee Hall in May, he and Tom volunteered to be on George Lansbury's campaign team, canvassing for the ILP candidate in Bromley-by-Bow in east London. Clem, now twenty-seven, wrote Lansbury's election song, to the tune of 'All the Nice Girls Love a Sailor'. When Lansbury won a seat in December 1910, Clem walked down the Bow Road to Mile End with a huge placard with the numbers of Lansbury's majority on it.[61] Lansbury was in Parliament as the Liberal government began to embark on another round of welfare legislation, with plans to bring in National Insurance, payment of MPs, and the development of Infant Welfare Centres.[62]

By this stage, east London was crackling with radicalism. The ILP was just one of a number of new groups seeking to assert themselves locally. Stepney had its own branch of the *meschuggena*, an anarchist group who became famous for the Houndsditch murders of 16 December 1910, when three City of London Police officers were shot dead after trying to prevent a burglary. It was the hunt for the killers that led to the notorious Siege of Sidney Street on 3 January 1911. Attlee watched from the crowd as the Home Secretary, Winston Churchill, sent in the army to root out the *meschuggena*.[63]

It is tempting to make a lot of this scene: aristocratic Churchill, hyped-up and enjoying the stage, ordering military manoeuvres in the streets of London, a stranger in this world with his top hat and cane; Attlee, adopted son of the local manor, who had learned of the commotion from a friend at the Haileybury Club, and strolled down to see it for himself. Yet this would be to stretch the point too far. Attlee still enjoyed certain privileges. He had the family home in Westcott to escape to and a secure income to rely on from his father's will. He continued to take relatively exotic holidays. There were walking tours in France and Belgium with Tom and Mig and a visit to Italy in the summer of 1911, where he took in Florence, Siena, Pisa and Lucca. Tom also ran a cooperative holiday for the Poplar Labour League in France which Clem joined, sharing in the cooking and housework.[64] Nonetheless, even among the anarchists and communists, Attlee gained respect for his stump work and presence in the constituency. 'In the old days rich folks would sometimes come down here giving us clothes and money but saying how sorry they felt for us,' recalled one prominent local Communist Party activist. 'But Clem was different. He came down here and he stayed. He worked with us and showed us how we could help ourselves. Nothing showy about Clem, same as there is about Winston, but he's genuine!'[65]

While the poverty of the East End and the reputation of men like Lansbury meant that the ILP had a naturally sympathetic audience, other ingredients complicated local politics. Stepney was also known for racial and religious tensions. Irish and Jews made up the greater portion of the non-English community. In 1903, the government had appointed a Royal Commission on Alien Immigration in response to requests from Major William Evans-Gordon, the Conservative MP in Stepney, and from local trade unions. Aliens Acts were passed in 1914 and 1919, which further inflamed tensions by trying to root out illegal immigrants, particularly Jewish refugees from Russia and Poland. At constituency meetings of the ILP, Attlee recalled being shouted at in Yiddish (of which he knew a few phrases). At one such event, in 1911, an orthodox Jew in a top hat, long black coat and long beard leapt onto the platform shouting and waving an umbrella – only for Attlee to shove him off and carry on speaking.[66] Much worse was to come with the invasion of Mosley's fascists and rival communist factions in the 1930s.

In some cases, socialist solidarity could trump these divisions. During the 1912 labour disputes, for example, Jewish tailors – protesting against the sweatshop owners – and Irish dockers raised money to support each other.[67] Attlee saw these efforts first hand, collecting food for the children of those striking. Despite moments of solidarity, tensions would still flare up.[68] Overcrowding and competition for housing and space only added to the problem. One Jewish resident described steering clear of Commercial Road on Sundays as there were so many Catholics that one might think he was in Ireland, Spain or Italy.[69] Within ethnic groups, there were clashes too. Irish Protestants and Irish Catholics were known to fight in the bars. That the Dutch Jewish community tended to be less orthodox than those from Russia and Poland was a source of friction, often leading to fist fights between them.[70]

Attlee believed that his experience in this ethnic tinderbox helped add another layer of realism to his political make-up. He drew upon these precedents when dealing with India, Ireland and Palestine as prime minister – though not always with the greatest success. While ethnic and religious divisions sometimes exasperated him, he was frequently reminded of their importance. As he later observed, it was believed for many years in Labour circles that racial and religious difficulties were fostered and encouraged by the privileged class for the purpose of dividing the workers, and as soon as the people were sufficiently enlightened, these divisions would evaporate. The history of Stepney did little to support this theory. 'Race, language, colour, religion and history are stubborn things that do not disappear with the waving of a Marxian wand.'[71]

Meanwhile, a strong sense of citizenship provided Attlee with a centre of gravity. In March 1911, after giving a series of ten lectures on trade unionism at Ruskin College in Oxford, he wrote an article for the Ruskin College magazine, which said much about the journey he had made over the previous decade. It took the form of an imaginary conversation between a master from a public school and a Labour man. In Attlee's dialogue, the public school man lauds the 'justice, good form, and fair play that you find in our public school boys, and above all, the power of taking responsibility'. Once the boys were taught how to look after themselves, there was nothing to stop them ruling great tracts of country in India or Egypt. The Labour man agrees that these boys had many advantages, but were not yet equipped with 'the necessary lantern "knowledge" to shew [sic] them the right path'. It seemed to him that the public schools, which were supposed to be training the future rulers of a vast empire, 'carefully avoid teaching the boys anything of citizenship'. Thus, it was regarded as a greater achievement for them to produce one county cricketer than one hundred local councillors.[72] Citizenship had to be about more than training for imperial service and sporting success.

By the same token, class conflict was anathema to Attlee's credo. He was commissioned by the government as an 'explainer' of Lloyd George's National Insurance Act of 1911 (which provided for limited health and unemployment insurance – funded by the state and compulsory contributions from employers and workers). This was the crowning achievement of New Liberalism, though Attlee saw it as a prelude to more concerted efforts. Liberalism was not enough. He believed that workers should not have to pay anything at all, given the challenges that they faced already. This did not prevent him from supporting gradual measures. Having crossed the street already, he was willing to do so again. Those who met him halfway were to be greeted warmly. Indeed, Attlee described how he 'admired the public spirit of the country notables, mostly Tories who had been bitterly opposed to the Act but who were most co-operative, once it had become law, in helping the work of information.'[73]

Such campaigns helped build one's profile, but they did not amount to a career in themselves. In January 1912, Attlee was finally granted a foot on the professional ladder when he was appointed as lecturer in a newly established Social Service Department at the London School of Economics. Sidney Webb secured Attlee the lectureship, though he was not an obvious candidate to explore the full intellectual parameters of socialism. He beat a young Cambridge economist, Hugh Dalton, to the post. Typically, Attlee believed that this was because he had more practical experience of social work; Dalton, a talented but famously vain man, attributed it to the fact that he had not yet qualified as a barrister. There was nothing else that Attlee had over him, so he thought. Dalton always believed that the moment would arrive when would overtake Attlee. As with many others who underestimated the incumbent, that moment never came.[74]

Tom, always more romantic and sentimental than his energetic activist brother, fell in love with Miss Kathleen Medley, a six-foot-tall classics graduate from Oxford who was entering the Fabian fold. Wanting to be closer to her – he was living in Putney at the time – he suggested to Clem that they rent a small flat in Brightlingsea Buildings in Limehouse in May 1912.[75] Kathleen, as a secretary of one of the government's Labour Exchanges, had political ambitions of her own. Engaged to Tom in May 1912, she continued to agitate for a position on the borough council in Poplar. Her campaign demanded a minimum wage for council employees, a 48-hour working week, improvements in housing, special courts to arbitrate on rental disputes, school meals and clinics, and better amenities such as lighting, baths and wash houses. She was elected on 1 November as the first and only woman on the council and one of only nine Labour members, all outweighed by a large Conservative majority. The family were now firmly embedded in local Labour politics. Will Crooks, the East End Labour MP, was at Tom and Kathleen's wedding, which took place on 6 May 1913. Attlee described with amusement how some of his snootier aunts were rather horrified to find themselves sitting beside Crooks and other Labour activists.[76]

Tom was fully formed. He was married and moved out to a larger flat nearby. Kathleen became pregnant. He was content lecturing and running an Oxford University Extension syllabus, and had no political ambition of his own. His 1914 essay, 'The Influence of Architecture on the Condition of the Worker', won him the Silver Medal of the Royal Institute of British Architects and reflected his devotion to Morris.[77]

Clem, thirty years old at the start of 1914, still had some developing to do. He shared some of Tom's literary tastes but was not an aesthete to the same extent. He had yet to find love and was lonely. While he had carved a niche for himself in London left-wing politics, there was no expectation of a revolution on the horizon. The flat that he had shared with Tom was taken over by two members of the Young Conservative League. They found prints of Marx and Engels which had been left behind. These were of no great interest to Clem, and were most likely Tom's.[78] 'The Red Flag' might be sung on the streets of Stepney, but it would not fly over Westminster any time soon. There had been nothing inevitable about his journey from Putney to Stepney, and nothing inevitable about the future. 'I was not a scientific person and was never attracted to Marxism,' he later reflected, 'I have never had much faith in the inevitability of socialism. I used to think in my youth: "What is the good of standing hours and hours at street corners if the whole thing is inevitable?" '[79]

4

The Soldier

If I should die, think only this of me:
   That there's some corner of a foreign field
That is for ever England. There shall be
   In that rich earth a richer dust concealed;
A dust whom England bore, shaped, made aware,
   Gave, once, her flowers to love, her ways to roam,
A body of England's, breathing English air,
   Washed by the rivers, blest by suns of home.

And think, this heart, all evil shed away,
   A pulse in the eternal mind, no less
      Gives somewhere back the thoughts by England given;
Her sights and sounds; dreams happy as her day;
   And laughter, learnt of friends; and gentleness,
      In hearts at peace, under an English heaven.

Rupert Brooke, 'The Soldier', 1914

I *Gallipoli, November 1915*

Just after 6 p.m., on Friday, 26 November 1915, the ominous dark clouds that had been forming over Gallipoli burst. Captain Attlee had been sitting in his sparsely covered dugout when the rain started. Within minutes, swirling winds and torrential rain had turned the sand on the beach into a dirty stew. As the makeshift roof started leaking at the edges, he piled his kit into a box, placed it in the driest spot he could find and went to the larger canvas awning at headquarters – which looked like a circus Big Top tent – where his fellow officers were huddling.[1] The lads in the kitchens at the back told him that the water had burst through and was up to their knees. Looking down at the ground, Captain Attlee watched as water quickly spread across the floor of the rest of the tent and soon it began to flow over his boots. It was no better here, he concluded. Leaving the tent, he could barely stand up against the torrent as he returned to his trench, where he found most of the dugout flooded and collapsed. He wrapped himself in what he could find, propped up the makeshift cover as best he could, and then hunkered down for the rest of the night.

Sleep was impossible in these conditions. The storm was relentless. It continued through the whole of the following day, unchanged through sunrise and sunset. Then, at around 2 a.m. on Sunday, 28 November, conditions deteriorated even further. The temperature dropped below freezing and flurries of snow began to fall. The 6th Gurkha Rifles, sitting in the trenches on a more exposed part of the hill, and still wearing their kit, bore the brunt. Over the course of Sunday prostrate bodies were carried, one by one, back down to headquarters with signs of frostbite and in a state of collapse. A fire was started and their commanding officer bustled round the tent, making sure the doctor got to all the men who had been most exposed.

Captain Attlee recognised the danger to his own company and took immediate action. To warm up his men, who stood shivering, he ordered them to run on the spot, and permitted them to make use of their rations of rum. He set them to digging new dugouts, issued fuel and petrol and got some fires going in old tins they had picked up on the beach. He then ordered a foot inspection and made all the men with sodden feet rub them with snow to make sure that the blood was circulating. With his fellow officers, Captains Lindley and Bayspoole, he requisitioned some old sandbags and made a sort of shelter about six by six feet in which the three spent the night. The Turkish army under Mustafa Kemal Atatürk, who had the beach surrounded, had also been exposed to the storm, but there was no retreat. The officers soon realised that they were on a more exposed part of the bay. As they lay down in their newly built trenches, Turkish bullets would occasionally go 'Plunk! Plunk!' into the shelter, just above their heads. They were too tired and cold to worry.[2] By the time the blizzard blew itself out on 30 November, the full damage of the storm was laid bare: 200 men had drowned on the shore and 5,000 were suffering from frost-bite, with some on sentry duty found frozen stiff, their rifles still wedged in their hands.[3]

II

Fifteen months earlier, in the first week of August 1914, Clement Attlee had been in very different surroundings. He had joined his brother Tom and his new wife Kathleen for a holiday in Seaton, a small seaside town in Devon. It was there that he learned that Britain had declared war on Germany. The international situation had been deteriorating rapidly since the assassination of Archduke Franz Ferdinand of Austria in Sarajevo on 28 June. This had set in motion a fateful chain of events during which Germany and Austria had declared war on Russia and France. On 4 August, following Germany's violation of the neutrality of Belgium, which Britain was treaty-bound to protect, Parliament voted to declare war on Germany. When looking back on the Diamond Jubilee of 1899, Attlee had only understood its significance in hindsight. It had taken a writer of Jack London's brilliance to portray the existence of two nations in Britain at the dawn of the Edwardian era in 1902. In 1914, however, there was no doubt in anyone's mind that the world was being transformed before their eyes. As Attlee later wrote, the start of the war 'marked the close of an epoch . . . The Victorian certainty in progress passed away and the secure position of Britain in the world was gravely shaken, as was the social system . . . Years of uncertainty lay ahead.'[4]

The onset of war was a particularly sad day for socialists across Europe. It exploded the dream that the solidarity of workers would bring an end to imperialist conflicts. As Attlee later reflected in unpublished private reflections, the idea behind the First Socialist International, founded in the 1860s, had been that 'differences of race, creed, history and habit of mind were minor matters which would shrivel up in the fire of the class struggle.' Nationalism was supposed to be a mere 'device of the capitalists to keep the workers divided'. Yet, when war came, the majority of socialists had found themselves, once again, volunteering in defence of their own countries. The Second International had been dissolved by 1916. The majority of socialists, Attlee included, chose their country first. They 'recognised not only solidarity with their fellow countrymen, but also the need for preserving intact the field on which they fought their particular battles.'[5] National survival became the first priority.

The same pattern could be seen across Europe. After much acrimony, a majority of the German Social Democratic Party, the largest socialist party in Europe, voted to support the Kaiser's war budget. The war split the British left too, beginning with the intellectuals. Of the Fabians, H. G. Wells supported the government's decision to go to war.[6] George Bernard Shaw railed against what he saw as British hypocrisy. Herbert Asquith's government claimed to be fighting a war for liberal democracy, while preserving its empire at all costs. Were the British really so different from the Germans they condemned for their militarism and expansionism, he asked?[7] Yet Shaw and many opponents of the war underestimated the strength of nationalist feelings in the country. For many, including Attlee, socialist solidarity and patriotism went hand in hand.

Another young socialist who was of a similar cast of mind was Rupert Brooke, a dashing young poet, and a leading member of the Fabian Society at Cambridge University, who volunteered in a flush of patriotic enthusiasm. His famous sonnet, 'The Soldier', was the fifth in a series of sonnets that were brought to the attention of Winston Churchill, the First Lord of the Admiralty in 1914. The war was a spur for Attlee to further develop his own poetic repertoire. Though not in the class of Rupert Brooke, poetry helped him weave his way through the complex range of emotions that the conflict produced: from fear of death to solidarity with his fellow soldiers, and a longing for home. As he was later to write, 'the issues presented by war are seldom as clear-cut as the theorists imagine.'[8]

The outbreak of the war presented a particular problem for the Labour Party. The fact that it had always been a coalition of so many disparate groups meant it was unprepared, and unable, to speak with one voice. In 1914, it had no agreed platform on foreign policy and its members were free to adopt their own positions. This created the conditions for what became an acrimonious split.[9] The party's founding father, Keir Hardie, was horrified at the collapse of international socialism and opposed the war. But the majority of the MPs who organised under the Labour Party banner decided to support the government, forcing the resignation of Hardie and another rising star in the movement, Ramsay MacDonald. Divisions opened up across the country. In east London, George Lansbury, a lifelong pacifist, backed Hardie. In doing so, he was followed by Tom Attlee, whose Christian socialism led him to the same conclusion. The oldest of the Attlee brothers, Bernard, enlisted as a military chaplain. Attlee met him in Alexandria in 1916 on his way to Mesopotamia.[10] The youngest, Laurence, with whom Clem had visited Stepney in 1905, also volunteered to join 'Kitchener's Army', named after Horatio Kitchener, the Secretary of State for War who had called for 100,000 volunteers. It was thus that the two youngest Attlee children, born into the self-confident world of late Victorian Britain, ended up on the blood-soaked beaches of Gallipoli.

Although his 'whole instincts as a socialist were against war', Attlee had no hesitation in enlisting. There were reasons why this would have seemed the most natural path for him to take. At Tom's Christian Socialist boys' club in Hoxton, there had been no corps or drilling. Since taking over from Cecil Nussey at the Haileybury Club, however, Clem had already spent almost ten years as a second lieutenant in the 1st Cadet Battalion of the Queen's London Regiment. He was a veteran of the Territorial Army. Many of the young boys he had trained were going to go to war.[11] How would it look if the man who drilled them decided that his conscience could not allow him to join them on the front line? The alternative was unconscionable. 'The outbreak of the war brought great heart-searchings in the ranks of the Labour and Socialist Movement, especially in the membership of the Independent Labour Party' he later explained, 'My brother Tom was a convinced conscientious objector and went to prison. I thought it my duty to fight.'[12]

In fact, Attlee went out of his way to serve. At thirty-one, he was already over the age limit for new recruits and was initially refused a commission. Still determined to enlist, he sought another avenue. First he drilled with the Inns of Court Regiment Officer Training Corps but no official commission came. Then he made a special request to a relative of one of his pupils at the London School of Economics who was commanding a battalion in Kitchener's Army. On the last Sunday of September 1914 he found a letter waiting for him, telling him that he had been commissioned as a lieutenant into the 5th Battalion of the 6th South Lancashire Regiment (which later became known as the Prince of Wales's Volunteers). He was to report to the garrison at Tidworth in Wiltshire, about eighty miles west of

London. There was 'plenty to do', as he soon found himself in temporary command of a company of seven officers and 250 men. The lads he commanded were 'excellent material' – from miners to errand boys – mostly from Wigan, Warrington and Liverpool.[13]

Over the course of the winter, the men trained in Tidworth, Winchester and Blackdown. On 8 February 1915, Attlee was appointed to captain, in charge of B Company.[14] The same month, Tom's first child with Kathleen, Christopher Attlee, was baptised at All Saints Church in Poplar, with a number of prominent pacifists in the congregation. Tom was already involved in the No-Conscription Fellowship and the Fellowship of Reconciliation, umbrella groups for those who were determined to resist enlistment on pacifist grounds. By the summer of 1915, however, as the war continued to escalate, they met with growing criticism, and sometimes violence, as protestors asked why the men on stage were not in uniform.

In Western Europe, the main theatre of the war, the trenches were already dug deep. A stalemate had developed by early 1915 between the Allies and the German and Austrian empires. Some of the bolder British strategists turned their thoughts to reinvigorating the war effort and breaking the stalemate by shifting the focus of the attack. An opportunity to do so was presented by the fact that the Ottoman Empire, allied to the Central Powers from October 1914, had blockaded the Dardanelles, the narrow strait that linked the Black Sea and the Aegean (through the Sea of Marmara). This prevented the British and French from supplying their allies in Russia, who were already suffering from German assaults. Following his embarrassment at Sidney Street in 1911, where he was widely deemed to have overreacted to the anarchist threat, Churchill had been moved out of the Home Office to the Admiralty. From this vantage point, he was well placed to exert a steering influence on British military strategy. Churchill now recommended an attack on the Ottomans to break the blockade and knock them out of the war. As well as relieving the Russians, it would have the added advantage of pre-empting any challenge to British interests in the Mediterranean and Middle East, where oil reserves and the Suez Canal were regarded as crucial.

While professing a horror of war, the truth was that Attlee had always been a keen student of military history. In the barracks he read Charles William Oman's three-volume history of the Peninsular War.[15] Initially, he expected to be sent to France, having been given large-scale maps of Western and Central Europe to study. In late spring of 1915, however, the men were issued with lighter, tropical kits. He realised then that his destination was either Gallipoli or the Middle East. On 13 June 1915, the 6th South Lancashire Regiment set sail from Avonmouth. On the voyage, they stopped in Malta, where there was time for fishing and some billiards (the one game for which Attlee had any real aptitude). From Malta, they travelled on to the huge British garrison at Alexandria. After extensive briefings they left Egypt in the last week of June. From there, they sailed into the Aegean, stopping at the island of Lemnos, where they spent two nights in the port of Mudros, sitting in a vineyard in heavy rain, and contemplating their fates.

At Gallipoli, the first phase of Churchill's campaign was already well underway. On 25 April 1915, the British and French had begun to land forces at Cape Helles, the southernmost tip of the Gallipoli peninsula, at the western end of the Dardanelles. The goal was to seize the forts guarding the approaches to Constantinople, the Turkish capital. The troops immediately came under heavy bombardment from German-made artillery, fired by a large Turkish defensive army, and were unable to move beyond their landing place on the beach. For a small strip of sand, it was a high cost to pay, with 2,000 men falling in the first assault. There were portents of other dangers. Two days earlier, Rupert Brooke, who was supposed to be part of the original landing party, died in a French military hospital moored off the Greek island of Skyros, after getting sepsis from a mosquito bite. As one of Attlee's fellow officers commented on the conditions, 'I don't think that anybody can stand this climate for very long . . . unless he has the inside of a rhino . . . It is not a health resort for the young.'[16]

It was at 6 p.m. on 1 July that Captain Attlee and his men set sail from Lemnos towards Cape Helles on two destroyers. Entering the bay, they transferred to the *River Clyde*, a bulky battleship which was being used as a makeshift pier from which the men could reach the shore. It was a treacherous manoeuvre, given that the surrounding hills were under the possession of General Mustafa Kemal Atatürk, the future president of Turkey.[17] They were greeted by a barrage of artillery and a hail of machine-gun fire.

Having unloaded their provisions on the shore, they secured enough of the beach, close to the cliff face, to keep themselves sheltered from the shelling, though they were vulnerable to lone Turkish snipers taking speculative shots from nearby hills or dunes. One Turk, who had jumped into a British trench, was swiftly stabbed in the guts with a bayonet. As Attlee's fellow officer, Captain Baxter, described in a letter to his mother shortly after the landing, 'John Turk' was an elusive creature. 'I have been in command of a bit of trench only 30 yards from him, when he used to amuse himself by bomb-throwing or attacking every second night or so, but I have not seen him. Such is modern war.' That having been said, there was a general feeling that the Turkish army was the most chivalrous fighting force in the conflict. Despite the fact that hospital ships were in range, they were not shelled. 'I expect you have noticed how charitable we all feel to Brother Turk. You see if he does use liquid fire or other such devices of the Middle Ages (he has not yet attempted gas) we put it all down to his German officers. He is . . . very sporting . . . far surpassing his "cultured" allies.'[18]

As the death of Rupert Brooke had indicated, if enemy bombardment was not enough, the natural environment contained its own perils. It soon became apparent that the troops faced another enemy, in the form of the weather. The heat was unbearable and brought legions of mosquitoes. There were also snakes, bats, grasshoppers and locusts of three to four inches.[19] Sitting alongside Attlee, Captain Baxter listed his complaints in order of seriousness, in a letter to his mother. First, the heat 'makes it more like hell than anywhere else I know as Kipling says', and from 10 a.m. to 5 p.m., 'one is absolutely prostrated'. Second were the millions of flies who hung like clouds above their heads. Third came the 'quenchless thirst'. Fourth, and of least irritation, were the evening's shells, which 'came shrieking overhead and sometime spray shrapnel about'. Among the list of requests were louse killer, Bovril, matches and waterproof sheets. There was also some annoyance that the French seemed to be living in comparative luxury and were better stocked. This was the first of many complaints against the generals in charge of the mission.[20]

Hemmed in on a narrow strip of sand, and under constant fear of attack, this made for an oppressive atmosphere. It was in his first three weeks at Gallipoli that Attlee wrote 'Stand To', which captured the grim conditions, and conveyed the first pangs of nostalgia for home:

From step and dug-out huddled figures creep
Yawning from dreams of England; bayonets gleam . . .
And rat-tat-tat, machine guns usher in
Another day of heat, and dust, and flies.[21]

Although boredom was a persistent feature of life at Gallipoli, Attlee was surrounded by like-minded men for whom poetry provided some light relief. Sitting beside him, Captain Baxter recited one of Kipling's more sardonic stanzas about the fragility of human life:

It's like a book, I think, this bloomin' world
Which you can read and care for just so long,
But presently you feel that you will die
Unless you get the page you're readin' done
An' turn another – likely not so good
But what you're after is to turn 'em all.[22]

By the end of July, predictably, disease had swept through the camp. Attlee fell ill with dysentery and collapsed. He was evacuated from Cape Helles, and it seemed his war might be over, as doctors suggested he should be sent back to England. At his insistence, however, he was taken to recover in a British military hospital in Malta, with a view to rejoining his men as soon as he was fit. Though he did not know it at the time, his timing was fortunate. As he lay on his hospital bed in Malta, he missed one of the major missions of the Gallipoli campaign. The Allies attempted to break the stalemate with an August offensive at Sari Bair, to take the ridge of land which lay above Anzac, the other landing spot on the peninsula. Three battalions of the Lancashire Regiment landed at Suvla Bay to open a second beachhead. It was there that Attlee's men had their first taste of battle, fighting alongside a battalion of Gurkhas.

As the attack began there was, as one of Attlee's fellow officers described, 'a Dickens of a noise', the 'flash of the warship guns and the bursting of the shells and an incessant crackle of rifle fire'.[23] Having captured a vital hill on the ridge, three battalions of Lancashires were isolated and overwhelmed, losing around 1,500 men and forty-one officers.[24] A few days later, from his trench, Captain Lindley could see the bodies of thousands of Turks and British soldiers – including countless numbers of Gurkhas and fighters from Australia and New Zealand – lying on the hillside in no-man's land, impossible to retrieve and therefore left to decompose.[25]

This was the end of any prospect that the Gallipoli venture would yield strategic success. Stranded on the shore, an uneasy stalemate followed, and boredom set in. At the end of August, news reached Gallipoli that Italy had joined the war against Germany, and they began to hope that their mission would be brought to a close.[26] But it was hard to know the real state of the campaign elsewhere. They received newspapers on the beach – *The Times, Daily Mirror, Morning Post* and even the satirical magazine *Punch* – but these were nearly three weeks out of date. There was a print passed around called the *Peninsula Press* but this only gave the barest facts.[27]

Churchill had already left the government in May, his plan in tatters. Of the 100,000 men now left on the peninsula, it was estimated that half were unfit for duty by the early autumn. For those stuck on the beach, there was a shortage of artillery support, and rifle barrels and bullets became worn out as winter approached. As the season changed and the wind picked up, waves started flooding dugouts on the shore. General Charles Monro visited Helles, Anzac and Suvla on 30 October, reporting back to Kitchener that the situation was dire. The troops held the merest fringe of the coastline, were exposed to artillery fire on the beach and effectively encircled.[28]

Stuck in these miserable conditions, with little hope of salvaging anything from the operation, irritation began to focus on the generals in charge of the mission. Among the volunteers of the Sixth Lancashire, there was also some feeling that they were looked down upon by professional soldiers. By early October, Baxter complained that they were sick of talk of 'wars of attrition'. Owing to 'the noted quiescence of that extraordinarily hibernacious creature – the British General' the men were none the wiser as to their next move.[29] With senior commanders occupying headquarters, officers slept in the trenches with the men, covering their faces with handkerchiefs and putting their hands in their pockets to avoid insect bites.[30]

III

In early November, by the time Attlee rejoined the regiment at their new location in Suvla Bay, the temperature had dropped considerably. Though this meant fewer flies, the mood was souring. Patience was fraying at the failures of the generals to do anything to lift the stalemate or, failing that, evacuate the beach. Attlee was there in time to see a barrage of Turkish shells on 5 November which, Baxter joked, was a happy reminder of Guy Fawkes Day.[31] As the military command continued to debate the merits of evacuation, the men did their best to keep their spirits up with humour, often at the expense of the growing number of generals who arrived at headquarters to discuss strategy. 'We are living in all the horrors of peace,' wrote Captain Baxter, 'Generals invade us daily, not from any useful purpose, but merely to find a stray jam pot, or to grouse because the officer (i.e. me) is not wearing a collar at dinner time.' The senior commander now insisted on weekly kit inspections, which was 'too annoying' for those who had been there for months.[32]

Having been bored and lonely in Malta, Attlee was just happy to be among the men again. He enjoyed the camaraderie. He discussed trade union politics with some of his men but found the officers' mess to be a less permissive environment for his socialist views. 'We used to have a merry time at headquarters where I used to go frequently of an evening,' he later recalled, 'The CO [Commander Officer] would say "let's have a good strafe, send for Attlee!" and after dinner we would discuss some broad proposition such as, "All socialists are scoundrels." '[33] A fellow officer was heard to remark, 'Just going to play bridge with this damned, democratic, socialist, tub-thumping radical.'[34]

By mid-November, only a fortnight after his return, conditions had become treacherous. Gale-force winds whipped up swells in the shallow bay at Suvla, making it impossible to land supplies. The booming guns at sea, the sudden glare of a ship on the cliffs at Anzac, the tugging of ships straining at their anchors on the shore, and the gathering clouds made a doom-laden atmosphere.[35] 'Yes we all live in holes out here,' commented the normally cheerful Captain Lindley. Living in trenches was safer than building up sandbags that could be easily blown apart by shells but the price was being constantly sodden and chilled to the bone.[36]

Finally, after negotiations with the French, the government in London made a decision to evacuate by 19 December. With so many men on the shore, this was a hugely complex operation in its own right. In total, 83,000 men, 186 large guns – not to mention thousands of tonnes of stores – had to be evacuated from Anzac and Suvla, from a small strip of land sandwiched between the enemy and the sea. Thankfully, the winter had caused a hiatus in Turkish attacks. Those on the beach, however, knew that previous periods of quiet had been followed by heavy bombardment. The more time that passed before the next assault, the more it weighed upon their minds.

Having missed the major operation of the campaign, Captain Attlee was delighted to be given a starring role in the evacuation which began on 19 December, under the cover of darkness. He was ordered to hold the last line around the cove of Lala Baba, against a Turkish assault, from where tens of thousands were due to board transports to take them off the shore. Under his command were 250 men and six machine guns. He dispatched Captain Lindley and another officer, Wakeford, with two subalterns, sixty men and two of the machine guns to hold the road to the sea. The remainder he put in trenches closer to the enemy to act as a first line of defence. He then joined the Company Sergeant Major and the signallers in a dugout to watch over the operation, communicating to his superiors at Lala Bala with a clunky portable telephone. Four of his officers were on duty protecting the telephone wire at intervals. To Attlee's irritation, one of these officers was 'rather barmy' and caused much irritation by waving his revolver around manically, sparking concern that the sleeping Turks might be alerted to the evacuation.

Over the next two hours, under the cover of darkness, hundreds of men began to pass through the gap created for them from the beach to Lala Bala. About 3.30 a.m. on 20 December, word came through that the last men had left the beach. Attlee warned his men to get their possessions together to join them on the last few transports out of the cove. Apart from the occasional shot heard in the distance from Anzac, it was quiet. As a Turkish sentry realised what was happening, machine-gun fire began. Attlee and his company brought up the rear and ran down to the pier where the last few boats remained. There he saw Lieutenant General Frederick Maude – an aloof character with a distinctive Victorian moustache – shepherding the last few men onto the boat. In the distance, Attlee could see flames from Anzac, where evacuation plans had not gone so smoothly.[37] Attlee and Maude were the last men off the shore.

Gallipoli alone had cost 43,000 dead and 250,000 wounded (many from the Dominions). It cast the war effort into crisis. Attlee's assessment was typical of many fellow officers. Churchill's idea was a good one, but the military planners had failed the mission: 'The Gallipoli campaign will always remain a vivid memory. I have always held that the strategic conception was sound. The trouble was that it was never adequately supported. Unfortunately, the military authorities were Western Front-minded. Reinforcements were always sent too late. For an enterprise such as this, the right leaders were not chosen. Elderly and hidebound generals were not the men to push through an adventure of this kind. Had we had at Suvla generals like Maude, who came out later, we should, I think, have pushed through to victory,' he later argued.[38]

In the short term, it was relief enough just to be off the shore. On 20 December, as the sun rose, Attlee and his company sat on board the *Princess Irene*, on their way back to the island of Lemnos from where the mission had begun. In the circumstances, they felt it a job well done and were proud that no casualties had been taken.[39] After a brief rest, they travelled to Port Said in Egypt where, just before Christmas 1915, Attlee saw Laurence, his younger brother, and exchanged stories about Gallipoli. The 6th South Lancashires were put on duty at the Suez Canal in January 1916, before they learned that they were to be sent to Mesopotamia as part of the mission to relieve Major General Townshend at Kut.[40]

IV

Attlee's shrapnel wounds, received at Kut in April 1916, brought an end to his war in the Middle East. Through sickness and then injury, he had missed two major assaults – at Gallipoli, and then in Mesopotamia – in which many of his comrades died. From Kut, he was taken back down the Tigris to Basra, and then to Bombay. He did not see much of the country as he was hospital-bound, though his wounds were healing well.[41] He was then transported to England, arriving at Southampton on 6 June. Doctors kept detailed notes on his recovery. Although he could stand, he had pain in his knee and his muscles had been weakened during his convalescence.[42]

By mid-1916, the war entered its darkest phase. On 1 July 1916, the British and French attacked the Germans over a twenty-mile front just over the River Somme in northern France. The Battle of the Somme put Gallipoli into perspective, with 21,000 men dying on the first day alone. It was a terrible blow to the British war effort. The prime minister, Herbert Asquith, who was to be replaced by Lloyd George in December, pushed through the Military Service Act, conscripting all men between eighteen and forty-one years old into uniform.

Conscription was organised through local authorities. In June 1916, Tom made an application for exemption to the Poplar Military Service Tribunal, on the grounds of his conscientious objection. On 18 October, he was offered non-combatant service, but refused this, also on grounds of his pacifist principles. Across the country, 16,550 registered as conscientious objectors. Most accepted non-combatant service, leaving only 1,300 absolutists willing, as Tom was, to 'go the whole hog'. 'War doesn't work: to kill one devil you can call up seven new ones,' he explained to his sister Mig. 'I think the growth of envy, hatred, malice, pride, vainglory, hypocrisy and certainly all uncharitableness is enough to drive me crazy.'[43]

There was no question of taking the easy option. Tom was prepared to suffer for his convictions. On 22 November the *East London News and Chronicle* reported how he had been targeted at a suffragette peace meeting at the gates of the London docks by anti-pacifists, who asked why he was not with the troops and rushed the stage. Another protestor threatened to throw Sylvia Pankhurst, the suffragette leader, who had been seated beside him, into the Thames.[44] In December, Tom learned that his appeal to the Tribunal had not been successful. He spent Christmas 1916 awaiting arrest, with Kathleen pregnant with their second child. He was finally arrested on 22 January and sent to Wormwood Scrubs, where he spent the first month in solitary confinement, forced to sleep on a plank and given only bread and water.[45]

Meanwhile, by the autumn of 1916, the scar on Attlee's buttock had almost fully healed. He could ride a bicycle for ten miles and march another eight without too much difficulty.[46] With his regiment still in the Middle East, he was transferred to the Tank Corps. On 1 March 1917, he was promoted to major in the 5th Battalion of the South Lancashire Regiment.[47] He spent the summer training in Dorset. He enjoyed the rural landscape, the setting for the novels of Thomas Hardy, and took time to visit the graves of the Tolpuddle Martyrs, transported by the government for engaging in 'combining' (early trade unionism) in 1834. But, for Clem, radical causes would have to wait until the end of the war.

As a major, Attlee was given more responsibility for training and instructing new conscripts before they were sent to the Western Front. He had two brief sojourns in France and Belgium – from 15 to 29 March 1917, and 10 to 24 September 1917 – but no prolonged campaigns on the front line. On his second visit he witnessed the preparations for the Battle of Poelcappelle in October, a successful assault on the German lines near Ypres.[48] He longed to be in the heat of battle himself, and felt somewhat undervalued by the commanders on the ground. He suspected that his commanding officer wanted a full-time soldier in his service, rather than one of Kitchener's volunteers. Indeed he refused a promotion to the staff on the grounds that this would mean he would never escape headquarters. He bemoaned the fact that he was regarded as an Eastern-front man and had not yet had a chance to demonstrate his valour. Nonetheless, while his visits to the front line were short, he saw scenes that would etch themselves onto his mind for the rest of his life. At Belgium and Ypres he witnessed 'the hideous scar of no-man's land'. It was the 'abomination of desolation itself'.[49]

In March 1918, Major Attlee was given an infantry regiment to train in Walney Island, Barrow-in-Furness in Cumbria, a highly industrialised area just south of the Lake District. He was still annoyed not to be in France, and felt no affinity with his new surroundings in the northwest of England. There was an element of Ruskin and Morrison in his description of Barrow as a 'crude, modern, industrial inferno'. He had never before seen the effects of the 'terrible masses of industrialism' in Tyneside, the West Riding, the Black Country and Lancashire. In France and Belgium he had seen a huge stretch of country 'smashed to pieces' by guns and artillery, a 'hideous sight', but he confessed it was 'not much worse to my mind than the district round Wolverhampton and the stretch of country seen from the train between Wigan and Widnes'. In the same language he had used to describe 'no-man's land' he described Lancashire as 'an abomination of desolation and . . . crude ugliness'.[50]

The Surrey-born man missed the south and longed to see cities like Salisbury, with its mellow old brick houses clustered around its cathedral spire, the little towns of Somerset and Dorset 'set in the gaps of the gently sloping hills half drowned in apple blossom in April', or the settlements on either side of the Thames such as Burford, Eynsham and, fairest of all, Oxford. His heart also longed for Cornwall, south Devon, Surrey, Sussex, the 'great garden of Kent and East Anglia with its tall church towers, rising from flat landscapes made famous by the paintings of Constable'.[51] This preference for more genteel scenery was also reflected in his fondness for Vita Sackville-West's poem, 'The Land', a nostalgic celebration of Kentish countryside across four seasons, published in September 1926. So fond of it was he that he later made Sackville-West a Companion of Honour during his first year as prime minister.[52]

Yet, once again, Attlee's instinctive affection for unspoilt rural England only went so far. He was an East Londoner now and had grown fond of its different qualities. Moreover, he was never an aesthete, and was not quite willing to submit to Morris's utopian fantasy of England as a rural arcadia in *News from Nowhere*, or the pre-industrial fourteenth century celebrated in *A Dream of John Ball*. He missed the urban chaos of London too. The England he loved was not only 'the true England of Nature, the trees, hedges, grass and the lie of the land, but even the transitory England of the C20th with its railways, towns and lighted streets, above all, the lit pavements shimmering and wet with rain'. The nation's capital combined 'beauty and ugliness in its great warm heart'.[53]

One thing that had been underlined to Attlee by the war was the fact that the Labour Party needed to maintain a national perspective. Of the Labour MPs elected in 1906, two were from London and the southeast; one from East Anglia and the Midlands; two from the northeast; two from Scotland; two from Wales; three from Yorkshire and there were eight from the northwest. Attlee might have felt industrial Lancashire was an eyesore, but it was also the engine room of the Labour movement. This simple fact was something that many in London Labour failed to recognise. Attlee absorbed the lesson, notwithstanding his personal preference for the south.

Stuck in Barrow in April 1918, waiting eagerly for another opportunity to go to the front line, he paused to reflect on what he had learned in the intervening years. On the one hand, the experience of the trenches had injected an element of cold realism into his worldview. Having drifted from agnosticism to atheism, he had less respect for organised religion than ever before. He confided to Tom his contempt for the Church of England, which he regarded as 'the blind leading the blind'.[54] In another letter, he mocked the suggestion by a senior Anglican bishop, writing in *The Times*, that one of the most tragic incidents of the war was that the Germans continued to attack during Holy Week in the east. This was a 'fine example of clerical fatuity'. Lives lost during religious holidays were no less important than those lost at any other. When conversation turned to Tom's religiously inspired pacifism, Clem was uncharacteristically contemptuous. 'I think your objection to taking life is fallacious,' he told Tom, 'in that it is at times necessary to take life.' He did not like the nature of war any more than Tom. But the scruples of conscience, he explained, 'cannot weigh with me if the work has to be done'.[55]

More than anything, he was left with a greater appreciation of how powerful a feeling was patriotism:

> It was not until the Great War that I fully understood the strength of the ties that bind men to the land of their birth. Although I had travelled from time to time on the Continent of Europe and had even crossed the Atlantic, always feeling on my return to England a keen sense of pleasure, yet the strength of the love of the land of my birth was not realised until I was ordered to leave it. A year in the East gave life to that unrecognised affection. The Greek islands are beautiful and on Gallipoli I could, even in the trenches, admire the bright colours and sharp outlines of the hills in the crystal clear light of morning, but I soon felt the want of the soft greys and greens of England.[56]

As Attlee told Tom in April 1918, he had seen no evidence that life in Britain, or the rest of Europe, would be freer, or better, under German dominance. Yet this should not lead to complacency, or an uncritical acceptance of the status quo. If anything, the experience of the trenches intensified the sense of moral urgency which underlay his determination to work for his fellow citizens. 'We live in a state of society where the vast majority live stunted lives – we endeavour to give them a freer life,' he wrote.[57] There was no apter description of the political battle that Attlee was determined to return to as soon as the war was brought to an end.

IV

Major Attlee finally got his wish to join the front line in France, arriving at Givenchy in May 1918. By this stage, it was clear to him that the war was reaching its end. This was made obvious by the reluctance of the

Germans to attack after the failure of their Spring Offensive of 1918, into which they had thrown everything as a last stand. In August, after moving units to replace a wounded major elsewhere, Attlee was with the 55th West Lancashire Division as they made their way into Artois in pursuit of the retreating Germans. Attlee's profound sense of duty and responsibility was undiminished by the prospect of victory. At one point, he was faced with an officer whose nerve had gone and who was weeping and refusing to go over the top. 'I said, you bloody well will go, and drew my revolver,' he later recalled. A few minutes later, as Attlee returned to check the lines, he found that the officer had fainted.

As the 55th West Lancashire Regiment was advancing towards the German lines at Lille, Attlee was carried off the battlefield for the third time in the war. Although the details were vague, it seems that he was floored when a flying piece of timber hit him in the back as his division made a dash out of their trenches towards the German lines.[58] Evacuated to England, in November he celebrated the news of Germany's defeat in a hospital in Wandsworth. Just a few miles away, over the other side of Wandsworth Common, sat his brother Tom in a prison cell. As children, they had cycled the distance between the hospital and the prison many times, with little thought to the circumstances that might see them end up in either. Ellen, their mother, remarked, 'I don't know which of these two sons I am more proud of.'[59]

On 11 November, the Armistice was concluded and thoughts began to turn to a future not defined by the war. After the huge sacrifice made by the British working classes, Lloyd George promised a 'fit country for heroes to live in', leading to a huge victory in the general election of December 1918. The Labour Party had withdrawn from the wartime coalition the previous month and was left unprepared for the election, though a return of fifty-nine seats meant that it had its strongest representation in Parliament to date.

While Britain had changed considerably over the previous four years, this was nothing compared to the transformation that had occurred on the European Continent. There were revolutions in Germany and Russia, and the fall of two of Europe's most powerful empires. For socialists, this was an exciting time. As Attlee later recalled, on a visit to Moscow fifty years later, 'we believed at the end of that war that we had achieved something. The old Europe had passed away.' Of course, the formation of a Bolshevik government in Russia was of particular interest. When the newspapers arrived in the mess in the last year of the war, his junior officers used to ask, "How are Major Attlee's Russians getting on?" '60 The red flag, which he had joked about carrying over the top in 1916, now flew over St Petersburg and Moscow. In fact, Attlee's view was that the Russian Revolution of 1917 was 'rather appalling' though 'quite explicable' given the suffering of the Russian people. The tyranny of the Tsarist regime was its root cause. Yet he had no affection for Vladimir Lenin, Leon Trotsky or the Bolsheviks. They seemed to him to be in the same mould as the Socialist Party of Great Britain (SPGB), an extreme Communist faction, or 'wilder types' in the Socialist Democratic Party (SDP), who were the main rivals of the Independent Labour Party in east London. From what he knew of the Whitechapel branch of the SDP, Attlee shuddered to think about the state of the country if they ever took charge.

If anything, in what was to became an important theme in his career, Attlee looked west rather than east in search of inspiration. While he viewed at events in Russia with a feeling of ambiguity, he was delighted by America's entry into the war in 1917. He believed that US President Woodrow Wilson was 'an enormous moral asset on our side'. He felt Wilson's Fourteen Points, his stated aims for peace negotiations announced in January 1918 – which included free trade, open agreements, democracy and self-determination – raised the Allied war effort to another moral plane. This was all the more important for Attlee as he regarded David Lloyd George's premiership as 'essentially vulgar', and too narrowly focused on traditional British imperial interests; his own view was that such great sacrifice could only be justified if it was turned towards the benefit of humanity as a whole. Attlee found many things in the United States to criticise. Nonetheless, this firm faith in the progressive power of America was something that remained with him throughout the rest of his life. It was to be particularly important at the time of the Second World War because it meant that the Anglo-American alliance was based on broader foundations than the friendship between Franklin Roosevelt and Winston Churchill.

Closer to home, Attlee was pleased to see the Labour Party perform its part well in the wartime coalition. The pacifists had been forced to step aside and, for the moment, the leadership was in the hands of men like Arthur Henderson, J. H. Thomas and Robert Smillie, all of whom shared his stance – 'ie. socialist pro-war'. The Labour Party's statement of war aims – which followed Wilson and took their inspiration from the Fourteen Points – had been well received. He believed that this marked an important advance in its efforts to appear as a truly national party.[61] It was to this end that the rest of his life was to be focused.

Part Two

The Making of a Politician, 1918–1931

5

Looking Backward

All thoughtful men agree that the present aspect of society is portentous of great changes. The only question is, whether they will be for the better or the worse. Those who believe in man's essential nobleness lean to the former view, those who believe in his essential baseness to the latter. For my part, I hold to the former opinion. *Looking Backward* was written in the belief that the Golden Age lies before us and not behind us, and is not far away. Our children will surely see it, and we, too, who are already men and women, if we deserve it by our faith and by our works.

Edward Bellamy, Postscript, *Looking Backward 2000–1887*, 1887.[1]

I *Boston, Massachusetts, 2000*

An America man, called Julian West, wakes up in Boston, Massachusetts, in the year 2000. Born in 1857, West is a native of the city. In 1887, on his thirtieth birthday, he undergoes hypnosis at the hands of a quack physician, Doctor Pillsbury. After sleeping for what he thinks are twelve hours, he awakens to find himself in the first year of the twenty-first century. Needless to say, it is a world transformed from that which he had known.

As West comes to his senses, he learns that he is in the care of a young man, Doctor Leete, who will act as a guide to this strange world in which he finds himself. Some things are reassuringly familiar. Despite the passage of time, for example, the two men share a fondness for the work of Charles Dickens. Other aspects of this new world are disconcertingly futuristic, straight from the realm of science fiction, such as the musical telephone that begins to ring in West's room. These technological changes, however, are nothing compared to the political revolution that has taken place in the intervening years. Doctor Leete explains to Julian West that he has awoken in a truly free and equal society based on socialist principles. Working conditions are closely regulated by the state, workers only toil for a few hours of the day and have ample time for holidays and leisure. Food is free for all, goods are equally distributed, and everyone retires at the age of forty-five.

This is the story told in Edward Bellamy's 1887 novel, *Looking Backward*. It envisages a utopian socialist commonwealth that is consciously, almost defiantly, modern. Bellamy's imagined future is not a rural Arcadia but a huge, sprawling, urban metropolis. Machinery, mechanisation and industrialisation play a crucial part in social progress. They have been utilised as assets for the common good, controlled and managed by a large but benevolent state. Advances in productivity, combined with an equal distribution of material wealth, ensure that the population can pursue a full and free life. So long as the citizens perform the duties required for the maintenance of the modern commonwealth of which they are part, they do not have to worry about wages, employment or food. Everyone contributes; and everyone shares the rewards. Bellamy's vision of the future may not have been perfect, but it was – in spirit at least – practical. This explains its appeal to Clement Attlee.

Infused with optimism about the potential of the future, Bellamy's book soon became a bestseller. By 1897, ten years after its publication, 400,000 copies had been sold in the United States, making it one of the most successful socialist novels in American history.[2] Its influence was felt further afield too. Leo Tolstoy called it 'exceedingly remarkable', and 50,000 copies were sold in Russia before the revolution in 1917.[3] That Attlee stumbled upon it is no surprise. His library contained 'quite a large collection of Americans of one kind or another', and he was impressed by other American socialist writers such as Upton Sinclair, known for his exposés of corporate corruption in the meat-packing industry and in Wall Street. Through such works, Attlee was impressed by a strong sense of the American progressive spirit, which later translated into his admiration for Franklin Roosevelt's 'New Deal'.[4]

As Attlee understood better than most, however, one man's utopia was another man's nightmare. As he once put it, 'we should be very unhappy in each other's paradises.⁵ The good life for one was not the good life for all. Given his admiration for Bellamy, it was ironic that he discovered *Looking Backward* through reading another work that had greatly influenced him before 1914: William Morris's 1897 book *News from Nowhere*. William Morris believed Bellamy's vision of the future was deeply flawed, and should be resisted by true socialists. Morris took to the pages of *Commonweal* to write a critical review of the book when it first appeared. He rejected the version of socialism that Bellamy envisaged, with its optimistic embrace of modernity. In Morris's view, Bellamy's was the type of socialism that 'makes its owner . . . perfectly satisfied with modern civilization, if only the injustice, misery, and waster of class society could be got rid of'. For Morris, this was only 'half-change'. The only ideal life on offer was that of 'the industrious *professional* middle-class men of to-day purified from their crime of complicity with the monopolist class'.

Morris considered this false progress. He continued to see himself as a disciple of the revolt led by John Ruskin, 'against the philistinism of the triumphant *bourgeois*'. His was a challenge to the very idea that civilisation and commonwealth could be achieved in a modern industrial society. Adjusting the machinery or mechanics of the economy or redistributing the wealth so that everyone could enjoy it, as Bellamy suggested, was merely to make peace with a perverted socio-economic system. The 'economical semi-fatalism' of some socialists in accepting commercialisation and industrialisation was both 'deadening' and delusional. What was more, Bellamy's ideas of life were 'curiously limited' to the urban world of Boston, and he had 'no idea beyond existence in a great city'. To Morris, true socialism would see the state, nationalism and war effectively dissolve.⁶ It was, in essence, an anarchic vision, which had no place for the big benevolent state of the future that Bellamy depicted.

Such was the extent of Morris's disgust that a critical review was not enough. *News from Nowhere* was actually written as a direct riposte to Bellamy's *Looking Backward*. In Morris's alternative utopia, heavy industry was abolished, the natural world was allowed to breathe again and beauty came from the worker's devotion to the means of production. Before long, the state would wither away. For Morris, this was a truer representation of Karl Marx's vision in *The Communist Manifesto* when he described the organisation of society after the overthrow of capitalism. While Marx had been vague about the future, men like Morris provided the aesthetic bridge to this prospective world. For this reason, he was initially courted by Marx's confidant and co-author Friedrich Engels, who encouraged him to establish *Commonweal*. Before long, however, even Engels had grown impatient with Morris's purism and unwillingness to play practical politics. He became frustrated by a man whom he saw as 'a very rich but politically inept art lover'. As Morris drifted more and more towards anarchism, Engels gave up on him as a 'sentimental dreamer pure and simple'.[7]

For Attlee, British socialism had a pre-history which long pre-dated the theories of Karl Marx. In his view, the first prophets of radical reform had been those poets of the late eighteenth and early nineteenth centuries whose unease at the effects of industrialisation had begun to impinge upon their work 'after the long sleep of Georgian artificiality'. Thus John Keats's misgivings about the industrial world had crept into poems like 'Isabella, or the Pot of Basil', in which he described 'torched mines and noisy factories'. At first the Romantic poets had highlighted these things rather than making any calls to action, but then Percy Shelley adopted a more militant tone. In 'The Masque of Anarchy' and other poems, one could see 'the spirit of revolt against social injustice, not intruding on the poet's vision, as in Keats, but animating and inspiring all his work'. Then came Ruskin and Morris, who went even further than Shelley: Ruskin had 'seceded' from the study of art to focus on 'bread and butter for the multitude'; and then even Morris moved from the world of art 'to the uncongenial duty of street-corner agitation'.[8]

Nonetheless, while Attlee was never a follower of Marx and Engels, he would have recognised the latter's critique of William Morris as something of a dreamer and an impossible purist when it came to achieving political change. It also reflected a tendency on the British left that he became increasingly frustrated with: a rather self-righteous assumption that a certain version of the 'good life' was superior to others.[9] Attlee retained a great fondness for Morris's writing, but he thought it a hopeless guide to political action. Aesthetic or idyllic socialism could only take one so far. The nation and the state could not be wished away; in fact, Attlee came to see them as positive instruments of change. In this respect, Bellamy was the better guide. Many years later, in 1948, when Attlee was prime minister, he was introduced to Edward Bellamy's son in London. In that brief meeting, he made an extremely revealing comment, describing his government, Britain's first majority socialist government, as 'a child of the Bellamy ideal'.[10]

Years later, in the late 1950s, the Marxist writer E. P. Thompson would criticise Attlee's government for failing to live up to the revolutionary potential of William Morris's ideas. Thompson blamed this omission on a 'hostile national culture both smug and resistant to intellectuality'.[11] Thompson assumed that Labour's leaders had simply forgotten Morris, if they had read him at all. In this respect, he completely underestimated the man who had led that government. If Morris did not provide the script for the Attlee administration, it was not because Attlee failed to appreciate him. He consciously chose a different path. It was the one outlined by Bellamy that held that the 'Golden Age lies before us and not behind us, and is not far away'.[12]

II

Up to 1914, Attlee had made his name in the Labour movement as an activist and a campaigner rather than a thinker or an intellectual. In the *Minority Report* campaign or in his support for George Lansbury, he had put his energy to good effect: licking envelopes, buttering bread, collecting tributes, writing election leaflets, or painting placards. His record in the war cemented his image as a man of action, rather than a man of thought. Yet, as we have seen with his reading of Morris and Bellamy, there was more intellectual depth to Attlee than has sometimes been appreciated. When stationed in Barrow-in-Furness in the spring of 1918, one of his great complaints was that he had been deprived of any new books – a 'great deprivation'. With no fresh material to tackle, he compared his mind to a horse running a racecourse going round the same track time and time again. The advantage of this was that it gave him time to reflect on what he had learned so far. There was no revolution in his thinking. But there was a greater tolerance and breadth. 'I do not find my outlook very much changed during the war though I think I have attained slightly more catholicity,' he explained to Tom.

This choice of words was revealing. Catholicity and tolerance were not things Attlee thought were in abundance among British socialists, particularly the intellectuals. For Attlee, fads and fashions of thinking were to be treated with scepticism. Through Tom, in the final months of the war, he had heard about a new idea within the Labour movement that was gaining momentum.[13] Guild socialism, partly inspired by the ideas of

Morris and articulated by the Fabian economists, G.D.H. Cole and J. A. Hobson, advocated a return to pre-industrial modes of workers' organisation, whereby guilds of artisans would practise a form of democratic control within their trade.[14] Attlee did not object to the idea entirely. He felt it had 'a great deal of practical value' in some trades, though much less application to manufacturing industry. His own view was that 'we shall have to have in the society of the future very many organisations in different bases' – from local government to trade cooperatives, as well as guilds.[15]

Here one can see the influence of Edward Bellamy shining through. In the socialist utopia depicted in *Looking Backward*, there were some guilds and some worker democracy, but the state was needed to exert overall control. Ultimately, hierarchy and central authority were required for the effective functioning of production. Attlee also stressed the importance of the role of the state 'as a referee between the contending demands'.[16] As he argued in 1920, advancement meant that human societies had the means of producing 'all the material necessities of a good life, food, clothing and housing in abundance'. Luxury and the means of art and literature could be open to all.[17] Each citizen, therefore, could pursue his own version of the good life, in his own time.

Setting aside the specifics, there was also something about the manner in which the guild socialists made their case which Attlee found objectionable. Once they had stumbled upon a philosophically elegant idea, they wanted it to supplant all others. There was a certain obsessiveness in this. Fabians had a 'tendency to erect all such schemes into complete social systems'.[18] The way they argued was also off-putting. In another letter, addressing J. A. Hobson's advocacy of the subject, he complained that some of the arguments he deployed were 'puerile, mostly of the non-sequitur type and the book informed throughout by petty malice'. A number of challenging questions, such as how a Britain based on guild socialism would trade with other countries, were entirely ignored.[19]

Another mistake that socialist intellectuals made was assuming that something extremely distasteful to oneself would be equally so to others. Certain forms of work and certain occupations, which seemed dull or monotonous – such as a doorkeeper or liftman – were perfectly interesting to some people. Karl Marx had written about the 'alienation of the worker from the means of production'. Both John Ruskin and William Morris had stressed the importance of the worker feeling proud of his craft. Here, again, Attlee dissented. The fact was that 'most of the work that has to be done to-day is on the whole dull'. Indeed, he identified him with those social reformers who placed increasing importance on the role of the state in ameliorating social conditions. Improving conditions for workers, such as wages, working hours, insurance and healthcare, was the first battle that the Labour movement should fight. This he described as 'the better apportionment of all the things that make up a good life'.[20] 'I think there was a danger in our movement in pre-war days of taking too narrow a view, in that we conceived that what appeared to be the ideal life for us was the ideal life for everybody,' he explained to Tom.[21]

If every individual insisted on the sanctity of his conscience what would this mean for the prospect of building a new society? In this, Attlee was not prepared to spare his brother's pacifism from criticism, notwithstanding the fact that he admired his bravery. 'I do not see how your principles can be applied in practice in the actual carrying on of the community. Don't they logically lead to anarchic individualism?' he challenged Tom, who was still in prison. The British nation, as a community, had decided that it thought the war was just. Once it had done so, just how much non-acquiescence to its general will could it tolerate? When did non-acquiescence become disloyalty? In Ulster, Sir Edward Carson had threatened violent resistance and civil war in opposition to Irish Home Rule before the war. Ulster Unionists had effectively rebelled against Parliament, while insisting that they remained loyal to the Crown. There had even been a mutiny at an army base in Curragh by soldiers sympathetic to their cause. Would Tom's principles also have him endorse the Carson approach?[22]

Not all Fabians advocated anarchic individualism, of course. For example, there were significant divergences of opinion between them on the role of the state in society. Another voice, which had gained in influence over the last decade, was that of H. G. Wells. Wells's socialism was defined, as much as anything, by a desire for order in a chaotic world. As we have seen, Attlee shared the same admiration for Kipling that Wells expressed in his 1911 novel, *The New Machiavelli*. For Wells, too much individualism meant 'muddle, meant a crowd of separated, undisciplined little people all obstinately and ignorantly doing things jarringly, each one in his own way'. What Kipling spoke of the need for was 'order and devotion' and 'collective vigour'. And it was in this spirit that Wells evoked 'an ideal state, an organized state as confident and powerful as modern science, as balanced and beautiful as a body, as beneficent as sunshine'. He spoke of a 'Scientific Commonweal, King'.[23]

'One has only to compare his Utopias with that of William Morris to see the difference between the scientific and aesthetic appeals to social service,' Attlee explained. Once again, we can see that he was able to navigate through these contending theories of socialism, without simply picking one side or the other. On the one hand, he understood that the desire 'to see the machinery of society running smoothly and cleanly' was almost a 'distinct motive in itself' within the broader movement for social reform. As Attlee recognised, Wells exhibited 'the disgust of an orderly and scientific mind' at the wasteful and chaotic nature of the existing social and economic system.[24] On the other hand, the danger of the Wellsian approach was that it lacked humanity. As Attlee explained, while he believed that it was necessary to insert some science into socialism, there was a danger that it would become too mechanical and systematised, and lose sight of the citizens it was supposed to liberate. 'The besetting sin of the scientific type of social reformer is his failure to make allowance for the idiosyncrasies of the individual.'[25]

Something similar could be said about the work of the Webbs and their attempts to quantify social progress. Before 1914, he now concluded, in a damning phrase, 'we were too Webby – I'm sure I was, having a fatal love of statistics and a neat structure of society.' It meant that 'our schemes for the future attained a certain rigidity which made them unpalatable to the general public.'[26] Many years later Attlee wrote of Beatrice Webb that she 'never understood that the New Jerusalem must be built with human beings and not institutions'.[27] On one occasion he recalled her suggesting that socialist change must be brought about by an intellectual vanguard: a 'dedicated cadre of workers in the Jesuit model which would be the mainspring of the new order in society'. To his mind, this was a typical Fabian conceit, which betrayed a 'lack of confidence in what ordinary men and women could do in a democracy'.[28]

Going forward, the Labour movement would 'have to allow for greater variety'. The 'main principles stand and must stand, of course'; it was 'the application that must be various'.[29] 'I think then if life is to be action not contemplation – if we are to do things – we must necessarily make sacrifices.' Any great measure of reform would contain details that would offend someone's conscience but these had to be sacrificed for the greater good.

He was convinced that the genius of the British political system, for all of its flaws, was that it could be changed without recourse to violence.[30]

This faith in gradualism, constitutionalism and pragmatic reform was not his alone. It chimed with a deeply ingrained political culture in the country that 'emphasised a common citizenship'. The prevalence of such views in Britain explains why Marxism or Leninist vanguardism never found much of a home there.[31] Attlee was no utopian visionary but he had a better sense of the mechanics of life and politics than many who were. He read the books that a socialist was supposed to read, and he set them against his experience as a soldier in the trenches.[32] Rather than simply following a script set for him by Morris, the Webbs or H. G. Wells, he took elements of each and arrived at an independently formed worldview. What emerged was not some sort of pinkish blend or vanilla compromise but an unambiguous and clear-sighted political creed. His socialism was not scientific but it was practical; it was not aesthetic but it was nonetheless humane.

III

On 16 January 1919, Major Attlee signed his demobilisation papers and left Wandsworth hospital. His army pay would be stopped within four weeks, and he was eager to restart his life.[33] He took the tube to Stepney and went straight to the Haileybury Club, where he hoped to take up residence again. He found it was boarded up and had fallen into disuse. Speaking to old friends who lived beside the club, he learned that part of the building was open in the evenings for younger children but that it was not the thriving institution it had been before 1914. Many of the boys he had known had fallen in the war. He would have to find alternative accommodation, though he was pleased to learn that he would be able to resume his lectureship at the LSE. With jobs likely to be in short supply, they expected to welcome a flood of students returning from military service.

Attlee spent that evening back in Putney reuniting with his family before returning, once again, to Stepney the following day. This time he carried a suitcase. On 17 January, he walked into the chemist's shop of Oscar Tobin, a Jew of Romanian descent and one of the most important Labour Party operators in London. Attlee followed Tobin through his shop to the backstairs and up to his flat on the first floor. Tobin unveiled his plans for the Labour Party to take control of the Stepney borough council. He urged Attlee to stand for one of the two Mile End seats in the forthcoming London County Council election. Attlee took his leave and said he would need a few hours to consider. The following day he agreed to run as the candidate of the recently established Limehouse Labour Party.[34]

These nascent constituency organisations were creatures of their locale. The one in Limehouse was formed when Irish Nationalists, led by the local political operator Matt Aylward, united with the Independent Labour Party in the area. On 1 May 1918, the Stepney Trades Council and Labour Party had also been formed, with Oscar Tobin as secretary. Within a year, twenty-seven more unions had affiliated with it.[35] Aylward and Tobin decided strategy between them. Both saw the potential appeal of 'Major Attlee' who had served his country so faithfully in the war, and hoped that he might be able to pick up voters who had never before supported Labour.

In March 1919 Attlee contested a Stepney seat for the London County Council elections. He missed out to a Liberal candidate by just eighty votes. Despite not being elected, he was now part of an influential network of Labour organisations. He was co-opted as a member of the Limehouse Board of Guardians in April and made chairman of the Stifford Children's Home, which looked after local orphans. All of this was intended to strengthen his hand as Labour's prospective parliamentary candidate for Limehouse.[36] He needed some effort to raise his profile. When mentioned in the local press, his name was frequently misspelled as 'Atlee' (just as it was in parliamentary records for the first few months of his Westminister career).[37]

With the Haileybury Club uninhabitable, Attlee needed an alternative base. Not for the first time, his father's bequest gave him an advantage. He leased a building, 'Norway House', at 638 Commercial Road, in the heart of Limehouse. It doubled as a home and a constituency office. Attlee took the top floor and employed an ex-member of the Haileybury Club, Charlie Griffith, as a batman to run his bath and his errands. The two were to remain lifelong friends.[38] There was a billiards table at which the two men would while away the very few free evenings they had, but conditions were far from luxurious. Years later, at the time of the winter fuel crisis of 1946–7, Attlee recalled how he had stockpiled coal under his bed in his Limehouse days, as was the local custom, which created a 'hump like a camel' in his mattress.[39]

Norway House also served as the Labour Party headquarters for the borough council elections that were forthcoming in November 1919. As he had now been chosen as the parliamentary candidate for the next general election, Attlee did not stand himself. But it was a sign of his growing influence that he wrote the election address for those that hoped to win a seat on the Stepney borough council. This called for open spaces, free milk for schoolchildren and better sanitation. Labour did not have it all their own way in Stepney. Their opponents were well organised and well established in the area. Of particular importance was the Union of Stepney Rate Payers, which had the support of the *East London Observer*. It was led by Major Earl Winterton, a local Conservative MP. Though he became a great friend of Attlee in later years, and spoke at the launch of his autobiography in 1954, Attlee's early experience of local politics was often bruising.[40]

The Union of Stepney Rate Payers feared that a Labour victory would be followed by crippling taxes being imposed on local business owners. Eighty per cent of the city's inhabitants were classed as 'very poor' and the estimated 16 per cent of residents who were lower middle class (shopkeepers and engineers) could not support them from their own pocket. As the *East London Observer* complained, the Labour programme for the borough did not 'err on the side of modesty' with its calls for the municipalisation of food supplies, markets, cinemas, theatres, meat, milk and dairy commodities, on top of other demands such as improved roads, the building of more public libraries, art galleries and museums.[41] The Conservative MP for nearby Bow and Bromley, Major Reginald Blair, went further still. The London Labour Party were 'the brothers of the Russian Bolsheviks, and had done everything to protect the Bolsheviks in their attempt to found a Russian Socialist State'. They had no sense of economy or efficiency and just wanted to plunder the area and to 'convert the Borough Councils into a sort of Selfridges, Harrods, and Whiteleys combined'.[42]

The result of the borough elections transformed the area. Of the sixty seats for Stepney – which was divided into Whitechapel, Mile End and Limehouse – forty-three Labour councillors were returned. There had been none before. In the Limehouse division, for which Attlee was to stand as MP, the Labour Party won all fifteen seats, which demonstrated his growing strength. Although he had not won a seat to the borough council, the victorious Labour members proposed to make him mayor of Stepney. With the few remaining Conservatives complaining about the unprecedented move, Attlee was effectively co-opted into the position by the unanimous support of the Labour councillors.[43] Oscar Tobin's guess, a wise one, was that Attlee was in fact the mayor likely to be the least provocative to disillusioned ratepayers.

A year to the day after the armistice, on 11 November 1919, Attlee stood outside the Stepney Borough Council Chamber in his three-piece suit and bowler hat. Inside the chamber, his Labour colleagues, who now had complete control of the council, went through the process of appointing him. Councillor J. R. Raphael, seconding the nomination, pointed out that Attlee brought to the office a family tradition of many years of public service. After a unanimous show of hands, Attlee entered the room to deafening cheers. The mayor approached his 'throne' and politely declined to don the mayoral robes, but submitted to the ceremony of having the insignia of office circled on his breast. It was a rousing scene. Stepney Borough Council, declared the new mayor in his victory speech, was 'now in the hands of workers'.[44] Across London, Labour was making strides. Attlee's old friend George Lansbury was elected mayor in neighbouring Poplar.[45]

As the victorious heads of the London Labour Party prepared to meet in Essex Hall following their victory, the ratepayers looked on nervously. US President Woodrow Wilson had declared his intention of making the world safe for democracy. But was Labour safe for London, asked the *East London Observer*. The Fabian headquarters on the Strand was 'a building odorous from conscientious objectors, cranks of every pattern, and all the "ists" and "isms" of the time'. These coming men had no interest 'in the history of local government, or the theory and practice of civic politics'. They did admit an exception in the case of Attlee, however. The new mayor had made a good first impression, even among his enemies. The first-ever newspaper profile of him, in the *East London Observer*, illustrated the way in which he could appeal to those who were otherwise political enemies. He had 'procedure to his finger-tips', a mind rapid enough to see what was correct and to act swiftly on that basis. His voice was 'penetrating, and he never makes hushed whispers nor swallows his words'. He spoke in 'intensely concentrated, firm – almost curt – precise, and unmistakable sentences'. His style resembled the slamming of a railway carriage door, 'so that the person on the wrong side is nonplussed, and before he can recover mental balance the opportunity has passed and he is left, the Mayor hurrying on with the next items on the agenda; to continue the metaphor, as a rapidly restarting train.' Above all, he was an 'out and out neutral' in the chair.[46]

In fact, the staccato style was a cover for shyness. Attlee's abruptness was a quality that some could appreciate. But it was also in danger of stunting his career. As one colleague warned him early on, 'the public don't want a stick, Clem; they want a man.'[47] That he had no wife was something of a drawback in this respect. There were rumours among his supporters that he had once made a proposal to a young lady, but his personal life remained something of a mystery, even to his closest friends. When there was a need for a mayoress for official ceremonies, he called upon the goodwill of his sister Mig to make the journey in from Putney.

Attlee remained connected to a wider world of socialist politics. He attended the 1917 Club, a group of progressive intellectuals (many of them pacifists) formed by Ramsay MacDonald, which met on Gerrard Street in Soho. He was a committee member, often lunching there. But most of his energies were focused on Limehouse, rather than becoming a darling of the Labour Party's emerging elite. One thing he did get from the 1917 Club was a recommendation for an election agent, John Beckett, whom he paid £6 a week and gave rent-free board at Norway House, along with his wife. The couple were to have a child there, in the flat they shared with Attlee. Beckett later broke with Labour and became a follower of Oswald Mosley, but he found a close companion in Attlee at that time. Every morning, the Major would sit and listen to a queue of people who came to him with concerns about the area. Beckett would screen the visitors. If help was impossible, the case never reached Attlee. 'I was the Hyde to Clem's Jekyll, and there were many who lamented that if only I had let them go to the Major, things would have been different.' Beckett's other innovation was to print a propaganda sheet, the *East End Pioneer*, which reached 5,000 readers in Limehouse.[48]

With an eye on the next general election, Attlee had been determined to make his mark in the borough as mayor. Although he only held the post for a year, he built up a reputation as an even-handed administrator, as well as a considerable power base for himself. He became chairman of the Valuation Committee, which gave him greater control over both rents and rates in the local area.[49] By increasing taxes on the ratepayers, Attlee built five prenatal and child welfare clinics, appointed professional health visitors, and provided free milk for more than 6,000 families. Regular rubbish collection, rebukes to slum landlords, improved roads, and expansion of public libraries were other features of his reign – as well as an increase in pay for council employees.

When it became known that Attlee was going to stand as a prospective MP for the Limehouse constituency, the other thing that helped him was his war record. The tensions between 'conchies' (conscientious objectors) and returning soldiers were still raw. While remaining deeply opposed to Labour, the *East London Observer* could at least express respect for a man who had served his country bravely.[50] Local newspapers were full of the plight of those – crippled and maimed – who had come back from active service. Attlee presided over a medal ceremony for veterans. A pacifist would have been overwhelmed quickly in this atmosphere.[51]

In his first parliamentary campaign, the Major's core message was a simple one. It was captured in a pamphlet produced by Beckett and distributed around the constituency. 'The Great Betrayal' decried the way in which the promises to those who had fought for their country in the Great War had been broken. They had been betrayed in two respects: materially (by a lack of financial support on their demobilisation); but also morally (by the apparent abandonment of the democratic aims that they were told they were fighting for). Thus, speaking on Armistice Day in 1920 at a meeting of the Union of Democratic Control in Kingsway Hall, Attlee denounced Lloyd George's government for failing to follow through on Woodrow Wilson's Fourteen Points of 1917, which had called for democratic self-determination and more democratic control of foreign policy. When victory had come, they had reverted to the old methods of secret diplomacy, vested interests and imperialism. 'When I was in the army I used to take occasion to chat with the men and with the officers, particularly with the men, and I have often asked the men what they went to fight for. I always got the same answer: they were fighting for something far bigger than King or Country. They believed, and we believed, that they were fighting for the good of the whole world. That is where the government betrayal comes in.'[52]

As mayor, he temporarily refused to take part in a recruiting campaign for the Territorial Army, of which he had once been a local linchpin. 'After four years of active service I have seen every ideal I fought for betrayed in the Paris Peace Conference,' he explained.[53] At his most over-exuberant he went so far as to say that 'Personally I think the time has come when we ought to do away with all armies and all war.'[54] There was an element of excitability and electioneering in this. The fact was that Attlee had admired those who had kept Labour in the wartime coalition more than he did the pacifists who had refused to serve. Now Labour's wartime leader Arthur Henderson told Attlee that his position was 'absolutely absurd and futile'. When tabling a motion at the Labour Party conference in 1923, pledging to vote against all military expenditure, he was 'well and truly answered' by Henderson, and rather chastened by the experience.[55] He retreated from his position – that he would never support a capitalist government on the question of armaments and conscription. Indeed, Attlee later credited Henderson for his faith in the concept of 'collective security', which was to be the basis of Labour's foreign policy by the time he became leader.[56]

On questions of material welfare, he was on firmer ground. This was something that all strands of the Labour Party could unite around. During his tenure as mayor, he focused his energies on urging the government to find employment for the thousands of ex-servicemen who had flooded back into the East End. In July 1920, he began planning for a major campaign on this issue. The Conference of Local Authorities of London called for government intervention in the form of vast public works which would improve national infrastructure. They also agreed that a committee be formed – consisting of the mayor of each of the metropolitan borough councils, and representatives from the Comrades of The Great War, the National Union of Ex-Servicemen, the National Federation of Discharged and Demobilised Sailors and Soldiers, and the London Trades Council – to convey their resolution to the prime minister.[57]

In private, Attlee was not convinced that public works were the best means of tackling unemployment. He also believed that a lowering of rates might relieve some of the burden on local communities.[58] Stepney Borough Council, however, was brimming with radicalism, and he kept his reservations to himself. In the summer of 1920, his colleagues tabled motions expressing support for the strikes of miners in the north and railwaymen in London. Expressing sympathies with the Communist government in Russia, they also articulated strong opposition to any prospect of Allied intervention against the Bolshevik government in Russia.[59] Sitting in the mayoral chair, Attlee kept his counsel for the moment. The *East London Observer* cast a nervous eye on these developments. Syndicalism – the radical trade union movement – was making its presence felt. Following a major strike in New York, there were rumours that London could also be brought to a standstill by militant trade unionists.[60]

By 1920, Labour had embedded itself in the poorest areas of London, particularly to the east and south. In these pockets of strength, different characters dominated. In neighbouring Poplar, Attlee already knew the mayor, George Lansbury, from well before the war. He began to deal more frequently with other forceful personalities and rising stars such as the mayor of Hackney, Herbert Morrison, five years his junior, and chairman of the Brixton branch of the ILP. Morrison, a chirpy cockney wit and master mobiliser, was to become a giant of London Labour. Along with Ernest Bevin, in fact, he would be one of the most important figures in setting Labour's national strategy in the 1930s, 1940s and 1950s. Yet, despite years of cooperation and a similar political outlook, a distance remained between the two. Morrison later said that he could not claim to have really known Attlee; nor indeed, could he name anyone, 'living or dead, in the Labour Party who has managed a real degree of intimacy with him'. There was a 'remoteness' about Stepney's mayor.[61] In return, Attlee got a taste of the behaviour of one of the major egos in the Labour Party. Morrison had approached him and offered him a position as a Labour alderman on the London County Council in 1919, only to renege on the offer and give it to a personal friend. Morrison swiftly forgot the incident; Attlee never did.[62] He came to the conclusion that Morrison was a colleague not to be trusted. The suspicion, it would later prove, was not without justification.

IV

On Monday, 18 October 1920, Attlee joined Lansbury, Morrison and nineteen other London Labour mayors in leading a deputation to Downing Street to protest against unemployment. They had been granted an interview with David Lloyd George, the prime minister. They were accompanied on the walk along the Embankment by well-drilled columns of unemployed men, mostly former soldiers, from each borough, marching in formation.[63] The mayors went into Number 10 and passed on their petitions to Lloyd George, who promised to give them consideration. Outside, however, a boisterous section of the crowd edged closer to Downing Street, broke ranks, and began to throw stones at the police. The mounted officers drew their batons and charged the crowd.[64] The mayors left Number 10 just in time to see what appeared to be the early stages of a riot. Attlee jogged round to George Street and found his men had moved from their resting place and were marching, in perfect order, towards the fight. As he recalled the story, he stepped in front and raised his hand. 'Stepney, Halt!' he shouted, then ordered an about-turn.[65] From there, he led them back to Stepney, 'thus saving some broken heads'.[66]

The following day, a meeting of the London County Council (LCC) was convened so that the mayors could report on the summit with the prime minister. Protestors thronged the galleries waiting to hear the outcome of the previous day's discussions. It was announced that the government would fund the LCC with a grant to begin a public works scheme to build arterial roads in London. The news did little to calm the atmosphere. The men in the gallery repeatedly chanted, 'We want grub, grub, grub.' Three days after 'the Battle of Downing Street' the newly formed Communist Party of Great Britain made its presence felt by occupying the offices of the Poor Law Guardians. With 20,000 unemployed in Stepney alone, Labour needed to find an answer.[67]

In 1921, Lansbury, the leader of Poplar Borough Council, broke ranks. Due to the severe conditions in Poplar, one of the poorest areas in the city, he refused to pay the contributions legally required of the borough by the London County Council and the Metropolitan Police. The Labour Party had campaigned for an equalisation of rates across London but the Poplar leaders took an independent course on the grounds that the situation it faced was more urgent. More moderate party leaders were irritated at what was perceived to be Lansbury's renegade behaviour. There was also a feeling that his campaign was misdirected. The LCC, despite its Conservative majority, was running services across the city and had been hoping to equalise rates. Any refusal to cooperate with it would only hold up the provision of education, school meals and medical treatment.

Typically, egos were at stake. Attlee made it clear that he was not happy with the Lansbury line because 'the real people we were after were in the government.' But he refused to condemn his old friend in public. This was left to Herbert Morrison, on the London Labour Party Executive, who denounced the Labour leaders of Poplar for their recklessness. Morrison was incandescent when Attlee visited him to complain that Lansbury had been singled out by a comrade in this way. To Morrison's fury, Stepney's mayor delivered 'a needle-pointed and rather superior lecture, in the manner of major-to-private'.[68] For Morrison, this was the first example of what he saw as a pattern in Attlee's political career: a failure to lead, and a willingness to let others do the dirty work. For Attlee's defenders, his unwillingness to condemn colleagues and friends, even when he disagreed with them, was something that inspired admiration and loyalty. 'You could be in a Limehouse pub and run down the Tories, and you could run down the Labour party,' recalled his batman Charlie Griffith, 'but if you ran down the Major, somebody might come up and give you the old one two.'[69]

There were other occasions when the Mayor of Stepney's passions got the better of him. Speaking in Oxford at a conference on social welfare, he showed that he had imbibed something of the radical tone of Poplarism, if not quite to the extent of endorsing anything unconstitutional. Shaking with anger he had denounced the self-comforting monologues of the rich and comfortable philanthropists he had heard speak. 'I sit on a man's back, choking him, and making him carry me,' he declared, quoting Tolstoy's *Writings on Civil Disobedience and Nonviolence*, 'and yet assure myself and others that I am very sorry for him and wish to ease his lot by any means possible, except getting off his back.' The passionate outburst shocked the assembled guests. 'Who would have thought it of him? He looked such a little gentleman,' remarked one shocked countess from Berkshire.[70]

Nonetheless, as his term as mayor came to an end, even the ratepayers of the *East London Observer* were rather wistful at his departure. In their view, the local Labour Party could not be grateful enough at the way in which he had upheld standards of common sense and decency in the office. They feared his successor, Joseph Cahill, was a firebrand.[71] Such practical experience of local government was the perfect rebuttal to the idea that Labour was irresponsible or revolutionary. At the end of his tenure in 1920, he published a Fabian Tract on 'Borough Councils', which was full of practical good sense about the role of local government and civic responsibility.[72] In this regard, he was certainly prepared to give the Webbs credit for the training they had offered him and others. Through such Fabian pamphlets, young citizen soldiers had been armed for the fight. 'The Socialist, unable to make more than a small breach in the citadel of power at Westminster, got elected to the local council and, thanks to the Webbs, was far better instructed in the problems of municipal administration and far more alive to its possibilities than his opponents of the old parties.'[73]

V

Having been chosen as the Labour candidate for Limehouse, a career in national politics seemed to beckon. Yet this did not translate into personal happiness. These were trying years for the Attlee family. On 19 May 1920, cancer took Ellen Attlee, who was now seventy-two. With both parents dead, the family home was sold. Then, on 30 June, the eldest Attlee sister Dorothy – just forty-two – also died. Mig went to look after Dorothy's seven children, meaning that she was unable to act as Stepney's unofficial mayoress. Tom and his wife Kathleen had already moved to Cornwall, building a small cottage in the countryside between Truro and Falmouth. The youngest Attlee, Laurence, was married in July 1921. This left Clement lonelier than ever. He had not only lost his parents but he no longer had the same companionship from his three closest siblings, who had moved out of London and were starting families. His poetry had often adverted to the loneliness that he had felt, particularly during the war: 'My lamp is burning but in vain, in vain.'[74]

At thirty-six years old, he might have given up on finding love. He had shown little interest in women before, and might have resigned himself to life as a bachelor. This was perhaps because he lacked any aptitude for the showmanship that such courtship required. In his long evening discussions with Attlee over the previous eighteen months, his election agent John Beckett noted that Attlee's usual calm deserted him on this subject. If anything, he seemed suspicious of the fair sex. 'The few occasions when his humour became caustic were in his discussions about feminine methods and their effect on masculine life. Never a young woman came near a friend without his instant realisation that she was "gunning for poor old so-and-so".'[75]

In need of some cheer in the summer of 1921, he agreed to take a holiday to Italy with Tom and Edric Millar – a close friend of Tom's from Oxford, who was now working at the Treasury. In the travelling party was Edric's mother and his younger sister Violet. The Millars were a genteel, Conservative-supporting family from Hampstead Village in north London. Born in 1896, 25-year-old Violet – the shier and less outgoing of a set of twins – was thirteen years younger than the rabble-rousing socialist from Stepney. She had volunteered as a Red Cross nurse during the war but had no professional ambitions of her own. She had been outshone by a prettier and more vivacious twin, who had a place at Cambridge. The contrast between the meek Violet Millar and Tom's outspoken suffragette wife, Kathleen, could not have been more profound.

Over the course of a few weeks these two shy souls were given an opportunity to open up that the bustle of Attlee's normal life would never have allowed. What followed, as Attlee later described in his personal memoirs, was a 'never to be forgotten' holiday which, over five weeks, took in Milan, Florence, Cortona, Orvieto, Perugia and San Marino.[76] He took the lead – first by acting as a tour guide, making the best possible use of his knowledge of Italian history. The two became inseparable. Rather than making any effusive declarations, they were rather dazed by the experience of falling in love. At one stage, young Violet woke up during an overnight train journey to find her besotted tour guide gazing at her. She later recalled to her daughter that this was when she knew that her future husband was in love with her. 'Of course, I was in love with *him* already.'[77]

It was to John Beckett's surprise that his housemate and employer had returned from his continental tour so enchanted with the sister of his friend. 'In response to a query whether she had been "gunning",' like all the other girls, Attlee seemed like a changed man. He opened up unexpectedly about how much he feared that she was unattainable: 'he spent some time telling me how difficult his task was, and how fortunate he hoped to be.'[78] In fact, now presented with an opportunity, Attlean efficiency was put to great effect. The courtship was remarkably swift. Within a few weeks of their return, they were engaged and then married, in Hampstead on 10 January 1922, the week of Clement's thirty-ninth birthday. Presiding over the service were Bernard Attlee and Violet's eldest brother, who was also a clergyman. They were to have three daughters and a son over the course of a devoted marriage. As he confessed to his siblings, he was 'mad as a March hare with joy'. Mary, the eldest sister, reported that he was 'transformed' and 'tremendously in love'. When the news was reported in the *East London Pioneer*, Attlee joked that there was a similarity between his love life and the Labour movement: 'waiting some time, before it came unto his own'.[79]

Violet did not have her husband's sense of adventure, or robustness, and he was eager to cocoon her from the harsh world in which he operated. Having devoted his public and private life to Stepney, he now drew up a

wall between these two worlds. There was no question of Violet ever joining her husband in grimy Limehouse on the top floor of Norway House,
with its lumps of coal under the bed. They moved to a modest house in
Woodford in Essex, which was five miles and a direct train journey away
from Stepney. There would be difficult years ahead – not least because
Violet could not match her husband's seemingly unshakeable capacity for
cheerful stoicism and succumbed to depression at various points in her
life. Clem saw no flaws in his wife, only someone to cherish and protect,
and to whom he was eternally grateful for her willingness to be his companion. It was a relationship girded by mutual adoration. This was to prove
an essential foundation for the career in national politics that Attlee was
about to begin – an arduous slog, a test of nerve and endurance.

6

Building Jerusalem

And did those feet in ancient time
Walk upon England's mountains green:
And was the holy Lamb of God,
On England's pleasant pastures seen!

And did the Countenance Divine,
Shine forth upon our clouded hills?
And was Jerusalem builded here,
Among these dark Satanic Mills?

Bring me my Bow of burning gold;
Bring me my Arrows of desire:
Bring me my Spear: O clouds unfold!
Bring me my Chariot of fire!

I will not cease from Mental Fight,
Nor shall my Sword sleep in my hand:
Till we have built Jerusalem,
In England's green & pleasant Land.

William Blake, 'And did those feet in
ancient time', 1808, quoted by Clement
Attlee in *The Social Worker*, 1920[1]

I *West End of London, 16 November 1922*

On the evening of Wednesday, 16 November 1922, the West End of London was packed with thousands of spectators as the general election results were flashed up on specially installed giant screens in Piccadilly Circus, Trafalgar Square and the junction between Tottenham Court Road and Oxford Street. Huge floodlights shone down on the packed crowds. A reporter for the *Daily Herald* compared the scenes to one of H. G. Wells's science fiction stories. There were cheers when 'Labour gain' flashed across the screen.[2] Just a few hundred yards away, at the 1917 Club in Soho, Clement Attlee was enjoying a glass or two with the leaders of the Labour Party, as his constituency would not be declared until the next day. He would have to wait for his own fate to be decided. That evening, he celebrated with friends instead as the results flooded in from elsewhere.[3]

The following morning, back in Limehouse, Attlee learned that he had become the first Oxford graduate to represent the Labour Party as a Member of Parliament.[4] It had been a close contest, but eventually he defeated the sitting Liberal MP, William Pearce, a supporter of the Lloyd George-led coalition, by 1,899 votes. His election address was a bold appeal to the tradition of the socialist commonwealth movement through which he had entered the Labour Party. 'I stand for life against wealth,' he told his rapturous supporters, 'I claim the right of every man, woman and child in the land to have the best life that can be provided. Instead of the exploitation of the mass of the people in the interests of a small rich class, I demand the organization of the country in the interests of all as a co-operative commonwealth in which land and capital will be owned by the nation and used for the benefit of the country.'[5] This was just what Edward Bellamy had demanded.

'Splendid – but we'll do better yet,' was the headline that greeted the final declaration of results in Labour's *Daily Herald*. The Conservatives had a majority of eighty-five seats but the Labour Party had gained sixty-eight seats to take it up to 137 (and 29.7 per cent of the overall vote). It was now the largest party in Scotland and its vote in London was up 128 per cent, from 146,468 to 333,035.[6] The two factions of the Liberal Party – ravaged by the war – were split almost exactly, with fifty-eight MPs who had broken with Lloyd George over conscription and fifty-seven for the National Liberals (those who had remained in the wartime coalition). One notable scalp was Winston Churchill, defeated in Dundee by a prohibitionist.[7] There was one Communist returned to the House, J. T. W. Newbold from Motherwell. In Scotland the political atmosphere was generally more radical, particularly in shipbuilding towns.[8]

The result meant that the Labour Party was the second strongest party and became His Majesty's official opposition in Parliament. On 22 November 1922, a celebratory rally was held for Labour activists in London at Kingsway Hall. The hall was overflowing and the speakers could barely make themselves heard as 'The Red Flag' was sung with gusto. 'Whenever we fought on the full programme of the Socialist movement, there we won,' Attlee told the crowd. Their boldness had been rewarded. There were many people who had suggested that Labour would have done better 'if it had temporised', or taken up the position of 'gentle critics of the present system', like the Liberals. It had refused this course and would instead bring a new formula to Westminster, one that combined 'reality and principle'.[9] In the excitement of that meeting, a number of the new MPs had become rather over-excited, noted the *East London Advertiser*. For example, George Lansbury, returned for Bromley and Bow, had said that 'every man should be his own House of Commons.' Major Attlee had sounded more radical, offering forthright denunciations of the government's betrayal of the working man. By the time he took his seat in the House of Commons, however, the *East London Advertiser* guessed that the new MP for Limehouse would be likely to stay on the path of 'legislative rectitude', no matter how much he might wander on the platform.[10]

Looking back on his early political career, Attlee later admitted that he had let himself be carried away by the febrile atmosphere of the immediate post-war years. It was a time 'where I sowed my wild oats – besides, until we got in office, there wasn't much else to do.'[11] But he also had learned important lessons that were to shape his approach to national politics, which he addressed at length in his 1920 book, *The Social Worker*. The book, which was 286 pages long, has not been given the attention it deserves. Principled, pluralistic and humane – rather than utopian or absolute – it is the forgotten script of the twentieth-century Labour Party.[12]

In the book Attlee set out the challenge facing the Labour movement in a way that reflected his own journey. He identified three developments that had transformed British politics and were to shape the decades that followed. The first was the recognition, beginning at the time of the Boer War, that social conditions among the poor were intimately connected to the health of the nation as a whole. The self-confident Victorian belief in progress, that 'evolution inevitably moves towards a higher and better state', had been checked by the emergence of imperial rivalry, and British fears of national decline. As Lloyd George had noted when introducing the New Liberal welfare reforms after 1906, Britain could not produce an A1 nation from C3 conditions. Victorian political economy, which held that the state must not interfere in social questions, was not only inhumane and inflexible; it had been rejected by the ruling classes as damaging to the future of the nation. In a revealing passage he quoted the work of Professor Urwick, his head of faculty at the London School of Economics, where he continued to lecture. Urwick was a student of T. H. Green and another alumnus of Toynbee Hall. His 1912 book *A Philosophy of Social Progress* bemoaned the way in which Victorian political and economic theory had undermined traditional British notions of citizenship and commonwealth. It was because of the emphasis on individual liberty in the prevailing economic theories of the nineteenth century that 'the pervading duties of citizenship are lost sight of in the wilderness of interests of both individuals and groups'.

The second major change had been brought about by the mobilisation of the country for total war after 1914. Every citizen had been asked to make sacrifices for the community. It had been argued, 'and by none so loudly as by those whose conception of citizenship had not previously been highly developed, that it was the duty of every man to do services in the trenches or munition works' in order to serve the national cause. Those who had refused to fight on the grounds of individual conscience, such as his brother Tom, had been excluded from the community. After the war, however, it was no longer acceptable to argue that citizenship was passive or dormant except in times of crisis. The population had rights as well as duties, but these had been betrayed by their government after 1918.

The third major change since the war, and the greatest opportunity for Labour, was the advent of democracy. The 1918 Representation of the People Act had increased the voting roll from 7 million to 20 million, effectively tripling it. The poor were no longer 'an inert mass on which the kindly disposed may exert moral or material pressure, or mould to their own liking'. They now claimed full citizenship. Society was built upon a series of rights and duties, expressed or implied. They may vary at different stages of human development and between different social classes, 'but at our present stage of development in which all do at least lip-service to democracy, our ideal is the fullest opportunity for the development of the human soul.' The days of a political system devised on the basis of class were passing. Whichever group one belonged to, all were united as members of the same society.[13]

The citizen ideal was one which the state and the individual needed to serve, in the name of a broader democratic community. This must begin at the local level. One of the greatest services that one could perform for one's community was getting elected onto local bodies 'to help create civic feeling and local patriotism'. Socialists may have remained deeply unsatisfied with the situation in post-war Britain, but the point that Attlee was making was that they no longer had any excuse for failing to participate. He threw down the gauntlet to those who believed they were 'above the rough and tumble of a local election', or above the need for compromise in politics. He condemned the 'revolutionary idealist' who rejected democratic participation. This type of extremist would 'criticise and condemn all methods of social advance that do not directly square with his formulae and will repeat his shibboleths without any attempt to work out their practical application'.[14]

So, even before he entered Westminster, he had come to understand that two principles must guide the Labour Party going forward. The first was patience, 'because things move very slowly, and years of effort are needed before any results are obtained'. The second was tolerance, 'because you will have to work with people who do not see things as you do, young people in a hurry and old people who have outgrown their enthusiasms and their capacity for receiving new ideas, and all sorts of cranks who will misunderstand and possibly misrepresent you'.[15]

A quarter of a century before he became prime minister of the first majority socialist government in British history, the essence of his message was that 'the dreamer must keep his feet on the earth and the thinker must come out of his study.' Yet it would be wrong to see this as some sort of plea for dry pragmatism. It was in the first few pages of *The Social Worker* that Attlee made use of William Blake's 1808 poem, 'And did those feet in ancient time', as an illustration of the idealism which drove him on.[16] The poem had been set to music in 1916 and had become a well-known patriotic hymm. The way that Attlee invoked it on the eve of his career as a national political figure says much about his brand of patriotically infused, sentimental socialism. On the one hand was Blake's unease with the 'dark Satanic Mills' that were springing up across the English landscape in the early nineteenth century – which represented the scourge of industrialisation. On the other hand was a promise of a better world to be built. The idea of building a 'New Jerusalem' was to become a centrepiece of the Labour Party message in the twentieth century. Thirty years later, Attlee announced the 1951 Labour manifesto with the call to arms, 'Let's go forward into this fight in the spirit of William Blake.'[17] The hymn was also sung at his funeral in 1967.

In the early 1920s, it remained unclear as to what that 'New Jerusalem' might look like in practice, or how it would be reached. For one thing, the Labour Party remained an uneasy coalition of different interest groups – from trade union representatives to intellectuals – from across the country, and had not yet fully developed a national identity. For much of the next two decades, it was to continue to debate strategy, tactics, ideas and economic theory and struggle to settle upon a shared programme.[18] Ultimately, it was an Attlean path that delivered it success.

II

With the electoral breakthrough of November 1922, a new phase in the history of the Labour Party began. The diffuse nature of Labour's support – with separate strongholds in northwest England, Scotland and London – created dilemmas as well as opportunities. If localism was one potential obstacle, another was factionalism. As Attlee had already recognised, an obsession with the sanctity of one's own ideas – a politics which took, as its starting point, the primacy of individual conscience – would hinder the creation of a broad appeal to different communities and different regions. Pacifism had split the party during the war, and those wounds were still raw. Thus the first thing the post-war party had to do was to articulate a coherent foreign policy. Labour's commitment to internationalism – support for the League of Nations and the ideas contained in Woodrow Wilson's Fourteen Points – gave it an idea, albeit a vague one, to cohere around.

The MPs of the party assembled at noon on Tuesday, 21 November, with two stated priorities. The first was to pressure the government to tackle the scourge of unemployment. The second was to push them to articulate an alternative foreign policy – a democratic internationalism working through the League of Nations. Many of those who had led the party before the war were returned, including J. R. Clynes, J. H. Thomas and Will Thorne. Also returned were a number of the pacifists whose stance had seen them defeated in the patriotic atmosphere of 1918 – chiefly Ramsay MacDonald, Philip Snowden and George Lansbury. The Labour benches were supplemented by two former Liberals in the ranks with experience of government – Charles Trevelyan and H. B. Lees-Smith. Of the new MPs, a number of them were well known for long service to the party at the grass-roots level. These included Sidney Webb, John Wheatley, Thomas Johnston, Emanuel Shinwell, William Whitley and Attlee himself.[19] As new appointments were made within the party, the *Daily Herald* urged unity, stressing that the movement had to be based on broad principles rather than personality.[20]

It was immediately clear that there were divisions among new members. Labour's success in the north was largely reliant on mobilising the financial power of the major trade unions, particularly in mining, transport and manufacturing. The MPs for these constituencies tended to be more moderate and cautious. They were usually less ideologically driven and set their sights on practical gains on trade union rights and unemployment welfare. Having fought in a Lancashire regiment during the war, this was something that Attlee understood better than many. The most radical MPs were the 'Clydesiders' from the shipbuilding districts around Glasgow, led by Jimmy Maxton of the Independent Labour Party. Maxton kept his independence from the mainstream Labour Party, though he supported it on most issues. In London, where the party had also performed strongly, the trade union presence was less pronounced. In east London – where Labour had taken Poplar, West Ham, Whitechapel and Stratford, as well as Limehouse – casual workers, many employed on a day-to-day basis at the docks, had formed the core of the Labour vote.

As a London Labour MP, Attlee was no bland moderate. In his history of the Labour Party, the Fabian intellectual Douglas Cole pointed out that Attlee sided with the radicals over the moderates on most debates within the Independent Labour Party in 1921 and 1922.[21] What he did have, however, was a greater sense of the plurality of the Labour movement. This plurality was a potential asset, if handled correctly. As Attlee observed, a typical Labour party supporter might be a member of the Notts and Derby Miners' Union, a casual labourer in the London docks, or a middle-class intellectual. It may be that he 'follows Tottenham Hotspur or Sheffield Wednesday at football, belongs to the Utility Rabbit Breeding Society, or plays the big drum in the Silver Prize Band'. Socialism was a secondary consideration at best to most citizens, even if they fitted the profile of a natural Labour supporter. 'Much of our trouble today comes from not seeing that England is mapped out into a very large number of conflicting and overlapping circles, and from expecting that each man will be interested in the same set of activities.'[22]

Ramsay MacDonald, a founding member of the Labour Representation Committee in 1900, was widely regarded to be the most charismatic figure in the Labour movement. As the new Labour MPs assembled, there was at least agreement that they should be represented in Parliament by their most capable leaders. J. R. Clynes had been acting leader in the absence of Ramsay MacDonald. After a vote of the parliamentary party, he was replaced by MacDonald as chairman; Clynes became deputy leader, while Arthur Henderson was made chief whip. MacDonald, a former schoolmaster, had previously led the party from 1911 to 1914, before resigning over the war. In what were to become prescient words, Clynes accepted the vote in good grace but warned – with an eye on MacDonald – that the cause was greater than those who led it.

MacDonald's undoubted talents as a parliamentarian, and his appeal to the public, came with an ego and a sense of superiority that annoyed some of his colleagues. Among some Labour veterans, there was a sense that he should be watched with care. This suspicion was not shared by Attlee, however. Although he did not hold with his pacifism, he was drawn to the leader's emphasis on political gradualism and moderation. Stopped by the lobby correspondent of the *Daily Herald* just after his election, MacDonald said that it was a 'magnificent thing' to have such support around him, including men who had 'already proved themselves in the fight'.[23] In fact, he was concerned about the influence of the more radical new MPs, particularly the Clydesiders. In order to balance against them, he turned to Attlee when filling one of two positions to act as his parliamentary private secretary (PPS). 'I have heard good accounts of a fellow named Attlee; do you think he would do it?' he had asked Clynes.[24]

The new MP for Limehouse had no hesitation in accepting. 'I had been a great admirer of many years,' he later recalled.[25] He was to work alongside Jack Lawson, a trade unionist and the representative of the Durham miners. Crucially Lawson was also a veteran of the war. The acquisition of these two had the additional advantage of giving MacDonald political cover in an area in which he was vulnerable to criticism because of his pacifism. Lawson had been in Parliament since 1918 and acted as a mentor to Attlee. This was the beginning of one of Attlee's most important political friendships. It was based on mutual fondness but it gave Attlee the benefit of being plugged into the beating heart of the trade union movement. 'The personal pronoun doesn't exist for him. He is objective; and appears to be free of many common human weaknesses . . . And loyalty is the very core of him.' Lawson wrote of his new colleague, 'Speaking as one who knows him as intimately as anyone outside of his household, I can say he is the most selfless man I have ever known, unshakeable in his loyalty to friends and colleagues and motivated by a deep and profound sympathy for the humble men and women who do the ordinary tasks of the world.'[26] A reputation for these qualities was to stand him in good stead.

III

On 23 November Attlee made his maiden speech. Reverting to the theme that had seen him win the seat for Limehouse, he referred the government to the awful state of unemployment in his constituency. 'The true wealth of the country and its finest asset are its citizens,' but under the present system, thousands of them could not even find homes. In Limehouse, two-thirds of the dwellings were beyond repair. In London as a whole, 600,000 people occupied one-room tenements. Many of those suffering were 'the same men who saved us during the war. They are the same men who served side by side in the trenches.' There had been full employment during the war. What was required was the taking hold of the purchasing power of the country, by 'directing the energies of the nation into the production of necessities for life, and not merely into the production of luxuries or necessities for profit'. In a flourish he finished with a plea: 'As the nation was organised for war and death, so it can be organised for peace and life if we have the will for it.'[27] Though much was to happen in the intervening years, the very same sentiments were at the heart of Labour's election message in its greatest-ever victory, in May 1945.

Following Attlee in the debate, MacDonald referred to the march that his new parliamentary private secretary had led to Downing Street two years before. Was there not something wrong with a country in which the Strand could be blocked with the Rolls-Royces of the wealthy one week, and processions of the unemployed the next? There was another intervention of note at the end of the debate, when Newbold, the single Communist MP, rose to speak and members rushed back into the chamber. Speaking with a booming voice and making animated gestures, he expressed his pride at speaking as the 'sole representative of the scarlet banner of Mr Nikolai Lenin', though – at the Speaker's insistence – he withdrew his claim that the opening of Parliament was a 'tomfool show'. There was ironic laughter when Newbold insisted that if the demands of the unemployed were not met in Parliament, they would be achieved outside, to which he reddened and bit back fiercely: 'You may laugh today, gentleman of England and Scotland, but they laugh best who laugh last.'[28]

It was an indication of Attlee's growing stature in the Labour Party that he was profiled by the party newspaper, the *Daily Herald*, in December 1922. 'Slight figure, delicate complexion, lofty brow and gentle manners – his personality wins you from the first, but you would hardly guess what work this man of 39 has done as scholar, soldier, and administrator.' He was a one-time imperialist who had been through a personal revolution, even before joining the ILP. Now he was best known as a champion of the abandoned heroes of the war. What drove Attlee was his dream of a 'Cooperative Commonwealth' but he was a firm parliamentarian in the MacDonaldite mould. 'The essence of democracy,' he was quoted as saying, 'is government by discussion.'[29]

Certainly, MacDonald saw him as a kindred spirit. He confided in his parliamentary private secretary that he thought George Lansbury, at one point Attlee's mentor, was a rather 'noisy fellow'. As Attlee moved into national politics, it was clear that he too left some of his old post-war radicalism behind him. This was simply a matter of necessity, he made clear. George Lansbury was 'a man of his time' with 'the moral earnestness of the Victorians', he later reflected, but 'It was not for him to plan in detail the New Jerusalem, but by example as well as precept to show people the way of life which they must follow if a new society was to be built on firm foundations.'[30] In other words, the ethical core of the Labour movement had been established by its pioneers. But an aspiring party of government needed a vision of the state: some practical ballast to go with its idealism.

One reason why Attlee regarded such clarity as so important was that he recognised the importance of establishing Labour as the genuine national alternative to the Conservative Party, at the expense of the Liberal Party. This had a tactical as well as an ideological dimension. In an article in *Socialist Review* in March 1922, he had suggested that it was best for Labour to avoid cooperation with the Liberals in certain constituencies (as it had done in the pre-war era). It was far wiser for the party to establish its independence.[31] Just as important for Attlee was his desire to emphasise the deep ideological differences between the two parties. Many Liberals joined the Labour Party after 1918. There is no doubt that it benefited from the acquisition of many 'New Liberal' progressives, such as the Webbs. A number of the prominent New Liberal thinkers saw Labour's development as a testament to the influence of their ideas. Indeed L. T. Hobhouse made this case by referring specifically to Attlee's political vision in 1924, as grounded in the same trinity of 'Liberty, Equality and Fraternity'. It was a revived idea of citizenship, which he traced back to the influence of T. H. Green, 'which gave raise to the social liberalism of recent times and to its twin, the ethical socialism described by Major Attlee'.[32]

In fact, Attlee went out of his way to reject the idea that his ethical socialism had anything to do with the social liberalism that Hobhouse referred to. From the moment he came into national politics, he was eager to contradict any suggestion that twentieth-century British socialism was the next stage in the evolution of nineteenth-century liberalism – that Edwardian Labour was the heir to the Victorian Liberal Party. In January 1923, he published a review essay in the *New Leader* arguing that the Liberal interpretation of the nineteenth century underlined the yawning chasm exposed between these two different creeds. 'His conception of society and its ends is different from ours. Our gods are not his gods,' he wrote of New Liberals like Hobhouse. At various points, he was prepared to give Liberals credit for their efforts on social reform. Yet the rise of the Labour Party was in itself a demonstration of their ultimate bankruptcy.

In the Liberal, or Whig, version of events, the nineteenth century was the age of great enlightenment and progress. It witnessed the rise to power of the middle classes with whom, of course, the Liberal Party was principally identified. As a reflection of this, its chief achievements made much of political reform, such as household suffrage, colonial self-government in Canada and the disestablishment of the Irish Church. The Industrial Revolution made modern Britain, though it was accompanied by some 'disadvantages', such as child labour, sweatshops and slums. To the Liberal, these were the inevitable 'birth pangs of a new and glorious state of society'. Attlee referred to G. M. Trevelyan's 1922 book, *British History in the Nineteenth Century (1782–1901)*, as a classic example of such a viewpoint. While he admired Trevelyan's attempt to achieve balance, his argument was based on the assumption that capitalism and landlordism were the best instruments of social progress. Thus, while Trevelyan acknowledged the miseries of industrialisation, he also claimed that, by the time of Queen Victoria's Golden Jubilee in 1897, most of the victims of the Industrial Revolution had escaped their bondage. Parliamentary reform, initiated by a benevolent governing class, had provided the necessary palliatives to mitigate its effects.[33] (It is worth noting that, many years later, Attlee was more impressed by Trevelyan's *English Social History*, as a corrective to his earlier work.[34])

The socialist reading of the nineteenth century rejected Trevelyan's core premise. The Industrial Revolution was but the 'first act of the tragedy'. It set in motion the change from 'an order of society in which each person has a definite status in the community to a system in which the vast mass of the population are proletarians, wage-slaves with no right or position in industry.' Liberalism had won the day in the nineteenth century. It had achieved its aims and it had no more worlds to conquer. That, above all, was why it was flailing and failing to find a programme. Socialism, which regarded the previous century as a failure and a tragedy, was 'beginning to come into its own'.[35] There were a number of core tenets from liberalism that Attlee thought valuable, but he entirely rejected the economic system that came with it. In fact, he believed that the best qualities of liberalism were ultimately incompatible with capitalism. 'I think myself that socialism must take the vital parts of liberalism with it . . . the realisation of the value of the individual and the value of variety', he later elaborated, 'but I consider that can only be achieved through socialism.'[36]

In rejecting liberal economics and the liberal interpretation of history, Attlee made sure to stop short of adopting a narrowly Marxist or determinist version of the past in its stead. It was too limiting to assume, as many

Marxists did, that economic forces were the main agent of historical change. 'There are people who try to reduce all human activity to one plane, who rule out all other motives save those of material gain,' and who 'read into the past the conditions of the present', he wrote. The socialist historian must not focus solely on economic history, but must deal with every side of human activity. He should be no less interested in 'the struggle of mankind to gain freedom of thought and escape from the bondage of superstition than with his various contrivances for gaining economic freedom'.[37]

This rejection of Marxism also gave Attlee the room to make another argument which was central to his conception of why Labour was starting to achieve national success. The party rejected the rapacious imperialism which had infected a number of European states in recent times. But this was because imperialism had become an extension of capitalist greed, 'merely the extension of exploitation to a larger field'. It was the duty of the socialist to uncover the profit motive behind this false nationalism. This meant uncovering 'the Wernher Beit and Co. behind the Rudyard Kipling'.[38] Wernher Beit and Co. was an easy target. It was the company of Sir Julius Charles Wernher, a German-born aristocrat and art collector, known for ruthless acquisition of gold and diamond mines in South Africa before the First World War. By the time of his death in 1912, he was one of the richest men in Britain, with huge investments in the diamond and gold trades in Africa. This was a flash of that crude anti-German sentiment that Attlee was not immune to using at various points in his career. But it was employed to illustrate a crucial point: Labour was the most genuinely patriotic of the three main parties. It was a theme to which he would often return.

IV

These were eventful years, in professional and personal terms. As Mac-Donald's PPS, Attlee served a useful apprenticeship behind the front benches, and became an expert on parliamentary procedure. He also learned about the toll that such a demanding job could take upon a young family. After their first child, Janet, was born in February 1923, Violet suffered from a condition which was most likely a form of post-natal depression. As she entered a clinic for a number of months, her husband was left as the principal carer of the child, though both their families provided support given the demands that his career placed on his time, even during the summer recess of 1923.

Events in Westminster required his full attention, and the lecturing job at the London School of Economics was given up, even though it provided a useful source of additional income. By the autumn of 1923, as Violet returned home, the Conservative prime minister, Andrew Bonar Law, had resigned due to ill heath. His successor as Conservative leader, Stanley Baldwin, believed that drastic measures were needed in order to lift the economy out of recession. Bonar Law had been a free trader; now, in October 1923, Baldwin announced his preference for protection in order to boost consumption of domestic products. Notwithstanding the differences between them, one thing that the Labour and Liberal Parties were agreed upon was their commitment to free trade. The mainstream of the Labour movement, including Attlee, shared the belief that it kept down the costs of living for the worker.

At the general election that followed the dissolution of Parliament in October 1923, the Conservatives lost their outright majority. In Limehouse, Attlee cemented his hold with an increased majority of 6,000. Nationally, Labour only made minor gains, winning 191 seats in total. Yet the supporters of free trade, including both factions of the Liberal Party, had a parliamentary majority. This meant that they could prevent Baldwin from taking office, even though neither Labour nor the Liberals could form a majority government on their own. A coalition between Labour and the Liberals was rejected by Labour. However, the Liberals suggested they would support a pro-free trade Labour administration. Though the conditions were far from ideal, Ramsay MacDonald took the decision to form a minority government.

On 21 January 1924, Ramsay MacDonald became the first Labour prime minister of Britain. Privately, as he left Buckingham Palace after seeing the king, he told Philip Snowden, his closest ally, that he was appalled by the poverty of talent around him. According to Herbert Morrison, the new MP for Hackney South, he was already showing signs of that 'remote and defensive attitude to those around him that in the end left him with virtually no friends in the real sense of the word'.[39]

Certainly, MacDonald had no great estimation of Attlee's talent. He was no mentor to the Major. But Attlee was regarded as sufficiently steady and reliable to be invited to enter the government in February 1924, serving as Under-Secretary of State for War, working alongside Jack Lawson, who was financial secretary. The minister they reported to was Stephen Walsh, another Lancashire miner known as 'Wee Stee' because of his small stature. A number of the under-secretaries and parliamentary secretaries from the last Parliament were also elevated to the second rank. Arthur Greenwood became a junior minister at the Department of Health, Margaret Bondfield at Labour, Willie Graham at the Treasury, A. V. Alexander at the Board of Trade and Emanuel Shinwell as Secretary of Mines. All were to play important roles in the party thereafter.[40]

Was Labour fit to govern? The former Liberal prime minister, Lloyd George, took to the *Daily Chronicle* to suggest that Ramsay MacDonald would be a responsible prime minister. For this, however, there would have to be some curtailing of socialist ambitions. At a meeting of the London Labour Party at Shoreditch Town Hall in January 1924, supporters were warned that there would be no 'millennium in a moment'. Yet already the Clydesiders were drifting towards a more radical position. Members of the Independent Labour Party, who were not fully incorporated into the main Parliamentary Labour Party, used the opportunity to express their independence. MacDonald would have a difficult task in keeping his minority government together.[41]

Though he was not a particular favourite of the leader, Attlee remained a committed MacDonaldite at this stage. It was perhaps a measure of his own lack of confidence that he was unperturbed by his leader's unwillingness to promote him to higher office. He shared MacDonald's faith in gradualism and the belief that the party had to display a sense of national responsibility at this moment. Initially, this seemed justified. MacDonald managed the competing expectations within his party with some skill. The ILP MP for Glasgow, John Wheatley, for example, was brought into the government as Minister of Housing. Despite the tightening of purse strings, some public funds were freed for the building of houses. The Wheatley Housing Act was particularly popular in Stepney as it allocated subsidies to local authorities in order to build houses for rental, and protected tenants more effectively from eviction. Other reforms were more in the tradition of previous Liberal legislation. The Minister of Education, Charles Trevelyan (who had joined the Labour Party from the Liberals in

1918 and was the elder brother of G. M. Trevelyan), established a commission that insisted that every child in the country was entitled to a state-funded secondary education. In a similar vein, there were further increases in old-age pensions and unemployment benefits.

On foreign affairs, the Labour government was also able to establish its reputation for competency. Its professed aim was to breathe fresh life into the League of Nations, which was floundering, partly because of America's decision to stay aloof from it, but mostly owing to resurgent tensions between the European powers. There was also a willingness to soften the harsh terms imposed on Germany at the Treaty of Versailles. The difficulty was that it went against the prevailing mood in France, which remained Britain's most important ally in Europe. In January 1923 France had occupied the Ruhr, Germany's western industrial heartland, in response to a late repayment of reparations, causing German inflation to spiral rapidly out of control.

While never a pacifist, Attlee had been involved in the 'No More War' movement after 1918. In the intervening years, he had proposed a resolution at conference to commit the party to vote against all military and naval estimates, only to be defeated. Now that he was at the War Office, he immediately resigned his membership of the Union of Democratic Control. World disarmament would have to wait.[42]

In truth, it was a difficult balancing act to keep his credibility in the Labour movement, while adjusting to the realities of office. Another anti-war radical, Josiah Wedgwood, had rejected a position at the War Office, a place in which 'red tape and officialdom' reigned. As Attlee mused:

> No more the old street corner
> Where the busy traffic lies
> No more the dear old platform
> And the cause that never dies
> I've got a government job now
> Propaganda isn't wise.[43]

In his first month in office, when the Clydesiders put forward a motion that the army be reduced to 100,000 men, Attlee remained studiously quiet during the debate. Although the government did reduce the army estimates by £7 million, these were cuts that had been instituted by the previous government. In an ideal world, Attlee would have liked to have done more in the War Office to encourage promotion from the lower ranks. He also wrote a memorandum proposing a reduction in the number of offences in which the death sentence was applicable to soldiers who were subject to a court martial. Neither initiative materialised.[44]

Nonetheless, the experience of office was another building block in the profile of a national politician. According to Jack Lawson, Attlee's greatest asset was his mastery of detail and clear-headedness. 'There was steel in him,' he reflected, 'and the spirit of service and integrity which is far above ambition.'[45] Both men had the considerable practical advantage of being respected by the military high command, having distinguished themselves in service. It was as under-secretary at the War Office that Attlee went on a tour of the battlefields and war graves of Europe, by car, from Boulogne to Amiens and Ypres. Along with Lawson, his other travelling companions were Sir Fabian Ware, the founder of the Imperial War Graves Commission; Harry Gosling, the London trade unionist, Labour MP and member of the Imperial War Commission; and also Lieutenant Colonel Reginald Applin, a veteran of the Boer War, and a pioneer of machine-gun warfare, who had stood as a candidate for the far-right Nationalist Party in 1920.[46] The following summer Attlee visited the Middle Eastern theatre. Most of his travelling companions were relatives of fallen soldiers and other ex-servicemen.[47] Alongside him was Laurence, who had also fought at Gallipoli. This time, they had made it through the Dardanelles and stopped at Constantinople.[48] He would continue to study books about the campaign, 'thinking of the lads with whom I trained in 1914, so many of whom lie there in the Peninsula'.[49]

It was a foreign policy crisis that cost the Labour government in yet another general election, the third in two years, in October 1924. As the election approached MacDonald took the decision to recognise the newly formed Union of Soviet Socialist Republics (USSR). With the country preparing to go to the polls, a letter was leaked by the Foreign Office to the *Daily Mail*. It purported to be by Grigory Zinoviev, a senior Russian official in the Communist International, urging the British people to revolt and suggesting that the soothing of diplomatic relations would encourage the radicalisation of British workers. Attlee believed that MacDonald had hesitated and should have denounced the Zinoviev letter as an obvious forgery at the outset. In hindsight, in fact, he began to see this as the moment that MacDonald started to steer in the wrong direction. He seemed to have been embarrassed by the episode and over-compensated by spending too much time in the company of aristocrats.[50]

Liberal Party attempts to use the Zinoviev letter against Labour back-fired, as the Conservatives won a large majority in the fevered atmosphere, gaining 419 seats. In the event, Labour won almost a million more votes than it had in 1923 but was down to 151 seats, a loss of forty. Although Labour were back in opposition, the experience of government had been valuable. Attlee was now established as a consistent and reliable parliamentary performer. He continued to build a reputation as an advocate of milk-and-water socialism, a scourge of cronyism or monopolies and a good parliamentary colleague. In the 1922–3 session, his first year in Parliament, he made fourteen speeches, followed by five in 1923–4, which was disrupted by another election. As a junior minister in 1924–5, this number had risen to forty-eight. In the 1925–6 session he spoke forty times from the opposition benches.[51]

Gradually his name became better recognised in some of the Labour heartlands. On 25 May 1925, the *Darlington Evening Dispatch* reported how he had posed a question to the prime minister, Stanley Baldwin, about ethics in public service. He referred to the practice of persons holding positions in the government, then resigning their appointments and accepting lucrative positions in companies with which they had been in contact during their official careers. He warned Baldwin that such behaviour gravely damaged the confidence that the public had in government servants and urged him to set up a committee to explore the restrictions that should be placed on such behaviour from civil servants after they left government.[52] He also went after the dividends and profits of private companies. He demanded that those firms that had received taxpayer support during the economic crisis should return half their profits as soon as it was clear that they were making a surplus again. He was appalled by the idea that this money would otherwise be distributed to shareholders as dividend payments.[53] It was about time, he said in Parliament in November 1925, that the government did 'something for the working classes in the towns'.[54]

No one saw Attlee as a rising star, however. 'Just an ordinary person, nothing spectacular, hardly going far,' said one fellow MP, Emanuel Shinwell.[55] Nevertheless, Attlee valued the time spent on the opposition benches. He relished not only the camaraderie on his own side but also the relationships that could be built across the floor, even with those with whom he vehemently disagreed. He counted Winston Churchill as a friend from the time he returned to the Commons in 1924 after a two-year exile. Looking back at these years, he reflected that one of the great virtues of Parliament was the continued process of talking and debate, by which 'people can learn to discover that there are virtues in other people's ideas'.[56]

V

The prospect of Britain succumbing to European-style radicalism and disorder reared its head again with the general strike of May 1926. Churchill's decision, as Chancellor of the Exchequer in 1925, to put Britain back on the gold standard had injured the export trade, particularly in coal. The Dawes Plan had also undercut British industry by opening up the German export economy too, as free German coal was sent to Italy and France under the arrangement. The mining industry had failed to keep pace with modernisation in Poland and America, which were both producing cheaper coal at a faster rate. In order to avert collapse and improve output, the owners of the industry demanded that the miners should work a day longer, with less pay. After the breakdown of negotiations, the Trades Union Congress (TUC) called a general strike on 3 May in support of the miners' cause and, the following day, almost 2 million workers went on strike. They were marshalled by a man who was already a massive figure in the Labour movement. Ernest Bevin was the general secretary of the Transport and General Workers' Union, a juggernaut of an amalgamated union. Brusque, thickset and combative, he was the bastard son of a servant girl from Somerset, who had left school at eleven before working on the Bristol docks.[57] It was during 1926 that Attlee first encountered him.

As prime minister, Baldwin framed the strike as an attack on constitutional government. Attlee shared the concerns of the Labour Party leadership that radical, particularly communist elements, might manipulate the crisis in a way that would damage Labour's hard-won reputation for constitutional propriety. But they had to tread carefully over an issue that was a litmus test of Labour's bona fides as the party of the workers. Attlee's own Limehouse constituency, hugely overcrowded and with the unemployed ambling through the streets, looking for work, was one of the most politicised in the country. Joe Jacobs, a local communist activist in Stepney, recalled how there was a different group on every street corner, engaged in some kind of gathering or protest. There were meetings of the Labour Party, Communist Party, various trade unions, anarchists and even a group who followed someone called 'King Anthony', a former police inspector who claimed to be the rightful king of England. Other public spaces were controlled by criminal gangs, drug dealers and unlicensed bookmakers, who ran games of dice and cards. Police flooded the area with special constables, although the locals could normally spot them a mile off because of their poor command of local banter. It was almost as if East Enders spoke different dialects, which combined more or less Yiddish or Irish slang depending on which group one came across.

The communists were a growing presence in the mid-1920s, and saw an opportunity to assert themselves on the national stage at the time of the general strike. They tended to organise in cells, operating in a local ward. The ideal was to have one cell in every street. The Communist Youth League would take boys as young as twelve, and anyone who could read was handed the works of Marx, Engels, Lenin and Trotsky. They also embraced a range of literature, including Émile Zola, Jack London, Thomas Mann, Leo Tolstoy, William Morris, H. G. Wells, J. B. Priestley and Arnold Bennett. On 1 May, every year, they would make their presence felt by singing 'The Red Flag' and marching with their banners down to Hyde Park. Although he was only fourteen at the time of the fall of the Labour government in 1924, Joe Jacobs described hearing about people called Attlee and Lansbury. But in many ways they seemed remote from the action: well-intentioned mainstreamers who would never liberate the workers.[58]

The general strike began on 3 May 1926, following the news that wage cuts would be enforced and that the government refused to continue subsidising the miners' wages. Baldwin recruited special constables and called the army in to keep order. On the day it began, Joe Jacobs witnessed the commotion in Limehouse as people ran toward Commercial Road from all sides, on their way to block the entrance to the docks. Truckloads of soldiers and special constables – volunteers with peaked caps and armbands instead of helmets – passed them by and tried to get there first, hotly pursued by ambulances and fire engines. When Jacobs reached the edge of the entrance to the docks, he saw police on horseback with long truncheons hitting down at the crowd, while the police on the ground tried to force the crowd to get back onto the pavements. There were bloodied heads and scuffles everywhere.[59]

On 11 May, the TUC was faced down. It called off the strike and went back to the negotiating table, once promises were made to reorganise and modernise the failing coal industry. There followed the Trade Disputes Act of 1927, which curtailed the power of the unions – condemned by Labour as another Taff Vale judgement. Attlee had not supported the strike but was cast into the front line by it. As alderman in the area, he was chairman of Stepney's electricity committee. This meant he negotiated with representatives of the TUC during the strike to ensure that a minimum supply was maintained to light Stepney's hospitals, while all non-essential supplies were cut. It was a costly decision. When one local engineering firm, Scammells, refused to cooperate in the arrangement, strikers pulled their fuses. In response, they took up a legal case against Attlee for loss of earnings. The courts supported the claim and, initially, he was ordered to pay £300, which could have almost bankrupted him – a backbench MP received £400 a year – and ended his career.

The next few years were taken up by a lengthy appeal during which the fear of bankruptcy loomed over the family. Attlee was a father of two children under four. Following Janet's birth in 1923, Felicity was born in 1925. Violet was pregnant with a third, Martin, who was born shortly after the general strike. In a long and busy career, he enjoyed those moments when he was able to devote the weekends to his family. But the Scammells case cast a long shadow over the sanctity of a home that he had always tried to insulate from the vissicitudes of politics. It was at this point that he seriously considered retirement from public life.

As one local trade unionist later put it, 'he bore it all on his own shoulders. Before that, we knew he was our friend. Then we knew he was also our champion.'[60] While they remained unimpressed by the Labour Party, even local communists could see some merit in their MP. 'When Clem says a thing you know he means it,' ventured Joe Jacobs, in 1945. 'It always has been like that with him, and we reckon up here it always will be.'[61]

7

Fame is the Spur

Fame is the spur that the clear spirit doth raise
(That last infirmity of Noble mind)
To scorn delights, and live laborious dayes

John Milton, 'Lycidas', quoted in
Howard Spring, *Fame is the Spur*, 1940.

I *Baildon, Yorkshire, November 1889*

Tall, handsome and with no shortage of self-confidence, Hamer Shawcross had been a stalwart of the socialist movement in Lancashire for many years, long before the Labour Party had even been founded. At the general election of 1889, he travelled to Baildon in Yorkshire to help a more hapless comrade try to win election to Parliament. Standing on the platform on election day, it was Hamer who stole the show. He was a man on a mission. He held aloft a sabre in front of the crowd and recited William Blake's poem 'And did those feet in ancient time'. 'This is the sword of oppression,' declared Hamer Shawcross, as he denounced landlords and greedy rentiers, 'I shall tell you how it is being used against us today.' The first time this had happened, it had caused great mirth in the Conservative press. But they soon learned their lesson. The trick worked. As the fortunes of the Labour Party rose, so the country came to know the name of Hamer Shawcross.

More than three decades later, Hamer was a minister in Ramsay Mac-Donald's minority Labour government of 1924. He was still handsome; he had aged well and he had lost none of his powers of oratory. As a minister in the government, however, Hamer's radicalism had been somewhat diluted. He liked government, in truth, and some of the perks that came with it. Indeed, he enjoyed the ceremonial dress that he was sometimes required to wear in Parliament. The sabre he had kept from his early days looked particularly elegant when he donned his robes or put on a white tie for a state occasion. Now, as he sat down in his office to attend to his papers, he sent a servant for coffee and sandwiches. As a minister, he faced pressure from some of his old radical friends to do more to help the poor. Politics, he explained, was not so simple as this. 'They didn't understand,' he mused. 'They thought a government, even a minority government, was an almighty juggernaut that could plough down the tremendous facades that had been built up through the centuries. Blow the trumpets and down comes Jericho! Ah! If it were as easy as that.'

It was not until midnight that Hamer finished his ministerial work and got up from his desk. He yawned and sat down on one of the couches beside the fire to record his day in his diary. He smiled to himself tiredly as it struck him for the first time that the couches were the same colour as the seats in the House of Lords. They were very comfortable. And even though Hamer had gone out of office when the government fell at the end of 1924, he learned valuable lessons from the experience. Two years later, during the general strike of 1926, he had refused to march with the workers. Such an act would be a gift to the enemies of Labour, he told his union friends. The association with communism and hardline trade unionism was one that Labour could not afford if it was ever to win a majority.[1]

Hamer Shawcross was a fictional character but his life was based on real events. He was the anti-hero of the bestselling 1940 novel, *Fame is the Spur*, by Howard Spring, which Attlee bought on publication and read within a matter of days. Without noticing the irony, he completed it while staying at Chequers, the prime minister's residence, having recently joined Churchill's wartime coalition.[2] As Attlee knew, the life of Hamer Shaw-cross, who started out as a socialist radical but became entrapped by the temptations of the Establishment and betrayed his former comrades, was largely based on Ramsay MacDonald. Having begun his parliamentary career as MacDonald's PPS, Attlee had continued to support his leader through the minority government of 1924 and the general strike of 1926. But MacDonald's betrayal of his party in 1931 was to be the lowest and bitterest moment in Attlee's time as a politician. It made him wonder if the journey he had been on for almost a quarter of a century had been worth the effort, and whether the movement in which he had invested so much might be heading for oblivion.

II

Such was the extent to which Attlee remained a faithful party man, that he began to risk looking like a stooge to more ambitious men. At best, he came across as no more than a steady all-rounder. He made a number of contributions to *The Encyclopedia of the Labour Movement*, published the following year with a foreword by MacDonald. The compendium – essentially a collection of essays – summarised Labour policy across a range of issues. Attlee wrote the entries on the air force, army, conscription, compensation, nationalisation, electricity and local government.[3]

In MacDonald's estimation, Attlee was a reliable foot soldier, and a competent colleague, but did not quite have the talent to demand a place at the top table. Nor was he a threat. Thus, the Labour leader nominated the MP for Limehouse to the Indian Statutory Commission, better known as the Simon Commission (after its chairman, Sir John Simon), which was formed in 1927. The reason given to Attlee for his selection was that he 'had a virgin mind' on the subject of India.[4] The truth was that MacDonald could also do without him on the front line. This posting was far from ideal for Attlee, who was now the father of three young children. Given Violet's difficulties with post-natal depression in the past, the prospect of Clem spending months away, travelling through India and Burma, was not something that was welcomed. The sense of uncertainty was compounded by the fact that he was still appealing against the compensation he was due to pay Scammells.

The aim of the commission was to review the effect of the 1919 Government of India Act, and assess India's progress towards self-government. This act had given the vote to a proportion of wealthy Indians – on a highly restricted franchise – and established a national parliament, though the colonial authorities still controlled the police and army, as well as taxation and foreign policy. Lord Birkenhead, the Secretary of State for India, judged that it had yet to make sufficient progress to allow for further measures of devolution. In fact, the Conservative government had growing concerns about the breakdown of law and order and increased protests against colonial rule. It was soon clear that, while they sought to do this under the auspices of an all-party commission, the intention was to put a brake on the country's evolution to self-governance, which the 1919 Act had promised. Sir John Simon, a Liberal lawyer who was notorious in Labour circles for declaring the general strike illegal, was chosen to lead the commission, which was dominated by a Conservative majority (reflecting their parliamentary strength). This was not a role that endeared Attlee to the Labour rank and file, who were generally more supportive of the cause of Indian self-government.

Attlee set off with the rest of the commission in the new year of 1928. They travelled through a clear but cool Mediterranean and stopped in Cairo, where they lunched with the British high commissioner.[5] One glaring weakness of the commission was the fact that it had no Indian representatives on it. Ostensibly, the reason for this was that it was extremely difficult to find a balance of all India's various political, cultural, religious and regional groupings.[6] When the commissioners arrived in Bombay on 3 February 1928, they found themselves boycotted by local politicians. Both the Indian National Congress (which was mainly Hindu) and the Muslim League refused to cooperate. As Attlee reported in a letter to his brother Tom, the *Indian National Herald* singled him out for criticism at the commission's first press conference. He 'cut a very sorry figure when tackled by the press people'. He was so 'hopelessly flabbergasted by the volley of questions that his hand began to shiver as he tried to light his pipe.' In this hostile atmosphere, the best hope for the commission was to get a better understanding of the state of the country.[7]

In the first of two visits, Attlee and the commissioners covered over 7,000 miles through February and March. On a train journey from Jaipur to Lahore, he described visiting the foot of the Himalayas and seeing Kashmir. After Lahore he was to move further northwest to attend, to his pleasure, an Old Haileyburian dinner to be held in his honour at Rawalpindi. Attlee believed that the first visit had gone well. He spoke of a 'tremendous reception' in the Punjab and reported that the Legislative Council had declared for cooperation with the mission.[8] The commissioners believed that there was enough local cooperation – outside the main parties – to return for a second, longer, visit after the summer. Thirteen provinces were to be covered, including Burma. This time, they were permitted to take their wives, so Violet joined the delegation, arriving in Bombay on 13 October 1928. She was to stay with him through to Christmas, before returning home to the children, who were staying with her parents in Hampstead.[9]

It was on this visit that they received the news that Clem's appeal against the compensation he had been ordered to pay Scammells had been upheld. It was a huge weight off his mind and both he and 'Vi' were more relaxed on this trip than they had been for many years.[10] Moving from Karachi to Kulachi, however, Attlee revealed that he was increasingly pessimistic about the prospects for India; he remarked that the growing evidence of communal strife 'gets depressing after a time'.[11] After a long train journey at the end of November, arriving in New Delhi, he confessed that the Indian question was 'very difficult'. Solutions did not present themselves. 'I don't think one can devise effective safeguards' in a way which would prevent the destabilisation of the country. 'The real trouble is that India's disabilities are social and economic and we have to deal with political change.' Although the commission's work was stalling, he and Violet were still having 'quite a good time', with pleasant hosts. They had seen the Khyber and were planning a visit to the city of Peshawar. In early December they had lunch at the Viceregal Lodge, dining with Lord Irwin, the viceroy, later better known as Lord Halifax.[12]

Violet, for whom the trip had been a 'chance of a lifetime', left for England on 24 January, just as the commission prepared to leave Burma for a fourteen-day visit to Calcutta and then, via sea, Rangoon.[13] By March, Attlee confessed that he was growing tired of the repetitiveness of the evidence he heard. He was 'sick of the same old story'. It was not the framing of a constitution for India that was the real challenge, so much as getting the various factions to support it. 'I fear it will be difficult to make people at home understand that we are not dealing with a tabula rasa, but a paper that has been much scribbled over,' he explained to Tom. More specifically, Attlee was concerned about the reaction to his pessimism of people in the Labour Party who championed Indian independence. Genuine self-government seemed much more difficult than he had once believed. 'Our people, like many out here . . . are apt to make a ready-made government for India, often on some model used elsewhere, without trying to see how far it will fit and how far it will be suitable to work in.'[14]

For the moment, he shared the view that the obstacles to self-government in India were, for the moment, insurmountable. The first was the question of what to do with Indian states – such as Hyderabad – that wanted to retain their independence and did not want to be incorporated into a larger political unit. Some of these states had de facto independence guaranteed by treaties with the British government, which was threatened by nationalist demands for a centralised state. The second was the position of the armed forces of India, which were still led by a British military command: there were very few Indian officers who had been promoted to positions of authority, which meant the troops were not deemed ready to take responsibility for the internal stability and external security of an Indian state. Leaving British troops at the disposal of a government not responsible to the House of Commons was politically impossible.[15]

Attlee showed little inclination to revolt against his fellow commissioners. He had not yet developed the boldness and decisiveness that later characterised his approach to Indian affairs as prime minister. Yet, even if he had, it would not have made any difference. Before they could report, the work of the commission was undermined by the viceroy. In order to satisfy the nationalists, Lord Irwin called for all-party talks in London – thus starting an entirely new diplomatic track and making the commission's work effectively redundant.[16]

Attlee began to wonder why he had been sent to India at all. To his increasing irritation, MacDonald was not even prepared to let him assume the mantle of Labour's spokesman on Indian affairs. MacDonald considered himself an expert on India – on which he had written two books – and barely acknowledged the work of the commission.[17] Attlee later claimed to have learned much on the trip that was to be valuable to him later. In the short term, however, he was frustrated that the drafting of the committee report – which urged relatively minor increases in self-government at provincial level but no prospect of Indian self-government at the centre – kept him out of parliamentary action, and far away from MacDonald's front bench.[18] It was only in hindsight that he recalled, with some unease, that MacDonald had often been contemptuous of many fellow colleagues back in 1922 when Attlee had first begun to work for him: 'I thought it quite wrong.' Increasingly this memory began to play upon his mind.[19]

III

To compound these frustrated ambitions, Attlee's visit to India nearly cost him his parliamentary seat. By the time Attlee returned home to fight the general election, called for 30 May 1929, he found that his absence had been used against him by his rivals in Limehouse. *The Times* suggested that the mishandling of the general strike would damage the Labour vote in the East End, by alienating moderates. Yet Attlee also faced a challenge from the left, as the Communist Party managed to field a candidate, Walter Tapsell, against him for the first time.[20] A new policy of all-out opposition to Labour targeted more obviously moderate candidates like MacDonald, Morrison, Clynes, Bondfield and Attlee. Tapsell was one of four Communists running in east London alone.

With the election just weeks away, Attlee needed to take urgent action. The members of the commission arrived back at Victoria station on the last Friday afternoon in April. Attlee was back in his constituency the following day and canvassed all weekend. On Sunday, conscious of the need to rally support behind him, his constituency party organised a demonstration in his honour at Limehouse town hall. Local Communists were also out in force, which made for a boisterous atmosphere when Attlee took to the stage, Violet by his side, to make his speech, with his 'stewards' providing muscle to keep his path clear. He praised the party for keeping the flag flying at the borough elections while he was away and rejected the allegation that he had been having a 'joyride' in India. If this was a joyride, he said, anyone was welcome to take the next one for him. He reminded the audience that he had been closely connected to the area for more than two decades. The men and women who had done the 'drudgery and donkey work' to build the Labour Party were not going to give up overnight. The Labour Party did not depend 'on a wizard from Wales' – as the Liberals did with Lloyd George – or a single charismatic individual, but the rank and file. 'I am a democrat,' he said, in a pointed turn of phrase, 'and I believe in democracy.'

At this point a commotion began at the back of the hall as supporters of Tapsell shouted out that he had abandoned Limehouse. Attlee raised his voice and declared: 'I am not prepared to take my orders from any superman, or from people I do not know or from people abroad – Russia,

Europe, France, or Italy, or anywhere else.' He did not care whether his opponents came from the left or the right. A Labour victory would never be based on the 'dictatorship of one man or a few men' but the support of the people. To a crescendo of cheers from his supporters, he said that the only way to change the world was to change minds. The communist way 'was the way to slavery' and would prevent men and women 'living the lives they should live in peace and comfort'.[21] Tapsell, his Communist opponent, condemned Attlee for not being willing to debate him directly. The *East London Observer* defended the sitting MP's decision, even if it did not support him. This was a country where 'extreme men or measures cannot prosper and East Enders, as a body, are built in the average English mould.' The country had not yet abandoned 'thoughts and ideas of God, truth, justice, love, loyalty and mercy, all of which are denied by Communistic principles and practice'.[22]

With memories of the general strike still fresh, the Conservative government campaigned under the slogan of 'Safety First'. MacDonald also continued to stress the need for a pragmatic, responsible course. Of the three main parties, in fact, the Liberals offered the boldest programme to deal with the high rates of unemployment. In an attempt to win back the ground it had lost over the previous decade, and influenced by the ideas of the economist John Maynard Keynes, Lloyd George's Liberals – with their 'Yellow Book' – made an ambitious pitch for working-class support, with proposals for public works schemes to modernise the economy and create jobs.[23]

MacDonald had successfully withstood the desire of some in his party to take a radical turn after 1926, particularly in response to the new Liberal programme. He had stuck to the party's strong support for free trade. The results of the election vindicated his strategy. Labour took 8.3 million votes and 288 seats against 5.3 million and fifty-nine for the Liberals. With the Conservatives receiving 8 million votes and 260 seats, Labour was in a position to form a government again. It did not have an overall majority but it was, for the first time, the largest party in the Commons. Attlee performed well, gaining 13,872 votes and a comfortable majority of 7,288. Tapsell received a mere 254 votes.[24] The *Observer* reported how he was the first to arrive at the count at Stepney's Great Assembly Hall, looking 'well satisfied with himself'.[25]

Into Ramsay MacDonald's Cabinet went the least radical members of the Labour movement – J. R. Clynes, J. H. Thomas, Arthur Henderson and Philip Snowden. Herbert Morrison became Minister of Transport. Attlee had seen Morrison rise through the ranks faster than him. Although there was no doubt that he was a highly capable administrator and party mobiliser, he had much less parliamentary experience. As MacDonald explained, Attlee was overlooked on the grounds that he was still involved in the writing of the Simon Commission report. Having cast his lot in with the leader, however, he was somewhat cut adrift between the party establishment and the rank and file. There was no real home for him amongst the backbenchers, 'an army of clamorous soldiery . . . officered by wild doctrinaires' such as Jimmy Maxton.[26] In some ways he was intellectually closer to the Independent Labour Party but, despite his growing frustrations, he thought that their strategy, increasingly detached from the mainstream Labour movement, looked self-defeating.

The biggest challenge facing the second Labour government was unemployment. Their task became extremely difficult because of events outside its control. In the last week of October, the bottom fell out of the international economy, beginning with a monumental panic on the New York Stock Exchange on 24 October that saw traders leap from windows in despair. With exports from Europe to the United States collapsing, Europe felt the effects immediately.

By March 1930, the Labour government was presiding over a massive hike in unemployment. The number out of work was 1.6 million, the highest in a decade, and rising fast. In Parliament, the constellation of forces was disturbed. It was Lloyd George, the Liberal leader, demanding public works, while MacDonald and his chancellor, Snowden, tried to steady inflation through spending cuts. The government took a battering from all angles. The Liberals, who seemed to have more innovative ideas on economic planning, took aim. After one particularly brutal debate on the economy, Herbert Morrison confronted Lloyd George in the chamber of the Commons, and said 'L. G., you gave us a very rough time this evening. Even Winston said we are the victims of a world economic blizzard.' 'L. G.' looked back and smiled. He recalled how the London Labour mayors had forced him back to Number 10 from a holiday in Scotland in 1920 in order to hear their demands for help for the unemployed. 'Young man, I seem to remember that the London mayors chased me to the Highlands on one occasion and gave me a rough time too!'[27] This was the price of office.

Talks of splits within the Labour movement emerged. Jimmy Maxton of the ILP launched into an attack on the Unemployment Insurance Bill for failing to offer any substantive increase in support to those out of work.

The effects of the economic crisis were particularly acute in Limehouse. Despite winning the recent election, Attlee was not immune to these pressures. 'We had a Labour Government,' commented Joe Jacobs, 'and as far as I could see they were not much better than their predecessors.' Radicals saw their opportunity. The *Daily Worker* was launched on 1 January 1930 as the official organ of the Communist Party in Britain. Its opening meeting was held at Shoreditch Town Hall, which underlined its growing presence in east London. The Communist Party and the Young Communist League took it upon themselves to sell the newspaper and spread the word with notice of events, rallies and gatherings across Limehouse.[28] In the *Stepney Citizen*, a short-lived publication designed to counter communist propaganda, the MacDonaldite line was still maintained. Gradualism was the only choice. Even Labour members who agreed that the government was going too slowly would be fools to want to turn out MacDonald only to put in Baldwin. 'Is there any way of obtaining heaven on earth quickly?' asked a columnist called 'Moonraker', who may well have been Attlee himself.[29] The answer, for the moment, was no.

These pleas for patience were falling on deaf ears. As he completed work on the Simon report, Attlee at least had the consolation of being out of the firing line as a spokesperson for the government. He spoke only twice in the Commons from July 1929 to May 1930. That changed at the end of May when Oswald Mosley resigned from his post as Chancellor of the Duchy of Lancaster, precipitating another major crisis in MacDonald's Labour Cabinet. Mosley had begun his political life as a Conservative before becoming an Independent, and then joining Labour in 1926. The fact that he had risen up the ranks in such a short time was a source of frustration and suspicion to many in the party, like Attlee, who had been overlooked for office.[30] His resignation was in protest at the government's failure to do more to tackle unemployment, which now stood at nearly 2 million. MacDonald and Snowden, the chancellor, had vetoed Mosley's suggestions that the government adopt a programme of public works. In hindsight, Attlee saw the episode as a cautionary tale, caused by MacDonald's penchant for young earls and 'queer fish'; and his tendency to disparage loyal servants of the party. As for Mosley, he was 'an effective and bitter speaker, but he seemed rather hopeful – a bit too much ego'. Attlee had not had much contact with him in previous years, save for a game of tennis at a Labour gathering at Lady Warwick's country estate.[31]

With the government reeling, MacDonald now turned back to his trusted former parliamentary private secretary to fill the void as Chancellor of the Duchy of Lancaster. The contrast between Attlee and Mosley could not have been more profound. Attlee was not impressed by his aristocratic predecessor; he thought Mosley had a habit of speaking to his colleagues 'as though he were a feudal landlord abusing tenants who are in arrears with their rent' (a comment that was leaked to the press).[32] As Attlee was announced as his replacement, Mosley – the 'perfumed popinjay' of the London drawing-room scene – was still giving interviews to the press from the office of the Chancellor of the Duchy of Lancaster that Attlee was due to enter.[33] Much was made of the physical difference between the men. Mosley was handsome, 'lithe and black and shiny'. He looked like a panther but behaved like a hyena. Attlee was bald, small and unsure of himself on stage. The only concession he made to flamboyance was that he occasionally wore a pinstriped shirt with his dark-grey suit. It was suggested that MacDonald was so fed up with Mosley that he looked around him and chose the 'most uninteresting, unimaginative but most reliable among his backbenchers to replace the fallen angel'.[34]

Contrary to what one might have expected, Mosley was not ungenerous in his assessment of the man who replaced him. On the one hand, Mosley felt there was more to Attlee than Churchill's famous epigram, that he was 'a modest little man, with plenty to be modest about', suggested. He had 'a clear, incisive and honest mind within the limits of his range', and he was apparently a competent chairman of committee in preserving the balance between conflicting forces within the party. On the other hand, he felt that Attlee was no improvement on MacDonald and Snowden and their overcautious approach to solving unemployment. In agreeing to take his job, Attlee 'must be reckoned as content to join a government visibly breaking the pledges on which it was elected'.[35]

Initially, Attlee had hoped to do more. He was brought onto the Economic Advisory Council, a fifteen-man body set up after Mosley's resignation. Intended to bring the best and the brightest minds to bear on the economic crisis, it became the scene of bitter battles about the future economic direction of the country. While he was mainly a spectator, he witnessed the clash between Montagu Norman, Governor of the Bank of England who wanted to keep government interference in the economy to a minimum, and the economist John Maynard Keynes, whose influence was growing but whose ideas were still treated with some suspicion. He also got to know the qualities of Ernest Bevin of the TUC first hand – his pragmatism and capacity to deliver on promises made through his control of the unions. Attlee was particularly suspicious of Montagu Norman, who never tired of telling people how delicate and complicated finance was. To Attlee, as he wrote in his private notes, this was obfuscation. Politics required moral clarity rather than intricate mathematics.[36]

Attlee's own memorandum of July 1930, on 'The Problems of Industry', made little mark on these internal government debates. What it did demonstrate was that he was inclined to support economic planning on Keynesian lines, but was as yet unprepared to oppose MacDonald and Snowden. He urged the creation of a Ministry of Industry in order to direct the modernisation and rationalisation of key industries.[37] Hugh Dalton, who was emerging as an influential critic of MacDonald, described the memorandum as 'not a very distinguished production', though he did approve of Attlee's idea of a new ministry – largely because it seemed to him to be a concession to his ideas on planning.[38]

Frustrated by the lack of interest in his work on economic planning, Attlee complained to Tom that he was used simply as a functionary, a 'tip-horse' brought in to 'pull various wagons'. He bore some resemblance to Boxer, the tired old shire horse in George Orwell's *Animal Farm*, whose goodwill and capacity for hard work are exploited until he is ready for the glue factory. As his colleague Ellen Wilkinson put it, more generously, 'Major Attlee . . . [is] too fastidious for intrigue, too modest for overmuch ambition, and yet with a mind that makes it worthwhile for a Prime Minister to discuss problems with him.' But he lacked confidence in his exchanges with MacDonald, expressing concern that his suggestions on policy might come across as 'too argumentative and tendentious', and apologising for his bad typing. In one exchange with a Conservative colleague, he joked, at his own expense, 'The Hon. Member did not see me; I am too small.'[39] It was only in private, in letters to Tom, that he expressed irritation at the 'timidity and conservatism' of some of the government ministers, particularly at the Treasury and Board of Trade.[40] Yet he still backed MacDonald in a clash against Mosley in Parliament in October

1930 and also helped his leader with the London Imperial Conference of 1931. In this, he followed MacDonald and Snowden in asserting his continued preference for free trade rather than imperial protection.

A more fruitful working relationship was built with the Minister for Agriculture, Christopher Addison. Attlee was impressed by Addison, a former Liberal minister who had joined Labour in 1918. Likewise, Addison regarded Attlee as 'most useful and clear-headed'.[41] Addison acted as something of a mentor to Attlee for many years, and was the leader of the Labour Party in the House of Lords after 1945. 'One of the most influential men in my time,' Attlee later reflected. 'No orator. No art. Patience, friendliness, common sense – these were his virtues.'[42] These were qualities not in abundance in the Labour Party in 1931.

V

It was Attlee's misfortune that the higher he went up the ladder of government, the more the government looked likely to fall. In March 1931, following a reshuffle, he was given some reward for his loyalty. This came in the form of his first departmental posting – as Postmaster General.[43] Symbolically, the protection of the Post Office from privatisation was an important issue for those who had invested in the slow and steady approach of the Labour movement.[44] Although he had barely five months in his post, he pushed forward with a public relations campaign to increase the use of the telephone.[45] One lesson that he learned – and which he took into his own government – was that ministers should be given more autonomy. The tight rein that MacDonald and Snowden kept on all departments had become a source of some irritation to a number of members in the government, who complained that they were being micro-managed from the centre.

By the early summer of 1931, hyperinflation in Germany began to infect the British economy too. As the German government started to default on its debts, Britain's massive investment in German industry in the previous years was suddenly made worthless. By July, foreign investors in Britain began to withdraw their money, fearing that Britain would be the next to fall. The Bank of England pressured the government to make cuts to restore confidence before there was a run on the banks. MacDonald felt that the only option was to cut spending, with a 10 per cent decrease in unemployment insurance. In July 1931, the Committee on National Expenditure, established by Parliament and headed by the Liberal MP Sir George May, released its report on the economic situation. It urged cuts in public expenditure, particularly unemployment benefits, and increases in taxes to save the British economy from disaster. Though the Labour government officially rejected its proposals, its publication precipitated a political crisis with grave consequences for the party. Some economists, notably John Maynard Keynes, suggested that devaluation of the pound might mitigate the worst effects. Brandishing a German Reichsmark note, a reference to the hyperinflation that had beset Germany, MacDonald rejected this, and insisted that the Labour Party must retain the gold standard. In order to avert financial disaster, therefore, MacDonald and Snowden argued that it was necessary to make whatever cuts were needed to restore a balance to the budget. They had a majority in the Cabinet but the minority – including Labour stalwarts such as Arthur Henderson – signalled their intention to resign if the proposed cuts were made. Most importantly, the Trades Union Congress voiced its displeasure, which meant that MacDonald would be unable to carry his policy before the Labour Party conference. Taking the majority of the Cabinet with him, MacDonald unilaterally brought the government down rather than face defeat by his own party.

Attlee was on holiday in Frinton-on-Sea, on the Essex coast, when he learned that the government had split. Beyond the rumours, he knew little of the details. He immediately travelled back to London for a meeting called by MacDonald on 24 August, at which the prime minister addressed his former colleagues. Leaving Violet, 'very much in her prime', and the children, including the newest Attlee addition, by the seaside, he set off for Westminster. 'God knows' what would happen next, he wondered.[46] Unbeknown to Attlee, the crisis was worse than he had assumed. What transpired in the next twenty-four hours was that those in the Cabinet who supported the cuts – MacDonald, Snowden, J. H. Thomas and Lord Sankey – had not only broken with their colleagues but formed a coalition with the Conservatives and a small rump of Liberals. MacDonald and Snowden would remain in situ but would be working alongside the Conservative leader, Stanley Baldwin, who was to be Lord President of the Council. The new National Government would go before the electorate to seek a mandate.

On 24 August, as he returned to London, Attlee discovered that

MacDonald had written to him from Downing Street, expressing thanks for his assistance in the government which he was now bringing down. 'It was a very painful decision that has had to be taken, and I wish you to have no doubt at all about what it was.' Britain was on the verge of a financial crisis that would have brought down the whole financial system, 'with the most dire results to the mass of the working classes'. It would take time for people to understand the issues, and the lack of alternatives. If they had stayed in, and debated things like unemployment benefits, 'We should have been fiddling beautiful music whilst Rome was burning.' They had to pursue this line for the preservation of everything they stood for. MacDonald argued that the party would have been ruined if it had presided over the disaster, 'swept away in ignominy before the end of this week by popular clamour'. The public, when free from panic, would then have the opportunity to turn to Labour again when things 'have become more normal'.[47]

To the horror of the majority of the Labour Party, its best-known leaders had simply deserted the party – without any consultation. The result was the bitterest acrimony in the Labour movement's history. At lunch with Hugh Dalton, all Attlee's anger came to the surface. He denounced MacDonald for his 'indecision and inferiority complex', especially in economic matters. As the two men ploughed through a bottle of Burgundy, Attlee showed himself to be equally angry at Snowden, for the way he had blocked every positive proposal of the last two years, because of a misplaced fidelity to laissez-faire economics.[48] To his credit, in fact, Attlee's memorandum on the problems of British industry had raised some concerns about the government's blind attachment to this economic orthodoxy, but he had not had the status to make himself heard.[49]

As the party convened later that afternoon, MacDonald put on a performance which Dalton described, mockingly, as Christ-like, making a great pretence of self-sacrifice. The bottle of Burgundy seemed to have had its effect on Attlee, whose bitterness flooded out in the meeting. Why was it that the workers and the unemployed were to bear the brunt again and not those who sat on profits and grew rich on investments? 'What about the rentiers?' he asked, heckling his fallen idol, in a phrase of which the young Hamer Shawcross would have been proud.[50] MacDonald was a man who had 'shed every rag of political convictions he ever had'. His so-called National Government was a 'shop-soiled pack of cards shuffled and reshuffled'. This was 'the greatest betrayal in the political history of this country'.[51]

What made the situation worse was that MacDonald had convinced the majority of the Cabinet to agree to the cuts, before deciding that he would be unable to carry this policy with the rest of the party. That he used this fact against former colleagues in subsequent arguments was a source of genuine outrage. The good faith of men such as Christopher Addison and Arthur Henderson had been turned against them. 'There was, in fact, no split,' Attlee later wrote, 'but only a shedding of a few leaves from the top of the tree, and a few parasitic appendages.' The question was whether the trunk and the branches could weather the forthcoming storm. In late August, as the National Government was formed, Attlee made sure that MacDonald was in earshot when he commented, as he walked through the Houses of Parliament, that 'Esau sold his inheritance for a few pieces of silver.'[52] It was to the familiar theme of betrayal that Attlee now returned. He appealed directly to those MPs who had fought alongside him in the war. 'Some of you have been soldiers,' he remarked. 'No doubt you will know that there is only one occasion when a soldier is justified in disobeying orders. That is when his senior officer goes over to the enemy.'[53]

What was left of the Labour Party was in despair and disarray. The majority of MPs, who had not been part of the Cabinet discussions, were cast adrift from the leadership. Thank God, remarked the *Daily Herald*, that the football season was returning to cheer up the Labour rank and file, and give them something else, other than politics, to focus on.[54] Where this left Attlee's career was another question entirely. To compound the personal humiliation, MacDonald had not even tried to take Attlee with him. Others had been offered posts in the new National Government. Stafford Cripps – a brilliant young bespectacled lawyer, educated at Winchester, who had been Solicitor General and was the rising star in the party, despite only joining it in 1930 – had prevaricated over the offer for a week. The same was true of Herbert Morrison, who had been Minister of Transport.[55]

At the end of August, the *Daily Herald* had identified eight men who mattered in the Labour movement and might lead its revival. They were Arthur Henderson, who was now acting leader, George Lansbury, Willie Graham, Arthur Greenwood, William Adamson, A. V. Alexander, Tom Johnston and Christopher Addison. Once again, Attlee was conspicuous by his absence.[56] Labour prepared an emergency policy in response to the proposals of the new National Government but, again, Attlee did not feature as a leading voice in the deliberations. He was completely overlooked in another *Daily Herald* article about the Labour men who had made sacrifices for the cause in these desperate times.[57] On 2 September 1931, he wrote to Tom to express his despair at the 'damnable' situation. 'I fear we are in for a regime of false economy and a general attack on the worker's standard of life,' he wrote.[58]

The election that followed in the autumn of 1931 almost killed the Labour Party. As the National Government went to the polls in November seeking a 'Doctor's Mandate', its old leaders – MacDonald and Snowden – dismissed the new Labour programme as 'Bolshevism run mad'. Henderson, who did not relish leadership, was not equipped for such a brutal fight. There had been no opportunity to prepare. Much of the party's propaganda literature still featured MacDonald's image. Once again, MacDonald made much of the fact that a majority of the last Cabinet had supported the cuts he had outlined.

The results were catastrophic. Some believed they were fatal; not only to the Labour Party but also, potentially, to the Westminster system. The National Government took 554 seats out of a total of 615. Labour's share dropped from 288 to forty-six (supplemented by five MPs from the Independent Labour Party, who were drifting further from the mainstream). In total, 14,150,915 had voted for the 'Doctor's Mandate' and 7,215,842 against. Labour formed the smallest opposition in the history of the House of Commons. Cascading out of Parliament went some of the biggest names in the movement. In Gateshead, Ernie Bevin lost a 17,000 Labour majority, defeated by the National Government candidate. Henderson lost his seat, along with nearly all the former Cabinet ministers of the Labour government who had not joined MacDonald, including Morrison. The one exception was the 72-year old George Lansbury, who was also the last member of the National Executive Committee left in Parliament.

Attlee was one of the lucky ones, narrowly clinging on to Limehouse by 551 votes. The vote in his constituency was now split five ways. In addition to a Communist candidate, Oswald Mosley's new creation, his 'New Party', had fielded a candidate too. The Mosleyite was Herbert Hodge, a local taxi driver who saw the New Party as an attempt to 'break away from the old doctrines and prejudices, from rigid orthodoxies of all sorts, both capitalist and communist, and re-plan Britain on a basis of human values – an opportunity for men and women of goodwill in both classes to work together for a classless society'.[59] It was an indication of the sense of despair that John Beckett, a friend of Attlee's for many years, who had followed him into the House of Commons as MP for Peckham, was tempted by Mosley's allure, after becoming exasperated with the failure of the Labour Party to advance the interests of its natural supporters in the working classes.[60]

Attlee's commitment to the constituency had stood him in good stead. And suddenly, against all expectations, his importance to the Labour movement was greater than ever before. Thirty-two out of the forty-six MPs returned were trade union-sponsored, and few of these were renowned parliamentarians or had mastery of any specific briefs beyond their region. The *Manchester Guardian* remarked that the opposition would be 'less gifted in the arts of Government than any group of men who could readily have been chosen'.[61]

As the few remaining Labour MPs drifted back into Westminster – devasted, dazed and confused – Attlee found a note waiting for him from Arthur Henderson, informing him that George Lansbury, his old comrade from the East End, would be leader of the parliamentary party, and Attlee would be proposed as his deputy.[62] Working alongside him would be Stafford Cripps, who was elected for the first time as MP for Bristol East.[63]

Henderson conceded that the result was a 'shattering blow' but hoped the party could resurrect itself. Experience had shown the importance of a strong opposition and thus Labour remained 'the only effective bulwark against reaction and revolution'. Sir Samuel Simon, the leader of one of the two Liberal factions, declared that the Labour Party was finished, 'perhaps permanently'. As the *Manchester Guardian* described, British politics had been transformed for ever. As the cyclone passed, having 'flattened out the accustomed landscape', one had to strain one's eyes to see the survival of a 'few fragments of the English political scene'.[64] If there was any cause for optimism, reflected Beatrice Webb, it was that the Labour movement 'may discover a philosophy, a policy and a personal code of conduct, all of which we lack today'.[65]

MacDonald's leadership had promised much but ended in catastrophe. That Attlee had attached himself to his project made the experience even more bitter. But an even bigger blow had been dealt to the sense of mission and momentum which the Labour movement had worked so hard to create since the early 1900s. In a newly established left-wing journal called *New Dawn*, the former Labour MP Ellen Wilkinson, who had lost her

Middlesbrough East seat, argued that, to have any chance of survival, the Labour Party would essentially need to start all over again. The New Jerusalem that Attlee had hoped to build, as described in *The Social Worker* in 1920, had evaporated into thin air. 'It was no good building Jerusalem in perorations,' wrote Wilkinson on 7 November 1931, 'the average voter wants to see the blue print of the city.'[66] For Labour to thrive again, it would have to return to its foundations.

Part Three

Albion's Troubles, 1931–1940

8

The Bullion Family

Ramsay Bullion of Albion Lodge prided himself on being a cultured Christian gentleman. He was always saying how hard up he was. He said that he could not afford to give the children in the family more than two shillings a week for their clothes, food and everything, but he would do a lot for art, culture and religion . . . Mrs Bullion who was born of the Neville Tories was also very kind hearted . . . but she would never give anything to her own family until she had tested their means . . .

Clement Attlee,
'Chapters from the life of the Bullion Family', undated.[1]

I *Albion Lodge, Abundance Avenue, November 1931*

The inhabitants of Albion Lodge, the Bullion Family, were moving up in the world. Having once lived in the Town of Scarcity, they had moved to Abundance Avenue. The Bullions liked to keep up appearances. Unfortunately, like many middle-class families, they had poor relatives who sometimes asked to borrow money. The Bullions had two family cars. One was an old 1844 Bank Charter, driven by their chauffeur, Monty Norman, who always called it his car, even though it was the Bullions who owned it. He also made sure he was paid a handsome salary. One day the car would not start. Monty filled it with petrol, 'Standard Gold', but it turned out it would not start unless it was oiled at every joint and bearing with 'Private Profit'. When they ran out of Private Profit, and the car failed, the Bullions were forced to seek alternative transport. Rather embarrassingly they had to travel about on an old donkey called 'Barter'. They did not care much for Barter's well-being, and piled their possessions on his back until he could barely walk. Though they now relied on Barter, they thought him 'low and socialistic'.

The head of the family was Ramsay Bullion, who always prided himself on his own sense of decency. He was always saying how hard up he was, despite appearances to the contrary. He insisted that he could not afford to give the children in the family more than two shillings a week to survive, but he had not forgotten his duties to the world of art and culture. His wife, Mrs Bullion, was born of a wealthier family, the Neville Tories. She too liked to pride herself on her kind-heartedness. When she visited the local butcher, she was told that her family was almost his only customer these days because no one else could afford meat. Mrs Bullion therefore told the butcher to raise his prices, given that times were hard. She even offered to stock more meat than her family needed so that his prices would not fall. The family friends, the Rentiers, were delighted at this, as they lent money to all the shopkeepers and butchers and bakers and had been afraid of losing their investments. Mrs Bullion was also very generous to some beggars she did not know who had fallen upon hard times. They had made a bet that Mr Dollar would stay where he was, but he did not. So she bailed them both out with a loan. When it came to her own family, she was not so generous. She would never give anything to her children until she had tested their means.

This unpublished satire, written by Attlee sometime in 1933, captured his disgust at the National Government formed after the 1931 election. The name Bullion came from Bullionism – the economic orthodoxy that held that it was a disaster to devalue the pound and abandon the gold standard. Ramsay Bullion was of course the prime minister, MacDonald. Mrs Bullion was Neville Chamberlain, the Conservative Chancellor of the Exchequer. Attlee's distaste for the National Government's budget of April 1932 shone through his tale of Mrs Bullion's visit to the butchers. In particular, he objected to the decision to raise wholesale prices to protect those selling goods, and the Import Duties Act that prevented cheap goods coming into the country, just as unemployment benefits were cut. Monty Norman, the chauffeur, was Montagu Norman, the head of the Bank of England, who was an influential advocate of economic orthodoxy and a balanced budget to ride out the storm. In the satire, Attlee also mocked 'Simple Simon' (Sir John Simon), the leader of the Liberal grouping in the

National Government, who now agreed to break with his party's commitment to free trade and support the policy of raising tariffs on goods coming into the country. The Rentiers were the speculators and traders who had been bailed out by the government after losing their money in the Wall Street Crash. The hapless donkey, Barter, was supposed to represent British workers, who were asked to bear the load but were treated with nothing but contempt.[2]

There was a certain irony that Attlee chose a wealthy suburban setting for his satire. Albion Lodge was closer to home than he would have cared to admit. In April 1931, he and Violet, having recently welcomed their fourth and final child (Alison), moved from Essex to a larger suburban home, a two-and-a-half-storey villa in Stanmore, Middlesex. It stood back from the road with a long half-acre garden behind it, along with apple trees and a tennis court. At the bottom, there was a tool shed and wood store. In the house he would walk around in well-worn slippers. He loved reading to his children, or playing with them in the garden. He was unfailingly good humoured with his family, though he often felt guilty about not spending enough time with them. Attlee had his own study, where there was a typewriter and shelves stacked full of books.[3]

This upward move brought pressures of its own, however. Violet had been suffering from another illness after the birth of Alison, which manifested itself as sleep apnoea, and she spent months recuperating in a clinic. This encouraged Attlee in his efforts to make a more comfortable home and a settled environment for his family. The decision to move was made when he was on a ministerial salary, but the collapse of the Labour government had deprived him of this. Running the household was difficult in these circumstances. Money was always stretched. Attlee sought alternative sources of income from journalism, or broadcasting. The furniture in the house was shabby, and Violet was always talking of the need to redecorate. A reporter who visited the day after Attlee became prime minister was surprised to see coupon cut-outs for slip covers and bedsheets.[4]

Even in leafy Stanmore, the effects of the economic depression could make themselves felt. In 1932, the home was burgled – the first of two such incidents in this period. Two men climbed through a window, ransacked Attlee's office and made away with two of his war medals.[5] There was a similar incident in 1936. Janet, the eldest child, had gone downstairs and saw a light on in the dining room, which was switched off as soon as she opened the door. She rushed upstairs to tell her father, who came down in a hurry to find the study in disorder, with papers on the floor and the desk ransacked. He gave chase but could not catch the offenders.[6]

In the 'Chapters from the life of the Bullion Family', it was the children of the family – the working people of Britain – who suffered most at the hands of the parents, MacDonald and Chamberlain. But there was another theme running through Attlee's satire that was to become of even greater concern over the following years. The Bullions of Abundance Avenue had problems with their neighbours. Tensions with their cousins the Pats (the Irish), could be put down to an old family dispute. Having lived in Albion Lodge for many years, they had moved to Erin Cottage and now shut their windows and doors to their former relatives. (This referred to the fact that the Irish government of Éamon de Valera rejected efforts to include Ireland in a revived British Commonwealth at the Ottawa Conference of 1932.) There were much more worrying developments in world affairs, meanwhile. The Marks (Germans), Franks (French), Liras (Italians) and the Yens (Japanese) were all causing problems with the Bullions and each other. That was not even to mention the Roubles (the Russians), who were a law unto themselves, or the Dollars (Americans), who lived far away and wanted to keep out of these disputes. As tensions rose, the different families began to throw missiles over the fence. The Bullions put up walls and netting but, as soon as they thought they were safe, more missiles would follow.

At the dawn of the 1930s, the inhabitants of Albion Lodge were ill at ease with themselves, struggling to keep harmony in their extended family and increasingly concerned about the world around them. The decade that followed was to prove that these fears were well founded.

II

Back at Westminster in November 1931, as Parliament reconvened after the election, Winston Churchill – who was not given a position in the National Government – confided to Attlee that he had 'seldom been so nervous' about the state of British democracy.[7] The size of the majority that the government boasted was unprecedented in British history. The supporters of the National Government held 554 seats out of a total of 615. Labour, as the official opposition, had only forty-six MPs. For those opposed to the National Government, the prospects of influencing it seemed hopeless. This was a spur to radicalism. Outside Parliament, the Communist Party sought to use the opportunity to assert itself, as did Oswald Mosley's British Union of Fascists, formed in 1932. If one cast one's eyes to other European nations – Germany, Italy and Russia – one could be forgiven for believing that the age of democracy was passing. 'In every sphere, economic and political, antagonisms and conflicts are advancing to bursting-point,' wrote the half-Indian English Communist Party writer, Rajani Palme Dutt, in his book *World Politics*. 'On all sides the world is felt to be drifting to catastrophe without control; yet the majority of political leaders and statesmen have no answer.'[8]

In these unpropitious circumstances, Labour was faced with two tasks, which were not necessarily complementary. The first was to provide the official parliamentary opposition that was essential to the effective functioning of British democracy. The second was to rebuild itself in the country after its crushing defeat. Labour still boasted certain organisational assets – chiefly its trade union links – which meant that it could exert pressure on the government outside Parliament. But there was a danger in this. The general strike had been a painful experience. Moreover, there were fears among the remaining MPs that the centre of gravity might shift from the parliamentary party to the Labour's National Executive Committee (NEC). On the NEC sat a number of prominent figures such as Hugh Dalton, who had lost his seat in 1931 but had little faith in the rump of MPs who had been left at Westminster.

For the leader of the parliamentary party, George Lansbury, now seventy-two years old, this presented an unenviable task. Lansbury, white-haired, with his bowler hat and mutton-chop sideburns, seemed to belong to a different era. The two years after he became leader were the busiest of his entire life. He managed to combine almost daily attendance at the House of Commons with a breathless itinerary across the country, speaking on the stump to keep up Labour morale. Deeply pious, he was even forced to give up his day of rest on Sunday.[9] 'I never considered myself leader,' he admitted, though he grew into the role and was rather less willing to give the position up once he had it in his hands.[10] Most of the time, Attlee was by his side. Indeed, Attlee's diary for these years reveals a dinner or speaking engagement almost on every single evening. There were also an ever-increasing number of speeches in the Commons. In 1933 he made forty-six, rising to seventy-eight in 1934, and ninety in 1935.[11] After the parliamentary exile imposed upon him by his duties on the Simon Commission, he was now one of the most active MPs in the Commons.

Making up the leadership triumvirate was the slim and bespectacled Stafford Cripps. Cripps's rise had been meteoric, having only become a Labour Party member in 1930. But he provided a welcome connection to the intellectuals in the movement, such as G.D.H. Cole – and was able to ameliorate the inevitable criticism from that quarter. Attlee warmed to Cripps immediately, and the feeling was reciprocated, though their relationship was to become strained. For the moment, Cripps respected Attlee's seniority. He also continued his legal practice, which meant that the main burden of parliamentary work fell upon Attlee.

The team assembled was small but dynamic. 'We put up a fair show,' Attlee wrote, after the National Government opened the new Parliament in mid-November 1931. It was difficult to get a sense of the House, 'the benches full of unknown quantities'. MacDonald himself was beyond redemption, of course. He had made a 'ghastly speech' with 'no grip at all'. From the outset, Attlee was more impressed by the Conservative Party leader and Lord President of the Council, Stanley Baldwin, who 'wound up really well'. Like Churchill, Baldwin was concerned about the imbalance in the House. His speech 'recognised the points made in our amendment and inferentially admitted much of their validity'. Stafford Cripps, meanwhile, was a 'tower of strength and such a good fellow', Attlee was pleased to report.

It was in these circumstances that Attlee's mental resilience and sharpness of mind stood him in good stead. His workload would have broken the backs of others. He would master numerous briefs on topics of which he knew little, speak in the chamber, then hurry off to committee after committee, with his paperwork overflowing into the weekend. There were some consolations, notwithstanding the catastrophe that had befallen the party. Not least among these was the sense of solidarity that was felt in adversity. Outside Parliament, Attlee also reported that a number of working groups had been established to revive the party's sense of mission. MacDonaldite gradualism had proved fatal. The intention was to 'get the party away from immediates and on to basic Socialism'. In hope rather than expectation, he expressed his view that 'the shake up will ultimately prove the salvation of the party.' In the short term, he recognised that he had been thrust to centre stage and would have to abandon some of his reticence about self-promotion. He intended to write articles for the *New Statesman*, the weekly political magazine of the new Labour intellectuals. Finding time for such endeavours was another matter, however. He had all sorts of committee work, which consumed his evenings. 'It's a funny position being one of the seniors in the House now,' he wrote.[12] As he told Kingsley Martin, the *New Statesman* editor, there was precious little time that could be 'scratched from political work'.[13]

Lansbury, Attlee and Cripps shared the opposition leader's official room behind the Speaker's chair. MacDonald was contemptuous about the stature of the new triumvirate across the floor from him. He regarded Lansbury, dating back to the days of Poplarism, as a silly old radical. The hostility led to some ugly clashes in the Commons.[14] 'I feel J. R. M. has completely gone,' Attlee wrote of MacDonald in December. His tone when discussing his old leader was unfailingly bitter. MacDonald revelled in his new aristocratic friends, but they would turn on him before long. He would have a 'rude awakening soon I think'. The government was still without 'any coherent plan for dealing with the situation'. It merely 'threw sops to sections of its following'. Attlee said he would almost prefer a genuine Tory protectionist government to deal with the crisis than this 'crossbird animal'. Lansbury, by contrast, 'makes an excellent leader'. He had 'far more idea of team work' than MacDonald ever had. 'We are quite a happy family, GL, Cripps and I.' As for his own role, Attlee told Tom, just before Christmas 1931, how he had had 'a very strenuous time' during the session, having to 'speak on something or other nearly every day'. Opportunities to write articles for the press kept passing him by. 'The devil of it is to find time.' In the new year, he hoped to do some broadcasting or write an impartial report of Parliament for one of the newspapers. But while Violet seemed to be feeling better, the pressures on family life were undeniable.[15]

Into 1932, as MacDonald's health began to suffer from the pressures of the previous two years, Baldwin started to take the lead in the National Government, assuming many of the prime minister's responsibilities. As he was a natural conciliator, this helped to soothe the mood. He kept the majority benches in line and spent time in the Commons bar with the trade unionists (who made up about a third of Labour's remaining contingent). 'I liked him,' recalled Attlee, 'although he would never look at foreign affairs.'[16] Behind the front line, in the backrooms of the Commons, important relationships were formed that were to ensure the country did not veer to the extremes of other European neighbours. Writing about Baldwin's chief whip, David Margesson, Attlee later said that he would always recall his 'unfailing courtesy and consideration to our small band, whose difficult task he recognised'. Attlee, as Margesson's successor James Stuart also noted, understood the necessity of keeping the machine running smoothly or, at the very least, 'grinding over the hard places'.[17] Sir David Hunt, later Attlee's private secretary when he was prime minister, also commented on the similarity between Baldwin's and Attlee's characters. Hunt believed that Attlee had learned from Baldwin's 'deflationary' tactics in the House in these difficult times.[18]

There were other connections made across the floor of the House which mitigated the effects of Labour's marginalisation. A figure of growing importance on the Conservative benches was Harold Macmillan, a wartime hero, MP for Stockton-on-Tees in the northeast, and something of an old-fashioned Tory paternalist. As unemployment rose to more than 20 per cent in early 1932, Macmillan made no secret of his distaste for those on his own benches who he thought were too close to the City of London. The group around Macmillan, which included the similarly minded Robert Boothby, was mocked by some Conservatives as the 'YMCA'. They countered by calling those MPs whom they believed had benefited financially from the last war as 'the Forty Thieves'.[19] Nonetheless, Attlee noted how the Labour attacks on the National Government front benches had struck a chord with this group. 'We get some support for our views from the YMCA group Macmillan, Boothby, and Co. who are in pretty strong enmity to the Diehards,' he wrote in February 1932.[20]

While it was heartening to have some sympathetic ears on the Conservative benches, this did not amount to a strategy in itself. Down to such a small number of MPs, Labour had to consider more drastic measures. With MacDonald gone, Labour had lost its centre of gravity and direction. A process of self-examination was a prerequisite to any revival. From the autumn of 1930, Attlee had been involved in a discussion group established by the Fabian intellectual G.D.H. Cole, whose ideas on guild socialism he had read (and dismissed) many years before.[21] Along with Lansbury and Cripps, he took part in the Society for Socialist Inquiry and Propaganda, established by Cole in June 1931. In the first instance, the SSIP was mostly composed of 'loyal grousers': those who remained loyal to the leadership, but who began to put forward the idea that Labour's future might be best served by a new 'socialist unity'. In theory, this would bring together all the parties of the left – potentially even the Liberals and Communists – into a broader coalition to oppose the National Government. There was a precedent for such a coalition in France, led by the socialist leader Léon Blum, who had managed the balancing act while retaining a moderate course. The fear, of course, was Communist skulduggery and contamination. Since 1918, Labour had refused to work with the British Communist Party and banned its members from holding dual membership. To do so now would be to court controversy and perhaps internal subversion.

SSIP meetings were convened at the Essex home of the Labour patroness, the 'Red' Countess of Warwick, where Attlee had once played tennis against Oswald Mosley many years before. For the moment, they aimed to funnel their views into the party apparatus rather than setting themselves up against it. Initially they were joined by Ernest Bevin, secretary of the Transport and General Workers' Union, who became SSIP chairman and who, despite his involvement in the general strike, was known to be a moderate. Attlee also joined forces with Cole in creating the New Fabian Research Bureau.

As much as anything, the leadership needed intellectual guidance and support, given the weight of work which now fell into their lap. On economic affairs, in particular, Attlee did not always inspire confidence. As he confided to Tom, after replying to the chancellor's budget in April 1932, it had been an ordeal. 'I do not move easily amid the arcana of exchanges, gold standards, etc.' he confessed. Another weakness was the clumsy way in which he approached media work, an increasingly important part of politics in an age when the methods of propaganda were being transformed. The challenge of simplifying his message for the wireless was particularly vexing. He also found it difficult to take a clear and unambiguous line on the main events of the day, without offending individuals in the House of Commons at the same time.[22] Such gentlemanly behaviour was not without appeal to the British people. But at some point he would have to bare his teeth.

III

Attlee was relieved when the parliamentary session ended for the summer recess in 1932. He had delivered ninety-three speeches in the House, putting him second only to Cripps. It had been strenuous and challenging, not least because Violet had suffered a minor relapse into depression. Overall, the party had done 'extraordinarily well' in difficult circumstances. Significantly, the parliamentary party had found a new sense of cohesion. He had bonded with a number of the former miners such as George Henry Hall, Tom Williams and David Grenfell. Williams and Grenfell had been promoted to the front bench and had made themselves conversant with all kinds of subjects, such as foreign affairs, that formerly they would have left to others. Many of the backbenchers – Charley Brown, Joe Tinker and Ted Williams – had 'risen nobly to the occasion'. Looking over at the government benches, Attlee felt that MacDonald was 'worn out'. The government had no 'constructive ideas' but were clinging to the 'miserable ... stunt' of presenting themselves as the saviours of the economy. It seemed that they feared their own back benches. Two titans, excluded from the National Government, also caught his eye. Lloyd George and Churchill were colluding, he suspected. Although Lloyd George professed to be on the left and Churchill on the right, Attlee guessed that 'they anticipate that as we get deeper into the mire, a change of leadership of the coalition will be called for and that they will come in.'[23]

The prospect of a redrawing of party boundaries hung in the air throughout the 1930s. In the short term, however, Labour had much work to do in getting its own house in order. 'We have been hard at work defining programme and policy of action.' Lansbury, Cripps and Attlee were working closely with 'sundry pundits' such as Cole, Dalton and Harold Laski of the London School of Economics. He believed that they had 'fairly well clarified our views'. He gave considerable thought to the effective functioning of the state in an era of great economic and political change. In October he told Tom he was busy preparing a broadcasting series on the machinery of government departments. He had considered writing a small collection of essays in the summer but did not know if he could produce 'anything worth having'.[24]

By necessity, Attlee also sharpened his understanding of economic affairs following the Ottawa conference, which took place in July 1932. Britain's abandonment of free trade meant that the question of imperial preference had been on the agenda among the Commonwealth nations. Attlee rejected the 'wild imaginings' of those who believed that the empire could be turned into a cohesive economic unit (with free trade within it, but tariffs to protect it from external markets). Nonetheless, he did feel that 'closer cooperation' between countries within the empire might be a step towards 'that planned economy which . . . must sooner or later replace the present chaos'. Britain needed outlets for iron and steel and the Dominions needed to sell foodstuffs. This could not be left to the markets to regulate, however. For, as he wrote in notes in his private papers, in a theme which he also came back to in his satire on the Bullions, 'capital knows no patriotism and investors look for their return in hard cash not soft sentiment.'[25]

Attlee was disparaging about the activities of the Independent Labour Party, who were increasingly fractious and refused to cast their lot in with the mainstream Labour Party opposition. As a man who had come into the Labour movement through the ILP, their unwillingness to cooperate upset him. His old friend John Beckett, who was now with the ILP (but was to soon associate himself with Mosley), criticised him personally in the Commons. He expressed deep sadness that 'a kind, gentle, loveable man' like Attlee had been corrupted by the parliamentary system.[26] The trouble with the ILP, Attlee believed, was that they had 'no ideals on which to work'. Fenner Brockway and Jimmy Maxton, its two agitators-in-chief, had 'the appearance of revolutionaries but nothing more'. Attlee predicted a further accession of strength to the SSIP, as the new vanguard of the left. He visited the Cripps family's ancestral home, Goodfellows, a large estate in Gloucestershire, for further discussions on strategy in August, and to prepare for the party conference in the autumn.[27]

The political formula that the party settled upon, at its October 1932 conference in Leicester, was the immediate implementation of socialism the next time they came to office. This would begin with moving the Bank of England into state ownership, followed by transport and electricity.[28] Yet this general agreement could not disguise the tensions that were emerging within the party on other issues. The various forces which made up Labour were pulling in different directions. Bevin, Walter Citrine and the leading trade unionists preferred gradual changes to raise the standard of living for workers, whereas there was a more theoretically inclined element, including Cripps, who insisted that socialist ideas should be applied wholesale in a process of rapid transformation, as soon as conditions were right.[29]

While Bevin had acted as chairman of the SSIP when it was founded, he now became concerned about the direction in which Cole and Cripps were taking it. He was particularly suspicious of their decision to form the Socialist League, a new organisation funded by Cripps, to try to bring ILP supporters back into the party. As Bevin understood it, the Socialist League was being used as a Trojan horse for a new strategy that Cripps was trying to enforce upon the party. In what was to become known as the 'unity front', Cripps urged the Labour Party to lead a new coalition of all left-wing parties, including the Communist Party. This was unthinkable to those trade union representatives who had spent so many years in conflict with Communists. An almighty row was brewing. For the moment, Attlee bided his time.[30]

Different centres of power started to emerge on the left. The National Executive began to try to assert control. In 1932 Dalton complained that the parliamentary party was a 'poor little affair', by comparison with those who sat in the Executive. Nor was he an admirer of the SSIP. He complained that Attlee and Cripps, who were still in touch with Cole, would sit in Lansbury's room at the House all day and all night, and 'continually influence the old man'. Dalton believed he was superior to both the leader and deputy leader, but that the unfortunate electoral result of 1931 had deprived him of his rightful place. Attlee, in particular, was in a 'purely accidental position' of authority.[31]

Given these pressures, Lansbury and Attlee had no easy task in keeping the attentions of the Labour Party focused on Parliament, and preventing a drift to the National Executive. Cripps too played an important role, but as he continued with his legal practice, and focused so much energy on the Socialist League, the main burden fell elsewhere. The work of Attlee and Lansbury is more important to the course of 1930s British history than has been recognised. To their credit, some Conservatives appreciated the significance of their efforts. 'When the history of Parliament is written,' Baldwin told MacDonald that year, 'see that Lansbury gets his due.' He had kept the 'flag of Parliamentary Government flying in the world'.[32]

This was a matter of striking the right balance. On the one hand, Attlee's trick was to turn the tables against the National Government by claiming it represented a serious threat to democracy. In Britain, it was the democratic socialists who were 'the true preservers of Western ideas', he claimed in Parliament on 25 November 1932. In its current form, capitalism was 'incompatible with the ideal of social justice'. If the capitalist system did not transform itself, he warned, 'what I myself hold to be most precious in our Western civilization will go down before the irresistible rush of the discontented.'[33]

On the other hand, the truth is that Attlee did flirt with radicalism in these years in a way that belied his later image as a studiously moderate parliamentarian. To some extent, he appears to have been slightly dazzled by Cripps and the gatherings at Goodfellows, through which the great and good of socialist society would pass.[34] It was an indication of the mood of the times that the Attlee of 1932–3 was as radical as he had ever been. Communism and fascism never tempted him but he was not immune to the excitement and the instability of the era of the Great Depresssion, and the new ideas that came with it.

In 1933, Cripps published a collection of essays in which he offered a fuller exposition of the views of the Socialist League. The professed aim of the book was an attempt to answer the question: 'Can socialism come by constitutional methods?' Cripps's answer was in the negative. He argued that the story of the twentieth century thus far had been to show that the nineteenth-century system of democratic government was incapable of adaptation to the economic and social conditions of the day. In the pre-1914 period, the theory of gradual advance seemed plausible enough. But the crisis of capitalism brought about by the Great Depression had meant that purely democratic change was no longer plausible. The one precondition for a socialist government was that it had to receive a popular mandate from the electorate. From that point, however, it would be necessary for that government to take revolutionary measures. The first would be to abolish the House of Lords; the second would be that it would have to assume emergency powers, for a short period at least, to enforce its methods.[35]

This was bracing stuff. Bevan and other moderates in the Labour Party baulked at the unconstitutional suggestions which the Socialist League made. At this moment, however, Attlee continued to associate himself with Cripps. In fact, he wrote his own essay in Cripps's volume, which contained its own radical suggestions. There was a plan for the

reorganisation of local government in the country in the event of a socialist government coming to power. He had not abandoned his humanism.
Any plans must be worked out with due regard to the fact that men and
women were not 'pawns in a game'. Yet, in a loaded phrase, Attlee insisted
that the important thing was 'not to do things with the most scrupulous
regard to theories of democracy or exact constitutional propriety, but to
get on with the job'. He proposed local government be divided into large
units within which commissioners would be appointed to make sure that
the government's overall plan would be implemented.

Attlee was aware that this sounded 'at first very autocratic'. In his conception, the idea of socialist commissioners bore comparison to the way in
which Cromwell had deployed his major-generals to run the country in
place of Parliament and spread the word of the English Revolution. He was
also well aware that his plan sounded like the Russian model of Communist Party commissars running the country. 'I am not afraid of the
comparison! We have to take the strong points of the Russian system and
apply them to this country,' he said, in a phrase from which he would later
recoil. He caveated his article by insisting that such methods would only be
temporary. 'It will be seen, therefore, that though I may seem to have
strayed into autocracy to some extent in the period of transition, I return
to a full exercise of democracy, as soon as the Socialist State, which I have
not space to discuss, is established.'[36]

Such was the mood of the Labour Party in 1932–3. To provide some
context, Attlee and the SSIP were not the only ones to depart from established positions in this period of excitement and flux. Lloyd George, for
example, also swung leftwards, partly with the intention of detaching
those Liberals who had joined the National Government. Attlee suspected
that the former prime minister would also like to rally the forces of the left
to his banner in some sort of popular front, but would never go far enough
to commit himself to 'the essentials of a new order of society'. Nevertheless, he did find it telling to see the extent to which men like Robert Horne,
a Liberal stalwart and Lloyd George's Minister of Labour in 1920–1, now
accepted 'the kind of things we preached at the street corner years ago',
such as the need for a rational organisation of industry and the principle of
planning instead of competition.[37]

Some of this was a simple question of efficiency. In his short tenure as a
government minister, he had seen enough to convince him that the British

system had 'anachronisms' in an increasingly treacherous world. To govern effectively required 'the power of taking energetic and rapid decisions'. The vice of the modern Cabinet was in allowing 'things to drift because of differences of opinion instead of bringing matters to the decision of a vote'. In a personal memorandum in his private papers, he recommended that a smaller group of ministers with no specific departmental responsibilities should take charge for the overall direction of state activity.[38] Speaking to an audience of Manchester United fans in Salford, he expressed this vision a different way. For a socialist government to be truly effective, there must be cooperation 'between the forwards and the backs, the right wing and the left wing'.[39]

Whatever spin was put upon it, the direction of his train of thought was increasingly radical. Along with Cripps, he submitted a paper to the National Executive Committee, which spoke of the need to strike at the heart of capitalism within months of taking government. 'The blow struck must be a fatal one and not merely designed to wound and to turn a sullen and destructive opponent into an active and deadly enemy.' On his copy of the document, the unimpressed Dalton wrote 'feverish' and 'no detailed plan'.[40] Privately too, Attlee admitted that he was impressed by Harold Laski's *Democracy in Crisis*, which he found 'amazingly good'; he felt it 'brings one right up to realities'.[41] Laski's book raised serious questions about the survival of democracy in a capitalist system. He wanted to impress upon the reader 'how close our feet lie to the abyss – the usual point at which Englishmen are stimulated to consider principle'.[42] That moment was indeed approaching.

V

In February 1933, Attlee reported with pleasure that 'everywhere I go I find reviving enthusiasm and great meetings.' 'George, Stafford and I all endeavour to give them the pure milk of the word.' It was a relief that the 'booming gradualism and palliatives' of the MacDonald era had passed.[43] There was newfound hope in the party, and the response seemed to be favourable. MacDonald had posed as 'the Weary Titan or the good man struggling with adversity'. Lansbury was a 'standing reproach' to such conceit.[44] After one mass rally at Hyde Park, Clem told his leader how the rest of the movement regarded him as 'almost a Gandhi'.[45]

Yet this was a passing phase. Europe in the 1930s was no place for a British Gandhi. It was developments in international affairs that caused Attlee to begin to check his radicalism in early 1933. Along with almost everyone in the Labour Party, Attlee remained convinced that the League of Nations – established after the Treaty of Versailles in 1919 – remained the best hope for the avoidance of war. The question which was to begin to divide Labour, however, just as it had divided Tom and Clem in 1914, was whether or not the League of Nations should use military force to enforce its authority.

In his satire on the Bullion family, Attlee suggested that the National Government had no coherent approach to dealing with the unravelling of international order. 'The Bullion family for years and years engaged in quarrels with their neighbours,' he wrote. Each family on the street had access to an orchard and a hen run. Unfortunately, each of them, the Bullions included, tended to stockpile these apples and eggs to use them as missiles to throw at their neighbours' windows. The result was that the children all went short of food and yet still their windows were smashed. The apples and eggs were armaments, and the wire netting represented the shifting defensive alliances that each nation explored. Their failure, and the reason why their disputes were interminable, was their inability to use the League of Nations to build a broader peace.

After Ramsay MacDonald, it was the foreign secretary, Sir John Simon, who bore the brunt of Attlee's satire. 'Simple Simon' had done nothing when Mr Yen (Japan) flouted the rules of the orchard in attacking Mr Tael (China). This referred to Japan's invasion of Manchuria in January 1931, a flagrant breach of international law. Simple Simon had made a great fuss but had failed to assert any authority. In the satire, he set up a neighbourhood watch and, the first time he was on the beat, he heard a commotion in Mr Tael's house and looked in to see that Mr Yen had Mr Tael by the throat. When he consulted with the neighbours, he went back to find Mr Tael on the ground, dazed, and Mr Yen helping himself to Mr Tael's watch and making himself comfortable in Mr Tael's front room. 'It looks to me,' said Simple Simon, 'that they are coming to an agreement.' Meanwhile, Simple Simon had also got into a great row with Mr Rouble (Russia) and said 'unless you agree with me I will shut my door against you and your family.' He was tricked into believing that the Roubles were to blame for everything, particularly by Mr Mark (Germany), who seemed particularly inclined to point the finger elsewhere.[46] In failing to act over Manchuria, Attlee later admitted that the League of Nations had failed its 'acid test'.[47]

Other developments in international politics were more concerning still. In January 1933, Adolf Hitler became Chancellor of Germany and began the process whereby he ended the Weimar Republic, installed one-party rule, and created the Third Reich. These events made a significant mark on Attlee. In a letter to Tom, written on 15 February 1933, one can see the two competing instincts which shaped his view of international affairs for the rest of the decade.

On the one hand, Attlee remained firmly committed to the ideal of the League of Nations, even as its authority began to wane. 'I am being forced to the conclusion that nothing short of a world state will be really effective in preventing war,' he wrote. 'I want us to come out boldly for a real long range policy which will envisage the abolition of the conception of the individual sovereign state.' In the first instance, this required a revision of the post-war peace treaties, including the Versailles settlement. Like many others, he believed that its harsh terms on Germany had created a destabilising imbalance. The world was being 'asked to sit down prematurely on a fantastic map of Europe'. Speaking to his old regiment at Catterick, he apprised them of his belief that internationalism was the next stage in political evolution, after nationalism. The difficulty that the world faced was that nationalism had not been allowed to run its logical course in the nineteenth century, as the successor to dynastic imperialism. It had been squeezed, subverted and flattened by autocratic or imperial regimes. This meant that it was bursting out in the twentieth century, in an uglier form, just when economic and technological developments should be breaking down the barriers between sovereign states.[48]

On the other hand, if a peaceful resettlement of international affairs proved impossible, he was prepared to consider more realistic alternatives. It would make sense for Britain, in the short term, to pursue a close alliance with America and France. If Russia could also be brought into this alliance, he hoped this might curtail the ambitions of revanchist governments in Germany, Italy and Japan.[49] Seven years before they joined together in government, this position bore striking similarities to Churchill's idea of a 'grand alliance' with France, and, if possible, America, which would encourage the Russians to stick their lot in with the Western powers.[50] Years later Attlee even claimed that 'we always believed that with a proper line-up of what Winston called the Great Alliance, we could have got rid of the war.'[51]

In Attlee's private letters there were the faint strains of a realistic and unsentimental approach to international affairs. The difficulty was that his two closest allies in the Labour Party at this time, Cripps and Lansbury, were pacifists. In the short term, over the first few months of 1933, Attlee urged the taking of a tough line with Hitler. Thus he argued that the League of Nations should intervene with a 'stern warning' to stop Nazi officials interfering in Austria, even though he expressed some sympathy with German frustration about the Treaty of Versailles. He also spoke strongly against Benito Mussolini's suggestion of a Four-Power Pact, whereby European affairs would be controlled by the four major powers – Britain, France, Germany and Italy – over the heads of the smaller nations.[52]

In the east, meanwhile, Attlee also believed that force – if not necessarily military intervention – was required against Japan. Thus he advocated an international navy to patrol the seas, which, of course, would be dominated by Britain and America. Indeed, Attlee went so far as to suggest that an international air force was necessary to police the globe. 'This may sound visionary,' he wrote, 'but I am convinced that unless we see the world we want it is vain to try to build a permanent habitation for Peace.' Above all, Attlee believed that Britain had a crucial role to play in world affairs – either as the champion of the League of Nations, as an arbiter between states, or as the leader of a new Western Alliance. Otherwise, the international order that had been established to prevent conflict at the end of the Great War was in danger of collapsing. These 'temporary structures' left from 1919 'will catch fire very soon if we wait any longer'.[53]

9

The Anti-Cromwell

Oliver Cromwell has long passed beyond the mists of calumny . . . By common consent he stands in the first rank of greatness, but there is little agreement on the specific character of that greatness. He is admired by disciples of the most divergent faiths . . . Constitutionalists claim him as one of the pioneers of the parliamentary system, though he had little patience with government by debate, and played havoc with many parliaments . . . Modern devotees of force have seen in him the super-man who marches steadfastly to his goal amid the crash of ancient fabrics, but they have forgotten his torturing hours of indecision. He has been described as tramping with heavy boots relentlessly through his age, but they have forgotten his steps were mainly slow and hesitating and he often stumbled.

John Buchan, *Oliver Cromwell*, 1934[1]

I *Cambridge, 22 February 1933*

The whole southwest of England was blanketed in snow and more was forecast for that evening. On 22 February 1933, Aneurin Bevan, the eloquent and radical young Welsh Labour MP, was due to debate with Sir Oswald Mosley, the former Labour rebel and leader of the British fascist movement, at the Cambridge University Union. Thickly built, wide-jawed, brave and full of rhetorical fire, Bevan seemed to have the ideal personality to take on Mosley, the engaging, handsome aristocrat who saw himself as Britain's answer to Mussolini, or a new Oliver Cromwell – speaking for the people but prepared to shake up the system, kick out the Establishment and, if necessary, use force.

In the early afternoon, Bevan pulled out of the debate. He had caught the flu and was bed-ridden with a fever in his Westminster flat. His flat-mate, Frank Owen, former Liberal MP for Hereford and now a reporter with the *Daily Express*, made his way to the office shared by Lansbury, Att-tlee and Cripps, to tell the Labour leader that Bevan was ill. Owen was a graduate of Cambridge and had heard that the students were 'all steamed up for the clash', with standing room only. 'Whom shall we possibly send?' asked Lansbury when he heard the news, 'It's important to answer Mosley in front of these young chaps.' 'I'll go,' said Attlee, without hesitation. Owen warned Attlee that the train would not get him there in time and that the snow was beginning to fall again. As he was intending to cover the debate, he offered Attlee a lift in his open-top car. Attlee grabbed his coat and they set off immediately, in hats, scarves and goggles, 'skidding over an ice-bound road, with the snow freezing on the windscreen and blanket-ing the headlamps'. In the course of the three-hour drive, they twice came off the road and into a ditch.

The two men arrived in Cambridge 'looking like a couple of snowmen' and just in time for the debate. There was no time for dinner, or to thaw out. Owen gratefully accepted a large dram of Scotch, while Attlee declined and entered the chamber. 'I was happy to report that Attlee had extin-guished the (debating) lights of Sir Oswald Mosley,' wrote Owen. Such was Attlee's schedule that they were forced to make the journey back home that same night – the deputy leader of the Labour Party was due to open a telephone exchange in Mile End in the morning. They clambered back into their snow chariot and set off again. Owen could not think of any other frontbench or even backbench politician who would step out on a freezing night at ten minutes' notice to drive sixty miles through a snowstorm to keep a colleague's appointment.

Six years later, when Britain declared war on Germany, Owen was the editor of the *Evening Standard*. Alongside Michael Foot and Peter Howard, he was also one of the authors of *Guilty Men*, the anonymous 1940 polemic which denounced the men behind the appeasement of Hitler. When the war began, he gave up his editorship of the *Evening Standard* and estab-lished a publication for the British forces in the South East Asia Command. The story of Attlee's self-sacrifice against Mosley first appeared in an article Owen wrote for the armed forces magazine, the *Phoenix*. It was also told to US Secretary of State James Byrnes, as an indication of the fibre of the man who led the Labour Party in these difficult years.[2]

The anecdote was all the more powerful because it was not an isolated story. The debate at the Cambridge Union was in fact Attlee's third speech that week, though it was certainly a highlight. Attlee was rather pleased with himself for besting the man he had replaced in MacDonald's government in 1931. 'Mosley talked pretty fair rot to a crowded house. I laughed him to scorn pretty effectively and got a good majority,' he told Tom. 'He has not any coherent ideas. It really is Mosley and nothing more.'[3]

Over the course of the previous year, Attlee had allowed himself to be carried along with the vague but radical idea, put forward by Cripps and Harold Laski, that the democratic process might have to be jettisoned, albeit temporarily, in the building of a socialist state. As a student of Renaissance history at Oxford, Attlee had confessed a fondness for the 'strong men' of history. Increasingly, however, he began to retreat from this position. The rise of men such as Mussolini, Hitler and – though he was laughable by comparison – Mosley, demonstrated the dangers of playing fast and loose with the democratic system. At various points Attlee had expressed admiration for Oliver Cromwell. However, as Mosley posed as the new Cromwell, Attlee came to a fuller appreciation of Cromwell's flaws.

The following year, Violet Attlee gave her husband a copy of a recently published biography of Cromwell by John Buchan, a Scottish Conservative peer, former Governor-General of Canada, prolific writer, and author of the bestselling adventure novel *The Thirty-Nine Steps*. Attlee found it a 'most well balanced life and admirably written'.[4] In the mid-1930s, Mosley sought to assume the Cromwellian mantle, as the populist strongman of the era. Buchan set out to debunk this at its source. Cromwell had been eulogised by the modern 'devotees of force' who had presented him as 'the super-man who marches steadfastly to his goal amid the crash of ancient fabrics.' But this was based on only a partial picture. For one thing, Cromwell had shown doubt and anguish over the difficult decisions he had taken. There was much more to his emotional and political make-up than a belief in the use of force, and there was much more humility and self-doubt in him than the neo-Cromwellians of the 1930s were prepared to admit. For another, Cromwell had made major strategic errors. His temper had got the better of him. The ideals he fought for had been compromised and the Cromwellian project contained within it the seeds of its own destruction.[5]

Such analogies were not lost on contemporaries. Reviewing the book in the *Spectator*, an impressed George Trevelyan wrote that Buchan was keenly alive to Cromwell's mistakes, which he listed: the execution of the king; the massacre of Irish at Drogheda; and the dissolution of the Rump Parliament. Perhaps most significant was Cromwell's experiment of governing the country with his major-generals. For Buchan, this had been a disaster. One can only imagine the effect that reading this on Christmas Day in suburban Stanmore had on Attlee, just a year after he had floated the notion himself in the name of establishing a socialist state. Yet there were other aspects of Cromwell's personality that he would have warmed to. In Buchan's hands he appeared 'a more attractive person and a subtler and more complicated psychological study' than Napoleon, Frederick the Great or any other 'Carlylean super-man'. This was reflected in 'his real humility of soul in presence of God; his desire to establish the political liberty on which he was forced to tread; the tenderness and pity which alternated with his iron moods . . . his humour, good fellowship and craving for quiet, domestic, country life . . . his opportunism and distrust of hard theorists.' It was these qualities that made him an 'essentially English hero, though it was his fate to ride rough-shod over Englishmen.'[6]

Did Attlee also read H. G. Wells's interview with Josef Stalin, published in the *New Statesman* just after the release of Buchan's book? In justifying his repressive tactics within the Soviet Union, Stalin had used the example of the English Revolution when, in order to get rid of the old system, it had required 'a Cromwell to crush it by force'. When Wells suggested that Cromwell 'acted on the basis of the constitution and in the name of constitutional order', Stalin offered a revealing reply: 'In the name of the constitution he resorted to violence, beheaded the king, dispersed some and beheaded others!'[7]

Just as the limits of Lansbury's Gandhism became clear, so Attlee began to become more apprehensive of Cromwellianism and unconstitutional behaviour. One could appreciate the personal qualities of Cromwell without getting carried away with the myth, or seeking to apply his methods. Years later, when reviewing the second volume of Winston Churchill's *A History of the English-Speaking Peoples*, Attlee noted that Churchill too, had come to a balanced assessment of Cromwell. He could appreciate Cromwell as 'a man of action and a soldier' while condemning the sack of Drogheda and his establishment of a dictatorship. In the final assessment, Attlee was to agree with Churchill that Cromwellianism was 'in lasting discord with the genius of the English race'.[8] Thus, along with Stanley Baldwin, the Conservative leader, Attlee was to be one of the most effective antidotes to the neo-Cromwellians whose flames burned brightly in this decade but ultimately faded.

II

In April 1933, Hitler did something in Germany that had a disconcerting echo of Attlee's own idea of splitting the country into administrative units run by commissars or major-generals. He divided Germany into forty-two new Nazi-run local authorities, each headed by a gauleiter who reported directly to him. This followed his Enabling Act a few weeks before, by which the German Reichstag granted Hitler the power to make his own laws without consulting it. Watching these events, Attlee was deeply uncomfortable. In Parliament that March he had condemned the Nazi use of violence.[9] By the time the Enabling Act passed, he warned that fascism promised the 'reintroduction of death in the near future'.[10]

Viewed as a whole, Europe looked increasingly prone to extremism, and possibly war. As Attlee put it, there was 'so much loose powder lying about and one cannot tell where the match will be applied'. He feared that the German Social Democrats had been flattened for a generation and that Austria was also likely to be subsumed by the Nazis before long. This would mean that all of Europe east of the River Rhine – with the exception of Czechoslovakia, for the moment – would be lost to anti-democratic forces. This had serious implications for the Labour Party, and in particular the idea of the Socialist League. How could they push forward with a 'world plan for socialism' in these conditions? German socialists were likely to be driven underground, or turn to communism for want of any alternative. The long-term trajectory seemed to suggest a war against Russia by the fascist powers, turning Europe into a battleground between far-left and far-right governments.

The question of how to confront fascism presented a tactical as well as an intellectual dilemma for the British left. In France and in Central and Southern Europe, the socialist strategy had been to build a broader coalition with all forces across the left-wing spectrum, including communists. It was a version of this strategy that Cripps and the Socialist League wanted to adopt. This was reflected in the idea of a 'unity' front, which would see the Labour and Communist parties affiliate, and seek alliances with unity fronts in other countries such as France.

It was on this issue that Attlee began to indicate his dissent from Cripps and the Socialist League. To divide Europe into the forces of left and right was counterproductive and potentially poisonous. Instead, his view was that the British Labour Party should define itself as standing for democracy over totalitarianism. Whether that totalitarianism was fascist or communist was essentially irrelevant. When it came to foreign policy then, once again Attlee looked west rather than east. 'It may be that we shall have to look for a time more to a movement working on the lines of Western democracy in the British Empire and U.S.A.,' he reiterated in April 1933. Socialism was most likely to become 'increasingly national' in the next few years, which meant that international socialist solidarity would remain a pipe dream. Russia, he felt, had given up on the idea of world revolution and was mainly concerned with pursuing its national interest. Even if world capitalism experienced another crash, there was no viable form of international socialism that could take its place. In fact, Attlee suspected that capitalism would adapt itself sufficiently to survive the crisis. Predictions of its imminent collapse were much overstated.[11]

Specifically, he felt that the League of Nations, 'an instrument of very great potential power', was not being utilised. He felt that Britain was the only nation that had the moral authority to lead it. In an early critique of appeasement, he also expressed his disquiet about 'a policy of buying off militarism by concessions'. And yet, he still remained vague about the alternatives. For example, he continued to oppose rearmament and only went so far as to urge economic rather than military sanctions against Japan over Manchuria.[12] Like many liberal internationalists in the inter-war era, his arguments were not yet fully formed. He was torn between a faith in peaceful international arbitration and a growing recognition that institutions such as the League of Nations were noble endeavours, but ultimately useless without the threat of force ('collective security') behind them.

By the summer of 1933, more broadly, Attlee had come to the conclusion that the National Government was suffering from a severe lack of leadership and had lost its sense of direction. A number of Conservative MPs were grumbling under the premiership of MacDonald, but in Stanley Baldwin they lacked a strong leader of their own. Baldwin had 'a modern outlook', Attlee wrote, but he was 'lazy and undynamic'. One alternative was Churchill, whose moves Attlee followed closely, but who had done himself no credit by adopting a hardline position on the India Bill of March 1933, effectively alienating his party. This bill had merely established a Joint Select Committee to discuss a government White Paper on Indian self-government. Churchill misjudged the mood of his own party by railing against it as a concession to Indian nationalists. 'Winston was a complete failure,' reported Attlee, who told him as much to his face after the debate.[13]

By the time of its conference at Hastings in October 1933, serious cracks were also beginning to appear in the Labour Party. It was at Hastings that Attlee began to move his own feet, subtly but surely, away from the left of the party. He was eager to avoid an acrimonious split. He defended Cripps against critics, such as Ernie Bevin, who believed that his programme for the party was too radical. It was important to tell the party establishment 'that we mean to act and not to sit still and carry on.'[14] On foreign policy, however, he believed that the pacifism of Cripps and Lansbury was becoming a serious problem. They had gone so far as to table a motion in favour of a general strike if the government attempted to mobilise the country for war. For Attlee, this was a step too far. The party had to make up its mind whether it would take 'an extreme disarmament and isolationist attitude' or whether 'it will take the risk of standing up for the enforcement of the decisions of a world organisation against aggressor states.'[15]

It was one thing to be a conciliator and another to have the responsibility for guiding the party's overall direction. In December 1933 Attlee was unexpectedly thrust into a leadership position when George Lansbury fractured his thigh. In truth, over the previous months, Lansbury's attendance in Parliament had already been on the wane; he had been greatly upset by his wife's death in March. Attlee visited him at the end of the year at Manor House Hospital in Hampstead and recorded how he was 'very cheerful and going on well' but that his recovery would take a while.[16] His only possible rival, Cripps, was very happy for Attlee to assume the leadership, albeit on a temporary caretaker basis. Indeed, Cripps, who was making a considerable fortune at the bar and had also been born into money, donated £500 himself to the party for Attlee's salary. Attlee told Cripps on 1 January 1934 that 'any time you wish it I should always be ready to retire in your favour.'[17] That conversation hung in the air for a number of years.

As acting leader of the parliamentary party, Attlee's first task was to stop any further leakage of power to Hugh Dalton and the National Executive Committee. The issue here was not one of ideology but principle. In January 1934, the National Executive pushed forward with the publication of a pamphlet on 'Democracy and Dictatorship'. This denounced the Communist Party and rejected any possibility of the affiliation that Cripps and the Socialist League had called for. Without objecting to the content, Attlee criticised the timing of the publication as unnecessarily confrontational and a challenge to the parliamentary party. Indeed, he went so far as to suggest that he might resign as acting leader in protest, at which George Dallas, one of the National Executive Committee members, remarked to Dalton: 'Well, let him. If he does, he'll never get anything else!'[18]

Significantly, the parliamentary party was gradually fortified as some of its more prominent members began to find their way back to the Commons in a series of by-election victories.[19] Arthur Greenwood, regarded as a potential leader, was returned in early 1933. In addition to being the party's spokesman on foreign affairs, the return to prominence of the Indian question also took up much of Attlee's time. As the party's India expert, he was nominated to the select committee examining the government's new White Paper on Indian reform. The select committee held 159 meetings, and 120 witnesses were examined during the course of its eighteen-month sitting – a serious burden given the existing demands on his time.

When the select committee reported in the spring of 1934, it recommended an all-Indian federation of eleven self-governing provinces and the independence of Burma from India. This was a genuine increase in Indian self-government, though external affairs and security would still remain in the hands of the viceroy. Each of the four Labour members on the committee – Attlee, Lord Snell, Morgan Jones and Seymour Cocks – voted against its final report and produced their own alternative report, known as the 'Attlee Draft'. This argued for decreased powers for the viceroy, and more measures of self-government in the centre, rather than merely in the provinces. It suggested that the new Indian constitution should state that it was the intention of the British government to grant full Dominion status to India, within a defined period of years. This meant that complete control over Indian foreign policy was to be granted to Indians, as it was to Canadians. The Attlee Draft also criticised what it saw as the conservative elements in the government proposals, such as a two-tier parliament, which would grant more power to the princes, and a limited franchise. It called for more effort to ensure the Indianisation of the army, thereby removing a major obstacle to eventual independence.

More broadly, Attlee complained that not enough had been done to consult the Indian nationalists, or to win their support. Indeed, he suspected that one of the aims of the bill was to undermine the power of the Congress Party, the strongest Indian nationalist party, and to keep left-wing elements in check. Vested interests and regional elites, particularly the princes, were given too much power. 'It has been done by the creation of a reactionary and unrepresentative Council of State at the centre and by the creation of reactionary second chambers in the provinces, and also the formation of the British side of the assembly by the methods which set a premium on communalism,' he said. His underlying objection to the bill – with its elite-dominated second chamber and the veto power of the viceroy preserved – was that it was premised on a mistrust of Indians.[20]

While the government's bill passed Parliament and became the India Act of 1935, it was largely thanks to Attlee that Labour now had an agreed and coherent approach to the subcontinent. It was also a clear advance from Attlee's comparatively conservative line on the Simon Commission in 1931. Labour was now unified behind a support for full Dominion status, within a set timetable, and Attlee had taken the lead.[21] The way Labour had conducted itself was important for other reasons too. The party had respected the parliamentary process. Rather than refuse to cooperate in the select committee, it had made a full contribution, while recognising that the final bill would be somewhere short of its own demands. 'When it came to the point of considering specific proposals we had to take our part in them and we did, both in Committee and on the floor of the House of Commons.'[22]

The more Attlee saw of the rest of Europe, in fact, the more he became convinced that the Labour Party had a responsibility to follow a constitutional path, or risk creating the conditions for its own demise. Socialists across the Continent were squeezed between the left and the right. The few democratic strongholds in Europe, such as Czechoslovakia, were under siege. In July 1934, Attlee flew to Prague for five days to attend the Socialist Olympic Games, in a display of solidarity. He made his way into Germany and visited Leipzig, one of the few remaining anti-Nazi strongholds in Germany, where he found the atmosphere 'quiet and nervous'.[23] On a golfing holiday with Violet in Scotland in August, Attlee had some time to reflect on the differences between Britain and the rest of Europe, where extremism seemed to be on the march. He had spoken many times against Mosley over the course of the previous year, and felt that Britain remained resistant to cults of personality and lurches into left- or right-wing radicalism. 'Things look pretty black abroad but [here] there seems to be a considerable amount of optimism about and an idea that the thing will not be pressed to extremes.'[24]

It was at the Labour Party conference in Southport in October 1934 that Attlee emphatically distanced himself from Cripps and the Socialist League.[25] Cripps complained that the National Executive policy document, *For Socialism and Peace*, was too cautious and launched an attempt to win control over the party agenda by appealing to the constituency organisations over the head of the National Executive. First, he wanted Labour to pass a motion declaring that it would adopt dictatorial emergency powers in the event that it won a majority, so that it could implement an irrevocable change of the economic system. On this, he came up against the increasingly alarmed trade unions who saw this as a disastrous position to adopt in the year before an election. Second, the Socialist League also renewed its proposal to affiliate Labour with the Communist Party. Third, Cripps – who had the support of Aneurin Bevan – called for a new approach to foreign policy that grew out of the idea of a broad left-wing coalition against fascism. Instead of pinning its hopes on the League of Nations, a Labour government should make common cause with the Soviet Union in a new international front.

Against the Socialist League were Bevin and the Transport and General Workers' Union, Hugh Dalton and the National Executive, and Herbert Morrison, who had engineered a strong Labour recovery in the recent London County Council elections, and was desperate to preserve Labour's newfound respectability before a forthcoming general election. As they slugged it out between them, none of these heavyweights regarded Attlee as a central actor in proceedings. If anything, Morrison thought that Attlee was guilty of shirking the fight, still posing as a reconciler and chairman when the party needed a leader.[26]

Following the Southport Conference, the Oxford historian Godfrey Elton, a close ally of Ramsay MacDonald who had been recently raised to the peerage, commented that it had followed the usual cycle. There had been whispers of a takeover by the left – a revolt, or even a split – but each year saw the same result. The platform always got its way, as the 'ponderous Trade Union steam-roller' was rolled out to flatten any restiveness from the radicals at the back of the hall. There was Cripps, the 'much-photographed, but foredoomed protagonist of revolt' on the fringes. But as soon as the shadow of an election began to fall across the conference hall, 'the interlude of belligerent heroics draws to an end.' Some trade union officials did not even open their conference programme – having been instructed in a pre-meeting how to vote – and instead spent their time in the bar or the billiards room.

It was Bevin who 'cracked the whip' and restored discipline. The one mention that Elton made of Attlee was on his contribution to the foreign-policy debate. It seemed that the caretaker leader had 'latterly come out for League wars all over the world'. However, the party had yet to rid itself entirely of its stated goal of a 'co-operative world commonwealth' about which there was 'an unmistakable ring of fantasy'. While some of the 'cloudy idealism' was evaporating, a number of crucial issues had been skirted around in Attlee's speech. The question of whether or not Labour would support a rearmament programme – or the army estimates of the government – had been postponed for the moment.[27] It would have to be tackled soon.

On the surface, then, the moderates had won. Yet Elton, as a supporter of MacDonald, was not entirely convinced that Labour had shorn itself of its anti-democratic tendencies. It remained to be seen whether the party machine had fully repudiated the radicals, or 'merely trampled on them in the interests of discipline, whilst reserving an opportunity, within the strict limits of the year's resolutions, of turning half-Left', should it suit them at a later date. Was this just electioneering? Even in the new party manifesto, there were a few phrases that had 'a dose of the dictatorial' about them. The Labour mainstream was not ready to support a purge of the civil service or the establishment of regional commissions of party men 'on the Nazi model'. But it had 'caught and faintly re-echoed the rising note of hysteria'. It was being familiarised with the language of 'emergency plans'. Thus, Elton claimed that a 'quite unconscious taste for the dictatorial peeps out in the most unexpected yet revealing places'.[28]

That is not how Attlee saw it. 'Southport passed off very well,' he told Tom, though he wished people would 'not always want to be strangling their friends instead of their enemies'. As ever, the unity of the party remained foremost in his mind. To this end, he hatched a plan to publish a new collection of essays on the Labour movement that would bring the factions together: 'a judicious mixing of the older and newer wine.'[29]

III

Having been acting leader for a number of months, there was no sign that the position was one which Attlee particularly relished. His instinct for conciliation was valuable but not always fitted for every circumstance. While he consoled himself that his job was to soothe tensions, rather than browbeat others, he was quite aware that he was being consistently overshadowed by stronger characters in the party – such as Morrison, Dalton, Bevin and Cripps. Political life brought great pressure on his time, with scant financial rewards. Violet had suffered while raising the children in his repeated absences, and it seemed as though he might have reached the heights of his career. Unsurprisingly, he grew a little restless, though he was unclear as to where his energies would be better directed.

Thoughts drifted elsewhere. In October 1934 he admitted to Tom that he had been working on an idea for a motion picture that had come to him 'all of a sudden'. It concerned two 'Balkanised despotisms' simultaneously wiping each other off the map, to the horror of the civilised world. Arms dealers, Nazi Germany and Soviet Russia loomed large in the plot:

Extremely realist scenes of destruction to be filmed. War fomented by rival armaments groups who own the Press of the two countries. Son of chief armament monger sees wife and children killed most unpleasantly. Repentance of chief armament monger who gives away story of the workings of the ring to the D.H. [Daily Herald] just in time to turn general election. Follows creation of international World State, abolition of armaments etc. with a postscript some years afterwards illustrating new world conditions by conversations of members of World air communications at H.Q. aerodrome in Vienna. Love interest etc. can be added if necessary.

The film would also see 'a Hitlerite dictator' intent on war and stopped by the threat of force from an international coalition. Attlee genuinely hoped that the idea might sell and he received encouraging noises from Kingsley Martin, editor of the *New Statesman*, and Beverley Nichols, known for his bestselling 1934 pacifist tract, *Cry Havoc!*. Attlee hoped it might be 'valuable propaganda if done sufficiently crudely for the popular taste'.[30] Nothing came of the venture, unsurprisingly perhaps.

Indeed, Attlee's visions of a 'world state' were in danger of outlasting their utility in a rapidly deteriorating international environment which was not conducive to a liberal world order. Yet, while his position on international affairs had not yet reached full maturity, it was, at least, in tune with public opinion. The Peace Ballot, organised by the League of Nations Union at the end of 1934, revealed that 10 million out of 11 million households supported disarmament and the League of Nations. On the question of stopping an aggressor state with the use of force, 2 million abstained, 2 million opposed, and 6 million supported it.

These were dilemmas that could not be wished away. The first half of 1935 was dominated by international politics. 'Foreign affairs are pretty dicky right now,' he wrote to Tom shortly after Easter. He had met with a number of socialist leaders from Germany and Czechoslovakia, who were despairing about the stronghold that fascists had created in Central Europe.[31] In his view, the National Government was floundering. He guessed that the Conservatives wanted to get rid of both Ramsay MacDonald, whose health was now failing, and Sir John Simon, his Liberal foreign secretary.[32] When the Cabinet reshuffle came, Sir Samuel Hoare replaced Simon at the Foreign Office. Attlee felt that this would be an improvement, but also believed that Anthony Eden, the dashing Conservative MP, would have been a better choice.[33]

One thing that the government was particularly eager to avoid was a fascist alliance between Hitler and Mussolini. Samuel Hoare thus began courting the Italian dictator, which infuriated those on the Labour benches. Attlee led the chorus of disapproval in Parliament. His mocking of Mussolini prompted Captain Fanelli, an Italian fascist newspaper editor in Rome, to challenge Attlee to a duel. In declining the offer, Attlee said that Fanelli's challenge revealed everything one needed to know about how far Italy had left behind the noble traditions of the Renaissance and Risorgimento.[34] In Attlee's stead, one Edward A. Dickinson of Highbury in London offered to take on Fanelli himself. 'If this fire-eating Italian fellow wants to eat fire, I will give it to him to eat.' Dickinson, a fishmonger in Billingsgate market, was six foot tall, well built and fancied his chances.[35] The contest never took place but Anglo-Italian relations became increasingly problematic over the following months.

This was brought to a head by Italy's invasion of Abyssinia in October 1935, which presented the greatest challenge to international order since the Japanese invasion of Manchuria in 1931. Mussolini calculated that the League of Nations did not have the resolve to act against him, despite his flouting of its rules. The news of the invasion reached England on the eve of the Labour Party conference in Britain. Having recovered from his fractured thigh, George Lansbury had hoped for a triumphant return as leader. However, as the majority of his party called for League of Nations sanctions and a strong line against Mussolini, Lansbury's position was effectively rendered untenable.

In a famous scene, Ernest Bevin rose in front of the hall and accused Lansbury of 'hawking [his] conscience around from body to body' as the world about him caught fire.[36] The die was cast, and Morrison followed suit with a careful dismantling of the pacifist position. Attlee's personal fondness for Lansbury meant that he was uncomfortable with the ferocity of Bevin's attack (he believed Bevin had a tendency to bully). Yet he did now break firmly with his leader and sided with the majority: 'We are against the use of force for Imperialist and capitalist ends, but we are in favour of the proper use of force for ensuring the use of law. I do not believe that non-resistance is a possible policy for people with responsibility.'[37] The problem with a pacifist, he later reflected, was that he had a tendency to believe 'that other people must see the thing as he did if only the matter was put fully before them'.[38] As for Bevin's controversial intervention, Attlee explained that he 'despised leaders who wanted to cling on to their conscience with one hand and on to power with the other'.[39]

With Lansbury fatally wounded – and unable to support the majority decision due to his personal beliefs – thoughts turned to who might replace him as Labour leader. The impression left from the debate, in the view of the *Observer*'s parliamentary correspondent, was the 'dangerously forceful personality of Mr. Ernest Bevin, the neat Parliamentary precision of Mr. Attlee, and the growth in the stature of Mr. Morrison'.[40] The *Daily Mail* suggested that there might be some support for Attlee as leader, but only as a temporary replacement. There were more serious candidates to take the leadership in the long term – namely, Arthur Greenwood and Herbert Morrison. While Morrison was the most capable – he was free from the 'sentimental sloppiness' of other Labour leaders and could appeal to the 'middle vote in England which wins elections' – he had the great disadvantage of not being in Parliament, having lost his seat in 1931.[41] Stafford Cripps was lobbying in the background on the grounds that he was the only candidate who raised enthusiasm at meetings of the rank and file, but he had also alienated the party machine. Beatrice Webb commented that none of the leading candidates had any great talent for public speaking, including Attlee who, 'though gifted with intellect and character and also with goodwill has, alas!, no *personality!*' He was 'neither feared, disliked nor admired' but 'merely respected by Labour men and approved by the government bench'.[42]

On 8 October, the Parliamentary Labour Party met at Transport House to hear Lansbury's resignation speech and decide on his replacement. Before the meeting, the *Daily Mail* was 'almost certain' that Greenwood would be nominated as his successor.[43] The *Manchester Guardian*, with a better understanding of the Labour Party, suggested that Attlee was also a serious candidate, though only to keep the seat warm until Morrison returned as an MP. Greenwood had a 'more positive and interesting personality' but Attlee was not to be underestimated. He was well-regarded by the existing MPs and had been 'every bit as effective in debate as Mr. Greenwood', while covering a wider field. More broadly, the *Manchester Guardian* believed that the defeat of Lansbury might be a turning point for Labour. It had 'suffered greatly from the chartered libertinism' of Stafford Cripps and 'not a little from Lansbury's vagaries' on international affairs. The trade unions at Brighton had asserted their determination 'to withstand any more balloon excursions into the neo Marxian stratosphere'. They wanted a 'firmly based and plainly understood' policy at home and abroad.[44]

As expected, the final decision on a new leader was postponed. It was decided that Attlee, as vice-chairman, should carry on the duties of chairman for the rest of the parliamentary session. The *Daily Mail* suspected that this was because Labour was 'strongly divided by jealousies and differences on policy'. There was also a matter of simple procedure. The chairman of the parliamentary party was normally elected at the beginning of each parliamentary session but everyone expected that Parliament was about to be dissolved. After an election, Morrison and several other leading figures would likely be back in the race.[45] The *Daily Telegraph* noted that Attlee, the interim appointment, enjoyed the 'respect of his opponents as well as his supporters'. For the moment, the 'dark, black-bearded kings' of the trade unions had decided that he was the best choice to lead the party into an election, after which the composition of the party might be changed.[46] Labour's *Daily Herald* did nothing to challenge the perception that Attlee was a stopgap solution for the election.[47] It was widely agreed, according to the *Manchester Guardian*, that Attlee, though an excellent parliamentarian, had not yet shown the 'personality of a popular leader'.[48]

IV

At no stage had Attlee lobbied for the job. As he later described, 'When I heard in 1935 that they were talking about my becoming the leader of the party, I did not know whether I was going to be proposed, let alone know who was going to propose me.' It would have been 'unbecoming, improper, and ultimately ineffective, to try to find out, even if I had not been too shy to do so.'[49]

Those closest to him, however, felt that he had been somewhat underestimated. Jack Lawson penned an anonymous article in the *Manchester Guardian* about the new leader the day after his appointment.[50] No one could say that Attlee had the personality of Lansbury, the oratorical skills of MacDonald or the finesse of Stafford Cripps. Mindful of his previous association with Cripps, Lawson located Attlee in the centre-left of the party. Once he demonstrated his worth, Lawson predicted, he would be very difficult to budge. He would know how to win loyalty from colleagues. He would command the respect of his opponents and, before long, the electorate. He had never stopped learning since he entered politics and was free of 'vanity or the ardour to dominate'. The party 'will always know where he is leading it; the country will learn unmistakably where he stands.'[51]

While Attlee professed to eschew personal ambition, there were signs that he was growing in stature. He gained in confidence from the backing of his peers, even if it was on a temporary basis. Back in the House of Commons, Attlee's first act as leader was to walk up to the reporters' gallery and tell the press that he did not want to be referred to as Major Attlee.[52] This was in line with other non-professionals who had served in the army, such as Captain Anthony Eden. Now that he was in the public eye as the leader of the opposition he felt that this should be made clear.[53]

The next thing he did was to create a new Labour defence committee. On it sat Jack Lawson, A. V. Alexander and Emanuel Shinwell – all of whom were known to be comparatively hawkish on foreign policy. In his first article as leader, entitled 'Keep the peace – but no arms race', Attlee dealt with the suggestion that Labour had become more militaristic on foreign policy. Once again he laid the blame for the deteriorating international situation at the door of the government, for their failure to uphold the League. If an aggressor challenged a law in any community, the law must be enforced. That there was now a risk of war must be acknowledged. If Mussolini were allowed to flout international law, others would soon follow him.[54]

In truth, the inconsistencies in his position were still not quite resolved. In his first public speech as leader of the opposition, on 11 October, he declared that the party stood by its 'policy of making the League system effective', but also for disarmament rather than rearmament.[55] 'You don't get peace by piling up armaments,' he repeated.[56] One reason why Attlee was unwilling to rip up the previous policy entirely was that he had been so central in forming it. Another was that wounds from the conference were still fresh in the party. As the Observer noted, Labour was still 'speaking with many tongues' on foreign policy. More than a hundred of its constituency organisations had voted against sanctions, and there were rumblings of discontent in Scotland with the new policy.[57]

In an effort to present a united front, Attlee appeared alongside Lansbury on a platform in Great Harwood in Lancashire, showering his former leader with praise and not challenging Lansbury's pacifism. He rejected talk of splits and schisms in the movement and played down his own importance. 'Our movement has never depended upon leaders but on the work of the rank and file. We do not need leaders with pink, blue, or red shirts. We do not even need a wizard from Wales. What we need is the application in national and international affairs, by men and women of strong will, of the principles they apply every day in their life.'[58] Of course, to insist that Labour needed a charismatic leader would have been to undermine his own position.

Talk of 'commissars' and 'emergency measures' was definitively dropped. The substance of the party programme would remain the same as that agreed at conference. A Labour government would nationalise the Bank of England, coal, electricity, cotton and transport. Unemployment would be tackled and the means test for welfare would be abolished.[59] There were no more of the military analogies which had been used in the early part of the decade. In his 1935 book, *The Will and the Way to Socialism*, Attlee preferred to present the English version of socialism in the most non-threatening way he could think of. It was like gardening: 'In this gardening there must be some pruning, lest the coarser growths take all the light and air from the more delicate. The gardener wants variety. The garden, seen from a distance, reveals a general plan and harmony, but viewed closely, every plant is unique. This general harmony is not fixed like a mosaic pattern. It is always changing . . . The gardener's work is never done.'[60]

With Attlee at the helm, even the *Daily Mail* struggled to paint the Labour Party as dangerously leftist or radical. He did bear a striking resemblance to Vladimir Lenin – they could not resist pointing out – but he was no revolutionary. 'Courteous and hard working, he perhaps can never be an out-and-out extremist: when he speaks you feel that however much you disagree with him, it is what he thinks, and thinks sincerely about the subject.' His speeches were sometimes too long, 'rather tied to notes, and rather lacking in spontaneity' but well thought out, nonetheless. The House of Commons liked him and that was a good sign. Unlike other moderates he had not been churned out of the trade union machine to counter the intellectuals. This was the type of man Labour had 'badly wanted' for years.[61] That he was the *Daily Mail*'s preferred candidate did not, of course, necessarily endear him to his critics in the Labour Party.

As the election approached, there was a very real prospect of European war. When Parliament met on 19 October, for the last time before its dissolution, the *Observer* compared the occasion to the fateful meeting of the House of Commons on bank holiday Monday on 3 August 1914, when war on Germany had been declared. The international situation was no less menacing now. Attlee offered a calm and reasoned speech which belied the assumption that a Labour leader ought to have 'stentorian lungs'. After the election there would be 'more loud-voiced and forcible aspirants to the office' but, at the present, he was Labour's best parliamentarian. He remained 'curiously unostentatious' on the opposition bench, 'intellectual looking rather than demagogic'. His fellow MPs always listened to him with an attention that testified to the general recognition 'not only of his ability but his character'.[62]

Attlee was cheered by his party as he rose to speak. 'The contrast between the numbers on the Government benches and our small group playing Opposition was almost laughable,' wrote Lawson, 'Attlee, slight of figure, standing at the Despatch Box, must have felt almost submerged: but he showed no sign of it.'[63] Keeping a calm tone throughout, he offered an extended critique of the National Government's foreign policy over the course of the last four years. At the last election, the National Government had sought a doctor's mandate. This time they went before the country for an undertaker's mandate.[64]

The Labour Party leader realised that the League of Nations was on very weak foundations. Frail as it was, however, he still felt that it was the one thing standing between Britain and another world war. Crucially, while Labour was not prepared to give the government a blank cheque on re-armament, he now suggested that they would consider what arms were needed for the country's defence.[65] In a subtle but important shift of position, as the *Daily Mirror* highlighted, Attlee had actually broken with the policy agreed to at conference of 'sanctions, without armaments'.[66] The influential journalist J. L. Garvin, former editor of the *Observer*, now attacked Labour for having joined the 'jingo stampede' to war on the eve of an election.[67] Either way, thanks to Attlee's quick thinking, Labour went into the campaign with a more coherent foreign policy than it had had for many years.

V

Oswald Mosley described the general election of 1935, held on 14 November, as a 'competition in dullness between Baldwin and Attlee' that resulted, predictably, in a victory for the former.[68] In fact, Labour made significant progress, given the disastrous revolt of 1931. It won 8.3 million votes (an increase of 3 million) and 154 seats (an improvement of more than 100). The National Government, with 11.8 million votes, still had a large majority (with 432 MPs) but Labour had made a significant dent. It won twelve seats in London and restored its lead in the north of England with sixty gains.[69] Attlee increased his own majority in Limehouse by almost a third despite a gruelling schedule which meant he had barely set foot in his constituency.[70]

So, as the Labour Party's new MPs convened to choose their leader for the new Parliament, Attlee emerged as a serious candidate to retain the leadership. Herbert Morrison had won back his seat at the election and now, as expected, entered the race. As Attlee noted, Morrison had the support of the 'intelligentsia and the Press'. Francis Williams, the influential editor of the *Daily Herald*, also believed that he was the most likely to appeal to the middle classes.[71] He was backed by Stafford Cripps and Hugh Dalton; to his serious detriment, however, he was opposed by Ernie Bevin, with whom he had clashed on a number of occasions. This would cost him dearly with the northern and trade union MPs, over whom Bevin had great influence. Arthur Greenwood, the former Minister of Health under MacDonald, was the third candidate, but in terms of substance or style, there was not much to distinguish him from Attlee. He could count on trade union support, though it was well known he drank too much (and there was a damaging rumour that he was a freemason).[72]

Thus the cards all fell in Attlee's favour. It helped that many of the new MPs had won their seats under his leadership. His reputation for hard work, reliability and trustworthiness was undoubted. Those whom he had worked alongside since 1931, such as David Grenfell and Tom Williams, came out strongly for him. This meant that he could afford not to push his own case in a way that belied his apparent disinterestedness. Morrison's lobbying – or more accurately, Dalton's lobbying on Morrison's behalf – raised suspicions. In the first round, Attlee won the ballot with fifty-eight votes, with Morrison on forty-four and Greenwood on thirty-three. In the second ballot, all but four of Greenwood's supporters turned over to Attlee, giving him an emphatic victory. As far as the parliamentary party was concerned, this was an obvious choice, not the surprise that it has often been made out to be. Attlee was a moderating influence and a natural conciliator who had already proved that he had a capacity to appeal to voters. George Hicks, general secretary of the Amalgamated Union of Building Trade Workers wrote to congratulate him, 'You are now in a position which will make the world know of the capacity, persistence, quiet strength and quality of leadership of Clem Attlee, as yet known only to your Parliamentary colleagues and a limited circle outside.'[73] *The Economist* suggested that he had 'undeniable ability, judgement and integrity' even if he lacked the 'conspicuous attributes of a leader'.[74]

Morrison never quite got over the snub. He claimed that only the 'spiritual and psychological' effects of the 1931 betrayal could explain why Attlee was preferred to him. It left the party with a feeling of distrust for natural leaders, and 'a determination that for the time being there should be no more great men, and seeking to tie up the leadership with conditions and checks of one sort and another'. After the vote, he noted that Attlee, in his victory speech, was 'diffident' about the importance of the position, acting almost as if it was thrust upon him. He stressed that it was for just a single session, in which time much could change. Morrison, writing many years later, felt certain that Attlee, in his own mind, intended to hold on to the reins in his 'ostensibly unwilling hands'. The grip was never loosened, though Morrison tried to exploit this apparent diffidence with challenges in 1939, 1945 and 1947.[75] For the moment, he damaged his future prospects by refusing an offer to serve as Attlee's deputy – allowing Greenwood to take the post – and instead resumed his leadership of the London County Council.[76]

The malcontents and grumblers were to be ever present under Attlee's leadership. He simply had to accept that fact and learn to deal with them. 'There are many who find it impossible to believe that men lead others by such things as the example of moral or physical courage; self-discipline; altruism; and superior capacity for hard work,' he later wrote.[77] Aneurin Bevan, who was to emerge as another rival on the left of the party, later complained that Attlee was guilty of 'bringing to the fierce struggle of politics the tepid enthusiasm of a lazy summer afternoon at a cricket match', and was 'determined to make a trumpet sound like a tin whistle'.[78]

Others, who had felt that they did not have sufficient support to run in 1935, but who believed themselves to be superior talents, bided their time. 'A wretched and disheartening result! And a little mouse shall lead them!'[79] Dalton suggested that the anti-Labour press all supported Attlee because he was the weakest candidate. In doing so, he missed an important fact about Attlee – that he had a strong appeal for those who did not count themselves as diehard Labour Party supporters. Beatrice Webb found it hard to object to the 'irreproachable and colourless' Attlee, and felt the decision was, 'on balance, a wise one'. Given the divided state of the Labour Party, Attlee 'the neutral and least disliked member of the Front Bench' seemed to fit the bill. She had no idea that the 'somewhat diminutive and meaningless figure' chosen to lead the Labour movement would be in the seat for twenty years.[80] The anti-Cromwell was to prove harder to shift than anyone had imagined. There was no hint of personal triumph, of course. Yet to say that he fell into the leadership of the Labour Party, or was merely handed it by fortune is to stretch plausibility. What distinguished him from the pack was not ambition – though he was not without this – so much as a self-awareness lacking in many of his peers. 'Men who lobby their way forward into the leadership are the most likely to be lobbied out of it,' he wrote, years later, and those who talked too much 'soon found themselves up against it'.[81]

10

The Major Attlee Company and the Clenched-Fist Salute

Yo, heave ho!
Yo, heave ho!
Once more, once again, still once more
Yo, heave ho!
Yo, heave ho!
Once more, once again, still once more
Now we fell the stout birch tree,
Now we pull hard: one, two, three.
Ay-da, da, ay-da!
Ay-da, da, ay-da!
Now we pull hard: one, two, three.
Now we pull hard: one, two, three.
Yo, heave ho!
Yo, heave ho!

'The Song of the Volga Boatmen', sung by
the International Brigades, December 1937

I Teruel, Aragon, 17 January 1938

'On every hill-top, Fascist or Loyalist, a knot of ragged, dirty men shivering around their flag and trying to keep warm . . . often I used to gaze round the wintry landscape and marvel at the futility of it all.' So wrote George Orwell, in *Homage to Catalonia*, describing the scenes he saw in the Spanish Civil War during the winter of 1937–8, when fighting resumed, despite blizzards and snowdrifts covering most of the central and eastern parts of the country.[1] The battle for the provincial town of Teruel, 200 kilometres due east of Madrid, had been raging since November 1937. Another foreign chronicler, the American novelist Ernest Hemingway, saw the fighting first hand, as a reporter for the *New York Times*. On 15 December 1937, Hemingway described how troops on both sides huddled in 'zero degree weather, with wind that made living a torture and intermittent blizzards'.[2]

By 7 January 1938, after weeks of attritional warfare, in which the Republican forces advanced street by street, then door by door, the armies of General Franco surrendered the town to government forces. Ten days later, however, on 17 January, Franco's Nationalists launched a massive counteroffensive that began with artillery and aerial bombardment, and was supported by Germany's Luftwaffe. Over 100 aircraft were involved in a dogfight over the Alfambra valley in which Teruel sat. Having asserted their supremacy, the Nationalists began to bomb Teruel into submission again. Two days later, on 19 January, they attacked from the north, vastly outnumbering the beleaguered Republicans who were left in the town.[3]

Depleted, freezing and running out of food and ammunition, the Republican defenders resisted as best they could. Alongside the 5th Navarese Division were the members of the XI International Brigade. This was a unit made up of foreign volunteers who had flooded to the cause of the democratically elected Republican government when the Spanish Civil War had begun in the summer of 1936. Among those commended for their bravery were two Britons, Bill Alexander and Walter Tapsell, who were also the commissars of the brigade.[4] Tapsell, who was from east London, had joined the Young Communist League as a boy in Stepney before studying at the International Lenin School in Moscow. It was Tapsell who had stood against Attlee in the Limehouse election of 1931 as the Communist Party candidate. In a strange twist of fate, one of the units he now presided over in the XI International Brigade was the 'Major Attlee Company', named after the man who had defeated him in that election six years before. The Nationalist assault on Teruel, on 19 January 1938, was a dark day for the XI International Brigade, and particularly its British volunteers. Twenty-one were killed in action. Thirteen of them were from the Major Attlee Company, which had borne the brunt of the artillery barrage.

It was a tragic start to the life of the Major Attlee Company, which had been created just a few months before, in the weeks before Christmas 1937, following a visit from the Labour Party leader. It was as the head of a Labour delegation which included three other senior Labour MPs – Philip Noel-Baker, Professor of International Relations at the University of London; John Dugdale; and Ellen Wilkinson, 'Red Ellen', of the left wing of the party – that Attlee had visited Spain between 2 and 8 December. The delegation flew to Barcelona (and saw the aftermath of an air raid in which thirty people had been killed in a cafe), then on to Valencia and Madrid, meeting representatives from the Republican government, viewing hospitals, schools and other bomb sites.[5]

In the capital, Attlee talked not only to government officials but also to volunteers and schoolchildren, who were still studying despite being only a few kilometres from the fighting, and under constant fear of attack. Ellen Wilkinson noticed that he was moved to tears by their plight. The Spanish were 'really marvellous with their cool courage under the conditions which they endure in Madrid and in the other towns', he told Tom. He was especially enamoured of the foreign fighters from Britain – 'good lads who had graduated over here', and who now held important positions in the Republican army.

The memory that stuck with Attlee most was his visit to the front line to review the XI International Brigade. Arriving in the dark in a bitterly cold wind, he had found the men standing in order in the square of a village, with torches held all around them. The officers he talked to included a Polish divisional general, a Yugoslav brigadier, an Italian colonel, and American and British company commanders. The Yugoslav had a particularly fine voice and sang the 'Song of the Volga Boat Men' after dinner, a traditional Russian folksong. 'It was a real international meeting,' reflected Attlee, and the song was an enjoyable alternative to 'The Red Flag', ownership of which was contested between the British Labour Party and the communists.[6] With regard to Spain, in fact, Attlee felt that the Republican cause had been weakened and damaged by factionalism on the left. In the face of the fascist threat, he believed that it was a tragedy that 'all the time the Communists were intriguing and seeking to divert the contest into a battle for Communism.'[7]

Despite the disaster that befell them at Teruel, the Major Attlee Company fought on to the end of the war. It was to be led by another Labour man, Jack Jones, a Liverpudlian dock worker. Before he left for Spain in 1936, Jones had fought fascists bare-fisted in the streets of Liverpool. Now, as the company commissar, he engaged in what was to become an ideological struggle for the soul of Europe. He was wounded at the Battle of the Ebro in 1938 before the eventual defeat of the Republicans. Years later, Jones took great pleasure in handing Attlee a copy of the history of the XI International Brigade, signed by all the members of the Major Attlee Company who survived.[8]

Tapsell and the communist commissars were dismissive of the moderate social democrats in the British Labour movement. Jones, who became general secretary of the Transport and General Workers' Union in later years, was more appreciative of Attlee. Back in London, he helped Jones raise money for the families of men killed fighting for the Republicans in Spain. As Jones noted, when Attlee was elected leader he was 'regarded by many as pedestrian and lacking in glamour'. Yet his subsequent career belied the 'hasty judgment of the faint hearts'.[9]

II

Almost exactly two years before this rousing scene, in December 1935, shortly after his election as Labour Party leader, Attlee was visited at his home in Stanmore by an American journalist from the *Literary Digest*. He was depicted as the epitome of the English suburban man, with a wife and four children, a collection of pipes, a bag of golf clubs and a shed full of gardening implements. No labourer's sickle had ever raised a blister on his palm; the closest he got was a hoe. Labour's new leader was fifty-two, 'slight, graceful, getting balder by the year, and the streak across his upper lip is a moustache clipped alarmingly close'. Not for the first time it was said his skull was 'as bulbous as Lenin's'. He was 'far from being an extremist', though his record in the First World War suggested he was made of stern stuff. His 'mocking brown eyes' had 'shattered some of the most cultivated poise in England'. He was no 'striking personality, nor a popular or inflaming orator', yet he had taken the reins at a time of great international crisis. 'Some day he may very easily be Prime Minister of Britain.'[10]

As soon as he became leader, in fact, he had quickly shown more mettle than his rivals thought he had in him; demonstrating he was not quite the

Left: Attlee followed in the footsteps of his older brothers when he went to Oxford in the autumn of 1901, where this photograph was taken. He studied Modern History at University College and was at this stage of life, 'a good old-fashioned imperialist conservative'.

Below: In March 1907, eighteen months after his first visit, Attlee became the resident manager of the Haileybury Club in Stepney. He taught the boys parade and discipline, refereed their football matches at the weekend, and began his conversion to socialism.

5th December 1915

Dear Richard

Thank you for your letter which has only just come as it has been chasing me all round the place.

I am writing this in a little shelter made of sandbags on three sides and waterproof sheets on the other. The roof is made of three poles with wire netting on the top and waterproof over it. If it was put on one side it would make a good rabbit hutch. It is about 6 foot broad & 6 foot long and four of us use it during the day. Isn't it a squash.

I had a place to myself much bigger dug into the ground with a window made of an old box but it rained very hard one night and part of the wall which was made of sandbags gave way and the water came in over my knees so I had to go out. All the men's things got stuck in the mud and then it froze hard. We had to dig the blankets out with a pickaxe. How would you like to wash in a biscuit tin with water out of, a puddle?

A rat has just come to live in our shelter. I have to hunt him away with a stick. A large centipede – as long as this paper called in today but we told him we could not receive visitors. He was like this

~~~~~~~~~~~~~~~~~~~~~

We have a fine view from our place. a great bay like in the middle and a long line of hills turn as high as Laverstock down and then the sea and out of the sea sticks a great big island called Samothrace – you can find it on the map. it is very high 5 or 6000 feet at least. This country is full of little trees with holly leaves and acorns on them.

I hope you are all well at Salisbury. Give my love to everybody. I hope this will reach you in time for Christmas. Thank mother for her letter.

your loving uncle
Clement Attlee.

Above: A letter written by Attlee to his godson during his service as an officer in the Sixth Battalion South Lancashire Regiment (38th Brigade, 13th Division) at Gallipoli, 5 December 1915, describing the construction of his dugout, the harsh weather conditions experienced on the Peninsula and infestations of rats and centipedes.

Above: Officers of the Sixth South Lancashire Regiment, (38th Brigade, 13th Division) pictured before the Battle of Sunniayat, Mesopotamia. Clement Attlee is seen fourth from the right, middle row. He was badly wounded on 6 April 1916 after charging an enemy trench, carrying the red flag of his regiment.

Left: Attlee, centre, pictured in 1917, having achieved the rank of major. After Gallipoli and Mesopotamia, he saw action on the Western Front, and was wounded for the second time during the war. Meanwhile, his pacifist brother Tom was imprisoned as a conscientious objector.

Above: As Mayor of the London borough of Stepney, Attlee led a deputation of unemployed men to see Prime Minister David Lloyd George at Downing Street on 18 October 1920. As he left the meeting, a riot was starting. He shouted, 'Stepney, Halt!' and ordered his men to turn away from the fight.

"THE LIMB OF LIMEHOUSE."
King Henry VIII., v. 3.
MAJOR ATTLEE.

Above: A cartoon from *Punch* magazine in 1932, when Attlee began to rise to national prominence following his appointment as deputy leader of the Labour Party. In the period following the 1931 election, at which Labour suffered huge losses, Attlee was at his most radical and some more moderate colleagues regarded his views as 'feverish'.

Above: Attlee speaking at the Cardiff and District United Peace Demonstration in Cathays Park, Cardiff, in 1935. He was a strong supporter of the League of Nations, but was extremely wary of Adolf Hitler and feared his intentions.

Below: Attlee, as leader of the Labour Party, on holiday at Nefyn, North Wales, with his daughters Janet (left) and Felicity (right), 2 September 1938.

Above: Attlee at the family home in Stanmore, Middlesex. In his 1935 book, *The Will and the Way to Socialism*, he presented the British version of socialism to gardening: 'The gardener wants variety. The garden, seen from a distance, reveals a general plan and harmony, but viewed closely, every plant is unique . . . It is always changing . . . The gardener's work is never done.'

Above: Men of the Major Attlee Company, British Battalion, 15th International Brigade, on the Ebro front in 1938. They were led by Jack Jones, later General Secretary of the Transport and General Workers' Union, who was wounded at the Battle of Ebro.

Above: Attlee and 'Red' Ellen Wilkinson touring the ruins of Madrid as part of a Labour Party deputation to Spain to view conditions during the Spanish Civil War in December 1938. He was moved to tears by the plight of children under bombardment.

Above: Another photograph of Attlee visiting government troops during the Spanish Civil War. Behind him is General Miaja, Commander of the Central Front Army. Attlee's decision to give the clenched-fist salute in support of the Republican side caused controversy back in London.

Above: The wartime coalition government formed in May 1940: standing, from left to right, Sir Archibald Sinclair, Mr A.V. Alexander, Lord Cranborne, Herbert Morrison, Lord Moyne, Captain Margesson and Brendan Bracken. Seated, from left to right, Ernest Bevin, Lord Beaverbrook, Anthony Eden, Clement Attlee, Winston Churchill, Sir John Anderson, Arthur Greenwood and Sir Kingsley Wood.

Right: The Deputy Prime Minister visiting troops of the 1st Polish Independent Parachute Brigade at Cupar in Scotland, on 20 April 1942. Despite Attlee's smile, this was one of the most testing phases of the war.

Above: Winston Churchill, in the uniform of an Air Commodore, with Dr H. V. Evatt (Australian Minister for External Affairs), Clement Attlee (Deputy Prime Minister) and Air Vice-Marshal C. R. Carr during a visit to a Yorkshire-based Halifax squadron on 15 May 1942. Attlee backed Churchill in prioritising a heavy bombing campaign against Germany before opening up a front on land.

Above: 'All behind you, Winston!' The key members of the war cabinet walking in the garden of No. 10 Downing Street. Attlee is behind a puff of pipe-smoke, while Churchill is flanked (on his immediate left) by Secretary of State for Foreign Affairs, Anthony Eden; and (in the middle of the picture), the Russian Ambassador, Ivan Maisky.

Above: The Attlee family at tea in 1945, during the last few months of the Second World War. Left to right (excluding Clement Attlee himself): Felicity, aged 19 at the time; Martin, aged 17, a Cadet in the Royal Navy; youngest daughter, Alison, aged 15; and Violet Attlee in her Red Cross commandant's uniform sitting beside eldest daughter, Janet, aged 22, a Section Officer in the Women's Auxiliary Air Force.

'little mouse' he had been presumed to be. While Hugh Dalton was given the brief of foreign affairs, it was Attlee who led the attack on the government's foreign policy. In December 1935 he came out strongly against the pact between Sir Samuel Hoare and the French prime minister, Pierre Laval, which ended the war in Abyssinia and partitioned the country. By accepting Mussolini's invasion of the country, the government hoped that he could be discouraged from any efforts to disrupt British interests in North Africa and the area around the Suez Canal. There were concerns about forcing him into a fascist alliance with Hitler and the Nazis. However, the National Government had gone into the election having promised to re-invest in the League of Nations as the best guarantor of peace. The conscious decision to undermine the League by dealing directly with Mussolini was therefore greeted with horror. Duff Cooper, the new Secretary of State for War, wrote in his diary that he had never heard such a howl of disapproval in the House.[11]

It was Samuel Hoare, who had replaced the hapless Sir John Simon just a few months before, who bore the brunt of public displeasure. Shaken by the extent of the national outrage at his negotiations with Laval, Hoare cut a sorry figure. He arrived in the Commons on 19 December 1935 with his nose covered in plaster following an ice-skating accident. He came into the chamber and sat on the third bench below the gangway before delivering his resignation speech, his voice quivering at the end: 'I trust that my successor will have better luck than myself.' Attlee moved a motion of censure and Hoare crept out, 'a broken man'.[12] 'Ten little Neville boys sitting in a line,' quipped the Labour leader in one of his poems, 'Hoare met Laval and then there were nine.'[13]

The sacrificing of Hoare was not enough. In the same debate, as a sign of his growing confidence, Attlee made one of his most forceful attacks to date on Stanley Baldwin, a man he otherwise admired. As prime minister, Baldwin must bear ultimate responsibility for the breaking of the promise made to the British people. They trusted him, and believed that he stood for peace, but he 'wantonly threw that confidence away, and he will not get it again'.[14] In fact, such was the force of Attlee's attack that it was generally agreed that he had overstepped the mark by questioning the prime minister's honour. He certainly miscalculated by suggesting that many Conservatives might rebel against their own government. Faced with an attempt to divide them, they rallied round their leader.[15] Herbert

Morrison, still sore from defeat in the leadership election, thought that Attlee had misjudged the moment.[16] Nonetheless, he could no longer be accused of being too meek, having inflicted a serious bruise on the government.

With the League of Nations in disarray, Adolf Hitler also sought to seize the moment. In March 1936, he made his boldest move to date by ordering his army to march into the Rhineland, the industrialised corridor between Germany and France, in an outright violation of the Treaty of Versailles. The potential threat posed by Germany was much greater than that of Italy or Japan as it endangered the British Isles directly. Even some of those who had justified the appeasement of Mussolini on the grounds that it was part of a broader game, now expressed grave concern. One of them, Sir Robert Vansittart, the head of the Foreign Office, was adamant that Hitler could not be bought off with territorial concessions in the same way. Significantly, this was also the view of Winston Churchill and the group around him, including the former diplomat, and National Labour MP, Harold Nicolson.[17] As the threat from Germany loomed ever larger, Attlee's pronouncements on the sanctity of international law seemed somewhat desperate. An assessment of his position in the *Saturday Review* complained that the Labour leader's constant insistence on the need to revive the League of Nations was, by now, tantamount to 'flogging a dead horse'.[18]

In private, Attlee was more pessimistic than ever. As he told Tom, the international situation was 'pretty bloody all round'. He feared that Britain was 'in for a bad time'. The government had 'no policy and no convictions'. He had never seen a collection of ministers looking so hopeless so soon after an election victory. Yet he also confessed that he was exhausted himself by the responsibilities of leadership. It did not help that an Easter holiday spent golfing with Violet in Herefordshire was ruined by snow showers and bitter winds.[19]

Back in Parliament after the Easter recess, Labour moved a vote of censure against the government on 23 June 1936, for its betrayal of collective security and its surrender to Mussolini. The government had refused 'to take risks for peace . . . and they have increased the risk of war.' Above all, in what was to become a major theme for Attlee, he bemoaned the fact that 'this country's honour has been trailed in the mud.'[20]

III

In August 1936, Attlee visited Moscow, where he stayed at the Imperial Hotel, a few hundred yards from the Kremlin. The visit followed the invitation from Ivan Maisky, the Soviet Ambassador in London with whom he was on good terms. Maisky had been lobbying for an Anglo-Soviet alliance but as yet to no avail. In his satire on the Bullion family Attlee had attacked the government for their irrational fear of Russia. In truth, however, he remained suspicious of communists in general, not least because of an increase in their activites in his own constituency. Maisky cultivated an important relationship with Churchill in these years, but he was yet to make a breakthrough with Attlee. The Russians, of course, put on the best possible show. Attlee's visit coincided with a public holiday in the Central Park of Culture and Rest. The people he saw were 'quite happy and well mannered' and the children were 'delightful'.[21] He also visited the foreign minister, Maxim Litvinov, at his country residence outside Moscow, where Maisky was waiting for him. The three walked Litvinov's dogs round the grounds and fed the ducks in his private lake. After playing billiards with Litvinov's children, Attlee was taken to see some thriving local communities, quite conscious that these were 'showplaces and not in the least typical'.

In 1917, Attlee had regarded the Russian Revolution as justifiable if rather horrifying. Twenty years later, his overall assessment, from what he saw, was that 'its sum total justifies the revolution in itself.' He was struck above all by the cult around Josef Stalin, whose picture was plastered on billboards everywhere he looked. Taken around the national war museum, the guides were insistent that every success had been due to the heroism of Josef Stalin and every failure due to the traitor Leon Trotsky. Back in Moscow, he was taken to a meeting of senior Soviet leaders, including the Minister of Transport, President of the Moscow Union and Marshal Mikhail Tukhachevsky of the Red Army. Tukhachevsky explained to him the role of the commissars in the army. They were the purveyors of the Soviet message.

As we have seen, Attlee already had an interest in these commissars. In conversation, he made a comparison between their role and the way in which Cromwell's army chaplains had spread his political message among the troops. The analogy was lost in translation. Tukhachevsky was rather horrified at the suggestion that the Red Army would be dependent on priests for morale. Attlee tried to explain that he did not think much of priests either, having not been impressed by the Anglican padres who had been embedded with the troops in the First World War. His point about Cromwell's army chaplains was that they were ideologically committed to the cause – they had the 'root of the matter in them'. Attlee was 'pulling his leg' but no one seemed to get the joke.[22] Tukhachevsky's lack of humour was perhaps unsurprising. He was executed by Stalin ten months later in a purge of the military.

Moscow-trained communist commissars, such as Walter Tapsell, were to play an important role in the Spanish Civil War, which began in July, as General Franco's Nationalist forces started a rebellion against the Republican government in Madrid. It became a proxy war between the forces of the left and the right in Europe. The unfolding of the crisis in the late summer and early autumn of 1936 further radicalised an already tense political atmosphere in Britain. Membership of the Communist Party increased in response, rising from 3,000 to 17,000.[23]

The Communists were particularly strong in Stepney, where ethnic politics played their part. Many east London Jews felt that the local Labour Party was too dominated by an Irish Catholic hierarchy that was unsympathetic to their plight in the face of provocation from the far right.[24] Mosley's British Union of Fascists attempted to flood the area with surprise attacks and daubed anti-Semitics slogans, such as 'Perish Judah', on walls in Jewish areas. To stand up to the fascists, it was the Communists who took the lead in establishing the United Action Front. They also organised events in support of the Republicans in Spain. As the local MP, Attlee was forced into a difficult position. While not wanting to lend his weight to anything unconstitutional, he could not leave control of the streets to the communists or the fascists. For that reason, he attended a number of meetings in support of the Spanish Republicans that he was quite aware had been organised by Communist Party members.[25]

This set the scene for the the infamous 'Battle of Cable Street', on Sunday, 4 October 1936: a violent clash between the Mosleyites and an anti-fascist coalition from the area including Jewish, socialist, anarchist, Irish and communist groups. Mosley's Blackshirts attempted to march through the Jewish district of Stepney, only to be stopped by an estimated 100,000 East Enders. A riot ensued as the police tried to keep the factions apart. As the fascists retreated, the air was full of triumphant cheering. 'They did not pass,' shouted those who had blocked their way.[26] That was not the end of the matter. Labour Party meetings were frequently stormed by fascists over the following months. Stench bombs would be put through a window, doors would be kicked open, and fists would fly.[27] Frank Lewey, the long-serving mayor of Limehouse and a veteran of the local Labour Party, later recalled some of the wild scenes of this time. 'Believe me, it was tough going then. Did we have some rough houses!' One night, Mosley's men burst into a meeting at which Attlee was speaking. 'Are you game?' asked Lewey. 'Yes, I am,' said Clem. The Labour supporters jumped off the stage to force the intruders out. As the fists flew, 'Clem just went on talking, like he was in Parliament itself. What a night!'[28]

Privately, Attlee admitted his concern that Mosley's marches had undone years of work in the East End to soothe tensions between communities. For the first time, he confessed a very real fear of 'a situation like that which obtained on the Continent', with street gangs becoming part of the fabric of national politics.[29] Just a few months later, at the end of the year, Attlee sued for libel after being slandered by fellow First World War veteran, and fascist agitator, Lieutenant Colonel Graham Seton Hutchison. Hutchison, who it was later revealed was funded by the Nazi Party, had claimed that Attlee was secretly a Jew who was intent on causing another world war, as part of a dastardly plan to enslave the poor. The MP for Limehouse waived damages when Seton Hutchison publicly apologised.[30]

It was in this ugly atmosphere that the abdication crisis of late 1936 began to unfold. King Edward VIII had proposed to marry the American socialite Wallis Simpson. However, the fact that Simpson was a divorcee meant that constitutional objections were raised, as the king was the nominal head of the Established Church. Attlee behaved with the utmost propriety, underlining the image of Labour as a party that could be trusted to deal with major issues of state. Some of those on the left of the party, such as Nye Bevan, suggested that the Labour leader might be able to bring down the government by backing Edward VIII's proposed marriage to Simpson. If Parliament became divided over the issue, their suggestion was that king might then bring down the government on a constitutional technicality and ask a new group of MPs, a 'King's Party', to form an alternative administration. Edward VIII's concerns about social justice had been well publicised so there was a belief he might be sympathetic to Labour. Others saw an opportunity too. At the time, Churchill also flirted with the idea of forming a 'King's Party', something that damaged his reputation.[31] Attlee refused to engage in the intrigue for short-term benefit. He remained firmly behind Baldwin in his handling of the crisis and agreed that abdication was the only acceptable option. 'Mrs Simpson was out of the question.'[32]

For the next two years, some on the radical wing of the Labour Party complained about the fact that Attlee was 'so glacially constitutional' on this matter. Had he shown 'more push and sting and farsightedness', he might have been able to force an election on the issue.[33] On 11 December, he paid tribute to the departing king for showing a 'deep human interest in the unemployed and the people of the distressed areas'.[34] He felt Edward was a charming person but he agreed with Baldwin's private assessment that he would not 'last the course'.[35] In private, he relaxed the stiff upper lip, and revealed to Tom that his daughter Felicity had turned the affair into a ribald verse that was sung at the home during Christmas: 'Hark the herald angels sing/Mrs Simpson's pinched our king.'[36]

Attlee was able to distinguish between fidelity to the constitution and the excessive pageantry that sometimes surrounds the monarchy. After the coronation of Edward's brother, George VI, in May the following year, when it was revealed in Parliament that more than half a million pounds would have to be found to pay for the occasion, Attlee expressed the view that the king should not be expected to always live on parade. In recent times, there had been 'far too much boasting of royalty in the press and on the wireless'. He decried what he called a 'display of fearful snobbery' and 'vulgar publicity' in a large section of the press, and he thought it undesirable for British democracy that the public were 'indoctrinated with an entirely false idea of the importance of the throne'. There was a great difference between occasional displays of public ceremony and incessant observance of ritual. 'We don't make a god out of the ordinary man in this country,' he added.[37] On another occasion, he refused to wear court dress when dining with the Speaker, much to the delight of Dalton, who saw no need to dress up as 'peacocks with swords'.[38] One could be loyal without being a courtier or sycophant, or making the mistakes of Hamer Shawcross.

IV

At the party conference in Edinburgh in October 1936, it was clear that Labour remained dangerously divided on foreign policy. The party's official position was still that it would vote against the defence estimates of the government because of the latter's failure to sufficiently support the League of Nations. But there was little left of the League of Nations to support. Events in Spain – the British government had taken up a position of neutrality in respect of the Civil War – complicated matters further. Despite unanimous support for the Republican regime, only a minority of the Labour Party wanted to send arms to them, whereas the majority supported the government's position of non-intervention. The fact that the fascist powers, Italy and Germany, were offering assistance to General Franco's forces, made this position difficult to maintain.[39]

In front of party delegates, not for the first time, Attlee let others lead the fight for a tougher line on defence. Dalton, increasingly hawkish, went so far as to argue that the party should agree to support the government's rearmament plans in their entirety. Attlee thought that Dalton's position was 'stupid' and an unnecessary provocation to the party.[40] Instead, he supported the somewhat tortured compromise position which emerged from the conference – that rearmament should be supported but only under the auspices of the League of Nations. What this meant in practice was not fully clear. Once again, Attlee's first priority was to find some sort of formula that the party could agree upon, even if the end product was not quite coherent. On the question of Spain, meanwhile, Attlee distanced himself from the non-interventionists, who also included Dalton and Bevin. The National Executive wanted to endorse the government's support for neutrality but Attlee moved that this was to be conditional on the Germans and the Italians keeping their end of the bargain over the following months. If the fascists continued to intervene on General Franco's behalf, then the Labour Party would have to reconsider its position, he warned.

Very little was resolved at Edinburgh. Overall, Attlee conceded that it was a 'pretty rotten' experience. There was 'a good deal of scare feeling over Hitler', which was not without justification. In the absence of a clear strategy for international affairs, he felt that the government's armaments programme was 'futile and wasteful'. Yet, notwithstanding this somewhat purist critique of the Baldwin adminstration, he did not deny that the League of Nations was practically defunct as a force in international politics. His last remaining hope appeared to be that Franklin Roosevelt would win the US presidential election and then take a lead on the international scene, ending years of American isolationism.[41]

Thus Attlee began to drift back towards an idea which he had first floated in 1933: of a new western alliance as the best guarantor of security. In January 1937 he made a major speech at the Théâtre des Ambassadeurs in Paris warning about the fascist peril facing Europe. He urged closer cooperation between Britain and France and warned about the rise of anti-democratic forces across the Continent. In Russia too, he pointed out, democracy had been thrown aside. The creeds of fascism, Nazism and communism were 'essentially intolerant' of opposition and individuality. Attlee bemoaned the fact that, since 1918, none of the visionary leaders in Europe had been in power at the same time. Thus when France had tended to ignore the League of Nations, Britain had been enthusiastic, but when France had been enthusiastic, Britain was lukewarm. In the 1920s, when Germany under Gustav Stresemann had attempted to make a new start with the other powers, they were intransigent. By the time the powers had softened their line in the 1930s, they were faced with Hitler. While Attlee left the door open for Russia, he made it clear that a new alliance must be built in the west.[42]

The same day that Attlee had spoken in Paris, Mussolini gave an interview in the Nazi Party organ in which he declared that 'the democracies are done for' and were today, 'consciously or unconsciously, nothing more than centres of infection, carriers of bacilli, and handymen for Bolshevism'.[43] In response, others in the Labour Party, notably Cripps and Bevan, urged the leadership to look eastward towards a defensive alliance with communist Russia – an arrangement underpinned by a united front of all the forces of the left at home, bringing together the Labour Party with the Communist Party, the Independent Labour Party and the Liberals in a new left-wing alliance. Their so-called Unity Campaign was supported by a new weekly publication, *Tribune*. It was bankrolled by Cripps and became a source of incessant criticism during the rest of Attlee's leadership.[44]

On his return from Paris, the Labour leader was forced to shield himself from the suggestion that he had now cast his lot in with a government that was doing nothing but 'piling up armaments on the old competitive lines'.[45] In reality, his exasperation with the government only increased when Baldwin resigned in May 1937 to be replaced by Neville Chamberlain, formerly Chancellor of the Exchequer. Attlee had found Chamberlain impossibly aloof and condescending to the Labour benches, something that made any cooperation with the government even more problematic.

In Attlee's view, the Labour Party was performing well as an effective opposition force. They had the government on the rack regarding its policy towards Spain, had given it a tough time over its budget, and had introduced important amendments to recent legislation on factory regulation and the Civil List. Following the creation of *Tribune*, he was irritated that these efforts were not covered sufficiently by the left-wing press. The *New Statesman* was a repeat offender. He wrote to the editor, Kingsley Martin, following a question in Parliament asked by a Conservative MP, 'Why does the *New Statesman* which professes to stand for democracy against Fascism, hardly mention Parliament and never the Parliamentary Labour Party?' Attlee felt the aspersion not unjustified.

On his desk at home in Stanmore, he had the last three issues of the magazine with him and could only find one reference to Labour activities in Parliament (and this one was disparaging). *New Statesman* readers would surmise from its pages 'that the only Socialist activities are those of the Communists and perhaps the Left Book Club and one or two of the intelligentsia.' 'I am not putting in a grouse on my own behalf,' he insisted. 'I get all the publicity that I want, but I do want to point out that this does not do justice to the Parliamentary Party as a whole . . . Our people have the impression that all that they can expect from the *New Statesman* is either complete neglect or denigration of a mild type.' He thought it a pity if the magazine was to 'go so high brow that it entirely ignored the existence of Parliamentary institutions'.[46]

Unmoved by this complaint, Kingsley Martin compared Attlee to an ineffective schoolmaster 'in his study watching over the boys, some of them too big to handle when they are fresh'.[47] While there was not yet an open revolt against him, *The Economist* also agreed there were indications of discontent, and not just from *Tribune*.[48] As the summer recess approached, Lloyd George observed that the Labour Party was riddled with jealousies. Arthur Greenwood had not given up his ambitions to be leader, Herbert Morrison overshadowed Attlee, while Bevin repeatedly used his control of the *Daily Herald* to influence the party from the outside.[49] The former Liberal prime minister was not an admirer of Attlee, whom he described as a 'pygmy'. (In fact, Lloyd George was said to be able to impersonate Attlee 'with a vividness that was unsurpassed'.)[50] By July, even the speaker of the House openly suggested in a debate that Attlee could not control his men.[51]

Attlee's defence was that he would never be a leader in the mould of Ramsay MacDonald. 'I am not prepared to arrogate to myself a superiority to the rest of the movement. I am prepared to submit to their will, even if I disagree,' he insisted. 'I shall do all I can to get my views accepted, but, unless acquiescence in the views of the majority conflicts with my conscience, I shall fall into line, for I have faith in the wisdom of the rank and file.'[52] Yet he was in danger of taking this passive approach too far.

Labour's contorted position on rearmament was a symptom of the problem. In June 1937, the parliamentary party was still voting against the defence estimates, as they had done for years.[53] But by July 1937, the National Executive finally decided that voting against these was no longer sustainable. The 'rearmers' – Dalton and Bevin – won the day by exerting the power of the National Executive, even though they had not yet had their policy agreed to at party conference. This was a turning point. Now that the rearmament question had been dealt with, Attlee was freed up to take a more robust line on Spain. As Bevin and Dalton had pointed out, it was absurd to argue that the government should do more about Spain but simultaneously fail to back it on rearmament. Once they won the day on rearmament, however, Attlee was given the opportunity to attack the government over its Spanish policy. Almost immediately, in July, he denounced the 'farce' of the non-intervention policy, demonstrating his independence from the National Executive.[54]

It was in the summer of 1937 that Attlee finally began to really assert authority over his party. This began with his book *The Labour Party in Perspective*, published in August.[55] It rejected both the idea of a united front (an affiliation with the Communist Party, Independent Labour Party, liberals and radicals) as well as some sort of popular front (an anti-fascist alliance bringing in disillusioned Conservatives such as Churchill). Communists did not 'believe in the methods of the Labour Party and do not accept majority rule'. A popular front would be useful if democracy was in danger in Britain; but it was not. Communism and fascism appealed to the 'politically immature' but were distasteful to the British and the French who have had 'years of experience of personal freedom and political democracy'. The natural British tendency to heresy and dissent had 'prevented the formation of a code of rigid Socialist orthodoxy. Those who have sought to impose one have always failed to make real headway and have remained sects rather than political parties. As in religion, so in politics, the Briton claims the right to think for himself.' There was nothing more dishonest than arguing that Britain must go down the Moscow road unless she follows the example of Berlin or Rome. 'I am well aware how slight a hold the principles of democracy have on some of our opponents but I believe the vast majority of the people in this country reject such methods,' he wrote.[56]

The Labour Party in Perspective sold over 50,000 copies. As well as bringing in a profit of £600, it set the tone for party policy at the conference in Bournemouth in October 1937.[57] Just a week before the conference began, *The Economist* had warned that it was likely to be crucial for Attlee's leadership.[58] It was, in fact, the moment at which his fortunes began to turn. First of all, a resolution was agreed which condemned the 'so-called' Unity Campaign, effectively renouncing any association with Stafford Cripps and *Tribune*.[59]

Next, even Dalton gave the leader some credit for his work on *Labour's Immediate Programme*, an eight-page policy document adopted at the conference that called for nationalisation of the Bank of England (and joint stock banks), coal, electricity, gas and the railways.[60] There was to be an expansion of social services, with improved pensions and holidays. Public works and economic planning would be used to revitalise depressed areas such as the northeast. Attlee had been 'very helpful in providing a continuous thread of argument to hold the programme together', which was 'much better than a bare list of items'.[61]

Having feared a repeat of Edinburgh, Attlee reported to Tom that he was delighted by events in Bournemouth. The room had been full, the speeches were of a high standard and there was a 'good spirit of unity and determination'. Even the Webbs had turned up, nearly thirty years after his first Fabian meeting, and his book seemed to be well received by the delegates.[62] Trevor Evans, a former miner and the industrial correspondent for the *Daily Express*, recalled seeing the leader – who normally preferred sitting in the corner reading a detective novel – enjoying a drink with some of the most influential trade unionists: Will Lawther of the mine workers; Fred Smith of the engineers; and Charles Dukes of the general workers. He seemed more relaxed than in many years.[63]

Foreign policy had divided the party in previous years but now Attlee saw an opportunity to use it to give it a sense of cohesion and moral purpose once more. The wounds over rearmament were still raw. Dalton and Bevin had won the argument in the National Executive Committee, but Attlee also appreciated that their tough-minded realism had created smouldering resentment. In order to deflect from this, therefore, he went against both Dalton and Bevin and made a plea for an end to support for non-intervention in Spain. In effect, the Labour leader turned the conference into a rally for the Republicans. As Franco continued to receive arms from Germany and Italy, Attlee went so far as to argue that to acquiesce to a 'one-sided intervention' was to be 'an accessory to the attempt to murder democracy in Spain'.[64] This was a culmination of an argument that Attlee had begun at the Edinburgh conference a year before. Having heard the testimony of delegates from Republican Spain, it had been the Labour leader who had moved for a new resolution demanding that, if there were further violations, the party should end its support for non-intervention.[65] A year later, following his prompting throughout the summer, a unanimous resolution was passed which ended support for non-intervention and called for direct aid to be sent to the government in Spain.[66]

It was in the name of solidarity with the forces of democracy that Attlee now declared that he would visit Spain himself. There was an undoubted element of political theatre in this. The invitation to do so had been made by the Republican prime minister, Juan Negrín, in October the previous year and had yet to be taken up. Over the course of the year, Germany and Italy had made a mockery of non-intervention. Events such as the April 1937 bombing of Guernica in the Basque Country by the Luftwaffe's Condor Legion and the Italian Aviazione Legionaria had contributed to a sense of moral urgency. For some time he had suspected that there was a 'strong pro-Franco attitude' held by some in the government – an attitude that genuinely disgusted him.[67] But it was also the case that the Spanish cause was a useful one for the Labour Party – torn apart on foreign policy – to reunite around.

In Dalton's view, Labour's newfound obsession with Spain was something of an indulgence. What was happening here was a transferral of Labour idealism from the League of Nations to the Republican cause in Spain. Thus, he complained that his colleagues had switched 'eager enthusiasm and credulous optimism from Geneva to the Spanish front'.[68] But here Dalton missed something crucial. This was precisely what Attlee intended. So it was that on

6 December he saw the XV International Brigade at Modejar, shortly before their departure to Teruel on the Cordoba Front, heard the stirring rendition of the 'Song of the Volga Boatmen', and told the volunteers that the British Labour Party was behind them in their fight for democracy.

V

In the mists of the battle in Spain, Attlee had found both clarity and a cause. He had also saved his leadership. Two years earlier, the *Literary Digest* had pictured Attlee in suburban Stanmore in his slippers. Now Attlee returned to England as a hero of the International Brigades. Back in Parliament after the visit, he was subjected to a motion of censure from a Conservative backbencher who suggested that he should have his salary as leader of the opposition revoked for giving the clenched-fist salute. When Lord Halifax had visited Germany recently, by contrast, he had not given the Nazi salute. Neville Chamberlain, not eager to be drawn into a debate about Spain, evaded the controversy. 'I was much impressed with what I saw in Republican Spain,' Attlee told the press, 'but not much impressed with what is being said in London.'[69]

When leaving Spain, in Negrín's personal aircraft, the Labour delegation were pursued by an Italian plane and forced to nosedive to escape its guns.[70] They stopped in France and urged the socialist government there to abandon their support for non-intervention (which could be explained, as much as anything, by France's fear of provoking Germany). It was time for the democracies to unite. Attlee took care to broadcast to an American audience on behalf of the Republican cause. 'You have been told that the government is a dangerous Red, whose object is to put an end to all religion in Spain,' he told the American people. This was nonsense. What was at stake was democracy. Out in the field he had met scores of Americans fighting with the International Brigades. They were a citizen army like those raised in the English Civil War and the American War of Independence. These American boys, 'willing to give their all, even their lives, for the defence of freedom, dying for an ideal, were worthy sons of the land of Abraham Lincoln', or those who fought with George Washington at Valley Forge, 'so that freedom might live'.[71]

There was a deftness to Attlee which had not been seen before. As his travel companion Ellen Wilkinson had come to appreciate, while he had his flaws, 'he is a subtle strategist, understands people and plays with his team.'[72] *The Economist*, which had predicted his demise over the previous months, defended him against the allegation that he had acted improperly; he was now providing the government with some genuine opposition.[73] Even Bevan, one of Cripps's agitators-in-chief in the Unity Campaign, was prepared to give the leader his due. Attlee had 'enormously improved' his position following the visit to Spain. He had always had a clever mind but, until now, 'a certain lack of horse power had prevented him from "getting across" as he should.' Perhaps, suggested Bevan, Attlee was finally realising that his position as party leader was stronger than he had assumed.[74]

Indeed, Attlee's stock was high enough to be asked to contribute to *Tribune* for the first time. In an article titled 'My answer to those who condemn me', he took the opportunity to explain his views on how an opposition party should conduct itself. Since 1931, he argued, there had been a growing tendency to import ideas into Britain that belonged, essentially, to the totalitarian conception of the state. One of these was that, when it came to foreign policy, everybody should support the government of the day. Another was that Parliament should be a 'Council of State' – a supportive and advisory body, rather than a source of opposition and criticism. This term he attributed to Ramsay MacDonald but he noted that it had been used since by editorial writers at *The Times*. To him, the idea behind this seemed to be that 'even if the Opposition thinks that the Government is steering the Ship of State on to the rocks, it must lend a hand with the rest of the crew to help it on its way.' This was 'unhistoric', 'undemocratic' and 'unpatriotic'.[75]

With his clenched-fist salute, Attlee made the most of his new status as a patriot rebel leader, the champion of the citizen soldiers of the International Brigades. Spain did not so much radicalise him as simplify and clarify his line on foreign affairs. Among Labour supporters, his reputation had been bolstered considerably. At the end of the year he addressed a large rally at the Albert Hall, where he received a spontaneous standing ovation on the platform. 'The visit has done a lot for the movement and has also had a good effect internationally,' he wrote to Tom, putting his slippers back on at the family home in Stanmore and picking up his pipe, 'The session before Christmas has closed well for the Party.'[76]

11

A Word to Winston

Oft on a silly night,
When slumber's chain has bound me,
And strewn to left and right,
Sketch writers dozed around me,
And Gallery reporters moaned,
While Mr. Attlee droned and droned,

There'd come a sort of sigh,
Like waves upon a sea bar,
And footsteps hurrying nigh,
As men forsook the tea bar,
And faces that just now were bleak
Would smile and murmur 'Winston's going to speak.'

Hamadryad, 'A Word to Winston',
Saturday Review, 29 August 1936.

I *Pratt's Club, London, 16 March 1938*

On 16 March 1938, Winston Churchill went to Pratt's club to dine with
Harold Nicolson, the National Labour MP who had become one of the
most prominent critics of the policy of appeasement. Four days earlier, on
12 March, the Nazis had invaded Austria. Austria had been due to hold a
referendum on its independence in which, it was expected, it would vote
against incorporation into the Third Reich. At the invitation of the

Austrian Nazi Party, which only had minority support in the country, Hitler decided to send troops over the border to cancel the referendum and order his own plebiscite. This was to become known as the *Anschluss*, a forcible union between the two countries, given a veneer of legitimacy after the event by a Nazi-rigged vote that declared that Austrians were unanimously supportive. Churchill had been warning about Hitler's expansionist tendencies from the moment the latter had come to power in 1933. As Churchill's prophecies were proved true, those who despaired about the direction of foreign policy under Chamberlain began to follow Churchill's next moves closely.

Over the previous decade, Churchill and Attlee had differed on many issues, particularly in the realm of foreign policy and imperial defence. Attlee felt that Churchill's views on India were hopelessly old-fashioned and unworkable. While Attlee supported sanctions against Japan over Manchuria, Churchill had opposed them. Attlee also noted that Churchill was more supportive of efforts to deal with Mussolini and Franco, despite the atrocities with which they had been associated. 'I don't think he really judged the Spanish rightly,' Attlee later remarked, 'He wasn't much perturbed about Abyssinia either.'[1]

The Labour Party's position on Germany had changed considerably over the previous years too. As far back as June 1933, Attlee had urged that the League of Nations should act to give a 'stern warning' to curb the activities of Nazi officials in Austria.[2] However, there was a significant degree of sympathy for German demands within the Labour Party. The consensus Labour line on Germany was captured in a 1932 article by Victor Schiff, the *Daily Herald*'s Berlin correspondent, who declared that 'all Germany wants is fair play.'[3] Even after Hitler seized power, Schiff, a German Social Democrat, continued to argue that the German people were not truly behind him, and that he could be pushed aside.[4] While Attlee was privately more alarmed by Hitler, he thought Germany's opposition to the Treaty of Versailles was not unjustified.[5] When Germany invaded the Rhineland in February 1936, the Labour Party had opposed sanctions. It was at this point, ironically, that Churchill declared himself a 'convert' to collective security, having disparaged the League on a number of occasions. As embodied by Churchill and Attlee, respectively, the predominant 'realist' and 'idealist' approaches to foreign policy began to converge, in a pincer movement on the appeasers in the middle.[6]

By early 1938, the critics of the government's foreign policy began to sense that either the moment to strike had come, or that the war they feared was imminent. On 20 February 1938, Anthony Eden, foreign secretary since the resignation of Samuel Hoare (which made him the third foreign secretary in as many years) resigned himself. He had clashed with Neville Chamberlain, his prime minister, over the handling of Mussolini – though it was the details of the appeasement policy rather than its whole premise to which Eden objected. He was replaced by Lord Halifax, who largely concurred with the existing policy but who soon also found reasons to dissent.

Following the *Anschluss*, it was widely anticipated that Hitler's attentions would turn east, first towards Czechoslovakia (where a German-speaking minority in the Sudetenland wanted secession and incorporation into a larger Germany), and then Poland, on which the Nazis also had designs for expansion. Over dinner with Nicolson that March evening, Churchill sympathised that Neville Chamberlain had inherited a ghastly situation from his predecessor, Baldwin, after years of indecision. In general, however, he was disparaging about the state of the Conservative Party, which was full of 'blind and obstinate' men. Britain was in need of a policy around which the whole House of Commons could unite. Churchill had heard that there had been secret discussions between the leaders of the main parties (Chamberlain, Attlee and Archibald Sinclair of the Liberal Party) to find such a formula. He would wait on the outcome of those negotiations. But if no clear statement was issued within a week, he would refuse the Conservative whip, take some fifty MPs with him, and hopefully bring down the government. In Churchill's mind, the threat to Britain was much greater than it had been in 1914, for two reasons. The first was the vulnerability of the capital to attack by the fleet of German bombers that Hitler was assembling. The second was a lack of political will to confront him. 'We stand to lose everything by failing to take some strong action. Yet if we take strong action, London will be a shambles in half-an-hour.'[7]

When Attlee had become leader of the Labour Party in November 1935, only one man had predicted that he would hold on to the job: Jack Lawson, his old colleague from the War Office. It was not the only successful prediction that Lawson made. In April 1936 he wrote a column called 'Watch Winston' in the *Sunday Sun* criticising the National Government's policy of appeasement. In it, he predicted that a war was almost inevitable and that Churchill would become prime minister.[8]

It was against the backdrop of the looming prospect of war that 'A Word to Winston', was published in the *Saturday Review*. Its anonymous author (who appears to have had fascist sympathies) compared the flurry of excitement that was caused when news went round that Churchill was to deliver a speech on foreign affairs, with Attlee's droning voice.[9] Yet Churchill could do very little on his own. The majority of his party remained firmly behind Chamberlain. In public, Churchill had in fact begun to temper his criticism of the government, in the hope that he might be brought back into office in some capacity, and be able to exert his influence from within. It was Attlee, energised by his Spanish excursion, who led the criticism of the government in Parliament.

II

Following the resignation of Eden, the prospect of a redrawing of the political boundaries increased again.[10] But Churchill was just one actor in the firmament. Writing in *Tribune*, a few days after Eden's resignation, Cripps pointed out that – in the *Labour Party in Perspective* – Attlee left the door open to the formation of a popular front in the event of a great crisis such as a war. In response, Attlee said that this crisis had not yet arrived. While the government was losing authority, he was not attracted to the idea of another minority Labour government, helped over the line by the Liberals, and a rump of Conservative MPs under Churchill. 'Let us assume that Cripps is right and that a Labour-Liberal majority is returned to the House of Commons. Can it deliver the goods?' he asked. In Attlee's view, all this would mean was a repetition of 1929 – a minority government that would expend all its energy on just trying to stay in power.[11]

Though the course was far from pre-determined, the shifting constellation of forces began to push Churchill and Attlee together in 1938. Their first contacts were tentative. In March they exchanged letters about Lord Robert Cecil's efforts to establish an inter-party group to sponsor a campaign for a rearmament programme under the name of the League of Nations. Yet Churchill played a cautious game. He suggested to Attlee that they keep their involvement unofficial, 'as otherwise it would look as if there was a significance quite beyond anything which an educative campaign implies.' Attlee agreed and also had no interest in scheming at this stage.[12] When the moment did come in May 1940, Churchill had the authority and eloquence to grasp it. Over the next two years, however, it was Attlee who led the attacks on the policy of appeasement, and it was Attlee, working through the Labour Party, who was to be the kingmaker.

In the first half of 1938, as Churchill softened his criticisms of the government, an emboldened Attlee ratcheted up the rhetoric. While the details of Eden's resignation were not fully revealed, it was widely understood to be a protest against Chamberlain's efforts to influence his negotiations with Mussolini. Thus Attlee attacked the prime minister for what he saw as his desire to buy off Mussolini at any cost, and 'rush into a bargain at the very first offer'. By lifting sanctions on Mussolini, international law and morality were being cheapened by 'the precepts of Machiavelli'.

Picking up a theme which he had begun to develop, Attlee appealed to the honour of the nation too. In doing so, he showed himself willing to play a more nakedly patriotic tune than he had done in the past. Addressing the admirals and senior military men on the Conservative benches, Attlee told the House that he longed for a figure with the substance of a Lord Charles Beresford among them. Beresford, who had sat as a Conservative MP before the First World War, had been an admiral and commander of the Mediterranean Fleet. He was notable both as a strong supporter of rearmament in the Edwardian era and as a practitioner of gunboat diplomacy (famously responsible for the bombardment of Alexandria during the Egyptian war of 1882). A relentless self-promoter, Beresford had cultivated his image as a latter-day John Bull by walking round with a British bulldog on a leash.[13] If the country failed to see the 'bulldog spirit' on the Conservative benches, Attlee now warned, it would be forced to look elsewhere.

It was also in March 1938 that Attlee came to the conclusion that there 'must come a time when it is necessary to stand firm'.[14] Labour continued to lead the assault. On 20 March, to cries of 'shame' and 'Chamberlain must go' from the opposition benches, Attlee pointed out that Hitler had marched into Austria while the German foreign minister Ribbentrop had been in London for negotiations. Republican Spain, meanwhile, was being terrorised by aeroplanes poured into the country by the fascist states. The democracies of Europe were being attacked. 'If they allowed all the fortresses of liberty to be captured one by one did they think this country could ultimately survive?'[15]

There were two strands to Attlee's critique of appeasement. The first was that its architects – from Sir John Simon to Chamberlain – did not 'take their stand on a moral basis'. The second was that their boasted realism was anything but realistic. In fact, he warned, 'they ignored the greatest reality of all in the international situation – that was the mentality of the dictators.' For Hitler and Mussolini, honour was irrelevant. They had no interest in what Attlee called 'the British conception of justice, humanity and honest dealing'.[16]

In April 1938, under the terms of the Easter Accords, Britain effectively turned a blind eye to Italian control over Abyssinia in return for an Italian agreement not to disrupt the status quo elsewhere in the Middle East, and to uphold free access to the Suez Canal. In the subsequent Commons debate, Attlee began by waving a copy of the *Morning Post* from 1936, in which Chamberlain had first expressed his desire to apply 'realpolitik' to Mussolini: 'I should like to congratulate the Prime Minister on his candour in having made it abundantly plain where his real sympathies lie.' Yet Chamberlain's approach was flawed, as Machiavelli was 'the natural teacher of Signor Mussolini'. As soon as it suited him, he would make a deal with Hitler, and all would be undone.[17]

Shortly after this, Attlee confided to Tom his belief that the government was leading the country into war. 'We are really back in 1914,' he said. The government, he predicted, would continue to allow all the smaller democratic states of Eastern Europe to be swallowed up by Germany, 'not from a pacifist aversion to war, but because they want time to develop armaments'. Chamberlain was 'just an imperialist of the old school but without much knowledge of foreign affairs or appreciation of the forces at work'. It was, all things considered, a 'pretty gloomy outlook'.[18]

In the first week of July, Attlee managed a short family holiday to Taunton in Somerset. As during his visit to Cornwall in 1914, the prospect of war followed him there. Doorstepped at his holiday cottage by a reporter, he said, 'I wonder whether I am going to get any holiday this year.' The government stumbled from crisis to crisis. Hardly a month went by without Chamberlain having to shed one of his ministers. 'Sooner or later they will all have to go, some because they are too good and others because they are too bad.'[19]

III

In the summer of 1938, as expected, Hitler began to press his claims on the Sudetenland, destabilising Czechoslovakia by posing as the champion of its ethnic German minority. This tested a verbal commitment that Chamberlain had made in 1936 – that Britain would help protect Czechoslovakia in the event of German aggression. There had been no defensive alliance, as with Belgium in 1914, but, once again, British honour was at stake.

On 29 August 1938, Attlee and his wife and four children visited Criccieth in Wales, in response to an unlikely invitation from the veteran Liberal leader Lloyd George. The fact was that Lloyd George was no great admirer of Attlee. But he still regarded himself as a potential war leader, or deputy to Churchill. In convoy with their two families they motored through Blaenau Ffestiniog on the road to Dolwyddelan. They laid a picnic at the foot of the hills under the shadow of Snowdonia. In this scenic setting, Lloyd George made a prediction that Hitler would get all he wanted on Czechoslovakia without war, and that neither Britain nor France would put up a fight.[20]

By the second week of September, both Japan and Italy declared their support for Hitler's claims on the Sudetenland, while the Russian fleet was mobilised and put on a war footing. On 15 September, Chamberlain flew out to Munich to deal with Hitler directly. He was back in Britain the next day to discuss Hitler's demands with the Cabinet but was due to fly out again on 22 September. There was a cheer of relief that war had been averted and that negotiations seemed to be progressing. Churchill shook the prime minister's hand, and Attlee spoke to cautiously welcome the news.[21]

That Sunday, 18 September 1938, Dalton made a 'pilgrimage' to Attlee's 'little Victorian villa at Stanmore', which he had never seen before, to meet Jaromír Nečas, the Czech minister for social welfare. Nečas insisted that the Czechs would 'sooner die and be drowned in our own blood rather than become Hitler's slaves'. The following day Attlee issued a statement of solidarity with the Czech people. On hearing it, Churchill telephoned him directly to tell him that 'Your declaration does honour to the British people.' 'I am glad you think so,' was the Labour leader's curt reply. For the moment, there was unanimous consent among Labour leaders that they should steer an independent path, despite overtures from Churchill, who sulked about the perceived slight.[22]

On the afternoon of 22 September, as Chamberlain flew out to Munich for a second meeting with Hitler, Churchill was met by Harold Nicolson, who pulled up in a taxi outside his flat in Morpeth Mansions, half a mile from Westminster. In the lift together, Nicolson remarked, 'This is hell. It is the end of the British Empire.' As they sat down at 4.30 p.m., Churchill revealed that the government had finally toughened its line and would demand German demobilisation. Churchill had no expectation that Hitler would agree and expected that war would be declared. Would Chamberlain be left stranded in Germany? 'Even the Germans,' remarked Churchill, 'would not be so stupid as to deprive us of our beloved Prime Minister.' Then came a telephone message from Jan Masaryk, the Czech ambassador in London, giving the latest updates from the area, where Hitler was demanding that the Czech authorities withdraw from the Sudetenland. Shortly afterwards, there was a call from Attlee. He suggested that the Labour opposition was willing to come in behind Churchill if he broke with the government. Now it was Churchill's turn to play hard to get. Nicolson and Churchill decided that they would still support the prime minister provided he took a tough line. However, if it was perceived that Chamberlain 'ran away again', they would side with Labour.[23]

On 27 September, Attlee published an open letter to Chamberlain urging the government to leave the Germans in no doubt that Britain would unite with the French and the Soviets to resist any attack on Czechoslovakia. 'Whatever the risks involved, Great Britain must make its stand against aggression.' There was 'now no room for doubts or hesitations'. The letter was taken to Number 10 by John Dugdale, Attlee's private secretary, on the evening before publication and shown to the prime minister. Attlee and Arthur Greenwood also visited Chamberlain personally to urge him to stand firm. Churchill was another visitor during the course of the day, also urging Chamberlain not to yield to Hitler.[24]

War seemed imminent. On 28 September, the British fleet was mobilised as Hitler threatened to begin a military invasion unless the Czechs gave way by 2 p.m. that day. The Commons was due to meet shortly after the deadline. Outside Parliament there was a large group of peace campaigners, many laying flowers by the Cenotaph to commemorate those lost in the last war. The prime minister entered the chamber from behind the Speaker's chair to loud applause from supporters. The Commons came to a hush as Chamberlain spoke. The only noise was the footsteps of the messengers who were running into the chamber, passing pink telephone slips around. Churchill, watching closely, received so many notes that they had to be held together by an elastic band. Chamberlain spoke calmly, providing the House with a chronology of events and occasionally pausing, removing his pince-nez, and looking up from his notes to elaborate on a particular point. Opposite Chamberlain, Attlee sat with his feet on the table 'looking like an amiable little bantam'. As Chamberlain spoke for an hour, a note made its way along the government benches from the Foreign Office. Having read it, the prime minister revealed that Hitler had agreed to give the Czechs another twenty-four hours and would be willing to meet him, along with Mussolini and the French prime minister, Édouard Daladier, in Munich.[25]

The prime minister's opponents were thrown by the last-minute reprieve. The next day, with Chamberlain in Munich, there was an attempt to get an agreed telegram between Churchill, Attlee, Sinclair, Eden and Lloyd George, warning the prime minister not to betray the Czechs.[26] But Eden did not want to be seen to have a personal vendetta against Chamberlain, and Attlee refused to sign it without the approval of his own party. According to Harold Nicolson, even Churchill seemed to have lost his fighting spirit.[27]

In the early hours of 30 September 1938, the Munich Agreement was signed between Hitler, Chamberlain, Mussolini and Daladier. The other signatories would support Hitler's claim to the Sudetenland if he agreed not to attack the rest of the country. Czechoslovakia had the hopeless options of standing alone against the Nazis, or ceding to the demand. It was from this meeting that Chamberlain returned clutching a copy of the treaty, as he walked down the steps from the British Airways flight, announcing 'peace with honour' and 'peace for our time'.

Attlee reacted with incredulity. The Munich deal constituted 'one of the greatest diplomatic defeats that this country and France have ever sustained'. Without firing a shot, Hitler had achieved a more dominant position in Europe than the Kaiser had done after years of preparation and war from 1914 to 1918.[28] Yet, the truth was more complicated. The Munich deal was hugely popular in the country and was supported by a comfortable majority in Parliament. As one Labour MP confessed, 'if Attlee had been Prime Minister at the same time and had stopped war at Munich under exactly similar circumstances, he would have been hailed with sheer delight by our people.'[29]

On 3 October, as Parliament reassembled, Chamberlain had not only ridden the storm; he now seemed unassailable. Attlee, however, spurred on by a number of attacks by Churchill's followers – such as Duff Cooper – kept up the pressure. The prime minister had ended his speech by saying that Britain must continue to rearm. His declaration of 'peace for our time' was nothing of the sort. 'We have felt that we are in the midst of a tragedy. We have felt humiliation. This has not been a victory for reason and humanity. It has been a victory for brute force,' said Attlee. The terms of the deal had not been negotiated; they had been laid down after an ultimatum from Hitler. The Czechs were a 'gallant, civilised and democratic people betrayed and handed over to a ruthless despotism'. Not only had Hitler overturned the balance of power in Europe; democracy had experienced a 'terrible defeat'. What was more, British foreign policy had been infected by a combination of effeminacy and loucheness. Appeasement was the sign of the moral degeneration – or at least, amoral nature – of a governing class dominated by technocrats and aristocrats. They were 'the pleasure-loving people, the people who are pacifists because they will not take up any reasonable position.'[30]

Attlee told Parliament that his feeling about the Munich Agreement was eerily reminiscent of the sensation he had had the night he had been the last man off Suvla Bay in 1916. 'There was sorrow for sacrifices,' he recalled. 'There was sorrow over the great chance of ending the war earlier that had passed away. There was, perhaps, some feeling of satisfaction that for a short time one was getting away from the firing line, but there was the certain and sure knowledge that before very long we should be in it again.'[31]

In truth, Chamberlain had retaken the political initiative over Munich. Attlee suddenly looked weak again and questions were asked about his leadership. Cripps urged Morrison to run against him, but neither had a sufficient personal following to make good on their intrigues.[32] It also seemed that Attlee's flirtation with Churchill and Lloyd George had come to naught. Speaking at a by-election in Kent in November, Attlee now rejected all talk of setting aside party differences because of the threat of war. The National Government had made this plea in 1931 but its residues constituted the 'most incompetent Government in modern times'.[33]

Any hope of dislodging Chamberlain seemed to have passed. In Attlee's view, the real obstacle to a new coalition was that 'you could never get the revolting Tories up to scratch', to vote against their own government.[34] First, Anthony Eden refused to speak alongside Attlee at a League of Nations Union meeting because he thought it would endanger his chances of leading the Conservative Party.[35] Next, Attlee refused to sign a letter of protest against the treatment of the Czechs that Churchill had circulated and was hoping to gain support for.[36] Nonetheless, he did maintain his contacts with the principal anti-appeasers. He lunched with Harold Nicolson on 25 January 1939. 'Attlee is very silly and charming,' recorded Nicolson. 'A delightful man of course, but not a pilot in a hurricane.'[37]

As Attlee and Churchill continued their mating dance, others attempted to seize the initiative. In January 1939, Stafford Cripps swooped in from the left and publicly came out for a 'popular front'. Replacing his previous idea of a united front – of all the forces on the left – this would be built of those across the political spectrum, including Churchill, who shared the desire to confront fascism and preserve democracy. Socialism, which he had previously argued must be applied immediately, could now be postponed. As a matter of urgency, however, the new coalition would seek a defensive alliance with the Soviet Union. In January 1939, Cripps used *Tribune* to launch his National Petition Campaign in support of the idea.[38]

This destabilising intervention was too much for the Labour leadership to bear, at a time when such sensitive negotiations were ongoing. Their indulgence of the radicals ended. By the end of March, Cripps had been suspended from the party. His supporters, such as Aneurin Bevan, were issued a seven-day ultimatum warning them to end their support, or face expulsion from the party.[39] Attlee privately admitted that he was having a lot of trouble with the 'popular front' agitation. The Oxford historian and Labour supporter A. L. Rowse had written a series of 'infantile' articles in the *Manchester Guardian*, which, Attlee felt, took Cripps's latest scheme far too seriously (though not going as far as to support it). Attlee's own response had been to compose a simple but effective riposte in the *Daily Herald*, offering an amusing twist on 'The Red Flag' song that he had learned in his early days in the Labour movement:

> The people's flag is palest pink
> It's not red blood but only ink.
> It's sponsored now by Douglas Cole
> Who plays each year a different role.

Then raise our pallid standard high
Wash out all trace of scarlet dye
Let Liberals join and Tories too
And socialists of every hue . . .
With heads uncovered swear we all
To have no principles at all
If everyone will turn his coat
We'll get the British people's vote.[40]

Here was the problem with the self-styled intellectuals with whom he had once worked so closely in the SSIP. Harold Laski, the LSE professor, was a 'brilliant chap, but he talked too much'. GDH. Cole was similarly 'brilliant' but, once again, like Cripps, 'he used to have a new idea every year, irrespective of whether the ordinary man was interested in it or not.'[41] In a damning phrase, Attlee called Cole a 'permanent undergraduate'.[42] The great pity about Cripps was that he could convince himself that whatever policy he was putting forward at any one time was 'absolutely right' and he would listen to no counter-arguments.[43] Bevan and George Strauss, another MP who supported Unity, were expelled shortly after this, on 5 April 1939.[44] According to *Tribune*, 'Right Wing Labour leaders' had no strategy of their own, they were simply waiting for Chamberlain and the National Government to defeat them again, as an election was expected at any moment. It was alleged that they were 'afraid of power'.[45] Beatrice Webb was visited by an insolent and sulking Stafford Cripps, who complained that Dalton was the devil, Greenwood a drunk and Attlee 'of no account'.[46]

By mid-March 1939, German troops had rolled into Czechoslovakia and Hitler had also begun to make demands on Poland, flouting his previous promises. Chamberlain was forced to concede that the Munich agreement was indeed in tatters. On 31 March, Chamberlain announced that Britain would support Poland, should Germany invade it. Yet Attlee's refusal to support conscription in April 1939, on the grounds that it would be less effective than relying upon volunteers, was a sign that the old incoherence was in danger of creeping back into Labour policy.[47] In hindsight, he did confess that this position 'probably wasn't awfully wise'. His justification was that Labour wanted 'combined thinking on defence problems', with a coordinated plan.[48]

Setting aside the issue of conscription, there was a widespread feeling that the government had been disastrously slow to grasp the nettle on planning for war, that it needed to move to a wartime economy; and that the failure of a system of private enterprise to provide sufficient aircraft for a coming conflict was another practical indictment of its approach.[49] As an indication of the problem, Attlee had heard a rumour that British firms were selling aeroplanes to Finland that were equipped with technology that the Royal Air Force was denied. More broadly, Labour began to think more seriously about defence. Attlee headed a triumvirate, including Dalton and A. V. Alexander, who sought testimonials from military experts.[50] He solicited the advice of the British military strategist Basil Liddell Hart, who emphasised above all the critical importance of air-power in the event of a major European war.[51] But the clock was ticking.

In a stormy debate in the Commons on 19 May, Attlee argued for a 'firm union between Britain, France and the USSR as the nucleus of a World Alliance against aggression'. The government was 'dilatory and fumbling' and was in danger of letting Stalin slip out of their grasp and into Hitler's hands.[52] It was reported that Attlee had been seen shaking with rage at the incompetence of Chamberlain and his government. In fact, he was most likely suffering from a fever brought about by an infection in his prostate – something from which his elder brothers had also suffered. On the last weekend of the month, he felt unwell on the train to the party conference in Southport. He had stayed in his hotel room on Friday evening, missing the party's executive meeting, and was hospitalised the following day. As the prospect of war loomed, he was now forced to undergo two corrective operations.[53] It was, he confided to Tom, the 'family trouble'. He had got a chill on the bladder, which induced a temperature and a 'considerable pain' in the 'J. T.' (John Thomas).[54] Arthur Greenwood was to deputise for him. The timing of his absence could not have been worse.

IV

In the last week of August 1939, Attlee was continuing his recovery in a nursing home in Nefyn in North Wales. Ordered to relax, he read *Greenmantle*, a novel in a five-part series by John Buchan, Cromwell's biographer, set against the backdrop of the First World War. As he sat on the sand in a deckchair watching his children play he heard on a portable radio the news that Hitler and Stalin had agreed to a non-aggression pact. On 1 September, the German army rolled into Poland. Its 'secret protocol' with Moscow provided a guarantee that the Soviet Union would not react. Two days later, after having demanded an immediate withdrawal, Britain declared war on Germany. Once again, Attlee heard the news via the wireless, in the very same location.

The Russian 'defection' had been expected for a number of months. Attlee was convinced this could have been avoided if the government had, to use one of his favourite cricketing analogies, 'played straight' with Moscow over the previous years, and sought an Anglo-Russian alliance. He recalled, 'without satisfaction', having told the government more than a year before that they were leading Britain straight into a war in which the country would be 'left to face the music with only France to help us'. Now the Luftwaffe could fly over the English Channel at any point. The children were evacuated to the countryside and the family planned to let the house at Heywood. Violet was going to return to nursing and first aid, and Clem himself predicted that he would be 'fully occupied'. They planned to rent a flat in the centre of London.[55]

On 2 September, it was the acting leader, Arthur Greenwood, who was in the limelight, as MPs assembled in the Commons to hear Chamberlain's statement on the ultimatum he had issued to Hitler demanding that he withdraw his troops from Poland. Greenwood walked in alongside the prime minister, and the chamber hushed as Chamberlain began to speak. He was a defeated man. There were no pink notes passed to him on this occasion; no last-minute reprieve. Greenwood's reply, in which he savaged the government, was cheered by the Labour benches. More significant were the noises of approval which came from the growing ranks of Conservative rebels. Among them was Leo Amery who rose to address the Labour front bench with the words: '*You* speak for Britain.' As the House adjourned, Harold Nicolson recorded that the lobby was so dark that a struck match 'flamed like a beacon'.[56] The following day, on 3 September 1939, Britain declared war on Germany.

Greenwood's statesmanlike handling of the occasion, in Attlee's continued absence, raised his status considerably. In Dalton's view he was doing 'pretty well – better than poor little Rabbit ever did'.[57] The same cast of rivals, including Herbert Morrison, began to position themselves, but a leadership election never came.[58] Greenwood's refusal to run against his leader effectively lanced Morrison's campaign before it began. In a mock

Yorkshire accent, which he was known to affect when he was being earnest, he refused to stand: 'Nay, it wouldn't be fair to Clem.'[59] Greenwood's drinking problem may have influenced his decision too. On some days, even when Parliament was sitting, he would not rise from his bed until the late afternoon. But Attlee also had the firm loyalty of the majority of the backbench MPs who had come into the Commons after 1935. His steadiness and trustworthiness were particularly important to the new intake of self-described 'cloth cap' MPs, 'horny-handed sons of toil' such as James Griffiths, MP for Llanelli, former miner and future Minister for National Insurance. It was to Labour's disadvantage, Griffiths observed, that the cloth cap was later replaced by the 'cap and gown' – those who were richer in academic talent but poorer 'in the character moulded in life's struggles'.[60]

By the second week of October, Attlee was sufficiently recovered to be back at Westminster. His first job was to articulate the Labour Party's war aims. 'It would be an error to think changes are only needed in dictatorship countries, or after the war the Western democracies can return to their pre-war positions unaffected,' he made clear. War was the 'forcing house of change' and the First World War had already seen 'an intense speeding up in social evolution'. Between 1914 and 1918 there had been gigantic advances in the public control of industry, 'bold experimentation in the role of socialization', and the mobilisation of labour. This progress had been checked by the attempt to return the clock to pre-war orthodoxy in the 1920s. The Labour movement was fighting for 'liberty, democracy and the spirit of man against the forces of evil embodied in Hitlerism', and to make 'the world safe for the ordinary man and woman of whatever creed or colour', and for the 'fundamental decencies of life'.[61]

In his October 1939 broadcast to the nation, Attlee reiterated his belief that the citizens of the democracies, 'who are accustomed to act and think for themselves', would 'stand the strain far better than the men and women who are subject to repression and to the regimentation of dictatorships'.[62] Others regarded this optimism as misplaced. Poland had already surrendered, and Chamberlain had yet to reorganise his Cabinet effectively for the war. Basil Liddell Hart wrote to the Labour leader to express his concerns that the government had not yet grasped the seriousness of the situation and was over-optimistic about Britain's ability to defend itself. 'If I were a bookmaker, I should be inclined to put the odds as at least 3–1 against either victory or defeat, and 3-1 on stalemate,' he warned. Modern warfare involved the mobilisation of the whole state, rather than tinkering with the military. 'The worst of our dangers today is that there is so little understanding of war, in the deeper sense, as distinct from its technical apparatus. And without such an understanding, no one can be expected to carry us through it and reach a safe landing on the far side.'[63]

It should have been easier for the Labour Party than other parties, to argue that the mobilisation effort required a transformative shift to economic planning. After all, this was something that it had demanded for the last ten years, regardless of war. It is surprising then that it was slow to grasp this opportunity. On 14 and 15 November 1939, John Maynard Keynes published two letters in *The Times* on 'Paying for the War', which he also sent directly to Attlee. Keynes argued for a percentage of all incomes to be paid directly to the government. This was partly to fund the war and partly as compulsory savings to prepare for its aftermath, when inevitably high levels of inflation would have to be tackled.

This plan was greeted with some dismay in Labour circles as a potential assault on working-class living standards. This grew out of the old suspicion that it was always the poor who bore the brunt of war. Bemused by Labour's objections, Keynes appealed directly to Attlee, on the grounds that his plan would protect the working classes from the worst of the postwar slump. But Attlee did not seem particularly interested; in fact, Keynes was unconvinced that Attlee even understood the economics behind it. The same applied to Bevin and Greenwood, who were wary about what they saw as an attack on the purchasing power of the working classes. Keynes was so exasperated by his failure to win over the Labour front bench that he complained to Harold Laski, the party chairman.[64] Eventually, Keynesian economics was to become one of the foundation stones of the Labour government of 1945–51. But the marriage was not as straightforward as one might have presumed.

Once again, as he had done with the Spanish Civil War, Attlee talked in terms of a struggle between 'Western values' – liberalism and democracy – and totalitarianism. This was in contrast to those from the Unity campaign, who preferred to see the war as a struggle between left and right. Bevan and Cripps had been right to stress that more could have been done to court the Soviet Union in an anti-fascist alliance before 1939, and Attlee agreed with them on this. However, when the Soviets used the cover of their non-aggression pact with Hitler to invade Finland in 1939, Attlee could not hide his disgust. He therefore backed the government in its offer to support Finland by sending arms. Speaking at Durham on 18 December, he was heckled by communists in the audience after he accused the Russians of imperialism. He responded emphatically. 'I object to aggression,' he told them, 'even if it is by people who call themselves Socialists.'[65] Attlee took his firm line against Stalin, aware that not everyone in his party agreed. On 22 December, Bevan announced his opposition to the sending of British arms for the defence of Finland, on the grounds that all efforts should be focused on the war against the fascist powers.[66]

By this stage, Attlee had little faith left in any form of international socialist solidarity. When he had been ill in 1939, a public letter had been sent to the Labour Party from Friedrich Adler, the Austrian socialist leader, urging them to consider reviving the Socialist International. This was a hangover 'from the romantic days of the movement', when the idea of coordinated revolutions across all European countries and 'overturning capitalist governments and creating the millennium was still realistic'. The Third International, established in 1919, and better known as the Comintern, had become more of 'a weapon used by the Russian State than a true revolutionary instrument, the common possession of socialists in many lands'. Its insistence on absolute loyalty to Communist Party decisions had ruined the idea of genuine solidarity on the left. In Britain, the idea that a party would pledge to obey the orders of an external actor was simply unacceptable. Now his own view was that the socialist ideal was one that had to be worked out in every nation 'in accordance with the native genius of the people of that country'. Genuine peace required not close relations between particular sections of opinion in each country, but between peoples as a whole. In this war, the relationship between Russia, France, America and Great Britain must be worked out on the international field between states, not between parties within those states. As Attlee put it, in private notes, the ideal for which the war was being fought was 'the freedom of every nation to manage its own affairs subject to the good of the human race'. He rejected the type of 'ideological imperialism which seeks to *force* every nation to accept one specific kind of economic, social and political structure', whether it came from left or right.[67]

Writing in *Tribune* in January 1940, Bevan deflected the criticism aimed towards him by launching an attack on the leadership for its failure to hold

Chamberlain's government to account. 'If one can speak of a general mind in Britain right now,' he complained, it was 'sodden and limp with the ceaseless drip of adolescent propaganda'. The *Daily Herald* was the worst offender. It had the 'intellectual astringency of a parish magazine', the 'skepticism of a Holy Roller' and the 'sycophancy of an eighteenth-century placeman'. Labour must abandon its political truce – based on a misconceived sense of patriotic duty – and seize this 'splendid opportunity' to collapse the government.[68]

Attlee responded immediately. When Leslie Hore-Belisha, the Minister of War, resigned in mid-January, Attlee pressed the prime minister for an explanation. He suggested that the War Cabinet was constructed 'on a wrong basis' and should not be composed of busy departmental ministers. Sir John Simon, for example, had the separate responsibilities of finance and coordinating economic policy. Why, even more alarmingly, were there still such high levels of unemployment when every man should be mobilised for war?[69]

This was not enough for the critics of the Labour leadership. 'Speak Up, Mr. Attlee!' the headline of *Tribune* boomed two days later, on Friday, 19 January.[70] More worryingly, at the end of the month more attacks were made on Attlee's leadership at several Labour Party constituency meetings, though some of this was attributed to Communist Party infiltration.[71] In February, the party hierarchy was forced to issue guidelines demanding that its members uphold the political truce.[72] The National Executive issued a document entitled 'Labour, the War and the Peace', which replaced Attlee's November 1939 speech, disparaged by Dalton as 'the Rabbit's Peace Aims', as official policy. Attlee was now relegated to the position of one of a number of essayists; others included Greenwood, Morrison and Harold Laski, the party chairman.[73] Dalton complained that Attlee's draft had been too flimsy, envisaging a 'Vague New World' that might come out of the war. Attlee preferred his own version but was forced to cede the point.[74] The rebels on the left agreed that the revamped version simply put a gloss on the first and largely 'echoed what Attlee had said some months before'.[75]

When Beatrice Webb went to hear the Labour leader present the new war aims at the London School of Economics, she complained that he was rather unfriendly to her. Clearly piqued, she wrote that his lecture was pitiable: 'he looked and spoke like an insignificant elderly clerk,

without distinction in the voice, manner or substance of his discourse.'
His address was 'in fact meaningless', there were no 'statements or arguments you could take hold of, whether to accept or deny; it was a string of
vague assertions about an international authority . . . [and] abuse of all
totalitarian governments, whether Fascist, Nazi or Communist, as inconsistent with "political democracy".' Webb's hostility can be partly explained
by her closeness to Cripps and Attlee's critics on the left. That same night,
in fact, she was visited by the Russian ambassador Ivan Maisky and his
wife, 'in excellent spirits, confident that the Red Army is going to win in
Finland'.[76] Attlee could not bear such apologias. He later felt that Webb's
'failure to understand the importance of the human factor in society as
against the mechanics' had led to her indulgence of the Soviet regime.[77] But
a Labour Party led by Bevan, Cripps or Webb in 1940 would have seriously
misplayed its hand. Attlee's steady patriotism may have infuriated many in
his own party. Viewed over the long term, it was an asset without which
Labour might have damaged itself fatally.

V

By spring 1940, as the 'phoney' phase of the war came to end, it became
clear that the Allied strategy was in ruins. France and Britain had been
planning to seize key ports in Norway and Denmark, and use these as
platforms to attack Germany from the north. Attlee had heard these plans
discussed on two visits to Allied headquarters in January and February. He
had taken the opportunity to visit Tom's son, Pat, a soldier in the British
Expeditionary Force, and was pleased to report back on his maturity. 'At
his age,' he confessed, 'I should have been petrified with shyness.' Attlee
also visited some British units in the field and seemed pleased with their
overall position. He liked the atmosphere of headquarters 'very much and
had much good talk'.[78]

Allied plans for Scandinavia were an open secret. On 18 March, the
prime minister raised hopes of a successful manoeuvre by telling MPs that
a force of 10,000 had also been readied to go to Finland as part of the mission. The Nazi regime took pre-emptive action. On 9 April 1940 Hitler
launched a surprise invasion of both Norway and Denmark. The Royal

Navy was caught completely unprepared. With no support coming, neither the Norwegians nor the Danes had any chance of successful resistance.

For Attlee, this finally laid to rest any notion that remained of seeking a negotiated settlement with Hitler. Talk of making peace was like 'proposing to make an agreement with a criminal lunatic', he said in a broadcast by the BBC on 13 April. The only possible approach was to 'round him up'.[79] Others came to the opposite conclusion. In fact, a division was emerging in the Cabinet between Lord Halifax – who still thought Britain might be able to cut a deal with Hitler, possibly with Mussolini's help – and Churchill, who had returned to the government as First Lord of the Admiralty on the declaration of war (the post he had also held in 1914). The debate was to continue for the next two months, and Attlee was to play a crucial part in its final issue.

Either way, the reality had to be faced: Britain desperately needed allies to stand any chance of victory. The ideal scenario was to bring America into the war, or at least to seek her financial support. In the short term, however, there was no prospect of American intervention. In these circumstances, as a leader of a major national party, Attlee understood that he would have to explore the prospect of a re-setting of relations with the Soviet Union. If he was to join a wartime government in the near future, this might well be a prerequisite.

Despite the non-aggression pact signed in August 1939, the Soviets remained deeply suspicious of Hitler's intentions in Eastern Europe. Maisky, the Russian ambassador in London, was on good terms with Churchill, but relations with the Labour Party had deteriorated considerably over the previous months, largely because of Attlee's disgust at the Soviet invasion of Finland. Maisky had told Beatrice Webb that the Labour Party was more of an obstacle to rapprochement than the Conservatives. Desperate measures were now required, however.[80] On 15 April 1940, two days after Attlee had broadcast to the nation rejecting the idea of any peaceful settlement with Hitler, he and Greenwood made a visit to Maisky at the Russian Embassy in west London. This time, however, they made no mention of the quarrel over the Soviet invasion of Finland and 'expressed their ardent desire to improve our relations and promised their assistance'. Greenwood did most of the talking, constantly addressing Attlee with the words: 'Isn't that so, Clem?' To this Attlee kept answering, 'Oh yes, absolutely.' Maisky got the impression that Attlee was more favourable to the

Russian position, despite Greenwood's nervous energy. 'Greenwood drank a lot, as is his wont, while Attlee merely sipped his cherry brandy,' Maisky noted, wryly, as the two men left. 'Facts are stubborn things, and the power of the USSR is undeniably one of them.'[81]

Churchill had grasped the absolute necessity of the Soviet alliance and had already made a similar pilgrimage. Now that Attlee had set aside his scruples, the two men edged a step closer to finding the common ground on which a new government could be formed. On 7 May, Chamberlain faced a stormy House of Commons for the beginning of a two-day debate on the debacle of the failed defence of Norway. While Greenwood had led the way over the declaration of war, it was Attlee who now launched an excoriating attack on the government for its failures. The debacle in Norway was just the 'culmination of many other discontents'. Britain had been led to the brink of defeat by a government that had had 'an almost uninterrupted career of failure'. Chamberlain's Cabinet had 'no plan, no intelligence, no concentration on essential objectives'. They had been 'over-optimistic and over-complacent' since the declaration of war. The Labour leader tore chunk after chunk off the government's record, going right back to the early days of appeasement.

At one point, Chamberlain rose to correct Attlee on a technicality. This was a mistake, as Labour MPs howled him down for his pettiness in the face of such grave danger. The government was 'blind and deaf', replied Attlee, if they did not realise that there was widespread anxiety in the country that the war was not being prosecuted with 'sufficient energy, capacity, drive and resolution'. Instead, Attlee picked up one of Chamberlain's phrases – a throwaway line about 'missing the bus' on Norway – and used it against the prime minister to devastating effect. 'Everywhere the story was "too late". The Prime Minister talked about missing the bus. He and his associates missed a number of buses since 1931. They missed the peace buses and caught the war buses.' Not for the first time in a foreign policy debate, Attlee picked up a newspaper and waved it for dramatic effect. It was *The Times*, which had run an editorial saying that the prime minister's greatest weakness was his devotion to colleagues who were either failures or past their best. Reaching a crescendo, Attlee said that 'In this life or death struggle we cannot have our destinies in the hands of failures or people who need a rest.' In order to win the war, he told the House, 'we want people at the helm other than those who now lead us.'[82]

The damage was done. For the rest of the debate, Chamberlain was subject to shouts of 'missed the bus!'[83] Leo Amery, the Conservative MP who had urged Arthur Greenwood to 'speak for England' in the debate over Munich, saw his moment to follow. Attlee's speech set up Amery's own famous interjection, in which he rose to address Chamberlain and quoted Oliver Cromwell's words (spoken when he dissolved the Long Parliament): 'You have sat too long here for any good you have been doing. Depart, I say, and let us have done with you. In the name of God, go!'[84] Harold Nicolson was not particularly impressed by Attlee's attack, but his real scorn was reserved for Chamberlain, who had been so severely rebuked that he was reduced to making a 'little, rather feminine gesture of irritation'.[85]

The next day, 8 May, the public galleries were overflowing and the late spring sunshine warmed the crowds that gathered outside Parliament. Before the debate recommenced, Attlee told a meeting of Labour's parliamentary party that it was time to break the truce they had agreed to at the start of war, and bring a vote of no confidence against the government.[86] Before the vote was cast, the 77-year-old Lloyd George spoke to urge the prime minister to resign. As First Lord of the Admiralty, it was not for Churchill to deliver the final blow. In fact, the debate wound up with the somewhat odd sight of Churchill offering a defence of Chamberlain's personal conduct. The government actually won the vote by 281 to 200 votes. But the abstention of 134 of its own MPs indicated the extent to which it had haemorrhaged authority.

After the vote, it was clear that drastic changes were essential if the government was to restore its authority. A new national government would have to be formed, at the very least. Attlee and Greenwood called on Chamberlain at Number 10 immediately after the debate. Halifax and Churchill were present, and they heard Attlee tell the prime minister that they would not serve under him in any circumstances. By this stage, it was believed that Churchill was more acceptable to Labour as a potential prime minister. This was because he had been such a strong critic of the government on appeasement, though it was noted that he had clashed with Labour MPs himself when defending Chamberlain.[87] Another possibility was Lord Halifax, the foreign secretary, who was preferred to Churchill by some in the Labour Party. For the moment, Churchill was unwilling to stick the knife in himself. Thus Chamberlain made an offer to Attlee for the Labour Party to come into government. He sent him away with two questions with which to address his party, which was convening for its conference in Bournemouth. Would Labour be willing to join a wartime coalition government? Would they be willing to serve under Chamberlain as prime minister?

After months of secret intrigue, now that a firm offer was on the table the decision would have to be made swiftly. On Friday, 10 May 1940, the news reached London that German forces had invaded the Netherlands, Belgium, Luxembourg and France. This meant, in effect, that most of Europe's northern coastline now looked like a launch pad for a Nazi invasion of England. France was in danger of being completely overwhelmed and Hitler seemed to be in a position of almost unassailable dominance on the Continent. Attlee made a statement, written by Dalton, which called for an urgent restructuring of the government that went beyond changes in personnel.[88]

That evening, as the Labour Party assembled for its conference in Bournemouth, the party chairman Harold Laski wrote that 'We are at a turning point in the history of the world.' Ellen Wilkinson added that Chamberlain, clinging on to office, was like 'an old widow in a boarding house, jabbing at critics with knitting needles'. In a special issue of *Tribune*, which reached the Labour delegates as they convened, G.D.H. Cole expressed his disappointment with Attlee's radio broadcasts on the crisis. After having said 'what every decent person must wish to say about the Nazis', Attlee thought he could leave it at that. It was not the place of Labour to wear a muzzle at a time of national crisis.[89]

Earlier in the day, Attlee, Greenwood and Dalton had travelled to Bournemouth to discuss with the party's National Executive Committee the details of Chamberlain's offer for Labour to join the government. They agreed to go into government but would not serve under the incumbent prime minister. Before they left to return to London, Chamberlain's private secretary telephoned the lobby of the Highcliff Hotel at 5 p.m. and left a message for the Labour leader. Attlee called back a few minutes later to confirm what he had told the prime minister the previous day. Labour would come into government but Chamberlain would have to resign. Attlee and Dalton immediately jumped into a taxi and went to the train station to travel back to London. In his diary Dalton remarked that 'the last blow which dislodged the old limpet was struck by us at Bournemouth this afternoon.'[90]

Chamberlain was dislodged but it was still not clear who would serve in his place. Most Labour leaders (Attlee, Dalton, Morrison and Cripps) had seemed to be more inclined towards Lord Halifax over the previous weeks. The preference was not a matter of left or right. As recently as 6 May, Stafford Cripps had anonymously published an article in the *Daily Mail* that described his ideal Cabinet. It had Halifax, rather than Churchill, as the prime minister, with Attlee as chancellor. Cripps's idea of a popular front had anticipated the collapse of Chamberlain, but he had failed to notice the growing importance of Churchill in the picture.[91] Dalton recorded that Attlee considered Halifax as an alternative contender for prime minister, possibly ahead of Churchill, a view Dalton shared himself.[92] Leo Amery also noted that Attlee had said weeks before, at a dinner in Oxford, that Churchill might be too old.[93] In fact, as Attlee would have known already from his visit to Number 10, Halifax did not want the job and was more than willing to step aside for Churchill.[94] By the time that Attlee and Morrison were picked up in a government car at Waterloo station, they learned that Chamberlain had resigned. They were told that Churchill wanted to see them at the Admiralty. In effect, the choice had been made for them. Attlee never dwelt on it. 'Queer bird, Halifax,' he later wrote. 'Very humorous, all hunting and Holy Communion.'[95]

There were those in the Labour Party who had their own doubts about the men they had sent into action at this critical moment in the nation's history. 'I feel,' wrote Laski as Attlee and Greenwood announced that Chamberlain was resigning, 'as though the cook and the kitchen maid have been telling us that they sacked the butler.'[96] The grumbling was not just confined to the left of the party. As leader of the London County Council, Herbert Morrison had remained in London and missed the National Executive Committee because of widespread fears that the Germans would launch an air attack on the capital that evening. He was woken early in the morning of 12 May with the news that the government was being formed. 'These aren't the right people to represent the party,' he groused. But the deal had been done. Attlee travelled back to Bournemouth on Sunday, 12 May, with news of the offer to serve under Churchill, and the Labour National Executive voted in favour of them joining the new coalition.[97]

Before the assembled conference that evening, Attlee broke the news to the delegates in this most 'tremendous moment'. The Labour Party had done all it could to avoid the war but it was now time to take a stand. 'You cannot dither in a crisis,' he said, an archetypal Captain Mainwaringism. The party delegates agreed to support the decision to join the government by a large majority, though the conference hall was not without its dissenters. Pacifists and a hard-left fringe made their presences felt with noisy protests.[98]

The *Manchester Guardian* described Attlee's speech as 'one of his best' in helping Labour to overcome its 'opposition complex' after spending almost a decade out of government. But it also noted that there had been an element of stage-management behind the proceedings. Very few opponents of the decision were heard as Hugh Dalton marshalled an absurdly long queue of delegates behind the speaker's rostrum to speak in favour of the decision.[99] Almost immediately, the radical left of the party began to use various committee meetings to put pressure on the hierarchy to make firm promises about what gains they would get from being in government. In fact, in the bar that evening there were some scuffles between trade unionists and communist infiltrators.[100] The *Daily Herald*, the voice of the party leadership, omitted these details as they described how Attlee left the conference hall, with 'almost unanimous' support, and shouts of 'Good luck' and 'God bless you' as he headed to London. It announced that its editorial policy would be to support any efforts on behalf of the new government towards victory in the war. National survival must come before anything else. Just beside this editorial was an advert for a new carbonated energy drink called Lucozade, which promised 'Remarkable Staying Power'.[101] Britain was going to need it.

As spring turned into summer in 1940, dark clouds began to gather over the British Isles. Back in his garden at Stanmore, Attlee reported cheerfully that the flowers were blooming and his daffodils were doing particularly well. But there were other symbols of the coming struggle. As the country stockpiled its resources in expectation of a siege, Attlee handed over control of the garden to the local allotment committee, of which he was chairman, before digging it up and replanting it with potatoes. There was in this an eerie echo of the way in which he had compared socialism to gardening in his 1937 book, *The Labour Party in Perspective*. Yet the sharing of allotments would not go far in countering the clunking fist of the German war machine, of course. 'Things are not going too well generally I fear in the world,' he confessed.

In the last week of April 1940, with fears of German invasion growing by the day, Attlee had visited George Lansbury at Manor House Hospital, where the old man was entering the last few weeks of his life. Lansbury reminisced about Tom, his fellow pacifist from the days of the First World War.[102] After being forced from the Labour Party leadership in 1935, he had devoted the final years of his life to touring Europe in what Attlee called 'a pathetic effort to try by sweet reasonableness to convince toughs such as Hitler and Mussolini to see the error of their ways'. He died on 7 May, three days before Chamberlain's resignation. Attlee thought it a blessing in disguise that Lansbury, his comrade from the earliest days in the movement, did not live to see the destruction of his beloved East End by the German bombers that were soon to arrive in the sky.[103] On 19 May, he was the principal speaker at a memorial service for Lansbury at Poplar Town Hall. As 'The Red Flag' was sung, the whine of air-raid sirens rang out across east London.[104]

Part Four

Finest Hour, 1940–1945

12

All Behind You, Winston

ALL BEHIND YOU, WINSTON

(David Low, *Evening Standard*, 14 May 1940)

I *Oxford and Cambridge Club, Piccadilly Circus, London, May 1940*

The Lord Privy Seal spread the papers in front of him as he ate his break-fast. This formed part of his morning routine for the first few weeks of the new government, in the interlude between May and September, when the Blitz of Britain began in earnest. While Violet remained in the house at

Stanmore, her husband took up temporary residence in Number 11 Downing Street (at Churchill's request) where he soon fell into a role for which he was naturally suited: the clearing house for government business and, in effect, though not yet officially, Churchill's deputy in government. His responsibilities involved keeping the new coalition harmonious, processing the government's domestic business efficiently, and surveying the international scene, as Britain girded itself for the enemy's onslaught. One of his very first acts in the new government was to ask for fuller summaries of the foreign press, having been unsatisfied by the abridged versions given to Cabinet.[1] Armed with a leather satchel, he would take his breakfast at the Oxford and Cambridge Club in Piccadilly, where he had a private phone installed for him to keep in contact with Whitehall in the event of an emergency. After walking back through St James's Park that summer, he would work all through the day and eat in the canteen of the War Office, sometimes ignoring the air-raid drills as his staff hurried downstairs to shelters.[2]

On 14 May, as the public learned that Labour would come into government under Churchill, the New Zealand-born cartoonist David Low captured the event with a famous print in the London *Evening Standard*. Low's cartoon, 'All Behind You, Winston!' depicted Churchill marching into battle with his sleeves rolled up. Alongside him, from left to right, marched the leading figures in the Labour Party, all in exactly the same pose – rolled up-sleeves, determined expressions, fists clenched, ready to confront the enemy. First by Churchill's side was Attlee; next was Ernest Bevin, the new Minister of Labour and National Service who had, just weeks before, been parachuted into a parliamentary seat for Wandsworth Central so that he could serve in the new government; and third was Herbert Morrison, the leader of London County Council, who became the Minister of Supply. This trio made up Labour's 'big three' in the government.[3]

That they were in the front row symbolised the sense of cohesion and purpose behind the new government. Their responsibility was for the home front – mobilisation of manpower and industry and preparation for national defence. These were things that Bevin and Morrison had been considering for years, as Chamberlain's foreign policy had foundered. They were to work closely with Sir John Anderson, who had been the Lord Privy Seal in the National Government. Anderson was home secretary and then, from October, appointed as Lord President of the Council, meaning that he chaired most of the home affairs committees. He was known as the 'Home Front Prime Minister'. Nonetheless, it was Labour, blessed with Bevin's trade union contacts and Morrison's experience of running the London County Council, who exerted the most leverage.

Behind Churchill and Labour's Big Three, in the subsequent rows of Low's cartoon, were the other key members of the government. A number of senior figures were retained from the National Government. Intitially, Chamberlain remained in, as Lord President of the Council, though ill health (he was suffering from stomach cancer) soon saw him replaced by Anderson. One of Churchill's suggestions to which Attlee had objected was the idea that Chamberlain would be leader in the House of Commons. Attlee understood that this would be deeply unpopular with the Labour Party. After Chamberlain, the most important figure retained was the foreign secretary, Lord Halifax (though he was appointed ambassador to the United States in December 1940).

To broaden the base within the Conservative Party, Anthony Eden – who would bring a significant number of followers – became Minister of War, responsible for the army. Leo Amery, one of the 'glamour boys' around Eden, became Secretary of State for India (a position of ever-growing importance in the context of the war). Churchill also brought in a number of his closest allies. Duff Cooper became Minister of Information. Lord Beaverbrook, the proprietor of both the *Daily Express* and the *Evening Standard*, was brought in as the minister responsible for aircraft production, though he was not shy about interfering elsewhere. Sir Kingsley Wood, formerly Minister for Air, was made chancellor. So that all parties were included, the Liberal Party leader Sir Archibald Sinclair replaced Wood as Minister for Air. The position of First Lord of the Admiralty went to a Labour man, A. V. Alexander, who had held it during MacDonald's government and was to grow in stature during the war. Arthur Greenwood, Attlee's deputy leader, was appointed minister without portfolio, though he was to become increasingly marginalised over the next eighteen months.[4]

The War Cabinet – which decided overall strategy in cooperation with the chiefs of staff – was composed of just five members: Churchill, Chamberlain, Halifax, Attlee and Greenwood. A larger Cabinet, responsible for general governance of the nation during the war, was created in which Bevin, Morrison and Alexander also sat. They were joined by Hugh Dalton, who became Minister of Economic Warfare, and was in addition given the brief for special operations and subversion in Germany. This was secured for him through special pleading by Attlee, after Dalton expressed the view that such work – subterfuge and appealing to German workers and soldiers to disrupt the Nazi regime – 'needed to be done from the left'.[5]

Dalton had never been a great admirer of the 'little Rabbit' Attlee, but his respect for him grew over the course of the war. 'He does quite well in his own little way,' he remarked in his diary. He was grateful that Attlee intervened on his behalf on a number of occasions during his periodic power struggles with Brendan Bracken, a Churchill favourite, who replaced Duff Cooper as Minister of Information in 1941. Dalton complained that Bracken was always running down Labour, as well as trying to usurp his own responsibilities. Attlee would listen calmly to these complaints on a number of occasions, then take Dalton's concerns to Churchill.[6] One of his undoubted skills was to navigate round the larger egos surrounding him, without letting disputes over personality get in the way of swift execution of government policy.

In all, sixteen Labour ministers were spread across the government. To maintain a balance between the left and right of the party, respectively, important posts were also handed out to 'Red' Ellen Wilkinson (private secretary in the Department of Pensions) and Sir William Jowitt, Attlee's former schoolmate, who was regarded as more moderate (Solicitor General). Labour representation in government also rose over the course of the war, increasing to twenty-two ministers in March 1942 and twenty-seven by 1945.[7]

Attlee was the only member of the government to sit on the three main wartime decision-making bodies: the War Cabinet, the Defence Committee (on which he was Churchill's vice-chairman) and the Lord President's Committee. It was the third of these that he had asked Churchill to create in order to address domestic issues during the war. This gave him close involvement with all the decisions on war strategy – though he chose his interventions carefully – and a steering influence on the home front.[8] Into his lap also came concerns about home defence in the summer of 1940. Some local government officials complained that while John Anderson was certainly efficient, he was 'blinkered' on some issues, and they doubted to what extent Britain was prepared for the bombing campaign that the Nazis were about to begin.[9] Attlee took to these tasks with relish, and urgency. 'It is no small part of his strength as leader that he is a tiger for work,' commented his friend, Jack Lawson. 'Incessant work. Labour from early morning to late at night. There are men more clever but none more selflessly devoted to his task. There are men more eloquent, but none who command more complete confidence in his integrity.'[10]

As a cartoonist, David Low was famous for his satires on the failures of appeasement. He was also particularly adept at capturing Churchill in his various guises – so much so that he confessed to growing tired of drawing him. Of the other big personalities in government, Low felt that the handsome and suave Eden had an 'unsensational formula', which was not difficult to depict; Bevin, rotund, combative and full of physical force, grew into Low's caricature to the extent that he almost became a real-life cartoon; and Morrison, with his large glasses and carefully cultivated quiff, loved to see himself in print so much that it almost took the fun out of depicting him.[11] Low's talents were respected across the political spectrum. Nye Bevan joked to him that his wife said only Low had been 'able to see me as I really am . . . you must have a strain of sadism in you and I therefore assume that you have seen that there is a strain of masochism in me!'[12] (As Bevan remained out of the government, his own strain of sadism was to become directed, with increasing force, at Attlee, from the moment the coalition was created.)

The Lord Privy Seal was another matter entirely. As Low admitted, 'Attlee I had never been able to get to know more than slightly, which accounted for my failure to abstract his essence.' From the day that he became party leader, Low's impression of him was 'of a tight-buttoned little man, shy of ridicule'. Someone had told Attlee that Low was Australian, so whenever they met Attlee confined the conversation to cricket, oblivious to the fact that Low did not follow the game and that he was actually from New Zealand.[13]

The best Low could do was to portray Attlee as a 'tough lamb', an evolution from 'white rabbit' or 'little mouse'. Yet Attlee certainly had a favourite from Low's collection. It was, in fact, 'All Behind You, Winston'. In the Low papers at the Beinecke Library at Yale University there is a letter from Attlee thanking Low for giving him the original copy of the cartoon. It was Attlee's prized possession, and for many years thereafter Violet would display it in their home any time they had visitors. When Low borrowed it for an exhibition, Attlee made sure that he did not forget to return it.[14]

Of all the moments of Attlee's public life – as a volunteer, soldier and politician – taking Labour into government under Churchill at Britain's darkest hour was his proudest act.

II

The day before Low's cartoon was published, on 13 May, Britain's new prime minister appeared before the House of Commons and addressed both Parliament and the nation for the first time. It was in this speech that he made the famous statement that all he could promise the British people was 'blood, toil, tears and sweat'. Many years later, when Churchill was honoured in Westminster Hall on his eightieth birthday, Attlee reminded him of the words that had been used to announce the formation of his government. 'You offered us only blood and sweat and tears and we gladly took your offer,' he said. 'I was very glad when Mr Attlee described my speeches in the war as expressing the will not only of Parliament but of the whole nation,' Churchill replied. It was the people who had the lion heart, remarked Churchill; it only fell upon him to give the roar.[15]

The importance of the personal relationship between these two men cannot be overestimated. That Attlee was in Churchill's campaign at Gallipoli was particularly important in setting the tone for the wartime coalition. That he believed it was a sound plan, ruined by poor generalship, was even more significant. In fact, Attlee went so far as to say that there was 'only one brilliant strategic idea' during the last war, 'and that was Winston's; the Dardanelles'.[16] He always spoke warmly about Churchill in the company of other Gallipoli veterans, who wondered what it was like to serve alongside him in 1940.[17] This was one reason why he maintained faith in Churchill's strategic vision in 1940–2, when others, including some of the prime minister's most important allies, despaired that he had taken the wrong course, and was leading the country to glorious defeat.

There were other lessons from the First World War on which Churchill and Attlee were agreed that hung over the coalition in the early months of the Second. Both believed that the chief failures of the last war were not ones of vision but of politics and planning. It had been the troops who had suffered because of the failures of communication between the last War Cabinet and the military high command. Winston 'knew what war meant in terms of the suffering of the soldier, high strategy, and how generals get on with their political bosses'. Most important of all, he understood what was required in terms of the 'setting up of the intra-governmental machine'.[18] Thus, as soon as Attlee won the support of his party to enter government, he had no interest in playing games over its composition. Churchill had a list of potential Labour ministers that he deemed acceptable. Attlee agreed the list without question. 'I was an old Gallipoli man and had the strong impression that one of the reasons for the failure of Gallipoli was that at the crucial moment the Liberals and the Conservatives were squabbling over the allocation of seats in the coalition Government,' he later recalled. 'And I said "I will not haggle about certain seats." Churchill proposed a certain number and I agreed, and we settled that night the main positions of the Government.'[19]

No other senior figure in the Labour Party could have built such a strong personal relationship with Churchill, or one that would survive the vicissitudes of the war. For many in the rank and file, Churchill was a hate figure. His tough line against trade union protestors in Tonypandy, Wales in 1910 – sending in the army to deal with riots when he was home secretary – was a long-standing sore point. The fact that Attlee's leadership depended on trade union support made this potentially more problematic. Indeed, Attlee had also witnessed a similar overreaction by Churchill in 1911 at Sidney Street. 'Trouble with Winston. Nails his trousers to the mast. Can't climb down.'[20] But no part of him believed that Churchill was hostile to the working classes; otherwise he would not have been so close to Lloyd George in his early efforts at introducing welfare reform before the First World War. When the coalition had first been formed, Attlee had jotted down some principles of conduct for his own guidance. 'We must certainly not play politics,' he had maintained. But one thing he had insisted upon, and now had to deliver, was a loosening of government controls on trade union rights.[21] The importance of this issue to Labour's power base is easy to forget, lost in the subsequent squabbles about welfare and healthcare which consumed Labour for much of the war.

This is not to say that there was perfect harmony between the two men. They had differed on a number of foreign policy issues in previous years and Attlee thought Churchill's opposition to Indian self-government reprehensible. By 1940, however, they had more to unite them than divide them. In particular, they retained a suspicion of Chamberlain and his followers. Initially, Churchill had no choice but to bring the Chamberlainites into government, owing to the fact that his own support base was limited. Yet Attlee watched with approval as they were dispatched to other positions – often to embassies – over the coming months. Chamberlain himself was killed by his bowel cancer in November 1940. A month later Halifax was sent to Washington, DC as ambassador, followed by Sir Samuel Hoare to Spain and Malcolm MacDonald to Canada.[22] Other potential spoilers were dealt with in a similar way. In an inspired decision, Stafford Cripps was simultaneously co-opted and sent out of sniping distance, when he was appointed ambassador to Moscow. This was in the hope that Stalin might be peeled away from his pact with Hitler and into a new alliance.

Although Cripps was temporarily muted by accepting a government job, he continued to fund the Labour left through *Tribune*. The weekly was used by Bevan as a stick with which to poke the new government at every opportunity. Sure enough, even before the ink was dry on the new Cabinet positions, *Tribune* suggested that Attlee had been outwitted in the negotiations with Churchill. The Labour ministers – charged with material and manpower – put petrol in the national car, but the Tories remained in control of the steering wheel.[23] Thus began the almost constant hounding of Attlee – along with Bevin and Morrison – which would persist for the duration of the war.

By bringing Ellen Wilkinson into government, Attlee momentarily took some of the sting out of the left-wing critiques. Wilkinson was a regular contributor to *Tribune*, but the fact that she was more of a follower of Morrison (who was rumoured to be her lover) than Cripps made her predisposed to work within the government. Writing in *Tribune*, she described the eerie scene on 'White Monday', 16 May, as the House of Commons assembled for its first-ever secret session, in which the details of discussions were to be kept from the public. It was odd to look down and see familiar faces on the front benches. Attlee, 'slim in figure, earnest in demeanour, put on a poker-face and kept it rigid'. A. V. Alexander, beside him, set his jaw like a bulldog and gazed steadily in front of him. Herbert Morrison sat at the end of the gangway and grinned cheerfully across at the Labour benches. Wilkinson, with whom Morrison did indeed have a long-standing relationship, could not help laughing back at him. The Independent Labour Party stalwart Jimmy Maxton was even more unforgiving of the new coalition than Bevan but was an isolated voice in Parliament in opposing the war. In this time of crisis, Wilkinson begged for time and leniency.[24]

The political machinations involved in the creation of the coalition faded into the background as the 'phoney' phase of the war drew to a close, and Britain readied itself for a life-or-death struggle. The day after Churchill addressed the House, Low produced another cartoon portraying the coming struggle as the 'Battle of All History'. He depicted two gods battling it out between the 'hope of freedom' in the West and the 'the threat of slavery' in the East.[25]

It was an indication of the gravity of the situation that previous quibbles about the use of force evaporated. When the War Cabinet met on 15 May, Attlee was among the strongest advocates of the decision to approve an aggressive bombing strategy against Germany, even in those areas where civilian casualties might be high. That very night, Bomber Command launched its first large-scale raid, with a hundred bombers attacking industrial sites in the Ruhr. Every measure available would be used to ensure national survival. With no sign of protest, Attlee was personally tasked with stocking up tonnes of poison gas to be used in the event of a ground invasion.[26] In later years, he made it clear that he would have had no hesitation in using it.

Throughout the 1920s and 1930s, Attlee had repeatedly condemned successive British governments for their lack of morality in international affairs. By 1940, however, he was convinced that Britain was on the right side of a battle between good and evil, against a rapacious and dark-hearted foe. Not only was the bombing of Germany strategically sound, Attlee regarded it as entirely morally justified. Indeed, he went so far as to suggest that there was a strong element of poetic justice in the RAF bombing campaign. It was thus that he quoted John Milton's *Samson Agonistes* as British bombers took off for Berlin:

> With winged expedition
> Swift as the lightning glance he executes
> His errands on the wicked.[27]

On 22 May, it also fell to Attlee – who was to lead government business in the Commons owing to Churchill's many absences – to introduce the

Emergency Powers Defence Bill. The government was to be given complete dictatorial powers for the foreseeable future. This would allow it to begin conscription – something Attlee had opposed just a year before – and mobilisation of the national economy for the sole purpose of victory in the war. In just under three hours, between 2.36 p.m. and 6.09 p.m., the bill passed the Commons, then the Lords, and was given royal assent.[28] As Attlee explained in a broadcast to the nation, the government had full control over all persons and property. 'Our ancient liberties are placed in pawn for victory; nothing less than a destruction of Hitlerism will redeem them.'[29]

Sandbags and machine guns were set up across Westminster. Lady Diana Cooper, Duff Cooper's wife, witnessed the scene as she arrived outside Parliament to hear the reading of the bill. Though Attlee read 'in a colourless voice – his voice', she 'nearly toppled out of the gallery in astonishment', such was the extent of the powers granted to government. The next day she lunched with H. G. Wells – who had envisaged a huge neo-Machiavellian state many years before, designed for a global game of survival of the fittest – who said, happily, 'The revolution in England has now begun.'[30] What that revolution might look like was unclear. Some of those on the left, including Victor Gollancz of the Left Book Club, made the point that war could only be won by socialist methods, such as economic planning and state control of vital industry. Churchill was a patriot, first and foremost, and if turning Britain socialist was the price of victory, it was one he might be willing to pay.[31]

After Hitler's surprise invasion of Denmark and Norway, the news from the Continent became progressively worse. Within just a few weeks of his massive and lightning-quick invasion of Holland, Belgium and France, it was clear that Hitler had scored his greatest victory yet, as the French divisions melted away in the face of *Blitzkrieg*.

The last flush of appeasement played itself out in heated discussions within the war cabinet between 26 and 28 May. It was precipitated by a suggestion from Paul Reynaud, the French prime minister, that Mussolini, who was still neutral in the conflict, might act as an interlocutor with Hitler in a final attempt at a 'grand bargain'. Hitler had made speeches that hinted that peace with Britain was something he would consider. Halifax, with tentative support from Chamberlain (who was a sick and broken man), pushed forward the idea that a new deal could be negotiated with

Hitler to save the Allies from total destruction. At this point, France had fallen and British troops were encircled at Dunkirk. In a meeting of the five-man War Cabinet, Churchill fought off Halifax by arguing that such a peace would be, morally and strategically, worse than defeat. Both Greenwood and Attlee sided with Churchill. Attlee warned Halifax that the British people would not take such a deal and it would be 'impossible to rally . . . [their] morale' if they got wind of negotiations. Greenwood added that the industrial north would regard any 'weakening' of the British position as a disaster.

Attlee and Greenwood had done enough to keep Churchill afloat against Halifax. But the debate was not yet won. If anything, the indications seemed to be that Halifax might sway the rest of the government in his favour, defeating the War Cabinet and dumping Churchill out of office. It was only when Churchill brought the question to the larger Cabinet, of twenty-five ministers, that the strength of his personality and his convictions ensured an emphatic victory. In full Cabinet, which met at 6 p.m. on 28 May, the force of Churchill's rhetoric won the day. 'If this long island story of ours is to end at last, let it end only when each one of us lies choking in his own blood upon the ground.'[32] There was to be no peace with 'that man'. Ministers cheered and banged the table, stood up, shook hands, and hurried around Churchill, patting his back.[33]

On 31 May, Attlee accompanied Churchill and the Chief of the Imperial General Staff, Sir John Dill, on a dash to Paris, escorted by Spitfires. They stayed in the British Embassy that night, where papers were being burned in the garden as the Nazis were expected to arrive within days. Attlee later recalled 'the curious silence and almost deserted look of the city, which had obviously already decided on surrender'.[34] As the Anglo-French Supreme War Council convened for the last time, General Ismay, chosen as Churchill's staff officer, described how a dejected-looking old man in civilian clothes shuffled towards him, offered his hand and introduced himself as Marshal Pétain, France's great hero of Verdun during the First World War. Attlee sat on the British side of the table, absorbing the news of the catastrophe that had befallen France. Recalling this scene, as darkness closed in, Ismay commented admiringly that Attlee was 'brave, decisive, and completely loyal to Churchill. His integrity was absolute and no thought of personal ambition seemed to enter his mind.' Although he looked somewhat meek, he had hidden fortitude and a strength of character by which he had distinguished himself in the First World War. He was, as Ismay later put it, a 'grand chief to serve, and a great servant of his country'.[35]

The next priority was getting the remaining British divisions out of France before capture, or worse, at the hands of the German forces. This led to the hastily drawn plans for Operation Dynamo, the evacuation of Dunkirk, which began on 27 May and lasted until 4 June. In desperate scenes, British troops took any transport they could, including fishing boats, to make it back across the Channel. More than 300,000 troops were saved.

As the government scrambled to avoid total catastrophe, Attlee was asked what Churchill was doing to win the war. 'Talk about it,' was his simple reply.[36] The Battle of France, and the looming prospect of what was to become the Battle of Britain, were addressed by Churchill in three famous broadcasts to the nation in late May and June.[37] 'Had I at this juncture faltered at all in the leading of the nation, I should have been hurled out of office,' he later reflected. 'I was sure that every minister was ready to be killed quite soon, and have all his family and possessions destroyed, rather than give in.' In this they represented the House of Commons and almost all the people. 'It fell to me in these coming days and months to express their sentiments on suitable occasions. This I was able to do because they were mine also. There was a white glow, overpowering, sublime, which ran through our island from end to end.'[38]

Outside the world of Whitehall, Attlee's presence in the government did not inspire in the same way. While the Ministry of Information listed him as a 'category A' speaker, it was perhaps telling that they misspelled his name, as Atlee, in official records.[39] Monitoring early wartime broadcasts at cinemas across the country, civil servants reported that Attlee's flat cap 'is said to have had a depressing effect on picture goers' when propaganda films were shown on cinema screens. Nor was he, with a German invasion believed to be imminent, one to gloss over the reality of the coming struggle. In July 1940 it was reported that his references to 'the "coming zero hour" (with its implication that we wait for Hitler's pleasure) fell on stony ground'.[40] Attlee's own concerns show that he was not unaware of his failings in this regard. He was worried about the BBC retaining its class voice and personnel and pushed for more working-class employees.[41] He was also involved in plans to reorganise the Ministry of Information, which he thought was outdated compared to the Nazi propaganda machine.[42]

One criticism that was sometimes made of Attlee was that he was unwilling to stand up to Churchill on critical issues. Given the way that Churchill had nearly been bounced out of office at the end of May 1940 over a negotiated peace, and that Attlee and Greenwood's support had been crucial in stopping the prime minister being overridden in the War Cabinet, Attlee could be forgiven for thinking that squeezing Churchill might not have been the best use of his influence in the first few months of the coalition. Ironically, the greatest purveyor of the claim that Attlee was too weak against Churchill was the man who posed as Churchill's greatest friend and ally, Lord Beaverbrook. Beaverbrook was not alone among Churchill's friends in pointing out the prime minister's flaws – not least his temper and dogmatism. However, Attlee had a way of expressing his own frustration at Churchill without directly confronting the prime minister himself. From the outset, Beaverbrook seems to have wanted to use Attlee as an outlet for his own frustrations with Churchill, developing an irrational hatred for the Labour leader. At a dinner in August 1940, General Sir Frederick Pile, the General Officer Commanding the Anti-Aircraft Command, described how Beaverbrook turned aggressively on Attlee after the Labour leader had offered a mild criticism of the prime minister (regarding a point on which Beaverbrook concurred). After what Pile regarded as a throwaway remark by Attlee, he was subjected to repeated hectoring by Beaverbrook, 'Well, why did you not put it right? Why did you not do something?'[43]

Contrary to the myth propagated by Beaverbrook, Attlee was no lapdog. He was not afraid of pointing out Churchill's flaws when he felt it was justified. He felt Churchill was a poor judge of men (Beaverbrook being a case in point) and a bad chair of Cabinet. He was also overrated as a parliamentarian. His speeches were magnificent rhetorical performances but they were 'too stately, too pompous, too elaborate to be ideal House of Commons stuff'.[44] Though he never regarded it as a quid pro quo arrangement, there were advantages for Attlee in making it clear that he was behind the prime minister on most key issues in the conduct of the war. For one, Attlee believed that Churchill talked to him more frankly than many of his colleagues in the Conservative Party. For another, having established his trustworthiness at the outset of the war, he was able to extract concessions from Churchill in its later stages. Beaverbook and Cripps – who regarded themselves as rivals – both huffed and puffed at various points, to much less effect.

Yet there was something more important than this. Quite simply, Attlee felt Churchill's leadership was the best asset that Britain had in trying to win the war. It was Churchill's decisiveness that he came to value most. He felt that it was dangerous if either ministers or generals allowed themselves to get 'bogged down in detail'. The job of the government was to provide decisive political direction. In this regard, Attlee believed that the relationship between the civil and military powers was smoother than it had been in 1914–18. One reason for this was that the set-up was much improved – with a Minister of Defence and a Defence Committee of the Cabinet on which the Chiefs of Staff sat. He also saw himself as an important cog in the machine, in the quick and efficient issue of business. Nonetheless, crucial to the functioning of the whole system was the personality of Churchill. Many of those in the 1940–5 government had fought in the last war. This was one reason why they pushed back against the generals. 'We knew what phrases like "If necessary, switch the attack to . . ." meant in terms of bloodshed and miles of mud struggled through.'[45] So while Attlee may have seemed to be too firmly in Churchill's camp on some occasions, this was a conscious calculation, rather than sycophancy. As Morrison later reflected, 'I imagine Attlee had decided that Churchill should have his head and so he rarely disagreed with him.' His custom was to nod in approval while Churchill was still making his proposal, or to say 'Yes, yes!'[46] Part of this was to bring the business of the Cabinet to issue. 'We used to let him get it off his chest and not interrupt,' Attlee later reasoned, 'indeed, it was extremely difficult to interrupt him because not only had he no intention of stopping, but frequently had no intention of listening. His monologues sometimes went on for very long periods indeed.'[47]

On those occasions when he deputised for the prime minister, Attlee thought it futile to attempt to mimic him. He joked to Tom that he preferred to achieve a 'mean between dignity of language and dullness'.[48] Inevitably, this caused some to disparage him by comparison. The journalist Trevor Evans recalled a discussion he had about Attlee one evening on a train leaving Liverpool Street for Cambridge in the autumn of 1940. The lights had been turned out as air-raid sirens screamed across London. In the carriage were Harold Laski, the Labour Party chairman, and Jack Corrigan, a stock market financier and Conservative donor who was known for his hatred of the left. Straining in the dark to read a copy of a newspaper on which Attlee's faced appeared, Corrigan asked Laski why the

Labour Party had chosen that 'colourless nonentity' as leader when there were so many better men available. Evans, an admirer of Attlee, objected to the slur – he may have been colourless but he was not a nonentity – and turned to Laski for support. Laski offered a less than spirited defence. He suggested the main reason why Attlee was in charge was that he was so unlike Ramsay MacDonald.[49]

As chairman of the Labour Party, Laski set out to improve Attlee's profile in the press by organising regular luncheons for him with journalists from the *Manchester Guardian* and *The Times* in the summer of 1940. Almost immediately, however, Attlee brought a halt to these meetings as an unnecessary distraction from his real duties. The truth was that he found it difficult to talk intimately and without restraint to almost everyone except his very closest friends and colleagues. 'They can accept or reject me for what I am – not for what ballyhoo and publicity can make of me.'[50]

For the moment, Laski held his tongue and kept his criticism of Attlee's leadership relatively muted. Month by month, however, he began to increase the pressure on the Labour members of the government. On 19 July, he used *Tribune* to pose twelve questions for Attlee and Greenwood, asking them what they intended to get out of the coalition. They must always remember that they were waging a war on two fronts. They were fighting fascism but also the profit-making system that made fascist tyranny possible.[51] This was a mere prelude to the almost incessant griping from Laski that Attlee was to face over the course of the next five years.

In the meantime, Attlee was focusing solely on the war effort. The situation was critical. On 22 June 1940, Paul Reynaud, the French prime minister, agreed to an armistice with Germany, leaving Britain completely isolated. On 3 July, at Mers-el-Kébir, on the coast of what was then French Algeria, the Royal Navy bombarded the French fleet to prevent it falling into German hands. Worse still, Mussolini now went into an alliance with Hitler.

The storm clouds that had gathered over Britain in the previous few months now looked set to burst. In July, the Luftwaffe began bombing British ships in the English Channel, as the opening salvo in the Battle of Britain. On 6 July, Attlee broadcast to the nation about the coming 'zero hour'. He expressed deep regret at the attack on the French fleet by the Royal Navy. But, if the 'one remaining citadel of liberty in Europe is to be preserved, its defenders must not shrink from taking those actions which the situation demands.' The country had to prepare for a 'war of nerves' with Hitler. France had fallen not only because of the force of arms but the 'destruction of unity of confidence and morale of a people, resulting in the paralysis of will power at a critical time'. Nation after nation had been deceived because they had refused to face the facts about the nature of the beast they were confronting. Short-sighted and selfish ideas of self-preservation had 'prevented the essential unity of spirit of the civilized nations of Europe from being translated into action'. That was why, he told the millions listening, 'we face the barbarians alone.'[52]

The fact that Hitler was now allied with Mussolini raised concerns in Moscow that the Germans might drive eastwards and break the non-aggression pact. Attlee remained deeply suspicious of Stalin, partly because he suspected that the Soviets were responsible for an increase in communist activity in Britain at a moment of such grave danger to the country. Both he and Morrison closely monitored the Communist Party's newspaper, the *Daily Worker*, and considered shutting it down.[53] Yet Attlee's squeamishness about dealing directly with Moscow would have to be jettisoned. When he met Stalin's ambassador Ivan Maisky in the House of Commons in August 1940, he could not stop himself from berating the Russians for their bullying of Finland and the Baltic States. Maisky asked him if this meant he wanted to end Anglo-Soviet negotiations. Attlee was stumped and quickly backtracked. 'No, no! You've misunderstood me.'[54]

Courting the United States was more to his taste, and, indeed, his skill-set. Increased American involvement on the world stage was something that Attlee had long wished for. He followed Churchill in lavishing praise on Franklin Roosevelt, the US president, as he decided to run for an unprecedented third term in the November 1940 election. He thanked Roosevelt for the hope he had given Europe in ensuring that 'the cause of civilization will in the end prevail.'[55] This was not simply opportunistic. The Labour Party also admired Roosevelt as the architect of the 'New Deal', whose faith in economic planning, as well as his broader worldview, tallied with their own. When President Roosevelt successfully held on to his position, Attlee wrote to Laski expressing his delight at the outcome:

Is not the result in the USA magnificent? Quite apart from the fact that any change of personnel at the White House would have meant confusion and delay for months in the war effort, the retention of Roosevelt means we have there a man with real understanding of European problems, strategic and economic as well as perhaps above all ideological. Only a man who sees the interrelationship between home and foreign policy can really give the required hand.

Laski, who was well connected with the American left, made sure the letter was passed on to Roosevelt.[56]

For Anglophile voices in the US, the broad composition of the British Cabinet was helpful in making the case that Britain should be given considerable financial support in its war efforts. Nazi propaganda had been suggesting that 'the British Government is made up of a bunch of aristocrats who are forcing the Cockneys to fight so that England can go on loafing,' wrote the London correspondent of the *New York Times*. The presence of Bevin, Morrison, Greenwood, A. V. Alexander and Attlee proved that this was a lie.[57] Expressions of fellow-feeling were welcome of course but they were insufficient in their own. As the nights got longer, the German bombers came in ever growing numbers.

III

One night in late September 1940, J. J. Mallon, warden of Toynbee Hall – Attlee's old comrade from thirty years before, when they had both worked on a national campaign to improve factory conditions – made his way up to the highest roof in the building as dusk settled on a blacked-out city. Nothing prepared him for the sights and sounds he was about to behold. First came the ever louder hum of Luftwaffe aircraft, then their flares, designed to light the turret-lined landscape of one of the most densely populated areas in Britain, and finally the awful screech of their bombs, directed at targets ranging from munitions stations to the Port of London Authority. Anti-aircraft guns rattled incessantly as explosive and incendiary missiles 'came to earth and blasted buildings and lighted fires along the line of the docks: a line against which one could see in faint silhouette the figures of a thousand fire fighters tussling with the flames'.

How did anything in east London survive the evenings on which 'our world became one of flame and smoke and sparks', wondered Mallon. Toynbee Hall was 'ringed on these awful nights with what seemed to be an all-embracing and quickly climbing and ever-spreading conflagration'. The Germans showered 40,000 bombs on the 1,903 acres of Stepney. Thousands of its 34,000 buildings, from tenement houses to crumbling factories and Victorian-era poorhouses, were flattened and very few escaped unscathed.[58] On 29 October 1940, the first bombs hit Toynbee Hall directly, killing two people. Further attacks were to cause even more damage over the course of the winter and into the spring. Before long, the building was also being used as a refugee centre for nearly a thousand refugees, most of them Jewish, from across Eastern Europe.[59]

Attlee had spent the weekend with his family in the village of Bibury in the Cotswolds when the Blitz had begun in earnest on 7 September. He rushed back to London with his daughter Felicity and arrived back to Stanmore in northwest London in time to see a 'livid orange sky' form over the city. He went straight to his constituency the following morning, 'watching while the digging went on among the rubble and talking to a pathetic queue of people waiting for the news of their next of kin'.[60] While it was some consolation that one of the first bombs had hit the old headquarters of the Mosleyites, the scene was one of desolation.[61]

By the end of the weekend, 1,211 civilians across Britain were dead. By June the next year, that number had risen to 43,000.[62] When Attlee spoke at the London Fire Brigade Headquarters during the attacks, he told them that the battle they were fighting might one day be regarded as one of the most important of the war.[63] As he reported to Tom, things were 'pretty hairy' in Whitehall too, as the bombs rained down on central London in late September 1940, the same month that Mallon had watched the bombers fly in across the docks. He had been in his office in Downing Street when a bomb landed 200 yards away, breaking some of the windows. In these conditions, it was decided to move the Cabinet out of the firing line. Attlee spent the first week of October at Chequers, with Violet and the rest of the government ministers and their wives. It was his first visit to the prime minister's official residence and they slept in an Elizabethan four-poster bed.[64]

The Attlee children were moved out of Stanmore before the worst nights of bombing, as the dark winter nights set in, giving the Luftwaffe a longer window in which to strike. Janet, the eldest child, turned eighteen in 1941 and volunteered as an anti-aircraft artillery officer in the Auxiliary Territorial Service (ATS), putting aside her studies in psychology for the moment.

Felicity, who was training as a nursery school teacher, travelled back and forth from London to the country, with thousands of evacuated children. The youngest two, Martin and Alison, were sent to boarding school in Salisbury for the duration of the war.[65]

Attlee returned to Stepney after each major attack. He saw the damage done to Toynbee Hall in November 1940. 'We are losing a lot of beautiful things in London . . . [along] with a great deal of rubbish.' Yet he revelled in the wartime spirit and the humour of the locals.[66] In January 1941 he took a delegation of senior American politicians around the bombed-out areas of his Limehouse constituency. Among them was Harry Hopkins, President Roosevelt's speechwriter and confidant on diplomatic affairs. Attlee described him as 'a first class man' and was delighted to find out that, in addition to being an architect of Roosevelt's 'New Deal', he had also been a social worker in his early career. More interesting still was the friendship he struck up with Wendell Willkie, the defeated Republican presidential candidate in the recent election. Willkie was a moderate but also, crucially, an internationalist, who opposed the isolationist tendency within the Republican Party. Attlee found him to be 'a very genial Mid-westerner', and enjoyed introducing him to the members of the Limehouse Labour Party, who belied his conception of socialism as a self-indulgent pursuit of bourgeois elites, or wealthy Jews in the Upper West Side of New York.[67] Whether their origins were Jewish, Catholic, Protestant, Polish, Irish, or English, the East Enders were made of stern stuff.

From the family home in Stanmore, Violet had helped establish a refuge centre for those bombed-out in Limehouse. As the local Red Cross commandant for the area, she also gave lectures to volunteers on first aid. Every Tuesday evening she could be found in Harrow at a rest centre for bombed-out persons, while most other nights she drove a mobile canteen to reach those without access to food. At one point, a bomb fell in a field outside the back of the home and she was the first out in the search party. She made sure the pressmen knew that she had been meaning to decorate the house for years, but when the bombs began to fall she thought it best postponed.[68] Violet played her part as the average citizen in extraordinary circumstances. Just like everybody else, she would cycle down to the local shop and queue with her ration cards.[69] There was no question of her using her husband's status to claim special treatment.

For some relief, Attlee and Violet went to see a play by Emlyn Williams, set against the backdrop of the air raids. 'I suppose in no other country would an audience stand the reproduction of bombing etc. in a play without getting the wind up.' The moral of the story, 'that one must serve others' was, he thought, very apposite for the day.[70] On a visit to Pontypool in Wales a few weeks later, he was deeply moved by how, in times of strife and shortage, people from different social classes worked so closely together.[71] These were simple emotions, but they were strongly felt by Labour's wartime leader.

IV

By early 1941, with the immediate threat of invasion receding, it was safe to ask a different question: how strong was Labour's influence within the government? In a series of articles for the *Washington Post*, this was something that Harold Laski attempted to answer for an American audience, whose interest had been pricked by Willkie's visit and the Blitz broadcasts of other American Anglophiles in London.[72] Laski argued that much of Labour's influence was 'screened from public view', something which was particularly true of the Lord Privy Seal. Labour ministers had a full share in all the central decisions of the War Cabinet, and in this, Attlee's voice was most important. It was an open secret, for example, that he had played an important role in securing the imminent publication of Britain's war aims – and in shaping them. Of the individual ministers, Attlee appeared least in public view but was 'quite definitely the most influential'. This was high praise indeed, coming from Laski. 'Shy, undramatic, and without a trace of egotism,' the Labour leader preferred to work behind the scenes. He was slow to make up his mind, but once he did, he had a persistence that carried great weight in the governmental machine. His fault, Laski suggested, was 'undue diffidence', which made him silent where speech was called for. But anyone who had seen him in action would 'yield no primacy to any minister but Mr Churchill himself for the value of the counsel he has brought to the war effort'. It was characteristic of Attlee that 'neither bad news can perturb him nor good give him undue confidence.' While his assessment was favourable, Laski did sound a warning that the Labour ministers still faced a battle to make their voices heard.[73]

The Blitz had raised Attlee's profile and improved his reputation. In February, he was described by the *Washington Post* as 'cautious Clem',

Britain's second in command, who could pass for the principal of a high school. He had always steered a cautious course between the left-wingers, like Stafford Cripps, and the right-wingers, like Ernest Bevin, but he was the unifying force in his party. Daring innovations in the strategy of the war would never come from him, but on issues on which he had insight, he was always prepared to 'stick to his guns'. This kind of man had a strong appeal to the British people, 'inclined to distrust too much brilliance and who like to chuckle over the idea of a socialist deputy acting as a brake on Tory Churchill's daring'.[74]

While generic praise about his character and reliability was not unwelcome, Attlee believed that the government was slacking in two respects. The first was to make a clear statement about what it hoped to achieve in victory. What were the goals for which British citizens were being asked to make such sacrifice? This came under the umbrella of 'reconstruction'. As early as July 1940, Attlee had let it be known to colleagues – through his parliamentary private secretary, Arthur Jenkins – that he was unhappy about the failure of the government to articulate a clear set of war aims. This created the impression that the Germans were fighting a revolutionary war for definite objectives. Britain was fighting a conservative war, for the status quo, and had thus far failed to put forward anything positive for the future. It was time to talk about a new world order, at home and abroad.[75] The second issue of concern was the resistance of some elements in the Establishment to a full shift towards socialist-style economic 'planning' (at least for the duration of the war). Only a month after joining the coalition, he urged the dismissal of Sir Horace Wilson, the Permanent Secretary at the Treasury, on the grounds that he was resisting decisions reached by the coalition on planning. Indeed, he believed that resistance to reforming the state was 'not only wilful but instinctive and habitual in the ranks of higher Civil Servants'.[76]

By early 1941, Attlee was satisfied that some progress was finally being made on the home front. In the first instance, this was manifested in a change in the intellectual atmosphere. He told Tom that there was 'a lot of movement of thought on reconstruction in all kinds of circles'.[77] This fed into the conviction – shared by Bevin and Morrison – that it was counterproductive to try to extract symbolic victories from the government. The transformation of the wartime economy would be the prelude to more comprehensive and revolutionary changes in the whole governance of the country, to take place after victory.[78] He shared Victor Gollancz's conviction that socialist methods were the only way Britain could win the war. He also noted growing influence of the ideas of John Maynard Keynes. To his surprise he now received memoranda from a number of grandees from the city of London and the banking world that he regarded as 'remarkably advanced'.[79]

In economic terms, then, the effects of the war seemed to herald a revolution. This was to be welcomed and ushered in. And yet, for all of this, Attlee did retain a conservatism that was almost unconscious. He never saw socialism as something to be fought for on the basis of class or culture. This was demonstrated when Rab Butler, the Conservative Minister of Education, went to see him about the future of the public school system. He was pleased to report that Butler was both reasonable and 'impressionable'. Attlee felt that this was an area in which Labour might make some quiet, steady progress without causing ructions in the coalition. That said, Attlee, ever the sentimentalist about Haileybury, expressed the view that 'like most of our institutions', the public schools 'should not be killed but adapted'.[80]

At this point, evidence of progress on reconstruction was sufficient for Attlee to feel confident enough to take the fight directly to his critics on the far left. He went to speak to the Oxford Labour Party Club at the end of January 1941 and had a good time answering the pseudo-radicals among its ranks.[81] In February, speaking at Tonypandy, the radical Welsh mining town, he condemned the 'gratuitous asses' of the Communist Party who were the unconscious tools of Hitler.[82] There was, Attlee was quite clear, no Fifth Column in Britain.[83] But the critics still had to be answered. In February 1941, James Chuter Ede, a trade union MP whom Attlee had brought in as a parliamentary secretary at the Ministry of Education, warned that there were tensions emerging in the party. A small minority was trying to create the impression that the leaders were isolated from the rank and file, as MacDonald had been. This would have to be monitored closely.[84]

In early March, as the Luftwaffe ratcheted up their campaign over the last few weeks of winter, Attlee told Tom that he was practically living underground, in a bomb shelter on Great George Street. When he finished going through his official papers, he read. He was impressed by *Forever Freedom*, a recently published anthology edited by his onetime colleague on the Labour front bench, Josiah Wedgwood, alongside the American progressive historian Allan Nevins.[85] It was a collection of poetry and prose celebrating the shared Anglo-American heritage of liberal democratic values, which included Roosevelt's recent speeches. Wedgwood was an old friend of Attlee and was offered a peerage by Churchill for his efforts to build the Anglo-American alliance.[86] These ideas were being tested as never before.

At the end of March 1941, Attlee was finally able to give the country some good news. They were now emerging from the long nights of winter, which had given the German bombers more time in the comparative safety of the dark. As all of Europe collapsed around it, Britain had stood firm through the first phase of the peril.[87]

V

Two things happened in the spring and early summer of 1941 that were to change the course of the war, though their effects would not be felt immediately. The first came in March 1941 when the US Congress approved the Lend-Lease Act, proposed by the president at the end of 1940. In addition to huge loans (over $30 billion loaned to the British by the end of the war), this authorised Roosevelt to lease or lend equipment to any country 'whose defense the President deems vital to the defense of the United States'. This gave the Allies (including the Russians and Chinese) a number of crucial material advantages in the supply of military hardware: munitions, transports, tanks and aeroplanes. The next was Hitler's decision to invade the Soviet Union in June 1941. Operation Barbarossa began with great success as the Nazis conquered huge swathes of territory. But it also provided the opportunity Churchill had wanted – to create an alliance with Stalin, and open up another front in the east to bleed the Nazis. It was Attlee who announced, two days after the invasion began, that Britain would assist the USSR's war effort. Stafford Cripps signed an Anglo-Soviet alliance on behalf of Britain in Moscow on 12 July, though the question of whether it should send its own men into that fight – rather than just material support – was to become a source of bitter controversy within the government over the next few months.

Britain still faced a grave threat, but the momentary reprieve after the Blitz meant that focus swung around again to domestic politics. Into the summer, under pressure from his party, Attlee began to push Churchill for a restatement of war aims, and to adopt a greater emphasis on reconstruction. As the worst of the Blitz had passed, Laski thought it time to end his ceasefire on the Labour leadership. 'Don't keep us waiting, Clem', was the title of an article he penned in *Tribune* on 9 May. 'Mr. Attlee has got to make up his mind about the future of our domestic policy. He must know that if you want to keep up the spirit of the people you must give it . . . hope and exhilaration.'[88]

In August 1941, Churchill and Roosevelt met in a secret summit in Newfoundland. It was from there that they issued the Atlantic Charter: a joint statement of their aims for the war (even though America had not yet officially entered it). Back in London, Attlee understood the significance of the moment, and acted swiftly. He saw it as another opportunity to entrench, on a grander scale, the spirit of change he had detected in Britain. Churchill's primary goal was to secure more material support from the Americans, particularly for the Battle of the Atlantic. The trade-off for this had been the emphasis on shared goals for the post-war world. In the Atlantic Charter, Roosevelt pushed Churchill further than he wanted, with provisions on national self-determination (with its obvious implications for the empire) and social welfare (reflecting Roosevelt's domestic priorities). As acting prime minister in Churchill's continued absence, Attlee took the opportunity to craft the document even more in Labour's image. He hastily summoned his Labour colleagues and they took the decisive step of shouldering responsibility for a redraft, which was cabled back to Churchill and Roosevelt following a midnight meeting of the Cabinet called by Attlee.[89]

Thus Labour were credited with the insertion of 'Freedom from Want' in the fifth aim of the Charter: that 'they shall bring about the fullest collaboration between all nations in the economic field with the object of securing, for all, improved labour standards, economic adjustment and social security.'[90] It was an example of Attlee's quick thinking. Churchill saw the trick, but he was hamstrung by two facts that prevented him from raising objections: his overriding desire to bring Roosevelt into the war; and the fact that Roosevelt's language on reconstruction, and on imperialism, was more in tune with that of the Labour Party. If he wanted one, he would have to accept the other.

As Churchill made his way back across the Atlantic, it fell to Attlee to announce the provisions that had been agreed. Despite his deft manoeuvre in Cabinet, he could not quite convey the achievement in a public session of Parliament. 'I had to take the place of the PM last week,' but it was 'no easy thing to follow such an artist', he confessed to Tom. He 'eschewed embroidery' and 'stuck to a plain statement'. It was no use 'trying to stretch the bow of Ulysses'.[91] 'Attlee spoke instead of Winston,' recorded the Conservative MP Cuthbert Morley Headlam in his diary. 'He read out a statement which told us nothing more than we already knew and he read it badly . . . bad voice, bad delivery.'[92]

This was a missed opportunity. Likewise, government surveys of public opinion suggested that Attlee's broadcast on the Roosevelt–Churchill meeting, in which he read out the provisions of the Atlantic Charter, was met with some disappointment. This was due to two factors. The first was 'the dashing of raised hopes' – based on wild rumours – of military rescue by the US, or an immediate armistice. The second was 'the vague wording of the declaration, which hid from many people that this was the Government's long-awaited statement of peace aims'. The most common reaction in Mass Observation Surveys was one of 'distinct anti-climax'. Embarrassingly, it was found that it was more popular among the 'middle class than artisan and working class people'. Among the latter, typical remarks were 'They do love talking don't they?', or 'too much yap'.[93] It was only when the prime minister returned that the Atlantic Charter was given 'the punch and clarity which Mr Attlee's broadcast lacked'.[94]

Attlee, however, proved more adept at selling the Charter to other members of the Allied family, particularly within the empire. Privately, Churchill thought that 'sovereign rights' for many colonies in the Far East, for example, could be postponed even after the war. The Colonial Office had no intention of letting go of Gibraltar, Malta, Cyprus, Aden or Gambia, Borneo, Malaya, Hong Kong, Bermuda, Fiji, the Falkland Islands and British Honduras. Those in charge of war propaganda were instructed not to make too much of the Charter.[95] In this respect, it was important that Attlee, unlike Churchill, was free from the taint of imperialism. This meant that he had an important role to play in addressing those not only in the Dominions (Canada, Australia, New Zealand and South Africa) but also in other portions of the empire (in West Africa, for example), who were to become increasingly important to the war effort, but who remained suspicious about British intentions after the war. Thus, he could reassure a group of West African students in London that the Roosevelt–Churchill principles – as expressed in the Atlantic Charter – applied to all races. He promised British support for self-government around the world, as part of the goals of the war. The Labour Party had always been conscious of the 'wrongs done by the white races to races with darker skins'. Its presence in the government – and Attlee's own record on these questions – helped ensure that an older conception of colonialism was making way for 'more just and nobler ideas'.[96]

Such messages played out well in America too, where Roosevelt's Atlanticism was checked by his suspicion of Churchill's proclivity for traditional imperialism. Indeed, it was also felt that Labour's presence in the coalition was something that should be stressed to the workers in Germany who had previously supported the Social Democrats. Here was a version of patriotic social democracy that was free from the brutality of Hitler's 'national socialism'. Attlee received reports about the effects of Labour Party propaganda in Germany. It was reported that the Nazis were particularly sensitive to this and were engaging in counter-propaganda through the summer of 1941.[97]

That Britain's American ally was the architect of the 'New Deal' made the coalition much easier to stomach for Labour. As the scaffolding of the Anglo-American alliance was put in place by Churchill and Roosevelt over the course of the summer, Attlee immersed himself in American history.[98] This was in preparation for his visit in October 1941. Just before he left, Churchill gave an impromptu speech at a private dinner in the House of Commons in honour of Attlee, praising him effusively.[99] It was in contrast to a meeting of the Parliamentary Labour Party just a few days before at which Attlee clashed with Emanuel Shinwell, a figure of growing importance on the left of the party, who complained that the Labour ministers had not taken the opportunity to bring the mines under public ownership. 'Anyone who would serve in a Wartime Government for fun would go to hell for pleasure,' remarked an exasperated Chuter Ede after the meeting.[100]

Flying to New York for the International Labour Conference, Attlee found the city 'unexpectedly beautiful' from the air. In a speech at Columbia University in Manhattan, he reported that the shortage of labour and manpower in Britain had been one of the severest difficulties the country had faced in the early months of the war. As America also entered a period of mobilisation for a likely war, Attlee returned to one of his favourite themes – the need for socialist-style planning for patriotic ends.[101] He toured a large aircraft factory in New Jersey as well as the Navy Yard in Philadelphia. He was impressed by the scale of American heavy industry, and the natural advantages on which it could draw such as large, sheltered harbours, which contrasted to the smaller docks on Tyneside and Clydeside.[102]

Given the crucial role of the American alliance, Attlee was very careful not to say anything that would upset Roosevelt. He sidestepped questions about the ongoing miners' strike in the US, despite attempts by the American Federation of Labor to get him to declare his support.[103] Attlee was 'as spry as ever', reported the *Manchester Guardian*.[104] Privately, in fact, he felt that American trade unionism 'seemed to me to suffer from a lack of the idealist spirit that adherence to the Socialist creed brings with it'. As for the leader of the miners, a temperamental Welshman called John Lewis, he felt, quoting Kipling, that there was 'too much ego in his cosmos'.[105]

More broadly, in his speech in New York, Attlee expanded further upon the provisions of the Atlantic Charter which referred to social welfare and post-war economic problems. Prosperity and stability could not be achieved by 'a return to an anarchic free trade competition'. These would require 'international agreements made not on the basis of scarcity and restriction but with the endeavour to promote the full production necessary to satisfy human wants and to ensure that such production is obtainable by all those who require it at prices which will give such a return to the producers as will enable them to maintain labour standards and conditions comparable with those enjoyed by workers in other fields of activity'. One weakness of the League of Nations was the failure to build an organisation that ensured cooperation in the economic sphere. 'If order is to replace anarchy and if cut throat competition is to be avoided the question of the wide divergences of the standard of life and the cost of living in different countries must be faced,' he warned. Price controls would be necessary and a fair distribution of resources must be ensured. 'Undoubtedly,' he concluded, 'the evils from which we are suffering today are to a large extent due to the economic conditions of the last two decades which by destroying the security of millions made them ready . . . to listen to the promises of gangster dictators.'[106]

Once again, however, when thrust into the limelight, Attlee was not an inspiring sight. The American press were rather bemused by the reticence, almost rudeness, of Britain's second-ranked politician – having grown used to the grandiloquence of Churchill. The British Foreign Office tried and failed to get Attlee to do more to project himself. They had arranged for Marquis Childs, a prominent American journalist and Labour sympathiser, to have an informal discussion with him. Childs visited him in an elaborately decorated hotel suite in New York, where Attlee sat in a chair, shifting uncomfortably. On the table beside him was a large basket full of fruit covered in cellophane. Attlee, remarked Childs, with his monosyllabic answers and guardedness, gave the impression that he was also under cellophane, being suffocated and short of air. 'Are you sure this isn't an interview?' asked Attlee, after a few minutes' probing. 'I'm afraid it is an interview,' said Childs, at which point Attlee got up and left.[107]

From New York, he took the train south to Washington, DC, which he described as a 'very fine city', though 'infested' with motor cars. He had a 'jolly' trip up the Potomac River on the president's yacht, alongside Lord Halifax, now British ambassador. The riverbank was wooden brown with scarlet maple trees and Roosevelt was 'excellent company'.[108] It was at this meeting that Roosevelt pulled an atlas from the shelf, pointed at Algiers in North Africa, and said, 'That's where I want to have American troops.' Attlee was impressed by the president and felt his mind 'took a broad sweep of world strategy'.[109] In reporting back directly to the prime minister, he informed Churchill that he was able to further explain the British strategy in the Middle East, and respond to 'specific points of criticism about it'.[110]

Eventually, Attlee let his guard down with the American press, in a way that offered an insight into his deep admiration for Churchill. He spoke of the prime minister's 'extreme sensitiveness to suffering'. Attlee remembered some years before how Churchill's eyes filled with tears when he talked of the sufferings of the Jews in Germany, and, more recently, his genuine pity for London's poor on a tour of homes damaged by the Blitz. This was a side of Churchill's character that was not always appreciated, he ventured. Another was his intense understanding and awareness of history. He saw all events 'as taking their place in the procession of the past as seen by the historian of the future'. Things such as the gallantry of the Greeks against the Nazis, the heroism of British people in the Blitz, or the 'moral break down of the French were always seen in perspective'.[111]

At the same time, his view of the American political scene was favourable. There was a reactionary group that detested Roosevelt but supporters of the New Deal had 'the right ideas'.[112] As soon as he returned home – via

Ottawa, where he met with the Canadian government – Attlee asked his civil servants for more information on general issues of reconstruction and Roosevelt's economic policy.[113] The Anglo-American connections on the left, between Labour and 'New Deal' Democrats, flowered under the umbrella of the Atlantic Charter. While their importance was sometimes underestimated by Attlee's critics on the left, they showed their worth in other ways. The following summer, when a strike by Durham miners was threatened, Attlee prevailed upon John Winant, the American ambassador in London, to make a personal appeal to them. Winant, another New Deal Democrat, had toured depressed areas in the 1930s at Labour's invitation. He was well respected by the union men. 'You who suffered so deeply in the long Depression years know we must move on a great social offensive if we are to win the war completely,' he told them, standing alongside Attlee in the Durham miners' union hall. 'We must solemnly resolve that in our future order we will not tolerate the economic evils which breed poverty and war.'[114]

While the groundwork had been carefully put in place over the previous years, the official entry of the US into the war in December 1941 was the turning point that the British government had dreamed of. Japanese forces had attacked not only the American fleet at Pearl Harbor but also British ships in Malaya and Hong Kong. They were expected to attempt a land invasion of the British territory of Burma at any point. On 8 December, Britain and the US declared war on Japan, and on 11 December, Germany and Italy declared war on America. These were trying times for the government. The House was 'fractious', Attlee confided to Churchill on 20 December, there was 'an undercurrent of opposition to the government generally'. The war in the east was going badly. The opening of the Russian front and British operations in North Africa were 'bright spots in a rather gloomy landscape'.[115] An uncertain future remained but at least Britain was no longer to face it alone.

13

The Hunting of the Snark

The crew was complete: it included a Boots –
    A maker of Bonnets and Hoods –
A Barrister, brought to arrange their disputes –
    And a Broker, to value their goods.

A Billiard-marker, whose skill was immense,
    Might perhaps have won more than his share –
But a Banker, engaged at enormous expense,
    Had the whole of their cash in his care.

There was also a Beaver, that paced on the deck,
    Or would sit making lace in the bow:
And had often (the Bellman said) saved them from wreck,
    Though none of the sailors knew how.

There was one who was famed for the number of things
    He forgot when he entered the ship:
His umbrella, his watch, all his jewels and rings,
    And the clothes he had bought for the trip.

He had forty-two boxes, all carefully packed,
    With his name painted clearly on each:
But, since he omitted to mention the fact,
    They were all left behind on the beach.

The loss of his clothes hardly mattered, because
    He had seven coats on when he came,
With three pair of boots – but the worst of it was,
    He had wholly forgotten his name.

He would answer to 'Hi!' or to any loud cry,
    Such as 'Fry me!' or 'Fritter my wig!'
To 'What-you-may-call-um!' or 'What-was-his-name!'
    But especially 'Thing-um-a-jig!'

While, for those who preferred a more forcible word,
    He had different names from these:
His intimate friends called him 'Candle-ends,'
    And his enemies 'Toasted-cheese.'

'His form is ungainly – his intellect small –'
    (So the Bellman would often remark)
'But his courage is perfect! And that, after all,
    Is the thing that one needs with a Snark.'

Lewis Carroll,
The Hunting of the Snark (An Agony in 8 Fits), 1876.

I *War Cabinet Room, Whitehall, February 1942*

Two days after Christmas Day in 1941, Attlee described to Tom how he was 'busy carrying the baby', with the prime minister in America again.[1] This meant chairing the War Cabinet in his absence. Attlee did this with great skill and no pomp. Whereas his parliamentary performances left some cold, even his critics regarded him as an extremely effective chair. As one colleague put it: 'When Winston presides at Cabinet we feel we are in the presence of history, the monologue goes on for hours and we come away as from a feast. When Attlee takes the chair it is a business meeting and we get home for dinner.' The journalist and MP Frank Owen, who had known Attlee for many years, suggested that he took a 'perverse pleasure' in making himself dull against the 'gold and purple of his captain'.[2]

The Labour leader had given the business of government much thought over the years. But his effectiveness as a chairman came from a natural intuition, which allowed him to gauge the collective mood of his colleagues. What some mistook for diffidence, or a lack of independent thought, was actually the process by which he read the room and made sure a firm decision was arrived at. As he summed up those decisions, he left no one in doubt of their responsibility once the meeting was over. He would sit on the edge of his chair, looking down but listening intently, and often drawing shapes or doodles on a piece of paper. His parliamentary private secretary later suggested that one could tell the general mood of the Cabinet by Attlee's designs. Floral patterns meant boredom, sharp edges meant conflict, but a combination of the two in a neat circle implied harmony.[3]

In one of Attlee's more apocalyptic doodles from the War Cabinet of 1942, he had drawn a miniature map of Britain, only to superimpose Russian cities and the great battles of the Eastern Front onto it: Kiev, Moscow, Odessa and Stalingrad.[4] This dystopian vision emerged from one of the major strategic debates in the War Cabinet, which was to have a spill-over effect into Labour politics – putting in doubt Churchill's leadership of the nation, as well as Attlee's leadership of the Labour Party.

The Anglo-Soviet Alliance negotiated by Stafford Cripps in July 1941 prevented both parties from engaging in hostile acts against each other, freed up trade and shipping between the two, and spoke in vague terms about further cooperation. As Hitler launched a huge assault into Soviet territory, in what was to become the bloodiest theatre of the war, the question facing the War Cabinet was to what extent Britain was willing to join the fight. It was agreed to send Stalin weapons and munitions so that he might halt Hitler's advance. But Churchill was reluctant to send him men or to open a 'second front' against the Nazis with British troops on the European mainland. One reason for this was Churchill's suspicion of Stalin. One of Stalin's demands was for Russia's 1941 frontiers – when it had used the non-aggression pact with the Nazis to execute a land grab in Finland, the Baltic states and a large portion of Poland – to be formally recognised. Another, more pertinent, objection was that it did not fit Churchill's grand strategic vision for the war.

The British Army was far smaller than its German and Russia counterparts and therefore could not spread itself too widely. For the moment,

Churchill preferred to focus on the Mediterranean – concentrating efforts in North Africa and the 'soft underbelly' of Europe, securing vital British interests, tying down German divisions and trying to get a stranglehold on Hitler's ally, Mussolini. Attlee concurred that this was 'entirely in line with the strategic lessons of our past' from the First World War. He also believed that Churchill was right to wait for the bombing campaign in Germany to take its full effect before landing a major land force in northern Europe (particularly as the Americans were not yet ready to commit their own army in this way).[5] The question was when that strategy would be brought into its next phase, in the form of a second front in Europe.

Having been sent to Moscow as ambassador, Stafford Cripps had been out of Attlee's way for over a year. Now Cripps arrived back in Britain as the man who had brought Stalin into the war on Britain's side. Not only was he to become a popular figure with the public; he would also be a key player in the defining debates in the War Cabinet over the following year. Cripps was an advocate for offering more support – including troops – to the Red Army, whose heroism was becoming the stuff of legend in the British press. This ground up against the considerable weight of Churchill's strategy. In fact, within a few months, as the war effort stalled, some began to float Cripps's name as a potential replacement for Churchill, who was said to have lost his Midas touch. It was Cripps's refrain that the prime minister's mind was 'ingenious rather than scientific', and if the war were to be won it needed greater planning, rather than the charismatic leadership of one man.[6]

It was an indication of the stakes involved that even some of Churchill's most important Conservative colleagues began to question his strategy. Anthony Eden, echoing the views of some of the senior military commanders, supported the idea of a 'second front' being opened up; so too did Beaverbrook, who was impatient for Britain to take the initiative in the fight against the Germans. In this Beaverbrook enjoyed the temporary support of Ernest Bevin, with whom he had struck up an unlikely friendship.

In the midst of these wrangles, Attlee was in a minority of those behind Churchill. In a lighter moment amidst the ongoing ructions, he reminded Churchill of Lewis Carroll's famous 1876 poem, *The Hunting of the Snark*, with its eerie echoes of the situation they found themselves in.[7] This was a farcical fantasy tale about a group of men who set out to sea in search of a mystical animal called the Snark. All the while, however, they fear that the Snark they are searching for might well turn out to be a Boojum, a dangerous beast one would be ill advised to get too close to.

The Snark, of course, was Stalin, and the various members of the British government were the crew of ten who set out on the dangerous mission to find it. In Carroll's poem, the crew of the ship were led by a Bellman (whom one can presume was Churchill). It may even be that Attlee saw himself as Boots, the only character without an illustration in the published version of the story (and therefore somewhat overshadowed by the others). There was no mistaking the resemblance that Carroll's characters bore to other colleagues in the War Cabinet. For Beaverbrook, always impatient and intriguing, there was a 'Beaver, that paced on the deck', or would 'sit making lace in the bow'. The Beaver was valued by the Bellman but the rest of the crew could not see his worth. There was a Barrister, 'brought to arrange their disputes', which no doubt made Attlee think of Cripps, recently returned from Moscow and enjoying his role as a saviour. There was also a Butcher, who previously only killed beavers, but becomes an unlikely ally of this Beaver in their hunt for the Snark. Without pushing the parallels too far, this seemed to echo Bevin's unlikely friendship with Beaverbrook.

Churchill was amused by Attlee's literary reference. He knew the poem well and quoted back a line from it immediately. Eventually, he would 'walk paw in paw' with a Russian bear, but not just yet.[8] Both men were mindful of the sinister twist that came at the end of Carroll's poem. 'For the Snark was a Boojum, you see.'

II

By the first week of February 1942, Churchill was reported to be 'very grunty' about the demands of his ministers that he should send Stalin men as well as weapons. Attlee backed the prime minister against Eden and Beaverbrook. Sir John Sinclair was regarded as floating between the sides but both Bevin and Morrison were said to be coming round to the idea that troops should be sent.[9] Pressure on Attlee also came from the left of the Labour Party, who condemned a ban on the *Daily Worker*, which Morrison had decided to implement. Bevan complained that this might upset the Russians and that, in any case, it was highly illiberal. At a meeting of the parliamentary party, Attlee replied that 'old-fashioned defenders of that view in other countries had lost their liberty.'[10]

With both sides' opinions entrenched, the matter became a question of personalities. Attlee threatened to resign if Russia was awarded control over the Baltic states. Having condemned the British Communist Party so strongly for turning a blind eye to Stalin's treatment of Finland, suddenly acquiescing to these demands was something that he could not stomach.[11] He also objected to a proposal, made by Beaverbrook, to make Cripps the leader of the House of Commons (thereby undermining Attlee's authority). Beaverbrook saw Cripps as an ally on the 'second front' debate and, for all of his doctrinaire socialism, as a superior talent to the Labour men already in government. Attlee was equally furious at a suggestion that Arthur Greenwood – who had not been one of the more active ministers – should be pushed out of government to make room for Cripps. As Dalton warned, the elevation of Cripps, who had after all been expelled from the Labour Party, would cause a 'riot' among its members.[12]

Churchill was not averse to bringing in Cripps, though he suspected that he had designs on his own position. But he was not prepared to see Attlee resign and therefore bring down the whole coalition. For the moment Beaverbrook had been outflanked. Unlike Attlee, he had newspapers but no party behind him. He complained that 'Attlee's resignation [when] in the wrong' was 'more important than mine when in the right'. He also thought, justifiably, that Attlee's resistance to Cripps coming in was less to do with protecting Greenwood and more to do with the fact that Attlee could not trust him. 'Having excommunicated Cripps in the peace, he is not going to make him assistant pope in the war,' a furious Beaverbrook complained on 17 February 1942.

On 18 February, Beaverbrook was summoned to Churchill's annex in the war rooms under the Treasury building. After telling Churchill that he should consider retiring, Beaverbrook launched a ferocious attack on Attlee, and urged his sacking from government on the grounds that he was not up to the job. His contribution towards fighting the war had been nothing, save bringing in his party; and he was only interested in seeking honours and a place for his followers. 'We want tougher fellows at a time like this. Fighting men.' Churchill told him that he would bring in Cripps but it would be Beaverbrook who would lose his place as a minister in the rebalancing. As they moved into the cabinet room itself, Beaverbrook saw that Attlee, Eden, Brendan Bracken and James Stuart were in conversation, and had obviously been given advanced notice of the decision. He repeated his objections, shouting at Attlee and shaking with rage. 'What have I done to you to treat me this way?' asked Attlee. 'Why should I not talk frankly?' Beaverbrook replied, 'You criticize me and I make no objection.' 'I never did,' replied Attlee, quietly. He was clearly wounded. Beaverbrook walked out in a fury, shouting down the corridor. The truth was that, unwilling to vent his frustration directly at Churchill, he had again displaced it onto Attlee.[13]

In the ensuing reshuffle, Cripps was made Lord Privy Seal, replacing Attlee. So that he was not seen to be demoted or replaced, Attlee was made deputy prime minister and Secretary of State for the Dominions. This was a deliberate elevation of the Labour Party's standing in the coalition. With Cripps and Attlee acting as general coordinators, Arthur Greenwood was dispensed with. Having previously threatened to resign if Greenwood was replaced by Cripps, Attlee accepted Churchill's counter-offer. In truth, both Attlee and Dalton had become frustrated by Greenwood's 'slowness and inertia', and now he paid the price.[14] Nonetheless, he had received no indication that the axe was about to fall, particularly after Attlee had been so vociferous about protecting him just a few days before.

This was uncharacteristically ruthless and Attlee's role in the reshuffle was criticised by Anthony Eden. Eden had advised Churchill that drastic changes were needed in order to win the war. But the game of musical chairs between Beaverbrook, Cripps, Greenwood and Attlee had barely changed anything. 'I'm afraid it shows Attlee to be what I've always thought him, a little man,' wrote Oliver Harvey, Eden's closest ally. The mood within the government was sour. Churchill was facing mounting criticism too, with concerns about his health and his 'lamentable' performance in the House of Commons. Eden was upset not to be consulted more and felt that Attlee and Churchill were shoring themselves up against criticism by attempting to 'fix it up' between themselves. If Attlee was being 'very petty' about Cripps, Churchill was more than happy to see Cripps's wings clipped too.[15]

Of the new seven-man War Cabinet, five members – Churchill, Attlee, Eden, Bevin and Anderson – had sat in it before. They were joined by Cripps, nominally as an independent, and the Conservative Oliver Lyttelton. With Beaverbrook dropped, both Attlee and Labour suddenly appeared to be in a much stronger position. Beaverbrook had overplayed his hand, even going so far as to suggest a coup in which he, Eden and Bevin would form a three-man government. That Churchill bore no grudge against Beaverbrook was something that Attlee could not quite comprehend. Bevin rationalised it in a memorable phrase: 'Well, you see it's like this: it's as if the old man had married an 'ore. He knows what she is, but he loves her.'[16]

'I had a pretty damned week fixing up the changes in Government,' confessed Attlee on 25 February. Removing Greenwood had been painful. These questions were 'the very devil owing to inevitable conflicts of loyalty'.[17] Nonetheless, it was agreed that the changes immediately restored some order. Even Oliver Harvey, an Attlee critic, was pleased to report that the Cabinet was already more businesslike, with the prime minister 'no longer getting away with it undisputed'.[18] As for Attlee, Churchill now ordered him to work with Eden on army reform, in view of recent failures, and this led to a thawing of relations between the two.[19]

With Cripps in government, and Bevan showing no signs of relenting in his hounding of the leader, it was not long before the pressure on Attlee from his party began to mount again. In March 1942, he warned the National Executive that Labour ministers should not attempt to bring in socialist measures by stealth, under the cover of war.[20] Laski wrote to Bevin at the start of the month trying to encourage him to push for the leadership 'I say again that unless you become the first man instead of the second the confidence of the masses in the movement will rapidly die . . . It is time for a fighting leader and you are the right person for that place.'[21]

Attlee wrote to his old friend Jack Lawson in the same week, confessing, '[we] are going through pretty difficult times which seem to me to test very much the spirits of our people. With most of them, like yourself, the dross disappears and the gold remains.'[22] Lawson himself declared that he would support the coalition until the war was won, and do so without quibble, but the loyalists' voices were drowned out by those of the rebels. Attlee's growing exasperation was visible in another difficult meeting of the parliamentary party on 17 March. Bevan 'indulged in a long windy diatribe' against the government, arguing that the people's morale would collapse if Britain did not offer Russia effective support.[23] While Churchill believed Bevan to be a 'squalid nuisance', Attlee reassured Lord Moran, Churchill's doctor, that he was no more than an irritant and could not destabilise the government from the outside.[24]

Cripps was another matter entirely, and Attlee watched him closely. Nonetheless, when the issue of India reared its head again, the two old friends found some common ground. From the early 1930s, Cripps had hosted most of the senior Indian leaders of the Congress Party, from Gandhi to Nehru, at his home in Gloucestershire. He had always included Attlee in these discussions. Even as they had fallen out over the Unity Campaign, the two had maintained civil relations when it came to Indian affairs.[25]

Indian nationalists had reacted furiously in 1939 when the viceroy, Lord Linlithgow, had unilaterally declared that India was at war with Germany, without consulting the Indian leaders. Thus followed a campaign of civil disobedience which threatened to destroy Britain's war efforts, given its reliance on India for manpower. A major effort was needed to soothe relations. For Cripps and Attlee, the best way to do so was to offer meaningful concessions towards Indian self-government. As the new Dominions secretary, Attlee now chaired the Cabinet's India committee. The other members were Leo Amery (the Secretary of State for India), John Simon (the Lord Chancellor), John Anderson (Lord President of the Council), and P. J. Grigg (Secretary of State for War). Attlee called the committee 'pretty good' but talked of their 'constant struggle' with Churchill, who had retained the right to resume his chairmanship of it at any point.[26]

Even before Cripps returned to government, Attlee had suggested to Amery, on 7 February, that it was necessary to establish 'a mission to try to bring the political leaders together'. He was not impressed by the performance of Lord Linlithgow as viceroy. A difference emerged between those – chiefly Attlee, supported by Cripps – who believed that the war effort would be better served, in strategic and ideological terms, by the full co-option of nascent democracies such as India, on the basis of an appeal to their demands for self-determination; and those, such as Churchill and Linlithgow, who believed that this was not the time for political experiments or attempts to reconstitute the basis of empire. Amery was caught somewhere in between. Within India, there was renewed support for the formation of an interim national government. The concern in London, however, was how the Indian Congress would react to this, and whether it would seize the moment to push a nationalist agenda in a way that undermined the war effort.

However complicated Anglo-Indian relations became, Attlee felt that they boiled down to a fundamental question of trust. He believed the Indian people, including the nationalists, could be trusted with more devolved powers. Lord Linlithgow had warned the War Cabinet that feelings of solidarity for Britain in India were scant and could not be relied upon. For Attlee, this might well have been 'an extract from an anti-imperialist propaganda speech. If it were true it would form the greatest possible condemnation of our rule in India and would amply justify the action of every extremist.' In a memorandum for his colleagues, Attlee stated that it was 'quite impossible to accept and act upon the crude imperialism of the Viceroy, not only because I think it is wrong, but because I think it is fatally short-sighted and suicidal'. There was not simply the question of India's status; there was also the need to maintain the support of China, the Soviet Union and the United States, none of whom were comfortable with British imperial pretensions. It was on these grounds that he repeated his call for someone to be sent out with broad powers to seek a negotiated settlement in India.[27]

In mid-February, following the reshuffle, Attlee saw an opportunity to push ahead with this. With Churchill consumed by the Russian question, Attlee convened seven meetings of the India committee in eleven days, drawing up drafts for a declaration to be made by the prime minister. On 2 March, Amery complained to Churchill about 'being rushed by Cripps and Attlee'. A draft declaration was drawn up which offered India the promise of independence within the Commonwealth. This was blocked by the Cabinet on 10 March. However, a compromise was reached by which Cripps would be sent to India in order to seek a negotiated agreement between local political leaders as a prelude to a new declaration. This new plan could appeal to both factions within the government, albeit for different reasons. For the status quo group, there was no guarantee that Cripps would succeed. For those who wanted independence, there was clear logic in seeking consensus within India rather than simply decreeing the new arrangement from London.[28]

In the event, Cripps's mission failed. The leading Indian nationalists had adopted a more uncompromising tone than he had expected. While it might have been seen as an asset once, the perception that Cripps was too close to the Congress Party damaged his credibility with the Muslim League. Once again the question of Indian independence was put aside until the end of the war. Attlee had acted assertively with Churchill over India and had got his way over the mission. Faced with growing unrest in India in the aftermath, he now took full responsibility and personally gave the controversial order for Gandhi to be arrested on 9 August and interned until the end of the war.

With the Indian question in incubation, arguments over the policy towards Russia spilled out of the War Cabinet and into the press. Once again, it was Attlee who did more than any other senior member of the government to shield Churchill from the growing criticism. It fell to the deputy prime minister to defend the war strategy in a stormy parliamentary debate on 19 May, in which he refused to say when a new front against Germany would be opened. Attlee became the lightning rod for discontent. John McGovern, the Independent Labour Party MP, accused him of being afraid to 'express a thought of initiative'. There was a 'paralysis' in government because of the unchallenged dominance of Churchill, the 'great white chief'. Oliver Stanley also suggested that Churchill's control over strategy be lessened, urging that more decisions should be moved to a new committee of combined general staff.

Tellingly, the Beaverbrook press now threw their weight behind this campaign for a new front to be opened immediately. An unlikely coalition between left- and right-wing critics of Churchill's strategy was formed. Around Parliament, posters were pasted to walls announcing a mass meeting in Trafalgar Square on 24 May, at which Labour's Emanuel Shinwell was to lead calls for an immediate invasion of Europe. Attlee's cautious response, in which he had called for 'sober' optimism about the future, was compared to a 'schoolboy essay' by some disgruntled MPs leaving the chamber.[29]

Worse was to come at the end of June with the news of the fall of Tobruk in Libya and the capture of most of the garrison there, which had consisted largely of troops from India and South Africa. This was to become the symbol of the flailing command of General Auchinleck in the Alamein campaign, and he was dismissed shortly afterwards. Attlee made a statement in the House on the defeat, reading a series of telegrams from Auchinleck in which he described the progress of the Eighth Army, before disaster befell Tobruk on 20 June.[30] His tone was neutral and he stuck to the details. This infuriated some of those in the House who felt that he had failed to do justice to the gravity of the situation. Yet it was typical of Attlee that he refused to scapegoat Auchinleck, despite widespread criticism of his command.

With the exception of India, on the big strategic questions of the war – from the bombing of Germany to the emphasis on a campaign in North Africa – Attlee agreed with the prime minister. Yet he did not do so uncritically or meekly. While he stoically bore the brunt of the public criticism over the defeats in North Africa, he expressed serious disquiet about the current military strategy. On 10 July he sent Churchill a 24-page memorandum, in which he vented his own frustrations. 'I have, I admit, put the matter somewhat controversially and bluntly to stimulate inquiry,' he wrote. Significantly, while he said that he had shown it to three colleagues in the Cabinet (most likely Bevin, Morrison and Dalton), he did not want to put it before a meeting of the full Cabinet, so as not to encourage mischief.

The bulk of his criticism was directed at the military high command, who he felt lacked dynamism and flexibility. They had been bested by superior German strategists. Defeat in Libya had taken place 'due mainly to the shock tactics of a comparatively small number of highly trained troops operating effective armoured vehicles under brilliant and enterprising leadership'. This had not been a problem of supply or organisation. Britain had almost equal numbers of tanks and men engaged in the fight. 'We seemed to be unable to concentrate effectively at the vital point,' and 'failed to seize the initiative.' Attlee felt that the British had invested too much in artillery, whereas the Germans benefited much more from aerial support – particularly from the use of dive-bombers but also from supply and transport aircraft. Likewise, defeats in the Far East by the Japanese – who had run the British out of Malaya, Burma and Singapore (the crucial naval base, which fell on 15 February) – had followed a similar pattern. The enemy had been more effective in its use of aerial support 'in conjunction' with its navy, while 'on land they sacrificed everything to mobility'. Lightly armed troops, equipped with the minimum of weapons and transports, operated in jungles and overcame obstacles thought impassable by British military experts. The enemy 'were highly trained guerrillas: ours were heavily armed troops, encumbered with all the impediments of European warfare.'

Returning to North Africa, Attlee asked whether any lessons had been learned from the embarrassment. 'Are we not still bound by conceptions of fighting before the present war which express themselves in the establishments and equipment which we maintain?' he asked. The features of the German successes had been 'speed, hitting power, mobility, maintenance of forces in the field and effective command'. British commanders, however, still thought in terms of numbers of troops and divisions. The latter was a 'huge mass of men (40,000) cumbrous to a degree, provided with an immense litter of ancillary services which almost swallow up the fighting men'. The staff structure grew out of the attritional methods of the last war. One of the biggest mistakes was the failure to incorporate airpower to its maximum effect. Attlee's emphasis on the importance of fast manoeuvre, as opposed to replicating the traditional European model of huge land armies, reflected – once again – the influence of the strategist Basil Liddell Hart.[31]

In many ways, Attlee thought it unfair that Auchinleck had taken so much of the blame. He was dealing with a military culture that was 'establishment-bound' and beholden to an 'over elaborate' chain of command. 'Have we the right type of man in command?' Attlee asked. His distaste for generals who did not fight with their troops – an old bugbear from the First World War – shone through again. Rommel had reverted to an earlier method of command in his leadership of Germany's feted Afrika Korps. Like Cromwell and Marlborough, he was actually with the troops at the front. With the vastly increased speed of modern war and with the facilities for communication, this was, in the eyes of Attlee, a basic requirement.[32]

Before long, Britain would have to open up a second front. While he stopped short of outright defiance, he now challenged Churchill's core strategy more forthrightly than he had done before. Was it really true that the war there could be 'won by the big bombers'? Attlee knew the importance that Churchill placed on this, so he chose his words carefully. 'I believe in the bombing of Germany but as a method of winning the war it must be viewed as only part of the necessary action,' he said. Ground troops would have to play a significant part in any scenario. Yet he feared that the military command still thought in terms of approaching in lines, even though linear warfare had been largely stultified by the aeroplane and the tank. 'If an attack on the Continent is to be a Blitz and not a siege, have we not got to sweat down our swollen divisions and concentrate on necessities to attain mobility?'[33]

Recognising the importance of Attlee to his government, Churchill responded carefully, though he could not hide some irritation. Many of the points that Attlee raised were now 'commonplaces', he suggested, and others were already under discussion. On a number of questions, such as Attlee's insistence that more should be made of commandos, Churchill was in agreement with him, against 'the orthodox school'. The biggest problem, however was that the Germans had been preparing for a war for at least ten years, while the British Army 'was grudged and stinted in every way'. In this, there was a subtle dig at Attlee. Compulsory military service, Churchill pointed out, was introduced only a few months before the outbreak of the war. 'It must also be remembered that Britain for the last twenty years was hagridden by pacifism and haunted by the craven fear of being great.' The prime minister welcomed Attlee's suggestions on ground transport and urged him to use the new Cabinet committee over which he presided to help 'comb the tail in order to sharpen the teeth'.

On the bombing campaign, specifically, Churchill was not prepared to cede to Attlee's growing doubts about its utility. 'Continuous reflection leaves me with the conclusion that, upon the whole, our best chance of winning the war is with the Big Bombers.' It would be several years before British and American land forces would be capable of beating the Germans on even terms in the open field. Britain was stretched already. 'The more we can bomb Germany, the better for all concerned.' To withdraw Bomber Command 'from the cities, factories, and seaports of Germany to be a mere handmaid of the Army, bombing airfields and railway junctions behind the hostile front, would be a great relief to the enemy'.[34] When the matter came before the full Cabinet and Churchill talked about 'wiping out German villages (three for one) by air attack', Attlee asked whether it was useful to 'enter into competition in frightfulness' with the Germans.[35] This was a refinement of his previous position in 1940 – in which he had been unambiguous in his support of RAF retaliation against German targets.

Despite the difficulties in North Africa, and even after the entry of the Americans into the war, Churchill continued, into the autumn, to resist pressure to open up a second front. After airing his concerns privately, Attlee continued to back him when the question reached Cabinet.[36] For this reason alone, Churchill was wise enough not to dismiss the views of his key ally in the War Cabinet. In fact, on 12 June, the very day he sent his memorandum to Churchill, Attlee publicly criticised 'attempts to separate the Prime Minister from Parliament, to try to make out that when something goes wrong the Prime Minister alone accepts responsibility'. Just a few weeks later he suggested that the idea of a 'second front' had become 'something of a catchphrase'. The government was constantly working on this, and there was no need for them to be constantly 'prodded' from the outside. This was typical of Attlee's approach – notably independent and challenging in private conversations; while remaining loyal to the prime minister in every comment he made in public.[37] Of course, it went largely unnoticed outside the government.

In August 1942, Churchill flew out to Egypt to visit the army and then went to Moscow with General Alanbrooke. Attlee covered for him in Parliament and Cabinet once more. This was no easy feat and caused him more stress, given the difficulties in the war effort. His mood was not helped by a serious injury to his daughter Alison, who suffered a fractured skull and torn artery after falling off her bicycle.[38] Simultaneously, Harold Laski griped about 'Whitehall's weary titans' and complained about 'the paralysis that seems, alas, to have settled down like a blight on the leaders of the Labour Party in the Cabinet'. National unity would not last long if Labour continued to be treated like a junior partner, he warned.[39] On the domestic front, the main complaint was the inadequacy of the government's provisions for old-age pensions. Yet the Labour left also repeated calls for a second front to be opened. Laski returned from a visit to Moscow with stories of the nobility of the Russians left to face the Nazi war machine alone.[40]

On Churchill's return from Moscow, the prime minister called for Attlee and Eden immediately. They met in the cabinet room, where they were joined by James Stuart and Brendan Bracken. Churchill talked for an hour and a half about the frank conversations he had had with Stalin. He was encouraged by the Russian determination to keep fighting, despite the heavy loses they had suffered. Stalin, noted Churchill, was the greatest 'realist' he had ever met. By and large, their discussions had been comradely. 'As for all this talk about Russian drinking – there is nothing in it. I drank twice as much as they,' he boasted.[41] The two had struck up a rapport, which did more than anything to bring about a thaw in Anglo-Soviet relations. This was enough for the deputy prime minister to relax his suspicion of Russia once more. In August 1942, Attlee was the government's representative at an event organised by the Russian Embassy in Earls Court to celebrate one year of the alliance. His old sparring partner, the Russian ambassador Ivan Maisky, also invited him and Violet to a private lunch at the Embassy.[42]

As a long-time champion of the League of Nations, it was particularly pleasing to Attlee that, out of the meetings between Roosevelt, Stalin and Churchill over the course of 1942, the idea of the creation of a 'United Nations' organisation began to emerge. While Churchill turned his mind back to military strategy, Attlee happily assumed the role of champion of the nascent United Nations. He called this 'collective defence', to distinguish it from the failures of 'collective security' in the 1930s. The idea was 'sneered at' before 1939 by people like Neville Chamberlain, he later noted, but it was now, he was delighted to say, 'orthodox doctrine'.[43] He visited Ottawa in September, trying to drum up support.[44]

For the moment, Churchill continued to prioritise winning the Battle of the Atlantic – making sure that the crucial convoys, of food and munitions, between America and Britain were unmolested by German U-boats – and gaining a decisive upper hand in North Africa, where the Allied armies had turned the tide. On 23 October 1942, General Montgomery began a massive assault on the Germans at El Alamein in western Egypt. This was followed shortly after by US General Dwight Eisenhower's invasion of western North Africa, to form the second point in a pincer movement against the Germans.

Attlee demonstrated an appreciation of the problems of fighting with allies that was missed by others; or, at least, an appreciation of Churchill's genius for this, which he felt that the chiefs of the general staff were apt to underestimate. Montgomery and Eisenhower were to clash at later points in the war but Attlee praised them both for different reasons. Eisenhower, he felt, was the better team player, with a greater understanding of the sensitivities of coalition warfare. Of all the British commanders, however, Attlee was most attracted to Montgomery's personality. He was 'great fun, with a delightful sense of humour, of a rather boyish kind'. There was a 'democratic' quality to him; and he was free of prejudice. Just as Cromwell preferred the 'plain russet-coated captain' so Montgomery had 'no use for the old school tie or the old boy network'. As a veteran of the last war, the Labour leader particularly enjoyed reading his battle orders. His description of these as 'a curious mixture of romanticism, tough

Officer-Commanding talk, and prep school slang' – with phrases such as 'we shall hit them for six' – might have been used to describe Attlee's own way of speaking. Above all, Montgomery was not guilty of the kind of behaviour that Attlee had been so disparaging of in the First World War – the way in which, 'whenever the mud and blood were flying, the generals would be well behind the lines'. Montgomery had led the Eighth Army into battle and transformed the whole mood of the campaign in North Africa.

Attlee was not one to begrudge a hero; nor, however, was he one to elevate a hero to the status of an untouchable. Thus he qualified his praise of Montgomery by pointing out that he had benefited from much more effective support and improved coordination on the civilian front than his predecessors had experienced. He got everything he asked for from London. Attlee also emphasised the importance of General Alexander as commander-in-chief of Middle East Command, after Auchinleck. Contrary to the perception that Alexander was some sort of 'glorified quartermaster' back in Cairo, Attlee believed he was, in fact, a 'great soldier-statesman' under whose guidance and control Montgomery flourished. The distinction between a great soldier and a great 'soldier-statesman' was one to which Attlee was to return.[45]

III

Much of Attlee's work went under the radar. In September 1942, a poll was released which asked the British public who they would most like to see as prime minister if Churchill left office. Eden had a rating of 39 per cent, Cripps was on 24 per cent, Bevin 4 per cent and Attlee commanded just 2 per cent. This was remarkably low for a man who was to become prime minister in less than three years. Yet it also meant that Attlee was free from the sense of destiny which periodically infected pretenders to the throne. Cripps, having risen to 24 per cent because of his work in crafting the Anglo-Soviet alliance, was a case in point. He returned from his failed mission to India – where he had been unable to broker an agreement between the various Indian parties – in a sour mood and full of complaints about the war strategy. Churchill remained suspicious of Cripps and refused to budge in the face of his renewed demands to open up a second front. On 1 October, Attlee and Eden witnessed a showdown between the two at Downing Street, during which Cripps signalled his intention to resign.[46]

Attlee urged Cripps to reconsider, as Operation Torch, the British invasion of French North Africa (Morocco and Algeria) was about to begin. It was to no avail.[47] With the War Cabinet so divided, Churchill feared for his own position. When Eden went to see Churchill at Downing Street as Torch began, he found Attlee already there. 'If Torch fails,' he told them both, 'then I am done for and must go and hand it over to one of you.'[48]

At Churchill's weakest point, both Eden and Oliver Harvey reiterated their complaint that Attlee and Bevin were too blind in their faith in the prime minister. 'What blimps!' complained Harvey. This was a reference to David Low's cartoons of the fictional Colonel Blimp, which mocked his good-hearted but simplistic jingoism.[49] Others may have agreed. Not long after Harvey's admonishment, Attlee was sent a special invitation to the Odeon in Leicester Square to see the premiere of the comedy film, *The Life and Death of Colonel Blimp.*[50]

In early October 1942, at the most sensitive time in the war effort, and just before the Labour Party conference, Cripps's *Tribune* came out in open rebellion against Labour's leader. 'Mr Attlee is a gentleman. He has none of the blustering and tough qualities which normally contribute so much to the success of an ambitious politician. Mr Attlee is loyal to the point of self-effacement – but Mr Attlee is no longer the spokesman of the movement which carried him from obscurity to the second position in the land.' This was 'not a personal issue', insisted a joint statement by the board of the *Tribune*. In truth, the attack was highly personal, and had a bitterness that previous criticisms had not. Attlee was a gentleman, but only in his relations with capitalists. Yes, he was loyal, but only to Churchill. He had failed to stand up to him on India, and also failed to secure any improvement on the terms of the pensions bill, which was due to come before the Commons. The MacDonald allegation was also raised. Here was the 'passing of yet another Socialist into the limbo of collaboration'.[51] Adding to the mischief, Beaverbrook – whose hostility to Attlee knew no bounds – decided to use his own newspapers to suggest that Herbert Morrison, no doubt a talented minister, would be an excellent replacement for Attlee as Labour leader.[52]

Attlee and Bevin joined forces in a joint letter to the National Executive on 19 October 1942, which made pointed reference to 'the benefits that had accrued to the working classes as a direct result of the presence of Labour Members in the Cabinet'. Harold Laski thought such piecemeal benefits did not go far enough for a truly socialist party. They 'point to a long list of social reforms, the "guaranteed week", the increase in old age pensions, the virtual abolition of the means test, and so on', but they had 'acquiesced in a policy which refuses to their doctrines the status of fundamentals' and they accepted 'methods of social organization incompatible with the kind of society to which they are committed'.[53]

Along with Bevin, Attlee had already been pushing Churchill to take the home front more seriously – or, at least, to allow the Labour ministers a freer hand on post-war planning. Taking the initiative, he now wrote to Churchill urging the creation of a reconstruction committee. Mass Observation Surveys had shown that there was a considerable desire for legislation on pensions, employment, housing and healthcare. Attlee insisted that a greater degree of post-war planning had become a pressing need. This was not some sort of ideological game; it was a recognition of reality. The war had brought about full employment and a transformation in the role of the state in the economy and in social matters. How the wartime economy was to transition into a peacetime economy was a matter of grave importance. Attlee's letter to Churchill argued that the government must be as courageous in fighting for the peace as it had been so far in the war. The people of the country, especially the fighting men, would not forgive the government if it failed to make suitable plans.[54]

Notwithstanding his desire for more activity on this front, Attlee had no doubt that important work on 'reconstruction' was already being done within the government. Whereas some Labour partisans wanted to score public victories, he detected the origins of a new consensus, which was not exclusive to one party. He singled out the work of Sir John Anderson, chairman of the Lord President's committee, 'a great man and a very good friend'.[55] Nonetheless, it was becoming clear that such careful gradualism was unacceptable to many Labour MPs. At a meeting of the parliamentary party in November, Attlee was subjected to another 'bitter attack' from his backbenchers, one of whom suggested that he tell the prime minister 'to go to hell'. Attlee replied that, when it was appropriate, 'he did tell the P.M. where he should go'.[56]

Mercifully, for both Churchill and Attlee, who were at their lowest ebb, in the first week of November there was a breakthrough in western North Africa, which helped to release some pressure. On 11 November 1942, Armistice Day, the extent of Montgomery's victory over Rommel had become clear. The Germans had suffered heavy casualties and the threat of the Axis powers taking the Suez Canal or reaching the oil fields of Persia was averted. It was a boost of huge significance for symbolic as well as strategic reasons, after a difficult year in the war during which the whole premise of British strategy had come under attack, inside and outside government. As Attlee reflected, 'what [Montgomery] did was important, but tremendously important was that he did it at a critical time. We badly needed a victory.'[57] Almost simultaneously, it was revealed that Operation Torch had also been a success, with landings across Algeria and Morocco. The Allies now had firm control over most of North Africa, something which had been crucial to Churchill's whole strategic conception of the war.

By 1 December, all attention turned to the report by William Beveridge – an alumnus of Toynbee Hall and now a senior civil servant – on *Social Insurance and Allied Services*. Beveridge famously declared war on the five 'giant evils' of Want, Disease, Ignorance, Squalor and Idleness. For Beveridge, the arrival of state-driven economic planning and full employment provided a unique opportunity. If this could be sustained into the postwar era, it would allow both the state and its citizens to make sufficient contributions to maintain an expansive system of welfare and social insurance. If Britain could beat Hitler, it could beat unemployment and poverty, he argued. Rather than means testing the poor, Beveridge proposed that the benefits of this 'cradle to grave' system would be universal.[58]

Struck by the massive popularity of the report – trumpeted in numerous languages by the BBC – the government decided to have it translated into French and German and dropped across Nazi-occupied Europe, including the major German cities, as an explanation of Britain's war aims, alongside the RAF's bombing campaign. The established organs of Labour support rowed in strongly behind its provisions. Indeed, the Trades Union Congress (TUC) demanded an election if there was any attempt to shelve it until after the war.[59] Beveridge himself was given free rein of the pages of the *Observer* to argue that his proposals could indeed be adopted in peacetime, and his articles were reproduced in the *Daily Herald*.[60]

The enthusiastic reception of the Beveridge Report does suggest that something had been lacking in Attlee's cautious approach. The bold shock of idealism galvanised those who had argued that the war must be fought for a new order, at home and abroad. 'War is temporary,' Beveridge argued, 'while peace should be planned to endure.' Such was Beveridge's popularity that he even turned his hand to international affairs – arguing that the establishment of the United Nations would be the expansion of the same idealism on a global scale.[61] In seizing the initiative in this way, he entirely outstripped the leader of the Labour Party. Attlee was in danger of being left in Beveridge's slipstream.

In early 1943, with the author and his wife sitting in the gallery, the Beveridge Report was the subject of a three-day debate in Parliament. On the eve of the debate, Arthur Greenwood – who had appointed Beveridge as the minister formally responsible for reconstruction – was the first MP to endorse it officially. This put the government in an extremely difficult position. Labour MPs demanded that Beveridge's principles be adopted, without delay, as government policy. John Anderson was forced to plead for additional time to be allowed to examine its provisions, while Greenwood countered that a ministry of social security should be established immediately. The normally cautious *Daily Herald* editorial board suggested that the government had made its gravest error yet in not supporting the report outright. It had been 'plugged to the world' as an achievement of British democracy – even dropped on Nazi Germany – and now the government was dissembling and stalling.[62]

That the Labour leadership had lost the support of the *Daily Herald* over the Beveridge Report said much about its impact. Attlee, Bevin and Morrison did not want to risk a split in the government on this issue. But they were given a bloody nose by their own MPs. This time it was not just the usual malcontents but studiously loyal figures who had grown impatient with the lack of action on reconstruction. On 18 February, as an amendment from Greenwood, supported by the backbenchers, was defeated, ninety-seven Labour MPs rebelled. The government still had a more than comfortable majority but the Labour Party was dangerously divided.

The debate was 'not a good show', Attlee reported to Tom. Too many on the Labour benches 'tend to use their hearts to the exclusion of their heads . . . I fear our people cannot ever understand when they've won. In fact they really prefer a "glorious defeat" in the lobbies to a victory. However, no doubt it will all blow over.'[63] In truth, the government had been lacklustre in the debate. James Griffiths, a usually loyal Labour MP who was to become Attlee's Minister for National Insurance, had intended to support the government line but, after Anderson's uninspiring speech, he had switched sides and moved the amendment instead. Morrison, not for the first time in his career, bore the brunt of the criticism on Attlee's behalf. He spoke for an hour with his hair tousled, and papers all over the despatch box, but it was a giant performance – the type of which Attlee was rarely capable.[64] The government, he reassured the party, did not 'wish to double-cross' the people and had worked hard on the preparation of the report. They were merely asking for an opportunity to explore how it would be implemented without committing themselves to every detail.[65]

Attlee acknowledged that Morrison's contribution had been 'first class' in preventing an open rebellion.[66] Yet his own leadership was in serious danger again. This was one reason why Morrison was happy to accept centre stage. He was deliberately fulfilling the role of conciliator and unifier once perfected by Attlee.[67] Nonetheless even Morrison was taken aback at the scale of the rebellion. At a meeting at Number 11 with Attlee and other ministers, he remarked that Labour's parliamentary party was a 'suicide club' and would sooner have a glorious defeat than victory. When the MPs met the following evening in the Commons, Attlee made his own plea for unity, which, according to Chuter Ede, 'did not make much impression'.[68]

Party officials warned Attlee that the predominant feeling in the National Executive was that the leadership had been responsible for a 'series of blunders'.[69] In fact, the executive formed a subcommittee that delivered a rather unflattering report on his overall performance. 'Attlee must consider most seriously his own public appearances and utterances . . . he appears in public much too infrequently and does not arrange for proper publicity when he does appear.' He was encouraged to make more speeches and employ a publicity officer.[70] A few weeks later, he was forced to issue a statement to members defending the party's record in government, and reassuring them that they were already working on reconstruction.[71] Such was the discontent that old trade unionists warned that the Communist Party was attempting to recruit again on the factory floor, even in comparatively conservative towns like Southampton. The Labour leadership had better 'stir their sticks'.[72]

By May, when the government's Old Age Pensions Bill passed the House of Commons on its second reading, harmony had not yet been restored. Of the 110 Labour MPs who voted, forty-eight rebelled on the grounds that it did not go far enough. Again, Arthur Greenwood made the opening speech with a row of Labour rebels lined up behind him. Now some of them began, once again, to question the validity of the electoral detente with the Conservatives.[73] The National Executive Committee was forced to produce a pamphlet justifying the continuance of the coalition until the war was won. This received the endorsement of the TUC, but only after intensive lobbying by Bevin.[74] Again, Morrison took the lead in making the Labour leadership's case.[75]

Bevin did manage to regain some control over the *Daily Herald*, which stopped short of calling for an end to the truce. The truce was 'no more congenial to Labour than are Army boots to the average citizen soldier'. It was the 'battledress' of British democracy; 'ugly, ill-fitting and irksome'. Nonetheless, it had to be maintained so long as the war was being fought.[76] In truth, largely thanks to Morrison again, the Labour Party arguably did more to plan for the end of the electoral truce, by laying plans for the commencement of battle long before the Conservatives did. This was apparent when the question of redrawing constituency boundaries arose. Both the Liberals and the Conservatives were encouraging boundary changes but Morrison urged Labour to spoil these efforts by refusing to cooperate until after the war. Frankly, as he explained to Attlee, this was a question of narrow party political advantage.[77]

For his own part, the Labour leader was upset by the volume of discontent. He complained that too many in the party remained silent when achievements were made. He regarded this type of sullen behaviour as deeply counter-productive.[78] In a brilliant illustrative metaphor, Attlee decried the way in which some within the Labour movement, such as Bevan and Laski, were demanding a caesarean section, rather than a natural birth.[79] If they waited a little longer, the war would leave them with a healthy child, with a full life ahead of it.

IV

If the Second World War had ended differently, Operation Torch might have been viewed as Churchill's last throw of the dice. It was just as important to Attlee's political survival. It had begun on 8 November 1942, at the conclusion of the Alamein campaign. The idea behind it was to retake the whole of French North Africa from the Axis powers and therefore gain complete control of the Mediterranean. This would then provide a platform for an attack on Italy and a possible invasion of France, opening up two fronts as thoughts turned to a war on the European Continent. October, just before Torch began, had been the most difficult month of the war so far. By Christmas Eve, there were signs of progress as Churchill, Eden and Attlee assembled for dinner at Downing Street. The prime minister emphasised the centrality of Roosevelt in holding together the wartime coalition. Meanwhile, in Britain, whatever happened to Churchill, 'or all three of us', there would be enough 'resolute men to see the business through'.[80]

This was unusually self-effacing from the prime minister – a recognition of the loyalty that Attlee and Eden had shown him over the previous months. As the war began to turn in favour of the Allies in early 1943, Churchill's star rose again. On 20 January 1943, when Churchill and General Alexander were at Casablanca – in negotiations with Roosevelt and Eisenhower about the Allies' next move – it fell to Attlee to deliver the government's assessment of the state of the war. 'The year 1943 has opened auspiciously,' he told the House, but he urged severe caution and continued resolve.[81]

Not for the first time, Attlee's inability to convey drama took away from what otherwise was a moment of vindication for him, for his steadfast support of Churchill. 'He is so dull and puny,' complained Harold Nicolson. Despite the initial success of Operation Torch, everybody filed out of the chamber feeling deflated.[82] With Axis forces in Tunisia on the brink of surrender in May, Attlee also undercooked his statement describing events to a secret session of the House. 'I cannot convey to you the absurdity of that man,' Nicolson complained. It was difficult enough to make a defeat sound like a victory, but to make a victory sound like a defeat was a 'masterpiece in human ingenuity'.

It was certainly a critical moment in the war. The very next day, in fact, Rommel's Afrika Korps surrendered and 250,000 troops were taken prisoner by the combined Anglo-American forces. Having asserted control of North Africa, the British troops were able to start planning for the invasion of Sicily and then – it was hoped – Italy itself. This would give them their first foothold back on the Continent since the evacuation of France. Meanwhile, the Germans were retreating in Russia. And yet Attlee stood at the despatch box 'like a little snipe pecking at a wooden cage'.[83] In a more friendly assessment, Chuter Ede thought his performance was respectable. 'He spoke quietly, with no attempt at drama, but the story itself is too dramatic to be made humdrum.' At least the House had cheered.[84] There was no point in pretending he was something he was not. As Attlee confessed to Tom, not for the first time, 'it is not easy to sub for the P. M. It is obviously futile to put on Saul's armour.'[85]

Meanwhile, after so many doubts about his leadership, it would be difficult to overstate the personal stature of Churchill as the war began to shift in the Allies' favour in the spring of 1943. In March 1943, the historian Hugh Trevor Roper, then an officer in the Secret Intelligence Service, commented in his diary on the prime minister's immense personal standing. This foreshadowed Churchill's own self-serving narrative that he had been vindicated after years in the 'wilderness', marginalised by the National Government (when writing the history of his esteemed ancestor, the 1st Duke of Marlborough):

> Him surely the gods love, for he has lived fully and learnt widely; he has learnt the bitter taste of disappointment from long experience, and has discovered its antidote in life and literature; and the sweet, intoxicating taste of success he knows also. In his exile he wrote . . . a great work which Destiny itself seemed to have reserved particularly for him; and his exile lasted long enough for him to complete it; and then the prophet was summoned from the wilderness to save his country, and it seems, he has saved it; not, unlike Lloyd George, leaving rancour and recrimination in his wake, but healing divisions, obliterating enmities, forgetting injuries.[86]

Despite his own travails, Attlee was far from begrudging Churchill his moment. If he had lost the pulse of the Labour Party, momentarily, Attlee understood the significance of the epoch-defining moment he was living in. At Easter 1943, with the prime minister always more statesmanlike and benevolent when he was basking in glory, Attlee took Violet and the children into Number 10 for a personal visit. Winston was at his glowing best. He and Mrs Churchill gave the children a personal tour of the air-raid shelter and Violet and Clementine struck up a close friendship that lasted many years.

Such was the improvement in the national mood that Attlee even permitted a press photographer to visit the family home in Stanmore, who pictured Violet and the children with two goats they had adopted for the common allotment. He and Vi also went to see *Watch on the Rhine*, a play by the American writer Lillian Hellman, in which the hero was a German anti-Nazi. He found it deeply moving. Like many in the Labour movement – particularly Bevin and Dalton – Attlee had expressed anti-German sentiment on a number of occasions since the First World War. The play reminded him that Germans, too, had suffered at Hitler's hands; and many had been extremely brave in their opposition to him.[87] (Hellman was later blacklisted by Joseph McCarthy's House Un-American Activities Committee during the early years of the cold war.)

Attlee now had more time to reflect on the bigger questions that might arise from victory. Some of his idealism had been doused by the brutality of war. He mused – in a rather philosophical memorandum for the War Cabinet – that there was nothing inevitable about the triumph of democracy as a political system. Britain's own path to democracy had been difficult enough. 'We are apt to forget that behind our present comparative political calm lie the storms of the Stuart period and the violent political factiousness of the Whigs and the Tories of the early 18th century.' Tolerance, on which democracy was based, was 'a plant of very slow growth'. The latest war proved, more than anything, that the successful working of democracy did not require 'the framing of paper Constitutions and the acceptance of dogmas, but an attitude of mind on the part of the citizens'. With this he had in mind not only post-war Germany but also those portions of the British Empire, outside the Dominions, that were still searching for functioning forms of government. Attlee's own view was that the 'Westminster model' could only go so far. It had worked in Britain and the Dominions, after trial and error, but it would not work in other European states; and he was convinced that it was also not the right system for India.[88]

In the short term some order was restored at the Labour Party conference in June, as a large majority voted down a proposal to admit Communist Party members.[89] Morrison led the way in seeking to soothe the tensions created by debates over the Beveridge Report.[90] Attlee joked that the British 'never know when they are beaten, and British socialists never know when they have won.' More seriously, he believed that the British people would remember the patriotism of the Labour Party. They had proven themselves 'fit to govern'. Had Labour remained 'merely a body of critics who left others to do the work, the Party would not have gained the respect and confidence of the country which I know it has today.'[91] Cheered by the attitude of the party membership he criticised the parliamentary party for its failure to convey any appreciation for the 'very considerable instalments of party policy which have been obtained, while every criticism, however minor, is fully stressed.'[92]

Labour's big three emerged from the conference with a renewed determination to begin making some progress on reconstruction. On 26 June, they submitted a memorandum to the War Cabinet on the 'need for decisions'. Here was an urgency and purpose that had not been present before. Uncertainty about the state of the economy after the war could not be used to block serious planning on housing and employment for those who had served the country. Employers and workers would need to know where they stood. The government had refused to commit itself to the Beveridge Report without having considered other demands. The principle of avoiding piecemeal decisions was agreed, 'but the moral cannot possibly be to make no decisions at all.' Planning of reconstruction had to begin now. Decisions 'in principle' were not enough. Legislation took time to get right and the passage of measures through Parliament had to begin. Rather than waiting for everything to pan out after the war, it was 'wiser to accept the risks of acting upon our convictions and to bid for the advantages which normally accrue to the man or nation who faces the future with mind made up on fundamentals.'[93]

On one level, it is true that Attlee remained the meekest of Labour's big three. Morrison and Bevin both had a certain force of personality that was better at deflecting criticism, even though all three were usually in agreement on the party's strategy. Yet Attlee was also the most adept at handling the internal politics of the coalition government. Positioning was everything.[94] Before they circulated the paper he wrote a separate note to

Churchill asking whether the prime minister thought this an appropriate way of bringing the matter forward.[95] Churchill was willing to let it be discussed in the War Cabinet but insisted that the paper should not be shown to a wider audience.[96] The chancellor, Kingsley Wood, then pushed back against Labour's big three, suggesting that their views were inconsistent with the prime minister's recent broadcast on the post-war situation. They responded with another paper on 20 July, which denied that they were causing any disruption to the government.[97]

Military advances ran parallel with this renewed emphasis on reconstruction. In July 1943, as Sicily was invaded and taken by the Allies, Attlee took the opportunity to stress the advancement that socialist ideas had made in the previous three years. In the *Daily Herald*, he insisted that Labour had not laid aside its core convictions. But, in what was to become a growing theme in the post-Beveridge Report era, Attlee stressed that the ground was shifting beneath the government. 'When I look back 36 years to the days when I first entered our movement, the most striking thing is the contrast between current conceptions of society then and today.' He saw the acceptance, by people across society, of the views of Keir Hardie, John Bruce Glasier and other early leaders of British socialism. The same even applied to foreign policy where, once again, the public also supported post-war ideas for international brotherhood that had been derided when socialists first articulated them. Labour was right to propagate its views but this was not the time for the adoption of lazy slogans. The war had to be seen through to its end.[98] At Transport House, preparation got under way for another pamphlet outlining Labour's achievements in the coalition.[99]

After Attlee was able to restore some control at the party conference, the trade union machine also rolled in behind him, marshalled by Ernest Bevin, who had become by far his most important sponsor and protector. Attlee was selected by the National Executive Committee to attend the Trades Union Congress in Blackpool in September, in order to boost his standing. When he arrived early with his parliamentary private secretary, Arthur Jenkins, an equally shy former Welsh miner and the father of Roy Jenkins, Attlee took his seat on the panel. Rather than make small talk in the corridors, he remained in the same spot as the delegates slowly filled the hall.

This would not do. George Gibson, chief of the Mental Hospital and Institutional Workers' Union, whispered to Jenkins to take the leader out and bring him through the main entrance at the back of the hall once the room was full. A few minutes later, as Attlee poked his head into the back of the room, Gibson took the microphone and announced, 'Let's give a good reception to our political leader, the Deputy Prime Minister.' As he walked down the middle of the hall he got one of the loudest and most genuinely warm standing ovations of his political life. 'Was that really necessary?' Attlee whispered to Jenkins, 'That should be normal, not unusual,' Jenkins replied.[100] Attlee's defenders were finding their voice. At exactly the same time that Attlee was being lauded in Blackpool, James Chuter Ede dined with a number of backbenchers who suggested that Labour could not win with Attlee and the party needed someone more brilliant. Ede replied that the country 'distrusted brilliant men' and that the Liberals, in 1906, had won their greatest victory under Henry Campbell-Bannerman, 'a plain steadfast man'.[101]

Party issues could still flare up with no warning, on issues of personality as well as principle. At a party meeting on 3 November, Attlee and Greenwood joined forces against the rebels who had voted against the government over the Workmen's Compensation Bill – for the familiar reason that it was piecemeal and did not go far enough – and had 'vituperatively attacked' their colleagues on the government benches.[102]

At the end of the month, there was also a storm of indignation when Oswald Mosley, arrested under emergency powers at the start of the war, was released on compassionate grounds. The decision had been made by Herbert Morrison, the home secretary, with Churchill's support, but the Labour backbenchers were up in arms.[103] Bevin, quick to anger when it came to Morrison, was 'kicking' and threatening to bring the whole government down. Attlee telegrammed a bemused Churchill about the crisis when the prime minister was in the midst of tense negotiations with Roosevelt and Stalin in Tehran about the invasion of Europe.[104]

Overall, however, there were signs that the emphasis on reconstruction was beginning to bear fruit. In December, Attlee declared himself very pleased with the first draft of the Education Bill which was due before the house early the following year. It provided free secondary education up to the age of sixteen and also created the grammar school system. He believed it was a good example of the work that the coalition had done behind the scenes, and reflected great credit on Rab Butler and James Chuter Ede.[105] Consensus was no bad thing; where it existed, it was to be encouraged. But there was no mistaking the fact that bigger battles were brewing on the home front.

V

To portray Attlee as an inadequate 'yes man' to Churchill, as Beaverbrook had done at the beginning of 1942, was unfair and misleading. It fails to appreciate that Attlee had a broader sense of what was required of the country's senior politicians during war. He chose his battles carefully, but he had sided with Churchill at critical moments during late 1942, when the prime minister's position was at its weakest. As the handling of India demonstrated, Attlee could push back against his prime minister on issues of fundamental importance.

Ultimately, the fact was that Attlee viewed Churchill as the greatest war leader the country had ever had. By this he did not mean that he was the greatest military strategist; he was not in the same class as Cromwell. He also doubted that, if put in command of armies, he would have ever been as successful as his ancestor, Marlborough. But a war leader in the democratic age must be more than a warrior. He must be a beacon for a country's will to win. In this respect, Churchill's popularity made him superior to William Pitt, the 'pilot who weathered the storm' in the French Revolutionary and early Napoleonic Wars. In the First World War, Lloyd George had an instinct that the generals were doing something wrong but no military knowledge to tell them what was right. Churchill did not always overrule the generals; but he usually had enough grasp of the situation to be able to hold his own against them. Attlee was quite aware of the fact that the chiefs of the general staff were often infuriated by him. 'Some of the generals out in the field thought he was like Big Brother in Orwell's book,' he wrote, 'looking down on them from the wall the whole time.' What Churchill really did, in Attlee's mind, was keep everyone on their toes.[106]

This faith in Churchill's methods did not endear him to everyone. In September 1943, as Attlee chaired the Cabinet, Field Marshal Alanbrooke remarked in his diaries how different it was: 'In many ways more efficient and more to the point, but in others a Cabinet without a head.'[107] Attlee was aware of the low opinion that Alanbrooke, Chief of the Imperial General Staff, had of him. He was not embittered by it. He regarded Alanbrooke as one of three great soldier-statesmen to emerge in the war, along with the American generals, George Marshall and Douglas MacArthur.[108] Yet, when reading, in later years, Alanbrooke's diaries about the autumn of 1943,

Attlee remarked that the generals too often failed to see the bigger picture in the way that Churchill did.

In Attlee's view, the chiefs of staff were slow to grasp that this was a war of alliance in which Britain was, in many ways, the weakest of the big three powers fighting Hitler. Alanbrooke's diaries made much of the tensions in global strategy between the three main allies, as attention turned to the invasion of Europe from late 1943. As Chief of the Imperial General Staff, he wanted everything that could be spared from the building up of the invasion force in northern Europe to be used in Italy. He also wanted to make sure the Germans remained concerned about their vulnerability all along the south coast of France, Italy and the Aegean, so that they would be unable to reinforce either their troops along the English Channel, or those holding off the Russians on the Eastern Front. The American high command, meanwhile, looked eastwards at this point. They were continually pressing for a campaign in Burma with a view to reopening the land supply route to Chiang Kai-shek in China, in order to bolster him against the Japanese.[109] Churchill, however, wanted something else, which Alanbrooke saw as reckless, adventurist and a distraction – an invasion of Sumatra by Mountbatten, to take it back from the Japanese. Alanbrooke was furious that in early 1944 both Eden and Attlee backed him on this scheme.[110]

As the Americans put more and more men, money and hardware into action over the course of 1943, Attlee reasoned it was inevitable that they would exercise more control over the conduct of the war. Attlee understood that Churchill was anxious for a campaign where Britain could dictate the action, and excel without American support – a classic piece of power projection, or politico-military theatre. It was for this reason that he put forward the Sumatra scheme. For Alanbrooke, the military strategist, this was of course irresponsible and 'absurd', as it was a distraction from the main theatre. But Attlee felt that Churchill's broader political perspective on the winning of the war – and the maintenance of British stature – needed to be understood. The fact that Churchill could not afford to take so narrow a military view was something that was not always considered by the generals.[111] Thus, for Churchill, the British role in leading the invasion of Italy in September 1943 was important as a means to prove to the Americans that Britain was an effective fighting force. They 'have high respect for us now', he explained, to Attlee and Eden.[112]

By late 1943, with the Germans having suffered huge losses at Stalingrad and Kursk, the tide began to turn on the Eastern Front. In December, now that Eisenhower appointed as the Supreme Allied Commander of the Allied Expeditionary Force, planning for Operation Overlord, the invasion of northern Europe, began. On this question, too, Attlee felt that Alanbrooke's political radar was poorly tuned. Alanbrooke was not overly impressed by Eisenhower's capabilities. He found him a 'charming personality and good co-ordinator' but no real commander, in the mould of Montgomery, over whom he was placed in charge. Again, Attlee felt that the choice of Eisenhower could only be understood in its broader political context. Over the course of 1942, the Americans had been persuaded, with some reluctance, to divert resources from the Far East to North Africa. Among the Allied commanders in the field, therefore, there had been a need for great diplomacy and care in handling relationships. It was because of Eisenhower's skills on this front that he came to the fore. As attentions turned to Europe again in late 1943, the fact that the Americans were bearing so much of the military burden meant that an American commander had to be chosen. The choice of Eisenhower also helped counter the efforts of Admiral Ernest King, as the head of the US Navy, to make Japan and the Pacific the main focus of American military efforts.[113] Attlee felt that the egotism of Alanbrooke and Montgomery was sometimes in danger of jeopardising the hard work that Churchill had put into bringing the Americans on board. It was easy for them to caricature the deputy prime minister as a lapdog to the prime minister in such events. Yet Attlee's faith in Churchill was not to prove so blind as some had suggested.

Ironically, but entirely rationally, it was when Churchill was in the ascendant from late 1943 that Attlee thought it more appropriate to challenge him. Just as the sycophants gathered around the feet of the prime minister again, so his deputy decided that this was causing an imbalance. After one lengthy Churchill speech before the War Cabinet, with everyone listening expressionlessly to his opinion, the prime minister declared, 'Well, gentlemen, I think we can all agree on this course.' Before anyone had a chance to nod assent, Attlee responded, 'Well, you know, P.M., a monologue by you does not necessarily spell agreement.'[114]

By the end of 1943, in fact, opposition to Churchill on key issues came from an unlikely combination of Attlee and Eden. Having overcome suspicions of each other earlier in the war, they became effective partners in countering some of Churchill's proposals. In December 1943, for example, Attlee wrote to Eden raising serious concerns about Churchill's desire to jettison General de Gaulle, leader of the Free French, with whom the British had been working closely. It was necessary to do more to maintain this relationship, as they were 'the best elements in France', objected the deputy prime minister.[115] While Eden's memoirs were sphinx-like in avoiding character judgements, he noted that Attlee's 'modesty in expression conceals a firmness of purpose'. He 'trusted him completely as a colleague'.[116] In an off-guard moment with Hugh Dalton, Eden once remarked that Attlee had been likened by Churchill to 'a terrier, who, when he gets hold of an idea, will not let go'.[117] The prime minister was soon to feel the full force of his deputy's bite.

14

The Invisible Man

There is no doubt whatever that Attlee exists
(Once head of H.M Opposition)
But in Government circles the rumour persists
That Attlee's a mere apparition.

As the Premier's Lord President Attlee is real,
But not as the Premier's double,
For the Deputy P.M. Crown lawyers reveal,
Is a mere Constitutional bubble.

The Deputy Premier is powerless to act,
Like colleagues in Government offices,
So Attlee, as Premier, was never a fact,
But only a working hypothesis.

But Labour say Attlee is really alive,
And give vent to their righteous vexation
That the Deputy Premier cannot survive
Constitutional clarification.

So Attlee has stood in the Premier's place,
All Members may well be indignant
If he's just faded out without leaving a trace
As a mere Constitutional figment.

The Premier's argument does not allay,
But only increases confusion,
If Attlee appears as the Premier one day,
And the next as a visual illusion.

And only the Tories can now understand
This weird Constitutional riddle –
Why Attlee is sometimes seen leading the band
And sometimes must play second fiddle.

Roger Service,
'The Invisible Man', *Tribune*, 30 March 1945.[1]

I *A urinal, cabinet war rooms, sometime in 1944*

The prime minister and deputy prime minister walked into the lavatory together during a break in a meeting of the War Cabinet. Lest there be any awkwardness, Churchill went to the far end of the urinal, leaving Attlee plenty of space in the middle. 'Isn't this unusual modesty for you, Winston?' quipped Attlee. 'Not at all,' responded Churchill, 'I'm just suspicious of you Socialists.' This story, most likely apocryphal, was to live on for many years. It became known to a wider audience through Dean Acheson, the US Secretary of State under President Truman from 1949 to 1953, who dealt extensively with both men.[2]

Through many of the tensest moments of the war, Attlee had demonstrated his loyalty to the government. This was often to the frustration of his fellow socialists, who wanted to extract more, in the name of 'reconstruction'. Attlee could have played to the gallery – to associate himself with great victories, or to take private disputes over the direction of policy into the public domain. Yet as Churchill acknowledged, he was 'not a self-seeking man and always tries to play the game and to do the best he can which is very much to his honour. I shall always assert that – except at times when we have special questions of difference.'[3]

Even as the prospect of victory seemed to increase, Attlee himself remained as scrupulous as ever in not wanting to destabilise the government. His New Year's message to the nation on 1 January 1944 was typically cautious. It spoke of testing times still ahead. 'There is always a danger of slackening when things go well,' he warned, deploying one of the many sporting analogies he enjoyed, 'How often have we seen football teams, with two or three goals in hand, let up for a few fatal minutes and lose the advantage they had gained? We must keep our eye on the ball.' In planning for the peace, the watchword of the government was 'First things first'. Plans had to be worked out before they were implemented.[4] Although he had been jostled along by his party, the Labour leader could justifiably claim that there had been progress on a number of issues close to Labour hearts by January 1944. This was not simply because the prime minister's eyes were diverted elsewhere; there was a genuine sense, as with education reform, that, in terms of how the state approached economic and social issues, the centre of gravity had shifted.

By February 1944, however, as the war began to swing decisively in favour of the Allies, the mood within the coalition started to sour. Churchill sounded the first note of discord, by exhibiting what Aneurin Bevan called a 'snarl' in a public letter to a Conservative candidate in a by-election in Brighton in February, in which he took a swipe at Labour. Not even Bevan could deny Churchill's popularity at this time. But he guessed that it was a depreciating asset and that the Conservatives would try to cash in on it at an election before long. Writing in *Tribune*, he warned that Labour must be prepared for the fight. With the Education Bill before the House, Bevan suspected that the Conservatives were trying to take the wind out of Labour's sails with piecemeal reforms. It was time for a counter-strategy. He argued that the party should reject any legislation on social insurance, health and welfare that fell short of a full implementation of the Beveridge Report, rather than accept the 'exhausted inspiration of a jaded Government . . . fixing the future pattern of our lives'.[5]

In March 1944, the Labour leadership announced that it would leave the coalition as soon as the war in Europe was over. Predictably, *Tribune* declared that this was a victory for its strategy.[6] In fact, it had been decided at a meeting in Attlee's office on 1 March, when Bevin had threatened to resign if the electoral truce was ended, and the parties started running candidates against each other at by-elections.[7] When the government suffered its first defeat in the Commons later that month – after trying to delay a motion on equal pay for female teachers – the Labour left began to smell blood again.[8]

By the first week of April, Attlee, Morrison and Bevin were condemned as the 'Three Blind Mice', bereft of a political strategy while the Tories strung them along for their own gain.[9] Attlee refused to cede to the demands of *Tribune* but there is no question that he read its editorials very closely. He understood that the government could not afford to ignore defeats in the House of Commons on health, education or social services. Nonetheless, he also went after those Labour MPs who played a short-term game by trying to 'spatchcock' socialist policies into government bills by stealth. 'Those who belong to a great party like ours,' he wrote, 'which aspires to power in order that we may bring about great changes, cannot tread the primrose path of the Independents. I do not wish to see the next Labour government go down through the individualism of professed Socialists,' he pleaded.[10]

Internecine Labour squabbles were in danger of descending into acrimony. In April, Attlee even threatened to resign if the party did not give the government full backing to the Education Bill, a battle he won. A pause in the momentum of the war effort had created the space for long-standing tensions to rise to the surface. 'The truth is,' wrote Dalton in his diary, 'that we are all showing various signs of disorder and strain as we wait the invasion.'[11]

In early May, Bevan was almost excluded from the parliamentary party – this time following clashes with Bevin and Greenwood – until Labour MPs voted (seventy-one to sixty) against this.[12] The move to exclude him had originated from the National Executive, which had tired of his constant criticism of their strategy. There followed complaints that the trade unions were exerting their pressure again and attempting to turn the parliamentary party into a rubber-stamping mechanism for their agenda.[13] Chuter Ede suspected that personal ambition played a strong part in Bevan's action. 'The only cure for Bevan's frame of mind was office,' he wrote. Attlee voted against expulsion but, according to Chuter Ede, 'appeared to have no influence one way or the other'.[14] *Tribune* now presented the leader's desire to keep the party united as a sign of weakness. He was mocked mercilessly as the 'invisible man', a 'mere apparition'.[15]

The irony was that the Labour leader's standing outside his party was increasing. Those with less partisan agendas could see that he was escaping 'the shadow of Churchill'. In May 1944, a full-page profile in the *Observer* described him as 'first-class captain of a first-class cricket side who is not himself a headliner'. He was 'equally an English worthy, though not a Great One'. He made men work together; he was a 'political catalyst' in a world that was becoming more suited to that type of politician.

More importantly, under the surface of the coalition, there were great structural and ideological shifts in British society, which seemed to fall in Labour's favour. As the *Observer* described, there was a 'deep surge towards progressive ways', which could be seen in the civil service (with the rise in the influence of men such as William Beveridge and John Maynard Keynes) and in changes in public opinion (manifested by the popularity of the Beveridge Report, which had sold hundreds of thousands of copies). While Churchill waged war, his deputy had recognised the significance of these changes at home. Attlee, though 'co-ordinator much more than creator', was 'at least as much a man of the times' as Churchill. It was the committee men and the collective bargainers – Attlee, Anderson and Bevin – who 'typify our state even more than the fighting Winston Churchill – road-menders, not road-builders, conservatives in the true sense of the word'. While Attlee might appear pedestrian, the future was likely to be more radical than people presumed. 'Clem Attlee is a Fabian; it is an infinite progress to the Brave New World he believes in. But his faith is at least real; he is a man of character.'[16]

Churchill, too, sensed that there had been a shift in the national mood. But either he could not quite put his finger on the nature of this change, or he was unwilling to follow it to its logical conclusion. When Clem and Violet dined with him at Downing Street a few weeks before, he remarked that the world was changing. 'The pomp and vanity must go; the old world will have had the honour of leading the way into the new.'[17] He was only half right.

II

Although the Allies were in the ascendant, there was still a war to be won. The Germans provided a reminder of their potency by launching a new weapon, the V-1 flying bomb, which was fired from northern France in June, causing thousands of casualties in southern England and London. Meanwhile, the opening up of a beachhead on the Continent involved ever-closer cooperation with the Americans. Attlee dined at Claridges at

314 | CITIZEN CLEM: A BIOGRAPHY OF ATTLEE

the end of May with the US Secretary of State, Cordell Hull, and Edward Stettinius, the Under-Secretary of State, against the backdrop of preparations for the Allied invasion of Europe.[18]

On 6 June 1944, D-Day arrived, and the Allies began their landings on the beaches of Normandy. 'We have been having exciting days lately,' Attlee wrote. He stayed awake through the early hours of the day before the invasion, sitting in the Admiralty and following the progress of 'the Armada'. After returning to Number 11 for a few hours' sleep, he then woke up to hear the sound of 'mighty wings continually beating overhead as the air-force went in.' Sitting in the War Office, as news of troop movements were telegraphed in, and scale models were moved across maps of France, he recalled the walking holiday that he and Tom had had through Normandy, Bayeux and Caen in 1919, just after the First World War. One memory that stuck with him was being told how the Huguenots had desecrated William the Conqueror's burial site in 1562. They had scattered his bones so that he could not take revenge from beyond the grave. Now it was the Nazis who were to be beaten, and scattered, so they could never rise again.[19]

Attlee believed that General Dwight Eisenhower, as the Supreme Allied Commander in Europe, showed great bravery to push ahead with the invasion, despite unfavourable weather. Once a bridgehead in France was secured, however, tensions between the Allied commanders resurfaced. Eisenhower favoured an attack along the whole length of the German line – combining forces with the armies under the control of Generals Omar Bradley, George Patton and Montgomery. Alanbrooke and Montgomery, however, wanted to strike a knock-out blow against the enemy through a concentrated attack at its heart in the Ruhr Valley. The British commanders were concerned that they were already stretched in terms of resources and felt that Eisenhower's conservative approach would prolong the war.[20]

When it came to Anglo-American relations in the field, Attlee repeated his criticism of both Alanbrooke and Montgomery. Once again, he felt that their haughtiness jeopardised the hard work that Churchill had put into bringing the Americans into the European theatre. On the fundamentals of the campaign, he believed that Montgomery was in the right in preferring a 'concentrated thrust' from the eastern flank in northern France, aiming directly at the Ruhr and Berlin and securing the northern French ports and those in Holland, Belgium and northwest Germany. These had always been regarded as the first priority in ensuring Britain's security within Europe. Yet, he could understand Eisenhower's position too. As Montgomery had confessed himself, the notion of a 'concentrated thrust' was badly explained to Eisenhower. It had actually been described as a 'pencil thrust', or a 'narrow thrust', by other senior officers, whereas Montgomery favoured something more like the big punch forward he had achieved at Alamein.

This was not the only source of friction. Over the course of the previous few months, the British had reluctantly agreed to Operation Anvil – the American-led invasion of France from the south. The British had preferred to strike further west, in the soft underbelly of Germany, concentrating on making their way through Italy and possibly up to Vienna.[21] Once Anvil was in place, however, the position of General Alexander, marching north through Italy, was not as strong as it might have been. It was the fact that most of the reinforcements were now coming up through France, and not Italy, that influenced Eisenhower's desire for a wider front against the retreating Germans. As Attlee understood, one strategic choice followed from another. In other words, Eisenhower's reasoning was not unsound, given the hand he had been dealt.

A related source of tension between the British and the Americans was the question of the Soviet Union, whose dominance over Eastern Europe now seemed unassailable. Attlee shared the view of Churchill and the chiefs of the general staff, that the Americans had yet to fully comprehend the nature of Soviet imperialism. But he also understood that strategic conceptions that seemed axiomatic in Britain – such as the balance of power in Europe – simply did not exercise the same weight or priority in the American mind.

British strategists were thinking in terms of lessons learned in the resettlement of Europe at the end of the Napoleonic Wars when – following Napoleon's defeat – Britain immediately sought to balance Russia's influence, by strengthening the Central European powers and allowing France to revive itself.[22] Simply speaking, the Americans had different priorities. In other circumstances, they might have prioritised the war in the Pacific – which many Americans (understandably after Pearl Harbor) believed remained a much graver threat. Montgomery's temperamental complaints about Eisenhower were counterproductive and short-sighted. He 'frequently showed so little sympathy with the difficulties of getting the Americans to put in major efforts in Europe, and not switch them to the Far East, that in any argument in which Anglo-American military relations were involved, his views were at something of a discount.'[23]

On this issue, Attlee arguably displayed even more sympathy for the American position than his prime minister, the architect of the American alliance. At this moment, in fact, Churchill was also furious about the American approach towards Operation Anvil. He was drinking heavily and took it out on the chiefs of staff in a 'frightful meeting' that began at 10 p.m. on 6 July and lasted until the early hours of the following morning. In quick succession, the prime minister fired barbs at Montgomery, Alexander and Alanbrooke. Then, at around 2 a.m., when the discussion turned to the Far East, he turned on Attlee, engaging in a shouting match with him over the future of India. The chiefs took the opportunity to leave the meeting 'under cover of this smokescreen', as Attlee bore the brunt of Churchill's anger.[24]

In July 1944, the American General Omar Bradley broke through the German lines, and cut off supply lines in the Cherbourg Peninsula. At the end of the month, Attlee revealed to Tom that it was likely that, before long, he would be going across to Normandy to see things for himself. The prospects for the war were good but there was more bloodshed and slaughter to come.[25] In Cabinet, he got the prime minister to agree to the visit on the grounds that there was a danger that those countries liberated from the Nazis in Southern and Eastern Europe would fall to the other extreme and install communist governments. There was a pressing need to 'encourage the development of democratic Left governments'.[26]

He made the journey over in the first week of August, taking a ninety-minute flight across the English Channel. He saw Bayeux – which had been preserved – and Caen, which was 'a good deal blitzed', with a large artillery hole in its cathedral. Many of the villages and farmhouses in the fighting zone had suffered badly. The saddest sight was the town of Saint-Lô, which had been flattened entirely. Its cathedral, of which Attlee had acquired a watercolour painting years before, was irreparably destroyed. More pleasingly, the Allied push was going well, with a constant stream of supplies coming onto the beach and lorries carrying men and provisions to support those on the front line packing the roads. Attlee travelled to the American sector in a jeep and was 'received with much kindness everywhere'. He believed the spirit of the French was good, with tricolores flying everywhere over the ruins, and refugees returning to their farms on carts – guiding cattle and waving at the troops.[27]

The day that he wrote this letter, 15 August 1944, Attlee was in the cabinet war rooms again, following the progress of Operation Dragoon on the large maps on the wall, which registered French and American troops landing on the south coast of France. He was in good spirits. Churchill's assistant private secretary, Jack Colville commented that 'Attlee, though not impressive, is very pleasant when not being official.'[28]

The breakthrough meant that there was good reason to be cheerful. At the end of August, the deputy prime minister travelled to the Mediterranean theatre to see the progress there. He flew in a Dakota, an American plane, and went via Gibraltar and Algiers, where he met French exiles at a party given by Duff Cooper to celebrate the liberation of Paris. After a night there, his party flew to Naples, which had many fine buildings but, Attlee felt, was also dirty and overcrowded, with a 'low grade population'. The Royal Navy was crammed into the docks. Attlee met up with Churchill in Naples, who insisted on travelling out to the island of Capri to see the famous 'Blue Grotto'. Attlee had to lie down on the bottom of the boat to enter the cavern but was suitably impressed by the network of caves and the crystal blue pools within.[29]

As Churchill bathed in the waters, Attlee chatted with Lord Moran, Churchill's doctor, for the first time. 'Most of these politicians are cool customers, who have spent their lives dealing with human nature, but Attlee does not appear to have any self-confidence,' wrote Moran in his diary. Attlee answered his questions in a quick, nervous manner, while repeating an Attlee family mantra of many years – that he never worried about anything. And yet Moran also felt that the nervous exterior obscured a hidden depth. 'I have a feeling . . . that there is a good deal more to him that this,' he wrote. 'Winston, I am pretty sure, underrates him . . . I have made up my mind to find out more about him.'

On their way back to the marina in Naples, having picked up Churchill, who was drying himself off on the boat, they came across a convoy of British troops who were about to set out for a landing in the south of France. Churchill told the captain to perform a few circles in the marina, while he stood in the stern waving and giving his famous victory-sign salute. Lord Moran noted in his diary that it was twenty-nine years before that another British convoy had travelled through the same waters on its way to Gallipoli. He thought of the men who were about to die and the 'futility of war'.[30] Attlee, beside him, kept his counsel. It did not occur to Moran that the deputy prime minister had made that journey himself in 1916 and had counted many of those young men among his friends.

From Naples, Attlee travelled to Rome by jeep, following the tracks of the Allied armies.[31] He witnessed the terrible aftermath of the Battle of Monte Cassino, which had recently seen the Allies suffer 55,000 casualties in the course of four assaults on the German lines. Cassino itself was completely ruined. He travelled up a hazardous spiral road to what was left of the monastery, desecrated by bombing. An old monk acted as his companion, whom he impressed by quoting Dante and speaking in his passable Italian. Arriving in Rome for a three-day visit, he met leaders of the Italian Communist Party, who now had political control of the city. He also called upon Pope Pius XII in the Vatican, whom he met after being guided through a succession of antechambers by guards in medieval uniforms. Attlee talked with him for fifteen minutes and liked him – 'a gentle idealist'. He saw St Peter's Basilica and the Sistine Chapel, before catching the Colosseum by moonlight. Moving to Siena, he met with General Alexander for the first time, whom he regarded as 'a very fine man'. With Alexander he flew to the Adriatic coast and went right up to the front line, where he talked with the US Eighth Army Chief of Staff, Major General George Walsh. He also travelled to the west flank of the front line, where he met with another senior American, General George Clarke, of the Fifth Army.[32] There he was shown some captured Germans, 'very young and unpleasant-looking – the products, I fancy, of the Hitler Youth Movement'.[33]

The homeward journey involved another stop at Algiers, where they arrived to the sight of a fierce red sunrise over the desert.[34] In Normandy and Monte Cassino, Attlee had seen, first hand, the extent of the damage that the fighting had left on the European mainland. His own constituency was deeply scarred too. In between these two visits to the Continent, he returned to Limehouse for the first time in a number of months, to survey the wreckage of the war there. Meanwhile, German bombers were still making occasional raids. He reported to Tom that the flat they had shared fifty years before had 'got it last week' in a bomb attack, though fortunately there had been no casualties. He had seen an old neighbour of theirs on the street who had been made homeless by the attack. The Haileybury Club had been damaged too, though it was still standing. 'One gets a most peculiar sensation going round Stepney,' he reflected. In place of the packed masses of buildings there were now open spaces and one could see wide vistas with trees in the distance, whereas previously the view was obscured by chimneys and factory blocks. So much had been flattened that the old nucleus of Stepney – the church and the high street – looked almost like an isolated village in the country. 'While one regrets the loss of an integral part of one's experiences, there is the gain in the disappearance of slum areas.'[35]

Among Attlee's close friends in the area was Frank Lewey, an orphan who had risen to become the Labour mayor of Stepney and was now the party's election agent for Limehouse. Attlee wrote a foreword to a book which Lewey had just had published, in May 1944, called *Cockney Campaign*. In it, Lewey – in his unfiltered, unedited, East End patter – vividly described the experience of Stepney during the Blitz, flooded by refugees, with Nazi and communist agents sowing dissension among them. Lewey estimated that the 'Black Hole of London' was home to twenty-six nationalities, speaking fourteen different languages, crammed into slums that had been utterly destroyed by the Luftwaffe. These men, women and children had been on the front line against Hitlerism. They had borne the brunt of the attacks. They were not beaten down or quiescent. Now there was a feeling of revolution in the air. There was an opportunity to find these heroes homes fit to live in, to get them amenities and restore the civic life of east London. If this opportunity was not taken, the country's leaders would never be forgiven.[36] Lewey's argument was straight out of the Attlee copybook of 1919–22. There could be no betrayal of those who had sacrificed themselves in this way.

This was the Labour message at its boldest – a radical patriotism that gloried in the fight but which would insist on the promises made to the people being fulfilled once victory had been won. Yet the raising of expectations also meant that the notion of a 'consensus' began to fray around the edges. A few days after this visit, Attlee officially ruled out the possibility of an 'agreed programme' with the Conservatives on economic reconstruction.[37] The Labour leadership reiterated that it would not continue the coalition into peacetime, despite the severe challenges that awaited the country after the end of the conflict.

If Labour's aim was to strive for a new socialist commonwealth, what would that look like in practice? As thoughts turned to rebuilding Britain's cities, some in the party urged the nationalisation and socialisation of the land. In July, *Tribune* urged the leaders to join the Labour rebels and vote down the second reading of the Town and Country Planning Bill – which made provisions for urban reconstruction – on the grounds that it did not go far enough in the socialisation of common land. *Tribune* was now in open rebellion. Their declared strategy was to bring the government down as soon as possible, and by whatever means possible. 'Over-simplified? We don't think so.'[38] In the event, the Labour rebels only brought fifty-eight members into the division lobbies but their determination to play tactics over the bill prevented the emergence of a coherent Labour line on an issue which would rumble on after the war.[39]

For Attlee, real reconstruction could not be achieved by set-piece battles which were doomed to fail. Ideological absolutism – the 'Primrose path of independence' – risked derailing the whole project. Tom's old friend A. L. Rowse, an Oxford historian and former Labour candidate in Cornwall, criticised the leaders of the Labour Party for their lack of boldness in a series of articles in the *Sunday Times*. Nonetheless, Attlee was pleased to note that Rowse offered even more criticism of the rebels. He was 'especially hard on the lack of compromise of the intelligentsia'.[40]

A similar point had been made by George Orwell, in his famous book of essays, *The Lion and the Unicorn*, written during the Blitz. Orwell mocked the self-regarding intellectuals of the left who ran down the national spirit at every turn, and who 'took their cookery from Paris and their opinions from Moscow'. 'The Bloomsbury highbrow, with his mechanical snigger', was as 'out of date as the cavalry colonel'. In 1940, H. G. Wells had commented that the revolution had already begun, as the government was forced to adopt what were essentially socialist methods in order to mobilise the country for war. Once it was proved that the state could play a steering role in the national economy – in ensuring that nearly every citizen was gainfully employed, fed and cared for – it was extremely difficult to reverse that idea in the public mind. Thus, Orwell also believed that a revolution was under way, even if, in predictably British fashion, it moved with 'glacier-like slowness'.[41]

In this respect, Attlee had a far superior feel for the mood of the electorate than many of those who complained about his cautious leadership. He had already used the analogy of a pregnancy to explain his strategy. Rather than trying to force the pace at every turn – demanding a caesarean section – patience would bring a natural birth. To extend the metaphor,

Labour was far better placed to be a midwife, rather than a surgeon. 'Although you are a theorist and I am only a working politician,' he told Harold Laski, pointedly, in one revealing exchange in 1944. 'I think that I give more and you give less attention to changes of conception than to legislative achievements.'[42] Dragging out concessions from the government was one thing; fostering and adapting to seismic changes in the public mood was the smarter course. Looking like a responsible party of government, with a truly national spirit, was part of this. In Attlee's view the party gained 'great stature' by going into government. 'I am told everywhere that there is a great swing to the left,' he told a Labour rally in Yorkshire in May 1944, 'among the workers, among the fighters, who had formerly refused to consider our views.' This swing was down to the fact that Labour men like Morrison, Bevin, and Alexander had taken on difficult jobs and had 'not been afraid to brave criticism by doing unpopular things'.[43]

As for evidence of a new 'consensus' among existing elites, in the civil service or across the leading parties, Attlee saw this as something to be welcomed. The laissez-faire economic orthodoxy of the 1930s, which accepted a high level of unemployment, was dead. This was not something for which Labour could take credit on its own. In fact, Attlee had singularly failed to grasp the nettle when John Maynard Keynes had tried to co-opt the Labour Party in support of his plans to pay for the war by an expansive new tax regime in 1940, as he feared it would take away the purchasing power of the working man. Keynes had been shocked by the conservatism of the Labour leaders. As Lord Privy Seal, however, Attlee had witnessed the successful adoption of what might be called Keynesian macroeconomic methods, which entailed greater government intervention in the economy, and encouraged full employment. The Keynesian revolution was an internal one, which took place within the state itself, much as the Beveridge report had been commissioned from inside the government. Even one-time critics of Keynes, such as the LSE economist Lionel Robbins, had explained to Attlee that Keynesianism had triumphed at the Treasury, which had once been the bastion of financial orthodoxy.[44]

Although he was not an economist, Attlee could at least grasp this much about the new dispensation. He told Tom about a jokey slogan he had heard from senior figures in the City of London: 'Bankers of the world unite you have nothing to lose but your Keynes.' Even more important, at a crucial moment in August 1944, as the post-war world was being made, he noted the influence Keynes was having at the Bretton Woods Conference, meeting in New Hampshire.[45] The meeting was designed to stabilise and regulate the international monetary system. It gave birth to what later became the International Monetary Fund (IMF). It also reconciled the American desire to maintain free trade with the British (specifically Keynesian) desire to maintain full employment after the war. Thus a synergy emerged which seemed to promise a more stable global economic system, and the conditions for the type of welfare system envisaged by Beveridge (whose plans for social insurance depended, as a pre-condition, on almost full employment, and a managed economy).

So, as Attlee toured bombed-out Stepney, he would have understood that somewhere amid the devastated areas of Britain were the ruins of the economic system that had created the great slums in the first place. The foundation stones of a new economic order were being put in place elsewhere. What Labour had to do was help bring it into existence. Now was not the time to rush the ramparts.

III

In the autumn of 1944, as Churchill travelled to Moscow for negotiations with Stalin, Attlee took the lead in the House of Commons and the War Cabinet in his absence.[46] 'I am, as you may imagine, fairly busy with the P.M. and Eden away,' he told Tom on 16 October, 'but things are going pretty well.' He was particularly pleased to have re-asserted some control over the party. At his insistence, the National Executive had announced that Labour would remain in government until Hitler was defeated. 'I drafted it myself and for a wonder it was accepted practically unaltered,' Attlee said, of the announcement. It had the 'true merit of brevity, a virtue not often found in the drafts of Transport House'.[47]

This sparked hysteria at *Tribune*. Was Attlee about to repeat the Ramsay MacDonald trick and form a new national government with Churchill, leaving Labour out in the cold?[48] There was certainly some evidence that this might be popular with the British people. A Gallup poll, conducted in November 1944, revealed that 35 per cent preferred an all-party government to take charge after the war, with 26 per cent in favour of a Labour government, against 12 per cent for the Conservatives and just 4 per cent for the Liberals.[49]

It was now nine years since the last general election – there were men and women in Britain who were thirty years of age and had never had the chance to vote. If these young people went any longer without exercising their democratic rights, *Tribune* claimed, they would never develop the democratic habit. The newspaper went so far as to claim that this would be a victory for Nazism.[50] Bevan made the hyperbolic claim that the British press was more servile than anything that might be found in Franco's Spain. He even denounced Greenwood, the champion of the Beveridge Report, for asking the government to implement its White Paper on Social Insurance before the election. A truly self-confident Labour would not bother about begging the Tories to pass 'this or that bit of ameliorative legislation'. Labour needed to rediscover its emotional drive – its sense of 'them' and 'us'.[51]

It was a sign that the war was nearly won that serious tensions between Attlee and Churchill finally surfaced at the end of 1944. In September, Attlee made a modest suggestion that service pay should be increased for those fighting in the eastern theatre, against the Japanese, where there was still much fighting to be done. When he received this note, Churchill suspected skulduggery. Labour was trying to pose as the champion of the serviceman, and Attlee, the little mouse, had graduated to 'a rat'.[52] This was just the start. In November, Churchill began to grumble that the Conservatives involved in the Reconstruction Committee – such as Butler – were consensus figures, whereas Labour were using their dominance to push a party agenda.[53]

A ceasefire between the two was put in place for the King's Speech on 28 November, which opened the new session of Parliament. Attlee proposed the prime minister's health and toasted him as 'a great leader and a great statesman'. Until the defeat of Germany 'we should remain united.' Churchill replied by saying that he had been greatly eased of his burdens by 'the loyalty and determination of his friend, Clem Attlee'. He had been able to leave the country 'with the certain knowledge that any difficulty that might arise would be met with great wisdom and undaunted courage'. The time for parting might come but he hoped 'the bitterness of party conflict would be assuaged by the knowledge we had all gained of one another's zeal in the cause and devotion to our country.' He also praised Morrison and 'his friend Ernie'. Labour ministers had shown 'great vision and revealed great capacities for handling momentous affairs'. Bevin, taking up the story, said they were glad to have the prime minister's tribute; it was a change, Bevin said, to laughter, from Churchill's old taunting query, 'Is Labour fit to govern?' As Churchill had begun speaking, Cripps whispered to Herbert Morrison and Chuter Ede, 'Now is the time for the V-2', referring to the V-1's successor missile. Within ten seconds a distant explosion was heard, before Cripps picked up the thread of his joke. 'The timing was good but the aim was poor.'[54]

In December 1944, the Germans launched their last major western offensive – in the Ardennes – but it soon petered out and the Western Allies and the Soviets began to close in around Hitler in a vice.[55] As Parliament was due to meet to debate the situation, Attlee accused Churchill of failing to brief the Labour members of the government fully on his return from Moscow, after he cancelled a planned Cabinet meeting. 'I think it would be helpful to you to know the points on which responsible members of our Party will wish to be enlightened,' he complained.[56]

By January 1945, lines were being drawn between the two main coalition partners. Attlee wrote a blunt note to the prime minister complaining about his conduct in Cabinet and attitude to ministers. He offered lengthy disquisitions on papers that Churchill had not read and accused him of relying too much on Brendan Bracken and Beaverbrook for counsel, to the exclusion of his ministers. Churchill's assistant private secretary, Jack Colville, commented, 'I am afraid there is much in what Attlee says and I rather admire him for saying it.' A number of senior Conservatives – and senior officials such as Sir Alexander Cadogan, head of the Foreign Office – agreed. Attlee had written the note in his own hand, and it was not intended for ciculation. Nonetheless, Churchill exploded at its contents and talked about a socialist conspiracy. That night, as news arrived of more Russian advances into Poland, he got uproariously drunk and told his staff, with a sarcastic slur, that soon they would have to bother 'about Atler or Hitlee'. The following morning, as he nursed a severe hangover, both his wife Clementine and even Beaverbrook – against whom the note was, in part, aimed – suggested to him that Attlee's concerns were valid.[57]

Another source of contention was the future of Greece after the Nazi withdrawal at the end of 1944. A civil war was soon to break out between the supporters of the Greek monarchy, and a communist insurgency. The government feared a communist takeover in Greece would give the Russians a steering hand in the eastern Mediterranean, an area that Britain was deeply invested in, and had fought so hard – in two world wars – to wrest from its enemies. Churchill and Eden flew to Athens, and took the decision that it was best to prop up the royalist government – despite its lack of popular legitimacy – against the communist insurgency. Privately, Attlee agreed. He had no time for Archbishop Damaskinos, who had been temporarily appointed as regent but whom he regarded as a left-wing agitator. Yet he still registered his concerns with Eden that the British Foreign Office was mishandling – and needlessly alienating – left-wing politicians in Greece. Eden replied that 'the leaders of these people are of the type of communists' that Labour had 'so roundly denounced' itself.[58]

Greece became the first of many new foreign policy causes for the left of the Labour Party, who pointed out that the royalist government was unpopular and brutal in their treatment of political opponents. 'Are we in Greece for war or politics?' asked the young Michael Foot, after the execution of a number of communist leaders in Athens. In his address to the Labour Party conference in London in the second week of December, Harold Laski urged Labour to articulate a new grand strategy for a planned world. Churchill, the gallant eighteenth-century imperialist, could only promise glories of the past.[59]

Attlee was willing to play this game but only to the extent of offering vague generalities. In his speech to the delegates, he laid out the case for an armed world police to maintain global peace. The League of Nations had not failed because its principles were wrong; but because it had no force behind it.[60] The following day, however, the party turned up the heat again on its leadership, voting for a resolution that called on it to take immediate steps towards an armistice in Greece. The resolution was moved by Arthur Greenwood, who, since leaving the War Cabinet, had taken up the (constitutionally necessary) role of the leader of the opposition. In the first sign that he was becoming Labour's key spokesman on foreign affairs, Bevin addressed the conference and told the delegates, with much more force than Attlee had done, that both of them had been party to the policy on Greece, and, what was more, supported it. If Labour was to win office, he warned, it would find that it could not carry out a policy on the basis of 'emotionalism'. It would have to ride the wave of criticism of its own policies too. Foreign policy could not be reduced to matters of black and white, or right and wrong.[61] Chuter Ede recorded that his argument was 'massive in its cumulative effect'. When Bevan rose to complain, he was met with shouts of 'What would you do?' which, he replied, he felt was not fair to ask.[62] Privately, Attlee confided to Lord Addison, the leader of the party in the Lords, that the party managers would have to play a careful game. If possible, they should avoid by-elections, 'with our people in a rather emotional state' on Greece, as discipline would be impossible to preserve.[63]

In early 1945, the last pieces were put in place for the final push in Europe and the Far East. Churchill, Roosevelt and Stalin reconvened at Yalta in the Crimea in February. The Russians were persuaded to enter the war against Japan and to participate in the formation of the United Nations. It was also decided that Germany was to be divided into four zones between the four main invading Allies (with the Big Three joined by a liberated France). As the minister responsible for drawing up plans for the treatment of post-war Germany, Attlee took a robust line – tougher indeed than Eden's – which urged an enforced settlement, and, to Dalton's delight, involved a measure of dismemberment of the state.[64] Attlee was opposed to the idea of post-Nazi Germany being entrusted to Germans and felt the country must be cured of militarism once and for all. On the other hand, he stopped short of supporting plans for the 'pastoralisation' of the country (envisaged by Henry Morgenthau, then US Secretary of State), which effectively entailed the dismantling of all heavy industry in Germany.[65] In any case, the future of Germany would be decided in the course of discussions between the Big Three as the war neared its end. It fell to Attlee to announce the results of Yalta to the Cabinet. He was pleased with this and backed the deal and was encouraged that Stalin had also agreed to free elections in Poland, while still remaining characteristically suspicious of long-term Soviet intentions.

In the first week of March 1945, Attlee visited the Continent again, escorted by Spitfires to Paris, where he stayed at the Embassy with Duff Cooper. He had an exacting itinerary, including a meeting with General de Gaulle at the Versailles Palace, at which the general – unaware that Attlee had protected him from the Churchillian sledgehammer – gave his thanks for all that Britain had done to help France. The main reason for the visit was to reassure the French that the British would help with respect to the supply issues they anticipated facing after the war.[66] The contrast with his two sorties to France in January and February 1940, when the Allied cause looked doomed, could not have been greater. He met a dozen ministers from the provisional French government – 'not a bad lot, some very able' – and found General de Gaulle in an 'unusually gracious' mood.[67]

From Paris he travelled on a night train to Brussels and stayed at the British Embassy.[68] Here the people, he noticed, were 'a little trimmer', having only recently been liberated. Meeting Prince Charles of Belgium, he was taken aback when he quoted a passage from one of Attlee's books, *The Labour Party in Perspective*. He visited Antwerp, which had been blitzed, as well as Walcheren and the town of Flushing, where the British had landed a few months before. There had been severe flooding but the local Dutch told him they would rather be flooded than enslaved under the Germans, who still held parts of the country.[69]

From Flushing, Attlee and his military escort flew to east Belgium and were driven in a jeep through local villages on Sunday – full of rural Belgians going to church – and then arrived in Maastricht, 'a fine town', celebrating the six-month anniversary of its liberation. He crossed the River Maas, on a bridge repaired by the Americans, and entered Germany. Attlee's chauffeur stopped at the Siegfried Line, originally built by the Germans in the First World War and then reconstituted, opposite the Maginot Line, in the 1930s. He was shown the fortifications that had recently been abandoned in the hasty German retreat. The party stopped and ate a picnic, washing down sandwiches with some claret given to them by the British ambassador in Brussels, which they drank from a soldier's tin mug. They went as far into Germany as the town of Aachen, which was in complete ruins, apart from the cathedral which housed Charlemagne's tomb, which remained intact. The few Germans he came across 'were going about their business quietly'. Indeed, the parts of Germany he saw seemed to him to be better preserved than what he had seen in France.[70]

Two hundred miles due north, Churchill was with Field Marshal Montgomery at his headquarters near Venlo, on the Dutch border. On the evening of 23 March 1945, Operation Plunder began, as the British Second Army and American Ninth Army began crossing the River Rhine at Rees and the River Leppe, south of Wessel. In the east, the Soviet army was already making progress towards Berlin. Eisenhower's decision to send a telegram directly to Stalin at the end of March, urging a joint assault on the German capital, was greeted with dismay by Montgomery and Churchill, who were already becoming concerned about Stalin's ambitions for post-war Europe. Attlee was more sympathetic than most to Eisenhower's decision – taken because of a desire to avoid further casualties and to end the war swiftly. But it was to have long-term consequences that would do much to shape the world he was about to inherit.[71]

IV

On 28 April 1945, a lift opened at the Mark Hopkins hotel in San Francisco, and two old neighbours greeted each other: Robert Collier and Clement Attlee, who had once lived side by side in Limehouse. Collier, a printer's apprentice and a member of the Independent Labour Party at the same time as Attlee, had written to Labour's leader when he had heard he would be visiting the west coast. Attlee had called him on arrival to arrange a meeting. 'When I knew Attlee,' Collier commented to the American press, 'it wasn't quite respectable to be a socialist.' Now his old friend was deputy prime minister, arriving to discuss the future of the world. He was in San Francisco for the United Nations Conference, convened to put flesh on the bones of the organisation that Roosevelt, Stalin and Churchill had conceived.

That night, Attlee, along with his private secretary, Captain John Dugdale, went to dinner in San Bruno, where Collier and his wife owned a cottage.[72] No politics were discussed; just stories from their days back in the East End. Collier's flustered American wife recalled how, after dinner, she suggested that the men should retire to the living room, while she washed up. Attlee just swung his legs out from the table and started washing the dishes, with Dugdale drying them.[73]

The fact that Attlee had been sent to San Francisco as the deputy to Anthony Eden was taken as a sign that the walls were starting to rise within the coalition. It was this snub, in which the deputy prime minister was placed under the command of a Tory foreign secretary, that caused *Tribune* to publish its poem on Attlee as the 'Invisible Man'. Bevan was apoplectic at what he saw as Attlee's wilful subservience. 'We do not ask Mr Attlee to lose his temper, for then he appears only querulous, but we do remind him that a capacity for indignation is not the least among the qualifications for public life.' At no point in the last ten years, had he 'stood so low in the estimate of his followers'.[74] Indeed, the *Manchester Guardian* went so far as to suggest that Attlee's days as leader might be numbered.

Either Bevin or Morrison would be 'manifestly superior' to the existing leader. It was deemed significant that Attlee put Bevin in charge in his absence, as it strengthened the latter's hand over Morrison as a likely successor.[75] The editorial board at *Tribune* had no great affection for either man but it took the opportunity to praise Bevin, on the grounds that he at least had some fight in him when it came to taking on the Tory press.[76]

On arrival in San Francisco, Attlee addressed 400 journalists from around the world, informing them that the British delegation arrived not as 'perfectionists but as grim realists'.[77] This came on the back of yet another exchange with Bevan, just before he had left. In an incredible statement, Bevan had compared the new organisation to the Holy Alliance constituted after the Napoleonic Wars. In an agile reply, Attlee commented that Bevan seemed to 'qualify everything with an adjective'. The Holy Alliance had 'unholy principles'. In San Francisco, he hoped, they were going to 'build an organisation or at least principles that we can all approve'.[78]

The American press were perplexed by the diffident Briton they saw in front of them. 'Say, he ain't a politician – he's a saint,' one remarked.[79] He was marshalled by Francis Williams, the former editor of the *Daily Herald*, who had taken up a senior position at the Ministry of Information when Labour had entered the wartime coalition. Williams, who became Attlee's press secretary later that year, described the great difficulty he had in selling the Labour leader's virtues to an American audience. His reserve made him appear 'sharp and brusque' or defensive. In San Francisco, Williams arranged a dinner with a group of American journalists so that they could get to know him. Similar arrangements had been made for Anthony Eden. Eden was frank, informal and persuasive. Attlee never succeeded in making anyone feel at ease. At the end of the dinner one journalist turned to Williams and said: 'Well, I feel I know a lot more about British policy and the British Labour Party, but I don't feel I know your Attlee at all.'[80] Ironically, Attlee believed these meetings to be a 'part success', though he was not afraid to poke fun at himself. An Australian journalist told him that his American colleagues had been divided by his performance. One had ventured that Attlee would be torn to pieces by a lion like Churchill in any election; another retorted, to Attlee's amusement, 'I'll bet this sucker eats lions.'[81]

One reason why Attlee sounded cautious about the prospects for the United Nations Organisation was that one of the chief driving forces behind it, President Roosevelt, had died unexpectedly from a stroke on 12

April. It was in paying tribute to Roosevelt that Attlee had stressed the importance of making good on his vision: 'the fact that we are realists does not prevent us from being idealists also.'[82] From San Francisco, he flew to Washington, DC to meet Roosevelt's vice-president, Harry Truman, who was to take his place. It was important that Truman took an immediate liking to the Labour leader, as their fortunes were to intertwine over the next five years, in ways that neither quite expected. As the US Under-Secretary of State Dean Acheson put it, Truman 'recognized Attlee as somebody like himself, a man with his feet on the ground, who spoke in simple, direct terms, and . . . whose thinking about politics was inspired . . . by identification with "the common man"'.[83]

In Europe, the war was approaching its conclusion. On 7 May, with Attlee and Eden still in San Francisco, General Eisenhower received Germany's unconditional surrender. In his victory speech on 8 May, Churchill studiously avoided mention of a general election. But the fact that Attlee was returning from the US and going straight to the Labour Party conference at Blackpool meant speculation was rife that an election would now be called.[84]

A series of Gallup polls suggested that the Labour Party had had a lead over the Conservatives since 1943; in some estimates, by early 1945, Labour were 20 points ahead.[85] Attlee and Bevin were not so sure. Their personal preference was to continue in government until Japan was defeated. This was not just a matter of party political advantage. Attlee's belief was that the 1918 general election had been rushed and had contributed to the severe difficulties caused by rapid demobilisation. This was a matter of patriotic responsibility. He asked for copies of the speeches made by Andrew Bonar Law and Herbert Asquith at that time, to help him guide his own conduct.[86] Meanwhile, some Conservative strategists urged Churchill to act now and terminate the government, capitalising on his personal popularity before the glow of victory faded.

On Friday, 18 May, as Attlee was about to leave London for Blackpool, he received a letter from Churchill offering two choices: an early dissolution or a continuation of the coalition government until victory over Japan. He hoped they could continue to 'work together with all the energy and comradeship which has marked our long and honourable association'.[87] At this point, Attlee also hoped to persuade his party that this was the right course. Two simultaneous developments made this impossible. First, the Labour

National Executive rejected the proposal at Blackpool. At exactly the same time, Churchill expressed alarm at the unconstitutional nature of Labour's relationship with its National Executive. Why should an unelected body be given control over a decision of such national importance? Why should unelected figures such as Harold Laski, the Labour Party chairman, hold sway?[88] There followed the first of a number of unpleasant written exchanges between the two leaders. As Attlee pointed out, Churchill had not complained when he had sought the approval of his party before joining the coalition in 1940. The result, however, was an unseemly dispute, made worse by Churchill's decision to make the correspondence public. The truce was well and truly over. Churchill confessed he was '[b]oiling with hate'.[89]

On 22 May, under pressure from Beaverbrook, the prime minister wrote a letter to Attlee that announced his intention to end the government. Before he did so, his private secretary rang Attlee and read out the text over the phone, which took forty minutes as Attlee insisted on writing down every word.[90] The furore over the letters, which were made public immediately, actually took the heat off the Labour leadership who, in the words of the Conservative chief whip, had been nervous of being blamed for the break-up of our 'not unhappy relationship'.[91]

So, by 23 May 1945, Britain looked like it was returning to some form of normality. In the Test match at Lord's, Australia beat England with the fourth ball of the last over and the public learned that there would be a general election for the first time in ten years. Churchill formed a caretaker government, to hold power until the dissolution of Parliament on 5 June. The election would take place on 5 July. The Conservative press expressed bold confidence, with the *Daily Mail* reporting how Churchill was chomping on Cuban cigars that Anthony Eden had brought him back from San Francisco, and was primed for victory on the home front.[92]

V

Before battle commenced, on 28 May Churchill held a celebration in Downing Street for the departing ministers at which everyone – Churchill included – seemed in very high spirits. Some of the former Labour ministers arrived, for the last time, in their official cars.[93] Churchill told the guests that this was a tea party rather than a cocktail party, although the drink was flowing. He eulogised Attlee's work and thanked his colleagues for their contribution to 'the most glorious five years in history'. Britain would have been 'wiped out if we had not been united'. Yet by the following morning, as MPs assembled in Parliament, the Labour leaders were back on the opposition benches and there were some fiery exchanges.[94] As the Minister of Education, Rab Butler had embodied the bi-partisan mood of much of the previous years. Appointed by Churchill as the new Minister of Labour in the caretaker government, he was surprised at how brusquely Bevin treated him as he arrived to replace him the following morning. Bevin blamed Churchill for breaking up the government, before turning to his secretary, and ordering her to, 'Fetch me my 'at.'[95]

Attlee had flown some 6,000 miles in the previous weeks. He now faced a gruelling campaign across the country.[96] Moreover, it soon became clear that proceedings would be anything but gentlemanly. The tone was set by Churchill's infamous election broadcast on the evening of 4 June. In an excoriating attack on Labour, he alleged that state socialism could not be established without some form of Gestapo to enforce it.[97] This idea had found its way into Churchill's speech via *The Road to Serfdom*, a 1944 book by the Austrian-born liberal economist, Friedrich Hayek, who had warned that states based on planned economies and state ownerships tended to eat away at political liberty. If the West was to convince communists and Nazis to abandon their ways, Hayek had argued, 'it will not be by concessions to their system of thought'.[98]

The imputation by Churchill that his coalition partners would even flirt with such methods was poorly conceived, and badly received. *The Economist*, which regarded itself as the home of liberal democratic moderation, commented of Labour that 'there are few groups of men less capable of moving in that direction than the leaders of the Labour Party, who have never been able to impose their wishes even on their own followers.' What was surprising was that Churchill thought this good electioneering.[99] A young Conservative supporter called Margaret Thatcher, a student at Somerville College in Oxford, later recalled listening to the nation's hero and thinking, 'he's gone too far.'[100] This impression was confirmed by the telegrams sent by the US ambassador in London, John Winant, back to Washington, DC. In private, Conservatives expressed their alarm at the tone of the speech. Most blamed the influence of Lord Beaverbrook on Churchill.[101] Harold Nicolson's wife, Vita Sackville-West, concurred: 'You know I have an admiration for Winston amounting to idolatry, so I am dreadfully distressed by the badness of his broadcast election speeches . . . If I were a wobbler they would tip me over to the other side.'[102]

The following night, Attlee made his measured response in a national broadcast. In denouncing Churchill's 'travesty', Attlee cleverly placed the blame elsewhere. While the voice was Winston's, the mind had been Lord Beaverbrook's. As for the prime minister's lurid descriptions of life under socialism, they were 'merely the second hand version of the academic views' of an Austrian professor, Mr Hayek. Here, as after the First World War, Attlee was not averse to playing on anti-German sentiment. 'Any system can be reduced to this kind of theoretical reasoning, just as German professors showed theoretically that British democracy must be beaten by German dictatorship.' British socialism owed very little to Continental European versions of the creed. Socialist theory had been developed in Britain by Robert Owen, the nineteenth-century Welsh utopian socialist, long before Karl Marx. While Attlee had kept a level tone for the most part, his voice quivered slightly with emotion when he addressed the claim that the Conservatives were the true defenders of individual rights. He recalled a time when children worked sixteen hours a day in sweatshops for pitiably small wages, and thousands died from poor sanitation. For years, every attempt to remedy these evils was blocked as an interference in the working of the economy. Labour had led that fight and was the real party of liberty in Britain.[103]

The Economist, while it was still sceptical about throwing its lot in with Labour, described the broadcast as everything Churchill's was not: 'moderate, sensible, constructive, [and] fair'. In elections, 'you cannot beat somebody with nobody' but they still had difficulty in imagining Attlee as prime minister.[104] 'Attlee, the "poor Clem" of the war years, did his piece tonight, and did it well,' commented Charles Moran. There was an ethical force in what Attlee said which reminded him of William Gladstone. 'At any rate, as I listened, it became plain that an ounce of Gladstone's moral fervour was worth a ton of skilled invective. And this in spite of Attlee's delivery.' It was clear to Moran that Churchill was on the wrong track. For the first time, said Moran, 'the thought went through my head that he may lose the election.'[105] Churchill was losing his self-confidence. 'I am worried about this damned election,' the prime minister remarked, with a sadness in his voice, 'I have no message for them now.'[106]

Churchill's missteps during the campaign were important in so far as they helped Labour reinforce its core message: that it was the truly patriotic 'national' party. A similar message had been put forward in 1918, but, at that time, the party's reputation had been damaged by the conscientious objectors in its leadership, and it also carried the burden of being an unknown entity. In the 1945 Labour manifesto, in fact, 'socialism' appeared just once, whereas 'nation' and 'people' were used repeatedly. The same patriotic language was also peppered throughout Labour's economic discourse.[107] Recognising this, the *Daily Mail* seized on unguarded comments that Attlee had made on the United Nations – that he had 'abandoned any idea of nationalist loyalty' – to suggest that he would not fight for Britain's interests in the world.[108] Attlee would have nothing of the sort. 'We hold that in peace no less than in war the national interest must come first,' he insisted.[109]

Another theme in the Conservative press was that a socialist government would be to the detriment of those who had been frugal and cautious with their money over the years.[110] Attlee responded on the election trail on 8 June, in Barry, Wales, that 'there was a whispering campaign by little, mean-minded people who crept around old women and little children telling them that wicked Socialists would take up their savings.'[111] Moving on to Cardiff he asked a Labour crowd, 'Why do you think Lord Beaverbrook likes the little trader when he stands by himself, but does not like little men when they join together in a cooperative society?' It was because little men were strong when they were united.[112]

As to what that cooperative society entailed, Attlee was duly cautious about how this was presented to the electorate. While acknowledging the great changes in public opinion, he understood that the country had not simply converted to socialism. Here the Labour Party had to check itself. In 1940, Keynes had regarded Attlee and Bevin as unduly cautious, and almost petty, in expressing concerns that his planned economy might be seen by the working classes as endangering those assets that they had managed to accrue, and generally reducing their spending power. That Attlee had talked about his own savings being 'crushed' by Keynes's proposals was regarded by the economist as a breathtakingly esoteric objection.[113] In fact, Attlee had given this question more thought than Keynes – who regarded Attlee's caution as typically suburban and small-minded – gave him credit for. In a memorandum in his private papers for

1945, Attlee made the point that the British working and middle classes had small but significant investments in insurance schemes, savings and property, as well as co-op shares and Post Office and savings bank deposits, which they were eager to protect. 'In the face of this it is time that the Labour Party ceased to mouth Marxian shibboleths about the proletariat having nothing to lose but their chains. It is just not true.' Thus, he warned, in a telling phrase, a 'silly speech by Aneurin Bevan might easily be used to stampede the electors away from Labour.'[114]

Although some of the evidence is anecdotal, there is reason to believe that Attlee's persona acted as a reassuring counterbalance to those who might otherwise have been put off by the Labour Party's penchant for factionalism and intrigue. As a schoolboy at Eton, the future Conservative minister William Waldegrave ran a political magazine, which denounced Bevan as a scoundrel, but was rather soft on Attlee as a reassuringly patriotic figure.[115] Likewise, the historian Paul Addison described how his grandfather was a committed Tory who detested the Labour Party. 'Only Mr Attlee commanded his respect as a decent Englishman who had somehow strayed into the wrong party.'[116]

Parliament met for the last time before the election on 15 June. It had been in existence for nine years, six months and twenty-six days, the longest of any since the eighteen-year Parliament during the time of the Restoration.[117] In one of the last pieces of business, Churchill announced that he had asked Attlee to accompany him to the meeting of the Big Three in Potsdam, on the southwest outskirts of Berlin. As a potential prime minister, it was important that he was party to the decisions that were reached. Predictably, Bevan strongly objected to the invitation. Ostensibly, this was on the grounds that, once again, the Labour leader was being led around on a leash. But it also reflected Bevan's opposition to the idea – insisted upon by Bevin and Attlee at the Blackpool conference – that the foreign policy of a Labour government would largely be based on 'continuity' with that of the wartime coalition. Churchill feigned outrage at another example of Labour factionalism. Attlee leaned back and rebuked his own backbencher with a fierce glare.[118] For the moment, *Tribune* was prepared to cut Attlee some slack. He was triumphing with 'calm logic'; this was in stark contrast to Churchill, the 'political glamour boy with a shrewd eye on the centre of the stage'.[119]

Early July saw another spat between the leaders, when Churchill suggested that a Labour government would share state secrets on foreign policy with Laski and the National Executive. Under the terms of Labour's constitution, he alleged, this would effectively give Laski, the chairman, control over foreign policy, despite the fact that he was not in Parliament.[120] This time Attlee was more forthright in his reply to the prime minister's 'vile humbug'.[121] Significantly, those sections of the press which normally supported the Liberal Party – for which Churchill had made a play – tended to side with Attlee following the broadcast. 'Something has happened to Mr Churchill,' suggested the *Manchester Guardian*. He had lost the 'broad, noble sweep of his war leadership and degenerated into the most partisan of politicians'.[122] Meanwhile, the *Daily Herald* complained that the *Sunday Times*, owned by the Conservative Lord Kemsley, effectively suppressed Attlee's reply by giving it almost no coverage. Beaverbrook's *Sunday Express* published it under the headline, 'It Makes Them Squirm', alleging that Attlee had been trying to 'hush up' Churchill.[123]

There were other signs that the mood was swinging in Labour's favour. Labour's manifesto, *Let's Face the Future*, sold a million and a half copies, thereby easily outstripping the Beveridge Report.[124] On 3 July, Churchill was humiliated when an attempt to hold a mass rally at Walthamstow Stadium in northeast London – firm Attlee territory – backfired spectacularly. For days the Conservative press had forecasted a crowd of 50,000.[125] Only a fifth of that number turned up and the great majority were Labour supporters, who sang and heckled at every stage of his speech.[126] 'Don't bite the hand that led you', scolded the *Daily Mail*.[127]

Now it was the Conservatives who were squirming. Three days before polling day, the *Daily Herald* ran with a photograph of Attlee drinking tea from a mug, surrounded by adoring children in his constituency. He had insisted repeatedly that the choice to be made was not between him and Churchill but between two contending visions of the country. The British election would not be decided on the Führer principle, foisted on the British people by Tory tacticians, he said.[128]

Yet the truth was that Attlee did indeed see the election campaign as something of a personal duel between himself and Churchill, and he was quietly confident that it might be scored in his favour. 'I can't find that my opponent is getting any support,' he wrote to Tom. 'Winston keeps slogging away at the silly Laski business, but I don't think that he gets the better of the exchanges with me.'[129]

Part Five

New Jerusalem, New Deal, 1945–1947

15

To Hope Till Hope Creates

To suffer woes which Hope thinks infinite;
To forgive wrongs darker than death or night;

To defy Power, which seems omnipotent;
To love, and bear; to hope till Hope creates
From it's own wreck the thing it contemplates;
Neither to change, not falter, nor repent;
This, like thy glory, Titan, is to be
Good, great and joyous, beautiful and free;
This is alone Life, Joy, Empire, and Victory.

Percy Bysshe Shelley,
Prometheus Unbound, 1820

I *Potsdam, Germany, July 1945*

On 30 April 1945, the day after Attlee dined with his old friend from Lime-house in San Francisco, Adolf Hitler shot himself in the head with a revolver. As he had instructed, his body was taken out of his bunker, doused in petrol and set alight, alongside that of his wife Eva Braun. A day later, the Soviet army entered the garden of the Reich Chancellery in Berlin where the ashes lay, climbed into the bunker and found dead bodies strewn throughout. Among the many files found in Hitler's bunker was a copy of William Beveridge's report on *Social Insurance and Allied Services* – one of the many that had been translated and dropped on Germany as part of

Britain's propaganda campaign. Nazi Party officials had pored over it and one commented that it was 'no botch-up . . . superior to the current German social insurance in almost all points'. Another even suggested that it seemed that the British had converted to the state-centred socialism promised under Nazism.[1] Toynbee Hall, where both Beveridge and Attlee had been employed in the early part of their careers, had been bombed three times by the Nazis during the war. It was a strange quirk of history that the work of its alumni echoed back into the epicentre of the enemy's war machine.

A week later, on 7 May, Germany announced its unconditional surrender. On the day that victory was confirmed, Robert Vansittart, the former head of the Foreign Office who had been staunchly opposed to the appeasement of Hitler, wrote a celebratory article in the *Daily Mail*, titled 'After the storm'. In the article, he quoted the famous lines from the epilogue of Percy Shelley's *Prometheus*, spoken by Demogorgon:

> . . . to hope till Hope creates
> From its own wreck the thing it contemplates.[2]

For Vansittart and many Britons, the words were emblematic of Britain's emergence from a six-year struggle that had been 'darker than death or night'. This was a battle in which humanity had emerged triumphant. The very act of endurance contained the seeds of something more creative and hopeful.

Attlee would have approved of the choice of poem, though perhaps for different reasons to Vansittart. There was a revolutionary message embedded in Shelley's poem, which did not sit easily with much of the other content of the *Daily Mail* in 1945, and which spoke to something more than military victory. Shelley himself had been a political radical when he wrote the poem. He had been fiercely hostile to the Tory government that had defeated Napoleon Bonaparte after being at war with France for more than twenty years. In 1815, however, after the Battle of Waterloo, this Tory government had hung on to power for another decade, despite the economic storms that hit Britain when the fighting ended. For those on the left of the political spectrum, the key figures in this government – such as the foreign secretary Lord Castlereagh – were regarded as the bogeymen of British history. This, in fact, was the government that Attlee had condemned for taking away British liberties in his first election broadcast in response to Churchill – a riposte to the idea that it was Labour who would create a Gestapo if they won power.

Prometheus Unbound was already an Attlee family favourite. In his 1920 book, *The Social Worker*, Attlee had celebrated Shelley as one of the 'prophets' in the movement for radical political reform. In Shelley's work, injustice did not just intrude on the poet's vision, but inspired his every work.[3] Thomas Attlee, his brother, had quoted the very same lines from *Prometheus Unbound* when writing about the formation of a first Labour government in 1924, after a quarter century of struggle: 'to hope till Hope creates'.[4] As we have seen, it was by adapting a line from another Romantic poet, William Blake, that Attlee had conjured up the idea of building a 'New Jerusalem'.

The first British soldier to enter Hitler's bunker was Hugh Lunghi, a 25-year-old fluent Russian speaker, who had been sent to Berlin on behalf of the British government in the final days of the war. Lunghi was with the Red Army troops who spilled over the German border and aimed for the heart of the Nazi regime, before storming the bunker. 'It was damp and nasty and there was a lot of dirty clothing,' he recalled, many years later, 'a horrible, grim place which smelt terribly.' Outside the door, he saw a distinctive and neatly organised pile of ashes. Lunghi asked one of the Russian soldiers guarding the door what this was. 'Oh, that's Hitler and his mistress,' came the reply. 'My God,' thought the young Englishmen, 'this is history.'[5]

Hugh Lunghi shared something in common with Clement Attlee. Both had been schooled at Haileybury. In fact, they had even been in the same house, though Attlee was thirty years Lunghi's senior. In many ways, Lunghi was more typical of the Haileybury type than the Labour Party leader. He was born into a diplomatic family in Tehran, where his father was posted, and had an aristocratic Anglo-Russian mother. He had also followed the well-worn route to Oxford University, where he played rugby for the first XV. When the war began he joined the army as an artillery officer, rising to the rank of major. In 1943, he was sent to the British Embassy in Moscow because of his fluency in Russian. Stalin and the Soviet leaders came to see him as a familiar face, and he had already met Churchill on several occasions. He was sent to Berlin in preparation for the conference of victorious Allies due to take place in the small town of Potsdam, just outside the city.

On Sunday, 15 July, Lunghi was among the soldiers who stood to attention at Berlin airport as the British delegation to the Potsdam conference touched down on the tarmac. At 6.12 p.m., Winston Churchill, who looked 'well and happy', stepped down from the plane in full military regalia, and the Royal Marine band put on a full display in response to his famous 'V' for victory. The prime minister was welcomed with warm handshakes and pats on the back by General Ismay and Field Marshal Montgomery. Not for the first time, Clement Attlee, the leader of the opposition, stuck out as so very different from the prime minister. He did not have any military uniform but wore his usual three-piece suit. Lunghi commented that his 'small civilian figure' appeared 'a little incongruous amidst this display of military splendour'.

The conference was due to take place at the Cecilienhof Palace, just outside Potsdam, set in attractive parkland by the side of a lake. Attlee described it as a sort of 'Stock Exchange-Gothic mansion' and noted it was full of English books.[6] In the middle of the large garden in front of the palace, the Red Army had planted a magnificent five-pointed red star with begonias. Soviet officers manned the entrances and exits, while Royal Marines and American soldiers patrolled the corridors. Anthony Eden had been given a graciously furnished office and Churchill, known to work all hours of the day, had made sure that a bed was installed in his. Overhanging both were bookcases and portraits of the German royal family. Attlee was given a study in the palace and the use of a nearby house, requisitioned from the locals, many of whom had fled the incoming Red Army. Attlee's villa, remarked Alexander Cadogan, head of the Foreign Office, was 'drab and dreary . . . very suitable . . . just like Attlee himself'.[7]

That evening, Lunghi was instructed to act as chaperone for the Labour leader on a tour of Berlin. He collected Attlee from his study at 8.45 p.m. and was introduced to his private secretary, Joseph Burke, a former intelligence officer with a deep knowledge of the history of art. As the sun did not set until late, they had a good view of the bomb-ravaged and deserted city, including the Reich Chancellery, which had been the nerve centre of the Nazi regime. The party walked across the grounds and saw the bunker where Hitler spent his last days.[8] At one street corner, they came across a group of British soldiers gathered around smoking. Attlee got out of the car, 'made a bee line' for them, and chatted away merrily, posing for photos. He was greeted with a beep and a cheer when, instead of Churchill's 'V' sign, he gave a thumbs-up to another passing car of British troops. Watching this spectacle, an unimpressed Lunghi commented that the Labour leader seemed 'almost pathetically anxious to endear himself to the common people'.

It was over a glass of whisky that night that Lunghi revealed to the Labour leader that he had been in the same house at Haileybury, albeit many decades later. As he returned to his quarters he jotted down his first impressions: 'Mr Attlee does not seem to possess a dynamic personality; he is small, almost insignificant in appearance, with a head bald save for a crown of hair around the temples, bespectacled, bookish, quiet, studious. His voice has a peculiar quality of quiet, slightly high-pitched softness. He puffs at his pipe reflectively, and takes it out to make some quietly-humorous remark. He has a nice wry smile, that savours of shyness.'[9]

Churchill enjoyed being the main attraction at Potsdam. On his tours of the city, he was followed everywhere by a convoy of reporters and photographers, and insisted on travelling in an open-top jeep – to the discomfort of the troops protecting him – on the grounds that it gave him a better view. Attlee remained aloof. When Lunghi dined with him and the British ambassador to Russia, Sir Archibald Clark Kerr, the Labour leader was overshadowed by Burke, who hit it off with Clark Kerr as they discussed the architecture of Moscow. Attlee's mind seemed to be on the recent election campaign. It was only late in the evening on 18 July, his tongue loosened by a few drinks, that he allowed himself to be drawn into conversation on the likely result. The result was to be announced within a week. Both sides had made bold predictions about victory. His own guess was that Churchill would win a majority of about seventy seats.[10] This mild pessimism was consistent with his other predictions. John Colville recorded that, even in his most 'optimistic dreams' he thought the best possible result Labour could get was to be within forty seats of a majority.[11]

During the latter years of the war, Attlee had led the government's planning for post-war reconstruction in Germany. In between the business of the conference, he asked to be shown something of the country outside the main urban centres, so he could get an idea of conditions. On the morning of Thursday, 19 July, Lunghi made arrangements for him to visit Sanssouci Palace, built by Frederick the Great in the 1740s, and now occupied by the Red Army. The Soviet commanders liked to have advance warning of distinguished visitors, so that they could switch on the fountains for dramatic effect. They were joined by another familiar face – Flight Lieutenant Greenwood, from the British mission in Moscow, the son of Attlee's close colleague and one-time leadership rival, Arthur Greenwood. The path to the Brandenburg Gate was blocked by the Red Army, so they instead weaved through villages such as Michendorf, Beelitz and Lehnin, stopping to ask questions of local inhabitants. They talked to a young girl who told them that her family had installed themselves in a house vacated after a family of eleven had poisoned themselves to escape the advancing Red Army.

Before the British delegation left to return to London, they were treated to an Allied victory parade, which culminated in a procession to Berlin's Olympic Stadium, the venue for the 1936 games, which Hitler had used to showcase the Nazi regime. To Lunghi's surprise, the British troops seemed to give Attlee an even louder cheer than Churchill. He thought nothing more of it. Bounding around in his colonel's uniform, Churchill seemed untouchable and looked buoyant and full of vigour. On the morning of Wednesday, 25 July, as the British delegation prepared to return home, he watched as Churchill harangued Poland's communist leader, Bolesław Bierut, whom he regarded as a stooge of Moscow, about his responsibility to hold fair and free elections. Everyone had to face up to democracy one day. 'Today I am returning to England to learn the results of the elections,' said Churchill, 'I do not know what the results will be, and maybe the people will not return me, nor do I care.' Of course, this was mere gamesmanship. Watching Churchill closely, Lunghi thought to himself: 'Yes, it's all very well for you to say that, but you are certain of victory in the elections, and you know that in your heart you do care very much.'[12] Shortly before he left, General Ismay described how the prime minister proposed a toast to 'the next leader of the Opposition in Britain, whoever that might be.' As he sat down, Stalin's expression seemed to say 'It won't be you; anyone but you, you old fox.'[13]

II

The odds on a Labour victory had shortened over the course of the campaign. Nonetheless, it was reported that investors in the stock exchange were confident of a Conservative majority, if one slightly diminished.[14]

This was generally reported to be the consensus at Conservative Central Office.[15]

Whatever the result, the termination of the campaign would be greeted with some relief, observed John Winant, the American ambassador. The public seemed shocked at the 'mud-slinging, vituperation and electoral tactics indulged in by all parties, coming so soon after harmony that prevailed during the coalition'. This had been accentuated above all by the antics of the Beaverbrook press, which had been 'particularly violent, inaccurate and personal'. Winant explained the difficulty of making accurate predictions with so many imponderables in play. First among these was the likely voting behaviour of those below the age of thirty. They amounted to one-third of a potential 30 million voters but had never voted before. Second was the uncertainty of the armed service vote. With the Liberals trying to engineer a revival – hoping to capitalise on the fact that William Beveridge was one of their number – there were large numbers of three-way contests. There was also the displacement and redistribution of population because of evacuations and the dispersal of wartime industries. There was one final wild-card question: would votes be cast for Churchill, the great national hero, regardless of party feeling?[16]

On 23 July 1945, three days before the result was to be announced, the *Manchester Guardian* speculated that there might be a stalemate, with no party winning an outright majority. In these circumstances, Attlee and Churchill might well be forced to form a coalition government once again.[17] The result would depend on the answer to a number of key questions. What were the effects of the war on the British political temper? How far had it 'gone Left'? To what extent were Continental political trends, such as the rapid spread of communism in the east, 'paralleled in our own unrevolutionary setting'?[18]

On 25 July, Churchill, Eden and Attlee made their way back to the airport in Berlin. They returned home, in convoy, on separate planes. The two party leaders arrived within an hour of each other at RAF Northolt, while Eden was taken to the Wiltshire aerodrome, so that he could head to his constituency to hear the count. Churchill was driven by chauffeur to Buckingham Palace to give the king a report on the conference, while Attlee was picked up by Violet in the same Hillman in which she had driven him round the country during the campaign. 'It was a pleasant and uneventful journey,' he told the reporters camped outside his home in

Stanmore. A photographer from the trusted *Daily Herald* was allowed into the home. On the eve of the election results, Attlee was pictured in his favourite armchair, with Violet and his daughters sitting around and gazing at him adoringly, while he caught up with a pile of official Labour Party papers given to him by his private secretary, Joseph Burke.[19]

Among those papers was an unpleasant surprise. One letter opened by Burke was particularly sensitive. He resealed it and scribbled on the envelope that only Attlee himself should see it. It was from Herbert Morrison. Morrison informed Attlee that, over the previous weeks, a number of colleagues had approached him asking him if he would be willing to accept the nomination for the leadership of the Labour Party, which traditionally elected its new leader before the parliamentary session. This he had accepted. 'That I am animated solely by considerations of the interests of the party, and regard for their democratic rights, and not by any personal unfriendliness towards yourself, I need hardly assure you.'[20] Attlee replied with his most famous one-liner: 'Thank you for your letter, the contents of which have been noted.'[21]

On Thursday, 26 July, on the morning of the election results, the *Daily Mail* warned that if defeated, as they expected, Labour must 'accept an adverse verdict like men and not like spoilt children'.[22] At 10 a.m. the first results came through from Salford, where there had been three Labour gains. Within a few minutes, it was clear that Labour had taken almost complete control of central Manchester and that there were other gains in Tynemouth, Peterborough, Dulwich and Bethnal Green. By 11 a.m., 150 results were in, with sixty of them gains for Labour. Then senior Tories started falling like 'ninepins'. Brendan Bracken, the First Lord of the Admiralty, was out at North Paddington and Harold Macmillan, Minister of Air, who was earmarked as a future leader, defeated at Stockton. Bevin had won Central Wandsworth, Morrison romped home in East Lewisham, A. V. Alexander held Hillsborough, and Cripps was back in with a massive victory at Bristol East.[23]

In the East End, as ever, things were more complicated. Mile End elected a Communist MP, Phil Piratin. This was of particular disappointment to Attlee given his battles against the Communist Party for so many years.[24] The electorate in Attlee's own seat, Limehouse, had been reduced to about 44 per cent of its pre-war size by the Blitz and he won comfortably against the Conservative candidate, Lieutenant Colonel Alfred Wood – 8,396 to 1,618.

Violet was a counting agent and had overseen the opening of the boxes. Attlee was cheered when he left Labour headquarters at Transport House, and arrived at the People's Palace in Limehouse to hear the declaration, with two of his daughters, Janet and Felicity, alongside him. 'Give us a victory smile, Clem,' shouted one woman, as he waved to the crowd.[25]

As they drove through the city, the Attlees picked up Alison at Waterloo station and moved on to Labour Party headquarters at Transport House, where there seemed to be much excitement, judging by the photographers outside.[26] Inside, a crowd gathered around a television monitor, as news flooded in of more Tory scalps. Duncan Sandys, Minister of Works and Churchill's son-in-law, was defeated at Norwood and Churchill's own son, Randolph, lost at Preston. So far, five Tory Cabinet ministers had lost their seats. Even Churchill, so supremely confident at Potsdam, had been given a scare. His opponent, an independent local farmer, racked up an astonishing 10,488 votes against Churchill's 27,688. It seemed as if no seat was safe. The Liberals fared disastrously, despite increasing their share of the popular vote. By 2 p.m. the Press Association flashed out a banner on television screens announcing 'Labour In'. The final result was announced at 7 p.m., and the scale of the victory was jaw dropping. Labour had gained 225 seats – up from 165 to 390 – and the Conservatives were down from 361 to 195, a loss of 166. The breakdown of the popular vote was 11,692,678 to 9,018,235. The Liberals were almost wiped out entirely, down to just twelve seats. All of Attlee's principal colleagues in the wartime government – Morrison, Bevin, Greenwood, Alexander, Dalton and Cripps – were returned.[27]

Labour now dominated almost 80 per cent of the northeast and London, 75 per cent of the Midlands, 70 per cent of the northwest and Wales, and 57 per cent of Scotland (where its advance had been the least dramatic). One of the most striking aspects of the result was the way in which it had asserted itself in the south and southeast, where it had taken 50 per cent of seats, and had even made significant breakthroughs in rural areas.[28] The composition of the new Labour Party in Parliament told another story too. It was a true cross-section of society. Of the 383 MPs, there were forty-four lawyers, forty-nine university lecturers or schoolteachers, sixteen managers and technicians, 150 manual workers, eight housewives and thirty-nine miners. The number of women in Parliament had doubled from fourteen to thirty. Nearly all of these were Labour.[29]

In Transport House, as the scale of the victory became clear, there were scenes of jubilation. Attlee was mobbed, slapped on the back, and squeezed so tight between admirers that the red rose on his buttonhole fell to the floor.[30] As the US Embassy reported, in a telegram sent back to Washington, DC, the victory 'startled Great Britain', and 'no one was more surprised than were the leaders of the Labour Party.'[31]

Meanwhile, a crowd had gathered in Downing Street. At 7 p.m., when the final result was announced, applause broke out as Churchill, cigar in mouth, left Number 10 and climbed into a limousine. He was driven to Buckingham Palace to tender his resignation to George VI. At 7.30, the Attlee family car trundled up the Mall to the palace, and drove in through the gate, past a cheering crowd. Violet, dressed in her Sunday best, had driven, though she was not allowed entry into the palace as the king wanted to see her husband alone.[32]

Back at Number 10, as he began to gather his possessions, Churchill seemed to take defeat with good grace. 'Well, you know what happened?' he asked when Lord Moran came to check on his health that night. He rubbished a suggestion by his doctor that Attlee might not stand up to Stalin with sufficient vigour when he returned to Potsdam. Perhaps, even, defeat might be a blessing in disguise. He was unsure whether the Conservative Party could have coped with the critical economic troubles that he saw looming like dark clouds on the horizon.[33]

That night, bonfires burned in the streets of east London, in a scene that was compared to the jubilations of VE Day. A reporter from the *Daily Herald* saw a burning effigy of Duncan Sandys being thrown onto a fire, and described how one dockworker walked along Commercial Road in Mile End, with a placard hung over his chest which read 'THIS IS THE HOUR OF TRIUMPH OF THE COMMON MAN'.[34] The *Manchester Guardian*, which had supported the Liberal Party, suggested that the victory was 'probably a much vaguer moment than some Labour left-wingers would like to think'. It was not a vote for a rigorous application of socialism, so much as an expression of mistrust of the Conservatives, combined with a desire to give Labour a chance. Many voters would now feel a little apprehension about having handed Labour a victory in such treacherous economic circumstances. Nonetheless, it was quite clear that the country had 'undergone a silent revolution' during the war. As a candidate for the Liberal Party,

William Beveridge had failed to win a seat in Parliament. Yet, it seemed, his 'famous plan goes marching on'.[35]

Throughout all this, Attlee appeared 'calm and discreet', and looked a little tired. Replete with fresh red-and-yellow flowers in his buttonhole, he read out a statement to the press in a cramped room on the second floor of Transport House with a view of Westminster behind him. Harold Laski, the source of such mischief as party chairman, sat beaming beside him. Attlee kept his eyes focused most of the time on the pipe he held between his hands. Occasionally he glanced up to emphasise one of the points he was making in a 'clear unemotional voice'.[36]

That night, Attlee addressed a celebratory meeting of new MPs in Central Hall in Westminster. When he entered the room there were five minutes of continuous cheering. He wondered what Keir Hardie would have made of the result, and thought back to those 'unknown comrades' who had toiled for the movement for so many years. Labour would not lose the confidence that the country had placed in it, he said.[37]

Morrison had been seen arriving at the rally with a large smile on his face, ready to make one last bid to snatch the leadership from Attlee's hands. First he tried to encourage Bevin to start a contest by suggesting he would be the ideal man to lead the party. When Bevin warned him to stop scheming, he continued to solicit support for a leaderhip bid, even approaching one MP in the lavatory before Attlee took the stage at Central Hall. He made sure to remind everyone that it was the convention for Labour MPs to elect a new leader at the start of a new Parliament. It was in this way that Ramsay MacDonald had replaced J. H. Clynes in 1922, despite the latter leading the party in the election.[38] For Attlee, there was no question of stepping down now. 'If you are invited by the King to form a Government, you don't say you can't reply for forty-eight hours,' he said, only to 'go back and say you can't and advise the King to send for someone else.'[39]

It was Ernie Bevin who put an end to the intrigue that night in Central Hall. He moved a vote of confidence in Attlee as leader, smothering any dying embers from Morrison's leadership challenge. It was a fine performance, delivered without notes. 'He spoke in telling phrases of Attlee's constant fidelity to principle and his unimpeachable personal integrity. The contrast between the two leaders during the election had enabled the country to realise who was Nature's gentleman.' Attlee's speech of thanks that followed was typical in avoiding triumphalism. 'Without a trace of emotion he alluded to the tremendous nature of our victory,' commented James Chuter Ede, who was set for a major role in the new government as home secretary. 'Attlee is no firework but the country find that Churchill had produced just the appropriate background' for the victory.[40] The meeting ended with the singing of 'The Red Flag' but Attlee, who handed over the microphone to Morrison, had already left with the cheers ringing in his ears.[41]

Outside Central Hall, the crowds had swelled. Whisked through the lines by a police escort, with his daughters by his side, he and Violet momentarily forgot where they had parked the car. The crowd surrounded him, backslapping and jostling him with effusive good will. Having located the motor, he stood on the running board. 'Speech!' someone yelled, and a hush settled. The new prime minister cleared his throat. 'Will you folks please let my daughters through.'[42]

The family were rather perturbed by the circus that followed them. 'Don't talk to me about it,' Violet had told a reporter, when asked how she would run the household at Number 10. It was a job enough taking care of the home at Stanmore. Despite the warm weather, she was seen clutching a crooked umbrella. With so many official occasions coming up, she could not afford to spoil her best hat, a scarlet boater. 'It's an old one but a nice one,' she commented, 'I can't afford new clothes these days with the coupon situation as it is and three daughters. It's been a hard war for all of us.' Would she be joining her husband when he returned to the Big Three conference at Potsdam, as Clementine Churchill had done? 'Goodness no! I'll be too busy. Besides, I'm not a great traveller.'[43]

The day after the result, the Attlee family gathered for a typically understated celebration – lunch and tea at the Paddington Hotel. Felicity, now nearly twenty, was due to graduate shortly from her training as a nursery school teacher. Alison, now fifteen, was still in school in Salisbury, while Janet, twenty-two, had got leave from her job as an ATS section officer. Martin had joined the Merchant Navy just two weeks before and would not be in touch until his ship had docked.[44] He sent his congratulations from the SS *Menelaus* via a telegram. 'Very glad to hear from you,' came the reply, 'Everything going very well. Family Send Love. Daddy.'[45] Felicity was to move in with her parents at Number 10, and would commute to work in Bermondsey, taking a bus from Whitehall every morning.[46] Janet, in addition to her ATS duties, had recently qualified as an assistant psychologist in a Bristol mental hospital, and would live there.[47]

On the night of the victory, as he prepared to return to Potsdam, the new prime minister announced who would fill the most important posts in his government. As well as being prime minister, he would act as Minister of Defence, following the precedent set by Churchill in the war. Morrison was made Lord President of the Council and Ernest Bevin was to be foreign secretary, Arthur Greenwood was appointed Lord Privy Seal, Hugh Dalton was made chancellor, and Stafford Cripps was brought back into the party hierarchy as President of the Board of Trade.[48]

The *Daily Mail* expressed alarm at the elevation of Dalton and Cripps to such senior economic positions. Dalton, they suggested, was incompetent, while Cripps was a 'doctrinaire socialist' who would cause anxiety in both the City and British industry. Bevin and Attlee were at least 'good Englishmen', and would take care of Britain's overseas interests.[49] In fact, Attlee had been leaning towards appointing Dalton as foreign minister, and believed that the home front was better for Bevin, who had himself asked to be chancellor.[50] When he had travelled to Buckingham Palace, however, the king had expressed a preference for Bevin, which, Attlee confessed, made an impression on him. Another consideration was the need to keep Morrison and Bevin apart. If Bevin were chancellor he and Morrison were likely to clash on the home front, so it was best to keep them in separate spheres.[51] Finally, the Foreign Office had also expressed concerns about Dalton's difficult personality.[52]

Morrison, too, had lobbied for the job but this was more with an eye on its seniority than a reflection of his interest in foreign affairs. By making him Lord President of the Council, and the leader of the party in the Commons, Attlee reassured him that he was, in effect, 'his number two'.[53] Meanwhile, The *Daily Herald* presented Bevin as the ideal heir to Churchillian robustness in diplomacy.[54] This view was also supported by the *Manchester Guardian*, which suggested that, though he had little experience in this arena, the 'root of the matter is in him'. He would make mistakes but he would never be without a strategy.[55]

IV

When the election results had been made known at Potsdam, the British delegation was reported to be 'dumbstruck' and 'aghast'. This was particularly true of the senior military figures, who could not reconcile themselves to the fact that Churchill, with whom they had been so intimately linked throughout the war years, had been given his marching orders. 'No one, in his wildest dreams, contemplated anything even remotely approaching this,' commented Hugh Lunghi.[56] Alanbrooke, who had clashed with Attlee at a number of points during the war, wrote that it was a 'ghastly mistake to start elections in this period in the World's History! May God forgive England for it.'[57] 'It certainly is a display of base ingratitude,' agreed Cadogan, 'and rather humiliating for our country.'[58]

Attlee was back in Potsdam on Saturday, 28 July. With him travelled Ernie Bevin, Sir Edward Bridges, secretary to the Cabinet Office, and General Ismay, with whom he had always had good relations. He was moved to the same house that Churchill had stayed in previously – known in the conference vernacular as 'Number 10 Downing Street'. Bevin was to have the first of a number of meetings with his Russian and American counterparts, foreign minister Vyacheslav Molotov and the newly appointed US Secretary of State, James Byrnes, respectively.[59] Ismay was confident that Attlee would perform well, as he 'knew all the ropes'. Bevin was an unknown quantity but Ismay quickly warmed to him. As soon as he arrived at the airport, the new foreign secretary had declared 'I'm not going to let Britain be barged about.'[60]

The British ambassador Charles Kerr noted that the Russians were 'utterly bewildered even gibbering with astonishment' at the fact that Churchill was gone.[61] The reaction to Attlee's election in *Pravda*, the organ of the Soviet government, was one of 'extreme reserve'. The Labour Party was regarded with profound suspicion by the Communist Party.[62] As Ivan Maisky, the Russian ambassador to Britain who was in Potsdam, observed, the Anglo-Soviet relationship pivoted around Churchill and the rapport he had struck up with Stalin.[63]

American officials at the British Embassy in London understood this well. They predicted that the Labour Party would be more likely to take a tough line with Stalin because of their hatred of the Communist Party at home, as much as in the international sphere.[64] Those Americans with less experience of British politics did not quite know what to make of this 'bald, stooped, and somewhat birdlike' figure who had replaced Churchill. According to the *Baltimore Sun*, the new prime minister was an odd fit in a world 'but lately run by Franklin Roosevelt of the cigarette holder, Winston Churchill of the chewed cigar and upheld V-sign, and Josef Stalin of the pipe and imposing moustache'. Yet, it was also clear that 'he was nothing of the shadow he has appeared.'[65] The *Washington Post* noted that there was something of a similarity between Attlee and President Truman, who had replaced Roosevelt following his death in April. Both men had taken over from larger personalities; both presided over restless and easily divided parties.[66]

On the evening of Saturday, 28 July, Attlee and Bevin attended their first plenary session, which lasted into the small hours of Sunday. By morning, Lunghi, acting as interpreter, began to adjust his previous opinion of Attlee. On the question of setting Poland's western frontier, it was instructive to watch the difference in technique between the new prime minister and the old. Lunghi was impressed by the 'sound, well-informed and realistic way in which Attlee, particularly, and also Bevin tackled the matter'. They got to the 'root of every question' and would not permit themselves to be distracted by 'red-herring digression' – a trap into which Churchill could sometimes fall. At one point, Bevin leaned his large frame across Attlee to Lunghi and said, 'Tell them, that in the Labour Party we call a spade a spade.' The interpreter did this with some relish, though, for the sake of translation, he substituted hoe for spade.

The following afternoon, on 29 July, Bevin and Attlee subjected the Polish communist leader Bierut to a 'regular catechism' on his responsibility to ensure free elections, freedom of press, and freedom of religion. While they were following the agreed Foreign Office line, they did so 'in telling fashion, tying their verbal opponents down to definite, committing, answers'. Sitting at Attlee's left, Lunghi watched in fascination as the new prime minister doodled a series of neat geometric designs, and also a caricature, though it was unclear of whom.[67]

At dinner with the British delegation on Monday evening, the Labour leader, sitting at the head of the table, seemed visibly more relaxed than he had been before the election. 'Mr Attlee was in elated spirits, and though his quiet temperament never gives way to boisterous display, he kept us all amused with joyful anecdotes and quips in a vein of political satire, showing that he has an excellent memory and a restrained but quizzical sense of humour.' The wine at dinner was good, and the food was passable, commented Lunghi, but 'all the spice was provided by the amusing conversation which revealed the P.M. as a good table-companion when in genial mood.'

There was no triumphalism. Attlee warned that Labour would not have it their own way, despite its huge majority. He suspected the Conservatives would likely perform well in the by-elections during the next Parliament. One reason for this was that so many of their heavy hitters had been voted out and would be aiming to regain a seat. In a telling phrase, he understood that the 'moderately-minded British electorate might feel a subconscious urge to redress the balance a little by opposing too violent a Leftish trend.'[68]

Some senior Americans, such as Admiral Leahy, had expressed concern that the Labour government would depart from Churchill's line on the essentials. Between them, Attlee and Bevin soon exploded the idea that Labour would adopt a softer approach. Indeed, Bevin surprised the Americans by his conservative suggestion that Germany might have been better off with a constitutional monarchy after the end of the last war, rather than a hurried transition to democracy.[69] James Byrnes, the Secretary of State, noted 'nothing of the actor' in Attlee. More importantly, President Truman thought highly of Attlee's performance at Potsdam, and his 'deep understanding of the world's problems'. At one point, they sat at the piano and sang bawdy soldier songs that they remembered from their time as junior officers in World War I.[70] The bonding experience was to be important, as Potsdam only sketched out the basic outline of the post-war settlement in Europe and left many other issues untouched, such as the future of Lend-Lease, by which American loans had propped up the British wartime economy, but which was due to expire after victory.

At noon on 2 August 1945, the conference came to a close in the main chamber of Cecilienhof. Attlee proposed a vote of thanks to General Stalin. That night, the new prime minister returned to familiar surroundings in the family home in Stanmore for the last time before their move to Downing Street. Once again, a press photographer was allowed into the home as Attlee, appearing almost like a tourist, opened a leather satchel and showed Violet and his daughters souvenirs from the conference. One included a signed photograph of President Truman, which he proudly put on a shelf in his study. There it sat alongside a photograph of Attlee and George VI, which Violet had had framed for him as a Christmas present.[71] Such was the mantelpiece of Britain's most successful socialist leader.

V

On 3 August, Attlee rose before 6 a.m. and made the final decisions as to who would be in his Cabinet. At noon, he drove again to Buckingham Palace, where he presented the king with a list of nineteen ministers. Clem and Violet spent their first night in Downing Street, though it was still full of many of the Churchills' possessions. As he returned, a bust of Churchill was being carried out of the building. Shortly afterwards, the chiefs of staff arrived for their first meeting with Attlee as prime minister.[72] They were followed into the building by the Attlee family kitten, Whiskey, and Ting, their old Welsh terrier. With three of their four children having reached adulthood, the Attlees took only one floor of the Downing Street flat. Churchillian grandeur was not on the agenda for Britain's suburban prime minister.[73]

Churchill reflected on the oddly English nature of this revolution in an account of a dream he had after his defeat. In the dream, as he painted in his studio at Chartwell, his father, Lord Randolph Churchill, appeared as a ghost of the past, and asked him questions about modern Britain. Churchill told his father that Britain now had a socialist government with a very large majority. 'Socialist!' exclaimed Lord Randolph, 'But I thought you said we still have a Monarchy.' Winston explained that in fact the majority of socialists were not republican at all, but looked upon the monarchy with great fondness. They were quite happy to go to parties at Buckingham Palace. 'Those who have extreme principles wear sweaters,' he explained. Meanwhile the new government might nationalise the mines and railways but it would pay full compensation to the oligarchs of industry. 'You know, Papa, though very stupid, they are quite respectable, and increasingly bourgeois.'[74] There was an element of truth in this. Attlee was to become very close to George VI. He enjoyed the king's informality. He noted how Queen Victoria had made her ministers stand in her presence whereas George VI preferred a cigarette and a gossip.[75]

The composition of the new government told a different story, however.

There were seven ex-miners in the Cabinet, most of whom had gone into the pits when they were barely teenagers. Of the twenty-six ministers, fifteen had been to state schools and only ten to university. Just two had been to Eton, compared to the nine in Churchill's Cabinet. These were Dalton and Frederick W. Pethick Lawrence – the Secretary of State for India, whom Bevan had once called a 'crusted old Tory'.

Nearly all of Attlee's ministers had served, in some capacity, in the wartime government. After Bevin, Morrison, Dalton, and Cripps, the next rank of ministers mostly came from the same generation as their leader: the home secretary, James Chuter Ede, a former school teacher, was sixty-four; George Isaacs, labour minister, who began life at a print works before he was a teenager, was sixty-two; Jack Lawson, war secretary, who had worked with Attlee at the War Office in 1924, was sixty-four; A. V. Alexander, returned to the Admiralty, was sixty-four. The oldest minister was 76-year old Lord Addison, the Dominions Secretary, a former Liberal with vast experience, who had been the Minister of Health in 1919. The youngest, and the most energetic person in the Cabinet, was born in 1897. He was 48-year old Aneurin Bevan, who took control of both Health and Housing. Contrary to what Bevan later claimed, Attlee insisted that it had been his own idea to put him in charge of Health. Despite his rebellious streak, Attlee believed Bevan could be a 'conciliator'. Far from wishing to hold Bevan back, Attlee made it clear that he now had a clean sheet and an opportunity to learn.[76] On the next tier down, other important figures included Philip Noel-Baker, Minister of State under Bevin at the Foreign Office, the colonial secretary George Henry Hall, and the only woman in the Cabinet, 'Red' Ellen Wilkinson, the Minister of Education, with whom Attlee had travelled to Spain ten years before.[77]

The Economist commented that the list of appointments aroused an emotion of 'anti-climax rather than exhilaration'. Some of the choices seemed odd, such as moving Chuter Ede from education, where he was an expert, to the Home Office, and swapping him with Wilkinson, who had spent the war in the Home Office. The average age of the Cabinet also drew some comment. It was higher than that in both the wartime coalition and Churchill's short-term government.[78] Seen from the outside, another striking thing about the composition was the weight of trade union influence in the government, heavier than that of the intellectual wing of the party.

Attlee was famously to comment a few months later that the 'old school tie' could still be seen in his government. But in other ways, his collection of ministers had more of a 'school of hard knocks' image.[79]

On 3 August at 10.45 a.m., MPs assembled in Westminster and went to take the oath of allegiance. Attlee gave the new Labour members of the House three pieces of advice: do not talk in the lobby of the Commons; do not loiter or dine in West End restaurants; and do not converse with Lord Beaverbrook. He was 'a magnet to all young men', but if they talked to him no good would come of it. 'Beware of flattery,' he warned. 'I am a very diffident man,' he also explained, 'I find it very hard to carry on conversation. But if any of you come to see me, I will welcome you. I will receive you and I will discuss your problems with you.'[80]

After so many years of criticism from his own party, Attlee was in no doubt about his weaknesses. He could not seize a moment with a great speech, and he had neither the force of personality, nor the appetite, to impose his will on others, nor to demand total loyalty. Nonetheless, having survived ten years as Labour leader, and having led the party to its greatest victory, there was more evidence than ever before that his methods had their merits. His comments on what qualities made an effective MP were partly a meditation on his own approach. An MP 'has to know his stuff; he mustn't talk too much; he must be good tempered; not conceited; and be known to be a decent chap.' Friendliness and common sense were necessary, while 'Machiavellian manipulators of men' were overrated. There was 'always a tendency for men with small minds, and a great deal of self-ishness in their nature, to assume that if one man succeeds in getting others to work with him, he is endowed with an even greater fund of self-seeking qualities' than them. In most cases, leadership required other traits: 'moral or physical courage; sympathy; self-discipline; altruism; and superior capacity for hard work'.[81]

Writing for the *Spectator* in early August, Francis Williams made the obvious assertion that the new prime minister would not be 'in the Churchill mould'. Williams was aware of Attlee's limitations in handling the media and he offered his services as press secretary at Number 10.[82] In the 1930s, as editor of the *Daily Herald*, he had seen Morrison as the ideal leader of the party. However, he had now corrected his view – not least because of Morrison's scheming. One reason Attlee had survived so many years was that he had 'great if unassuming gifts of integrity, moral and intellectual honesty and calm judgement'.[83]

Those on the right of the spectrum tended to see Attlee's success in less flattering terms. According to the *Daily Mail*, the post-war era was 'an age of understudies – unexpected, incongruous men who are suddenly thrust into the places of colourful and even flamboyant personalities'. Thus Harry Truman succeeded Franklin Roosevelt, just before Attlee succeeded Churchill. Yet it was agreed that the new prime minister had been somewhat underestimated. 'At first sight Attlee seems insignificant, but from one thing even his enemies – inside the party or out of it – have never even sought to detract, his integrity.' He had, after all, been the first man whom Churchill asked to join his government in 1940 and the work he did during the war, while 'inconspicuous . . . should not, in fairness, be underrated'.[84] Most bemused were Attlee's critics on the left. Jimmy Maxton of the ILP confessed that the result was 'totally unexpected'. Attlee was of 'clean, upright character' with 'undoubted brainpower'. But it was still hard to accept that he was responsible for such a victory. 'Even now I don't believe that Labour so much won the election as that Churchill and his most vocal colleagues lost it.'[85]

This view of Attlee as a passenger of history, carried along by the force of events, is highly misleading. If a revolution had occurred in British politics because of the war, surely the role of the man who presided over it deserves more serious consideration? First of all, there is no question that there was a leftward shift in British politics in the intervening years. One reason why Nye Bevan was so infuriated by the electoral truce was that he felt it gave the Conservatives a free hand to keep up their majority when the evidence suggested that they were losing support. Independent left-wing candidates who had stood against Conservatives in by-elections during the war had fared increasingly well, even though Churchill's personal popularity rarely dipped below 80 per cent after the end of 1942. Montgomery's great victory at El Alamein, followed by the success of Operation Torch, had effectively saved his position. Still, there was an appetite for a left-wing alternative. While Labour respected the truce, Sir Richard Acland's newly founded Common Wealth Party – which owed much to guild socialism – won seats in April 1943, January 1944, and April 1945. Although Acland joined Labour after the 1945 general election, and the Common Wealth Party faded into oblivion, it had clearly captured something of the change in national mood. Given its popularity, it was also the case that the party perceived to be most likely to deliver the Beveridge Report had an advantage.[86]

Attlee had watched these developments carefully throughout the war. With regard to Acland, he believed that 'a vote for a splinter candidate does not carry with it a support for an alternative Government.' As Attlee wrote in March 1944, there was no question in his mind that there was 'undoubtedly a left-wing swing, especially in regard to post-war problems'.[87] The key question was timing Labour's next move to ensure maximum possible effect. On this he was in full agreement with Bevin. In November 1944, they had come under pressure from the party to force the government to take the coal mines, and iron and steel industries, into public ownership in preparation for the post-war period. Both Bevin and Attlee believed that this would be a crucial measure in any future Labour government's economic plans. However, they felt that it must have the support of the public and could not be pushed through by skulduggery, or by threatening to bring the coalition down. 'To have a showdown on these matters seems to me to be the wrong tactics, which will be seen through quite easily.'[88]

Undoubtedly, Bevin and Morrison played a significant role in raising Labour's profile, and demonstrating that it was capable of office. They were widely regarded as two of the most dynamic ministers in the government, with much clearer briefs than the one Attlee was given. It was Ernest Bevin's clunking fist – girded by the support of the unions – which kept, just about, the rebels on the left of the party from outright rebellion. And it was Morrison who did more than anyone to determine Labour's political strategy. His mastery over the London County Council elections had taught him that Labour must also appeal to a significant portion of the middle classes to achieve a national victory: Morrison wrote the Labour manifesto, *Let Us Face the Future*, to this end. Aside from the content, two things are worth noting about it: it sold a million and a half copies; and it did not mention Attlee. This stands in stark contrast to the Conservative manifesto, which was called *Mr. Churchill's Declaration of Policy to the Electors*.[89]

There were other developments that played into Attlee's hands. The warm reception that he received from the British soldiers at Potsdam was revealing. Although it was not a decisive factor, the evidence suggests that the service vote – that of the 2 million Britons serving abroad at the time of polling – did tilt strongly in Labour's favour. As much as anything, this seems to have been linked to two considerations: employment and housing. The majority of those who served were from working-class backgrounds. They were raised on stories of the betrayal of those, like their fathers and uncles, who were demobilised in 1919: the government failed to provide 'homes fit for heroes', or do anything to mitigate the levels of unemployment which, in the worst years of the depression, were almost as high as the number who had been conscripted to fight. Raymond Williams, a tank commander who later became a Marxist intellectual, captured this perfectly when explaining the service vote in 1945. 'It was a vote for a job. This is how people talked about it. They associated the Tories with unemployment and depression. People knew what happened when the army went back after 1918.'[90] Once again, Attlee was quick to identify the significance of this to Labour Party strategy. 'I find intelligent Service men often of high rank and men in various walks of life who come to me and tell me that they have been converted to Socialism by what they have seen done in wartime,' he wrote to Laski, 'It is therefore in my view mistaken tactics to belittle what has been done.'[91]

If these were the most pressing concerns, then the Labour Party was best placed to deliver upon them. One might add that three of the traditional reasons why people tended not to vote Labour were also eroded by the experience of the war. The first was that the fear of the 'Red Menace', often used by the Conservative press against Labour, had been much diminished by the popularity of Russia in Britain in 1945 and the widespread admiration for the efforts of the Red Army at places like Stalingrad. The second – the impression that Labour were somehow weaker on defence and foreign affairs issues – was also exploded by the firm stance that the party had taken against appeasement. This was now widely seen as a Tory sin of the 1930s, a decade when, of course, Churchill himself had been marginalised by his own party. The third impression that the electorate was disabused of was that Labour was somehow inefficient on economic matters. In many ways, the conduct of the war on the home front – the mobilisation of manpower and industry – was a vindication of Labour notions of planning; Churchill's dependence on Bevin and Morrison in this area was the greatest possible compliment.[92]

It would be easy to play down Attlee's own role, given these wider trends pointing in Labour's favour. Yet one reason why Churchill's first election broadcast was seen as so counter-productive was the calm and reasoned way in which Attlee swatted it down. It is impossible to imagine Bevin or Bevan offering a more effective rebuttal. Attlee's steady hand, and lack of egotism, throughout the years of the war stood him in very good stead by 1945. He understood intuitively 'that it was quite useless for me to pretend that I was as colourful a figure as Winston'.[93] But he bided his time and made an impact in different ways.

As we have seen, he was subject to almost daily criticism, some of it verging on the hysterical, in *Tribune*, and undermined by Cripps, Laski and Bevan. At various points he could have used the trade union steam roller, as well as the fact that he had majority support in the Parliamentary Labour Party, to score a decisive victory over his critics. Instead, he let himself become a lightning rod for discontent in a way that prevented the rupture of the party. Ernest Bevin never had the patience for this game. No individual did more than Attlee to keep the Labour Party in the coalition without splitting. This was no mean feat in itself.

The underlying reality was that Attlee's political instincts were far subtler and more attuned to the mood of the country than those of his main critics, Bevan and Laski. He has been consistently underestimated as a practioner of these arts.[94] Bevan was a hero for a portion of the Labour Party, but was widely regarded as hysterical, disloyal and unpatriotic by those outside it. He turned a blind eye to the Soviet invasion of Finland in 1939, would have taken Labour out of the coalition at various points, and was constantly demanding the sacking of Churchill.[95] Attlee was proved right in refusing to follow the paths that both Bevan and Laski urged him to take. It was ironic, Attlee said, that for a professor of political science, Laski 'never quite got the hang of it'.[96] That Laski came to him, cap in hand, after the victory in 1945 and asked to be made ambassador to America must have been a sweet moment for the man he had tried to force out just a few days before.[97] It was typical of Attlee not to make anything of this, though Laski did not get the job.

While Attlee refused to regard himself as a 'political hero' and 'had not much idea of destiny', he was more responsible than any other individual for the position that Labour found itself in on 27 July 1945.[98] It was the Labour Party's patriotism which had earned it the position it now found itself in.

In a letter to Bevin at the end of the war, he wrote the simple but powerful line: 'In serving the country you have also served our movement.'[99] In the same spirit, but even more revealing, was a note he had written to Laski back in January 1941, when he first came under serious criticsm about his lack of strategy. 'I am sufficiently experienced in warfare,' he ventured, 'to know that the frontal attack with a flourish of trumpets, heartening, as it is, is not the best way to capture a position.'[100] Four years later, Attlee's strategy had indeed been vindicated.

16

English Traits, American Problems

And so, gentlemen, I feel in regard to this aged England, with the possessions, honors and trophies, and also with the infirmities of a thousand
years gathering around her, irretrievably committed as she now is to many
old customs which cannot be suddenly changed; pressed upon by the
transitions of trade, and new and all incalculable modes, fabrics, arts,
machines, and competing populations, – I see her not dispirited, not
weak, but well remembering that she has seen dark days before; – indeed
with a kind of instinct that she sees a little better in a cloudy day, and that
in storm of battle and calamity, she has a secret vigor and a pulse like a
cannon. I see her in her old age, not decrepit, but young, and still daring
to believe in her power of endurance and expansion. Seeing this, I say, All
hail! mother of nations, mother of heroes, with strength still equal to the
time; still wise to entertain and swift to execute the policy which the
mind and heart of mankind requires in the present hour ...

Ralph Waldo Emerson, *English Traits*, 1844[1]

I *Chequers, August 1945*

In later years, when he could afford to say it, Attlee used to claim that the
secret to his political longevity was that he did not take anything too seriously. After accepting the king's invitation to form a government, he had
turned to Violet and recalled a saying of Pope Leo X, 'As God has called us
to the Papacy, let us enjoy it.' One of the lessons of his life, he reflected, was
'to take things as they come. One should never worry and one should get

the greatest pleasure out of things.'² On Tuesday, 7 August, two days after his return from Potsdam, the new prime minister was at Lord's to see England make a spirited reply to Australia's total of 338 in the fourth 'Victory Test' between the two, reaching 139-3 by close of play.³

That weekend, 11–12 August, before Parliament began a new session, he went to the prime ministerial residence at Chequers for the first time as premier.⁴ While there had been a house on the grounds since the twelfth century, it took its present form in 1565; it had diamond-paned windows and Elizabethan paintings were hung throughout. Attlee had visited for the first time during the Blitz when the Cabinet was moved out of Whitehall. When he became prime minister he tried to spend as many weekends as possible there. He would stroll the grounds in a bright mustard-yellow suit, looking every inch the country gentleman, play tennis and croquet with the family, or cards beside the fireside with Violet in the winter. The staff found him to be a 'great raconteur, not in the majestic and elaborate style that Churchill favoured but pithy and epigrammatic'. Violet caused some comment with the way she drove her car round the winding lanes like a racing driver, earning a reputation as the 'worst driver in the home counties'. When she took the prime minister out, his private secretary and a detective would sit in the back, both with their eyes closed. Violet could be abrasive, but the warmth and openness between the couple was obvious, notwithstanding some gentle sparring. 'I know what I'm like,' she told the staff at Chequers many years later, 'I don't know what would have become of me if I hadn't been married to the best man in the world.'⁵

Sir John Colville, who retained his position as assistant private secretary to the new prime minister despite the election, observed that Chequers under Attlee was more formal than it had been under Churchill. At dinner 'a starched shirt and stiff butterfly collar was the order of the day.' In the mornings he could be a 'little astringent'. More than once, too, Colville noted how Attlee was predisposed to trust Old Haileyburyians over other candidates for senior jobs in the civil service. Yet 'none of this detracted from Attlee's virtues of total honesty, quickness, efficiency and common sense.' In Colville's view, he was the only prime minister of the twentieth century, with the exception of Alec Douglas-Home, 'who had no shred of either conceit or vanity'.⁶

When back at Downing Street, the prime minister also settled into the rhythm which he maintained for the rest of his premiership. He would wake up between 7 and 7.30 a.m., then read the newspapers over breakfast. The three chosen were *The Times*, *Manchester Guardian* and *Daily Herald*. He would glance at the sports pages – particularly during the cricket season – and sometimes make a start on the *Times* crossword. At least once a week, he and Violet, accompanied by a detective, would take the terrier for a walk in St James's Park.[7]

By 9.30 he was at his desk in the cabinet room, which also served as his office. He sat in the middle of the cabinet table with his back to a marble fireplace surmounted by a portrait of Sir Robert Walpole, the first prime minister. Opposite him, long sash windows gave a view across the small garden to Horse Guards Parade, and there was a view of St James's Park to the left.[8] On his desk he had three pipes neatly laid out, and smoked them successively over the course of the day. He would leaf through telegrams and state papers, and receive visitors, screened by his private secretary, parliamentary secretary and a small entourage. When making comments on the documents put before him, he maintained the clipped style he used in official conversation. 'C. R. A.' was a sufficient stamp of approval.[9]

Lunch was usually scheduled for 1 p.m. Most of these were working lunches but, when he had the opportunity, he would eat with Violet in the upstairs flat. The afternoon was usually spent in the Commons, with Question Time at 2.30 three days a week. (He rejected the suggestion of one of his MPs, Marcus Lipton, that it was advisable to have regular press conferences in the manner of the US president. Attlee replied that it was Parliament's job to scrutinise him.)[10] While the other MPs took to the division lobbies and bars, Attlee returned to the cabinet room to prepare for the next day – reading memoranda, and editing the speeches drafted for him. On those occasions when more concentration was required, he would retire to his private flat at Number 10, and use his old typewriter, employing only the index finger on either hand. 'I can say I have never signed anything I have not written myself or do not thoroughly agree with,' he joked.[11] Around 9.30 p.m., he would return downstairs for a couple of hours' more official work in the cabinet room, before returning upstairs, reading for an hour (something light – like a detective novel, a biography, or adventure), before getting into bed around midnight.[12]

The quaintness of Attlee's routine, and his calm exterior, sit oddly against the ominous backdrop of world events. Attlee's first six months in office were defined by a succession of three related crises in

Anglo-American relation. A strong alliance with the United States had been the bedrock of British strategy for five years. American support had been essential for the country's survival. It had been his relationship with Roosevelt that Churchill prized above anything else. At the end of the war, however, the certainties of the Anglo-American friendship were thrown into doubt, in a series of body blows to Britain, which threatened to plunge Attlee's government into crisis before it had even found its feet. The first was the termination of Lend-Lease on 19 August 1945. Without briefing London, President Truman unilaterally cut the umbilical cord on which Britain had depended to pay for the war. The second was the decision of the United States to step back from its wartime agreements on the sharing of nuclear technology, following its own success in building an atomic weapon. The third was an ugly row over the future of Palestine and the rights of European Jews to migrate there.

While Attlee's relationship with Truman could not be compared to that of Churchill and Roosevelt, he did have one great advantage over his predecessor when it came to Anglo-American relations. His anti-imperialism was a welcome contrast to the stances adopted by Churchill. Even Roosevelt had retained suspicions about British imperialism; and the last thing the American government wanted to be seen to do was to prop up the British Empire.

One of the great tragedies of the interwar period, Attlee believed, was America's retreat from the world. Any return to this pre-war status quo would be fatal for Britain. The UK would be left alone to shoulder the burden against an emboldened Soviet Union, as well as to try to manage Germany's security. America had acquired a number of huge bases throughout Europe and the Far East during the last phase of the war – as part of the price for its loans. Yet Attlee feared this might feed into an attempt to create a 'glacis plate' – a new security barrier far beyond its shores, behind which it would hide, waiving any commitment to the preservation of what Attlee called 'world order'. Another variable was America's likely attitude to the Soviet Union. In 1945, relations between London and Moscow were cooler than between Moscow and Washington, DC. But the situation was fluid. Would the United States now blunder into a broader confrontation, the ramifications of which would be felt within Britain's sphere of influence – particularly Europe and the Middle East?[13]

Attlee did not revert to Churchillian tropes, but ventured a subtler, less grandiose, vision of the unity of the English-speaking peoples. It was in this context that he evoked the words of the American writer Ralph Waldo Emerson, delivered on a visit to England in 1847, a hundred years earlier. Emerson had spoken at a time when Britain was suffering from an economic crisis and struggling to adapt to the rise of international competition. There were echoes of these problems a century later Nonetheless, Emerson's words also offered some hope that Britain was blessed with a 'kind of instinct that she sees a little better in a cloudy day' and was 'still wise to entertain and swift to execute the policy which the mind and heart of mankind requires in the present hour'.[14] It fell to Attlee and his government to ensure this was the case.

II

On 6 August 1945, the Japanese city of Hiroshima was flattened by the atomic bomb, followed by Nagasaki on 9 August. Initial estimates suggested almost 100,000 people were killed in the two attacks, though the death toll was to rise considerably over the following weeks. Churchill had been informed by Truman at Potsdam that America was preparing to use the weapon on Japan. When Attlee was asked in later years if he was also aware that the bomb was going to be dropped he offered the vague answer, 'Yes, I think so,' before elaborating, 'I was told by Harry Truman that they had this Bomb and he had already arranged with Churchill what was to be done and it was their campaign not ours.' When pressed further on whether he would have objected to the dropping of the bomb if he had known its effects, he was clear that he supported the decision. 'At that time our information was that the possibility or probability was that the Japanese would fight for another six months and we reckoned that the loss of life there and the whittling out all over Asia would be greater than any possible loss of life by an atomic bomb, which, after all, was really in essence not much more deadly than the bombing of Tokyo by ordinary means.' Was he surprised by the power of the weapon? 'I don't know. I am never surprised by anything.'[15]

The day after his return from Chequers, on 15 August, Attlee was closeted in a meeting with Lord Louis Mountbatten – the king's cousin and Supreme Allied Commander of the South East Asia Command, who had helped expel the Japanese from Burma – when the ticker tape machine brought news of Japan's surrender.[16] 'Let all who can relax,' he broadcast to the nation on that evening, as the Second World War was finally brought to an end. On Victory Japan day, Piccadilly Circus and Trafalgar Square became a carnival ground once again and, at midnight, trains and tugs on the Thames honked their horns. Extra police were deployed and soldiers marched in fours down Regent Street with girls in pyjamas and dressing gowns, while others in evening dress headed to swanky West End clubs. People waded into the fountain in Trafalgar Square, and others marched to Buckingham Palace and shouted 'We want the king!'[17] Victory was complete. At the opening of Parliament, on 15 August, Attlee paid tribute to Churchill's 'transcendent services' during the war. Even though he had not been in government when the final victory was declared, it had come about due to the plans that he had laid down. 'His place in history is secure.'[18]

Despite the prime minister's confident performance in Parliament, the new government had already been confronted with a grave crisis. The previous day, 14 August, Attlee had circulated to his colleagues an extremely gloomy paper by John Maynard Keynes on Britain's overseas fiscal prospects, which warned of a 'financial Dunkirk'. Spending on the war had almost bankrupted the country and the whole apparatus of the economy was still geared to the continuation of fighting. The country might not even be able to feed itself, or be forced to make a 'sudden and humiliating withdrawal' from the global responsibilities it had assumed during the war, and which it had nearly broken itself trying to maintain. Its survival depended on credit provided by the United States being continued into peacetime. Attlee warned his colleagues that the details of the report – and Cabinet discussions – should be 'treated as matters of the utmost secrecy'.[19]

Just as the scale of the financial crisis became clear, descriptions of the aftermath in Hiroshima and Nagasaki began to reach England. The bombs, attached to a parachute, exploded about 1,700 feet above the ground, causing a flash and white smoke, followed by circular ripples of heat rays. For five to ten minutes after the explosion there was a shower of 'black rain', with fires starting up around the city ten minutes after impact. Some who suffered what appeared only to be minor injuries grew extremely sick and died a few days later.[20]

As one of his first acts as prime minister, Attlee wrote a lengthy memorandum outlining his own thoughts on the implications of the advent of the atomic bomb in international affairs. He believed that the event called the whole premise of British post-war planning into question. This included both the plan to distribute industry across the country to make it safer from future aerial attack – now 'futile' in the face of atomic weapons – and Britain's whole grand strategy. Indeed, in what was to become a theme for Attlee – to the consternation of the military and diplomatic classes – he went so far as to suggest that the commitment to maintaining strategic bases in the Mediterranean or the Far East was 'obsolete' if the British Isles could be wiped out with just a few bombs. This vulnerability was 'the one fact that matters'.

The new prime minister was effectively ripping up conventional wisdom on British grand strategy, by playing down the importance of the 'periphery' (which had defined Churchill's strategy in two world wars). He had noticed at Potsdam that people still talked of waterways and rivers as strategic frontiers as if they were just as important as they had been in the nineteenth century. Attlee felt this was outdated. He believed that the implications of the advent of air power had yet to be grasped by the military establishment – an argument he had first made as early as 1938. Instead of the 'periphery', Attlee emphasised the overriding importance of 'deterrence' to the future of British foreign policy. In one respect, he was ahead of his time. But the conclusion he drew from this was a depressing one. The only response to an atomic bomb on London – or the only deterrent – was the expectation that Britain would not let such an attack go unanswered: 'Berlin and Magdeburg were the answer to London and Coventry. Both derive from Guernica.'

In other words, Attlee's instinctive and immediate response to the dropping of the atomic bomb on Japan was that Britain must have this weapon for itself. In a brutally realistic assessment, he came to the conclusion that there was no alternative. He had heard a suggestion that, in a new Geneva Convention, all nations might agree to abstain from the use of the atomic bomb. Yet while gas was forbidden in the First World War it was still used. Indeed, the British were quite prepared to use it on the Germans if they had landed on British beaches in 1940. Attlee himself had been the minister responsible for stockpiling thousands of gallons of poison gas against this eventuality. Now that one nation had the bomb, it was inevitable that others would do everything in their power to follow suit. The march of scientific discovery could not be reversed; nuclear technology would be of growing importance. Nor could Britain and America enforce some sort of worldwide ban with inspections of laboratories or plants in other countries. They could never penetrate 'the curtain' that concealed vast areas of Russia, for example.

Significantly, in the weeks that followed the end of the Second World War, the British prime minister continued to think of this as a shared Anglo-American problem. In a series of arrangements made by Churchill and Roosevelt during the course of the war, the British and the Americans had agreed to pool intelligence, science and resources in order to build the bomb before their enemies. While the Americans had made the breakthrough first – and Attlee was conscious that Britain needed to follow suit – he still approached this question as one that was the joint responsibility of London, Washington and Ottawa (as Canada had been party to those original agreements). He did not believe that the secret could be kept between the English-speaking nations. The most they had was a few years' head start on their rivals. The real question was what they would choose to do with that opportunity.

For Attlee, it was more important than ever to redouble efforts to make the United Nations viable. 'We should declare that this invention has made it essential to end wars. The new World Order must start now.' The work begun at the San Francisco conference had to be carried further. Much responsibility lay with the UK and US. No two governments had ever been placed in such a position, 'responsible as never before for the future of the human race'. This is where his reasoning began to break down. He expressed a hope that the Big Three could coordinate an agreed approach to world order, which would create a stable international system. To do so, however, the Soviet Union would have to abandon, 'if it still holds them, its dreams of revolution by force or intrigue'. All nations 'must give up their dreams of realising some historical expansion at the expense of their neighbours' and 'must look to a peaceful future instead of a warlike past'.[21]

There were two flaws in Attlee's approach. The first was that the behaviour of the Russians was not inspiring confidence that they could be a responsible partner in the policing of nuclear proliferation. Would this involve sharing the secrets of nuclear technology with them? The second, which was to become clear over the next few weeks, was that the

Americans were no longer prioritising Anglo-American cooperation as they had done. Now that the war was over, the US did not regard the Roosevelt–Churchill agreements about sharing technology as applicable. Having developed the bomb first, the Americans were in no rush to hand it over, even to their most important ally.

III

In fact, Attlee's victory had caused some consternation in certain sections of the American press. First were the predictable attacks from the Anglophobe newspapers such as the *Chicago Tribune* which – playing to its Irish-American constituency – was suspicious of British imperialism, no matter the government in charge.[22] It should be said that there were still plenty of pro-British voices in the US press. Carlyle Morgan, a journalist who had taken a stroll through San Francisco's Nob Hill district with the British prime minister, wrote that it was absurd to suggest Attlee was a dangerous man. Nonetheless, a number of influential voices in the US had already begun to question the need, in peacetime, to maintain Lend-Lease to the UK. That this would now be used to prop up a socialist government stuck in the craw of those on the right of the political spectrum, in particular. One Republican congressman was quoted saying that 'We must make sure that any American dollars loaned to England are used only for reconstruction and not to aid the leftist government in effecting its radical social and economic reforms.'[23] This was not helped by a number of boastful interventions by Harold Laski in the *New York Times*, where he talked of a 'revolution by consent', and lauded Britain's conversion to socialism as an example to America.[24]

The termination of Lend-Lease, within a week of the ending of the war in Asia, caused shock and consternation. The day before the announcement was made, *The Economist* warned about the effects of the scaremongering of the American right about British socialism, combined with a return of the American isolationist reflex.[25] Now there was no time for recriminations as payments would come to an end as early as September. While the British government did not think the arrangement would continue indefinitely, they had expected prior consultation. Even senior officials at the American Embassy in London had not been fully briefed, causing embarrassment for those who had been working on negotiations to find a new arrangement for Britain to continue to receive American support – in the form of a loan – to allow it room to transition back to a peacetime economy.

For his own part, Truman later expressed regret about the way the ending of Lend-Lease had been handled. He was influenced by a caucus of advisers within the US Treasury whose views were not shared by most officials in the US State Department.[26] 'It was a great shock. The tap was turned off at a moment's notice,' Attlee recalled. 'All we had was what was in the pipe line and even that looked like being in jeopardy when the news first came. We had not had a chance to reorganise ourselves on a peacetime basis. The Americans, I suppose, didn't realise what it meant.' Nonetheless, he absolved Truman from personal blame. The decision had been made on official advice. Apparently, 'from what we were told later, he didn't realise in the slightest bit what it involved. He thought it was an ordinary routine thing. If the facts had been fully put before him he might have got Congress to carry on. But they went by the letter of the law.'[27]

In the short term, the only response that was open to ministers was to seek to return to the US government with a request for a large loan – in effect a parachute payment – in order to avert complete economic collapse. On 23 August, the key figures in the Cabinet – Attlee, Morrison (Lord President of the Council), Bevin (foreign secretary), Dalton (chancellor) and Cripps (President of the Board of Trade) – met to discuss the approach to take in forthcoming discussions with the Americans. Also in attendance were Lord Pethick-Lawrence, Secretary of State for India and Lord Halifax, the ambassador to Washington, DC. Lord Keynes was to lead the negotiations and it was agreed that the Prime Minister would go to Churchill to seek his cooperation in presenting a united front to the Americans.[28] They were looking for a loan of at least $5 billion in place of Lend-Lease. Keynes was optimistic that his efforts would be successful and lead to a good deal for the UK. Bevin was not convinced. 'When I listen to Keynes, I can hear the money jingling in my pocket,' he said, 'I'm not sure it's really there.'[29]

In Parliament the following day, 24 August, Attlee informed the House and announced that Halifax and Keynes would lead the negotiations. As expected, Churchill agreed on the need for restraint in discussions of the matter until the issue was settled. Before going to the Commons, Attlee had telephoned Truman to announce the sending of the delegation. If they were unsuccessful in seeking a new American loan, he made clear, the British government would be forced to buy all its goods outside the dollar area. It would also launch an all-out export drive, which would mean huge cuts and controls on consumption of food, clothing, tobacco, petrol and luxury goods.[30] This would cause a further distancing between the two countries. It would be impossible for Britain to live up to the agreements it had made at Bretton Woods during the war, when it had agreed to open up the sterling area – the loose economic unit which included Commonwealth countries whose currencies were tied to the pound – to the dollar.

In order to survive, Britain would also have to close its markets to the Americans with tariffs and controls. In subsequent negotiations it was these two conditions that the Americans insisted must be part of any loan arrangement. First, they demanded that the pound should be made convertible to the dollar; second, they demanded access to markets in the 'imperial preference system' – a separate global economic ecosystem, based around the empire and Dominions, which was protected by tariffs.[31] The fact that America protected its internal markets through tariffs was a matter of some irritation. 'The Americans had a great idea. They believed in free trade for the rest of the world but not for themselves.' Nonetheless, there was little choice but to adapt to the realities of the post-war world, which was defined by US predominance.[32]

The first few weeks of government had been 'very strenuous', Attlee admitted to Tom on 30 August, at the end of his first full month as prime minister. He was happy to see Parliament go into recess for the summer. The government was 'still in the honeymoon period' in terms of public opinion. Many people had been personally kind to him, and his ministers had set to work very well. But the financial situation was on a knife-edge and 'no doubt storms will soon come.'[33]

After the end of Lend-Lease, the next most pressing problem was the demobilisation of the millions of servicemen who were still stationed abroad. This was a matter freighted with great emotional significance, given that so many families had yet to be reunited with their loved ones. Yet the government was equally concerned that if they rushed this process they would be unprepared for the flood of people returning with no job to go to, food shortages and a housing crisis. Fearing a repeat of the poorly handled demobilisation at the end of the last war, it fell to Attlee to justify the cautious approach. Inevitably, *Tribune* complained that his September broadcast on the subject lacked 'the warmth of hope that springs from vital, courageous action'.[34]

More worrying was the fact that the Trades Union Congress also condemned the policy on demobilisation at its conference in Blackpool in September. Even Bevin's insistence that the delays were the only responsible course of action was not sufficient to win the day. Worse still, Jack Lawson, the Minister of War, threatened to resign when the government released doctors from the service early, thereby violating the principle that age and length of service should be the determining factor in demobilisation, rather than profession.[35] It was only Attlee's personal appeals to his old friend that kept him in his post.

On this issue, the prime minister also took a tougher line with the US, after complaints that the Americans were using three British ships – the *Queen Elizabeth*, *Queen Mary* and *Aquitania* – to prioritise their own troop withdrawals. Attlee found this 'extraordinarily selfish' and appealed directly to the president on 3 October 1945. 'I shall speak with the utmost frankness,' he told Truman, 'I cannot continue to justify to the British public the use of our three biggest ships in the American service.'[36] 'They thought that every G.I. should come back before any of our people that were there for far longer,' Attlee later reflected, 'But old Truman came up at once. He understood,' and the ships were returned.[37]

IV

On 6 September, John Winant, the US ambassador in London, wrote a review of the Labour government's first few months in office. On the one hand, there had been some backbench rumbling over policy in Greece and Spain – with the government under pressure to sever ties with both right-wing dictatorships. On the other hand, Attlee's decision to pardon Indian leaders involved in civil disobedience, and early moves to deal with the Indian question, had made a good impression. It was noted that Ernest Bevin was trying to muzzle Harold Laski – who had written a number of provocative and boastful articles in the *New York Times* on British socialism – as negotiations concerning the American loan continued. On the home front, the leadership were attempting to reassure those in industry about their intentions for the nationalisation of coal, electricity and gas. This was depicted in one of David Low's cartoons. He drew Attlee, Morrison and Greenwood trying to teach captains of industry how to dance to their tune. 'Relax. Don't rush it. You will soon pick it up,' they said, reassuringly, moving slowly closer before they could exert a grip.[38]

Just a few days later, however, another difficulty arose, which caused an additional source of tension in Anglo-American relations and began to drive a wedge between Attlee and Truman. The full scale of the tragedy which had befallen Europe's Jews was beginning to become clear, now that the Allies had liberated the remaining concentration and extermination camps in Germany and Eastern Europe. This prompted a wave of sympathy in the US, where there was already a large pro-Zionist community, who advocated the rights of liberated European Jews to emigrate in larger numbers to Palestine (where Britain had been granted a mandate to govern by the League of Nations in 1922). To complicate the picture, many on the left of the Labour Party had long supported the Zionist cause, whereby Jews advocated the formation of their own self-governed nation in the territory. Attlee and Bevin were conscious of the danger, impressed upon them by the Foreign Office, of the effect that such a large increase in Jewish immigration would have in Palestine. First was the issue of stability in Palestine itself, which was increasingly fragile as rival Jewish and Arab groups vied for supremacy. The British mandate included responsibility for maintaining security. More broadly there was the traditional Foreign Office concern that this would alienate Arab opinion when the British needed the acquiescence of local Arab leaders to maintain their presence in the Middle East.

In the first instance, Attlee and Bevin said they had no intention of budging from a 1939 government White Paper that only made provision for 1,500 Jews to be granted certificates to arrive in Palestine each year. After the events of the Holocaust, however, it was clear that 1,500 was nowhere near sufficient to deal with the hundreds of thousands of Jews who now wanted to migrate to Palestine. President Truman became the champion of their cause. There is no doubt that Truman was seeking electoral advantage – courting the Jewish vote in the US – but this was underlaid by a strong personal conviction that European Jews deserved a homeland in which they could feel safe and secure.

On 14 September, Attlee was informed that Truman was planning to make an announcement, repudiating the British White Paper and demanding the immediate granting of 100,000 immigration certificates. The prime minister was furious and wrote to Truman immediately to express his concern. Such action 'could not fail to do grievous harm to relations between our two countries', he warned. The position in the Middle East was already one of 'great danger and difficulty' and such a move was likely to 'precipitate a grave crisis which would be a lamentable start to the work of reconstruction to which we are now devoting ourselves'.[39]

Truman's reply was brusque, reminding Attlee that the issue also caused political difficulties for him, and refusing to back down.[40] In a more emollient follow-up letter, Attlee offered a further exposition of the British position. The situation in Europe for Jews was dire but he insisted that 'we have the Arabs to consider as well as the Jews.' Attlee knew that many Arabs were likely to be dispossessed by such an increase in the number of immigrants. He reminded Truman that both Churchill and Roosevelt had made promises about the issue to various Arab leaders in the course of the war – the breaking of which would 'set aflame the whole Middle East'. Attlee confessed that an additional concern was the attitude of the 90 million Muslims in India, who were 'easily inflamed' by perceived slights against the Muslim world.[41] The issue was 'bristling with difficulty', he added.[42]

Tensions over Palestine made it more difficult for Attlee to make progress on a matter that concerned him more – the proliferation of nuclear weapons. He was torn between two instincts. The first was a genuine desire to build up the United Nations – the foundation stones of which had been put in place in San Francisco. He had an idealised vision of taking the issue of nuclear proliferation to the United Nations. If the UN could deal with a matter of such importance to global security, it would succeed where the League of Nations had failed. Inevitably, this would mean working closely with the Russians. At the same time, Attlee had another concern at the back of his mind – that Britain would be left behind in the race to develop an independent nuclear deterrent. If the Russians got there first, Britain would be in a position of catastrophic strategic weakness once again.

Attlee wrote to Truman on 25 September about the pressing need to come to some sort of agreement on the management of nuclear weapons in world affairs. He spoke in apocalyptic terms, about 'airplanes flying through the stratosphere dropping atomic bombs on great cities'. The letter was a reworking of his previous memorandum, written after the surrender of Japan. He reiterated his view that deterrence was the only defence, and that it would be impossible to prevent the proliferation of nuclear technology. In the light of these developments, he suggested that it now fell upon Britain and America to 'make a fresh review of world policy and a new valuation of what we call national interests'. While the US Secretary of State James Byrnes was due in London to discuss some of these matters with Bevin, Attlee pressed for a meeting with the president himself.[43]

At the same time, however, as he juggled these competing instincts in his mind, the prime minister was also confronted with worrying reports about Russian behaviour. On 25 September, he was forced to write an urgent telegram to Stalin after the first of many clashes between Bevin and Molotov at the Council of Foreign Ministers. The Russians wanted to exclude the Chinese government, who were fighting a communist insurgency supported by Moscow, from the discussions. The British preferred to conduct negotiations through the five members of the United Naitons Security Council, which included France and China, as well as the Big Three. Attlee told Stalin that the line taken by Molotov did not accord with 'my understanding of the spirit and intention of the decision arrived at in Potsdam'. Going back on agreements would throw into doubt the whole value of the Council of Foreign Ministers, cause grave offence to the French and Chinese, and force difficult questions for him in Parliament.[44] Stalin was unmoved.[45] Then, on 29 October, Attlee informed Stalin in a short note that he was going to visit Truman in Washington to discuss with the president, and the Canadian prime minister, 'problems to which the discovery of atomic energy has given rise'.[46]

Already the cracks in Attlee's nuclear strategy were starting to appear. After sharing his letter to Truman with the rest of the Cabinet, he also sent it to Churchill, on the grounds that it was Churchill who had made the original agreements with Roosevelt. As Churchill pointed out, Attlee's letter did not actually make it clear what he expected from the Americans, beyond asking them to 'act in good faith'. Was his implication that he wanted them to share the science of atomic energy with the United Nations, or with the Russians as part of a Big Three agreement? If so, he did not expect the Americans to agree; and, quite frankly, Churchill would think them entirely correct in refusing to do so. Pointedly, Churchill referred to the fact that 'we have a special relationship' with the Americans on this matter, as defined in his gentleman's agreement with Roosevelt. This 'almost' amounted to a military agreement with the greatest power in the world, and should be handled with care. Churchill would 'greatly regret if we seem not . . . to value this and pressed them to melt our dual agreement down into a general international agreement' consisting of 'pious empty phrases'. In other words, Attlee was making a mistake in trying to push the Americans to take the matter to the UN because he was jeopardising the headstart that Britain had on Russia. Getting the bomb before Moscow did was the real priority.[47]

The prime minister did not need a reason to be suspicious of the Soviets. Already, at Potsdam, he had seen that it was 'quite obvious they were going to be troublesome'.[48] Nonetheless, his officials made sure to remind him of this threat as the question of the sharing of nuclear secrets came to a head. On 1 November, he received an intelligence report that analysed German–Russian relations between 1933 to 1940, and including, the Hitler–Stalin pact. These were based on documents taken from the Nazi archives by British intelligence. Officials brought to the prime minister's attention two comments in particular. In August 1939, in conversation with the Nazi foreign minister, Ribbentrop, Stalin had denounced the 'ridiculous' fact that 'a few hundred Englishmen should control India'. His foreign secretary Molotov had also added that Russia would feel threatened by a British occupation of Greece, and was determined to prevent that eventuality.[49] Significantly, the intelligence was brought to him by Sir John Anderson, the former Lord President of the Council in the wartime coalition. Anderson was chairman of the British Atomic Energy Commission, and Attlee kept him in this position because of his expertise in Anglo-American cooperation on the nuclear issue.

By 5 November, as he made the final preparations for Attlee's visit to Washington, DC, on which Anderson would join him, it was clear that his thinking had changed considerably. In a new memorandum, he focused more directly on Britain's selfish strategic interests in this matter. Britain was particularly vulnerable to nuclear attack because of her geographic location – so close to other European powers – and concentration of population. The effects of bombing had already been felt in the Blitz. On this point, Attlee was adamant that the government would not renounce use of the weapon entirely. She needed it for her self-defence He still hoped to reinforce Truman's commitment to making the United Nations a 'living thing'. But he now abandoned the notion of committing the nations that held the bomb to any specific conventions, beyond a general commitment to the principles of the UN Charter.

Churchill's letter threw another bucket of cold realism over Attlee. He began to retreat from the idea that the Americans should be asked to take the issue to the UN. However, he did not backpedal fast enough. One reason for this was that he needed to keep his ministers with him. His first instinct – the conviction that Britain needed a bomb of its own – was not necessarily shared by all his colleagues. In a 5 November memorandum for the Cabinet, it was clear that he was beating a retreat from his previous position that the UN should decide these matters. This, he now explained, had been no more than a 'general thesis', rather than a specific demand. Sadly, he admitted, there was no evidence that an offer to share scientific secrets with Moscow would be 'likely to effect a change of attitude to world problems by the U.S.S.R.'. In a key passage, he now made clear that the establishment of better relations between the leading powers should 'precede the exchange of technical information'.[50] When the matter came before Cabinet three days later, on the eve of his departure, there was a certain degree of obfuscation in what Attlee said. He was careful to spend more time on his 'general thesis' about the need to support the UN and end power politics.[51]

Just before he left for Washington, Attlee addressed the United Nations conference in London. He told the assembled delegates, in a reworking of one his favourite socialist slogans, that the 'foundation of world order must be laid in the hearts of men'.[52] Multilateralism was something that he genuinely believed in. He even drew up proposals for a UN wireless service that could spread its message and offer global news, 'unbiased by national interests'.[53] Yet, while Attlee's heart was in the idea of collective security and multilateralism, his head told him that Britain's immediate future was to be secured by an even closer bilateral relationship with the United States.

He now had two main goals for the visit to Washington. The first was to come to some sort of arrangement on the sharing of nuclear technology which – however it might be dressed up – gave Britain access to scientific secrets. The second was to improve the diplomatic atmosphere in a way that would encourage Congress to sign off on the huge loan which Keynes had now negotiated. The national interest came first.

Cabinet agreement was harder to come by on the loan than it was on the nuclear issue. Keynes had negotiated the basis of a new $5 billion loan, but it came with a number of caveats and conditions that made it difficult to swallow. First of all, it was to be paid back at a competitive rate of interest (meaning the last payment was not made until the early years of Tony Blair's premiership). Second, Britain agreed to abide by the understandings reached at Bretton Woods, in which the imperial preference system would be gradually phased out, along with tariffs protecting Britain against an influx of cheap American goods. Third, within eighteen months of the agreement being signed, the British would agree to allow the convertibility of pound sterling into dollars. The latter was the most dangerous of all, risking a run on the pound if the British economy was not stabilised by the time convertibility kicked in.

When it was clear that this was the best that Keynes and the negotiators could get, a divide emerged in Cabinet, which foreshadowed later divisions. In a discussion on 6 November, Nye Bevan urged Attlee not to sign off on the proposed deal. He viewed it as a deliberate attempt to weaken the British economy and secure American predominance. With the prime minister remaining silent, Ernest Bevin said that he too would have preferred a much more straightforward loan, without so many conditions attached. In the end, however, the government had no choice but to accede to these conditions. The negotiating team had got the best they could get. 'Were we to reject these terms and demand these further sacrifices from the British people?' asked Bevin. Not for the first time, Attlee was happy to let others slug it out. The prime minister had written 'pro' and 'con' on his meeting notes but just filled the page with two nervous doodles.[54] The truth was that had already made up his mind.

V

At 6 p.m. on 9 November 1945, a grey and bracingly cold day, the British prime minister walked down the steps of his Skymaster plane at Dulles airport, outside Washington, DC, in a thick black overcoat. He was greeted by Lord Halifax and George T. Sullivan, Special Assistant to the Secretary of State. They took him into the warmth of the terminal where he shook hands with Secretary Byrnes, Brigadier General Harry Vaughan, military aide to the President, and two State Department officials. After an hour-long drive to the city, Truman greeted him in the portico of the White House. They linked arms and went inside, followed by Halifax. Canadian prime minister Mackenzie King also arrived at Union Station, having travelled down from New York.[55] A year previously, King had suggested that Churchill bullied Attlee in the War Cabinet .[56] But he had already begun to adjust his estimation, having visited Attlee in London a few weeks before.[57] The two were to have a good working relationship.

Attlee rested before lunch on the second floor of the White House. British officials, including Halifax, were given a conference room in the building so that they could brief the prime minister. As a sign of his changing priorities, Attlee dominated the discussion with his criticism of Stalin. He believed that the Soviets were becoming the largest obstacle to the effective working of the UN. He proposed that they should be asked to state their maximum demands. It was made clear at this meeting that the aim of the British delegation was to leave Washington with an agreed statement on the nuclear issue between Truman, Attlee and King. Ideally, this would be to the effect that they had no wish to monopolise nuclear technology, and hoped to discuss the matter further with the Russians in the context of the UN. In reality, this meant keeping the Russians at arm's length and redoubling efforts to get America to share secrets directly with Britain.[58]

The discussions began well. At a dinner that night, before fifty guests, Truman and Attlee both spoke of a shared desire for a 'universal foreign policy'. The next morning, Armistice Day, the three leaders travelled out to Arlington National Cemetery in misty drizzle and dark skies. Their route took them past the Lincoln and Jefferson Memorials. At Arlington, they were met with a gun salute. After laying wreaths, they stood, heads bowed, for the national anthems. From there they moved to the yacht of the

Secretary of the Navy, *Sequoia*, for a steak lunch. They then worked through to dinner when the vessel docked back at the landing spot at 8.35 p.m.[59]

The other rationale for the visit was, in effect, a public relations exercise, to reassure Americans that a Labour government would act responsibly with a $5 billion loan. On 13 November, to this end, Attlee made a major address to the United States Congress. As he stepped up onto the rostrum, one reporter said he looked like the treasurer of a children's aid society presenting his annual report.[60] Halifax had briefed him extensively beforehand about the mood of Congress. He recommended a neat phrase, a variation on the liberal imperial notion of colonial trusteeship, suggesting that Britain and America had a 'trusteeship of humanity' in the post-war world.[61] There was also sound advice from the Board of Trade, who urged the prime minister to reassure the Americans that Britain would remain an outward-looking trading nation, and reminded him that Americans generally did not like 'hard luck stories' and were 'only interested in forward-looking and not backward-looking statements'.[62]

Attlee had a difficult job, particularly given that most of those in the room had been present for Churchill's famous address of 1941. One reporter counted only three outbursts of applause – the loudest when Attlee paid tribute to Churchill.[63] Yet the message was well crafted. Attlee was clear that there would be differences in his government's approach. 'You will see us embarking on projects of nationalisation, on wide all-embracing schemes of social insurance designed to give security to the common man. We shall be working out a planned economy. You, it may be, will continue in your more individualistic methods.' But the basis of Attlee's message was that the Labour Party was a 'freedom-loving movement' that sat easily within a long Anglo-American tradition. 'We, in the Labour Party, declare that we are in line with those who fought for Magna Carta, habeas corpus, with the Pilgrim Fathers and with the signatories of the Declaration of Independence . . . We have much in common. We have the language of Milton and Shakespeare, of Burke and Chatham, of Lincoln and of Jefferson.'

When he turned to foreign affairs, there was a hint of Edward Bellamy's vision of a futuristic commonwealth in *Looking Backward* when Attlee spoke of his desire to create 'a world as orderly as a well run town, with citizens diverse in character but co-operating for the common good'. While he skipped the thorny issue of Palestine, he did make clear that his government was committed to self-government in its former imperial possessions.

As Britain moved from an empire to a commonwealth, he predicted that there would be 'ever closer friendship' between Britain and America. They were united by 'the things of the spirit' and a shared belief in the 'validity of the moral precepts on which our whole civilization is founded'.[64]

The *Manchester Guardian* believed that Attlee had performed well. Britons sometimes forgot that Americans regarded socialism as a 'kind of Red Death' from a ravaged Europe that had skipped over the Channel and taken hold in England. Attlee embodied the fact that 'when other nations were listening to Marx, we were paying more heed to Ruskin and Morris'.[65] The speech received a mixed reception in America. The *Chicago Daily Tribune* saw it as another attempt to get America to prop up the British Empire.[66] Others noted that it had been short on specifics. Attlee spoke on a 'high moral plane', while failing to mention that he was asking for a massive loan.[67] The *Washington Post* felt it was 'neat and uninspiring' but, at least, an 'unvarnished story'.[68] The *Wall Street Journal* suggested that Attlee had done as well as could be expected.[69]

On the question of the sharing of nuclear technology, however, the visit was a failure. Ironically, one of the things that Attlee had been praised for by the American press was his suggestion that the matter should be handed over to the UN. 'The peacemaking role is traditionally American. That role had slipped far out of Washington's hands this week,' wrote Joseph Harsch, the prominent diplomatic correspondent at the *Christian Science Monitor*.[70] It is also worth noting that influential voices within the US diplomatic establishment – notably Dean Acheson, Under-Secretary at the State Department – approved of Attlee's 'general thesis' and had independently recommended the same approach.[71]

In fact, Attlee had boxed himself into a corner on this issue. By suggesting bringing the matter to the UN, he had taken the matter out of the realm of the special relationship. What is more, American negotiators had used his own idea back against him. Instead of making good on the gentlemen's agreement between Churchill and Roosevelt, they instead signalled their approval for the 'general' thesis that the matter should be brought to the UN for discussion first. This was the perfect delaying tactic: it gave the prime minister what he said he wanted, but not what he really needed.

Attlee continued to put the best possible spin on this. As he reported to the Cabinet on his return, some preliminary discussions had taken place about the sharing of atomic scientific secrets directly between Washington and London. A Combined Policy Committee was formed after the summit, leading the British to believe that cooperation would be forthcoming. However, the Americans rowed back from making any formal commitment, suggesting that such an agreement would need to take the form of a treaty, which would then require the approval of Congress.[72]

By mid-December, Attlee was still confident that the American government would keep nuclear cooperation out of the public eye, and therefore sidestep the need for legislative approval.[73] Again, he was poorly informed. Increasingly anxious, he continued to impress upon Lord Halifax the need for any final agreement on nuclear secrets to be 'unambiguous' on pooling of information as well as materials. Cooperation should be 'full and effective over the whole field'.[74] Ultimately, however, the issue did come before Congress, which, under the Atomic Energy Act of 1946, forbade the sharing of technological information. Months later, in June 1946, Attlee wrote a long letter to Truman in which he expressed his disappointment that the cooperation he had hoped for had never materialised, and his view that this was inconsistent with the 'spirit' of the agreement they had come to. Truman never replied, on the grounds that it was no longer possible for him to make any statement on the issue.[75]

Once again, Attlee did not blame Truman personally, and understood that there was nothing he could do once Congress got hold of the issue. Not unjustifiably, he also complained that the deal that Churchill had made with Roosevelt was 'a rather loose agreement', which had made his task more difficult.[76] As much as anything, it was an indication of the shift of power between these two nations, and the beginning of America's accession to true superpower status.

As Attlee arrived back over Britain on 21 November 1945, winter had already set in. A low fog had descended across London, meaning that the Douglas C-54 plane in which he travelled was forced to divert to RAF Tangmere in Sussex. While he hoped he had made progress on the nuclear issue, the loan had been held up. On 26 November, he wrote to Halifax in Washington stressing the importance of completing the arrangement, on the grounds that the 'clock is ticking' on the British economy.[77]

Finally, at the start of December, the US government agreed a loan of $5 billion. Speaking at a Pilgrim's Dinner on 5 December in London, Attlee paid tribute to the US and restated his firm belief in the importance of Anglo-American relations.[78] Not everyone was happy. 'American capitalism has driven a savage bargain,' complained *Tribune*. Indeed, it was not just on the left that the terms were denounced. Lord Beaverbrook grumbled that 'We have sold the empire for a trifling sum. Henceforth the United States of America reaps where we have sown.'[79] The British might 'burn at the terms' but they were left with little choice, reported the *Washington Post*.[80] 'You can criticise the loan and the arrangements surrounding it – and we fought inch by inch throughout the negotiations – but the fact remains we couldn't do without it,' Attlee later reasoned. 'The critics could shout. We had to run things.'[81]

17

The British New Deal

Methinks I see in my mind a noble and puissant nation rousing herself like a strong man after sleep, and shaking her invincible locks: Methinks I see her as an eagle muing her mighty youth, and kindling her undazzled eyes at the full midday beam; purging and unscaling her long abused sight at the fountain itself of heavenly radiance, while the whole noise of timorous and flocking birds, with those also that love the twilight, flutter about, amazed at what she means . . .

John Milton, *Areopagitica*, 1644, quoted by
Clement Attlee at the Lord Mayor's Banquet, 9 November 1946.[1]

I *Hampstead, November 1945*

John Verney had married Elizabeth in 1938 but it was not until the winter of 1945 that he came to hate her steadily and fiercely. He was not a bad-tempered man, 'a look of fatigue and abstraction was the only visible sign of the passion which possessed him.' During the war he had served with distinction. He had never lost his temper with his men, though he did get irritated when they disturbed his reading by listening to political news on the wireless. Before the war began, Verney had stood twice for Parliament as a Liberal candidate. He lost both times. But the war had not changed his convictions. As a committed Liberal, he was suspicious of the large state which had grown up during the war, and thought it time to shrink it back to size. When he returned to England in 1945, he had both a badly wounded leg and a Military Cross to show for his bravery. This would stand him in good stead with the electors. And yet the England to which he returned was not the one he had left. The flat that he had lived in with Elizabeth in Belgravia had been requisitioned by civil servants. Elizabeth, who had joined the Foreign Office in the war, was living with his parents in their old Georgian villa in Hampstead, one of the most affluent areas in north London. But even in Hampstead things had changed. The wrought-iron railings had been torn away to be melted down for munitions. Worse still, the servants had all resigned or been sent to war.

In the general election of 1945, John Verney had made a third and final attempt to get elected to Parliament, for a constituency on the outskirts of London. Alas, he came last. To his disgust, the winner was a 'rancorous Jewish school teacher' from the Labour Party who topped the poll by a distance. The Tories had put up a Battle of Britain fighter pilot who claimed most of what was left of the middle-class vote, leaving John with little chance. He was defeated, disillusioned and disorientated. He complained about 'the vast net of government control which had been woven in his absence'. 'I know it's maddening, John, but you must realise it's the same for everyone,' said Elizabeth. 'That's what all you bureaucrats want,' he replied, 'Equality through slavery. The two-class state – proletarians and officials.' John's bitterness grew. Elizabeth was 'part and parcel of it. She worked for the State and the Jews. She was a collaborator with the new, alien, occupying power.' His mood darkened even more during the winter of 1945, as the gas burned feebly in the stove, and wind blew through shattered windows. He grew further apart from Elizabeth, whom he came to see as 'the archpriestess and maenad of the century of the common man'. He began to plot to kill her by putting poison in her coffee. What he didn't know was that she was planning to do the same.[2]

This tale was told in Evelyn Waugh's 'Tactical Exercise', a 1946 short story about an army hero struggling to adapt to Attlee's Britain. While it was a black comedy, it reflected the author's own mood. A nostalgia for the pre-war social order also ran through Waugh's most famous work, *Brideshead Revisited*, published in 1945. As he said himself, it was a reaction against price controls, officialdom, and meritocracy, 'the period of soya beans and Basic English'. As Waugh later reflected, his post-war work was 'infused with a kind of gluttony, for food and wine, for the splendours of the recent past'.[3]

The American-born writer Frederic Raphael thought these descriptions of England hysterical. 'The defeat of privilege did not appear to destabilise society. Only a posturing reactionary such as Evelyn Waugh could claim that Attlee's England made him feel as if he was living in an "occupied country".'4 Yet Waugh was not the only one to express such feelings of privation and alarm. The day after Labour's election victory, a young soldier called Peregrine Worsthorne, who was to go on to edit the *Sunday Telegraph*, wrote home to his mother about an unsettling experience that one of his fellow officers experienced at their camp just outside Hanover in Germany. Every morning his friend had grown accustomed to having his working-class batman bring in a silver jug full of hot shaving water to him, along with ivory hairbrushes, and his razor. This ritual had been maintained throughout the war in the most difficult of conditions, even under bombardment. That morning, the silver jug was nowhere to be seen. The officer did not raise a word of dissent. 'Having shown an aristocratic determination not to allow Hitler to alter his habits,' wrote young Peregrine, this officer was 'obviously not going to meet the challenge of Mr Attlee and his socialist cohorts with comparable sangfroid'. In the face of the foreign enemy he had not flinched; but 'in the face of the class enemy his nerve has gone before the battle is even joined.'

As Worsthorne later reflected, many misconceptions later grew up around the true meaning of the 1945 election. There was no political revolution, in a way that a Marxist academic would recognise or approve of. But what did change was 'nothing less than the Zeitgeist'. The result was a vote of no-confidence in the governing class. It was not that their privileges were taken away; what was ended was 'the ethos of hierarchy that made sense of those privileges. Everything about the class system was left intact except its *raison d'être*.'5

For Attlee's critics on the left, by contrast, this was precisely where he failed. Not enough changed about Britain in 1945. One of the earliest criticisms made of his government by *Tribune* was that he relied too heavily on the pillars of the old regime. For example, Sir John Anderson had been selected to travel to Washington with him, and was still closely involved in discussions on nuclear energy. Despite Laski's requests for the job, Lord Halifax remained in situ in Washington, DC.6 When in Washington, Attlee himself had reassured his American audience that 'the old school tie' could still be seen in government, and that the Labour benches represented a cross section of English society. Michael Foot's favourite story about Bevan was the efforts to which Attlee, and indeed Violet, went to get

Bevan to wear a dinner jacket to a royal banquet at Buckingham Palace. For Bevan and his wife Jennie Lee, the Attlees were guilty of 'vulgarity' and 'bourgeois values'.[7]

This cultural condemnation gathered momentum in later years. In a 1959 collection called *The Establishment*, the historian Hugh Thomas argued that the 'fusty Establishment, with its Victorian views and standards of judgement' had been left unchanged despite the great Labour victory of 1945. In the same book, economist Thomas Balogh argued that one of Attlee's failures was to have professed no interest in the political persuasions of anyone his government appointed to senior positions in the Church of England or the judiciary. Thus he missed the opportunity to change the culture of the Establishment at the very top.[8] Another essay in the same volume by the educationalist John Vaizey denounced the Attlee government's failure to abolish the public schools.[9] Ironically, Hugh Thomas later worked for Margaret Thatcher, and became Baron Thomas of Swynnerton, of Notting Hill; Thomas Balogh was gazetted as Baron Balogh of Hampstead; and John Vaizey, the scourge of public schools, became Baron Vaizey of Greenwich and sent his son to St Paul's.

The serious point is that Attlee never intended a cultural revolution, nor a purging of the Establishment. As Roy Jenkins noted, 'he confined his radicalism to politics' and 'liked and respected all the institutions with which he was ever associated'.[10] His government did, however, institute a British 'New Deal' – a new contract between state and citizen. The ideas that it drew upon owed much to those of citizenship and commonwealth that Attlee elucidated in the early part of his career, in the decade before the First World War, and in its immediate aftermath. They owed very little to Continental European models of socialism. If anything, they were inspired more by President Roosevelt's 'New Deal' of the 1930s, though in spirit rather than in legislative detail. On his 1941 visit to Washington, Attlee had praised the supporters of the New Deal for having 'the right ideas'.[11] The similarities were not lost on contemporaries either. As the American Embassy reported after the Labour victory in 1945, the British people wanted their 'own version of the "New Deal"'.[12]

The liberal American historian and future presidential speechwriter, Arthur Schlesinger – who was sympathetic to the Attlee government – made a similar point. During the Attlee government, when Schlesinger was a visiting fellow at Cambridge University, he wrote many essays in the

New York Times arguing that the British experiment in democratic social-ism was in fact the strongest possible answer to communism. And yet Schlesinger found that he had some difficulty in presenting the English 'revolution' as an exciting story, on a par with that of Roosevelt's 'New Deal'. This was partly because its architect-in-chief, Attlee, 'lacked high drama' and was 'altogether too bourgeois'. When Schlesinger managed to get himself into Number 10 for an interview, he found the prime minister 'entirely courteous, but he answered every question monosyllabically, ven-tured no remarks of his own and reduced me in fifteen minutes to despairing silence'.[13] Years later, Attlee expressed great admiration for the first book in Schlesinger's three-volume biography of Franklin Roosevelt, which addressed the origins of the New Deal.[14] 'It is interesting to contrast the working of democracy in UK and USA, the huge long jamboree that made Roosevelt the Democratic leader and the hour in a committee room in the House of Commons that made me Labour Party leader,' he also mused.[15]

With his suspicion of showmanship, Attlee was not the ideal man to dramatise events. Yet that should not blind us to the substance of what his government achieved, or the extent of the transformation over which he presided. Above all, Attlee set the ethical terms on which Britain's new social contract was founded. On one level, this was the reward that had been promised to the British people – a fuller definition of rights, which were the corollary of the great obligations placed upon them. It had been a promise made during the previous war but one not kept by Lloyd George. That betrayal had been the issue that had defined Attlee's early political career, from the moment he became Mayor of Stepney in 1919, to his maiden speech in Parliament as MP for Limehouse in 1922. Indeed, the promises that Attlee's government delivered upon after 1945 had an even longer heritage, which stretched back into his earliest years in the socialist movement. Specifically, some of the things that his government did on welfare and insurance were the culmination of campaigns which Attlee had fought since long before the First World War.

Attlee's overriding goal was to adapt the conditions of modernity in a way that served the best interests of the citizens within the commonwealth, in the spirit of Edward Bellamy's 1888 novel, *Looking Backward*. It was thus that Attlee called his government a 'child of the Bellamy ideal', and shared the conviction that the 'Golden Age lies before us and not behind us, and is not far away.'[16] By Attlee's own estimate, his government delivered upon its fundamental aims; in fact it had mostly done so by 1948. The standards by which he judged its success were the convictions he had held from his earliest days in politics, almost forty years before.

II

While the Attlee government had faced bankruptcy in its first few months, it retained one great asset: a parliamentary majority of 146 seats. This created a strategic dilemma for its opponents. In the first month of the government, when Labour announced its intentions to nationalise the mines and the Bank of England, Churchill said he was prepared to support these measures, if they were handled properly. He also claimed to have reassured the leaders of foreign countries that there was nothing to be alarmed by in Labour's immediate programme.[17] By the time Attlee returned from his visit to Truman, however, and the terms of the American loan were agreed, Churchill and the Conservatives had changed tack.

On 6 December, the Conservatives tabled a motion of censure at the new government for not doing enough to address the living conditions in the country. Demobilisation was happening too slowly and they were not making sufficient efforts to keep expenditure down. The motion held that the government was 'impelled by Socialist theory' and was prioritising 'the formulation of long-term schemes for nationalisation' over the best interests of the people – who wanted food, homes and work. Churchill led the attack, claiming that he had held fire during the American loan negotiations, in the interests of the nation, but he could stay silent no longer. He also claimed to have been provoked into action by the triumphalism of Herbert Morrison and Nye Bevan in recent weeks. Churchill, ever the showman, said that he was prepared to absolve Attlee from personal blame. The prime minister had 'not sought in any way to embitter or inflame our proceedings', but, of course, he knew very well himself what Morrison and Bevan were capable of.

Attlee began his reply by mocking Churchill's opening remarks, spoken in 'a quiet note of injured innocence'. It was the Conservatives who had driven the wedge between the parties at the end of the wartime coalition. 'I have not forgotten the right hon. Gentleman's broadcast at the beginning of the Election, nor have the people of this country.' As for demobilisation,

Attlee found it hard to believe that Churchill really wanted to leave Britain without sufficient troops to fulfil the requirements of its foreign policy. To cheers from the government benches, he delivered a surprising flourish in response to Churchill's suggestion that vultures were hovering above British industry. 'I have no doubt the right hon. Gentleman knows all about vultures. The vultures never fed on him because he kept alive, fortunately for us all; vultures feed on rotten carrion. Is it his view that our basic industries are so rotten that they attract the vultures?' The real problem, he suggested, quoting the Book of Job, was that the Conservatives had not yet adjusted to the fact they were no longer in power. 'Truly ye are the people and wisdom shall die with you.'[18]

Not for the first time, reported the *Manchester Guardian*, Attlee had proved that his debating qualities were underrated.[19] Officials at the US Embassy were equally impressed. As ever, he was 'statesmanlike' and 'sincere' in the face of Churchill's 'taunting tactics'. Yet he had also shown a spark and a self-confidence that had not been seen before. Having been 'generally considered to be lacking in personality on the platform', he had emerged as 'a politician quite capable of replying in kind to the invective so often used by his predecessor in office'. The prime minister was 'resoundingly cheered and given a remarkable ovation from his followers when he had finished'.[20] Even in Beaverbrook's *Daily Express*, a poll released just a few days after the debate suggested that 59 per cent of the public were pleased with the government so far. But an even greater number, 67 per cent, were happy with Attlee's performance as prime minister, and only 21 per cent unhappy.[21]

Recognising Attlee's personal popularity, Francis Williams – who had become his press secretary in October – urged him to take centre stage more often, rather than leaving things to his ministers.[22] Yet this did not fit his conception of how government should work. The functioning of a government was something he had given serious thought to following his limited experience of Ramsay MacDonald's ministry. In the early 1930s, he had written a memorandum on Cabinet government that he kept in his private papers but now returned to. The essential quality in a prime minister was that he should be a good chairman, able to get others to work together. He should have a 'permanent nucleus' of ministers around him and an 'architectonic sense' of the whole strategy of government. At some point, however, there must 'be someone to take a decision'.[23]

Years later, he elaborated on this approach in an interview with Francis

Williams. An effective prime minister could not afford to be 'egocentric' and 'must remember that he is only the first among equals . . . Some people will think he has a certain amount of wisdom. His voice will carry the greatest weight. But you can't ride rough-shod over a Cabinet unless you're something extraordinary.'[24] Thus, when discussions reached their conclusion, according to Jack Lawson, he would deliver judgement 'in clear terms, leaving you under no illusion as to what he means . . . We soon learned that he could give a "take it or leave it" decision without raising his voice. There is no bluster about him and he rarely shows temper but – well, we have known odd times when a whip would have been more welcome than his tongue.'[25]

There were drawbacks to this quick-fire style. For one thing, he could be abrupt and curt in a way that hurt his colleagues' feelings. Francis Williams noted that he could be 'sharply impatient . . . does not suffer fools gladly, nor is he tolerant of clever men in their foolish moments'. He was irritated if any colleague strayed from his fundamental point and would 'interject a frosty reminder' that the time was not for speeches.[26] In some cases, this was deserved. Konni Zilliacus, a left-wing agitator on the back benches, was given a classic Attlee rebuke: 'Thank you for your memorandum which seems to me to be based on an astonishing lack of understanding of the facts.'[27] After a lengthy monologue on post-war Germany, the backbench MP Richard Crossman received a famous put-down: 'I saw your mother last week. She is looking very well.'[28] Another habit, when growing tired of a visitor, was to put his pipe on the blotting paper in front of him, grunt and look at the clock.[29] He was unafraid to sack ministers who were failing: 'It's awkward to have to sack a man and tell him he doesn't make the grade. But I always think it's best not to rush around looking for some sort of cushion for him, like it isn't his fault.'[30]

While he was generally favourable to Attlee's style of management, Herbert Morrison suggested that he tended to side with colleagues on the basis of their seniority. His 'staccato and monosyllabic comments' to young ministers could wound. He could appear 'schoolmasterly' and even a little 'pompous' in his tendency to make 'pontifical judgments' in response to junior members.[31] Hartley Shawcross, the Attorney General, observed that, even when junior members of his government performed well, he struggled to give them praise.[32] Edmund Dell, a Labour MP in the 1950s complained that Attlee was biased against youth and depended too much on the old lags of the 1930s.[33]

There were times when the Labour Party needed more leadership from the top than Attlee was able to provide. Sometimes, Morrison was later to write, Attlee 'doodled when he ought to have led'.[34] And yet his ministers valued the leeway he gave to them, and the loyalty he showed. Ellen Wilkinson, his Minister of Education, had criticised Attlee on many occasions in the past. However, in her short time serving in his government (she died in 1947 from an accidental overdose of barbiturates, taken to combat asthma and insomnia), she came to re-evaluate her assessment, working with him at close hand. For one thing, he had a certain generosity of spirit. He was a great parliamentary prompter. He was the only MP who would give up his own best lines to colleagues, by whispering in their ear when they were engaged in parliamentary combat. She recalled how she once got much laughter and praise for a witty remark that Attlee had fed her just a few moments before. Such 'casual generosity' was hard not to warm to.[35]

More substantively, Attlee put his weight behind Wilkinson in her efforts to implement the 1944 Education Act, which had been drawn up by the Conservative Education Secretary, Rab Butler, working in close cooperation with Labour's education expert, James Chuter Ede. This committed to raising the school leaving age to fifteen by April 1947, and eventually sixteen, guaranteed free schooling for all children under that age, and created a tripartite system of secondary schooling based on merit (grammar schools, secondary technical and secondary moderns).

Within a few months of taking office, because of spiralling costs elsewhere in government, Wilkinson realised that the promise to raise the school leaving age by April 1947 was under threat. This was because of the extra funding required to help Local Education Authorities to cover the expanded school numbers, and because Bevan's efforts to build thousands of new homes had caused a shortage in building materials and manpower. (One feature of Wilkinson's short tenure were the temporary huts which sprang up in school playgrounds across the UK.) While he was sympathetic to Wilkinson's aims, Bevan expressed concern that his attempts to build more houses were being curtailed by the money spent on education.

Both Herbert Morrison, as Lord President of the Council, and Stafford Cripps, then the President of the Board of the Trade, came out against Wilkinson's insistence that the April 1947 deadline must be met. The costs were too high and the manpower was needed elsewhere. Before Cabinet on January 1947, only three weeks before her death, she made an impassioned plea, pointing out that, in times of economic difficulty, education always suffered first. The government should keep its promise, mindful that 'those to suffer most by deferment will be precisely those working class children whose education has already been so seriously interrupted by the war.' Bevan was swayed, but more importantly the prime minister came down firmly on her side, against Morrison and Cripps.[36] Still there was no attempt to abolish the public schools; but to condemn Attlee for this is to ignore the fact that he had never intended to pursue this course. 'I am myself in favour of an educational system which will break down class barriers, and will preserve the unity of the nation,' he had said in February 1945, 'but I am also in favour of variety and entirely opposed to the abolition of old traditions and the levelling down of everything to dull uniformity.'[37]

More than anything, Attlee's handling of Bevan as a minister exemplified the importance of his belief that tolerance was an under-valued virtue in political life. From the 1930s onwards, he had been bombarded with criticism from Bevan: some of it hysterical, and some of it damaging to the party. The diaries of James Chuter Ede and Hugh Dalton from the war years confirm that this was an almost weekly occurrence. On a number of occasions during the war, Attlee had opposed expelling Bevan from the parliamentary party, despite Ernie Bevin's desire to 'crush' him. In fact, he believed that Bevin's unwillingness to brook dissent was his greatest flaw. As leader, it was necessary to set aside one's own ego, and not to fall into the trap of thinking that 'the other fellow's a dirty dog.'[38]

On the making of his Cabinet, Attlee had commented on the need 'to have a certain number of solid people whom no one would think particularly brilliant, but who between conflicting opinions can act as a middle man'. Often these were trade unionists. One example he gave of this type of minister was George Tomlinson, a 'common sense' Lancashire man, who replaced Wilkinson as Minister of Education. Education, he reasoned, was a job for an administrator. Other positions required vision and the capacity to build upon that vision. The appointment of Bevan was inspired by a recognition of the need for talent and energy in other areas.[39] Thus Attlee gave Bevan responsibility for two of the most important briefs in his government – health and housing. Why did he appoint a rebellious and divisive character? The reason he gave was simple: 'He had great ability.' That said, he had given some thought to how he might be managed. As long as Stafford Cripps remained a key figure in the government – as a man whom Bevan greatly respected – Bevan never caused any trouble.[40]

Bevan's biographer, Michael Foot, did a good job of making Bevan appear even more graceless, and petty, about Attlee in government than he had been about his leader during the war. The prime minister was 'so solitary that no one knew he was there'. He seemed 'immune, almost disinterested' from the bruising ordeal of the political fights in which Bevan was engaged as he struggled to set up the National Health Service. He might complain that Attlee's version of leadership was insufficiently decisive at various moments, yet he could never complain that he was not given sufficient leeway and support to make his ministry work. Thus, as Foot wrote, 'the remoteness of the Prime Minister did have its advantages.' Bevan, 'new to a government department, was both surprised and gratified to discover how free he was left to make his own plans'. He appreciated that Attlee had shown towards him, in 1945, 'a conspicuous act of magnanimity, and the promise of a start with a clean sheet was honourably fulfilled.' That there were 'moments when the association between the two men trembled on the edge of a warmer friendship' was chiefly Attlee's doing, according to Foot. These moments would pass when Attlee 'would stress the need for teamwork in some excruciating cricketing metaphor, or he would seek to rally the Parliamentary Party with the moral uplift of a public school speech day.' Apparently these were the 'prissy exhibitions' and 'suburban middle class values' which Bevan detested. The story of Bevan refusing Attlee's request that he wear a dinner jacket to Buckingham Palace was given as the prime example of this.[41]

Without the patient and unegotistical way in which he was managed by Attlee, it is hard to imagine Nye Bevan having had such an influence in the course of British history. Ernie Bevin, with whom he had many bitter clashes, would not have had him in his government; and even Morrison would have struggled to handle him, as they fell on different sides on most issues. It is a testimony to Attlee's skills – and ability to see beyond issues of personality – that he was not only able to incorporate him, but to marshal his energies so effectively. He had no fundamental objection to Bevan being the leader in the future, and thought this was possible, if he learned to appreciate the 'sense of responsibility' that leadership required.[42] At no point did he see it as a problem that Bevan stole the limelight from him. 'Our new ministers are doing well, I think,' he reported to his brother Tom a few months into the government. He had no qualms about saying that the best performer was Bevan. The fact was that Bevan's force of personality and idealism were huge assets for the government, which faced serious professional resistance from the medical establishment to its proposals on health. When Bevan first outlined his vision for a National Health Service in October 1945, Attlee expressed delight that his minister had done well 'on a pretty sticky wicket'.[43]

This was not the last time that he would use one of the cricket analogies that so infuriated Bevan. A good leader was like a batsman. He had to be ready to go on the attack when the opportunity arose, or play a steadier, defensive game – even if he felt his groove was in. 'In cricketing language,' he said, 'he has to be ready and willing to go out and hook one off his eyebrows over the pavilion: but he has also got to move over and let a fast one go by the off-stump without nibbling at it, whatever the barrackers say.' A leader must be trusted and have guts. But grown men, 'who know the score, do not want their leader to be continually beating his breast and advertising his agonies'. As with every batsman, the longer he stayed in the more he learned about his game.[44]

III

With the immediate threat of bankruptcy averted, there were two overriding priorities on the home front. The first was the nationalisation of essential industries, and the second was the fulfilment of the promises made during the war, and in the 1945 Labour manifesto: the creation of an entirely new regime of social security and welfare.

Nationalisation was something that had been central to the Labour Party programme since 1937, drawn up by Dalton but, as he acknowledged, with significant input from Attlee himself. As expected, the first plank in this was the nationalisation of the Bank of England. This was largely a symbolic act. The bank was already, in effect, controlled by the Treasury. Nonetheless, in the eyes of *Tribune*, there was a value in such symbolism, as it removed an anachronism in the British economic system.[45] Attlee himself commented that he expected more controversy, but it passed through Parliament easily: 'rather odd when you think of all the row and trouble there used to be about it.'[46]

Following the Bank of England, during the parliamentary session of 1945–6, the government nationalised electricity, gas, civil aviation, cable and radio communications, and the roads and railways. This was followed by the coal industry in 1947. The case for steel and iron nationalisation, in the second half of the government, was to prove more contentious.[47]

Of these, nationalisation of the mines was a long-time Labour goal which dated back to before the general strike of 1926. The case was made on two grounds. The first was the treacherous working conditions, and scant remuneration, for those who worked in the mines. The second, arising from the first, was the need for greater efficiency in an industry that was crucial to so many others – as the main provider of energy – and which had been falling behind its competitors in other countries for decades. In this respect, the inheritance of a wartime economy, when the government had effectively taken control of the industry, undoubtedly made the transition easier.

As an American State Department analysis of the Labour Party programme in 1945 identified, Britain was 'already under a more or less complete system of government control and planning for war purposes'. This meant that the objective of a planned economy to ensure full employment was more easily attainable. Added to this was the acquiescence of the trade unions, particularly the miners, in making such changes. Longer term, however, planned nationalisation of iron and steel was likely to prove particularly difficult, as these were more complex industries, with many different tiers. For example, the main companies in the iron and steel industries also undertook ancillary activities – such as car manufacture – which the government did not want to nationalise. Transport was also to prove trickier than expected. While nationalisation of the railways was seen as a success, road haulage presented further management difficulties.[48]

Gaining control of credit and capital was the prerequisite of a planned economy. As Attlee reasoned, this 'wasn't just nationalisation for nationalisation's sake but the policy in which we believed: that fundamental things – central banking, transport, fuel and power – must be taken over by the nation as a basis on which the rest of the re-organisation of the country would depend.'[49] The next priority was to adjust the economy to peacetime, and, in so far as possible, global conditions. British industry had been geared to fighting the war. The country was not producing or exporting enough and was dangerously dependent on imports.[50] Correcting this imbalance – ensuring a 'balance of payments' – became something of an obsession for the government.[51] And it was something that had been achieved by the time of Stafford Cripps's death in 1951.

In making these vast changes to the economy, the government did face significant obstacles, nonetheless. The most immediate, connected to the demobilisation issue, was a manpower shortage. This meant that the coal industry, among others, faced problems of under-production, which had an effect on iron and steel and transport. The second was that, in taking these industries under control, they inherited long-term inefficiencies caused by mismanagement and under-investment. In 1944, for example, Attlee had observed to Tom that 'it is a vice in our industrialists to take immense pride in machines that ought to have been scrapped long since.'[52]

The science of 'management' became something of an obsession for Stafford Cripps at the Board of Trade. But for many who had waited years for changes, the results of nationalisation could be disappointing. The father of Raymond Williams described the disillusionment with the new regime he felt as a railway worker. 'Within six months, he, who had always supported it, was bitterly against the character of the new structure. It seemed to him the substitution of one kind of directorial board for another. He said that the immediate work discipline actually became harsher. The way he put it: "There used to be one inspector, now there are two." '[53]

The prime minister was conscious of this type of criticism. In truth, he admitted the limitations of nationalisation in changing the culture of the work environment. 'We tried hard to establish more joint consultation and things of that kind, but not with much success,' he later reasoned. 'A hang-over from the past . . . Some of them still had the old feeling of opposition to any administration. Others frankly said, "Well, look, management isn't our job." ' Attlee accepted the imputation that a lot of nationalisation simply meant 'the same old bosses with different hats on'.[54]

While the prime minister was disappointed with this, he was not particularly surprised. At the end of the First World War, much influenced by William Morris, he had carefully considered the ideas of 'guild socialism', which stressed worker democracy and smaller units of production. Yet Attlee had never been convinced by Morris's proposition that man needed to feel attached to the product of his labour, or that workers necessarily wanted control of the industries in which they worked. From the time of his campaigns against the practice of 'sweating' in factories, he believed it was more important to improve working conditions than to change the nature of work itself. It had been this that had led him away from Morris towards Edward Bellamy's ideal of a socialist commonwealth. In the latter, hierarchy and central control were an essential part of industrial efficiency. The pay-off was that the workers had shorter hours, better conditions, and more time and opportunity to pursue whatever activities they sought for fulfilment. Every man's version of the good life was his own domain; the point of government was to provide him with the space to enjoy it.

Above all, the greatest challenge facing the government in its management of the economy was its vulnerability to vicissitudes in the global market. From the moment that the American loan was agreed, Britain was tied into an economic system dominated by the dollar. Thus, it was in a race against time to stabilise the economy, and increase production and exports, before sterling was due to be made convertible to dollars in the summer of 1947. 'We had to move fast,' explained Attlee. 'We had to rebuild the export trade, and you can't build the export trade in a vacuum. You've got to have fuel and power, transport, finance and all the rest of it.' The most unpopular aspect of this was to be the controls which were maintained on consumer consumption. 'Very frustrating, but you can't avoid it . . . We had to get back to our international markets. We had to get back on our feet as an international power in order that our voice counted where it was needed.'[55]

This also pointed to a fundamental tension at the heart of the Labour conception of economic planning. At one level it aimed to stabilise international markets through multilateral cooperation (increasingly with the Americans, but also within the Commonwealth); at the same time, it practised a form of economic nationalism in its own efforts to control the domestic economy.[56] Significant advances were made in the modernisation of the economy. Production and exports did improve by the end of government. Yet ultimately Labour had a 'fragmented conception of economic policy' in which 'planning was a rhetorical reference as often as a coherent programme of action'.[57]

The economist Douglas Jay, who spent the first year of the government in Number 10 as Attlee's economic adviser, reflected on just how difficult it was to keep responding to changes in the global economy. 'My most vivid impression of all in these months at No. 10 was the falsity of the illusion, harboured by journalists, academics, and others that something called "power" resided in the hands of a Prime Minister. The picture drawn, or imagined, is of a great man, sitting down in his office, pulling great levers, issuing edicts, and shaping events. Nothing could be further from the truth in the real life of No. 10 as I knew it. So far from wielding great power, the PM at this time found himself hemmed in by relentless economic or physical forces, and faced with problems which had to be solved, but which could not be solved.'

In an echo of Evelyn Waugh's 'Tactical Exercise', Jay had gone into government with a picture in his mind of Attlee as 'the little military man, just back from the First World War, springing to attention on the pavement in Hampstead'. Working alongside him soon changed this impression. He admired Attlee's calmness and command of the levers of government. And yet, because of what happened beyond his control, the position of the prime minister was 'more that of a cornered animal or a climber on a rock face unable to go up or down, than that of a general ordering his troops wherever he wished around the landscape'.[58] The surprise was that so much was achieved in such restrictive conditions.

IV

On questions of nationalisation – and economic planning in general – Attlee was happy to leave the details to his ministers, particularly Dalton, Cripps and Morrison, who all claimed interest and competency in this sphere. In fact, Lord Longford, one of his ministers, claimed that he 'did not care a damn about nationalisation'.[59] Douglas Jay described how Attlee, when being asked in the Commons by George Strauss, a Labour MP and pedantic academic, 'whether nationalisation and socialisation are the same thing', Attlee had replied, 'Very much the same.' If Strauss was expecting an elaborate exposition of guild socialism, he would have been disappointed. While MPs roared with laughter at the quickness of Attlee's witty response, it actually demonstrated how such questions – the bread and butter of socialist economists – did not particularly exercise his attention.[60]

Questions of social policy, insurance and welfare, were a different matter entirely. In fact, Attlee was much more personally invested in these than in any other issue, with the one possible exception of India. Quite simply, as Attlee put it, it was 'not our policy to try to re-create an un-egalitarian society, but to work steadily towards a greater equality. Not a dead level, but fewer great differences, more opportunities and more social justice.'[61]

There were massive procedural and structural leaps to make from the vision to the realisation of such ideals. The most obvious example was the National Health Service, which began to take shape under Bevan. Its provisions included comprehensive and free care at hospitals; health centres; a general practitioner service; supplementary services such as midwifery, maternity and child welfare; ambulance services; and the supply of spectacles, dentures and dentistry, along with prescriptions and medicines. The difficult was that this new regime had to be superimposed onto an existing healthcare system that was locally conditioned and in the hands of different vested interests, many of whom were resistant to change. It would take three years of struggle with the medical profession before Bevan was able to make the crucial breakthrough.

On 7 February 1946, it was Attlee who led the debate on the second reading of his government's National Insurance Bill. This provided a comprehensive and universal basis for insurance provision. All persons of working age were to pay a weekly contribution, deducted from their salary, and in return were entitled to a wide range of benefits in times of unemployment and sickness. There were further provisions for orphans, widows, and pensioners. In the abolition of the 'hated means test', it broke clear ground from the New Liberal reforms of the early twentieth century. The principle of universality implied nothing less than 'a new concept of citizenship'.[62]

According to the *Manchester Guardian*, the prime minister was at his 'quiet, reflective' best in the debate. He hardly stirred a cheer, yet he had the complete attention of the Commons, as he offered a historical survey of the battle for social reform. He did justice to all the pioneers of welfare – Keir Hardie, Will Crooks, Lloyd George, the Webbs and Sir William Beveridge. With 'refreshing honesty', he also acknowledged the contribution of Tory ministers in the late coalition in shaping the new policy.[63] But he was not afraid of a little boast. He claimed that the passage of the National Insurance Act, along with the introduction of the new Industrial Relations Bill, which freed the trade unions from punitive restrictions on the right to strike, marked his government as the most radical and reforming in British history, in just the first year of its existence.[64]

In many ways, this was the fulfilment of much that Attlee had fought for from his earliest days in 'good works' at the Haileybury Club in Limehouse. As he had explained in his 1920 book, *The Social Worker*, he had gone into the Labour movement because he thought existing conceptions of charity inadequate. Before the First World War, he had not only given his life as a volunteer in the East End, but he had campaigned for the *Minority Report* on the Poor Law, alongside the Webbs. Many of the pioneers of welfare that he praised were the people that he had worked alongside. This was his cause. In an unusual act of sentimentality he made a special request to his minister for National Insurance, James Griffiths, to ask if he could personally move the death grant clause in the original, which included funeral benefits.[65] He wrote the speech himself, junking the version prepared for him by Douglas Jay.[66]

In a letter to Lloyd George's daughter, Megan, who joined the Labour Party in 1955, Attlee acknowledged that a great debt was owed to the liberal radical tradition to which Lloyd George had once belonged. Much of Attlee's government's work had involved 'extending and amplifying measures initiated by radicals', such as the National Insurance and National Health Acts. Yet there was a crucial difference. In the past, the struggle was largely one of 'getting for the underprivileged some crumbs from the rich man's table'. Nowadays, the emphasis was on universalism – 'providing for all the things which all should enjoy in a modern community'.[67]

In this respect, one cannot deny the influence of Beveridge's White Paper of February 1942. The Labour Party's legislation in this field followed the provisions that Beveridge laid out. One thing the Beveridge Report had bequeathed to Labour was the idea of universality. The transition from a welfare system based on means testing to one premised on universal provision – including a health system 'free at the point of use' – entailed an entirely new relationship between state and citizen. These were the grounds on which the British 'New Deal' had begun to take shape. There was, as the historian Paul Addison has argued, a significant degree of consensus about this which arose from the war, and which the popularity of the Beveridge Report underlined. Important developments such as the Education Act of 1944 and Family Allowances Act of 1945, the first to provide child benefits, were on the statute books. In many ways, then, Addison is right to stress the importance of the 'patriotic compromise' brought about by the war.[68]

Although he offered him a Labour peerage, which was refused, Attlee thought that Beveridge rather overestimated his own importance. 'Always a mistake to think yourself larger than you are.'[69] Moreover, one needs to consider the connections between what Beveridge prescribed and what Attlee had striven for throughout his own life. Attlee understood the world from which Beveridge had come. They shared the same frustrations about the limitations of isolated charity work in places like Toynbee Hall, where they had both worked. Both came to believe in the need for the state to intervene more proactively in questions of welfare. Both, moreover, took as their starting point a strong sense of citizenship. One thinks back to the quotation from Attlee's head of faculty at the London School of Economics, which opens this book, and which he used in *The Social Worker*. The citizen idea was 'the necessary and single basis of social duty and social morality'.[70]

While the passage of the National Insurance Act of 1946 was a watershed moment, it is equally important to note that this was just the first plank in a comprehensive system that the government continued to put in place over the following years. This, in other words, was an area of ongoing attention and concern for Attlee's government. The next building block came in the form of the Industrial Injuries Act of 1946, which provided compensation to workers who were left injured or unable to work as a result of work-related accidents. The National Assistance Act of 1948 completed the idea of 'cradle to grave' support and a 'safety net' for those who did not pay national insurance contributions, such as the homeless, handicapped and unmarried mothers, and offered supplementary benefits to pensioners struggling to make ends meet. It also made it a requirement for local authorities to provide accommodation for those who, through illness or old age, were in need of care and support. The jewel in the crown was the National Health Service, though this would require many more political battles to be won before it came into existence in 1948.[71]

No British government of the twentieth century was as active, in terms of legislation passed, as the Attlee administration of 1945–51, particularly when it came to changing the relationship between state and society. Historians of the Attlee government have tended to view these changes in one of two ways. There are those, such as Paul Addison, who stress the importance on many issues of the consensus which arose during the war, and pre-dated the victory of 1945, and which 'fell like a branch of ripe plums, into the lap of Mr. Attlee'.[72] By contrast, there are those, such as Kenneth Morgan, who place more emphasis on the agency of the Attlee government itself, in adding new elements to that consensus, in its 'social radicalism' and as 'a landmark in the history of the Labour movement'. Many of the economic ideas, for example, and the emphasis on nationalisation, appeared in Labour's *Immediate Programme* as far back as 1937.[73] In many cases, too, the government chose 'the most radical available option'.[74]

What does Attlee himself tell us about these historical debates? First of all, while certain elements of a new consensus existed already, it is worth pointing out that Attlee had been there at the creation of the ideas which were now adopted. What was remarkable to him was the fact that things which he had campaigned for in the wilderness for so many years could now be included in this so-called 'consensus'. This was precisely the point he made to Harold Laski, when he talked about the fundamental 'changes of conception' which he had seen over the course of his career. 'I have witnessed now the acceptance by all the leading politicians in this country and all the economists of any account of the conception of the utilisation of abundance,' he wrote, in a passage that was redolent of Edward Bellamy's writing. 'From 1931 onwards in the House I and others pressed this. It was rejected with scorn. It is now accepted and important results flow from it.' Another transformation was the 'acceptance of the "doctrine of full employment"', which 'colours our whole conception of the post-war set up in this country'.[75]

In other words, Attlee did not deny that a new consensus had emerged during the war. His essential point was that the new consensus reflected arguments that he and others had been making for decades. Another important observation that Addison makes is that Attlee's government was dominated by what he calls 'social patriots', whose worldview was embodied in the national unity required to fight the war.[76] Yet the idea of social patriotism was not born in 1940 when Labour entered the government. It was inherent in everything that Attlee did from 1906. It was embodied in his service for his country in the First World War, in circumstances very different to those in which he found himself in the Second World War.[77] The language and the logic behind it had a longer heritage which, in many ways, defined Attlee's whole career. One need only consider a sample of his pronouncements to see the continuity. 'We live in a state of society where the vast majority live stunted lives – we endeavour to give them a freer life.' That was the mission he defined for himself, as a soldier in 1918.[78] 'The true wealth of the country and its finest asset are its citizens.' As the nation was organised for war and death, 'so it can be organised for peace and life if we have the will for it.' The 'utilisation of abundance' could be brought about by taking hold of the purchasing power of the nation, by 'directing the energies of the nation into the production of necessities for life, and not merely into the production of luxuries or necessities for profit'.[79] These were words from Attlee's maiden speech in 1922, but could just has easily have appeared in an election address in 1945. What others have since seen as a consensus, Attlee saw as the successful fulfilment of a mission that he had embarked upon four decades earlier. In a way that undercuts many subsequent historiographical debates, however, he saw no need to claim such profound changes as some sort of sectarian victory for the Labour Party.

V

'Such a transformation came at a considerable financial cost, of course. 'The question is asked – can we afford it?' Attlee had acknowledged, when introducing the National Insurance Bill in February 1946. 'Supposing the answer is "No," what does that mean? It really means that the sum total of the goods produced and the services rendered by the people of this country is not sufficient to provide for all our people at all times, in sickness, in health, in youth and in age . . . I cannot believe that our national productivity is so slow, that our willingness to work is so feeble or that we can submit to the world that the masses of our people must be condemned to penury.' In the prime minister's view, a healthier population represented 'a true economy and [an] addition to the national wealth in the long term'.[80] Nonetheless, Attlee also acknowledged that the success of the new system was linked to two things: the maintenance of full employment; and an increase in overall productivity in essential industries.

Accordingly, just a few weeks after this speech, in March 1946, Attlee announced a 'prosperity campaign' to the nation. This was a coordinated burst of industrial activity, organised in conjunction with the trade unions, in which employees and employers would join together to ensure maximum efficiency of production. The trade unions had been brought on board by Bevin. This was social patriotism in its purest form. That said, as the *Observer* reported, there was a 'certain impatience' growing about the ministerial habit of lecturing everybody on the need to work harder.[81]

The first signs of internal discontent within the government also emerged in early 1946. Ellis Smith, a Lancashire MP, resigned as junior minister to Stafford Cripps at the Board of Trade. Smith felt that the government was putting too much emphasis on increasing its export quota. This was forcing it to maintain a tough policy of internal austerity, with price controls and the continuation of wartime rationing. Ben Smith, the food minister, also complained about Cripps's regime. Cripps – a vegetarian teetotaller – was to become the emblem of austerity Britain. As Trevor Evans, the trade union correspondent of the *Daily Express* observed, it seemed that the 'phase of toleration' was beginning to pass.[82]

One of the prime minister's favourite observations, to which he often returned, was that government was about 'priorities'. By the spring of 1946, however, not everybody in his Cabinet agreed what those priorities should be. Dalton and Cripps – supported by Emanuel Shinwell, the fuel minister – pushed for more movement on the plans to nationalise iron and steel. Morrison – and to a lesser extent Attlee – was sceptical, and also called for a relaxation on wartime controls. Significantly, Morrison chaired the Official Committee on the Socialisation of Industries, which meant that he had the casting vote.[83] Labour's vague plans for reforming the House of Lords were also postponed. For those who were more doubtful about nationalisation, there was a feeling that the Lords acted as a useful check, lest the Labour left get carried away with the party's huge majority in the Commons.[84] At the party conference in June, Attlee stressed the need for patience. Labour had made great progress in a very short time, but 'narrow dogmatism' would not serve its cause.[85]

By July 1946, as the Labour government celebrated its first anniversary, it had a number of undeniable achievements to its name. In the 1945 manifesto, *Let Us Face the Future*, Labour had pledged itself to the nationalisation of six industries. It had already begun the process in four of these (coalmining, transport, electricity and gas). Demobilisation had been carried out relatively smoothly, despite initial clashes over delays. Two and a half million had been mustered out of uniform, and unemployment still held at under 400,000 – less than 2 per cent of the working population. The prime minister was finally able to let Jack Lawson, who was suffering from ill health and needed to recover after an operation, leave his position as Minister of War.[86]

The same month, Ben Smith, the former food minister, was also replaced by John Strachey, from the intellectual wing of the party.[87] But it soon became clear that he had taken on something of a poisoned chalice. A global food shortage had been caused by droughts in Europe, New Zealand and North Africa, and famines in India and Burma. As well as responsibility for the empire, Britain had to foot a large portion of the bill to keep Germany fed, and secure. One of Strachey's first acts was to take the extremely unpopular measure of announcing that bread would have to be subject to further rationing.[88]

Speaking at the Durham Miners' Gala in May 1946, to celebrate the anniversary of victory over Germany, Attlee appeared a little defensive and piqued by the criticism. No responsible government wanted to ration bread, he pleaded. But the anti-austerity cry had been got up by the Tory press in order to 'mobilise the housewives'. The Tories had not cared much about these things during the depression. Nye Bevan, standing alongside his prime minister, also promised further progress on housing, claiming that there would be no housing shortage at all by the end of the government's term.[89] For all the successes of the last months, food and housing were areas of concern.

Meanwhile, back in London, Herbert Morrison had seized on a more optimistic memorandum circulated by Strachey – which suggested that Canadian wheat yields were up – and called a meeting of ministers to suggest that the measure be postponed. Attlee objected to this slight on his authority and called a mini-cabinet in Durham that night where it was decided that the only responsible course was to push ahead with the measure: 'we had these responsibilities to India and other parts of the world. We couldn't think only of ourselves.' As for Morrison, 'He thought he was in charge but he wasn't. I soon had him on the scrambler.'[90]

With Cripps and Morrison pulling in different directions, it was not always easy to maintain harmony. But a greater concern was the waning physical condition of a number of senior members of the government. Bevin suffered a number of health problems in 1946, as did Stafford Cripps, Ellen Wilkinson, and Jack Lawson. Surprisingly, perhaps, Lord Addison, at seventy-seven years, was one of the more robust members, said to be fit to lead the party in the Lords for another session. Lord Pethwick-Lawrence, working alongside him, was seventy-five, but also seemed to be better preserved than many of the Cabinet. It was the fashion to say that the back benches were full of talent. But the parliamentary correspondent of the *Manchester Guardian* was not so sure. The back benches were full of subject specialists but lacking those 'built to a more comprehensive mould, who at the same time stand out above the ruck'.[91]

Attlee did attempt to reshuffle the pack before the new Parliament began in the autumn of 1946. To reflect the transition to peacetime, the heads of the three armed services were to be represented at Cabinet by a new Minister of Defence. This position was to be filled by A. V. Alexander, though Attlee made sure to retain his chairmanship of the Defence Committee. George Henry Hall was replaced as colonial secretary by Arthur Creech Jones, an expert in this field and an obvious choice to pursue the 'new colonial policy' that Attlee was hoping to make progress on.[92] Philip Noel-Baker was moved from his junior ministry at the Foreign Office to become aviation minister, and Hector McNeil was appointed as Bevin's new adjutant.[93] By the autumn of 1946, the changes were in place. Most of the government's business for the forthcoming session would come from the Lord President's Committee, over which Morrison presided. The main focus was on housing (with a forthcoming Town and Country Planning Bill), exports (still regarded as the key to economic revival), and energy (with the nationalisation of electricity and gas to be finalised).[94]

It was as the new parliamentary session got underway in the autumn of 1946, that the prime minister turned to the poetry of John Milton again to reflect his pride at what had been achieved so far, and his optimism that Britain was beginning to realise that the foundation stones of the New Jerusalem really had been laid. 'Methinks I see in my mind a noble and puissant nation rousing herself like a strong man after sleep, and shaking her invincible locks,' he said, quoting Milton's *Areopagitica* in a speech at the Lord Mayor's Banquet, 'Methinks I see her as an eagle muing her mighty youth, and kindling her undazzled eyes at the full midday beam.'[95]

The domestic transformation of Britain had begun at pace. The new social welfare system had been crafted in the prime minister's image and had realised some of the goals which he had strived for from his earliest days in politics. But it was to foreign affairs that his attention would increasingly turn from late 1946; and where, after welfare, he felt the greatest personal sense of mission.

18

Empire into Commonwealth

Finally and fatally, Athens would not allow to other groups over which she had power, the liberty she had found admirable for herself. She was accused, not unjustly, by her allies and her enemies, of being a tyrant city. And in the fifth book of Thucydides there is written the eternal condemnation of a city which can refuse autonomy to her dependants when she has prided herself on attaining it for herself. The fall of Athens, in 404 BC, was directly due, not to the liberty she had attained, but to the attempts she made to limit her ideal to herself. There may be no moral in history; yet one more than half agrees with the Thucydidean conception of a Nemesis overtaking all who refuse to others what they believe most necessary for themselves. Athens won independence and used it; and then built upon her achievement an insolent claim to empire and a vulgar ambition for wealth.

Cecil Delisle Burns, *Political Ideals: An Essay*, 1919[1]

I *Luxembourg Palace, Paris, 26 July 1946*

The theatre of the Luxembourg Palace in Paris was lit by spotlight. There were so many cameras that it resembled 'opening night' at a Hollywood premiere. The delegates at the Paris Peace Conference, convened to set terms for reparations and borders for the post-war settlement of the world, sat in plush red chairs, each with a place name. The conference had been called to determine the remaining post-war issues in Europe and North Africa, settling state boundaries, making provisions for minority rights, and determining compensation. The former diplomat and MP, Harold Nicolson, who had lost his parliamentary seat in 1945, sat towards the back. He was there as an official observer, as he had been at the Paris Peace Conference of 1919 convened after the First World War.

The delegates sat waiting for the senior dignitaries to take their seats to hear a speech by Georges Bidault, the French prime minister. Just after 4 p.m., as expected, the leading cast emerged from behind the curtain, walked across the main stage and down the steps before taking their places among the stalls. First came the Russians. Soviet foreign minister Vyacheslav Molotov, and his deputy Andrey Vyshinsky, strode across the stage 'with all the consciousness of power'. They were followed by the US Secretary of State James Byrnes and his officials, who emerged with all the consciousness of 'great virtue'. Finally, the British – minus Ernest Bevin, who was suffering from a heart complaint and had been ordered to stay in London – made their appearance. As Nicolson saw it, it was a 'lamentable' entry: 'in trips little Attlee, hesitates on finding himself on the stage, tries to dart back again into the door through which he has come, and is then rescued by an official who leads him across the stage with a hand on his elbow . . . How insignificant they look there in their red plush stalls! How different from Lloyd George and Balfour – how terribly different from Winston.'[2]

Three unavoidable, uncomfortable, and interconnected, realities had confronted the prime minister and his foreign secretary, almost from the moment they had arrived in Potsdam the day after their general election win. The first was the fact that the war had left the United States in a supreme position in world affairs. Britain was not only financially tied to America through its loan – bound in a dollar-dominated financial system – it was also to become increasingly dependent on US military strength to preserve its own strategic interests. The second was the growing assertiveness and expansionism of the Soviet Union – in a way that seemed to directly threaten British security. Britain had not been through a war with Hitler to permit another threatening hegemon to gain control in central Europe, particularly given that it had now seen the damage that could be done to it by the air from attacks launched in Germany. If anything, the fates of Poland and Czechoslovakia now seemed more important than they had done in the 1930s. Furthermore, Britain had not invested so much in the campaign in the eastern Mediterranean, North Africa and the

Middle East to see the Russians become the dominant power there. This was a region of vital strategic importance to the country: with the Suez Canal, Persian oil reserves, and the northern flank of India suddenly appearing vulnerable.

The third, related, problem facing the government was that the British Empire was unsustainable in its current form. The war had stretched Anglo-Indian relations to breaking point, leading to the imprisonment of the Indian nationalist leaders – by Attlee's order – in 1942. Beyond India, could Britain afford to maintain large military or naval bases in places like Egypt, Aden, or further afield, in Singapore? Within a few days of Japan's surrender, Keynes had expressed concern that Britain had 'got into the habit' of maintaining large and expensive military establishments all over the Mediterranean, Africa and Asia. The commitment to 'police vast areas eastwards from Tunis to Burma and northwards from East Africa to Germany' could cripple the country, he warned.[3]

As Chancellor of the Exchequer, Hugh Dalton seized on Keynes's warnings. Even after demobilisation, there were still more than 1.5 million British service personnel posted round the world at the end of 1946. All had to be fed, housed, paid and armed. Defence spending was at nearly 18 per cent of gross national product. There was a manpower shortage in vital industries, with 18.6 per cent of the British male population still in the services by mid-1946.[4] There would be no use for these men at all 'if we come an economic and financial cropper two years hence.'[5]

There was another problem with maintaining the empire in its current form. Britain and its allies had fought in the name of democracy and self-determination. For that reason alone, it was difficult to ignore demands for independence in places like India. What complicated matters for the government was that it was never so simple as handing freedom to those countries that wanted it. Competing ethnic and religious groups – such as Jews and Arabs in Palestine, or Hindus, Muslims and Sikhs in India – had rival claims for nationhood and often irreconcilable territorial demands. Leaving these places without political agreement meant leaving those left to fight it out between themselves – often with bloody consequences. Shrugging one's shoulders was not a course to be taken by a responsible global power that sought to command respect. Nor was it wise in narrowly strategic terms. The danger of withdrawing was that others, chiefly the Soviet Union, were poised to fill the vacuum. Thus Churchill warned of the danger of 'scuttling' from imperial commitments for the first time in late 1946. Scuttle was a word that was to ring in Attlee's ears thereafter.

When approaching these problems, Attlee had certain preconceptions which pre-dated the last war. On the question of American predominance, for example, though it was sometimes hard to swallow, there was not much alternative. One lesson of the interwar years was that having the United States engaged in the world was far preferable to seeing it revert to anything resembling isolationism. Subservience to a dollar system was the price to be paid but there were consolations – not least the huge tranches of money that came from the American loan, and, from mid-1947, the Marshall Plan. The lessons of the 1930s, and the failures of appeasement, cast a long shadow on British foreign policy, particularly regarding the threat posed by the Soviet Union. Thus Attlee, following Bevin, became increasingly hostile to displays of what he called 'Russian imperialism'.

The close relationship between the prime minister and his foreign secretary in these years was in many ways the defining characteristic of the Attlee government. It was built not simply on personal affection but also on mutual respect. Attlee claimed to have 'never met a man in politics with as much imagination as . . . [Bevin] had, with the exception of Winston'.[6] 'Better get Clem's agreement,' Bevin was known to say, 'I value his judgement and if things should go wrong we will be better off if he has agreed.'[7]

To those outside the government, this seemed to convey complete unanimity on foreign affairs. 'If you've got a good dog,' Attlee once said, 'you don't bark yourself.'[8] Behind the scenes, however, there were profound disagreements between them on a number of issues. This meant that Labour's foreign policy did not follow a predetermined course. Part of this was due to a difference in mentality. In the foreign policy debates of the 1930s, Bevin had been the foremost Labour 'realist' in urging the party to support the government's rearmament programme – a position to which Attlee had been slower to convert. On the issue of Spanish intervention, Attlee had seized on the cause as a moral imperative, whereas Bevin had opposed intervention. The latter translated this idealism from the League of Nations to his hope for the United Nations; Bevin remained more cautious about multi-lateralism.

After 1945, the most important difference between the two was in how they talked about empire. When Bevin complained about the prospect of

Soviet expansionism in the eastern Mediterranean and the Middle East, he spoke like old-fashioned British imperialists. The Soviet Union was 'coming right across the throat' of the British Empire, and its 'lifeline' to India, he objected in November 1945.[9] This certainly endeared him to the Foreign Office and the chiefs of the general staff – the two key interest groups in the making of British foreign policy. It was not a sentiment shared by his prime minister, however. 'We ought to confront the Russians with the requirements of a world organisation for peace, not with the needs of the British Empire,' he had said at Potsdam. On the contrary, he expressed sympathy for the Russians in their desire to get control of the exits from the Black Sea, and to acquire a warm-water port in the Mediterranean. It was 'necessary for us to look at the matter from a Russian angle'. When it came to the Eastern Mediterranean and North Africa, moreover, the prime minister ruffled some feathers within the British Establishment with his suggestion that, 'Our claim that we occupy these positions as trustees for the rest of the world that can trust our disinterestedness is not likely to be generally accepted.'[10]

There was something else that motivated Attlee in these years, and did so more than anyone else in government: this was the conviction that the old British Empire, that of Queen Victoria and the Diamond Jubilee, had come to an end, and should not be supported beyond its natural lifespan. Ideally, he hoped that a new British Commonwealth would take its place. Yet he was equally clear that this would be the decision of those nations who would emerge from the old empire. As we have seen, Attlee did not repudiate every aspect of the empire. In his view, imperialism had a chequered past but the instincts that fed into it were not all malign.

If anything, Attlee's approach to imperial questions after 1945 can be seen as an attempt to end the empire on the right note, and to salvage something of its better side. More specifically, his aim was to make good on the promises of self-government that had been held out to those under British rule. He certainly did not see this transition in terms of British decline – more the fulfilment of an unwritten compact agreed to many years before. Repeatedly, he expressed the hope that something better might emerge from the foundations of empire. 'We are seeking everywhere to extend the freedom we enjoy to others,' he said. Based on the principles of self-determination and the rights of free association, perhaps the British Commonwealth might even become a 'United Nations in miniature'.[11]

When perusing the shelves one weekend at Chequers in 1949, Attlee's eyes fell upon the classic work by Edward Gibbon – *The History of the Decline and Fall of the Roman Empire*, published in six volumes between 1786 and 1789.[12] He read the whole thing. It is tempting to make much of this – to conclude that Gibbon provided the soundtrack for a declinist-minded British prime minister. That was certainly how the *New York Times* interpreted it when it was revealed that Attlee had become a keen student of Gibbon. The Downing Street press office was quick to play down the significance of this.[13] Moreover, no one was more enamoured of Gibbon than Winston Churchill, who had read all six volumes as a young man. The set that had been left on the shelves at Chequers was owned by him.[14]

What did Attlee take from this famous work as he set about making radical changes to the British Empire? Gibbon's basic thesis was that the decline of the Roman Empire could be explained by an internal degeneration of ideas of citizenship among its citizens. It lost the sense of duty, manliness and virtue that had been crucial to its rise. One symptom of this was the rise of Christian ideas of pacifism within its territory; and another was its reliance on mercenaries to fight its wars, on behalf of vested interests.[15] There was an obvious link here with the profound sense of citizenship which guided Attlee's own career. Moreover, as we have seen, Attlee returned home from the First World War as a modern citizen soldier in the Gibbon mould.

More importantly, the prime minister did not read Gibbon in isolation. As he revealed to Tom, at a crucial moment in the transition from empire into commonweath, he also studied the work of the London University professor Cecil Delisle Burns. While Burns was a well-known anti-imperialist, he had also expressed, as early as 1918, the Attlean belief that the independence of the colonies would not lead to a 'severance from the British Commonwealth of Nations'.[16]

Burns was also renowned for his work on ancient Greek notions of citizenship. Indeed, similar to Gibbon's thesis on Rome, he had argued that the fall of Athens in 404 BC had been due to the fact that she 'would not allow to other groups over which she had power, the liberty she had found admirable for herself'. To support his argument, Burns cited the fifth book of Thucydides' *History of the Peloponnesian War*. This warned of a Nemesis bringing retribution on all who refuse to others what they believe most necessary for themselves. Athens had won her own independence and liberty; but all she offered to others was 'an insolent claim to empire and a vulgar ambition for wealth'.[17] Once more, there were echoes of this in Attlee's approach to the empire question.

By the autumn of 1949, a more immediate concern was the 'iron curtain', which threatened to divide Europe once again. So he now turned to Burns's more recent historical work, *The First Europe: A Study of the Establishment of Medieval Christendom, A.D. 400–800*.[18] The book covered the period from the end of the Justinian period through to the rise of Charlemagne, the ruler who united most of Western Europe. In the preface to his book, Burns addressed those politicians striving to make a third Europe from the ruins of war. For Burns, in the era of Charlemagne was 'to be found the real basis of modern democracy – the assumption that all human beings have an equal right to derive benefit from the social system and all adults an equal responsibility for its maintenance'.[19] These words – which evoked a universal concept of citizenship that encompassed social and economic needs – might have come straight from the mouth of Attlee himself.

II

At the Labour Party conference of May 1945, which had taken place in Blackpool just before the general election, it had fallen to Ernie Bevin to articulate what a Labour foreign policy might look like. At the time, he had suggested that a socialist government in Britain might be able to act as a mediator between capitalistic America and communistic Russia. Long after Bevin had given up such hopes, many on the left of the Labour Party continued to cling to this idea. This was the theme of the 'Keep Left' faction, which emerged within the party to become the critics-in-chief of the Attlee government's foreign policy. Led by the young backbenchers Michael Foot, Richard Crossman and Ian Mikardo, this group argued that Britain should become a democratic socialist 'third force' in world politics. Bevin became their target.

In the early stages of the cold war, nothing encapsulated the growing distance between Soviet Russia and the Western Allies better than the relationship between Bevin and his Soviet counterpart, Molotov. In fact, the

American Secretary of State, James Byrnes, watched, with some bemusement, the bitter clashes between the two at the meetings of the Council of Foreign Ministers in the autumn and winter of 1945. In a good mood, Bevin would tell Molotov, the son of a respectable shop clerk, that he knew nothing about the proletariat. In a bad mood, he would accuse him of behaving like Hitler – a piece of provocation which forced Byrnes to intervene on Molotov's behalf.[20]

These tensions were about more than just personality. As American observers soon realised, the enmity between London and Moscow had a long heritage. What was more, the issues on which Bevin and Molotov clashed had more than a whiff of the imperial 'great game' about them. This was most obvious over the fate of the North and East African colonies that had been wrested from the Italians over the course of the war. The Soviet Union pushed to have the statelets Tripolitania and Cyrenaica (both in modern-day Libya) turned over to their care as protectorates. Bevin objected that this would be an incursion into an area fundamental to the 'lifeline' to India. The British government was already alarmed by the prospect of Greece coming under control of the communists. With Marshal Tito having taken Yugoslavia into the Soviet sphere, followed by Romania – creating a 'chain-mail' of satellite states – Greece was the last bulwark against Soviet control of the Aegean and Adriatic.[21]

Mallory Browne, the astute foreign correspondent of the *New York Times*, noted an unresolved tension at the heart of British foreign policy. On the one hand, no government was more enthusiastic about the creation of the United Nations, which it hoped to make 'an effective reality' where the League of Nations had failed. On the other, Britain was engaged in an old-fashioned battle with Russia over spheres of influence, which stretched from the Baltic to the Mediterranean and on to the Persian Gulf. America had little stake in this fight. In the Middle East and elsewhere, the British and the Russians 'were carrying on the age-old battle of balance of power' and a scramble for oil (particularly in Persia).[22]

In fact, in pointing out this contradiction, Browne had stumbled on something that had hitherto remained unknown outside the government. Privately, Attlee was highly sceptical about his foreign secretary's twitchiness regarding North Africa and the eastern Mediterranean. The prime minister's views ran directly against certain assumptions that had been ingrained in the British military and diplomatic establishment for generations. To the alarm of the chiefs of staff and the Foreign Office, he had suggested in September (during the London Council of Foreign Ministers) that, if the UN was to be effective, Britain would not be able to accept the colonial trusteeships which it claimed there. If the UN was to function as he hoped, 'it does not matter who holds Cyrenaica or Somalia or who controls the Suez Canal.'²³

Attlee's faith in the UN only went so far, however. In the immediate aftermath of the war, Attlee had spoken in almost utopian terms about the need to 'abandon all out-of-date ideas of power politics' and 'lay aside our nationalistic ideals'.²⁴ Yet, if anything disabused him of this faith, it was the behaviour of the Soviet Union. While he retained great hopes for the United Nations in the long term, as early as the autumn of 1945 he was alarmed and disappointed by Russian attitudes towards it. He suspected that Stalin was trying to circumvent the newly established UN Security Council – on which France and China (still under a nationalist government) sat – by aiming to keep the key international issues in the hands of the Big Three; and ignoring 'the spirit' of decisions reached at Potsdam.²⁵ By December 1945, Attlee's personal messages to Stalin had been reduced to basic formalities.²⁶

Churchill was mostly supportive of Attlee and Bevin in their approach to the Soviet Union. The one exception to this was that Churchill believed that another summit between the Big Three might have provided the opportunity to reset relations, whereas Attlee thought that this would undermine the UN.²⁷ Yet, by the time that Churchill made his famous intervention into the early stages of the cold war, in a speech at Fulton, Missouri in March 1946, there was not much to separate them. It was in this speech, made in front of President Truman, that Churchill suggested that an 'iron curtain' was being drawn from the Baltic to the Adriatic, and denounced any 'appeasement' of the Soviet Union. Not only did he evoke the 'fraternal association of the English-speaking peoples'; he argued that Anglo-American unity was more important than the United Nations in providing 'The Sinews of Peace'.

Labour backbenchers were outraged at Churchill's intervention, which had been coordinated closely with the White House. Yet Attlee refused to condemn or comment on the speech. In fact, despite later denials, he had been kept closely informed by Churchill and was given advance notice of its contents on 17 February 1946. As Churchill explained to the prime minister, he remained committed to the UN Charter. Yet he did not believe that this should come at the expense of Britain's 'special relationship' with the US. It was more important than ever to preserve this unity now that the combined chiefs of staff – the US and UK military hierarchies had been fused together in the war – had recently been dismantled.[28]

In early June, he followed Churchill in a House of Commons debate on foreign affairs and condemned the Russians for disregarding the 'spirit' of the Potsdam pact. One of the greatest difficulties was to 'get into the minds of our Russian friends some real understanding of the way we work things in western democracies'. This was to become something of a theme, in which he spoke of the early cold war in terms of darkness and light. 'We have to look at the Russian people, to some extent, as if they had been born in a dark forest; they did not seem to understand the sunlight, the wind and the air of the free democracies.' He parroted Churchill's phrase about this 'iron curtain . . . a curtain between minds'. Churchill applauded the government for their 'resolute denunciation of communism'.[29]

On 15 August 1946, the first anniversary of Victory Japan Day, Attlee hosted both Churchill and the wartime chiefs of staff for a celebration at Downing Street. To his amusement, each of his three daughters had a field marshal sitting next to her at the lunch. That night there were fireworks, which he watched from a vantage point in the House of Lords, sitting with the king and queen, whom the girls were meeting for the first time. The celebrations ended with a boat ride to Hampton Court, more illuminations and a late supper.[30] However, just a year after victory, trouble seemed to be looming once more. 'Public affairs grow no easier,' he grumbled to Tom on 30 August, 'but I suppose we shall get a ray of light sometime.'[31]

While Churchill had stressed the sanctity of the Anglo-American alliance, Attlee was presented with stark evidence of its limitations. A year after his visit to Washington, DC, it was clear that the relevant scientific information needed to build a nuclear weapon had not been forthcoming. It now dawned on the prime minister that his mission had failed. As he wrote to Bevin, Truman had given him the impression that the sharing of nuclear secrets was imminent. The problem, however, was there was not 'a definite pledge in so many words'.[32] The Combined Policy Committee, which had formed after his November 1945 visit, had urged full cooperation. However, Secretary of State James Byrnes had decided that this required the approval of the US Congress. Dean Acheson, Byrnes's

Under-Secretary of State, bemoaned this turn of events, and felt that the British were within their rights to view this as 'bad faith'.[33]

In Attlee's view, there was no sense in resorting to public recriminations, or risking his relationship with Truman. He appreciated that it was difficult to offer a full exchange of scientific information because of the objections of Congress. Nonetheless, the episode had demonstrated to the prime minister, even more than before, that Britain needed more independence. 'We ought not to give the Americans the impression that we cannot get on without them; for we can (though at some extra cost in time and resources) and, if necessary, will do so.'[34] This was the moment at which Britain began the process by which it was to build its own atomic bomb.

Attlee had kept the nuclear issue out of the public domain in his first year in office. Initially he hoped to bring the Cabinet along with him in his efforts to acquire the weapon. In a meeting on 25 October, however, both Dalton and Cripps raised their objections to the £30–40 million needed over five years to construct a plant for the production of uranium. It was at this juncture that Bevin made a powerful intervention. Again, following Attlee, he made the case that independence from the US was one of his main concerns. 'That won't do at all,' he said, 'we've got to have this . . . I don't want any other Foreign Secretary of this country to be talked to or at by a Secretary of State in the United States as I have just had in my discussion with Mr. Byrnes. We've got to have this thing over here whatever it costs . . . We've got to have the bloody Union Jack on top of it.'[35]

Despite Bevin's forceful pleas, the objections of Dalton and Cripps – two of the big four under Attlee (along with Bevin and Morrison) – were noted. The bomb was taken off the agenda after the October Cabinet meeting. Yet so important did the prime minister regard this issue that he took the highly atypical, and arguably unconstitutional, decision to circumvent the Cabinet entirely. Rather than have a lengthy debate with those Labour ministers who opposed the bomb – and risk news of the argument leaking out – he formed a secret committee (GEN 163) to begin work on it before objections could be raised. GEN 163 met for the first and only time on 8 January 1947, with Attlee presiding. Dalton and Cripps were excluded and the only other senior ministers were Bevin and A. V. Alexander, the defence secretary, who could also be counted on for his support. The work was to proceed with the 'utmost secrecy'.[36]

Attlee's decisiveness on this issue underlines the strength of his conviction that this was the right course. Two considerations overrode any other in making this a matter of urgency. The first was the fear that the Russians would get there first, through skill or skulduggery. (The case of Klaus Fuchs, the German-born British scientist who was exposed for giving information to the Russians in 1950 proved that this was far from a hysterical fear). The second, relatedly, was that America had not yet committed itself by treaty to the defence of Europe. In either scenario, Britain could be left alone – or with only a few West European allies – to resist the communist tide. If the Russians had the bomb first, Britain would be severely exposed, just as the US Congress rebuilt barriers to effective Anglo-American cooperation.

There was a third consideration at the back of Attlee's mind. In his letter to Bevin on 27 November 1946, the prime minister had dismissed concerns over the 'extra cost' involved. Nevertheless, the question of the cost-effectiveness of British defence was indeed weighing on his mind. In this respect, he had a different agenda. A nuclear deterrent, he hoped, might allay the need to keep up such a large military establishment overseas.[37]

It was on the latter issue – the size of the overall defence budget – that Attlee had already begun to run into serious opposition from both his foreign secretary and the chiefs of staff. Bevin's job was to keep Britain strong, secure and powerful in the world. Attlee, who juggled all these concerns as prime minister – domestic and foreign, short term and long term – felt he had to keep the broader picture in mind. He also believed, as he had told Churchill at various points during the war, that the chiefs of the general staff had not fully grasped how new technologies – particularly in aeronautics – had changed the nature of warfare. In North Africa and Burma, for example, the British had suffered losses to highly mobile German and Japanese units, who made innovative use of air support. In his view, these lessons had to be fully grasped.

As early as March 1945, even before the end of the wartime coalition, Attlee had raised doubts about maintaining a large military presence in the Suez Canal zone.[38] In February 1946, he once again questioned the need for Britain to maintain such a large military presence in the Mediterranean and the Middle East, as well as in the Far East. Naked Soviet opportunism over the future of the Italian colonies obscured what was an emerging division within the Cabinet about this issue. Even as he came to share Bevin's suspicions of Moscow, the prime minister retained his view that Britain was dangerously overstretched. It had 200,000 troops stationed across the Middle East, with the Suez Canal Zone garrison at 80,000 alone. Resources would be further strained if, as expected, India became independent (as the Indian Army formed a large portion of the overall military force).[39] 'The perfect plague of my life,' he later recalled, 'was to get those numbers down.'[40]

Attlee made sure not to bring these debates into the public domain, or even the Cabinet. It was to Bevin and the chiefs of staff that he directed his concerns, in a succession of memoranda. Nonetheless, both Bevin and the chiefs were deeply concerned about what they saw as an ill-informed challenge to the very basis of British security policy. They did not accept the prime minister's view that, first, aerial warfare, and second, the nuclear bomb, had transformed the premise of British grand strategy. Montgomery, now Chief of the Imperial General Staff, despaired at what he saw as the prime minister's naivety.[41]

The prime minister retained great admiration for Montgomery as a wartime hero. However, he felt that he made a poor peacetime chief of the services. 'I myself had to give him more than one good ticking off, and once I had to give him a really good raspberry.' Montgomery was used to getting what he wanted, and saw every major issue facing the Attlee government in terms of what it meant for the army. In other words, because social insurance took money away from the military budget, he was strongly against it. For Attlee, this reflected his inability to take soldierly thinking to a higher level. He did not have 'as clear an idea of the importance of morale and welfare in the larger socio-political field'. Nor was he much of a visionary. General Alexander had told Attlee after the war that he did not wish to have another military posting because of the danger that he would always be thinking of the last war. Montgomery, Attlee felt, had fallen into that trap. He still saw everything from the perspective of needing to draw on large expeditionary forces.[42]

It should be said that Attlee was not the only one to think in these terms. In May 1946, for example, he was sent a personal memorandum by the military strategist Basil Liddell Hart that argued that Britain was unnecessarily over-committed in the Middle East and that Africa should be a greater longer-term priority. Liddell Hart also suggested that the British presence in the Middle East was an unnecessary provocation.[43] The prime minister also considered alternative sources of manpower. He instructed the Colonial Office and chiefs of staff to investigate the possibility of raising an army from the African colonies, though he was told that it would take decades to train sufficient numbers.[44]

In response to the prime minister's demands that they contemplate a large-scale withdrawal from the Middle East, Montgomery replied that 'the basic principles of our strategy . . . will not be radically altered by new developments in methods or weapons of warfare.'[45] In mid-1946, the chiefs of staff tried to turn the prime minister's argument on its head by arguing that the Middle East provided the necessary airfields for a deterrence policy against the Soviet Union – if, as expected, airpower was to be the key determinant in future wars. This knocked the ball back into the prime minister's court. However, in December 1946, Attlee continued to insist to Bevin that he was unconvinced that the countries bordering the Soviet Union's southern flank – Greece, Turkey, Iraq and Persia – could be made strong enough to 'form an effective barrier'. By building up a British presence there, without sufficient resources to sustain it, this would just 'seem to them [the Russians] preparations for an attack'.[46] In other words, he felt the strategy – which was supposed to be defensive – was actually provocative, and, worse still, insufficient to hold these areas if put to the test. The greatest risk was that it would be exposed as bluff and bluster.

This argument between Attlee – essentially fighting a lone battle because of his unwillingness to deploy Dalton or Cripps on his side – and Bevin and the chiefs rumbled on for the next eighteen months. The matter came to a head in January 1947, just as he pushed ahead with the secret plans to build the bomb. On 5 January, Attlee made one last push against the chiefs of staff's 'strategy of despair', in a memorandum to Bevin, calling for renewed efforts to find a settlement with the USSR. At this point, the foreign secretary firmly rebuffed his prime minister, by evoking the precedent of appeasement. As Bevin replied on 9 January, 'A surrender of the type you suggest would only encourage the Russia leaders to believe that they could get their ends without war and would lead them into the same error that Hitler made of thinking that he could get away with anything by bluff and bullying.' Even if Attlee was right in terms of military strategy, such a move had to be seen in a broader context (and through the eyes of others). A full-scale withdrawal would lead the US to 'write us off'. Britain was decreasing force levels in Egypt and Greece, and seeking American support to hold the line. 'Your proposal,' he told Attlee, 'would involve leaving from weakness.' Now also, the chiefs of staff made their presences felt. As they prepared for a final discussion on the matter in Downing Street, Montgomery let it be known to the prime minister that he could expect the collective resignation of the chiefs of staff if he proceeded along the path he was suggesting. By the time they convened at Number 10 on 13 January, Attlee, having already seen Bevin and A. V. Alexander in person, had backed down. There were to be no more drastic withdrawals other than those already agreed under demobilisation plans.[47]

The issue was not raised again. There has been speculation as to what made Attlee retreat from his 'heresy'. In testing strategic assumptions at their very foundations, he was doing what a prime minister should do – leading on foreign affairs, but behind the scenes, so as not to let the argument spill out into the public domain. For eighteen months, he had been insistent on the issue. This was the most serious disagreement between himself and Bevin, and he had continued to send memoranda to the foreign secretary making his case. Bevin's reply of 9 January, comparing the drawdown of troops to appeasement, had been his most forceful to date, and may have had an effect. That the weight of the Foreign Office was behind Bevin was also significant.[48] Moreover, the threatened resignations of the chiefs of staff was also something that would have been hugely damaging. That Attlee conceded the point was probably due to the fact that he felt the weight of the foreign secretary, plus the chiefs of staff, was too much to resist. Beyond that point, however, he refused to be pushed around by the military high command. Six weeks later, Montgomery felt the force of the prime minister come down upon him. He had made a speech in which he appeared to take a sideswipe at the government, stating that it was 'vital that we should have leaders at all levels who were to dominate the events that surround us, and never let those events get the better of us'. At this point, Attlee finally lost his patience. He wrote to A. V. Alexander to warn him that Montgomery must be disciplined: 'if he gets away with this speech, he will follow it up with other outbursts.'[49] Attlee also brought Montgomery into Number 10 for a scolding.

Meanwhile, Bevin was able to point to other successes in January 1947, which gave the prime minister confidence in his foreign secretary's overall strategy. Above all, he was making progress in his attempts to persuade the

Americans to help shoulder the burden in the eastern Mediterranean – particularly Greece and Turkey, where thousands of British troops were garrisoned and which were both coming under Soviet pressure. Bevin's point to Attlee, that the Americans would 'write off' Britain if it was seen to scuttle from its commitments, may well have been what clinched the argument.

Sure enough, on 21 February 1947, the day after Attlee set a deadline for Indian independence, Bevin made it clear to the Americans that Britain could no longer afford to maintain Greece, still in the midst of a civil war between the forces of the Greek monarchy and the communist insurgency.[50] The Americans were asked to take more responsibility for the preservation of the Western alliance at its weakest points. From this was born 'the Truman Doctrine', signed off by Congress in March 1947, which offered American support to 'free peoples' who were resisting attempted subjugation by armed minorities (specifically, communist factions). The US provided weapons and other military equipment to Greece, to preserve the monarchy as the British withdrew. From this point on, Bevin set about pinning down the details of American financial and military support for Western Europe, to bolster it against further communist expansion. That Attlee did not raise the issue again suggests that he felt his foreign secretary had made the right calculation.

Significantly, Bevin found a willing partner in George Marshall, the US Secretary of State who, in January 1947, replaced James Byrnes, with whom relations had deteriorated. In a June 1947 speech at Harvard University, Marshall spoke of an urgent need to assist Europe in its economic recovery. Now Bevin, seizing the opportunity, became the champion of what became known as the Marshall Plan.[51] Attlee believed that it was his foreign secretary's greatest achievement to run with, and reinterpret, Marshall's ideas in a way that suited British interests. 'I don't believe that Marshall, when he made his speech, had any idea it would be taken up as Bevin took it up.'[52] The very day after Marshall delivered his speech, Bevin moved into gear, creating a programme which involved Britain taking the lead in the shaping of the Western European economy. Bevin's approach consciously struck the same note as the policy of 'containment' now becoming popular in Washington, DC. Bevin went even further in envisaging a 'Western Union', 'a sort of spiritual federation of the West'.[53]

So British grand strategy entered another phase, within the orbit of an expanded world role for the US. It was a strategy that was to come to fruition in the form of the North Atlantic Treaty Organisation, which took form in April 1949. Bevin's brusqueness had somewhat disguised the subtlety of his approach to Anglo-American relations, which now had the full support of his prime minister.[54] Evidence of firmness and fortitude was the best foundation for the relationship with Washington.

III

The most vexing foreign policy problem faced by the government, and which ultimately defeated both Bevin and Attlee, was the future of Palestine. One reason Palestine became such a problematic issue was that it cut across a number of overlapping debates. For instance, it fed into debates about the future of the British presence in the Middle East. If Britain was to maintain its garrison of 80,000 at the Suez Canal, could it afford to provide the forces required to stabilise Palestine?

More importantly, Palestine was the single most divisive issue in Anglo-American relations. As we have seen, President Truman was heavily invested – personally and politically – in pressing the British, almost from the moment that the Labour government was elected, to allow a large increase in Jewish migration to Palestine. There was a huge gulf between the existing British commitment to granting 1,500 immigration certificates a year, and Truman's demand that 100,000 be granted without delay, to accommodate the vast numbers of refugees.[55] In hindsight, it is clear that neither Bevin nor Attlee grasped the gravity of what they were dealing with. They failed to register the emotional force, arising from the Holocaust, which underlay the creation of Israel. The result was a perception of lost control, a series of broken relationships, and a legacy of ill will, which contrasted to the handling of India over the same period.

In November 1945, eager to avoid a rift with Truman, and to play for time, Bevin had established a joint Anglo-American commission to consider how best to manage the migration problem. In April 1946, it recommended that 100,000 Jewish refugees should be allowed to enter the territory over a phased period, and that it should be partitioned into two separate states, for Arabs and Jews. The British would continue to administer the area until this came to fruition. However, violence between various factions, and against the British forces in Palestine, increased considerably in the summer of 1946. The British government rounded up and interned 2,000 Jews – including a number of prominent Jewish political leaders – in June, following the murder of sixteen British soldiers and six policemen in Tel Aviv. They claimed that there was clear evidence of links between the Jewish Agency, and the Haganah, the biggest armed group operating in Palestine, which had worked closely with the British in the past. The Haganah, in turn, had an offshoot in the form of the hard-line Zionist paramilitary organisation the Irgun.[56]

The ability of the British government to fulfil its mandate duty to maintain law and order was in serious doubt. 'It is clear we can no longer tolerate this direct challenge to our authority,' Attlee told the House of Commons in July 1946, revealing that the High Commissioner for Palestine had been given all available powers to restore order.[57] Despite the rising violence, continued pressure came from the US to allow Jewish refugees into the country at a faster rate than the British felt they were able to process or manage. Many in the US State Department were much more cautious than President Truman was in making such demands. They felt that there was a danger of the US becoming too involved in what was a seemingly interminable problem. The danger of superpower status, warned Walter Lippmann, the influential journalist and foreign policy expert, was that one would soon become responsible for problems that sapped the energy, status and finances of others.[58] Sure enough, if the Americans wanted more interference, the British approach was to make them assume more responsibility. As Dean Acheson described it, Attlee wanted to move the US government 'from fluent advice to immersion in the tough details of the problem'.[59]

In British exasperation at the influence of the Zionist lobby in America, some ugly prejudices rose to the surface.[60] When Bevin came back from a visit to New York in December 1946, he complained to Attlee about the intense criticism he faced from Zionist groups. Attlee reported Bevin's anger in a letter to Tom. 'It appears that Zionism has become a profitable racket over there.' A Zionist, Bevin had said, 'is defined as a Jew who collects money from another Jew to send another Jew to Palestine,' with the collector taking a good percentage of the collections.[61] In fact, the situation was more complicated than this. As the Russo-English Jewish intellectual

Isaiah Berlin noted in a letter to *The Times*, the Zionist lobby had, for example, supported the American loan to the UK, 'despite their . . . deep disapproval of British policy in Palestine'. What was more, both Jews and Arabs could point 'to all too many occasions where, in their dealing with Britain, force has paid and patience, reason and goodwill have not'. Indeed, Mr Attlee 'honourably recognised that this is so'.[62]

Attlee had emerged from the ethnic and political tinderbox of east London, where both Jews and Irish represented powerful political caucuses within his constituency. The futures of Palestine and Ireland had been pressing issues in Stepney since his earliest days there. Not only had Attlee courted these interest groups in the past, he had also been on the front line against Mosley's British Union of Fascists, and was deeply saddened by the damage he and other such demagogues had done to community relations. As someone who placed such value in fraternity, however, Attlee had a surprising blind spot when it came to appreciating the force of ethnic and religious identity. One anecdote from 1942 reveals something about his mentality. As Lord Privy Seal, he was visited by the Irish ambassador in London, who pleaded for clemency on behalf of six men who faced hanging in Belfast for the killing of a Catholic police officer. As the ambassador reminded him, he had always relied on a large Irish vote to keep his parliamentary seat. He found Attlee 'cold and detached' in response to this special pleading, replying that 'there were probably two sides to that story.'[63] (In fact, five of the six men were later pardoned and one of them, Joe Cahill, went on to lead the Provisional IRA.)

By early 1947, it was clear that the British were making no progress towards a political solution in Palestine. Exasperation turned into defeatism. This explains the decision that was made in January 1947 to send the issue to the United Nations for arbitration. The most generous possible interpretation of this decision was that the British government was demonstrating its faith in the UN as a body which had been designed precisely to determine such disputes, and mediate between contending claims to statehood.[64] In truth, however, it was a sign of the further slippage of British authority in the Middle East. Even after the issue was sent to the UN, moreover, Attlee remained personally active in trying to slow down illegal immigration from Europe to Palestine. In March 1947, he told officials that he wanted the 'utmost pressure' put on the Italians, Greeks and French to 'stop this traffic at source'.[65] Yet another summer of violence followed in 1947, underlining the fact that Britain could not reassert control without a major military investment it was not prepared to make. That the issue was tied up with the ongoing debate about force levels in the Middle East complicated the matter further. When Cabinet convened to make a final decision on Palestine in September 1947, Dalton insisted that the three service ministers and the chiefs of staff be made to wait outside, so that the decision was made by the ministers alone. 'This, if we stick to it, is a historic decision. We are drawing in our horns in the Eastern Mediterranean.'[66]

At the crucial Cabinet meeting on 20 September, Bevin expressed his concern that any solution reached by the UN on Palestine would still fall upon the British to implement. If those proposals were unworkable, then British troops would remain stuck in an impossible position. He now recommended that, rather being left with a seemingly interminable problem, it was better for Britain to surrender its mandate entirely and, failing a satisfactory settlement, withdraw its forces. The prime minister commented that there was a close parallel between the situation in Palestine and that in India. He did not believe that it was reasonable to ask the British administration in Palestine to continue in these conditions, in which a political solution between forces on the ground seemed no closer. He repeated Bevin's rather hopeful argument – rejected by officials at the Foreign Office as entirely groundless – that withdrawal would have a 'salutary effect' on the realism of those involved in the conflict.[67] The Foreign Office urged Bevin and Attlee not to simply wash their hands of the question when it went to the UN, but to continue to push for a settlement.[68] However, in the context of all the other struggles in which they were engaged – on troop numbers, the building of the atomic bomb, and attempts to get America to invest in Western European security – Palestine was becoming the one battle they felt was no longer worth the fight. On this Bevin and Attlee were agreed.

On November 1947, the UN General Assembly voted for partition of Palestine and the creation of an independent state of Israel for Jews. This resolution also asserted that those Palestinians living within the borders of the Jewish state had a right to stay within its bounds. Bevin feared that this solution had the potential to inflame the situation still further and warned that the extent of Arab opposition had been 'underestimated'. 'The existence of a Jewish state might prove a constant factor of unrest in the Middle East,' he warned.[69]

The government's defence committee drew up a memorandum on the likely effects of British withdrawal from Palestine on the region as a whole. The prospect of a coordinated Arab attack on the Jews was not thought to be high. The British military had close ties with a number of Arab armies, and had warned them that an intervention from them in Palestine would be taken as an attack on Britain. Once again, however, there was concern that the British would lose their military missions in Iraq and Saudi Arabia, in addition to the loss of a major base in Egypt. This, in strategic terms, 'would be a severe blow to our influence', concluded the Defence Committee.[70]

In further discussions in November 1947, for which the chiefs of staff were brought in, it was clear that Bevin had taken on some of these objections. He now changed the terms of the debate. If British troops were moved out of Palestine, they could be better used elsewhere. Thus 'maximum use would be made of British territory' in the region, such as Aden, and some use might also be made of Transjordan. As a sop to the chiefs of staff, he pointed out that the number of troops in Egypt would increase as they were moved in transit out of Palestine.[71] Ultimately, though, there was now an acceptance that the issue had proved beyond the gift of the British government to solve. 'We have tried on numerous occasions in the past to put forward solutions for the settlement of Palestine. Each one has been rejected by one side or the other, or both. We have been suspected of ulterior aims in Palestine.' Withdrawal was the only option.[72]

The government faced strong criticism from across the political spectrum. The pro-Zionist group on the Labour left urged Bevin and Attlee to take more responsibility for the implementation of the roadmap decided at the UN to protect the nascent Israeli state from the likelihood of an attack from Arab armies.[73] From the Conservatives too, Labour faced an interrogation about the perceived 'scuttle' from empire when its White Paper on Defence was published in March 1948.[74] When the Argentine and Chilean governments began sabre rattling over Britain's possession of the Falkland Islands, Anthony Eden, the Conservative spokesman on foreign affairs, asked Attlee whether he was willing to be 'cheeked or chivvied out' of any more British territories.[75]

On 14 May 1948, the British mandate ended and the creation of the state of Israel was declared. Within three days, Bevin's optimistic assessment – that withdrawal would help increase the 'realism' of the main protagonists – was proved to be hopelessly inaccurate. Egypt, Iraq, Lebanon, Syria, and Jordan invaded the new state. In the war that followed, it was soon clear that the chiefs of staff had miscalculated the respective strengths of the forces in the Middle East. Attlee recalled Montgomery telling him that if there was a war in the Middle East, the Arabs would 'hit the Jews for six' into the sea. 'We soon saw who did the hitting,' remarked Attlee.[76] By January 1949, the Israelis had fought back ferociously, securing the territory given to it by the UN and winning substantially more from the new Arab state that the UN had created alongside it.

For many years Attlee was forced to rebut the allegation that the British scuttle had caused the power vacuum that led to the 1948 war. The essence of the problem, he argued, was that he did not believe the government could achieve a settlement by force – and that a political settlement, given the distance between the two sides, was impossible. Once the US had started to undermine the proposal on migration numbers put forward by the Anglo-American Commission, he felt there was no going back. There was some truth in this. But it was also the case that the government was hedging its bets. Withdrawal from Palestine was rationalised as a way of bolstering troop numbers in the Suez Canal Zone. And it had been enacted out of hope rather than any expectation that the giving up of the mandate would increase the likelihood of a political settlement. Whatever anyone said, it had always been likely that the power vacuum would result in war.

Above all, the government demonstrated a desire to move on from the ugly disputes over Palestine as quickly as possible. Given their irritation at Truman's interference, what was most surprising is how careful both Attlee and Bevin were not to let the matter disrupt Anglo-American relations. Neither of them showed any lingering irritation when they met the US ambassador in London on 25 May 1948, just ten days after Arab armies from Egypt, Jordan, Syria and Iraq had joined forces and invaded Israel.

They were now focused on two larger strategic objectives. The first was to ensure that peace was maintained in the Muslim world beyond Palestine, from Morocco to Indonesia, to avoid, as Montgomery put it, a 'holy war, or anti-Western campaign'. The second was to make sure that the Palestine question 'did not poison Anglo-American relations to the advantage of third parties who might wish to fish in troubled waters'. For that reason, they wanted to avoid placing any sanctions on the Arab regimes that had attacked Israel. A number of these were already weak and vulnerable to communist influence. It was thought that sanctions might also have a knock-on effect in Persia, where Bevin was inclined to 'let sleeping dogs lie' to prevent it also being destabilised. Once again, there was an element of wishful thinking here. Bevin expressed the hope that the Arab fighting would cease 'if the Arabs felt that they had a friend in the world and were not driven to desperation'. Both Bevin and Attlee indicated that they thought it possible the Arabs might even accept a Jewish state if the immigration problem was controlled and there was some sort of economic union linking Israel with the Arabs.[77]

British policy under Attlee had failed on two counts. One was a failure to grasp the impact of the Holocaust on the gravity and the geopolitical implications of the Jewish question. The second was the way in which Attlee and Bevin resorted to overly optimistic predictions to cover their tracks on withdrawal – suggesting that the local parties would be more likely to make a deal in this event. The third facet of their approach – to refuse to let it damage Anglo-American relations, or provide a window of opportunity for the Soviets – demonstrates just how precarious a position British foreign policy occupied in the post-war world.

In June 1948, as the Arab–Israeli War entered its second month, Isaiah Berlin denounced British foreign policy for its short-sightedness in simply leaving Jews and Arabs to fight it out. In a letter to Dr Chaim Weizmann, who was to become the first President of Israel the following year, he wrote that it was, 'leaving Jewish considerations out of it, crass blindness and stupidity on Bevin and Attlee's part, to drift into the position of international villains at once hypocritical and savage'. If there was a massacre of Jews in Jerusalem, for example, given what had happened in the Holocaust, Britain's reputation might never recover.[78] Over the course of the following year, Isaiah Berlin, as a naturalised Briton who was not unsympathetic to the Labour Party, also came to recognise the extent to which Britain now depended on America. 'My impression of our rulers is that they are like an acrobat on a tightrope with a large net cosily below them: they know that if they fall into the net (USA) they will suffer a loss of face but not of life . . . this takes away from the acute sense of crisis which would otherwise drive them dotty. They are like a son who knows that his debts will ultimately be settled by his annoyed and angry parents, with much humiliation all round, but that he will not go to jail . . .'[79]

IV

Attlee's approach to the question of Indian independence, which unfolded alongside the crisis in Palestine, was not without its flaws. However, it was superior in a number of important respects. First, the prime minister took personal responsibility for its future in a way that was lacking over Palestine. Second, the policy on India was proactive and decisive, which arose from a desire not to be caught in the drift of events. Third, the whole strategy was underlaid by both a moral authority, and a clarity that came from years of reflection and a deep sense of history.

In 1942, it had been Attlee – more than any member of the government – who had insisted that Anglo-Indian relations must be put on a better footing during the war. Utilising his membership of the government's India committee, he had created the space for Stafford Cripps's mission to India in 1942. When the mission had failed to win the support of the Indian nationalist leaders, it had been Attlee who had presided over their arrest and internment until the end of the war. But the issue had continued to exercise his mind thereafter. In fact, the vital role that India played in the war pushed him further toward firm support for Indian independence. His strong preference was that this would be within a newly reconstituted British Commonwealth. However, that was for India to decide by itself. In many ways, in fact, India's willingness to join the Commonwealth was the test that Attlee set for himself in his handling of the question after 1945.

The development of Attlee's thinking on India can be seen in a 1943 memorandum he wrote for the War Cabinet on the 'principles of democratic government'. The crises of the 1930s, the rise of totalitarian systems, had underlined to him the fragility of democracy. Where democratic tendencies did exist, they should be encouraged and allowed to develop. Thus, in a firm break from the position he had maintained on the Simon Commission, he now regarded it as absurd to insist on a specifically British form of democracy as the condition of self-governance in the empire. In particular, the Westminster system could not work in societies where race and religion were the dividing lines in politics; and where a minority feared the consequences of majority rule, at both the national and provincial level. Canada, with its British and French citizens, had been able to avoid the worst of these tensions. But the divisions in Palestine and India (and also Ceylon and Malaya) ran far deeper. Was federalism the answer, as some hoped in India? The problem with this was that federal constitutions were difficult to make work, particularly when states were in their infancy and there was doubt about where authority and power lay. External referees could certainly help mitigate the worst of the tensions. But the role of a referee was a thankless and ultimately unsustainable one: not only did it go against the very principle of self-government; the referee would always have the taint of imperialism attached to them.[80]

As soon as he became prime minister, Attlee set about reviving the offer made by Cripps in 1942. Self-government would be granted as soon as the leading parties in India could agree on the terms. He announced that a constituent assembly and an executive council would be established following elections, with the responsibility for drafting a constitution. The British government itself was 'determined' to do its 'utmost' to promote the 'early realization of full self-government'.[81]

Having witnessed many false dawns before, the Indian leaders responded with scepticism. Jawaharlal Nehru, the Congress party leader who had been imprisoned during the war, objected that Attlee's efforts were too vague. He was a 'well-intentioned liberal' but had failed on the specifics.[82] Devdas Gandhi, the youngest son of Mahatma Gandhi, was more generous, crediting Attlee with 'complete sincerity'.[83] But by now the greatest practical obstacle to independence came from within India itself. It arose from the tension between the Hindu majority (represented by Congress) and Muslim minority (who demanded their own independent state so that they would not be subject to majority Hindu government). The distance between Nehru and Muhammad Ali Jinnah, the head of the Muslim League, precipitated a rise in tensions, particularly in the Punjab and Bengal, in the north and east of the country respectively. Nehru wanted the British to impose unity; and Jinnah wanted it to guarantee the creation of a separate Muslim state (but one which included three provinces – Bengal, Assam and North-West Frontier – which still had Hindu majorities).[84]

On 15 March 1946, Attlee announced in the House of Commons that membership of the Commonwealth was what he wanted for India, but if she 'elects for independence, she has a right, in our view, to do so.'[85] 'The temperature of 1946 is not the temperature of 1920 or 1930 or even of 1942,' he asserted. When Indians attacked British rule, 'they base their attack . . . on the basis of standards derived from Britain.' How then could their demands be denied any longer by a democratic parliament? Of course there were immense difficulties in finding the appropriate arrangement. But, in what was to become the basis of his approach, he told the House, 'We cannot dictate how these difficulties may be overcome. Our first duty is to get the machinery of the decision set up.'[86] Nehru greeted the statement with some equivocation. 'Expressions of good will, even couched in friendly terms, do not take one very far by themselves,' he said. Jinnah denounced the plan as 'calculated to create misunderstanding', and warned there would be bloodshed unless independence for India also meant the creation of an independent state for India's 92 million Muslims.[87]

That same week three senior ministers were despatched on a new mission to India with instructions to encourage the writing of a constitution – preferably one which would keep India from being divided. It was headed by Cripps again. Despite the failure of his mission of 1942 he had a long-standing relationship with Nehru, which stretched back to the 1930s. A. V. Alexander was sent out to give consideration to the military and strategic implications of the move. The third minister was Lord Pethick-Lawrence, the 74-year old Minister for Colonies. They arrived to the backdrop of rising sectarianism, and rioting between rival ethnic groups. The impression was growing, as it was in Palestine, that the British could no longer keep India stable, or from slipping into civil war.[88] While the mission was bound to fail, it was Cripps who bequeathed the idea that British withdrawal should no longer be dependent on finding an agreement between the various Indian parties.[89]

The prime minister was concerned that the viceroy, Archibald Wavell, whom he had criticised at a number of stages during the war for his lack of trust in Indian leaders, was losing control of the situation. In his defence, Wavell was a military man rather than a politician. Attlee wrote to him in July 1946, expressing sympathy with the difficulties he was facing in trying to create a cross-party commission to discuss the future of India. One needed 'infinite patience in dealing with Indians'. The Indian mind was 'so apt to ignore the substance for the shadow'. 'I was always struck by the fact that our Indian friends, though politically minded and fully acquainted with the theory of democratic government had little or no understanding of its actual working,' said the prime minister. Nonetheless, he also expressed the view that British civil servants in India had been poor at interpreting democratic government in an Indian context. All his colleagues on the Indian Statutory Commission had come to feel that 'we were trying to introduce Anglo-Saxon democracy through the medium of men whose whole practical experience had been confined to working a system which was a combination of the Mogul and Continental systems of Government with an Anglo-Saxon face.' The prime minister suggested that his viceroy should take on a political adviser to help him in his efforts to establish the Constituent Assembly to oversee the drawing up of a constitution. 'We have to give you the tools if you are to finish the job.'[90]

Wavell was irritated by Attlee's letter, and resisted the attempt to control him from London. In August 1946, as communal riots got out of control, Attlee wrote to Wavell that he supposed 'there is just a chance that these events may serve to bring some sense of reality into the minds of the contending politicians.'[91] This was the same kind of hopeful attitude that had contributed to the failures over Palestine. Wavell responded by expressing grave concerns about what he saw as a policy based on 'no more than wishful thinking'. His view was that the priority must be to draw up plans for the evacuation of British civilians in a 'phased withdrawal'. The fundamental difference of opinion he had with the prime minister was that this should not be tied to a political timetable.[92] Though he did not use the word, 'scuttle' was the option that Wavell seemed to be proposing. With no central authority, there was a danger that India would fragment, which would endanger minorities across a number of its provinces.

By the last week of August 1946, after more than 5,000 deaths following rioting in Calcutta, and with violence spreading – with the Sikhs in Punjab particularly concerned at the prospect of subjection to a Muslim-dominated state – Attlee decided that a date for withdrawal had to be set, even if the Muslim League refused to enter the Constituent Assembly. Meanwhile, the Cabinet had agreed that Wavell's plan, of 'withdrawal by stages' would simply be an 'encouragement to fragmentation'.[93] As Attlee put it, the Indian problem was 'entering a new phase' and the government could not afford to have a viceroy who did not support his policy. In January 1947 Attlee summoned Wavell, who in any case had been asking for a month's leave because of exhaustion, back home to London.[94]

The first two months of 1947 were a watershed in the history of the British Empire. In January there were large-scale troop withdrawals from the

Middle East and eastern Mediterranean, though not from the Suez Canal. On 14 February, Bevin announced that the Palestine mandate would be referred to the UN. Then, on 20 February, Attlee announced that Britain would grant Indian independence no later than June 1948. It was up to Indian leaders to find a solution by then. Where Wavell had proposed a phased withdrawal, regardless of political progress, Attlee now provided a firm date by which agreement had to be reached. One Conservative MP commented that it seemed a 'tremendous gamble and a needless policy of despair . . . Shall we withdraw our troops and leave India to anarchy and chaos?' The announcement came as a 'shock to the whole of the House', and Attlee 'did not seem very comfortable about it himself'.[95] To add to Attlee's troubles, Bevin was taken into hospital with heart trouble at the end of January, Morrison was also ill, and Dalton was warning the prime minister about the seriousness of the economic situation. It was, he admitted to Tom, a 'rather troublesome' few weeks.[96]

A blueprint of sorts was provided by the precedent of Burma. In the 1935 India Act, Burma had already been earmarked for independence from any future Indian state. The Burmese nationalists had been crucial to the resistance movement against the Japanese, working closely with Lord Mountbatten, Supreme Allied Commander of the South East Asia Command. Mountbatten had shown considerable political imagination in building a close working relationship with Aung San, the leader of the Burmese Anti-Fascist People's Freedom League. Whereas the Foreign Office had regarded him as a dangerous extremist, Mountbatten appointed him war minister of Burma in 1943, in an attempt to co-opt him. The gamble had paid off and Aung San had established himself as a responsible leader, willing to work with the British as the Burmese moved towards independence.

When a Burmese delegation arrived in London in January, Attlee was impressed by what he heard. First, if Aung San could 'control his wild men', this raised hopes of a smooth passage to independence in India too. Second, it was clear that most of the Conservative Party were willing to accept Burmese independence, apart from its leader, who had coined the phrase 'scuttle'. 'Winston was the only objector in the House to the unconcealed distaste of his Party.' This suggested that Attlee was more likely to achieve the support of Conservatives for his approach to India.[97] Third, Burma's desire to be independent from the Indian state also created more sympathy for the idea of an independent Muslim state.[98] Fourth, the 45-year-old Mountbatten, a cousin of the king, had performed extremely effectively in dealing with the Burmese question. (That said, the fact that Aung San and his entire cabinet were assassinated in July 1947 demonstrated the potential difficulties.)

With Wavell now heading back to London, Attlee asked Mountbatten if he would be willing to replace him as the new viceroy for India. He accepted on 15 January 1947, at a critical moment, as Attlee announced a timetable for independence. The prime minister's mandate to him, delivered in February 1947, instructed him to secure 'the closest and most friendly cooperation between India and the UK', and, if possible, a 'military treaty'. While he did not want partition, partly because he felt Jinnnah's proposed independent Muslim state would be more vulnerable to Soviet influence from the north, he had now accepted it as an inevitability.[99] Mountbatten, based in Delhi during the war, had what Attlee called a gift for 'getting along with all kinds of people'.[100]

It was 'curious that that the Royal family should provide a Viceroy who is completely in agreement with Labour policy', the prime minister wrote, in a letter to his brother.[101] In fact, something about the fact that Mountbatten was a descendant of Queen Victoria appealed to Attlee's own sense that he was 'completing' the work of empire, rather than jettisoning Britain's imperial past. Having asked Rab Butler about Mountbatten's suitability for the post, Attlee provided a glimpse of his own sentimentality: 'I feel sure that the first Empress of India would be glad to see a descendant complete the last part of a century's work.'[102]

The Labour majority was big enough to pass any measure regarding Indian independence through Parliament. Yet the prime minister placed great importance on bringing as much of the Conservative Party along with him as possible. His main critic remained Churchill, with whom he clashed after the announcement that a date had been set for independence. Winston 'required a bit of correction', he told Tom, and was 'singularly inept as an opposition leader' when it came to Indian affairs. His scare-mongering about the end of the empire caused 'much discomfort in Tory ranks'.[103] It was also important to him that Lord Halifax spoke in support of the policy in the House of Lords. As Attlee later put it, the Lords knew that Halifax knew India, and that he would tell them the truth.[104] In conversation with the king, he was also confident enough to rebuke Churchill, commenting that the 'old man was really rather naughty in the House yesterday about India'.[105]

Attlee took the initiative on India policy in a way he failed to over Palestine. While Bevin and the chiefs of staff had beaten him back over withdrawing troops from the Suez Canal, he was unmoved by their concerns that he was being too hasty in setting a date to leave India. Just before the decision was announced, Bevin, after enlisting the support of A. V. Alexander, Minister of Defence, had written a memorandum listing all of his concerns. 'I am not a defeatist but a realist . . . If you disagree with what is proposed,' the prime minister told his foreign secretary, 'you must offer a practical alternative. I fail to find one in your letter.'[106] None was forthcoming. Partition and independence would go ahead. As Attlee put it after facing down Bevin and the Foreign Office, 'a scuttle it will be if things are allowed to drift.'[107]

On his arrival in India, Mountbatten soon realised just how treacherous the situation was. He had been given full political and military powers as viceroy to make good on withdrawal by June 1948. By the spring of 1947, he feared that the country was on the brink of civil war, as contending factions jostled into position in anticipation of the partition of states and redrawing of boundaries. He now urged that the government push forward its own deadline for independence to August 1947, or civil war would erupt. Attlee agreed immediately, pleased that Mountbatten shared his sense of urgency. While a complete breakdown of order was averted, matters remained bleak. Indeed, it might be said Attlee was sometimes in danger of overestimating the viceroy's healing powers. 'I have just been listening to Dickie Mountbatten's broadcast to the Indians,' Attlee said on 5 June 1947. 'I have hopes that something has really been brought to fruition at last.' He believed that Mountbatten and his wife Edwina had done 'wonderful work' in getting on personal terms with Indians of every point of view, including people who had never had contact with the government before. Even 'wild extremists' might be brought into the fold.[108]

At midnight on 14 August 1947, India became independent and an amalgamated Pakistan was also born, with Nehru and Jinnah as prime minister and Governor-General, respectively, of each country. Just a few days later, Attlee met Mountbatten's private secretary, who had given him an account of 'extraordinary scenes at the handing over'. Mountbatten, it was reported, was surrounded by about a quarter of a million Indians, 'all violently enthusiastic for him'. He had 'certainly captured the Indian imagination', Attlee wrote admiringly of him. By now, there was a sense of foreboding creeping into his consciousness. 'I doubt if things will go awfully easily now as the Indian leaders know little of administration,' he wrote to Tom on 18 August. In some respects, this was a startling admission from the man who had just granted independence. Yet, whatever the outcome, Attlee's fundamental belief was that 'at least we have come out with honour instead of, as at one time seemed likely, being pursued out ignominiously with the whole country in a state of confusion.'[109]

Mountbatten praised Attlee effusively. 'The man who made it possible was yourself. Without your guidance and your unwavering support nothing could have been accomplished here.' The former Conservative Secretary of State for India, Leo Amery, agreed, notwithstanding the clashes they had had on the matter during the wartime government. It was a 'personal triumph' for the prime minister.[110] The verdict of the *Manchester Guardian* was that Indian independence owed a huge amount to Attlee's 'creative zeal'. Attlee's approach to the question was 'no brilliant improvisation, the result of the impact of a fresh mind, on a stale problem'. It was the culmination of many years' interest and devotion to the Indian question. It was a policy 'triumphantly crowned' after a very long march.[111]

To leave with honour had always been the essence of Attlee's approach to the Indian question. An ignominious scuttle had been avoided. A full-scale civil war was averted partly because of the 'haste' which Churchill had described as 'appalling' when accusing the prime minister of 'scuttling' from Burma.[112] As Attlee had written in his 1937 book, *The Labour Party in Perspective*, a Labour government 'would always prefer to err in being too soon rather than too late in the grant of self-government'.[113]

While the decisiveness was laudable, it was also attended by grave consequences. A number of imponderables were left to chance. While partition and a new constitution had been agreed, borders and state boundaries had not. Owing to the tight timetable, this was done in a panicked four-week process led by the lawyer Sir Cyril Radcliffe. In the drawing of boundaries, the Muslim majority Pakistani state was further divided into East Pakistan and West Pakistan, on either side of a larger Indian state. In many provinces, minorities were left with an uncertain future, as ethnic groups scrambled for supremacy, and lines were hastily drawn on the map. As soon as partition began, a sectarian bloodletting followed. Although exact numbers have never been determined, approximately half a million people were killed after partition in August 1947. Millions more were displaced by the violence as they tried to find safe havens.

Another ugly legacy was the almost constant fear of a serious military confrontation between the new Pakistani and Indian states, of which there were four by 1971. In October 1947, Nehru wrote to Attlee about his deep concerns regarding the fate of Kashmir, which was contested between the two states. It was invaded by Afridis and other Muslim tribesmen, carrying automatic weapons, and flooding in convoy over the new border with Pakistan. In October 1947, the Kashmiri authorities appealed to Nehru for help, and possibly intervention, which would most likely lead to war.[114] Attlee sent an urgent telegram to Jinnah the following day urging him to stop the invaders coming across the border.[115] He also warned Nehru that intervention would cause 'incalculable tragedy'. Notably, the prime minister sent his telegram to Nehru's personal office rather than through official government channels, in order to make a personal appeal.[116] For many years, Attlee feared that the government of India was 'too much a one man show', and there would be difficulties once Nehru left office.[117]

The assassination of Gandhi in New Delhi on 30 January 1948 demonstrated just how uncertain India's future remained. Speaking the following day, Attlee commented that the ideals of brotherhood and peace for which Gandhi had stood could not be silenced. Yet, in calling Gandhi India's 'greatest citizen', he also observed that he 'seemed to belong to a different period of history'.[118]

Further tensions followed in the summer of 1948 as the Indian government attempted to blockade the centrally located kingdom of Hyderabad, a Muslim-ruled Hindu-majority state whose rulers wanted to maintain independence from India. In a bitter debate in Parliament, Churchill presented himself as the hero of Hyderabad and argued that it should decide its own future, just as other states had done. Attlee was genuinely outraged at what he saw as Churchill's efforts to act as a spoiler, now that Indian independence had passed. According to the *Manchester Guardian* Attlee answered him with a 'cold fury' unseen before. 'You don't like it, do you?' he shouted across the floor, several times, suggesting that Churchill had tried to pick at a scab which others wanted to see healed. In fact, the Indian government had already submitted the proposal for a plebiscite to the rulers of Hyderabad, just as Churchill had called on them to do. Attlee leaned over the dispatch box and asked Churchill to agree that he approved of their actions. Not for the first time, the reaction from the Conservative benches suggested that Churchill had misjudged the mood, and Attlee commanded the full authority of the House. 'What will the wits do now who have called Mr. Attlee "a sheep in sheep's clothing"?' remarked the *Manchester Guardian*'s parliamentary correspondent.[119]

Underlying this confrontation was something that is crucial to consider in making an overall assessment of Attlee's India policy: the process was managed with great moral certainty and authority. This was recognised by the Liberal politician and soldier, Alan Campbell-Johnston, who was acting as Mountbatten's press attaché at the time. Attlee's approach to India, he observed, in a telling phrase, was underpinned by 'a hidden fire' and sustained by a 'certain spiritual integrity'.[120]

That 'spiritual integrity' was something sorely lacking in the alternative strategies for dealing with the India question. Attlee had been willing to take the opprobrium for interning Gandhi and the other nationalist leaders in 1942. Having won the war, however, it was politically unthinkable to keep them imprisoned in the face of rising disorder. Repression was a finite and depreciating asset in statecraft, particularly by a country so eager to trumpet its democratic credentials. Reputation mattered even more in the context of the early cold war. As Attlee had said in November 1946, when he was about to turn his full attention to the Indian question, it was always better to answer one's critics 'by deeds not words'.[121] In this respect, he believed that the granting of independence to India was also the perfect riposte to the Soviet Union's complaints about British imperialism. On the contrary, he commented in May 1948, it was the Soviets who provided the 'supreme example of imperialism' in the modern age. The British had shown how an old empire could begin to grow into a commonwealth. 'In all the essentials of freedom', Britain was far ahead of those in Soviet Russia.[122]

The next alternative was Wavell's plan for a hurried evacuation. This was indeed a 'scuttle', which would have left an even bigger vacuum than the one that emerged in Palestine in 1947. There was good reason to believe – and this was certainly feared – that a move like this would create such uncertainty as to spark a civil war. Finally, what would a Churchill-led government have been able to do to control the subcontinent, while continuing to oppose independence? Years later, the future Labour leader, James Callaghan, went so far as to suggest that, if Churchill had remained in charge, Britain would have ended up fighting a vast insurgency in India, perhaps even a full-scale war.[123] It is worth noting that the most influential figures in the Conservative Party – Halifax, Eden and Macmillan – all thought Attlee had taken the most honourable course. Ultimately, Churchill had no answer to the single most important factor in India politics: the desire for self-governance shared by the vast majority of the people. Britain was ready to quit India; much more important was the fact that India was ready to quit Britain.[124] 'Attlee realised this,' as Lord Robert Boothby remarked, 'and . . . having realised it, he acted with his usual speed, courage and decision.'[125]

V

It was in the late summer of 1949 that the prime minister informed his brother that he had been immersing himself in Edward Gibbon's *The History of the Decline and Fall of the Roman Empire*. As we have seen, he did not see Britain's place in the world as characterised by decline and fall. There were elements of Gibbon's thesis, such as the importance of maintaining virtue and citizenship, which fitted with his own views. Yet, on closer inspection, it's clear that the prime minister read Gibbon's work with a critical eye.

While he admired the overall thesis, he was unconvinced by Gibbon's assessment of the Emperor Justinian, who ruled the Byzantine (eastern Roman) Empire from 527 to 565. Justinian was regarded as a successful leader, famous for the spread of a civil legal code beyond his dominions. This success presented Gibbon with a problem in his argument because it appeared to buck the trend of decline in the late Roman Empire. Gibbon's response to this was to stress the flaws in Justinian's rule.[126] Attlee, by contrast, thought that Gibbon did not quite do justice to Justinian. He admired the later emperors' commitment to spreading the values of the Roman Empire – such as the rule of law – to other nations, even as its territory and military strength receded.[127]

This observation was made in September 1949, just a few months after the May 1949 Commonwealth Prime Ministers' Conference. It was at that conference that the terms for membership to the Commonwealth were changed to allow republics to join, without declaring allegiance to the monarchy. This was the device by which India and Ireland, officially republics, were deemed able to join the Commonwealth. While the Irish refused the invitation, the Indians signalled their intention to join the Commonwealth shortly afterwards, becoming a member in 1950. This fact gave Attlee as much pleasure as anything else that his government achieved, with the possible exception of the National Insurance Act of 1946. Is it too much to say that Attlee, perhaps tongue in check, saw in himself a little bit of Justinian?

At the Paris Peace Conference in 1946, Harold Nicolson had despaired at the British prime minister's lack of stature compared to his predecessor. In January 1947, Nicolson had listened, unimpressed, to his radio broadcast announcing Indian independence: 'It is very thin and frail. Attlee is a charming and intelligent man, but as a public speaker he is, compared to Winston, like a village fiddler, after Paganini. It is all rather sad.'[128] Two years later, when Attlee announced that India would remain within the Commonwealth, Nicolson had changed his estimation entirely. He described the move as 'a fine piece of good sense' that would 'only enhance Attlee's growing prestige. People are ceasing to think of him as a "dear little man".' They now realised 'he has a vision and courage and intrepidity so compelling that it is a force in itself.'[129]

At the close of the previous century, as a young boy at the Diamond Jubilee, Attlee had been deeply impressed by the moral force of the British Empire. He had been taught to believe that civilisation, self-government and the rule of law were the great gifts that the empire would eventually bestow upon nations within its territories. Growing older, he had become more uneasy about the uglier side of imperial pride, and the sense of racial superiority that sometimes came with it. More than half a century later, as he presided over the birth of a new Commonwealth, his mind turned to the poetry of Rudyard Kipling, which he had always associated with the Diamond Jubilee, and the imperialism of his youth. Kipling had to be understood in context. In April 1949, as H. G. Wells and George Orwell had done previously, he criticised those who denigrated Kipling's poetry 'without appreciation of the period in which the subject lived'.[130] A few months later he revealed that he was reading Violet passages from Kipling's

Above: Josef Stalin, Harry Truman and Winston Churchill at the Potsdam conference in July 1945. Attlee, seen in the background, attended as an observer, before he and Churchill returned to hear the results of the general election.

Above: Attlee chatting to constituents in his Limehouse constituency in July 1945, during the election campaign. The Luftwaffe dropped an estimated 40,000 bombs on the 1,903 acres of Stepney during the war, transforming it forever.

Above: On 26 July 1945, Attlee and his colleagues celebrate their emphatic victory in the General Election at Labour Party headquarters at Transport House.

Above: Within days of Labour's great victory, Attlee was back at Potsdam where he now joined Truman and Stalin as a member of the 'Big Three'. Standing from left to right behind them are America's Admiral Leahy, British Foreign Secretary Ernest Bevin, American Secretary of State James Byrnes and Russia's foreign minister, Vyacheslav Molotov.

Above: Attlee and his Foreign Secretary Ernest Bevin photographed at 10 Downing Street at midnight on 14 August 1945. They had just announced, in a speech broadcast to Britain and the Empire, the news of the Japanese surrender. 'If you've got a good dog,' Attlee once said of his loyal ally, 'you don't bark yourself.'

Above: Talking to King George VI on a visit to Buckingham Palace, shortly after the election. The two men were very fond of each other and Attlee was deeply upset by the King's death in February 1952.

Above: The cabinet of the first majority Labour Government. Attlee is flanked by Herbert Morrison and Ernest Bevin. The average age of the cabinet was in the mid-sixties.

Right: The key members of the Attlee cabinet visit Buckingham Palace. Left to right: Herbert Morrison, Attlee, King George VI, Arthur Greenwood, Ernest Bevin and A.V. Alexander.

Above: Attlee in conversation with Stafford Cripps in August 1945. The two had a long and complicated relationship that stretched back to 1931 when they shared an office behind the Speaker's Chair with George Lansbury. Attlee admired Cripps but he questioned his judgement.

Above: Attlee and Hugh Dalton just before the Second World War. Attlee beat Dalton to a lectureship at the London School of Economics in 1912 and Dalton was often disparaging about a man he called 'the little rabbit'. However, after he served as Chancellor in Attlee's government, Dalton came to respect the Labour leader more and urged him not to retire.

Above: Attlee and his former minister of health, Aneurin Bevan, leaving London Airport on the first stage of their visit to China, on 9 August 1954. Attlee admired Bevan's idealism and force of character and the crucial role he played in the formation of the National Health Service. However, the two clashed repeatedly and Bevan once accused Attlee of 'bringing to the fierce struggle of politics the tepid enthusiasm of a lazy summer afternoon at a cricket match'.

Above: Attlee with American President Harry Truman, and Canadian Prime Minister Mackenzie King at the White House in 1945.

Above: Attlee is introduced to Stanley Matthews by captain Joe Mercer at an England football match at Wembley Stadium in January 1946.

Above: 1st Earl Attlee and his wife, Violet, at their home, Cherry Tree Cottage in Great Missenden, Buckinghamshire, where they moved after their time in Downing Street came to an end.

Right: Attlee reads the news of his impending retirement while waiting for a train at Marylebone tube station, 7 December 1955. He was once famously stopped by a commuter who asked him 'if anyone had ever said he looked just like Mr. Attlee'. 'Frequently,' came the reply.

Above: After retirement, Attlee was a regular visitor to America. He met President John F. Kennedy at the White House on 16 May 1961. Attlee criticised American actions on a number of occasions, yet, from the time of the First World War, he believed it was a progressive force for good on the world stage.

Above: Attlee and Churchill in conversation at Draper's Hall in 1956. In later years, when both men were retired, Attlee would take pleasure from sitting with Churchill and listening to his booming voice, unperturbed by the fact that Winston refused to use his ear trumpet and therefore could not hear anyone else talk. 'I knew my Winston,' he would say. 'What a career! What a man! We shall not see his like again.'

novels too.[131] These were not the reading habits of a man who saw the end of the empire as a repudiation of Britain's past.

In the same way that he saw the National Insurance Act of 1946 as the realisation of a lifelong goal of the Labour movement, so Attlee viewed Indian independence as a 'mission of fulfilment' for the British nation.[132] The United Kingdom finally delivered on the promise implicit in the imperial project. Something honourable was salvaged from a controversial and sometimes ugly past. 'We followed the policy which we have always preached,' he said in July 1949. Never before in history had there been such a freely given handing over of sovereignty from one country to another.[133]

Part Six

After New Jerusalem, 1948–1955

19

In Barchester All is Not Well

In Barchester all is not well.
The County People pine and sigh.
They wish the government in Hell
And long for happier days gone by
When the gloom did not obscure the sky.

At tennis parties, dinners, teas
They still keep stiff their upper lips.
Oppressed by petty tyrannies,
The lack of fun and food and ships,
They jibe at Attlee, Strachey and Cripps.

Orville Prescott, 'Books of the Times',
New York Times, 3 February 1948.

I *The County of Barsetshire, Middle England, 1946*

Barsetshire was an archetypal English county, like Wiltshire or Berkshire, set deep in the heart of Middle England. Its main population hub was a cathedral city, called Barchester. This fictional world was a creation of the Victorian novelist, Anthony Trollope. In his series of six novels, known collectively as the 'Chronicles of Barsetshire' and written in the 1850s and 1860s, Trollope addressed the changing political, social and economic conditions in mid-nineteenth-century England through the lives of the inhabitants of Barsetshire. In the 1930s and 1940s, the novelist Angela Thirkell picked up the story where Trollope left off. In her own series, also set in Barsetshire, she painted a picture of family and social life, set against the backdrop of the economic depression, the Second World War, and its immediate aftermath. She was famed, in particular, for her portrayal of Britain's middle-class housewives, struggling to keep their households afloat in the years of high unemployment in the 1930s, bereft of their husbands during the war, and continuing to manage amidst scarcity and rationing even after 1945.

The world of Barsetshire was well known to Attlee, who discovered it through his reading of Trollope. Indeed, it was an interest he shared with Winston Churchill, and the two would discuss Trollope's work in their later years.[1] In politics, Trollope was a liberal and a reformer. Yet, despite his liberal convictions, he showed a sympathy and respect for those with different convictions. There was something of this in Attlee's belief that 'toleration' was the greatest political gift of all.[2] While he mostly avoided 'the moderns', Attlee did enjoy Angela Thirkell's more recent portrayals of Barsetshire. During the Blitz, in fact, he would use the long hours in the bomb shelter to read Thirkell's novels to Violet. As he wrote in 1941, he found them 'uncommonly good' in their depiction of a typical English family.[3] By the winter of 1946, however, with Britain suffering from shortages in fuel and food, the inhabitants of Barsetshire were increasingly unhappy with Attlee's government.

Thirkell's novel, *Private Enterprise*, set in 1946 and published the following year, spoke to a feeling of disillusionment experienced by pockets of middle-class Britain a year into the Attlee government. As we have seen, the continuation of controls and rationing – to which bread was added in the summer of 1946 – caused much grumbling. More broadly, Thirkell hoped to portray the sense in which traditional English life was being stifled by bureaucracy and officialdom. *Private Enterprise* described 'a great increase of boredom and crossness, which made people wonder what use it had been to stand alone against the Powers of Darkness if the reward was to be increasing discomfort and a vast army of half-baked bureaucrats stifling all freedom and ease'.[4] Life was boring and 'there was really nothing to talk about but food.' The villains of the new regime were Stafford Cripps (President of the Board of Trade), Hugh Dalton (chancellor) and John Strachey (the Minister of Food, whose first act had been to put controls on bread), who presided over the 'Red Tape and Sealing Wax Office' and the 'Ministry of General Interference'.[5]

It was after reviewing *Private Enterprise* that the American writer Orville Prescott was inspired to write a poem about the discontent in Barsetshire. He described the griping of the bourgeoisie and minor gentry at the 'petty tyrannies' of government and the lack of fun and food that left them to 'jibe at Attlee, Strachey and Cripps'. Suburban England maintained its 'stiff upper lip' but the government bore the brunt of its grumbling, and was even blamed for the bad weather.[6]

Thirkell was not the only novelist to make such complaints. B. Ifor Evans, in *The Church in the Markets* (published in 1949), also told the story of a struggle for meaningful, individual life under socialism, where everything seemed 'stale, used-up and empty'.[7] In 1948, Anthony Bower, the cultural critic of the *New York Times*, suggested that the English literary scene in general was suffering under Attlee's government. A society, 'slightly underfed, very tired, rationed, restricted, and struggling desperately for economic recovery', did not encourage a vibrant cultural atmosphere, conducive to great literature. Where was the inspiration in the 'mild, gentlemanly and irksome social revolution being so politely carried out by the Labour Party – no bloodshed, no guillotine, no *tricoteuses* (consider the wool ration), and no *sans culottes*, only sans coupons'?[8] In his 1949 *Definition of Culture* in 1948, T. S. Eliot went so far as to suggest that British culture was in decay. He blamed this on the 'levelling' policies of the Labour government.[9] In her book on Eliot, the academic Helen Gardner singled out Attlee himself as the source of much of this discontent. The prime minister's appeals to the nation to work 10 per cent harder were sucking its life and energy out of it.[10]

Of course, there were some who would never be reconciled to Attlee's Britain. Those who expected their batman to bring them their shaving kit in the morning could be put in this bracket. Likewise, Evelyn Waugh and T. S. Eliot were clearly irreconcilables. The ivory towers of *Brideshead Revisited* were not the prime minister's concern. The inhabitants of Barsetshire were another matter entirely. Barsetshire was the type of place that had returned one, if not two Labour MPs, in the landslide of 1945. The disillusionment of its inhabitants was something that the Labour Party could not afford to ignore if it was to remain in power.

II

In January 1947, Clem and Violet celebrated their twenty-fifth wedding anniversary with a lunch at the House of Commons. Attlee's old friend, Jack Lawson, was asked to give the address.[11] It was a brief respite in the most critical month of Attlee's premiership to date. Major decisions on Palestine and India were on the horizon. On the home front, meanwhile, the government was seriously embarrassed as the effects of a winter fuel shortage began to make themselves felt. In one of the coldest winters in decades, supplies of coal ran out. Worst of all had been the over-confidence of Emanuel Shinwell back in the autumn of 1946. 'There will be no fuel crisis, I am the Minister for Fuel and Power and I ought to know,' he had said. This quotation was printed on the handbook given to all Conservative Party MPs in the remaining years of the Attlee government.[12]

At the end of January 1947, with the worst months of the winter still to come, Hugh Dalton warned the prime minister just how treacherous the situation was. As he confessed, all the ministers on the committee for economic planning – of which he was one – had failed to anticipate the shortage. The real reason was the continued shortage of manpower, with 1.5 million men still in the armed forces. It was no use asking people to work harder when there were not enough people to man the vital industries. Instead, Dalton proposed that the only way out of the crisis was a drastic reduction of numbers in the armed forces, followed by more planning, including nationalisation of steel and iron.

The chancellor's warning was stark: 'We are, I am afraid, drifting, in a state of semi-animation, towards the rapids. We have started our course since the last election, wonderfully well. But we look like finishing wonderfully badly – worse, perhaps, than in 1931.' In making his plea to the prime minister, Dalton asked him to consider their shared experience as members of Ramsay MacDonald's government. That government had 'failed, as I think you and I would agree, for lack of courage, of knowledge, of warnings in advance, and of a Parliamentary majority'. This government did not have the same excuses.[13]

In the midst of his own battles with Bevin and the chiefs of staff about force numbers, Attlee recognised the need for drastic measures. He was determined that the fuel shortage would not be repeated at the end of

1947 and announced plans for fuel economy measures for the spring and summer months. Britain needed to save 2,500,000 tonnes of domestic and non-industrial coal, which would mean a 10 per cent cut in train services, and increased restrictions on the consumption of gas and electricity. These measures were announced to the nation in March in a 'colourless recital', ending with the serious warning that if they proved insufficient, more dramatic action would be taken. 'A clerk reading the minutes to a parish council could hardly put less animation into it,' remarked the parliamentary correspondent of the *Manchester Guardian*.[14] It was hard to sell bad news.

Anthony Eden, leading the opposition as Churchill was on holiday, invited Attlee to reconcile his own seriousness with Shinwell's apparently 'derisory' attitude to importing more coal just a few months before. He also suggested that the emphasis on planning would be useless unless the Cabinet itself took executive responsibility for policy decisions. According to Eden, the government was moving too quickly for its own good. The clerks who produced Hansard, the official parliamentary record, complained that they were overworked to the point of breakdown because of the number of debates and committee meetings.[15] When Churchill returned to denounce the government's economic record in April, Attlee hit back at him, pointing to the mistakes that his opponent had made over the gold standard in the 1920s. He was the 'most disastrous chancellor of the century'. With some force, Churchill responded that Attlee 'must feel himself very hard pressed to have to go back a quarter of a century to find excuses for the mismanagement and blunders of which he evidently feels his own government is guilty'.[16]

No sooner had the government plugged a gap than a leak sprang elsewhere. In April 1947, there was a Labour rebellion on government proposals for peacetime conscription.[17] The National Service Act, which required eighteen-year-olds to take part in eighteen months of military service (extended to two years in 1949) was intended to compensate for the loss of the Indian army after independence.[18] Attlee himself – as a volunteer in the First World War – had a long-standing antipathy to the idea of conscription; but it was a necessary counter-balance to the reduction of the military establishment. Both enemies and allies watched these debates closely. Dean Acheson, the US Under-Secretary of State, was concerned that the government might fall before the end of the year, default on its debts, and become so weak that it would leave the US to face the Soviet Union on its own.[19]

In May 1947, against all expectations, the prime minister remained opti-mistic. 'The sunshine is cheering us up,' he wrote to Morrison, who was recuperating in France after suffering from a blood clot in his leg, and 'Poor old Winston gets deafer every day.' Changes were made in the gov-ernment to support a renewed emphasis on economic planning. Morrison was given more support as Lord President of the Council, with the econo-mist Hilary Marquand brought in as Paymaster General. Yet Morrison complained to Dalton that these changes were not sufficient to take con-trol of the situation. The prime minister was merely 'moving all these people round like pieces on a chess board'.[20]

By July, Attlee's personal popularity ratings had stabilised after a short dip. He had 51 per cent approval, according to a Gallup poll of July. This was down from 66 per cent in the flush of victory but there had been only 1 per cent slip-page since October 1946, when the fuel crisis began.[21] Dalton noted that he 'seems strong and less rattled now', having heard that any immediate threat to his position seemed to have passed. The only real criticism of Attlee that Dalton suggested was justifiable was that he had let Shinwell keep his job.[22]

At the party conference in Margate in June, the main issue on the agenda was Labour's commitment to continuing the economic programme out-lined in the 1945 manifesto. From the conference, the new American ambassador, Lewis Douglas (in position since February), reported that the party leadership was trying to avoid being pinned down on its plans for iron and steel nationalisation.[23] Attlee spoke in high moral terms, but was short on specifics. In the course of its first two years the government had put down a heavier amount of legislation than any before it. The Con-servatives complained about this but they lacked 'the essential inspiration' and the 'moral idea which shapes our policy'. Labour had 'gone far now in deciding fairer distribution of the national cake'. Its next task was to increase the size of the national cake through economic development. In other words, the prime minister was calling for consolidation.[24]

Attlee declared the party conference to be a great success and suggested that the newspapers had been hard pressed to invent stories of splits and dissent.[25] But at the end of July, a group of forty backbenchers signed a letter to their leader urging him to declare his determination to steer through the crisis with socialist solutions. Despite the heavy load of legis-lation, there was a significant minority on the left of the party who felt not enough was being done to implement socialism.[26] At a meeting of the parliamentary party on 30 July, Attlee made, 'of his characteristic kind, a good speech', which Dalton felt would have a positive effect.[27] By 4 August, however, the mini-rebellion had spread. A petition signed by 143 back-benchers was sent to him, demanding that he scotch rumours that he was no longer committed to the nationalisation of the steel industry.[28]

The timing could not have been worse. One year after the US Congress had passed its loan to Britain, in July 1946, the convertibility of sterling into dollars was imminent. Even though the government had had a year to prepare, the results were disastrous. The day it was due to take effect, 15 July 1947, passed without incident. But within a week, a huge flow of capital went out of the country as people exchanged pounds for dollars and sold stocks in British industry, causing currency reserves to haemorrhage. What was left of the American loan was rapidly losing its value. As an emergency measure, $150 million was withdrawn from circulation.[29] On 5 August, the prime minister broadcast to the nation and announced further measures of austerity. The nationalisation of steel would be postponed, as the backbenchers had feared. There was to be more 'belt tightening' and the five-day working week for coal miners was to be ended in order to drive up production. Work and investment would be directed mainly towards exports, and imports were to be restricted (particularly food and tobacco).[30] In front of a huge Conservative rally at Blenheim Palace, Churchill defined socialism as the belief that 'nothing matters so long as miseries are equally shared'.[31]

On 6–7 August, there was a two-day debate on the state of the nation, as the national emergency grew to 'gigantic stature'. Attlee's speech, commented one Conservative MP, was 'long, dreary and futile'.[32] 'That any speech of Mr. Attlee's would be arid and uninspiring is, unfortunately, to be taken for granted; he touches nothing that he cannot dehydrate,' commented Isaiah Berlin in a letter to the editor of The Economist.[33] 'We are, indeed, very tired', noted Dalton in his diary, who was taking Benzedrine, an American-made prescription drug which soldiers had taken to energise themselves before battle in the last war. Morrison was still recuperating from his blood clot, Bevin was in and out of hospital, and Cripps looked sallow and clearly overworked. The chancellor now complained that his warnings had not been listened to and that food and military cuts should have been instituted earlier. Among other things, the chancellor found it infuriating that so much money was still being spent on the upkeep of

Germany. He also continued to push for a running down of armed forces but was resisted by Bevin and A. V. Alexander, the defence minister.[34]

After a hasty agreement with the Americans, convertibility was postponed, and the government was permitted to continue to discriminate against the dollar. This was nothing more than a stopgap measure, and did not, in itself, provide a way out of the crisis. The country would have to be put on a new economic regimen. This was badly received. On 12 August, Lewis Douglas reported that Attlee's authority was slipping away. His 'fireside chat' to the nation on further measures of austerity was, at best, 'humdrum' and he was failing to deliver the 'requisite leadership'. This was also having consequences for British foreign policy. The withdrawal of troops from Greece and Italy was an example of how an economic millstone hung around the neck of the government's strategy. For all British protestations to the contrary, Douglas believed that drastic troop reductions 'must effect a change on the vigor of British foreign policy if not of the policy itself'. The government was lurching from crisis to crisis.[35]

Attlee was forced to break off from a family holiday in Wales to return to Downing Street in the third week of August, confessing that 'things are pretty difficult just now.'[36] He resumed his holiday at the end of the month, having already learned that a plot had been hatched against him. Cripps, who had also been warning about the coming crisis since March, now concocted a plan with Dalton to force the prime minister out. First they went to Herbert Morrison. However, Morrison feared that this had the whiff of a palace coup, and thought the matter should be placed before the parliamentary party (in which event, of course, Morrison would have a stronger chance of becoming leader). Cripps and Dalton then went to Bevin instead. This was somewhat ironic given the concerns that both of them had about Bevin's heavy drinking. Nonetheless, in view of his connections with the unions, they believed that he could act as an effective 'overlord' of a new planning drive. Attlee could then be shuffled sidewise from his position, perhaps to the Foreign Office. Bevin seemed to signal his assent to the move.[37]

On 9 September, the day after Attlee returned from Wales for the second time, Cripps went to Downing Street determined to ask for the prime minister's head. At some point, Attlee had been forewarned of the plot. With Cripps sitting before him, the prime minister picked up the phone and asked Bevin if he had any intention of leaving the Foreign Office to take over at Downing Street. Bevin rubbished the idea immediately.[38]

Cripps and Dalton had been played at their own game. They made their approach to Bevin on 17 August, and had presumed that he had given them the green light to proceed. Bevin had even complained about Attlee's leadership in a car journey with Dalton. But all the while he had been briefing the prime minister.[39] 'I have never betrayed a colleague, yet, and I have no intention of starting with Clem,' he now remarked. This was just a matter of that 'bastard' Dalton getting up to his old tricks again.[40]

Now, not only did Attlee call Cripps's bluff, he actually co-opted him. After hearing his complaints, he offered Cripps a new position in government, created specifically for him. He was to be a new of Minister of Economic Affairs, with overall responsibility for planning and exports. Cripps paused for just a moment at Attlee's offer, before accepting it on the spot. Having walked in with the intention of forcing Attlee out of office, he walked out with most of the responsibilities that Morrison had previously had as Lord President. This was a tactical masterstroke, which demonstrates that Attlee was far more determined to hang on to office than he would care to admit. Morrison, the strongest challenger to Attlee, now slipped a few rungs down the ladder, and had a diminished role.[41]

Cripps confessed to Dalton that he 'felt rather a dirty dog' for his part in the episode.[42] Morrison, learning the news while on holiday with his wife Margaret in Jersey, could not hide his anger when Attlee wrote to him informing that there were to be some changes in the government. 'I have been giving a lot of thought to Governmental reorganisation,' said the prime minister. There was to be a new emphasis on youth and ability, and the size of the Cabinet would be reduced. He had been too distracted by Indian affairs in the past years, he confessed, so he excused himself from some committee work. He would no longer preside over the Defence Committee on routine business but leave it instead to A. V. Alexander. As Lord President, Morrison would now be more of a deputy prime minister, leading the party in the Commons.[43] Stranded in the Hôtel Grandes Rocques, Morrison could only muster a few words by way of reply: 'I am sorry that once more – 3rd time! – you feel you must decide on Government changes when I am away. It puts both of us at a disadvantage.'[44]

The Cabinet reshuffle took effect in the first week of October 1947. Eleven ministers went out, including Arthur Greenwood, who announced his retirement. The most prominent of the casualties was Shinwell, who had performed so haplessly during the fuel crisis. Hugh Gaitskell, a

41-year-old economics professor and the rising star of the centrists in the party, replaced him. The rest of the inner team retained their places. Bevan also remained in control of health and housing, despite criticisms of his lack of progress on the building of new homes. (Attlee continued to push his minister to achieve more on this front. Bevan had taken the decision to create a Housing Production Executive in April 1946 but valuable time had already been lost and this was to be one of the areas in which the government did not perform as well as it had promised. It was not until 1951 that a new Ministry of Housing and Local Government came into being, an important, but tardy, step.)[45] The average age of the Cabinet was reduced from sixty-two to fifty-seven. Most importantly, the prime minister now invested everything in the Cripps approach – with its greater emphasis on planning – by giving him three handpicked senior officials to work under him in his new role.[46]

It would be a while before their measures would take effect. In October, William Gorell Barnes, a senior civil servant working as the prime minister's economic adviser, warned him that there was no easy way out of the country's economic difficulties. In two years in office, the government could claim some great successes. Unemployment was at a record low figure of 249,691, meaning it stood at 1 per cent of the insured population. This was lower even than Beveridge's definition of 'full employment', and meant that social insurance provision could be paid for. On the other hand, there were related problems caused by full employment, such as inflation in prices. Second, the improvement of essential industries through modernisation and mechanisation would most likely lead to a return to higher levels of unemployment in the future. Finally, it was increasingly clear that the Labour Party was divided on how to avoid the running of a dollar deficit. Some suggested closer integration with the European market; others, increased production within the Commonwealth, in a reworking of the old idea of imperial protection.[47]

As *Private Enterprise* was published in the autumn of 1947, another of Attlee's officials noted that there was also a problem of perception when it came to austerity. Many people 'seem to think that the Government want to see such a large proportion of home-produced goods exported just for the fun of the thing – because they are austerity or restrictionist minded'. It fell to the prime minister to explain that, when the government exported consumer goods, it was so that it could obtain essential food and raw materials.[48] There was no easy way to put a positive spin on this.

Ominously, it was not only Barsetshire that was showing signs of revolt at the new regimen. Mining unions began to baulk at the six-day week and the failure to increase the £5 minimum weekly wage. Bevin warned the prime minister that his authority over the unions could only be stretched so far.[49] A. V. Alexander was asked to push ahead on reductions in the armed services. But there was a press campaign against the cuts. Attlee suspected that the chiefs of staff had fuelled this with private briefings to select journalists.[50] Then, having drawn up an austerity budget, Hugh Dalton was forced to resign the morning after it passed, on 13 November, after leaking some details to a journalist in a throwaway comment. 'Perfect ass,' was Attlee's verdict.[51] Cripps replaced him, but did not give up the Ministry of Economic Affairs, meaning that finance and planning both fell within his purview.

On New Year's Day 1948, a year before George Orwell published his dystopian novel *Nineteen Eighty-Four*, the government unveiled a billboard poster that was put on advertising hoardings across the country. In true Big Brother fashion, it had a photo of the prime minister inscribed with his latest call to arms: 'This year let us all put into our work the spirit that has made our nation great. An all-out effort will increase our production by the 10 per cent we need to turn the tide.'[52] January 1948 also marked the halfway point of the government's parliamentary term. That month the railways finally passed into public ownership, followed by gas and electricity. Yet, as the bearer of bad news, Attlee was losing popularity across the country. A Gallup poll showed that he had now dropped down into negative popularity ratings for the first time – from 66 per cent in August 1945, to 51 per cent in July 1946 and 44 per cent in January 1948.[53]

Added to existing concerns about the balance of payments – in this instance, quite simply selling enough abroad to buy what was needed at home – was the continuing drain on gold and dollar reserves. This was the buffer on which the rest of Cripps's strategy depended. All eyes would be on his budget in April 1948, but the government had a tough few months ahead to prepare the ground.[54] Harold Wilson, the new Minister of Trade, was tasked with establishing new bilateral trade agreements, designed to swap goods and raw materials without losing more money on the dollar exchange. Exchanges were put in place with Denmark, Ireland and Belgium, which traded foodstuffs in return for coal. These were regarded as temporary solutions, however. There was a global shortage in coal, steel, locomotives, machinery and farm equipment. The challenge remained the same: to boost production for export faster than Britain consumed imports. As the *Manchester Guardian* put it, there was nothing in this programme to improve the national mood. 'We walk in the shadow of economic catastrophe and live month to month.'[55]

For those who had warned about the dangers of a planned economy – or the perils of socialism – the difficulties faced by the British government provided a salutary warning. The *Wall Street Journal* ran a long article on the 'education of Mr. Attlee' as a warning to those in America who had been impressed by the social democratic model. The British government had set out to correct 'disequilibrium' in the economy – through planning and price control – but every time they attempted to set one portion of the economy right, they had destabilised another. The British people had plenty of cash but very few goods available to buy. This meant inflation and high prices for those goods that were available. The first chance the public had, when the pound had been devalued, they had rushed to buy dollars. This had caused the government to try to control the exchange but this, in turn, had damaged exports. The government had nationalised industries but was responsible for freezing wages, meaning that workers were starting to wonder if it really did benefit them.[56]

As memory of the war faded, there were only a finite number of times that Attlee could appeal to a sense of patriotic duty. He did so again when a dock workers' strike began in east London in June 1948 – in protest at his announcement of another freeze in wages. As someone who had supported the dockers for many years, from the earliest years of his career, he was able to call on great personal authority in his appeal for them to go back to work, with more than 152 ships lying idle, and unpacked. In the current conditions in the country, this was a strike 'against your mates, a strike against the housewife, a strike against the ordinary common people who have difficulties enough now to manage on their shilling's worth of meat and other rationed commodities.' The prime minister's personal intervention with the dockers won him some credit with the press.[57] Others were not so forgiving. When Attlee dined at his old college in Oxford just a few weeks before the dockers' strike, the undergraduates deflated his tyres, took his hat from the back of the car and returned it with the notice 'Vote Tory Next Time' affixed to it.[58]

III

A lifeline presented itself in the form of the Marshall Plan, which had been put before Congress in December 1947. The prospect of a large cash injection into the European economic system was very welcome. In early 1948, as negotiations over the details of the plan continued, Attlee wrote warmly to Truman, praising the 'combination of vision and practical statesmanship' which underlay his proposals, and urging him to persevere.[59]

Yet the Marshall Plan also pointed to a dilemma which the Labour government was not yet ready to face. As part of his strategy for encouraging America to take more responsibility for the financial well-being and security of Western Europe, Bevin had offered much vague rhetoric about the need for Western European unity. The problem with this was demonstrated when the drive towards economic unity in Western Europe began to take on a momentum of its own. When France and West Germany began to make moves in this direction, the British came under pressure to follow suit.

Nary of economic integration, Bevin preferred a policy of defensive treaties and alliances, offering protection to Belgium, Holland and Luxembourg. Before long, however, the French government, like the Americans, began to complain about Bevin's 'artificial' support for European unity. They instead tried to draw out the prime minister, by citing his past favourable references to a European customs union. In the US Senate, for example, the Republican John Foster Dulles, who was to become US Secretary of State, pointed out that Attlee himself had said in 1940 that 'Europe must federate or perish.'[60] In truth, the prime minister had long since given up on this idea.

The issue of economic unity was set aside for the moment in February 1948, when a Russian-sponsored coup in Czechoslovakia brought in a new Stalinist regime. This extended the Soviet sphere of influence further west. That Czechoslovakia had been bullied into submission by a powerful neighbour once more – just as it had been by Hitler – was a source of genuine sadness. The coup had been followed by the alleged suicide of Jan Masaryk, the Czech foreign minister, who was very popular in London from his time as ambassador in the 1930s. 'It may well be,' remarked Attlee, in a public tribute, 'that he could not endure to live in the suffocating atmosphere of totalitarianism when all that he had striven for was being ruthlessly destroyed.'[61] Significantly, it was in response to these events that an influential portion of the 'Keep Left' group of the party also began to share the government's concerns about Soviet behaviour.[62]

The combination of these events was a further spur in Bevin's efforts to push through the Treaty of Brussels, signed a week later, on 17 March. This provided for mutual aid in the event of an attack on any of Belgium, Britain, France, Holland and Luxembourg. Attlee also ratcheted up his rhetoric against communism. It was a political ideology that had been 'bred on the continent of Europe in the atmosphere of authoritarianism and brought to flower in the soil of Tsarism'. Labour's socialism, by contrast, had its roots in 'European civilisation, in humanism, in Christianity and in our British traditions'. Once again, Attlee was willing to use Manichean imagery to describe what was happening in Europe. It was a 'conflict between two ideologies – the totalitarian ideology and the democratic ideology'.[63]

'Could it happen here?' asked The Economist, with reference to events in Prague.[64] In May 1948, MI5 submitted a report to the prime minister that raised concerns about the growing influence of the Communist Party. Around two hundred people in the civil service were estimated to be Communist Party members, with twenty at the policy-making level.[65] In response, a mini-purge began, which Attlee defended on the grounds that it was increasingly clear that the Communists were as 'ruthless and unscrupulous' as the Nazis.[66]

On 3 April, the next bolt was fastened into a new Western alliance when President Truman signed the Economic Cooperation Act, finally bringing the Marshall Plan to life. Attlee sent a joint message to Truman and Marshall praising them for their 'unparalleled act of generosity'.[67] Marshall, in particular, was considered to be much superior to 'little Jimmy Byrnes'. The offer was made to include those countries on the east of the Iron Curtain as part of a tentative gesture of rapprochement. But as Attlee later wrote, 'Stalin stamped on it.'[68] There followed a considerable escalation of tensions. In June, the Soviets began a blockade of west Berlin – under the control of the French, British and Americans, but within the Soviet-administered zone – after raising objections to the introduction of a new currency, the Deutsche Mark, in West Germany. The Russians effectively tried to force the removal of British, French and American troops by preventing any provisions from arriving in the city.

It was a source of some regret to Attlee that the United Nations had not been able to reduce these tensions, and that a new Western alliance had, by necessity, to be established in its place. Ultimately, however, he believed that the blame should be laid at the door of Moscow. On this issue, Attlee was happy to follow Bevin, who was the driving force in turning the Treaty of Brussels into a larger security arrangement with the Americans and Canadians. Thus, in the second half of 1948, the building blocks were put in place for the North Atlantic Treaty which was signed in Washington, DC, in April 1949. Before NATO was formed, there remained a British fear that America's tough line against the Soviet Union would not be matched by a willingness to take military action against it. Above all, the government was anxious to avoid another scenario like that of 1940, when Britain stood alone. Thus, as Attlee made clear, 'Europe came first. In the order of priority in world strategy that was Number One.'[69]

The diplomatic work on the North Atlantic Treaty coincided with a deft military manoeuvre in Berlin itself. This involved a massive airlift of food and medicine to the western portion of the city, which alleviated the shortages for the Allied troops and the civilian population among whom they lived. As during the war, there was grumbling from the combined chiefs of staff that the airlift was put under the command of a US general – Lucius Clay. Once again, however, Attlee and Bevin regarded military subservience as a small price to pay for continued US protection for Western Europe.[70] It was at this time that James Forrestal, the US Secretary of Defense, visited London, to make arrangements for the stationing of three groups of large bombers on British soil. There was no formal treaty to regulate this arrangement, which effectively made Britain a launch pad for America's nuclear deterrent.[71] Once again, Attlee chose to speak for Britain on this matter himself. He told Forrestal that there was 'no division in the British public mind about the use of the atomic bomb – they were for its use.'[72] Indeed, he referred Forrestal to a pamphlet by the Church of England which had justified the holding of the bomb on the grounds of 'defensive necessity'.[73] But the issue was kept from Cabinet and Parliament.

The prime minister witnessed the Berlin airlift himself at the start of March 1949, flying to the American aerodrome in the blockaded city, and meeting General Clay.[74] It was bitterly cold, with deep snow on the ground. The spirit of the Berliners was admirable, he commented.[75] In explaining the formation of NATO, he launched another strongly worded attack on the Soviets. Communists continued to 'mouth their old shibboleths' against British imperialism but the independence of India, Pakistan, Burma and Ceylon answered them firmly. The political system that the Communist Party had created behind the Iron Curtain was a 'ghastly travesty'. There was no freedom of speech; scientists, poets and artists were arrested for deviations from orthodoxy; even the footballers were supposed to be Marxist-Leninists.[76] Meanwhile, Britain mopped up aid from the Marshall Plan gratefully, receiving three billion dollars between April 1948 and December 1951.

IV

At the May 1948 Labour Party conference in Scarborough, Herbert Morrison reminded the delegates that vast cheques had been drawn on the assumption that national productivity and exports would increase. 'We must be careful not to under-estimate the bill we have to meet,' he warned. 'Don't let us think that we can meet the bill as a whole by squeezing the capitalists further, or by any other short-cut other than production.' In his speech before the conference, Attlee refused to 'enter into detailed questions' on economic affairs. Instead, he emphasised the 'spirit' of their efforts to build a new society. Whereas Attlee's ministers talked about the balance between supply and demand, the prime minister reverted to a familiar theme: the balance between rights and obligations. While his ministers addressed the immediate crisis, he talked in more general terms about the journey of the Labour movement to this point.

Above all, Attlee appealed to an ideal of citizenship as the foundation of all their efforts. That version of citizenship had brought many benefits but it required patience, solidarity and sacrifice too. 'Socialism is a way of life, not just an economic theory,' he explained, which 'demands a higher standard of civic virtue than capitalism.' He urged the party to appreciate the achievement of the 'many things for which we of the older generation have striven':

> There is, for instance, the ending of the Poor Law. I recollect joining up with the Webbs and George Lansbury nearly forty years ago in a campaign for the abolition of the Poor Law. It is now accomplished. And yet, some people say we move too fast. I recall at the street corner urging a

national medical service, urging a nationalisation of transport, electricity, and the rest. How formidable were the obstacles which faced us then. Yet they have been overcome . . . It is the greatest task which lies ahead of us all in the Labour and Socialist movement to see to it that the citizen's sense of obligation to the community keeps pace with the changes effected in the structure of society. We need to stress duties as well as rights.[77]

These were entirely genuine sentiments that captured the essence of Attlee credo – 'citizenship, enthusiasm, idealism and self-sacrifice' – and the sense in which he had presided over a transformation of Britain. But for impatient members of 'the younger generation' they were the same vague 'moral homilies' which had made Bevan so furious during the war; and a sign that the prime minister was slowing down in the second half of his government.

In a similarly cheery tone, Attlee stressed that his government was a united team, and bemoaned the tendency to talk about 'Cripps's economic policy', 'Dalton's financial policy', 'Bevan's health policy', or 'Bevin's foreign policy'. Behind the scenes, however, divisions were opening up in the Cabinet about the nationalisation of steel. On the one hand, Morrison advised the party to go slow and consolidate its gains before it faced the public in another general election. Nationalisation of steel needed to be postponed. 'We are getting to that very perilous stage in which previous revolutions have sometimes foundered.' Bevan and his disciple, Michael Foot, insisted steel and iron were the most important elements in the drive for efficiency. In this they were backed by Dalton, traditionally on the right of the party, but a man with great intellectual faith in the notion of a planned economy. In his view, steel nationalisation was the ultimate test of a socialist government.[78]

Morrison seemed to offer the prime minister a way out of this dilemma. He floated the idea of a compromise on iron and steel, which would allow for partial nationalisation. He was encouraged by Attlee to explore this idea with the Iron and Steel Federation (which represented the private industry). After discussions, Morrison came back with the idea that there should be an Iron and Steel Board to give the government some control over the industry, for planning purposes, but that this would stop short of full nationalisation. Morrison claimed that the prime minister responded by saying, 'Herbert, this scheme is good. I like these schemes very much, and I'll certainly support something on those lines.' When Morrison presented the plan in Cabinet, however, it was soon clear that he was not going to get a majority. Having remained silent throughout, the prime minister simply assumed his usual role as chairman and concluded in favour of the majority. This acknowledged that the weight of opinion was behind full nationalistion of iron and steel, but Morrison was furious. When the Cabinet meeting ended, he waited behind in the cabinet room and accused his leader of abandoning him in the discussion. Attlee did not say a word.[79]

For Morrison, this was yet another example of a lack of conviction, a failure to face down the majority, that he had identified in Attlee many years before when they were both borough mayors in London. Yet, viewing the bigger picture, the prime minister could justifiably claim that other developments that summer vindicated his style of leadership. The most profound example of this was in the creation of the National Health Service. As we have seen, he had handed Bevan free rein to implement his National Health Act, which had passed in April 1946. The difficulties that he faced in implementing it were profound. They arose from the fact that the new regime would have to be superimposed onto a tripartite system which existed already – of voluntary hospitals (traditionally supported by private donation), health centres (supported by local authorities) and general practitioners. The result was a patchwork quilt of a healthcare system in which various groups had competing interests. The voluntary hospitals represented one of the more noble aspects of the existing scheme. However, as Bevan put it to the House of Commons when moving the original Health Service Bill, he believed it was 'repugnant to a civilised community for hospitals to have to rely upon private charity'.[80] Some sections of the medical profession – notably surgeons – were amenable to the professionalisation implied in a new national service. Others – above all the general practitioners (GPs) – were deeply resistant.

It was the clash between Bevan and the British Medical Association (BMA), who represented the GPs, which defined the struggle to bring the new health service into life by the summer of 1948. A majority of GPs refused to cooperate with the scheme – demanding freedom to practise in the area of their own choosing, more control over their own salaries, and other employment rights – until the last few months before it came into being. After the worst of Bevan's public spats with the BMA in January 1948, the prime minister asked his health secretary to write a full report for the Cabinet. Bevan used the opportunity to attack Dr Charles Hill, the secretary of the BMA, for his campaign of 'sabotage' against the NHS. He was at pains to point out that even what he called the 'reasonable critics' of the scheme (including *The Times* and *The Economist*) did not support the BMA campaign against the bill. Attlee prepared a speech to intervene in the Commons National Health Service debate in early February, on Bevan's behalf. In the end, however, he decided against intervening.[81]

The prime minister was criticised for not being sufficiently vocal in supporting his health secretary.[82] It was a view that Bevan shared, complaining that he was not given enough support by the Cabinet. On the other hand, by remaining aloof from the ugliest moment in Bevan's dispute with the BMA – when the whole scheme seemed to be in jeopardy – Attlee left some room for compromise and further negotiation. Bevan softened his approach. Without retreating, he decided not to proceed with a full-on confrontation with the BMA. Thus emerged a space in which negotiations could continue in the short time before the deadline for the implementation of the new service. As with the School Leaving Age, Attlee had never for one moment considering postponing this, or pushing it back, as the BMA had hoped.[83]

In Bevan's view, it was only by 'stuffing their faces with gold', that he was able to get the doctors to acquiesce to the new system. This occurred when a majority of the BMA broke with their leadership and voted to cooperate with the NHS. To Bevan's irritation, it was Attlee who broadcast to the nation on 4 July on the eve of the new National Health Service coming into existence. Yet this was not a matter of taking the credit, so much as placing the most controversial part of the British 'New Deal' in a broader context, after so much acrimony. While this was the jewel in the crown, the government saw the NHS as linked inseparably to its three previous measures of welfare reform: 'The four acts which come into force tomorrow – National Insurance [1946], National Injuries [1946], National Assistance [1948] and the National Health Service – represent the main body of the army of social security . . . They are comprehensive and available to every citizen. They give security to all members of the family.'[84]

In the days following the creation, Bevan caused another storm by labelling those Conservatives who had opposed the National Health Service, or had attempted to obstruct it, as 'lower than vermin'.[85] Churchill demanded an apology. Indeed, he accused Bevan of creating needless antagonism with the medical profession, and delaying the implementation of a service

Churchill that the Conservatives had been happy to support during the wartime coalition. Addressing Attlee in the Commons, Churchill said that it was time the prime minister got rid of his troublesome minister.[86] Privately, Attlee did rebuke Bevan for his loose tongue. 'I love being the bugbear of the Tories,' Bevan told him. 'You can't be the bugbear of the Tories and be regarded as a statesman,' replied the prime minister.[87] In doing so, he explained his broader strategy. 'It had been agreed that we wished to give the new Social Security Scheme as good a send-off as possible and to this end I made a *non*-polemical broadcast. Your speech cut right across this . . . You had won a victory . . . but these unfortunate remarks enable the doctors to stage a come-back and have given the general public the impression that there was more in their case than they had supposed.'[88]

Despite these occasional flashes of exasperation, Attlee never for one moment thought of dispensing with Bevan. While Bevan claimed that he had asked to be appointed as the health minister in 1945, Attlee denied this and countered that the idea had been his own. Nonethless, when it was required at the crucial moment, Bevan displayed 'real gifts as a conciliator'. Attlee maintained this high praise even after reading Michael Foot's biography of Bevan in which Foot made much of Bevan's contempt for the prime minister. 'I admired much about him,' he insisted, 'to the extent that I thought he would have been a natural leader of the Labour Party if one was sure he would learn to keep his temper.'

Yet there was a sting in the tail of Attlee's assessment of Bevan. It was not Bevan's idealism or his impatience that were his downfall but two other flaws. One was his mistaken belief that 'people would not fight in any war except a class-war, not realising the Tories loved their country as well as their class'. This had the effect of alienating people who might otherwise have been favourable. The other was his tendency to 'speak contemptuously to party veterans who had been slogging away before he was born'.[89] Among them, of course, was Attlee himself.

V

Like many of his ageing Cabinet, the prime minister was showing signs of overwork. At the end of August 1948, after a two-week holiday in Ireland, he went into St Mary's Hospital in Paddington for treatment on severe eczema on his feet, only for doctors to tell him he had an early duodenal ulcer, which required an operation.[90] On Friday, 11 September he returned to Downing Street for a Cabinet meeting. He greeted the press cheerfully on his way into Number 10 but was forced to go back to hospital in the afternoon and stay there all weekend. Doctors advised him to keep away from the opening session of Parliament that was to take place a few days later, but Attlee went ahead and issued his usual invitation to new MPs to take tea with him the day before.[91] By early October, he was buried in work in Downing Street but avoiding public functions, raising questions about his fitness for the leadership once more, just as preparations for the Steel Bill began.[92] His doctors told him to cut his smoking to one pipe a day. So, he joked, he went out and bought the biggest pipe he could find.[93]

Now that he was approaching his mid-sixties, recovery sometimes took longer than expected. It was perhaps a sign of mental as well as physical exhaustion that he seemed increasingly inclined to nostalgic reminiscences. 'Whenever I want to brace myself to any of the tasks we have to face to-day I think of the people I used to know in Limehouse – the little chap who used to come out Sunday after Sunday, carrying the platform, doing all the heavy work of the movement. He had no hope of seeing the visions that he had realised,' he told the Cambridge University Labour Party in November 1948, 'He just doggedly set himself to serve his fellow-men.'[94]

Implicit in this story was that some of these dreams had indeed been realised over the previous three years. It was not only on the home front that the prime minister could point to great victories. The British Commonwealth, which he had done so much to create, began to take shape. Despite his recent operation, one reason he was so eager to get back to Downing Street was so that he could continue with a schedule of meetings with new Commonwealth heads of state. He saw D. S. Senanayake, the prime minister of Ceylon (which had become independent in January 1948), Liaquat Ali Khan, prime minister of Pakistan, and Nehru. He also hosted Seán MacBride, the Irish foreign minister, at Chequers in mid-October. While Ireland had rejected the opportunity to join the newly reconstituted Commonwealth, arrangements were already under way to facilitate the integration of India, Pakistan and Ceylon.[95] For all the difficulties in the international arena, Attlee also remained more personally invested in the United Nations than any other member of his government. He broadcast to the nation on the third anniversary of the coming into force of the UN Charter, and declared, once again, that Britain was determined to make it work. At the same time, however, George Marshall broadcast from Paris expressing the same sentiment but making clear that most obstructions were coming from the Soviets.[96] These bonds were tightened whenever possible. Marshall visited London at the end of October, and lunched with Bevin, Attlee and their wives, at the American Embassy.[97]

In January 1949, the *Observer* profiled the prime minister and suggested that his 'disciplined independence' should not be confused with isolation in his own administration. He was still strong and had ridden out every attempt to knock him out of government.[98] Yet speculation about his retirement resurfaced, and just a week later Downing Street was forced into releasing a statement emphasising that the prime minister had made a good recovery from his ulcer and that any worries over his health had been allayed.[99] When a minor scandal broke after it was revealed that two Labour ministers had accepted gifts from foreign dignitaries – thereby breaking Foreign Office protocol – Churchill could not resist the wisecrack that this would not have happened if Attlee had still been alive.[100] The press also noted that the prime minister had bought what seemed to be a retirement home near Great Missenden, in Buckinghamshire. It was a six-bedroom house – dating back to the sixteenth century – with about one acre of land, which they purchased from a stockbroker.[101] Did Barsetshire beckon?

Once again, these were minor tribulations compared to what had been achieved in the intervening years. Indeed, by February 1949, as he returned to full fitness, it seemed the prime minister was finally able to point to signs of economic recovery. The policy of 'firm and fair control' on the use of resources, and the building up of basic industries, was bearing fruit. With a brighter economic picture, the government's record looked increasingly strong across the board. As Attlee now pointed out, the government had 'won a unique distinction in British politics' – it had kept every promise it had made so far. It had introduced a social security and health scheme that was already 'the envy of nations'. It had built more new homes in proportion to the population than had ever been constructed by a government in any other country, and the overall health of the nation was improving. Now production and export figures for the second half of 1948 had risen considerably, he could justifiably argue that this was vindication for Britain's 'four-year plan' for recovery.[102]

For all the wear and tear of the previous four years, the economic upturn in early 1949 brought a greater sense of perspective, and allowed for a more favourable appraisal of the government's achievements so far. In early 1949, Francis Williams reissued Attlee's 1937 book, *The Labour Party in Perspective*, adding a new preface. As Williams wrote, the book showed, to a remarkable extent, how Attlee had anticipated nearly every major measure his government had taken in domestic and foreign affairs since 1945. He had foreshadowed the measures of colonial development and independence for India, Burma and Ceylon, as well as the programme of nationalisation.[103]

Those who presumed that Attlee had somehow run out of steam, or was drifting along like flotsam, were in danger of forgetting his personal role in the transformation that Britain had undergone in the short time since the war. Ferdinand Kuhn, the diplomatic correspondent of the *Washington Post*, observed that, following his health problems, 'a visitor to Downing Street finds Attlee a strangely unimpressive figure, hunched up like a gnome at the great cabinet table, shy and awkward in conversation, matter-of-fact to the point of dullness.' Never was it so misleading to judge a politician by external appearances. He had been hugely underestimated, particularly in the United States. Referring back to *The Labour Party in Perspective*, Khun joked that not even Hitler had given a more accurate indication of his ultimate intentions when he wrote *Mein Kampf*.[104]

Unfortunately, due to circumstances beyond the government's control, this was a short period of calm before another economic crisis. Once again, the fire began elsewhere, just as the balance of payments had been brought under control. In this case, a recession in the US meant American demand for British exports collapsed. This was combined with a rise in prices. With so much of the budget already spent on social programmes and defence – not least the Berlin airlift – the government was forced to announce cuts in domestic spending. Attlee was determined not be outflanked by Churchill on the issue of defence expenditure.[105] But the costs were to be felt at home.

Once again, it fell upon Attlee to appeal to notions of solidarity and citizenship when announcing further measures of belt-tightening. In April, the prime minister announced that the implementation of the new social insurance regime would have to be slowed. For once, the Labour left and the trade unions were united in their opposition. Just as the government began to consider the possibility of a general election at some point within the next twelve months, so the prospect that the pound might have to be devalued against the dollar – in order to kick-start exports again – was raised.

This was the unpropitious background to the April 1949 pamphlet, issued by the party leadership, *Labour Believes in Britain*, a plea for patience and another five years to complete the job they had begun. 'Acts of Parliament do not dig coal, plough fields or tend machines. It is the people of Britain who have, by hard work, good sense, and self-discipline, outfaced disaster and brought forth recovery.' On the last page, the party boasted that they had approached their task 'in the British spirit – the effort to find practical solutions to practical problems, but no less to aim at a high and comprehensive purpose'. That aim was 'to usher in the finest age in our history – a buoyant age of adventure, progress and initiative, of unity in common purpose and justified pride in our nation's greatness'.[106] From the 'patronising title on the cover to the patriotic back-slappery' of the last page, the *Manchester Guardian* was unimpressed.[107]

The patriotic back-slappery was the foil for a new emphasis on stability. More than ever, under these mounting pressures, the prime minister spoke of 'consolidation' rather than socialist advance. 'We are not the slaves of abstract formulae,' he insisted. At trade union meetings, he made a point of acknowledging that middle-class voters were struggling under the weight of taxation.[108] Once again, he returned to the same understanding of citizenship, as a dialectic between duties and rights. It was with deep regret that he was forced to announce further cuts in welfare spending. Equally, however, he made a pointed criticism of those who took the new benefit system and welfare state for granted, or abused the support it provided. 'Everyone who fails to contribute his fair share is as much a parasite as those who used to live on the backs of the people without working. The man who slacks at work is scrounging off his mate.'[109] For Attlee this notion was central to everything he had ever stood for. To his critics, it sounded like yet another 'of those sermons on ethical values' that the country was fast becoming tired of. That this condemnation came from the *Manchester Guardian*, the organ of the Liberal Party, but which had been relatively supportive of the prime minister in recent times, was an indication of the changing mood.[110]

The prospect of an election within the next twelve months weighed heavily on the minds of the Labour leadership. Morrison and Attlee tried to restore some discipline by calling the Labour Party MPs together at the end of May, before the end of the session, and warning them not to stray from the leadership's line during the summer. Foreign policy remained a sore point but mainly within the party. Two MPs had had the whip withdrawn from them after expressing pro-Soviet views and sixty-seven members had defied the government in a vote on NATO. There were some tough questions from the backbenchers but it was felt the party was patched up enough to see it through the summer. More worrying was the restlessness of the TUC. Having agreed to restrain claims for higher wages for its members, it sought an urgent meeting with Cripps, asking him to alleviate the pressure on living costs by lowering prices.[111]

Holidays for Attlee were increasingly snatched; cricket matches a rarity. Violet was once again ordered to take a 'complete rest' and entered a clinic in Surrey suffering from exhaustion in early May.[112] By June 1949, Attlee had given up hope of finding time for a vacation as he learned that it might be necessary to devalue the pound.[113] He did manage to get to Wimbledon, sitting in the sweltering heat with 17,000 others at Centre Court to watch the American title holder, Pancho Gonzales, defeated by the Australian Geoff Brown, known for his distinctive two-handed backhand.[114] Rather ungenerously, when he saw photographs of the party leader there, Hugh Gaitskell observed that Cripps had spent all weekend working from his sick bed. 'The P.M. is perhaps so successful because he is content to let others do the work.'[115] This was the first time that Attlee had been accused of failing to keep pace with the work ethic of his colleagues.

The prime minister attempted to address some of the mounting criticisms in front of a massive crowd of 11,000 Labour supporters at King's Hall in Manchester in July 1949. Any government after the war would have faced huge difficulties. But he also warned that those who had gone on unofficial 'wildcat' strikes, or expressed sympathy with the Communist Party, were endangering the whole project.[116] In response, *Pravda* took the opportunity to publish a lengthy article on the 'tribulations' of Britain's prime minister. The bourgeois press in England had long spoken of his supposedly 'tranquil, self-restrained and balanced character'. His speech in Manchester was 'emotional . . . hysterical . . . [and] fevered', accompanied by sobs and angry tears, while making 'filthy insinuations' about Communists.[117]

Although *Pravda*'s picture of mental collapse was greatly exaggerated, he was undoubtedly showing some signs of strain. 'He is not an impressive man in a crisis,' observed the Conservative backbencher Cuthbert Headlam, as Attlee introduced a new Finance Bill and justified the use of emergency powers – sending in the troops to disperse another dock strike.[118] An additional strain was caused by the fact that two of the government's most effective ministers were taken ill. Bevin was suffering from heart problems, and in July, Cripps, who was suffering from cancer of the abdomen, was sent to Switzerland to recuperate in a clinic.[119]

In August 1949, Attlee was told that a 30 per cent devaluation of the pound was unavoidable to counter the dip in exports caused by economic depression in America. As chancellor, Stafford Cripps had been determined not to take this course. In his absence, however, pressure for devaluation had mounted within the Cabinet. The *Spectator* explained the rationale behind it. It was hoped that 'the American buyer, confronted with an effective price reduction of 20 per cent, would certainly feel more disposed to buy; the flagging export trades would get a first-class fillip; [and] the forbidding problem of getting costs down to the competitive levels suitable for a buyers' market would be solved (for the moment) in a trice, without any of the painful concomitants of deflation.'

On the other hand, there were dangers in taking this course of action. As the *Spectator* warned, to lower the price of pounds to the American buyer of British goods also meant raising the price of dollars to the British buyer of American goods. This brought different pressures: 'Out of every category of goods which Great Britain now exports to America . . . more would have to be sent to bring home the same quantity of American cotton, tobacco and machinery . . . A merely proportional increase would leave us just where we were – the poorer, indeed, for the extra goods shipped across the Atlantic instead of being consumed at home.' There was also the danger that others would follow suit and try to engineer their currencies for competition, which would further undermine the pound. This risked creating an 'avalanche of competitive exchange-wrangling, throwing down all the painfully built-up fabric of international economic confidence, distributing gamblers' gains and gamblers' losses, and convincing the whole world trading community that dollars or gold are the only safe store of value.' To stand any chance of success, even more severe cuts in spending would have to be implemented.[120]

The recognition that further cuts in spending would eventually follow created a political dilemma about when to call the next election. Hugh

Gaitskell, the fuel minister and an increasingly important figure in the government, urged the prime minister to call an election in November 1949. Gaitskell believed that devaluation might buy the government a brief 'lull' in economic conditions (provided confidence in the pound did not entirely collapse). It might then allow the government to go to the polls before it had to put further controls on consumptions and imports (which would inevitably follow, and which was the greatest source of discontent). Thus, an early election would avoid the considerable problem of trying to pass another painful budget.[121]

Gaitskell's strategy was opposed by Morgan Phillips, general secretary of the Labour Party and a key figure in its national strategy.[122] Instead, Phillips urged the prime minister to go to the country in the spring of 1950. First, there was the question of honesty. If the government was to pursue devaluation, it should not disguise the costs that would come with it. Second, Phillips pointed to slight improvements in the polling figures and suggested that the party could be on an upward trend. This he attributed to a combination of a relaxation on milk rationing and good weather. Third, the Labour Party had always done better in spring elections. In any case, the constituency organisations were not prepared to fight a snap poll.[123]

Officials at the US Embassy followed developments with close attention, not least because the stability of the government in Britain was a central component of the Marshall Plan. Attlee and Bevin were 'physically and mentally tired', observed Samuel Berger the Labour attaché, and it remained to be seen whether they could impose such an unpopular policy of cuts on their party. Bevan was the elephant in the room, and had become the lightning rod for discontent. The public had not quite grasped the extent of the economic crisis that was likely to hit in the autumn. In Berger's view, Labour might be making a fatal mistake in not calling the election now.[124]

Following a parliamentary debate on devaluation in October, the Cabinet met to make a final decision on the date of the election.[125] It was decided to hold it in four months' time, in February 1950. This was to coincide with the Labour Party's fiftieth birthday, though, as the *Manchester Guardian* noted, this celebration would mean very little to the middle-class and liberal voters whom the party would need to keep on its side to remain in office.[126]

All this meant that Labour was left with the unenviable task of trying to win an election against the backdrop of immediate 8 per cent cuts in government spending. Once again, Attlee appealed for patience and solidarity. He called for greater collective effort on production. Speaking to the nation on the BBC on 24 October, he did not hide the fact that the position of the country was 'critical'.[127] Following a meeting of the Cabinet, two days later, Dalton commented that the prime minister looked 'very nervous' as the government sought to make further reductions in its expenditure.[128] Writing to Tom that night, Attlee complained again that the press was being 'particularly mendacious', by comparing the economic crisis to that of 1931. Indeed, he observed that the American papers were more generous on the government's management of the economy – specifically its attempts to take necessary measures in preparation for the Marshall Plan.[129]

As ever, Attlee acted with great integrity. The *Observer* praised him for his honesty in cutting spending before the election. He could not be accused of hiding from a difficult problem or trying to mislead the British people. He was honest to a fault, perhaps. The paper noted how British political cartoonists were having much fun with him, portraying him as a mouse, curled up on an empty stage, speaking timorously. Part of this was a matter of presentation. He still thought that 'the preparation of a broadcast is not so important as even a trivial committee.'[130]

In the midst of these tribulations, Harold Nicolson saw Attlee at a dinner at the Society of Socialist Journalists. He had recovered physically after his ulcer problem, at least. 'He is very well now, and seems to have gained nervous energy since I last saw him,' wrote Nicolson. With the party's support ebbing away and an election looming, the journalists at the dinner debated how to make him a more popular figure, and complained that his press officers refused to give them personal anecdotes of Attlee's life, such as what he ate for breakfast. 'Obviously he lacks glamour and is bad at self dramatisation, but couldn't we build him up as a "simple man"? What the public wanted was the human touch.' 'The nice little man took all this quite humbly,' recorded Nicolson, as Attlee reminded the journalists that even a prime minister had a right to privacy. 'Besides, I should be a sad subject for any publicity expert. I have none of the qualities which create publicity,' he said. This comment 'made all the decent ones among us like him even more than ever', wrote Nicolson, 'But what percentage are we of the whole?'[131]

The overlapping notions of citizenship, patriotism and ethical socialism had been absolutely integral to Attlee's belief system from his earliest years. The experience of two world wars – from the trenches of the First to the Blitz during the Second – had sharpened these convictions. The social patriotism of the Second World War had been the highest expression of the Attlee credo. This had been translated into a stunning victory in 1945. For the first four years of his government, the same core convictions had crystallised in the form of a new system of social insurance and healthcare which was beyond anything that Attlee could have dreamed of forty years before. When the battle was won, but other problems had to be confronted, the prime minister fell back upon the old script. No one doubted his dignity or the strength of his ethical convictions, but they showed increasing irritation at being reminded of their duties as well as their rights. As the sense of solidarity and shared sacrifice that had been so profound during the war faded, these words began to seem hollow.

'I wish I could wish Labour well, but they depress me too much because of the minor public school morality which [is] the tone Mr. Attlee adopts,' wrote Isaiah Berlin in December 1949, as the election loomed. 'No doubt he is a morally better man than any who has ever been Prime Minister of England, but the effect is too flat. People like to have something idealised as a goal for which to strive and the ideal citizen of the Labour government is too unattractive an individual.'[132]

20

Taxis, Teeth and Hospital Beds

'The Major's got a good one about Attlee,' said Mr Pontresoli, in his thick, adenoidal Italian cockney, his series of blue stubbled chins wobbling as he spoke.

'It's impossible to be as funny about this government as they are themselves,' said Trevor. He had *such* a quiet sense of humour. 'They're a regular Fred Karno show.' But they all begged to hear the story, so he gave it to them. 'An empty taxi drove up to No. 10,' he said 'and Mr Attlee got out.'

Beautifully told it was, with his monocle taken out of his eye and polished just at the right moment.

Angus Wilson, 'The Wrong Set', 1949[1]

I Number 10 Downing Street, December 1949

An empty taxi drove up to Number 10, and Clement Attlee got out. This joke, often mistakenly attributed to Churchill, was told in Angus Wilson's 1949 short story, 'The Wrong Set'. It was in fact a satire on the high-society types who, replete with monocles, double chins, and an ingrained sense of superiority, condemned the prime minister.[2] Nonetheless, it soon became a favourite in the Conservative press. Writing in the *Daily Express* on 28 December 1949, as the prospect of an election loomed, the anti-Labour polemicist Colm Brogan suggested that many of the Prime Minister's Labour colleagues hoped to hear a different version: 'An empty taxi drew up at 10 Downing Street – and Attlee got in.'[3]

If Francis Williams was Labour's most effective propagandist, Brogan was its scourge. Williams told of Labour's noble struggle as it approached a half-century of existence since its foundation in February 1950. In *Socialist Britain: Its Background, Its Present and an Estimate of Its Future* (1949), Williams praised the Labour leadership for their tactical skill, decisiveness, hard work and integrity in government.[4] In the *Fifty Years' March: The Rise of the Labour Party* (1949), he stressed that Labour was a party of moderate patriots – embodied by Attlee, Bevin and Morrison – from whom the middle classes had nothing to fear.[5] Brogan set out to rebuff this image in a series of books and pamphlets as a direct response. In *Our New Masters* (1947), *They Are Always Wrong* (1949), *Patriots? My Foot!* (1949) and *Fifty Years On: British Socialism, 1900–1950* (1950), he sought to paint a different picture. Far from being the loyal patriots they presented themselves as, Labour's leaders were dangerous ideologues trying to transform Britain by stealth.[6]

More than many in his own party, Brogan understood that the prime minister was crucial to Labour's appeal. While the party's left wing underestimated their leader, this was not a mistake Brogan would make. Attlee's rise was a story which would have delighted the Victorian moralists, who had little patience 'for brilliance or audacity, or any other dazzling quality', and preferred 'plodding characters' who rose slowly to eminence, while their brilliant rivals 'shot up like rockets and came down like Daltons'.[7] He was the tortoise who won the race, to the bemusement of all the hares. On the surface, he was the archetype of the English middle-class man. For Brogan, however, this made him all the more dangerous. Attlee's reassuring image disguised a man with a zealous and ideological commitment to socialism. As the election approached, the tortoise had to be deprived of his shell.[8]

By December 1949, another joke doing the rounds in Westminster was that Attlee was going to have peanuts for his Christmas dinner. This arose from an embarrassing episode that was seized on as a symbol of the government's failings. While India had been granted independence, the government had pursued a policy of economic investment in the remaining British colonies, particularly those in Africa. As early as September 1945, the prime minister had stressed that trusteeship of colonies required efforts towards economic development alongside gradual moves towards self-government.[9] Constitutional reform was instituted in Ceylon, Newfoundland and Malta, Malaya, the West Indies and Central Africa.

Simultaneously, emphasis was placed on economic stimulus, particularly in Africa, partly in the hope that this would tie export-orientated economies into the sterling area.[10] The more trade within the sterling area, the less vulnerable Britain would be to a dollar-dominated trading system.

Arthur Creech Jones, the Secretary of State for the Colonies, stressed that development was also a good strategy against the spread of communism in Africa.[11] In an attempt to pull together these various strands of policy, John Strachey, the food minister, hoped to relax food controls by bringing in more imports from British colonies. In other words, the hope was that development could be mutually beneficial. In one such scheme – run by the government-sponsored Overseas Food Operation – £3,000,000 was invested in peanut growing in Tanganyika in East Africa. After massive ground clearance and planting, it became clear that very few peanuts were arriving in England, raising serious questions about the business efficiency of state corporations. In the last debate in Parliament before Christmas 1949, Churchill had great fun with what he took as further evidence of the government's failures in planning.[12]

While Labour strategists hoped that the fiftieth birthday of the Labour Party would give it a boost of energy in the forthcoming election, its leader was rather more reflective. In some ways, he noted, when looking back, it was easier standing at street corners than it was dealing with the complexities of life in office. As a Christmas present, the minister for colonies, Arthur Creech Jones, had given him a biography of William Morris. He was delighted to discover some new poems written when Morris was a young man, which he had not previously known. Another old comrade, Margaret Bondfield, who had campaigned against sweated labour in the factories, and had become the party's first female cabinet minister, also sent him her biographical reflections. In a letter to Tom, Attlee revealed that one of the old volunteers from his days at the Haileybury settlement, Miss Scott, had died. The prime minister had tried to give her an official honour but she had refused. 'So do these links with the past disappear.' This was an old man speaking. 'I suddenly forget the name of people I know quite well whereas the past remains as distinct as ever.'[13]

That December, one of Attlee's favourite books was turned into a motion picture. *The Forsyte Saga* was based on the 1907 novel, *The Man of Property*, by the English writer John Galsworthy. It was the first in a series of three novels (and two 'interludes') which told the story of the socially aspirational

Forsyte family. Soames Forsyte was an Edwardian gentleman who styled himself a 'man of property' but who was deeply conscious of his family's status as 'new money'. No matter how many material possessions he acquired, however, he could not find happiness. Attlee had known the saga so well that, when he lived in Limehouse after the war, he had been able to draw out the whole Forsyte family tree on a blank piece of paper. Writing in the *New York Times*, Marquis Childs – an American socialist writer who was sympathetic to Labour – reported that the prime minister was a 'devoted' follower of Galsworthy's writing. When asked, Attlee revealed that he was not going to see the film, as he was worried that Errol Flynn would not quite fit his conception of Forsyte. Nonetheless, his fondness for Galsworthy's books told a bigger story. The prime minister was very much 'conscious of the history of the class from which he comes and of the contribution that class made to England's greatness in the last century'. Indeed, it was because he was so representative of the 'average Britisher' that Attlee was somehow immune from the worst attacks of the Tory press. Consequently in the forthcoming election, 'good old Clem' was likely to be Labour's most potent weapon.[14] When standing before the British people, no Labour leader had a more natural appeal.

II

After a brief break at Chequers, Attlee returned to Downing Street a week earlier than expected, on New Year's Eve 1949, to begin planning for the election. The press followed the government's every move in anticipation of an announcement of the election date. The evidence suggested that it was imminent. Bevin was on his way to Ceylon for a Commonwealth conference, but had refused an invitation to stop off in India and Pakistan on his way home. Nye Bevan had also cancelled a scheduled trip to India, where he had been asked to advise on the formation of an Indian national health service. Churchill, who had sailed to Madeira for some winter sun, was only due to have a three-week holiday, much shorter than the usual six-week sojourns that no one seemed to begrudge.[15]

On 11 January 1950, Attlee told the country that Parliament would be dissolved within a month, and that there would be a general election on 23 February. Campaigning began in the first week of February. On the grounds that he would be travelling the country as party leader rather than as prime minister, he refused official transportation. At 10 a.m. on 8 February, Violet Attlee drove out of Downing Street in a twelve-year-old black Hillman, which would be pursued everywhere it went by a carload of American reporters from *Life* magazine. The car had 44,493 miles on the clock already and bore the marks of some of Violet's previous scrapes. In the back seat were a special constable and a reporter from the *Daily Herald*. In the passenger seat was the prime minister, with a large brown attaché case on his lap.

There were no bands or flags as the Hillman pulled up at Watford Town Hall for Attlee's first engagement about an hour later. After a brief appearance, they drove straight to Birmingham, where the prime minister spoke to an audience of 15,000 Labour supporters, who greeted him with a rendition of 'The Red Flag'.[16] By the end of the first day, the Attlees had become friends with the journalists from *Life*, who were covering their every move. Among them was Patricia Beck, an aspiring journalist acting as assistant photographer, who was enamoured of the prime minister. At the end of the campaign, Beck brought to Downing Street a copy of William Blake's poems because they 'were relevant to his attitude to society'. Attlee met her at the door and the two became friends thereafter.[17]

Within a week, Violet had escorted her husband from London, through Birmingham, to Edinburgh and back to York. His reception on the road was almost always a warm one. As the *Manchester Guardian*'s special correspondent reported, he had that 'quality of ordinariness which is a good deal rarer than it sounds'. Even the dilapidated Hillman seemed 'the epitome of the family car that every home-loving man either has in his garage or would like to have'. Attlee's message was not to let 'small griefs' get in the way of the big picture. He was 'fundamentally appealing to hearts rather than heads' but it was a 'powerful appeal' too. As Childs had predicted, the prime minister was 'unquestionably one of Labour's greatest personal assets'.[18]

Churchill – who travelled in a chauffeur-driven limousine – also seemed revitalised by his holiday and galvanised by the campaign. The problem that the Conservatives faced was that the issues they had decided to focus on ahead of the election – austerity and economic competency – were not ones on which Churchill was particularly strong. As the campaign moved into its second week, Churchill therefore began to develop a theme he had been hinting at in previous months – the idea that only he had sufficient gravitas to deal with Stalin were there to be a new meeting of the Big Three.[19] Even Churchill's admirers, like Harold Nicolson, thought this somewhat opportunistic. His implication was that, in the event of a new international summit, 'Winston could talk to Stalin on more or less the same level. But if Attlee goes, it would be like a mouse addressing a tiger.' For Nicolson, now standing for the Labour Party, this was a 'stunt', unworthy of Churchill.[20]

Attlee focused on the inconsistencies in Churchill's position on the home front, and drew attention to his sporadic attendance record in Parliament. At one moment, the opposition leader would complain about extravagant public spending; at another he would complain about austerity. He had criticised the amount spent on defence but had not attended the Commons debates pertaining to it. Attlee also paid court to Britain's housewives, sympathising with their plight and asking them to trust his government to see Britain through the storm. One of his tricks on the platform, observed the *Manchester Guardian*, was to 'behave as if his audience has all the right ideas – ideas which he himself in his own modest way is trying to put into words.'[21]

In total, Attlee made thirty-four major speeches in the course of the campaign and covered more than 1,000 miles. Due to the redrawing of electoral boundaries, his old constituency of Limehouse had been absorbed into Stepney. The prime minister was given the relatively safe seat of West Walthamstow, a few miles north, where he spent the last few days of the campaign. Violet volunteered as an official counting agent and was present, knitting a bright blue sweater, on polling night on 22 February. Attlee's main challenger was a Liberal who might have come straight out of an Evelyn Waugh novel: a six-foot-three-inch former RAF wing commander who drove round the area on a miniature motorbike.[22]

On 26 February, the results were announced. While the prime minister won Walthamstow easily, Labour suffered a serious dent. Their majority fell from 146 to just five, with the Conservatives making ninety gains. Still, there were reasons to be content with the result; Labour still had an outright majority, albeit a small one, for the second time in its history. In terms of popular legitimacy, the government had a strong mandate to carry on. Turnout had been higher than in any election in British history and the party won an overall majority of the popular vote – 13,226,176 for

Labour and 12,494,404 for the Conservatives – which suggested that it had suffered from the redrawing of constituency boundaries. Within the Labour Party, there was a widespread feeling that this was a strong showing, given the depressing economic backdrop to the election. One of the more optimistic assessments was provided by the left-wing MP, Richard Crossman, who suggested that Labour had won a clear mandate from 13 million people to push ahead with 'pure socialism'.[23] Attlee's view was typically more sober. After receiving a congratulatory note from Jack Lawson, he replied, 'I think considering the weight of the attack our people did fine in the election.'[24]

On the evening of 26 February, Attlee returned to Downing Street, as the press pack descended on Number 10. Frederic Raphael, who was then a student shadowing a Fleet Street reporter recalled how Attlee stood, 'in his signature funereal rig', on the doorstep, with cameramen and reporters huddling round him. The British press 'were inclined to respect our Prime Minister's temporising' on the result. However, Raphael was surprised when an American voice was heard to say 'Make up your mind, Mr Attlee, you going or staying?' 'We shall carry on,' he replied, 'in a modest voice that was never going to inspire anyone to fight on the beaches.'[25]

There was some reason for optimism. If the government could stabilise the economy and consolidate its gains, then it would be able to call another general election within the year, at a time of his choosing. In the short term, Attlee was invited to form a new government by the king. 'We have been having a busy time,' he told Tom on 2 March, as the government took the seals of office. The first matter on the agenda was the 'distasteful business' of reconstructing the Cabinet. Two women were promoted to it, Peggy Herbison (Scotland) and Edith Summerskill (National Insurance). Most of the key ministers remained in situ. 'Our folk are in very good heart,' he was pleased to report.[26]

In the opening debate of the new Parliament, the prime minister insisted that, in the short time before the Easter recess, the government would prioritise only essential business. This meant continuing to implement the existing policy on the balance of payments and also pushing through the nationalisation of iron and steel.[27] He was rather piqued when the Conservatives put down an amendment on the steel bill almost immediately. This was the new reality, however. Having lost the cushion of a large majority, the government must prepare itself for a campaign of attrition from the opposition on every measure it put before the House.[28]

On 15 March 1950, Cripps circulated a report on economic policy among his colleagues. The forthcoming budget, due in April, was of critical importance to the government's whole economic strategy. On it would rest the future of the planned economy to which Labour had committed itself after 1945. To make his point, Cripps stressed how much had changed since 1939. Before the war, governments had accepted a high level of unemployment and the economy ran through cycles of booms and slumps. The first goal of a planned economy was to avoid pendulum swings between inflation and deflation. Price controls and adjustments to taxation were designed to prevent a situation of 'too much money chasing too few goods'. There had been pressure from Herbert Morrison and others to reduce taxation. In Cripps's view, this would be ill advised at this moment. Planning had succeeded in keeping employment high and improving exports. But it also meant that the government was less gymnastic and dynamic in responding to vagaries in the international market. It had to tread a steady and careful line, and maintain a tight rein on consumption.[29] In other words, ministers should prepare themselves for the fact that it would not be a popular budget with the public.

At the start of April, Cripps warned the prime minister there was a major division opening up in the Cabinet, caused by the need to curtail the increase in public spending, specifically on the National Health Service. He believed that limits on spending on health must be established before costs got out of control. One way of doing this was to introduce charges for prescriptions. For Bevan, this was a matter of principle, which undermined the whole commitment to a health service that was 'free at the point of use'. He threatened to resign if charges were introduced. A final decision on this issue could be postponed until after the budget, suggested Cripps, but could not be delayed indefinitely. 'I must make it quite clear that I could not agree to nothing being done,' he warned.[30]

The budget, delivered at the end of the month, had a 'fairly good reception', reported Attlee. However, he was aware that its provisions could be worn down and eroded with stalling amendments, 'if the Tories think it worthwhile'.[31] The government's majority was being tested all the time. It had survived by just five votes on two tax proposals (the doubling of petrol tax and a 33.3 per cent purchase tax on lorries). It fought off another Conservative motion in May, a bill censuring the government for its policy of bulk-buying food. Worse still, Cripps's health was failing. His stomach cancer returned aggressively and he announced his retirement shortly after the budget. The issue of Health Service charges was to be postponed to the next session.[32]

In these circumstances, unity was needed more than ever before. In May 1950, the leadership headed for a weekend retreat to Surrey in order to agree a strategy to keep the government going into the second half of the year, and with a view to calling a new election. Attlee, Bevin and Morrison had all come to the conclusion that the party had lost votes on the grounds of perceived inefficiency in business and administration, but that the public continued to prefer the values they stood for. Either way, there was no enthusiasm for more nationalisation. Against them Bevan adopted a motto of 'onward'; for him, consolidation of existing gains was not enough. Transport House estimated that an estimated 5 per cent of the middle-class vote had swung against Labour. But it also calculated that 29 per cent of the working classes still voted Conservative. Attlee reminded his colleagues that Labour had a long way to go when it came to converting the country to socialism.[33]

III

On an unseasonably cold day in May, the US Secretary of State Dean Acheson arrived at Chequers with a delegation of American diplomats and their wives. Having replaced George Marshall (who became Secretary of Defense) in President Truman's second administration the previous year, he was an important visitor. The Foreign Office urged the prime minister to give Acheson 'a specially warm welcome . . . not only because he is the guest of honour, and a vitally important figure from the point of view of our interests and policies, but also because he has recently been the butt of so much heavy, undeserved and indiscriminate criticism, mainly from his own countrymen'.[34] Acheson enjoyed the hospitality but could not understand why Violet had opened all the windows in the dining room on this wet, 'allegedly spring' day. Even the well-insulated Ernie Bevin retreated to the coal fire to warm his hands, while the shivering American female guests kept their fur coats on throughout.[35] (They were not the only ones to feel that the Attlees were rather puritanical when it came to hospitality. Some government ministers' wives would fear a dinner invitation on the grounds that they were only served half a glass of sherry at best.[36])

Courting Acheson was doubly important because of a divide that was beginning to open up between the Western European recipients of aid from the Marshall Plan. The Secretary of State had travelled from Paris, where he had heard the foreign minister, Robert Schuman, make an announcement that was to change the course of European history for ever. The Schuman Declaration of 9 May 1950, called for a 'supranational community' to be established in Europe. The first stage was to pool coal and steel resources in order to improve the efficiency of the European economy. From this would eventually emerge a project with the professed aim of establishing 'ever closer' political union in Europe.

As Acheson arrived in London, the British government was squirming at Schuman's proposal. Both Attlee and Bevin had paid lip service to the idea of greater Western European unity. Following the implementation of the Marshall Plan, the US had pressed for positive measures to be taken to ensure that there was greater coordination between the Western European economies. However, Attlee's government was deeply sceptical about the merits of pooling resources in this way. For one thing, it was incompatible with its own vision of a planned economy.

The prime minister was left walking a diplomatic tightrope. In mid-June, Labour's National Executive Committee issued a pamphlet that rejected the prospect of closer economic integration with non-socialist states such as France. The pamphlet was printed and released on the eve of a House of Commons statement that Attlee was due to make on the forthcoming negotiations in Paris, which had been called to discuss the Schuman Plan. The official position of the government was that it would not attend; Schuman had made attendance dependent on agreeing to certain preconditions which would have locked the British into a deal they did not want to sign. Attlee had hoped to keep the prospect of future cooperation open with an emollient public statement. However, the issuing of the pamphlet by the NEC effectively undermined his strategy. The lack of coordination was extremely embarrassing. To make matters worse, the chairman of the NEC was Hugh Dalton, who had returned to the Cabinet after the election as Minister of Town and Country Planning.[37]

In a stormy session in the Commons on 15 June, the prime minister offered the limp explanation that the pamphlet's publication that morning had been an unfortunate coincidence. This was met with roars of laughter on the opposition benches. Did the prime minister and his foreign secretary know when the next Labour pamphlet on foreign affairs would appear?[38] The political correspondent of the *Observer* suspected that there was more to the story than met the eye. Attlee had created the impression that he was 'a babe unborn', with no idea of the contents of the pamphlet or when it would emerge. Yet it was claimed in Labour circles that he had known about it. Was Dalton being used as a 'scape-goat'?[39] Dalton's view was that Attlee had indeed seen the pamphlet. When he called at Number 10, he found the prime minister 'in a bit of a fuss'. He claimed not to remember agreeing to the publication but did, when Dalton pushed him, concede that he had been in the room when it was discussed.[40]

The debacle did not play well in Europe or the United States. The French saw it as a symptom of a weak government torn between two instincts. In the recent budget, the prime minister had made some concessions to the critics of austerity and tight price controls. This was at the request of Morrison, in particular, who was attempting to woo back Liberal voters with a kind of 'milk-and-water socialism'. After the budget, Attlee had tilted the other way by making concessions to Dalton and the economic planners regarding the Schuman Plan.[41] In the US, the group of senators responsible for the administration of the Marshall Plan demanded a clear statement on his position from the prime minister. 'We want action,' they warned him, 'not mere lip service.'[42]

Within just a few days, however, the embarrassment of the Schuman Plan was dwarfed by a much graver international crisis, which was to dominate the rest of the Attlee government – and ultimately play a part in bringing it down. On 25 June 1950, a border conflict between North and South Korea escalated into a full-scale war when Kim Il-sung's Korean People's Army – backed by Communist China, and with the tacit support of the Soviet Union – flooded over the border and invaded the South, claiming that it was the legitimate government of all Korea. The same day the United Nations Security Council – which had been boycotted by Russia since January – unanimously condemned the North Korean invasion of the Republic of Korea. Two days later, on 27 June, the Security Council voted to send a joint force, under the US General Douglas MacArthur, former Supreme Commander of the Allied Forces in the South West Pacific Area.

By bringing the Americans into confrontation with the Chinese – and with the Russians in the background – the conflict had all the ingredients for rapid escalation. Attlee was kept apprised of the situation through a series of telegrams from MacArthur, forwarded to him by the US Embassy in London, and written in the general's inimitable style. 'Attack makes amply clear centrally directed Commie imperialism has passed beyond subversion in seeking [to] conquer independent nations and now resorting to armed aggression and war.'[43] Truman ordered his Seventh Fleet to prevent any attempt by the Chinese Communists to take the island of Formosa (Taiwan), for fear that this made the US vulnerable to attack on its Pacific coast.

As a member of the Security Council, Britain was committed to contribute to the mission. This would mean that the government would face additional costs for which it had not budgeted. A more immediate concern was that the conflict might turn into another large-scale war between the great powers. While Attlee was never one to play down Russian skulduggery, he thought that American hostility to the Chinese Communists was too extreme. Neither the US nor the UN would acknowledge the Chinese Communist Party as the legitimate government of the country. However, they had clearly gained a clear upper hand in the civil war against the nationalist forces. He believed they would have to be recognised before long. The prime minister also feared that MacArthur, who wanted to take the fight directly to the Chinese in the north, was in danger of exceeding the brief given to him by the UN Security Council. On the other hand, Attlee understood that Korea had presented the first real test of the UN's authority. If aggressive expansionism could be resisted, it would set a strong precedent in a way that the League of Nations had failed to do. As he wrote to Tom, these were 'anxious times with the Korean situation but I hope if this is nipped in the bud we shall stop other aggressive armed movements.'[44]

Parliament met for a scheduled debate on the Schuman Plan on 28 June. The Conservatives had brought a motion of censure against the government on the grounds of its incoherence on European policy. Churchill spoke for an hour, criticising Labour for its failure to involve itself more closely in the negotiations between the French and the Germans. Attlee, supported by Stafford Cripps, argued that no British government could put British industries at risk by accepting, as a precondition of negotiations, the principle of supra-national authority. In reply, Churchill raised a concern that was to echo into future decades. What if France and West Germany agreed terms for cooperation and Britain was left outside a new European market?[45]

All the while the Korean crisis hung over Parliament. 'The thunderclap of the invasion was reverberating strongly when the debate opened on Monday,' reported the parliamentary correspondent of the *Spectator*. Just as Churchill wound up his attack on the government over Schuman, a parliamentary clerk entered the back of the chamber, behind the Speaker's chair, and signalled to the government front bench. A note was passed down to Attlee, who read the details carefully. It consisted of President Truman's statement to the American people on Korea. When Attlee rose to reply to Churchill, he asked the Speaker for a moment to read Truman's statement. Memories of the debates over the Munich Agreement of 1939, when Chamberlain had been handed notes from the Foreign Office updating him on the situation in Czechoslovakia, flooded back. MPs listened in silence as Attlee read the statement. As soon as he had finished, and the debate turned back to Europe, the shouting and jeering resumed.[46]

Attlee felt that Churchill 'made a fool of himself over the Schuman Plan', plunging in 'without considering the consequences'. It was 'generally thought that we had the better of the debate', he claimed.[47] Labour narrowly defeated the motion of censure by ensuring that all its MPs turned up for the vote, but the debate had taken a toll. In fact, the party had only just avoided a rebellion by pro-European MPs who thought that the Schuman Plan should be embraced. With so small a majority, even the smallest signs of dissent could have brought the government down.[48] Forced to summon a number of MPs from their sickbeds – carrying them in bath chairs – the government was literally dragging itself into the division lobbies, surviving week by week.

The tightrope walk continued as Parliament broke for summer recess. In early July, the Attlee family managed to spend some time in a chateau in the Loire Valley. But there were rumours of another party revolt – with left-wingers in the party now challenging the legality of the UN decision to impose military sanctions on North Korea, as Russia had boycotted the Security Council since January.[49] The Korean crisis occupied the rest of the summer. Every time that Attlee left for Chequers, the press was informed that he would not be back in London for weeks. The next day, almost inevitably, he had to return to Number 10. Microscopic attention

was paid to his movements on the grounds that he was privy to vital information. Gearing the country up for another rearmament campaign was
the first obstacle, as he and Bevin pleaded with the trade unions to cooperate without making further demands on the government. Already some
ordnance factories were imposing double shifts to meet the demand
for new artillery shells. It was felt that Attlee needed to perform well at
a forthcoming meeting of the TUC in early September, particularly
after his 'lame speech' at Bridlington the previous year, on the eve of
devaluation.[50]

As the North Koreans made progress towards Seoul, the capital of South
Korea, the ability of the UN forces to stem the tide was now in serious
doubt. Just over five years after VJ Day, it seemed like Attlee might be cast
in the role of the war leader. Harold Macmillan, the former Conservative
Minister of Air, conceded that he was 'more definite and stronger than we
had expected', but still felt he lacked obvious leadership qualities. The
prime minister insisted that Britain's involvement in the campaign was
sufficient in meeting its commitments – 'we have done all that is expected
of us' and 'we are doing as much as anyone else' – but Macmillan thought
him rather defensive. This was 'rather an uninspiring attitude for the
Prime Minister of Great Britain'.[51] The wife of Lord Rochdale, the Conservative peer, joked that he might 'easily win a medal as the finest cradle
rocker in the country'. Whatever the situation, a broadcast by the prime
minister made one feel 'soothed and lulled by the stupefying illusion that
nothing was seriously wrong'.[52]

Not unreasonably, Attlee believed that the responsible course was to
keep warlike rhetoric to a minimum. At the start of September, he attacked
Churchill for reckless grandstanding. For the last twenty years, his opposite number had seemed to regard Parliament as a place where he made
speeches. He was seldom present for most business, until he 'comes down
like a *prima donna*, delivers his oration and then, except for an occasional
appearance at question time, is seen no more until the next occasion'. If
Churchill was so disappointed with the government's record on defence,
why had he not been in Parliament at any point over the previous five years
when defence estimates had been discussed?[53]

The prime minister comforted himself with the view that Conservative
attacks on Korea were not 'very effective'. With another election being
mooted, he saw no evidence that the Korean crisis would benefit

Churchill. Most 'decent people' had a 'strongly held fear that, if Winston got in, he would lead us into war'.[54] There was something in this argument. Isaiah Berlin suggested that the political world was divided between 'reputable mediocrities' like Attlee and 'flashing swords' such as Churchill and Stalin. When Korea flared up, he confessed he would rather be 'killed by attrition by them than struck down splendidly by the heroes'. There were things worse than 'pettiness and mediocrity'.[55]

Fears that MacArthur would exceed his brief were proved right when the UN forces pushed back into North Korea in October. In response, Chinese Communists, who feared that MacArthur had designs on China itself, flooded over the Yalu River. This was the most dangerous point in the war yet. On Tuesday, 28 November, after a serious reverse for the UN forces, MacArthur stated that the advent of 200,000 Chinese had created 'an entirely new war', with much higher stakes. Then, on Thursday, 30 November, President Truman told a press conference at the White House that the commander in the field was free to use whatever weapons he saw fit. Suddenly, the prospect that the US might resort to an atomic weapon against the North Koreans, or even the Chinese forces, was raised. A subsequent statement was issued which clarified that only the president could authorise the use of an atomic bomb (and that MacArthur did not have it at his disposal). Nonetheless, news of Truman's press conference reached London during a foreign affairs debate in the Commons, and there was great alarm as the word spread among MPs.[56] Dalton scribbled a note to Attlee across the front bench which insisted that the prime minister must go to Washington immediately.[57]

Within six hours of Truman's statement, about 4.30 p.m. in Washington, the American ambassador in London, Julius C. Holmes, wired to the State Department that the British prime minister wanted to see Truman in person about 'Korea and related matters of mutual interest'. Dean Acheson was at the Pentagon at the time, but returned to the State Department at 4.45 p.m. and told the president about the request. About fifteen minutes later, Downing Street was notified of Truman's assent to a meeting with a single-word message: 'Agree.'[58]

In private, Attlee was highly critical of MacArthur. He believed that it would be a disaster to get embroiled in a major land war against China. In fact, Attlee went so far as to argue that a deal could be made with 'Red' China if it was recognised as the legitimate government of the country.

One suggestion was that a defensive line be fixed across Korea, well short of Manchuria, to which the UN forces would retreat. This would be a preliminary to negotiations with the Chinese. However, it was a difficult case to make in the US, where anti-communist sentiment was intensifying.[59]

In taking these concerns to Truman, Attlee had the support of the French government. He met with the French prime minister, René Pleven, and Schuman, on the morning before he was scheduled to visit Washington. The European members of the Western Alliance feared that they would bear the brunt of another world war. If America was mainly focused on the Asian theatre, they would be particularly vulnerable to Russia. To complicate matters further, there were a variety of perspectives on the Korean crisis within the British Commonwealth. To the irritation of the Americans, the Indian government had warm relations with the Chinese Communists. Meanwhile, Australia and New Zealand were more sympathetic to the American position because of their fear of the spread of communism. As Attlee left Heathrow airport on 3 December, he told the press that he was looking forward to 'an exchange of views between man and man'. Bevin pushed through the crowd of photographers to talk with him, whispering in his ear right up until the moment he boarded the plane.[60]

On the morning of 4 December, a silver-and-white British Airways Stratocruiser emerged from the grey sky and touched down at the National Airport in Washington, DC, with a bitter wind pummelling the phalanx of reporters and photographers on the runway. Truman, in a thick dark coat, greeted Attlee with great warmth as soon as he stepped onto the tarmac. The prime minister made a formal statement over a battery of microphones. Yet as Attlee later recalled in his memoirs, the atmosphere between the two countries was more tense than it had been in a decade. Some Americans blamed Britain for 'not trying hard enough in the dark battle'; and some Britons blamed America for 'forcing the pace, for impetuous action and rash and reckless policies'.[61]

During the course of the flight, the situation in Korea had deteriorated considerably, to the extent that Attlee's prepared agenda was almost useless. When he had left, the priority had been to stabilise matters by establishing a buffer zone between the armies of the North and South, as a prelude to negotiations. By the time of his arrival, it was not clear that the line could be held at all. The main priority was now to save the UN forces from complete encirclement. The British delegation was taken straight to the cabinet room of the White House, and updated by General Omar Bradley about MacArthur's retreat. Further meetings took place on the president's yacht, the USS *Williamsburg*. It helped that Attlee got on with Truman at a personal level. That evening, the prime minister was afforded some light relief when he went to Constitution Hall to hear a concert in which the president's pianist daughter, Margaret, was playing (though some mean-spirited gossips suggested that this was not so much of a treat). The following evening, after another day of meetings, Attlee spoke at the National Press Club, 'flooded by klieg lights, interrupted by seven motion-picture cameras chattering like the undertone of locusts on a summer night'.[62]

This was the type of summitry of which Churchill was the master. So what did the hurried visit to Washington achieve? Herbert Morrison, never one to offer effusive praise of Attlee, believed that this personal rapport between the leaders was crucial in calming the situation and preventing escalation and potential nuclear conflict. If other men had been in charge at this moment, he ventured, another world war could have broken out.[63] In fact, the details of Truman's meeting with Attlee on 4 December suggested that Attlee's role in calming the situation might well have been exaggerated. Truman rebuffed Attlee's suggestion that a more emollient line might be taken with the Chinese. In the president's view, they were the satellites of the Soviet Union. 'The only way to meet communism is to eliminate it,' he said, at the end of the meeting. After Korea it would be Indochina, then Hong Kong, and then Malaya.[64] There would be no negotiations with Peking.[65]

Dean Acheson, who was present during the key negotiations, commented that the prime minister 'was a far abler man' than Churchill's description of a 'sheep in sheep's clothing' suggested. He also understood that Attlee had 'not come here for a lecture on current events', but to steer America away from a conflict with the Chinese. Attlee alerted the president to the growing fear that if America's attentions were turned elsewhere, it would leave Europe exposed to the Soviet Union. Thus, he successfully urged Truman to appoint a supreme commander to NATO, in order to provide reassurance. 'Mr. Attlee's method of discussion was that of the suave rather than the bellicose cross-examiner.' The president had a tendency 'to show concurrence or the reverse' on each of the issues on their agenda. This suited Attlee's business-like style, but it also allowed him to guide the negotiations so as to box the president into agreement. Framing his statements in such a way as to get a nod of assent from Truman, Attlee 'soon led the President well onto the flypaper'. Acheson stepped on Truman's foot under the table at their second meeting to alert him to the trick, and urge him to take more caution.

The fear that Western Europe would be left exposed by a new Asian war was certainly a major consideration for the British negotiators. Yet Attlee did think more broadly about the balance of power in the world as a whole, rather than focusing on Europe alone. One of his major themes was the need for the Western Alliance to maintain the good favour of other major powers in Asia. Chief among them was newly independent India, which had relations with the Chinese Communists, and were also treated with suspicion by the US. Pushing back against the British, Acheson made the point that it would look odd to take a tough line against the Communist advance in Europe – with the vast investment in NATO and the Marshall Plan – while turning a blind eye to it in Asia. On this issue, the president would not budge. Although he already had some concerns about MacArthur's command, he sidestepped Attlee's criticisms of MacArthur and stated that America would stay in Korea and fight. It preferred to have the support of its allies but 'if not, we would stay on anyway'.

Truman had remained firm on the fundamentals. As Dean Acheson recorded, however, Attlee had one more trick up his sleeve. While a joint communiqué was drawn up by officials, the two leaders retired to the Oval Office for an informal chat. They came out smiling and the president said cheerfully that they had been discussing the atom bomb, and 'agreed that neither of us would use these weapons without prior consultation with the other'. Acheson winced at the fact that the president seemed to have fallen into another agreement 'in principle'. Once again, Acheson intervened, warning that this could not be a formal commitment between the two nations without congressional approval. Attlee acknowledged this 'a little sadly'.[66] In the end it was decided that the joint communiqué would read that it was 'the president's desire to keep the prime minister at all times informed of developments which might bring a change in the situation.' In Attlee's view, this proved that they were 'partners, unequal no doubt in power, but still equal in counsel'. In fact, even this was a somewhat over-optimistic assessment. The prime minister had won his point on the appointment of a supreme commander to NATO, expressed his concerns about MacArthur, and had got reassurances from Truman that he would continue to consult him. In return, however, he had promised that Britain would remain firmly committed to the Korean campaign. This would require another push on rearmament.[67]

To fail to back the Americans in this instance would have been almost fatal to the UN, and would have risked a rupture over the defence of Europe at a critical moment. The prime minister believed it to be the right course. Yet the costs of the Korean War were to bedevil the rest of Attlee's time in office. On his return to England – via meetings at the UN in New York, and a visit to Ottawa – he broadcast to the nation, telling them that he had committed Britain to fight alongside the US in order to preserve the authority of the United Nations. The atom bomb, he reassured them, was not in the hands of men who would use it 'lightly or wantonly'. This gave him cover for the fact that he now rowed in strongly behind the US. 'You may be certain that in fair and foul weather, where the stars and stripes fly in Korea the British flag will fly beside them. We will stand by our duty.'[68]

V

Harold Macmillan had raised doubts about Attlee's leadership at the start of the Korean crisis. But as the prime minister announced that new cuts in domestic spending would have to be instituted to pay for an extended defence programme in January 1951, Macmillan reflected that the Labour leader had shown 'real political courage'.[69] More austerity and wage freezes were not a good way to begin a year in which another general election was expected. Thus, as the Conservative MP Cuthbert Headlam recorded in his diary, the prime minister opened 1951 with yet another appeal for miners and steel workers to work just a little bit harder, while the 'unhappy housewives' were 'beseeched to use less coal, less electricity, and less gas'.[70] The latter were by now in open revolt, mobilising themselves into organisations such as the British Housewives' League which were given much publicity by the conservative press.[71]

The idealised British citizen of Attlee's mind was also, if the truth be told, a consumer. On a visit to London that month, the Irish-American satirist Leonard Wibberley, who had been raised in the city, produced an assessment of Attlee's England for the *Los Angeles Times* by examining advertisements. Wibberley – author of the 1955 novel *The Mouse that Roared*, which satirised the cold war's nuclear arms race – observed that the few comforts of life were priced so high that only the richest capitalists and most successful black-market spivs could possibly obtain them. Cigarettes, even the cheap Three Castles brand, were three times the price they were in the US. The Jamaican cigars on sale were even more expensive than the much superior Cubans sold in America. Barely anyone in the country had a refrigerator and even if they did, there was no food to put in it. Wibberley picked up an excellent canary-yellow waistcoat for $11.20, which he wore as a protest against the puritans and 'hair-shirt brigade' now in charge of the country. As for the new National Health Service, he joked that it seemed to be making the country sicker. In the Britain he remembered as a child, it had been regarded as unpatriotic to admit infirmity.[72]

With steel nationalisation due to come into effect on 15 February 1951, Churchill saw an opportunity to stick a finger in an open wound in the government's side. This he did by goading Herbert Morrison, who was well known to be sceptical about the plans for the steel industry. By this stage, Morrison had made some revisions to the 1949 Iron and Steel Act – it having been twice rejected by the House of Lords – and was happier with the revised model for the nationalisation. A government-owned Iron and Steel Corporation would become the principal shareholder of eighty of the main iron and steel companies (a reduction of the number proposed in the original bill), rather than the outright owner of all their undertakings. When Churchill raised the prospect that the Conservatives might bring yet another vote of censure against the government, Morrison replied that the government would refuse to debate it. Churchill was swiftly on his feet again, scolding the socialists for their flouting of parliamentary conventions.[73] The government fought off a last-ditch Conservative effort to postpone the implementation of the 1949 Act in a ten-vote victory on 7 February. Churchill was heard to chunter, on his way out of the Commons chamber, that 'It looks as though these bastards can stay in as long as they like.'[74]

Once again, the walking wounded on the Labour benches had been brought into the division lobby to keep the government's majority alive. This was unsustainable, particularly as the government's most important ministers were falling by the wayside. Both Attlee and Morrison had spent considerable time in hospital over the previous two years. Dalton was pumping himself full of medication for various ailments, and Cripps had resigned in October 1950 due to his stomach cancer. The beginning of the end of the government came in March 1951 when it became clear that Ernest Bevin, Attlee's most important ally, was no longer fit enough to stay in the Foreign Office. While his mind was as sharp as ever, his heart and his lungs were no longer robust enough for the physical exertion required as foreign secretary. The heavy drinking – including a couple of pints of beer most lunchtimes – did not help. For a number of years, he had fallen asleep in the middle of meetings. On Korea, with Bevin in hospital, the prime minister had been forced to take over almost all his duties. With no sign of improvement, and with his attention required elsewhere, Attlee came to the conclusion that he had to be replaced.

The decision was made all the more painful for Attlee by the fact that his friend was deeply hurt by the imputation that he was no longer fit for the job. Nor was he placated by the offer that Attlee made at his bedside, which was to retain a position in Cabinet as Lord Privy Seal.[75] 'I am neither a lord, nor a privy, nor a seal,' he said, 'I was born into a poor little home, and went to a poor little school, and look what I have done in the world. There must be some purpose in it. And now they want to throw me on the scrap-heap.'[76]

Aside from his sadness about this encounter, Attlee was left with the immediate problem of finding a replacement. Once it became clear that the prime minister would not be moved, Bevin recommended one of his protégés, National Insurance minister James Griffiths, for the position. Yet Attlee was concerned that Griffiths did not have a sufficiently forceful personality to fill the vacuum. This left him short on alternatives. Though he was one of the few heavy hitters left in government, Dalton had a poor relationship with the Foreign Office. Dalton's own view was that the prime minister should continue to act as foreign secretary, as he had been doing for the previous four months. But Attlee believed that this was impossible given his workload.[77] The only other member of Labour's 'big five' remaining was Herbert Morrison. Morrison had expressed an interest in the position previously, and he had the personality and the gravitas to be his own man. 'It boils down to the fact you are the inevitable choice,' Attlee told him.[78] This was neither a roaring endorsement, nor – it was to be become clear – a good choice.

As the old Labour Party was reduced to a core of three (Attlee, Morrison and Dalton), the 'new generation' began to square up against each other for control of the party. Without Bevin by his side, and with his own health difficulties – manageable but fatiguing problems with his prostate and his stomach – controlling the party became more difficult for Attlee in the early stages of what was later to become a civil war in the party. Battle commenced over the budget of April 1951.

At the end of March, Cripps's replacement as chancellor, Hugh Gaitskell, wrote to Attlee about the need to cap the ever-rising spending on the NHS. The only way to do this, Gaitskell argued, was to introduce charges for dental work and optical services, as well as prescriptions.[79] Nye Bevan, who was not well disposed to Gaitskell in any case, would not react well to this. When moving the National Health Service Bill four years earlier, Bevan had placed great emphasis on the importance of these services. Indeed, he had said that the collective state of the British people's teeth was a national embarrassment.[80] By instituting charges in this way, he objected that Gaitskell was perverting the very spirit of a health service that was supposed to be free at the point of use and delivery.

There was no greater symbol of the fatigue of the government – and the passing of the baton from one generation to another – than that the prime minister himself now fell ill at the crucial moment. In the first week of April, he was forced to have another operation on a stomach ulcer. He was recuperating in his hospital bed at St Mary's in Twickenham when the issue came before Cabinet on 9 April. Gaitskell put forward his proposal for a new National Health Service Bill to allow for these charges, as a prelude to his budget. There had been agreement that Health Service expenditure would be subject to an upper limit of £400 million. With a scheduled overspend of £23 million, £10 million was to be saved in hospital administration and £13 million would come from the new charges on treatment of teeth and eyesight and prescriptions. Bevan, who was now Minister of Labour and National Service, stated his objection on the grounds of principle – refusing to abandon the concept of a free Health Service. This was an issue on which he was prepared to resign. Neither man would budge. At the end of the meeting, Morrison – deputising for the prime minister – agreed to relay the discussion to Attlee.[81]

That afternoon, Morrison sat beside Attlee's hospital bed in Twickenham and told him about Bevan's threat to resign. He took instructions from Attlee and returned to Downing Street as Cabinet reconvened that evening. This time the argument was more heated. Bevan once again refused to agree to a 'breach of Socialist principles', for the sake of £13 million. Morrison informed the Cabinet that the prime minister wanted his ministers to seek a compromise but that, if none was forthcoming, the chancellor must have the final say. Attlee had also pointed out that it was most unusual for a minister to resign on a budget issue and it would have a negative effect on the party as a whole. If the government fell now, causing an election, it would be deprived of the potential benefits of good weather in the summer, or an improvement in the international situation. Indeed, if the Conservatives got back into power, then Bevan would have no influence at all. Bevan commented that 'he was not surprised to hear that the Prime Minister took this view'. Yet he was starting to entertain the view that he could bring more influence to bear on government policy from outside the Cabinet than he could ever hope to exercise within it.[82] It seemed likely he would leave the government within a matter of days, though, with the prime minister in hospital, he would delay a final decision on his resignation.

In the midst of this wrangling, the prime minister was dealt a severe personal blow. On 14 April, when still in St Mary's, he learned that Ernie Bevin had passed away. Attlee paid a tribute to his closest friend in politics with a heartfelt note, written from his own hospital bed. Bevin was 'first and foremost a great Englishmen, forthright and courageous; an idealist, but an eminently practical one. He understood the people of this country which he loved, and I believe he interpreted the British idea with great fidelity.'[83] Bevin's death was something that continued to haunt Attlee, particularly as the former had felt betrayed at their last meeting. For many years later, when Attlee spoke of Bevin, his voice would soften and show signs of emotion.[84] In his letter to Flo, Ernie's wife, Attlee explained that one reason he had asked him to resign was so that his health could recover. His sadness shone through as he wrote of his 'wonderful friend, so loyal and courageous'.[85]

Now that he was in his hospital, Attlee's foremost skills – the management of Cabinet and the maintenance of party unity – deserted him. When Dalton arrived to see Attlee in hospital on 20 April, he saw Morrison, Gaitskell and Chuter Ede huddled around his bed, discussing Bevin's death and Bevan's likely resignation. On the way out of the door, Morrison remarked to Dalton that 'We must all keep a stiff upper lip now.' As Dalton sat down beside Attlee, the prime minister told him that he had sent Bevan, whom he now called a 'green-eyed monster', an ultimatum to agree to the budget or resign. He fully expected him to go. Attlee also confided in Dalton that – somewhat ironically, with Bevan ready to leave government over dentistry charges – he was now having problems with his teeth, and would have to stay in hospital to have part of his gum cut away.[86]

As expected, on 22 April, Bevan announced his resignation. He was soon followed by Harold Wilson, the minister at the Board of Trade. Wilson expressed his regret at giving this news to Attlee as he tried to recover his health.[87] Attlee was irritated by Wilson's letter and what he regarded as an 'inadequate' explanation for his resignation. Moreover, the prime minister made sure that Wilson knew that he was fully recovered and would be back in Number 10 within days.[88] He was sounding like a cantankerous old man. From the hospital in Twickenham he called up Alfred Robens, parliamentary secretary at the Ministry of Fuel, in his 'little barking voice' to offer him a promotion to fill the gap left by Bevan. 'Robens? Is that Robens? This is Attlee.' Would the Ministry of Labour suit him? As soon as Robens answered in the affirmative, the prime minister slammed down the phone without uttering another word.[89]

Back in his constituency in Ebbw Vale, Bevan was treated like a returning hero by the local Labour Party. They greeted him with a rendition of 'Guide Me, O Thou Great Jehovah'. Emboldened, he went on the attack against his critics. Francis Williams had suggested that the threat to resign had been 'the most persistent theme' in Bevan's ministerial career. Bevan blamed Attlee for this slur and accused him of bad faith in leaking private Cabinet discussions to press officers.[90] While he had not raised the issue in Cabinet, Bevan now began to criticise Attlee for the huge military spending commitments he had made in his meeting with Truman. Attlee dismissed this as opportunistic. 'I note that you have extended the area of disagreement with your colleagues a long way beyond the specific matter to which, as I understand, you have taken objection.'[91] That said, Attlee did complain, in later years, that the Americans had pushed too hard on this after the Washington summit of November 1950.[92]

Bevan did not have sufficient support for a leadership challenge at this stage. In Parliament, in fact, his resignation speech was a flop and he was met with stony stares from his fellow Labour MPs.[93] 'The Bevan business is a nuisance,' Attlee confessed to Tom at the end of April, 'The real miracle is that we kept him straight for so long.' He had hoped to rest over Easter at Chequers but it took all his energy to deal with the fallout within the party. Contrary to his claims that he was back to full fitness, he confessed to Tom that his stomach continued to trouble him.⁹⁴

Churchill was impressed enough to call the prime minister a 'lion-hearted limpet', stubbornly holding on to the rocks as the waves crashed around him. With a disgruntled phalanx of Bevanites, the government had effectively lost its majority. Attlee offered a mild sop to Bevan by insisting that the NHS cuts in the budget were only for a two-year term, and could be revisited later. For the moment, then, the government survived. But, as the Labour peer Lord Winster described, this was a 'patch-up job'. The Cabinet was sullen and increasingly sceptical about the war in Korea, which dragged on. There were other ominous problems on the horizon, particularly in the Middle East. Egypt's nationalist government rejected new British proposals for control of the Suez Canal; and there were growing concerns in Persia, where the Iranian government had nationalised the Anglo-Iranian oil company (raising fears of another 'Russian-inspired Korea'). It was a 'heavy load for Attlee to carry' without Bevin.⁹⁵

A few days later, officials at the US Embassy produced a lengthy assessment of a government that seemed to be nearing its end. Ironically, following the loss of Cripps (whose cancer was terminal), Bevin and Bevan, Attlee's personal authority had never been greater. Potential successors, such as Gaitskell, did not have sufficient support to run for the leadership. Despite the furore caused by Bevan's resignation, there were some small grains of hope for the government in the event of an election. Consumption was increasing and the party's standing in the polls had stabilised. Overall, the government had achieved much that it had promised in 1945, even if the 'utopia' had not been reached. On the one hand, it had found that many of the problems it faced – such as the unpredictability of global markets – were not susceptible to socialist solutions. On the other hand, it was fair to say that it had also been encumbered by huge challenges that no one could have foreseen, and perhaps no government could have handled better.⁹⁶

With Bevin gone, and Bevan having broken rank, the party was lacking in heroes. Increasingly, and somewhat to his bemusement, Attlee himself filled that void. When he addressed the Durham Miners' Gala in July 1951, an estimated 30,000 people turned out for the occasion. As he watched the parade, the prime minister was typically surprised to see two new banners unveiled with his own face on them.[97] It still bemused him that anyone would see him as a hero.

Everyone waited for the next move. In August, Gaitskell guessed that Attlee would call an election soon, 'partly because he is tired, and partly because the risks of hanging on are so great . . . and partly because he wants to get away from the conflict with the Bevanites'.[98] By late summer, foreign affairs presented a succession of crises that demonstrated the extent to which the government was treading water. After years of seeking the highest office, Morrison was showing his limitations. For all his immense capabilities elsewhere in government, he showed no aptitude for diplomacy. The sense of lost control was captured by an unintentionally revealing comment in his memoirs: 'One never knows what will turn up at the Foreign Office. Other countries often shape the agenda.'[99] This was particularly true in the Middle East where, as Britain's authority drained away, others vied to fill the vacuum.

The essence of British strategy in the Middle East from 1945 to 1951 had been to encourage the 'conciliation of moderate nationalists' and 'to preserve British power' by preventing local influence passing to 'anti-British extremists'.[100] In Egypt, Palestine and Persia, this approach began to unravel with alarming speed in the summer of 1951. The assassination of King Abdullah of Jordan in Jerusalem by a member of the Palestinian Husseini clan prompted the equally helpless statement by Attlee – as revealing as Morrison's in his memoir – that there was 'a good deal too much political murder about just now and generally the wrong victims'. Attlee had lunched with Abdullah at Chequers and found him very intelligent, 'a real statesman', and felt he would be a loss to the Middle East.[101]

Now a new generation of nationalist leaders was emerging, embodied by Mohammad Mossadeq, the prime minister of the new Persian government, whose National Party won power in the April 1951 general election. True to his promise, Mossadeq nationalised the British-engineered oil wells at Abadan without any consultation or discussion of compensation, seizing the assets of the Anglo-Iranian Oil Company. Aside from the further diminution of British standing, this had the potential to do more serious strategic damage. Iranian oil accounted for 31 per cent of Europe's oil imports and 85 per cent of the fuel used by the Royal Navy.

At Cabinet in September, Morrison urged the prime minister and his fellow ministers to take a tough line against Mossadeq and to consider a military intervention. To the surprise of his colleagues, he spoke, in almost Churchillian terms, against a policy of 'scuttle and surrender' in the Middle East.[102] Morrison presented two alternative plans: one called 'Buccaneer' (an armed intervention to take back the oil wells); and the other called 'Midget' (which would evacuate the 4,500 British technicians working there). Attlee was prepared to concede that the loss of Abadan Island would be 'humiliating' but he vetoed any intervention. Existing commitments in Korea meant that Britain was already stretched.[103] The prime minister suspected that the task of running the oil industry – refining it and transporting it – would make Mossadeq more willing to come to terms. But there was a deeper reason behind his unwillingness to intervene. The Americans had cautioned against a military intervention, partly on the grounds that this would appear like a naked instance of British imperialism. Attlee told the Cabinet that Britain could 'not afford to break with the United States on an issue of this kind'.[104]

Effectively, Morrison was sidelined from this point. Dalton complained that the foreign minister was acting like a latter-day Lord Palmerston, and suspected he was overcompensating for the fact he had been a conscientious objector in the First World War.[105] By September, the prime minister was complaining that Morrison's ignorance on foreign affairs was shocking. He had pressed for the job but it was clear he was not up to it, reading from a sheet of paper in Cabinet meetings. 'I am handling Persia,' Attlee told Dalton, making it quite clear that British troops would only be sent in order to rescue citizens if they came under threat.[106] He later called the appointment of Morrison as foreign minister his 'biggest mistake'.[107]

Was Attlee right to veto military intervention? Churchill and Eden discovered the details of these discussions when they returned to government and Churchill confided to Dean Acheson and General Omar Bradley that he was horrified that Attlee had allowed Britain to be 'kicked out of Abadan in a most humiliating way'.[108] In fact, nothing happened subsequently to make Attlee doubt his decision. He understood the desire to teach Mossadeq a lesson. He also thought military action would have been popular with the public in an election year. There was 'still a kind of combativeness in the people' and lots of people thought: 'let's give these people a knock.' But having leaned on the Americans to play by UN rules over Korea – and criticised the Russians for flouting them – the prime minister felt that it was hypocritical for Britain to take unilateral action when its own interests were threatened. As he put it, 'you couldn't do that if you were a faithful member of the United Nations.'[109] After all, it was precisely such renegade acts that he believed had caused the failure of the League of Nations.

More importantly, if Mossadeq was forced out, who would take his place? As he told Cabinet, Mossadeq had been 'able to form his Government owing to the support of Persians who were dissatisfied with former rule by a corrupt clique. We could not safely assume that if we succeeded in upsetting the present Government their successors would be less unsatisfactory, and we should risk identifying ourselves with support of an equally undemocratic regime.'[110] When Mossadeq was eventually forced out in a coup engineered by the British and Americans two years later, this was exactly what happened. One might say that he was blessed with a considerable degree of foresight when it came to Iran. Reading an account of the Cabinet discussions in later years, the historian A. J. P. Taylor commented that 'Clem as usual is the only one who comes out with his reputation enhanced – the best leader Labour ever had.'[111]

The problem, however, was that Mossadeq had set a precedent which others would soon follow. Sure enough, on 15 October, ten days before the general election, Morrison had another unwelcome surprise at a Labour campaign meeting in South Lewisham. A reporter handed him a slip of paper that revealed that Egypt's nationalist government had decided to abrogate the treaties that guaranteed British access to the Suez Canal. Morrison rushed back to Downing Street and summoned his officials from the Foreign Office. This time, in urging a 'stiff line' with Egypt, he was supported by the prime minister. The difficulty was that the government was in no position to take any military action with an election due to take place in just over a week. As British authority in the Middle East was given another dent, thus began the series of events that culminated in the Suez Crisis of 1956.[112] That said, the path from 1951 to 1956 was by no means set in stone, and Anthony Eden and his Conservative government were to make major miscalculations themselves along the way.

Watching the government from the Conservative benches in the autumn of 1951, Eden reflected that the strenuous efforts made by Labour ministers during the war years had finally taken their toll. The government was 'but a shadow of its former self' and its 'message was exhausted'.[113] In September, Attlee admitted to Tom that he was suffering from severe backache, on top of his other ailments.[114] Much of his cheeriness had deserted him. He was still sulking at Bevan and refused to be the one to initiate a reconciliation. As he told Dalton, 'he walked out on me; it's up to him to come and see me if he wants to.'[115]

This exhaustion partly explains the decision to hold an election in October 1951. The date of the last election had been the source of extensive discussion among the Cabinet and the Labour Party hierarchy. It was a reflection of Attlee's diminished faith in his colleagues that he spent much less time consulting them this time. One consideration in pushing ahead with an election in the autumn of 1951 was that he did not want to disrupt the arrangements for the king's tour of Africa in February 1952.[116] But Morrison, who for all his failings as a foreign secretary, was the party's best strategist, was not even consulted. In San Francisco for an international conference on Japan, he was furious when news reached him that a date had been set. He suspected that Hugh Gaitskell, who favoured an early poll, had exerted his influence in Morrison's absence. Yet, as much as anything, Morrison suspected Attlee was just tired after years of government.[117] The lion-hearted limpet was struggling to summon the will to cling on.

21

The Pilgrim's Progress

Who would true valour see,
Let him come hither;
One here will constant be,
Come wind, come weather
There's no discouragement
Shall make him once relent
His first avowed intent
To be a pilgrim.

Whoso beset him round
With dismal stories
Do but themselves confound;
His strength the more is.
No lion can him fright,
He'll with a giant fight,
But he will have a right
To be a pilgrim.

Hobgoblin nor foul fiend
Can daunt his spirit,
He knows he at the end
Shall life inherit.
Then fancies fly away,
He'll fear not what men say,

> He'll labour night and day
> To be a pilgrim.

> John Bunyan, 'To Be a Pilgrim', from *The Pilgrim's*
> *Progress from This World to That Which Is to Come*, 1678[1]

Scarborough, October 1951

'Let us,' said Herbert Morrison, looking over a huge display of red-and-yellow chrysanthemums at the Labour Party conference in Scarborough on 6 October 1951, 'let us not do things that play into Tory hands.' These were hopeful words. A Bevanite insurgency in the party was in full swing. The rebels topped the poll of constituency organisations for elections to the National Executive Committee. For the sake of the election, to take place in just over a week, there was one last stage-managed show of unity.

Attlee, 'in the star role now allotted to him', turned up with a red carnation on his lapel of such giant proportions that it was difficult to see him through the foliage. He entered through a side door with his family and took his place on the stage. Morrison sat to his right on a packed platform, chomping on his pipe, as Attlee rose to make his election speech:

> The crucial question of this election, on which every elector must make up his or her mind, is this, what kind of Society you want. We want a Society of free men and women, free from poverty, free from fear, able to develop in full their faculties in co-operation with their fellows, everyone giving and having the opportunity to give service to the community, everyone regarding his own private interest in the light of the interest of others, and of the community; a society bound together by rights and obligations, rights bringing obligations, obligations fulfilled bringing rights; a society free from gross inequalities and yet not regimented nor uniform ... Our opponents, on the other hand, regard the economic process primarily as giving an opportunity to the individual to advance his own interests; community interests, national interests, are regarded as a hypothetical by-product. Their motto is: 'The world is my oyster; each one for himself.' The result of that policy can be seen by all. There was the army of the poor; there were the slums; there was beautiful Britain defiled

for gain; there were derelict areas. The fruits of our policy can be seen in the new fine generation that is growing up, in the new houses – because we have done a great work in housing. You hear only of the people who are not satisfied. The people who are snug in a Council house do not write to you about it. The fact is that a very remarkable job has been done under great difficulties. You see our new towns, you see our smiling countryside. I am proud of our achievement.

Before the Labour leader sat back down, he finished with a flourish. 'Let's go forward in the spirit of William Blake,' he said, 'I will not cease from mental strife, nor shall the sword sleep in my hand, Till we have built Jerusalem, in England's green and pleasant land.'[2]

This was to be the last major speech made by Attlee as prime minister. It went back to very first principles. It was the clearest expostition of a belief system that had begun to take shape almost half a century before. Yet, it already seemed to belong to a past era.

As it ended, television cameras panned to stony-faced Bevanites in the crowd. Despite the pageantry, there was a feeling in the party establishment that the old guard were losing their grip. 'We cannot fight the Bevan glamour boys with old age,' one delegate confessed. Some of the older trade union stalwarts still gave a good account of themselves on the conference dance floor, reported the mischievous political correspondent of the *Observer*. Yet underlying all this was a timeworn story: of sons rebelling against fathers, of the young trying to knock the old off their perches. While the brass band played in the concert hall, one could almost hear another sound under the din of the trumpets and trombones, more commonly heard in the Scottish Highlands: the grunting and butting of young stags in the mating season, attempting to establish their primacy over rivals.[3] There was one poignant moment that reflected well on the old guard. A great-grandmother from Poplar, who had been in the Labour movement for forty-eight years, stood up in front of the conference hall and told how dear old Clem had come knocking on her door to canvas in 1907. Even Bevan was genuinely moved. The two men shared, as much as any others in their party, a sense of the moral purpose that was embroidered into the Labour movement.[4]

Away from the conference, the Conservatives had a narrow lead in the polls. Churchill looked revitalised, with the cigars out, the limousine serviced, and town halls booked up and down the country for what would most likely be his last election campaign.[5] At the age of sixty-eight, Attlee campaigned as vigorously as ever. Violet beat previous records for driving. In their new Humber, which replaced the Hillman, she covered 400 miles in one day, from Manchester to Cornwall, via Chequers. This time the cabinet secretary, Sir David Hunt, travelled in the Attlee car, so that Attlee could keep up to date with events in Iran and Egypt. Hunt would call the Foreign Office from the hotel lobby wherever they stopped. As in the previous campaigns, the prime minister was well received wherever he went. 'We have had a remarkable time,' he wrote to Tom, at the end of the campaign. There were large crowds and great enthusiasm on the roads, 'but what it will mean in votes I can't tell.' The result of the election was 'anybody's guess', said Attlee at the end of polling, 'depending largely on which way the Liberal cat jumps'.[6] The fact that there had been 478 Liberal candidates at the previous election was one reason that the government's majority had diminished. With the Liberals putting up far fewer candidates this time round, it left open a significant number of potential swing voters.

While defeat followed, it cannot be said that the British public rejected their government. In an odd way, the result was both a tribute to the Labour Party's great achievements over the previous six years, but also a recognition of its utter exhaustion. In fact, Labour received the largest number of votes of any British political party in history to that point, surpassing even the 13 million won in 1950 by nearly 200,000. However, its successes were not as widespread as they had been in 1945, or even 1950. Despite securing a larger share of the vote, the idiosyncratic nature of the British electoral system meant that the party only won 295 seats. With 321 seats, the Conservatives attained a workable majority. The Liberal cat had jumped right. Suburban swing-seats in the southeast – in places like Barsetshire – returned Conservatives, having been enthusiastically behind Labour in 1945, but increasingly dubious by 1950.

Attlee relinquished office on 26 October, the day the results were announced, driving to Buckingham Palace to offer his resignation to the king. A week later, Attlee's brother Tom wrote to their sister, Mig, saying that the family should not feel too disheartened by the result. Had there been a huge landslide to the Conservatives, it would have shown that the government's achievements had been entirely rejected. In fact, Labour's strong share of the popular voted showed just how many people in the country admired the principles that their brother had expounded. A new political consensus had emerged around health and welfare, and even the 'mixed economy', in which some industries were nationalised and others remained in private hands. Tom still feared that some attempts might be made to undo some of the work (on iron and steel nationalisation for example, or controls on consumption). 'Don't you think that after a revolution of such as has been worked for the last six and a half years there is bound to be a reaction? The benefits of the revolution are taken for granted but the imperfection of the working out of its implications is taken to heart.' Nonetheless, their brother's governments had moved the centre of gravity in British politics for ever. 'As far as Clem is concerned his work is safe – a bit of the backbone of history.'[7]

Of course, Attlee was sure to insist that the job was not yet complete. Thus, just a few weeks before he went out of government, he invoked William Blake's Jerusalem the way he had thirty years before when he had set out on a career in national politics. While they had built the foundations of Jerusalem, there was much more to be done. In the latter years of his government, he had been criticised by the left for slowing the pace of new legislation, for consolidating rather than insisting on socialist 'advance' at every step. Three years before, when the Labour Party had last held its conference at Scarborough, those who were impatient with his leadership had criticised his speech for offering vague 'moral homilies' rather than announcing new legislation. Yet others had judged progress in terms of legislation, or battles at Westminster. By contrast, Attlee warned that there was a danger that the original ethos that had driven the early foot soldiers of the Labour movement would be lost. 'We need today as much as in our pioneer days the idealism, the longing for a just social order, which aroused our enthusiasm and commanded our devotion in the days of adversity, and it is no less idealism for being married to knowledge.'[8]

In 1906, the year that Attlee moved to Limehouse, John Bunyan's famous hymn 'To Be a Pilgrim' – written as part of his epic allegory, *The Pilgrim's Progress*, during a twelve-year prison sentence for refusing to conform to the established church – was adapted to music to become a rousing hymn, which spoke of a long struggle to make progress towards the promised land. Though the hymn was sung at Churchill's eightieth birthday celebrations in 1954, it had already become something of a Labour anthem, recited at Ellen Wilkinson's memorial service in 1946. Attlee chose it, along with 'And did those feet in ancient time', for his own funeral service.[9]

Bunyan's *Pilgrim's Progress* was divided into two parts. The first told the story of a man called Christian as he travelled from the 'City of Destruction' to the 'Celestial City', overcoming many obstacles on the way. The second part told how Christian's wife and children attempted to follow in his footsteps, but came across many different challenges. Bunyan's language also inspired William Beveridge as he wrote his famous Report on Social Insurance. Just as Christian defeated the Giants Despair and Diffidence, so Beveridge had declared war on the five 'Giant Evils' of 'Want, Disease, Ignorance, Squalor and Idleness'.[10] Attlee's government had fought that battle more fiercely than any before it, in the spirit of Bunyan.

The journey taken by the first generation of Labour's pilgrims came to an end in October 1951. As it did, they took a moment to reflect on the distance that they had come. With less pressure on his time, Attlee turned his hand to a series of essays in which he discussed the stalwarts of the old Labour movement in the East End.[11] He began with a piece on George Lansbury in the *Observer* in December 1951.[12] It was only when looking back that one can get a sense of just how remarkable that journey had been.

Ellen Wilkinson once said that Attlee would have been equally determined if his own pilgrimage had never left the narrow streets of Stepney. Like Bunyan would not have flinched if that same road had led to jail or the scaffold.[13] That it had taken him to Downing Street did not mean that he had ever left this world behind. Visiting Limehouse for the opening of a recreation hut for the Haileybury Club in early 1952, the former prime minister was struck by the enormous physical improvement of the Stepney boys in the fifty years since he and his brother had first volunteered there.[14] Such changes, rather than set-piece battles at Westminster, were the means by which the success of the Labour movement was best judged.

II

After leaving Downing Street, Clem and Violet moved to the home they had been preparing for retirement: Cherry Cottage in Great Missenden, Buckinghamshire. On Saturday 27 October, they went first to Chequers, where they cleared out their last few possessions. They were met there by Hugh

Dalton, who travelled with them on the short seven-mile journey to Cherry Cottage. In 1938, Dalton had visited the Attlee's 'little Victorian villa' at Stanmore. On this occasion, he could not resist the observation that Cherry Cottage looked 'rather like a pensioner's cottage'. A few rather ugly trees blocked the light down the path that led to the house. It was an hour-long train journey into London. Violet was to live at the house and Clem was to commute, sleeping in London at a club when there was a late vote in Parliament. However, Violet now urged him to resign from the leadership.

With fewer of Labour's big beasts in front-line politics, those who were still involved were forced into close quarters with each other. In this they found some solace. Dalton had complained about Attlee many times over the years, and plotted to oust him as leader on three occasions. With the loss of Cripps and Bevin, and his own alienation from Morrison and Bevan, he had begun to write more fondly of Attlee in his diary. The 'rabbit' or the 'little man' was now referred to as 'Clem'. On his visit to Cherry Cottage, Dalton reflected on the role that they had both played in the Labour movement over the past decades, and how they had helped rebuild the party after MacDonald's betrayal in 1931. 'We've done all that now; written the first chapter of the Socialist story, in law and administration. What next?' he asked. In fact, Dalton now begged Attlee to stay on as leader. As yet, no clear winner had emerged among the new generation of stags seen locking their antlers at the party conference. Hugh Gaitskell was Dalton's preferred successor. However, he was not yet strong enough to be guaranteed to fend off Morrison, who seemed the favourite, or Bevan, whose support among the constituency organisations had soared. As Dalton returned to London that evening, he wrote that 'if Clem dies soon, or if Vi persuades him to retire, there'll be a problem.'[15] For the moment, Attlee agreed to stay on – partly, it must be said, because he did not want to see Morrison lead the party.

Defeat, at least, allowed more time for reading. As he told Tom, Attlee picked up Arthur Bryant's light-hearted *Historian's Holiday*.[16] Bryant's popular narrative histories were full of sentimental patriotism. He was, as Attlee was quite aware, an 'old Tory'. Attlee was pleased to learn, then, that Bryant had a genuine fondness for Labour's leader.[17] His own affection for British institutions, particularly the monarchy, had grown during his time in office. This was demonstrated once again after the death of the king in February 1952, by which he was greatly saddened. Now the leader of the opposition, he had gone with Churchill to see the queen to offer condolences. On hearing the news, he walked into a Labour Party meeting, 'looking as though he had had a stroke'. 'The King is dead; he was always very nice to me,' he remarked sadly. Richard Crossman, a voice of growing importance on the left of the party, commented that 'no one I have met genuinely feels anything about this, except for Clem Attlee.'[18] Indeed, when Attlee made his parliamentary tribute to the late king it was, he admitted himself, one of the few times that he had showed emotion in public.[19]

Now that he was free from the crushing pressures of office, Attlee began to enjoy parliamentary life again. An attaché at the American Embassy reported in March that he seemed to be relishing his return as leader of the opposition. After an initial hiatus following the election, Labour went on the attack in the spring of 1953. Their first target was the cuts in education spending announced by Rab Butler, and the second was Churchill's approach to the Far East, where the Korean War continued. These parliamentary assaults were 'shrewdly planned and conducted'. There was no challenge to Attlee's leadership from within the party either. Morrison's influence had waned considerably, particularly as Attlee was now dominating the foreign affairs brief once again; meanwhile, Gaitskell and Bevan continued to build up their support but both were content to shadow box at this stage.[20]

As yet, there was no attempt at a reconciliation with Bevan. At a meeting of the parliamentary party in January 1952 – at which Bevan made a speech about the need to take the fight to the government – Attlee and Morrison had simply left the room. Afterwards, in the Smoking Room, Attlee, who was drinking at the next table, did not acknowledge Bevan's presence. 'Not that this means very much with the little man who is shy to the point of incivility,' commented Richard Crossman.[21]

In these circumstances, it would be a challenge to maintain party unity. The Churchill government had inherited its predecessor's commitment to rearmament as part of its efforts in the Korean War. Attlee wanted to keep his MPs behind him in continuing to support that. This was partly because he did not want Labour to fall back into the position it had occupied in the 1930s, when it had voted against the government's defence estimates as a matter of habit. In order to keep the party with him, therefore, some positioning was required. Thus, he blasted Churchill – recently back from a visit to Washington, DC – for giving succour to 'dangerous elements' in American politics who wanted to extend the war in Korea into an offensive against China's Communist government. He was particularly disparaging about those who still clung on to support for the Chinese nationalist Leader, Chiang Kai-shek, whom he regarded as 'corrupt'.[22] In truth, however, there was no departure from the fundamental conviction that the Anglo-American relationship was key to British security – something underlined by an unofficial visit he made to the USA in Easter 1952, during which he was able to explore the country more widely.[23]

This was a difficult balancing act. Having blamed rearmament for leading to cuts to the NHS budget, Bevan and his followers refused to vote with the government on its defence estimates. Attlee won a three-to-one victory over Bevan at a meeting of the parliamentary party on the eve of a defence debate in March. In the subsequent debate, however, Churchill reacted to Attlee's suggestion that he was playing up to anti-China hysteria in the US with an unexpected counter-attack. Breaking parliamentary convention, he stretched the truth by claiming that Attlee had, in principle, agreed in his meeting with Truman in 1950 to support the Americans if they bombed Manchuria in the event of further Chinese incursions into Korea. The Bevanites exploded at this claim. 'There was pandemonium. I was sitting directly opposite Attlee,' wrote Harold Nicolson, 'He was sitting hunched up like an elf just out of its chrysalis, and stared at Winston, turning slowly white.'[24] Three days later, Attlee wrote an article in the *Daily Herald* in which he now tried to outflank Churchill on his other side, by claiming that the government was not doing enough to deliver on rearmament. 'The best way to peace in Europe,' Attlee wrote, was through strength. The Russians were not moved by moral considerations; but they did understand force.[25]

The debate rumbled on within the party. Before Parliament broke for summer recess, Bevan infuriated the leader by retrieving his February 1951 speech on rearmament. Certain 'precautionary words' had been inserted into Attlee's announcement at the time. He had made rearmament conditional on the availability of certain raw materials and machine tools, which would keep overall costs from spiralling out of control. Now that Churchill was ignoring these caveats, and costs were mounting rapidly, Bevan made the legalistic argument that those who had agreed to support the programme in the last government – after the issue had been debated in Cabinet – should be freed from that commitment. Attlee offered an icy rebuke of his former cabinet minister for disclosing Cabinet discussions. Bevan denied any impropriety and countered that Attlee had done the same to him, by leaking details of private discussions to Francis Williams, at the time of his resignation. Attlee, given the great stock he placed on propriety, was horrified by the implication.[26] Dalton believed that Bevan's 'shocking tactics' were 'rallying all moderates in loyalty behind Clem'.[27]

At the start of September – though he was now deprived of Bevin to marshal the unions – Attlee succeeded in getting the Trades Union Congress to support him on rearmament. Nonetheless, a showdown between Bevan and the leader was expected at the party conference in Morecambe at the end of the month. Lord Winster, the Labour peer and Attlee critic, contrasted the two personalities:

> Attlee's blood runs chilly, Bevan's is never far off the boil. Attlee has little genius for friendship. Bevan is warmhearted and feels and inspires affection. Attlee has little imagination; Bevan has too much. Attlee has no administrative achievement to his credit; Bevan put the remarkable and complicated Health Service Act on the statute book. Attlee evades argument by sticking to incontrovertible commonplaces; Bevin will dash into argument for the sake of using a clever phrase which has just occurred to him. Attlee never gets off the white line in the middle of the road.

Winster suggested that Attlee was suffering because he had not taken the precaution – as Churchill had done with Eden – of grooming a successor. Bevin's death had deprived him of a reliable lieutenant. Hugh Gaitskell was the most obvious candidate but he still suffered from a lack of popularity with the party base.[28]

Morecambe was not a 'happy experience', as Attlee admitted to Tom. The Bevanites won even more seats on the National Executive Committee, pushing themselves into a stronger position to set party policy. Moreover, the leader feared that there had been a 'considerable infiltration' of communists into the constituency organisations, tilting the party further to the left.[29] (This was becoming a reputational issue for the party, with Tory propagandists talking about a Trojan horse in the Labour movement and demanding that Attlee challenge it.[30]) Not for the first time, Attlee was grateful that Herbert Morrison took the fight to those on the left who sought to undermine the leadership. 'Morrison made a fine comeback,' he reported to Tom. 'He has been under the weather lately, but returned to form.' His speech also contained generosity, a quality that was 'generally rather lacking' in many of the insurgents on the left. Yet the fact was that the old guard were 'dropping out' in ever-greater numbers. Few of the new agitators on the left of the party had any knowledge of the early days, or the work that had gone into making Labour electable.[31]

To outside observers, Attlee's placidity in the face of Bevan's challenge at Morecambe was perplexing. One American observer sent to watch the proceedings joked that the Labour leader proved the rule that, in British politics, 'people never "run" for office; they simply "stand".'[32] Finally, as the new Parliament got under way, the leader's patience snapped. It was intolerable, he told a specially convened meeting of the parliamentary party, for a leader to have to put up with challenges to his authority on almost every issue.[33]

When Attlee was taken into hospital once again in March 1953, the liberal historian R. J. Cruikshank wrote a warm tribute to him in the *News Chronicle*, which read almost like a political obituary. Attlee retained great personal popularity in the country, but one feature of his career was that he had never really known how to capitalise on this when dealing with his party. It had been said of Lawrence of Arabia that he always managed to 'back very modestly into the limelight'. But there was nothing false about Attlee's modesty. Cruikshank described how, when there had been talk of a leadership challenge in 1948, a friendly crowd had gathered outside Downing Street to show him their support. Attlee had arrived from the House of Commons and observed the assembled cheerleaders with an expression of bemusement verging on alarm, before dashing into Number 10 like a man escaping his creditors. A few minutes later he had literally been forced out again by his officials to meet the crowd. Attlee had often been compared to the tortoise who ran the race against the hares. But, as Cruickshank pointed out, he was now a tortoise of considerable years, and showed unmistakable marks of ageing.[34]

III

After years of holidaying at Chequers – so that he could keep up with government work and be back in London in the event of a crisis – the former prime minister enjoyed the opportunity to travel more. In addition to yearly visits to the United States, much of this took place within the

Commonwealth that he had done more than anyone to bring into being. In the summer of 1952, he visited Rhodesia for a fortnight. He was very taken with the writing of Laurens van der Post, an early critic of the apartheid regime whom he described as 'a Boer with a great sense of mission to the negro people'.[35] On his return he reflected that the future relationship between black and white was a 'pretty difficult question', though he did not express any further thoughts on it.[36] He also visited Karachi over the Christmas holidays of 1952 for a Commonwealth conference where he warned against the dangers of extreme nationalism.[37]

Typical of many elder statesmen, it was international affairs that galvanised him most. Free from the constraints of office, he was more candid with his thoughts. His anti-communism and criticisms of Russian imperialism continued to win him credit with American diplomats in Europe.[38] However, he caused a minor controversy by criticising the role that the US Congress was playing in the making of American foreign policy, and suggested that the new president, Dwight Eisenhower, was 'not really master in his own house' because of this. This was seized upon by Republican Senator Joseph McCarthy, who was in the midst of his anti-communist crusade.[39]

In a specially convened press conference, McCarthy distributed a copy of a picture of Attlee 'reviewing Communist troops in Spain in 1937' alongside General Miaja and Commissar Anton, a leader of the Communist Party in Spain, all giving the clenched-fist salute. He also produced a copy of a letter, in Attlee's handwriting, in which he praised the communist brigade he had inspected and extolled its achievements to his fellow 'comrades' at home. Throughout the press conference, McCarthy referred to the former British prime minister as 'Comrade Attlee' – a 'Communist term meaning fellow Communist'. Attlee's response was that the British Labour Party had been in the vanguard of the fight against communism, at home and abroad, long before McCarthy was ever heard of. The idea that he had given a communist salute in 1937 was an old claim, long since discredited. The Spanish government had been republican, not communist, and he had reviewed troops of all political persuasions.[40]

Undaunted by his brief encounter with McCarthy, Attlee took up an invitation from General Josip Broz Tito, the Communist partisan leader who had become president of Yugoslavia in early 1953. Visiting Belgrade and Dubrovnik, he found the Yugoslavs full of humour, with nothing of the austere nature of the Russians.[41] He conferred at greater length with the Yugoslav leader at his summer residence at Bled. As with China, Attlee felt that there were certain countries within the Communist bloc who were more biddable, and could be peeled away from the Soviet orbit. Tito, he suggested, was developing a system 'very different from that of totalitarianism'. Attlee hoped and predicted others would follow suit and he saw hopeful signs of dissent against Communists in Hungary, Czechoslovakia and Poland.[42]

As the Korean War approached a conclusion in the summer of 1953, Attlee once again criticised the Americans for working to block India from regional peace conferences. In doing so they were alienating a 'leading democratic Asiatic state'. Meanwhile, he felt that it was mistaken to continue to exclude Communist China from the seat on the UN Security Council which the previous Chinese government had been given in 1945. A functioning government should be acknowledged by other powers, no matter its political creed.[43] Thus, despite his displeasure, his own government had acknowledged Franco's Spain in 1945.[44]

Some of these themes fed into Attlee's speech before the Labour conference in Margate in September 1953, in which he aimed to reassert his control. He spoke with authority on foreign affairs in a way that no one in the party could challenge. He also launched a broadside against the Conservatives' handling of the economy. In dispensing with planning, and relaxing controls on consumption, they were offering nothing more than 'optimistic and complacent drift'. After all the criticisms of his government over austerity, food prices were rising fast. By keeping inflation at a minimum, the Attlee government had been able to justify wage freezes. Now that prices were rising again, he came out strongly behind a TUC campaign to demand higher salaries.[45]

The strategy worked. A surprised Lord Winster suggested that the leader had not received such applause in years. There was no 'cleansing' ceremony, or any attempt to take on the rebels. Instead, Attlee had stolen Churchill's clothes. As the prime minister was in bed convalescing from an illness, Attlee appropriated his idea that there should be a summit with the Soviet foreign minister, Georgy Malenkov, to try to reset relations following Stalin's death earlier in March. The proposed meeting should go ahead, even if the prime minister could not attend personally. Winster counted three references to 'American witch hunting' – references to Senator McCarthy's investigations into 'Un-American activities' – which met with great applause each time. There was also cheering at his assertion that if a Labour government had engaged in what the Conservatives had been doing in Egypt – where they were withdrawing more forces in the face of a rising tide of Arab nationalist sentiment – they would have been accused of 'scuttle'.[46]

Attlee certainly felt that he had retaken the initiative. The conference was characterised by 'an excellent spirit' and 'an absence of personal jars', he told Tom. In particular, he noted that his comments on foreign policy had 'pleased all sections'.[47] American officials were disappointed by what they saw as a 'distinct shift' away from support of the US but they did not deny that the position had a strong consensus behind it.[48] It was clear that Attlee's 'reassuring competence' remained the party's best asset, particularly in its efforts to appeal to middle-class and floating voters.[49]

Even though he had cemented his place at the top, the Labour leader cut an increasingly lonely figure. At Margate he admitted that he felt like a Victorian among men of a new generation. Without Bevin to ease his passage with the trade unionists – and many friends within the unions long since gone – he breakfasted, lunched and dined every day alone, 'in icy aloofness'. On his way out of the dining hall, he would slip silently past with shoulders bowed and head sunk, not stopping at a single stall or table for a word, even with former colleagues. On the platform he set a good example by sitting religiously through every single session.[50] One of the few men whom he did count as a close friend, Jack Lawson, admitted that this was a weakness. 'It is said that he does not keep company with members – even of his own party. There is truth in that, but it is not deliberate. Now and then he does enter the tea room and joins the company at some table, but – time, time, time. It is precious to him . . . Some think he is shy and cannot easily make contacts. That may be part of the explanation: but only part. For the truth is that he is so absorbed in his task that he begrudges the minutes not given to it.'[51]

IV

In January 1954, Attlee celebrated his seventy-first birthday. The title of his autobiography, *As it Happened*, which appeared shortly afterwards, was already in the past tense. It was painstakingly guarded and inoffensive. There were no revelations or character assassinations. Attlee himself suspected it was not very interesting.[52] Most of the reviewers agreed. It was almost as if Attlee had gone out of his way to remove any hint of drama. The epoch-shaping events in which he had been involved were given no gloss. The description of meeting with the king after the 1945 election victory was typical: 'The King gave me his commission to form a government. He always said later that I looked very surprised, as indeed I certainly was at the extent of our success.'[53] The *New York Times* suggested Attlee displayed a maddening capacity for taking his readers to the brink of the cliff and leaving them there. There was nothing revealed, for example, of the details of his discussions with Truman in 1945 and 1950, when the world was under the shadow of potential nuclear war. Oblique references to 'other occasions' and 'certain persons' appeared throughout but Bevan was barely mentioned.[54] The *Manchester Guardian* quoted a review by Dr Crane Brinton, a professor of history at Harvard, who said that the book was 'not a history of the times, not a collection of his State Papers, not even – for it is not detailed enough – his memoirs'.[55]

Dalton found it 'unbelievably laconic. No statesman not an Englishman could have written such a book. Understatement exaggerates its emphasis.' Dalton also wrote about Attlee in the past tense, yet not without some grudging admiration. The party leader 'fitted with the requirements of the time; lacks all positive political vices; is honest and infused by rather drab goodwill'.[56] The contrast with Dalton's own memoirs, in which he saw himself at the centre of every event, could not have been more striking. The extent of Dalton's penchant for gossip and intrigue illustrated the distance between their personalities. As Attlee quipped, wryly, 'while I wrote the Acts, Dalton wrote Revelations.'[57] When Dalton told him he liked his book, Attlee replied, with effect, 'It's not nearly so interesting as yours.'[58]

While Labour was led by a 71-year-old, Churchill had entered his eightieth year. His party was becoming restless under his leadership, particularly as Labour was narrowing the gap in the polls. Very few of them dared to call for his head but there were demands for a reshuffle in the spring of 1954. Ironically, Conservative MPs praised Attlee for his comparative decisiveness in leading his party.[59] This was more credit than his critics within the party were willing to give him. In March he had another furious argument with Bevan over leaks to the press from the National Executive. Even a young Bevanite like Richard Crossman confessed that the party was 'utterly exhausted by all these alarms and excursions'.[60]

Sadly, some of the last major parliamentary clashes between the party leaders descended into acrimony, and left both of them bruised. Concerns had been raised about the new hydrogen bomb that the US government had tested on Bikini Atoll in March 1954. It was believed that the bomb was up to 1,000 times more powerful than the atomic weapon that destroyed Hiroshima. Attlee forced a debate and called for more transparency from the government on its policy in this area.[61] Churchill's response was to criticise Attlee's failure to make good on his own deal with Roosevelt, and his inability to get the US to share nuclear secrets in 1945. What was more, he reminded the Labour benches that it was their own leader who had kept his decision to proceed with the building of an atom bomb from them.[62] In being seen to impugn Attlee's character, Churchill had misjudged the mood of the Commons. The Labour leader was seen to be 'red in the face, quivering with rage', with 'the backbenchers shouting and booing'.[63] Shouts of 'Guttersnipe! Swine! Resign!' filled the chamber and even Churchill seemed to be shocked by the extent of the barrage. In the middle of the turmoil, Richard Crossman detached himself from the scene and reflected 'how nauseating we were, howling for the old bull's blood.' In his response, Attlee had 'behaved like an impeccable patriotic leader, putting country before the Party'. Indeed, this was 'the only way in which to hold the Party, once you've got the initiative'.[64] As Attlee neared the end of his career, so Crossman and many of those who previously criticised him began to understand his many strengths.

Writing to Tom, Attlee felt he had given Churchill the opportunity to make a 'just speech on a high level'. Instead, Churchill had 'plunged' into an attack, to 'everyone's disgust'. It would have been 'an eye opener' for the prime minister if he could have seen the uncomfortable expressions on the faces of his own MPs behind him.[65] Ironically, just a few days later, Attlee faced a similar problem when Bevan broke ranks again in a parliamentary debate on the Far East at the end of April. He flouted parliamentary convention by raising a point of order during his own party leader's speech. Bevan was hauled before the parliamentary party the following day and then stormed out when he was condemned by his fellow MPs. As Bevan exited, Gaitskell described how Attlee shouted after him in his 'Haileybury military accent', 'Why can't you be a man and face the music?'[66] At the next meeting of the parliamentary party, Attlee made 'an extremely long and conciliatory speech' in which he asked for a cessation of personal abuse.[67] The ceasefire would not hold long.

V

In July, in the last major debate of the parliamentary session, Churchill characterised recent comments by Attlee about America's approach to China as 'one long whine of criticism'. In particular, the Labour leader had infuriated the Americans by arguing that Formosa, which was held by the Chinese nationalists, should be put under UN control while relations were normalised with the Chinese Communist Party.[68]

When Parliament broke for recess, Attlee visited China as part of a delegation that included Bevan. He left London on 9 August, with a three-day stopover in Moscow, at the request of the Russians. Almost twenty years after his first visit to Moscow, in 1936, Attlee recorded that the city looked more modern, with many new buildings, more cars, and a better-dressed population. On closer inspection, however, he noted that the housing problem was appalling and there was intense overcrowding in the capital. As the Soviet hierarchy – Malenkov, Molotov, Mikoyan and Khrushchev – vied for supremacy after Stalin's death, his impression was that the foreign secretary, Georgy Malenkov, was the dominant personality.[69]

From Moscow they flew to Irkutsk, and then on to Peking, Mukden and Shanghai. Morgan Phillips, the party secretary, kept a diary of the tour. 'It is', he wrote, 'not only a Communist revolution – it is a Nationalist and an Asian revolution.' The Britons met Mao in Peking, whom they found 'fit and sunburnt; in good health and humour'.[70]

When the delegation arrived in Hong Kong on 2 September, Attlee was able to give his uncensored thoughts about what he had seen behind the so-called 'Bamboo Curtain'. He revealed how Chairman Mao had urged him to campaign for the Americans to change their foreign policy. In response, Attlee had asked Mao to campaign for a new approach from the Soviet Union. To Chinese concerns about Formosa, he raised Western European concerns about the Soviet Union's satellite states. (In fact, a Foreign Office account of the meeting suggested that Attlee pushed back firmly against Mao's criticisms of America.)[71] In Attlee's view, Mao and his followers were unlikely to budge from their hardline stance on Formosa and would only accept its peaceful surrender. As for his general impression of China, he found 'less rigidity' in the system than he had seen on previous visits to Russia. The Chinese Communists were 'incorruptible' when it came to their revolutionary principles. Nonetheless, Attlee found a desire for friendship and the opening up of trade. Denying that there had been 'excessive eye wash' during the closely choreographed visit, he believed that he had seen genuine progress in education and public health.[72]

Attlee moved on from Hong Kong to Singapore, where he met up with Violet, and then to Sydney and Auckland, taking in Australian and New Zealand perspectives on China. He travelled back through San Francisco: here he gave a press conference to the American media on 20 September, and warned that trying to encircle China would only push it into the hands of Russia.[73] When he touched down in London again on 22 September, after a 30,000-mile round trip, he managed to spark another controversy by suggesting, at a press conference, that it was the Americans rather than the British who were now viewed as imperialists in Asia. He also claimed that the Australians and New Zealanders he met were not as firmly behind US policy as had been claimed.[74] Some of this was positioning. The China trip – and the repackaging of Labour as a 'third force' in the world – was an attempt to outflank the Bevanites once again.[75] In particular, Attlee wanted the party to back the government in its support for German rearmament. This was brought about by the need to strengthen the Western European alliance against the Soviets, and for West Germany to take on some of that burden itself. However, the prospect of a remilitarised German state played on the neuroses of many of those in the Labour Party who had lived through the last two wars.[76]

By the time of the party conference at Scarborough in September, it seemed that this strategy was bearing fruit. The party voted in favour of continued rearmament, despite Bevan's decision to invite the West German socialist leader, Erich Ollenhauer, to make the case against. As a vindication of Attlee's strategy, some opinion polls now had Labour ahead of the Conservatives.[77] In fact, his success gave a momentary fillip to the old idea that British-style socialism represented a possible 'third way' in Europe. (Ironically, Ollenhauer was later described as a 'German Attlee' by some, despite their differences on rearmament.[78]) After Scarborough, the Labour leader travelled to Denmark for a conference with the moderate social democratic parties of Scandinavia, with whom he felt he had more in common. To his amusement, at one stage in the visit he found himself in a dodgem car with the Swedish prime minister, Tage Erlander.[79] Attlee admired what his counterpart had built, describing it as 'perhaps the most remarkable example of the successful development of Socialism through constitutional means'.[80]

In the autumn of 1954, with an election expected the following year, talk began to turn again to the likely retirement of the leaders of both main parties. Churchill had effectively been replaced already by Anthony Eden, who led most business in the Commons. In the Labour Party the only candidate who could command sufficient support for a leadership bid was still Herbert Morrison. Yet he suspected that Attlee was holding on just to stop him taking over.[81] Attlee's only remaining priority was to preserve unity until the next election, and thought that a leadership election now would do damage to its prospects.

There was another challenge in party management when the question of West German rearmament raised its head again in November 1954. Now it was the old generation rather than the young bucks who raised the loudest voice of dissent. Dalton, perhaps the fiercest anti-German in the party, threatened to resign if Labour supported German rearmament. He sought Attlee's support. 'He, having fought the Germans in WWI, is always more conscious than our conscientious objectors, Quakers, reserved occupations and youngsters, of the dangers of rearming them.'[82] The issue was to rumble on into 1955.

On 3 January 1955, Attlee celebrated his seventy-second birthday, and entered his twentieth year as Labour leader. To Morrison's growing frustration, he was still hanging on until an alternative leader emerged. It was the Conservatives who managed the transition first, as Eden, the heir apparent – whose looks gave him a boost in an increasingly televisual age – officially replaced Churchill as leader in April. Rather than waiting until the end of their five-year term, the Conservatives called an election in the hope that they could take advantage of an improvement in the public mood after the relaxation of food rationing. As another poll approached, Attlee continued to have trouble with the Bevanites, but he vetoed any expulsions from the party, so that a semblance of unity could be maintained in the forthcoming campaign. As the old man prepared for one more election, his knee joint was so sore that he could no longer walk upstairs.[83]

Part Seven

Mission's End, 1955–1967

22

Few Thought He Was Even a Starter

I vow to thee, my country, all earthly things above,
Entire and whole and perfect, the service of my love;
The love that asks no question, the love that stands the test,
That lays upon the altar the dearest and the best;
The love that never falters, the love that pays the price,
The love that makes undaunted the final sacrifice.

I heard my country calling, away across the sea,
Across the waves and waters, she calls and calls to me.
Her sword is girded at her side, her helmet on her head,
And around her feet are lying the dying and the dead;
I hear the noise of battle, the thunder of her guns;
I haste to thee, my mother, a son among thy sons.

And there's another country, I've heard of long ago,
Most dear to them that love her, most great to them that know;
We may not count her armies, we may not see her King;
Her fortress is a faithful heart, her pride is suffering;
And soul by soul and silently her shining bounds increase,
And her ways are ways of gentleness, and all her paths are peace.

'I Vow to Thee, My Country', Sir Cecil Spring Rice, 1922

Wolverton, Buckinghamshire, May 1955

An American reporter from the *Baltimore Sun* who followed Attlee in the final few days of the May 1955 general election campaign described how the Labour leader was greeted everywhere as 'good old Clem', an elder states-man and national treasure. He spoke with 'customary earnestness' but in hope rather than expectation of victory. Unlike Eden, he never looked at ease in television broadcasts, and preferred the hustings and town hall meetings. At one election rally in Wolverton in Buckinghamshire, just as he rose to leave the platform, a gust of wind caught his black homburg hat and blew it to the ground. Half a dozen hands reached to give it back to him but he walked gingerly down the steps, obviously embarrassed, and took it from a child who had been first to retrieve it. Five minutes later, back on stage, the hat blew off again. In Peterborough, where Violet drove him next, he stopped for tea at the house of an election agent. Just outside he encountered a lady with a baby in a pram. Faced with this classic election scenario, the Labour leader seemed somewhat uncertain what to do. Look-ing back at the reporters, he smiled tensely, bent down awkwardly, and kissed the baby's head, as the photographers' bulbs flashed behind him.[1]

In truth, Attlee was more adept in the arts of the modern election than this somewhat hapless portrait would suggest. He remained Labour's greatest electoral asset. Morrison, Gaitskell and Bevan – his potential heirs – were far behind him in terms of the affection for them and the public esteem in which they were held. Attlee had performed well in the polls over the previous year. However, an economic recovery, the relaxa-tion of food controls, combined with Eden's apparent deftness in foreign affairs – set against the backdrop of a potential rapprochement in Anglo-Soviet relations – played well. The Conservatives increased their majority to sixty, winning 13,310,891 votes to Labour's 12,405,254. Attlee had now led the party into five general elections over twenty years. The first, in 1935, had seen it recover from near annihilation four years previously; the results in 1945 and 1950 were the best in its history, and, even in 1951, despite losing power, Labour had won the largest share of the vote. Notwithstanding the tensions within it, it is hard to conclude that the party was in anything other than good health.

Attlee wanted to retire immediately. Once again, however, because of the uncertainty over the succession, the National Executive Committee persuaded him to stay on for a few months. Arthur Moyle, his parliamentary private secretary, described how the leader sank into his chair with complete exhaustion when he was told that the party hierarchy wanted him to remain. He was, it should be said, flattered by the warm declaration of continued support that Bevan gave him after the defeat. But he confided in Moyle that he did not have much strength to go on. 'Well, my boy. I do not know what to think of it all but I feel like someone who has been put in charge of a maternity clinic without the slightest knowledge of what the period of gestation is.' There were some who suggested that, once again, he was serving himself by staying in office, or doing anything in his power to prevent Morrison replacing him. To the very few who questioned his motives, he showed complete indifference. As ever with Attlee, he carried the responsibility with 'little fuss'.[2]

II

On 8 June, Hugh Dalton described how Attlee and Churchill were sworn in to the new Parliament, both looking worn and old. Attlee was given a cheer when he took his seat on the opposition front bench once again. But he signed his name very slowly on the parliamentary ledger, and hesitated before writing Walthamstow, rather than Limehouse, as his constituency. Dalton saw him puffing on his pipe in the Smoking Room a few hours later and thought the leader looked glum at the prospect of another parliamentary session on the front line. To Attlee's chagrin, Dalton continued to press him on the question of party policy on German rearmament.[3]

On a family holiday in Wales in August 1955, the Attlees took with them a German maid, whom Violet had employed at Cherry Cottage. Clem mentioned her as the 'very nice girl who has done something to mitigate my prejudices against that people'. Reading a book about a group of students from Munich who had been executed by the Nazis reminded him that there were 'still Germans with courage to stand out for freedom'. His views on rearmament were also softened by the fact that the international situation was 'distinctly brighter'. The Russians had 'come some way' while 'the Yanks are more reasonable'. Having generally 'cussed' him for going to China in the previous year, the Americans were now softening their line with the Chinese Communists. 'They generally are a year behind us,' he said. Attlee also expressed his admiration for *Socialist Commentary*, as a 'useful corrective' to the *New Statesman*, which had become the vehicle of the left-wing dissidents within the party. In his view, 'the so-called left have been consistently wrong on foreign policy.'⁴ *Socialist Commentary* was run by the Socialist Union, the wing of the party associated with Hugh Gaitskell and those centrists who set out to oppose Bevan's 'squadron'.⁵

The day after this letter to Tom, on 9 August, Attlee suffered a slight stroke, which left him bedbound for two weeks.⁶ As the contest to succeed him intensified throughout the autumn, Attlee saw the opportunity he had been waiting for. On 6 December 1955, he told Tom that he was to give up the leadership of the party the following day. There was an expectation that he would be elevated to a peerage in the Lords. This would at least have the advantage of softening his break with public affairs and allow him to see his friends in the House of Commons. After thirty-three years he suspected he would miss the Commons but he certainly did not want to carry on until he was senile.⁷

At 11 a.m. on 7 December, the Labour Party convened in committee room 14 of the House of Commons to hear their leader announce his resignation. He did so in classic Attlee style and was out of the room by 11.20 a.m. 'Who is going to believe that the man who was Leader for twenty years would finish his speech in under five minutes?' commented Crossman.⁸ Morrison, who was still determined to push for the leadership, jumped up to lead the tributes. Attlee was praised in glowing terms by representatives of the old guard, such as D. R. Grenfell, the 74-year-old trade unionist who recalled many years of struggle alongside him. On the announcement of his peerage, it was recalled that Earl Attlee had once joked, during the war, that, in such an event, he would call himself Lord 'Luv-a-Duck' of Limehouse.⁹ He instead chose Earl Attlee and Viscount Prestwood of Walthamstow.

At a press conference the following day at Transport House, Attlee refused to get drawn into the discussion about his possible successor. Asked why he was retiring, he simply said, 'Well, one has to watch the times, you know.' He was entitled to a £2,000 pension as a former prime minister. Commenting on the earldom that was about to be conferred on her husband, Violet told reporters that it would make no difference to her.

The main change in her life would be that she would no longer have to drive to Great Missenden station after midnight to pick up her husband as he returned from London. 'I shall be doing the housework and everything else, the same as usual,' she declared, though it would be nice to have a husband in the house for the evenings, after so many years of late-night sittings in the Commons.[10]

Conservative Party strategists told the *Daily Express* that Attlee's departure would deprive the Labour Party of two great assets – an ability to keep the party together, and an appeal to the floating voter. As for the mooted alternatives, it was felt that Morrison, sixty-seven, was an 'extinct volcano', Bevan, fifty-eight, was a 'wild cat', and Gaitskell, forty-nine, was a poor shadow of Attlee, though the closest to his image.[11] On 16 December, Gaitskell easily topped the poll of the parliamentary party, winning 157 MPs, against seventy for Bevan and just forty for Herbert Morrison who – just as he had done in 1935 – blamed Attlee for ruining his chances.

To Bevan's credit, even after his defeat, he wrote in praise of Attlee in *Tribune*. He credited the retiring leader with having the unique gift of intuition. So many decisions had to be made with little or no time for reflection; and intuition was not something that could be acquired by study or intellectual training. The party rank and file felt safe with him, though sometimes he seemed too slow, 'too modestly cautious'. The deaths of Ellen Wilkinson (1947), Ernie Bevin (1951), and Stafford Cripps (1952) and the illnesses of Morrison and Dalton could partly be attributed to the huge workload faced by the government after the war. Attlee looked the weakest of all these but it turned out that he was, physically and mentally, the most resilient. Notwithstanding their many quarrels Bevan spoke of the 'pleasure and gratitude' he felt serving under him.[12] Attlee, too, was happy for a ceasefire. As he later observed, a lieutenant was entitled to challenge his leader if 'he genuinely feels he should'.[13]

It has been claimed that Attlee would have preferred Bevan to be leader, given that he never endorsed Gaitskell. He was, perhaps, sentimental about Bevan – the nearest thing to an authentic big beast of yesteryear. He had no great enthusiasm for Gaitskell. As he told Bevan's supporters, 'Nye had the leadership on a plate. I always wanted him to have it. But you know, he wants to be two things simultaneously, a rebel and an official leader, and you can't be both.' In any case, he had long since 'cooked his goose'.[14] Attlee had come to the conclusion that Bevan was 'a horse that works best in harness'.[15] A leader must suffer fools in a way in which Bevan seemed incapable.[16] When later asked if he had ever regarded Bevan as a potential leader, Attlee commented that he had only ever considered this 'at long range'. It is important to note that this was not an ideological objection – he could see the merits of the party being led from the left – but one based on a reading of his character. Bevan never developed the necessary 'sense of responsibility' that Attlee had encouraged him to adopt when appointing him to government in 1945.[17] Leadership was out of the question now for Bevan; Gaitskell was the only viable choice.

III

As Labour's parliamentary party celebrated fifty years of existence in January 1956, Attlee was afforded some more opportunity for hindsight. The last year had seen the retirement from the National Executive Committee of Hugh Dalton, Emanuel Shinwell, James Chuter Ede and Herbert Morrison. This marked 'the passing of a generation that grew to manhood in the reign of Queen Victoria'. There was serious need for a 'flexible approach to the problems of a changing age'. Socialist principles 'must be applied to new conditions'.[18]

Attlee also feared that political leaders were less in touch with the man in the street than they were fifty years ago – despite the populism of mass media and broadcasting. Fifty years before, Labour MPs had wanted to be in Parliament because they were disturbed by the conditions they saw around them. 'Nowadays,' he wrote, 'there are quite a lot of chaps who are in the House because the idea of sitting in Westminster and helping to govern the country appeals to them.' Nor had they much experience of the long years spent as a minority party in the House, struggling for credibility, trying to survive in the 1920s and 1930s. 'It gave us a sense of pace and a sense of proportion,' he reflected.[19] Who in the Labour Party would remember these things now?

Just before his elevation to the House of Lords on 25 January 1956, Attlee hosted a dinner at the Commons to celebrate his sister Mary's eightieth birthday. He presented her with a moleskin coat, joking that there was always a chance she would give it away to a beggar. Mary had gone out to South Africa in 1910, working in the Railway Mission in Johannesburg and then setting up an organisation called 'Racial Unity', at Claremont, before returning home to live out her final years. Mig had devoted herself to charity work through the Church of England in Salisbury, and the care of her nephews and nieces, particularly the children of Dorothy, the eldest sister who had died in 1920. Of the brothers, Bernard had died in 1943, and Rob in 1953. Clem's two closest siblings – Tom, with whom he had entered the Labour movement – and Laurence – who had fought in Gallipoli – were also at the dinner. In widely divergent ways, this was family linked together by a shared sense of public service.[20]

In April 1956, Attlee was given a further bauble; he was made a Knight of the Garter, an honorary position bestowed by the queen. At the ceremony, he sat between Queen Elizabeth and Churchill, who, at eighty-two, was unsteady on his feet. Afterwards Attlee allowed himself an uncharacteristic boast at the two official distinctions he had picked up since retiring, to add to the Companion of Honour and Order of Merit. In a poem for Tom, he wrote:

> Few thought he was even a starter
> There were those who thought themselves smarter
> But he ended P.M.
> C.H. and O.M.
> An earl and a knight of the garter.[21]

Still, his calendar continued to pivot around the Labour Party, even if many of the old friends were gone. When he 'looked in' on the Labour conference at Blackpool in October 1956, it was clear that his loyalties were with Gaitskell, whose performance he described as 'excellent'.[22] Just a few weeks later he gave an incredible example of the sense of duty and stoicism that had defined him over the course of five decades' involvement in his party. On the way to a trade union dinner, Violet had skidded on ice and crashed the car into the side of the road. The couple turned up slightly late and sat through dinner, barely mentioning the incident. Violet had cut her head and blood had seeped into the back of her hair. Sitting beside Gaitskell, Clem said that he was no more than a little bruised as his pipe had been in his pocket on collision. The next day Gaitskell learned that he had broken two ribs.[23]

III

India continued to exercise Attlee's mind greatly as he and Violet prepared for a visit there at the end of 1956. Beforehand, he read two recent Penguin books on two of the uglier aspects of Anglo-Indian history: the Thugs (organised bands of bandits and assassins who used to roam the land); and the Indian Mutiny of 1857, which was brutally suppressed by the British colonial authorities in a way that left lasting resentment. While acknowledging the darker elements of the past, he continued to hope that the new relationship, within the Commonwealth, would be built from the healthier aspects of shared history. In this he allowed himself some sentimentality. Before leaving, he learned that his batman on his first trip to India had become a hugely successful businessman since the granting of independence. Nonetheless, the erstwhile batman had written to the Indian government asking to assume the role again for the former prime minister's visit. This was, for Attlee, 'a pleasing touch after twenty years'.[24] It was all the more pleasing because it was an expression of unforced solidarity.

Attlee hoped that such relationships could be replicated on a larger scale. His reception in India and Pakistan gave him more personal satisfaction than perhaps anything in his career. 'We had a wonderful time being greeted most warmly, cheering crowds often assembling.' Both countries, he was pleased to report, had been 'making great strides', especially in the villages, where schools and community centres were being introduced, along with electricity, irrigation and agricultural improvement. He and Violet saw the main cities and travelled up the Amber Way on an elephant, enjoying the Mughal architecture. He received an honorary degree from Madras University and also visited Kashmir, where the couple enjoyed a perfect view of the Himalayas.[25]

Indian independence and partition had been bloody and chaotic; Kashmir remained a sore point between India and Pakistan. From this, as much as anything, Attlee had grown to a greater appreciation of the power of nationalism. Those who played down its importance were misleading themselves. Before his visit he talked to Harold Nicolson about how 'he well remembered being told that Irish and Indian nationalism were artificial movements engineered by a handful of agitators.'[26] His fear was that nationalism could be excessive and aggressive. 'We all ought to have a measure of nationalism,' he told an audience in Pakistan, 'It gives us decent feeling about ourselves and pride in our own show, but in the present-day world we have got to go beyond that.'[27] Ironically, it was at the end of the visit that he was informed about the 'wretched' crisis developing over Colonel Gamal Abdel Nasser's seizure and nationalisation of the Suez Canal.[28] War was to follow shortly thereafter.

It was after his return that Attlee wrote an article for the *Spectator* about the 'two sides of colonialism'. As a young man, he explained, he had been an imperialist. But he had come to believe that the British Empire had taken a wrong turn. Once again, he made clear that the idea of the Commonwealth, which he had brought into existence in its stead, was not intended to be a repudiation of everything that had come before. Rather, it was designed to make good on the promises that had been contained in the imperial project from the outset – above all the reward of self-government. He was retrieving something noble from the mess, but without cleansing the record.[29] To a certain extent he was putting a gloss on history. Even Indian nationalism, he argued, reflected the pervasive power of British ideas of democracy and self-determination. As he had said in 1942, at the height of the Indian mutiny, 'We are condemned by Indians not by the measure of Indian ethical conceptions but by our own, which we have taught them to accept.'[30]

For some reason, Attlee was much impressed by *The End of Empire* – written by his old colleague John Strachey, the former Minister of Food and one of the party's sharpest intellectuals – which was first published in 1958.[31] The thesis of Strachey's book was that the decision to give up the empire could be attributed, as much as anything, to a change in domestic political thinking over the previous fifty years. A liberal democratic state could no longer reconcile itself to the measures required to defend the empire; the ugly nature of imperial rule had been exposed and there was no will to subject other peoples to rule that they did not want. Domestically, there were greater demands for welfare and a supportive state. Finally, there was a new future for British foreign and security policy, in a series of new partnerships with Europe and North America.[32]

This was very much how Attlee understood the generational shift that he had seen in his lifetime, since his personal awakening at the dawn of the century. The imperial movement had waned as the Labour movement had waxed – and the very nature of Britain had been changed accordingly.

Attlee had played a role in guiding Britain to that point. He did not see this as a feat that he, as a statesman, had brought about, so much as the conclusion of a national journey (for Britain as much as India). His decisiveness in office was based on the conviction that the moment of ripeness had come (even if the conditions were never going to be perfect). He was happy to share the credit with those who understood this too. Attlee was greatly saddened by Edwina Mountbatten's death in March 1960: he was deeply fond of her and believed that, like her husband, she deserved great credit for her handling of the transition.[33]

Further visits to Canada and Australia in 1959 allowed him to interpret these changes in a broader framework. The realisation of a Commonwealth raised the prospect of a wider community of like-minded nations, bound not by ethnicity but a shared conception of self-government. This was something he was to expand upon in his Chichele lectures of 1960, which were collected and published as *Empire into Commonwealth*. The lectures themselves were put together from scant notes. On this question, he spoke from the heart rather than as a master of the detail.[34]

This belief – that Britain was stronger as a partner in a community of like-minded nations – shaped his view of the Suez crisis of 1956. Back in 1951 he had opposed Morrison's suggestion that there should be an intervention against Mossadeq. This had been based on his view that Britain could not chide others for flouting UN rules, or behaving in an imperialist fashion, only to do so itself. He also believed it would be a mistake to break with the Americans on such a fundamental issue. During the Suez crisis of 1956, he felt that the Conservatives had made two major mistakes. The first was not keeping the US fully informed of its intentions; the second was not cultivating allies within the Commonwealth and the United Nations. Of course, Nasser was engaged in a 'purely selfish nationalist show', but the government had played into his hands.[35] He wondered whether Eden had been goaded into making a 'strong gesture' by his backbenchers.[36]

Not long after Suez, Attlee was reunited with Harry Truman for a joint radio broadcast on international affairs. Both recalled how at Potsdam they had urged the internationalisation of the world's canals to prevent these types of disputes. The idea had been rejected by the Russians at the time.[37] Attlee's ideal was to have a fully functioning UN that was more than a Western Alliance, or a diplomatic foil for NATO. In later years, he returned to this idea and indulged himself with the one-worldism to which he had always been inclined since first hearing Woodrow Wilson's Fourteen Points in 1917. 'I have become a supporter of World Government' again, he wrote. 'Impractical, they say, but not so impractical as trying to run a world of sovereign States equipped with hydrogen bombs.'[38] He became a champion of the World Parliament, travelling in a delegation to Moscow and making an appeal to Nikita Khrushchev and President John F. Kennedy to disarm at the time of the Cuban Missile Crisis in 1962.[39]

On occasion, Attlee had groused about aspects of American foreign policy. This was not simply a matter of deflecting pressure from Bevan and the left-wingers in his party. He had genuine criticisms of its approach to the Korean War, and its non-recognition of 'Red China'. On the fundamentals, however, he had made room for criticism because he was such a staunch ally. The commitment to rearm and to support America in the Korean War was one reason why his government fell in 1951. Ultimately, his flashes of irritation with America – cheering on Australians against Americans at Wimbledon, for example – did not run deep. He was always eager to repair any misunderstanding. When William Boyd ('Hopalong Cassidy' of the American cowboy films) came to town with a group of American boys as part of a scheme called 'Operation Friendship', designed to improve relations between the peoples of both countries, Attlee welcomed them to dinner at the Savoy Hotel. The boys and their British counterparts must remember, he said, 'that we all come from common stock and there are certain things we hold in common, and particularly our love for freedom and democracy.' The nations had stood together in two world wars and Attlee believed that it was just as important for the stability and the future of the world that they stood together in peacetime.[40]

After his visit to India, Attlee's next major tour was to North America in 1957, where he visited New York, Los Angeles, Miami, and Toronto. He and Violet travelled back and forth from university campuses in the south, warm and pleasant even in winter, and the north and Midwest, covered in snow. Hiring a car in upstate New York, Violet even managed to hit a stag in the road and broke the car radiator.[41] Despite six traffic accidents in five years she was always insistent that she was perfectly fit to remain behind the wheel. Clem, she reported, was 'always an absolute dear' about these scrapes.[42] His speaking tours were a relatively profitable business, which meant a return visit to the US in March and again in 1960, where he gave twenty-two lectures across the country. Attlee found the students he met in the university towns strikingly 'left wing' and receptive to his brand of democratic social-ism.[43] He was also delighted to report that American isolationism was dead and there were fewer objections raised to his call for recognition of Red China. On one visit, he took a helicopter ride over New York and joked that he had almost been able to shake hands with the Statue of Liberty.[44]

Back in the British Isles, with Vi driving, he toured County Cork in Ireland and Fife in Scotland. His daughter Alison and her husband Rich-ard took their children to Butlin's in Criccieth – and Attlee was full of praise about the idea of a holiday camp in which the parents could be relieved of children for a few hours.[45] On other visits to France, Germany and Italy, he also saw the rebuilding of Europe. He was pleased to see Ber-lin back on its feet, and the improvements in Aachen which he had seen, destroyed and starving, in the last few months of the war. He travelled to Italy where he met the grandson of Garibaldi, one of his heroes, and he and Violet visited Lake Como, where they had fallen in love.[46]

Attlee remained sceptical about further moves towards European unity in the 1950s and 1960s. This, perhaps, is unsurprising in a man who had lived through two world wars. 'We ought not to consider Europe as a con-geries of nations, each of which has a somewhat similar view of its position in the world. For this is to ignore history and geography,' he wrote. Europe contained certain nations that had traditionally looked 'outwards' (like Britain, Portugal, Holland, Belgium and Spain) and other nations whose dominating concerns had mainly been on the Continent itself (Germany, Austria and Russia). There were other countries that had only recently attained nationhood and had for the most part lost it again as they slipped behind the Iron Curtain (Czechs, Poles, Croats, Serbs, Bulgarians and Romanians); they understood little about citizenship. 'What is the idea which will make a united Europe? What are the ideas which will animate each of these nations?'[47]

IV

How did Attlee place himself in history? When visiting Oxford in 1960, at the invitation of the Conservative Association there, he was struck by how 'left wing' the students were on issues such as the Health Service and the welfare state.[48] The socialists of his generation, he noted, had been regarded as dangerous revolutionaries among the middle classes. In his day, he told the students, a young socialist lawyer would be ostracised by Tories and Liberals, or looked down upon by the parents of the girl he wanted to marry.[49] Attlee continued to see these changes in national rather than tribal terms. Rather than squabbling over their origins, they were to be welcomed as signs of progress in which all could partake. As he entered the last decade of his life, he took a perverse pleasure in writing for right-leaning magazines, such as the *Spectator*.[50] It amused him that the *Sunday Times*, once so hostile to his views, tried to entice him from the *Observer* as a columnist. He was surprised to be in such demand.[51] Fifty years before, he would have been regarded as a firebrand street radical in such publications. Was it he who had changed, or the country around him?

Attlee had come to know some of the most important figures of the twentieth century – Lloyd George, Churchill, Roosevelt, Truman, Stalin and Mao – on personal terms. While he had never been cowed in their presence, he viewed the events in which he had participated with something approaching a sense of detachment. Reviewing a book on Churchill, Stalin and Roosevelt, by Herbert Feis, Attlee conveyed an almost a lingering sense of wonderment that he had been an equal participant alongside these giant personalities. It was typical of Attlee to take mischievous pleasure from the fact that Churchill kept on sending him his books, 'despite my somewhat astringent reviews'.[52]

In truth, his fondness for Churchill only increased in later years. Just before Christmas in 1957, he and Violet lunched with the Churchills. Winston was by now very deaf but refused to use the ear trumpet designed for him. Attlee was full of warmth for his old foe, who had remarked 'with satisfaction, that he and I either as allies or as government and opposition leaders covered fifteen years between us'.[53] He enjoyed the anecdotes about Churchill in Alanbrooke's diaries: barking instructions at his generals in his vast Mexican sunhat, eating soup with one hand and swatting flies with the other; or getting ordered back to headquarters when crossing the Rhine in 1945. At the description of Churchill's pouting expression at not being allowed to go further into Germany – like a boy being called away from his sandcastles on the beach – Attlee wrote, 'I can just see that look.'[54] There were other things that brought them still closer in later life: a shared interest in military history but also, after their retirement, the novels of Anthony Trollope, which they would discuss at length.[55]

Nevertheless, Attlee had never been afraid to criticise Churchill – and to point out some of his uglier characteristics and flaws. In an interview given in 1958, he criticised the way the Conservatives had behaved after the 1950 election in hounding the government on every issue, to force it into submission. In his self-image, Churchill was always above party politics, until it suited him not to be. Attlee went so far as to say his behaviour in 1950 had been 'unpatriotic'.[56]

In his burgeoning journalistic career, Attlee also wrote about many of those who had been involved in the rise of the Labour Party. It was hard not to think about this in generational terms. When drafting an appreciation of Beatrice Webb, one hundred years after her birth, he commented to Tom, 'These centenaries of people one knew quite well make one realise one's age.'[57] He described how he went to a party to celebrate Fenner Brockway's fiftieth year in the socialist movement only to realise that he and Tom had preceded him as members of the Independent Labour Party by some months.[58] In 1959 he wrote articles on the centenaries of the births of George Lansbury, Sidney Webb and George Barnes.[59] Once again, as with the accession of India to the Commonwealth, there was an odd sense of circularity in this: a maturation of a movement that he had joined in its raw and infant state in the East End in 1906; and a mission fulfilled, albeit imperfectly.

V

Clement Attlee grew old with more time to reflect on the world around him than many others were given. Tom died in late 1960, just as Clem was preparing an eightieth birthday celebration for him. His very last letter to his brother referred back to the letters that he and Bernard, the eldest brother and an army chaplain, had written during the war. They had been given to him by Laurence, now in his late seventies.[60] The experience of the First World War was something that took up much of his thoughts in later years.

At the end of 1961 Attlee was admitted to Amersham hospital with a minor stomach upset – only for doctors to be forced to operate on his abdomen because of the severity of his ulcers. Violet was in the same hospital suffering from pain in her lower back. There were numerous tributes in the press when he reached his eightieth birthday on 3 January 1962. Still making occasional visits to the House of Lords, he spoke his mind, though the world was changing in ways he had never expected. He felt that the Americans drove Fidel Castro into the hands of the Russians by continuing to support the old regime that he had deposed, long after it was discredited.[61] He was disturbed at the 'extreme emotion' they had shown over the issue, and saw it as partly to blame for the Cuban Missile Crisis.[62] On Europe he came out as a strong opponent of the Common Market, an issue on which he and the 'old Beaver', Beaverbrook found themselves to be unlikely bedfellows.[63]

With the passing of nearly all the remaining big Labour ministers of his government (Bevan in 1960, Dalton in 1962, Gaitskell in 1963, Morrison in 1965), Attlee had much time to reflect on his own mortality. In 1963, in a series of radio broadcasts, he allowed some of his amateur poetry to be read out, and spoke more expansively than ever before about the Gallipoli campaign and how it had shaped him.[64] Asked what history would remember him best for, he simply replied, 'I don't know. India, maybe.'[65] In July 1965 he realised that it was sixty-four years since Queen Victoria died – longer than she had reigned, 'so I am in the eyes of youth the equivalent to the young bucks like Palmerston of those days.'[66] He was one the last prominent Victorians in public life to pass away.[67]

In June 1964, Violet died suddenly of a cerebral haemorrhage, collapsing in the kitchen of Cherry Cottage. Recognising the massive blow that this loss would be to Clem, who was already frail, his old friend A. V. Alexander wrote to him urging him to take care of his own health. In Violet he had lost 'a life-partner, who through her own care and work for you in Government and Opposition, served the Party and the whole nation, of which you have been such a loyal and faithful servant.'[68] Violet had even had a small bungalow built, in the expectation that Clem would die first, as Cherry Cottage was too large for one. Attlee moved to a flat in Temple in central London, and employed an old soldier called Alfred Laker to look after him. He sought some solace in the company of Patricia Beck, the American journalist from *Life* magazine, whom he and Violet had got to know during the 1950 election campaign. Her original brief had been to 'send him up' but she was completely converted to his politics. She remained a staunch friend and would often visit her 'Uncle Clem'. He would read, eat his dinner on his lap in front of a fire, make the odd visit to the House of Lords, or sometimes to Wimbledon or the Oval cricket ground.[69]

Aside from children and grandchildren, there were almost no familiar faces left. In 1965 he wrote to Jack Lawson about his occasional visits to the House of Lords. 'I miss you a lot for I seem now the only one in the Party of our generation who attends except Chuter Ede. There are lots of new Peers who I do not know. Our boys on the Front Bench do well, but I fear those in the Commons make a good many mistakes. I wish MPs would not raise all those silly points of privilege.'[70] Just a week later, he learned from Lawson's daughter that the old man was in hospital and unable to reply.[71] He died just a few days later. Attlee lived to see Harold Wilson's sweeping election victory the following year, though the truth was he felt very much detached from the new generation. This was the context for his famous interview with the BBC's Percy Cudlipp in which he left his interviewer stumped after answering twenty-eight questions in just five minutes.[72]

At Churchill's funeral in January 1965, the 82-year-old Attlee stumbled at the entrance to St Paul's Cathedral. He had insisted on taking a full part in the previous day's rehearsals, against the advice of his doctors, and was barely able to walk up the steps. The front page of the *Observer* captured the old man sitting on the bottom step at St Paul's, bent over his cane, with a member of the Horses Guards standing behind him in attendance, ready to help him get to his feet.[73]

Back at his flat, he was bordering on collapse. Alfred Laker put his slippers out and wrapped a blanket round him by the fire. Attlee refused a brandy but Laker slipped some into his tea. He suspected the old man knew what he had done, but drank it just to humour him.[74] How different things could have been if Churchill and Attlee had not been forced together by events in 1940. It was odd to think that, at one stage, it seemed as if Neville Chamberlain might be replaced by Halifax, who, in Attlee's words, 'had a curious conscience which could justify anything', and who wanted to sue for peace with Hitler.[75] As for Churchill's view of him, the Conservative MP Sir John Rodgers learned that while Churchill would occasionally make an off-hand remark about Attlee, he did not allow others the privilege. 'Mr Attlee is a great patriot. Don't you dare call him "silly old Attlee" at Chartwell or you won't be invited again.'[76]

After a minor stroke in late 1966, which temporarily reduced his powers of speech, Attlee divided the last eighteen months of his life between the flat in Temple and visits to his family. He reread his old favourites, from Jane Austen to John Buchan, as well as General Slim's account of the

HE WAS EVEN A STARTER | 545

Burma campaign.[77] One of the very last books he read, Alistair Buchan's life of Walter Bagehot, reflected the sensibilities of a man who was born a Victorian.[78] How different the world was now. When he visited his grand-children, he was bemused by the fact that they would immediately sit down in front of the television after returning from school.[79]

Clement Attlee died in his sleep on 8 October 1967 in Westminster Hospital, after contracting pneumonia. His ashes were buried on 7 November in Westminster Abbey. At his own request, Sir Cecil Spring Rice's 1908 poem, set to music in 1923, 'I Vow To Thee, My Country' was played. The other hymns he chose were 'And did those feet in ancient time' and 'To Be a Pilgrim'.[80] Each conveyed the sense in which he had been on a personal journey but one that had always related to the fate of the country he loved.

Two years before his death he had joked that, when hearing of his passing, most people would say 'I thought he died ages ago.' After surviving two world wars – and serving, in very different ways, on the front line – Attlee understood how lucky he had been. As he reached the end of his life, his thoughts turned back to those moments when events might have taken a very different course. In April 1916 he had been injured going over the top in Mesopotamia carrying the red flag of his regiment. Fifty years later, he recalled what one of his men had said to him just before they charged out of that trench: 'I have lived in the greatest country in the world for twenty-two years.' The young soldier who had uttered those words was killed the same day that Attlee was hit by shrapnel and carried from the battlefield. In contrast to his comrade, he had enjoyed 'sixty [more] years of memories of friendships and kindness'. 'I shall die with lots of poetry in my heart and perhaps on my lips.'[81]

23

Epilogue: The Promised Land

I pondered all these things, and how men fight and lose the battle, and the thing they fought for comes about in spite of their defeat, and when it turns out not to be what they meant, and other men have to fight for what they meant under another name.

William Morris, *A Dream of John Ball*, 1888.[1]

Depending on one's perspective, Britain has been blessed, or cursed, with an abundance of public school socialists. In one sense, Attlee might be seen as the most successful of them all. In another, he could not have been more different from the prototype. He did not recoil, or react with disgust, from his background or his schooling. His life did not equate to a lengthy dialogue with an imaginary right-wing housemaster. At the Haileybury Club, his mission was to teach the discipline and order that had been instilled in him in the Rifle Corps. Unlike many public school socialists, he was not repulsed by 'suburban values' or the country of his birth. Even as he came to see British imperialism as flawed and wrong-headed, he did not condemn Rudyard Kipling, so much as come to a more mature appreciation of his work. Even as he gave up on Christianity, he was not ashamed to acknowledge that it contained certain ethical principles that guided his conduct. The Victorian values inculcated in him by Richard and Ellen Attlee, his parents, were the ones which he took with him in his early career as a social worker. Attlee was uneasy about many aspects of British politics and society and felt that much needed to be corrected, improved, and reformed. But at no stage did he repudiate the world from which he came; or try to overcompensate for it by adopting fashionable positions to gain him the approval of 'Bloomsbury highbrows', or the dinner party set. The first thing to understand about Clement Attlee is that, for all his shyness, he was at ease with himself. The second is that he was tolerant of others who did not agree with him, in a way that many public school socialists were not.

It was a combination of these qualities that helped Attlee lead a fractious and often self-destructive political party for over twenty years, to its finest hour in 1945, and beyond. It was a position for which no one thought he was a natural fit, and yet who else could have held it together in this way over more than two decades? He cultivated no cult following, or power base – either among the intellectuals or the trade union movement – but he provided a bridge between these two worlds. At one Labour Party conference in the 1930s, Trevor Evans, the former miner and Labour correspondent for the *Daily Express*, recalled seeing Attlee enjoying a drink with some of the most influential trade unionists: Will Lawther of the mine workers; Fred Smith of the engineers; and Charles Dukes of the general workers. This was at the time when another public school socialist, Stafford Cripps, was threatening open rebellion. When the discussion turned to Cripps, Lawther blurted out: 'You know, Clem, you'll never do any good by playing up to those intellectuals and old school tie merchants. They don't know enough about the working class.' Lawther stopped suddenly when he realised what he had said, and everybody started laughing, none more so than Attlee. The eyes of the 'old school tie merchant' 'gleamed with pride' at being accepted in this way.[2]

It was through small acts over the course of a long career – more than half a century in the Labour movement – that Attlee's reputation was built. A perfect example was the story told by the journalist Frank Owen about Attlee's dash through the snow to the Cambridge University Union to take on Oswald Mosley in February 1933, when Bevan had fallen ill. A month after Adolf Hitler came to power, the MP for Limehouse thought that those who sought to mimic Hitler, ought to be answered. Attlee's outstanding quality, Owen reflected many years later, was that none of his qualities were outstanding. He was not a deadly debater, even though he had bested Mosley. His tone was 'metallic' and his sentences overly precise. Loquaciousness was not one of his chracteristics. With his tinny voice, he did not sound like a great statesman in the mould of Winston Churchill or Ramsay MacDonald. No legend was attached to him; nor did he have any of the attributes that the public expect from their 'great men'. He was 'not discernibly ambitious, egotistic, ruthless, exciting, or even superficially charming'. But he had hidden depths that those around him began to appreciate with age, and which shone in times of crisis. Above all, he had a firm conviction in his own beliefs. These were genuine and therefore unshakeable. To understand Attlee one had to understand that he did not follow the fashion of the moment. He had not converted to socialism on the basis of sudden emotion, or passion, 'for these are not the springs from which Attlee draws his strength'. Nor had he swallowed Karl Marx's theory 'as an intellectual diet, which deranges some folks' political digestions for years to come'.[3]

To say that Attlee has been underestimated is to ignore the accounts of those who knew him best. Some of the most enlightening fragments of the Attlee story took place a world away from Number 10 Downing Street, when the prospect of leading a large majority government was so unlikely as to almost seem like an impossible dream. In 1936, at the height of the depression, Attlee was visited in his constituency by James Griffiths, MP for Llanelli, one the trade unionists who arrived in the parliamentary party as it rebuilt itself following the catastrophe of 1931. When Griffiths joined the party leader in Limehouse that day, he noticed how Attlee seemed more relaxed among the dock workers of the East End than he did among his fellow MPs. 'How is our little man doing?' they asked Griffiths, who was to become Attlee's Minister for National Insurance nine years later, ushering in the welfare legislation that gave Attlee as much pride as anything else his government did. 'Behind that phrase, "our little man", was real deep affection,' Griffiths later reflected, when paying tribute to his former leader in the House of Commons in 1967. 'The little man with hidden greatness, the quiet man who created the Welfare State and began the transformation from Empire to Commonwealth; we in this House and in the country have cause to remember and bless the memory of the quiet man.' As someone who was to serve under him for nearly twenty years – in government and opposition – Griffiths appreciated that 'one could always depend on Clem.' Attlee's career proved that, 'in the long run, it is integrity and dependability which count most in life.'[4]

With the exception of Ernest Bevin, Attlee's closest friend in politics was Jack Lawson – another trade unionist, who had worked at a Durham colliery since the age of twelve and went on to serve with the Durham

Light Infantry. From the moment they were placed together in the War Office in 1924 – two former officers in Labour's first government – they struck up a rapport. When Attlee became Labour leader in 1935, almost every newspaper suggested that this would be a temporary arrangement while the party decided its destiny. Lawson was one of the few who understood immediately that Attlee was being greatly underestimated, and predicted he would maintain his hold for much longer. There was 'nothing brilliant or obvious about him' and he had none of Churchill's 'power of self-dramatisation'. But he had 'courage in abundance, endless doggedness, and a shrewd commonsense'. Few men were better judges of character. He had 'profound integrity' and was 'wholly devoid of jealousy or pose'. His convictions were unshakeable and he fought for them with 'a tenacity that one has to meet in order to appreciate'. Significantly, though, he was a 'Socialist sans phrase', a man who did not 'improvise his convictions'. Unlike many others, he was free of 'vanity or the ardour to dominate'. Here was a man 'one has to know to learn to appreciate'. In Lawson's memorable phrase, Attlee had 'the kind of solidity and integrity which responsibility turns into massiveness'.[5]

Even before the leadership election of 1935, there were elements of personal and political fortune in Attlee's story. From the two major battles he missed on the battlefield in the First World War – having been carried off the front line at Gallipoli with dysentery before the August 1915 offensive at Sari Bair, and then wounded in Mesopotomia in April 1916, the day before many of his good friends were killed in a follow-up assault at Kut – he was blessed with a certain degree of luck. It seemed strangely appropriate too, that his worst injuries were from friendly fire. Nonethless, while history favoured him at various points, Lawson's phrase is a telling one. Given the opportunity – in 1940 as the man who was asked to take Labour into the wartime coalition; and in 1945 as the beneficiary of an unprecedented landslide for Labour – his solidity and integrity did indeed turn into massiveness.

It is only when Attlee's life is seen in the long view that one appreciates just how remarkable the story was. This was a man born into the governing class of the British Empire and expected to serve it, but instead chose to embed himself in the East End of London to study and alleviate poverty, later confronting communists, anarchists and fascists on the streets. This was a young officer of the Territorial Army who became disgusted at

British imperialism but took great pride in fighting for his country in the First World War; who could admire the convictions of his pacifist elder brother, whom he loved dearly, but still tell him that he thought he was badly wrong, and that his duty to the community of which he was part outweighed his individual conscience. Like many others in the Labour Party, Attlee was a personal loser in the General Strike of 1926, and, given his loyalty to the leader, more personally hurt by the betrayal of Ramsay MacDonald than perhaps anyone else. His assertion that the only time one was permitted to rebel against an officer was when he went over to the enemy was a sign of the depth of his feeling.

In the early 1930s, it looked like Attlee might take a turn towards radicalism along with Stafford Cripps. But a combination of an almost innate constitutionalism and a recognition that pacifism was inadequate to deal with a treacherous world in which Hitler, Stalin and Mussolini operated shook him to his senses. He was also, from the mid-thirties at least, at the centre of the major events of the middle part of the twentieth century, from his visit to the front line of the Spanish Civil War to the march to war in 1938–9. As leader of the Labour Party, he was the man who took it into coalition at Britain's zero hour in 1940; who appealed to the nation for calm at the height of the Blitz, when Churchill was absent; who flew, flanked by Spitfires, to Italy, France and Germany at the end of the war, and saw the aftermath of the Battle of Monte Cassino, and Soviet flags flying in Berlin. As prime minister, he was the man who replaced Churchill and faced up to Stalin at Potsdam in 1945, and who secretly built the atom bomb while he publicly built the National Health Service.

Not only was Attlee there at these moments, his personal journey was also emblematic of larger trends in the British national story. In the different phases of Attlee's life, much more so than Winston Churchill's, there lies a clue to the path taken by the country as a whole: the pride in empire in the late Victorian period, with national self-confidence shaken by the Anglo-Boer War and the emergence of new and dangerous rivals; the feeling that the widespread poverty and social despair in the slums created by industrialisation were stains on the national character; the belief that citizenship was a right of every man, and woman, rather than the preserve of a propertied few; the conviction that Britain, for all its flaws, was still a better place than most, and boasted traditions of liberty that were (twice) worth fighting to preserve; the rejection of an economic orthodoxy which held that high levels of unemployment and poverty were an unavoidable part of the system; the conviction that 'the right to work' was as legitimate a demand as any other; the demand that, in the aftermath of two wars, there had to be a new deal between state, society and the individual; and the understanding that the nation-state was best when it acted honourably abroad, but sometimes it also needed to be firm in defence of its security and its values. What happened in 1945 was that Clement Attlee and the British people arrived on the same page in history – much as they had with Winston Churchill in May 1940.

To take Attlee as emblematic of the average Briton is to push the case too far. In his later years, when once travelling in a third-class carriage to Westminster, Attlee was once stopped by a commuter who asked him 'if anyone had ever said he looked just Mr. Attlee'. 'Frequently', came the reply. On his retirement in 1955, one American journalist reflected on the oft-made comment that he 'went about his business looking just like the sort of man who would vote for Attlee'. There were many Britons who looked liked him, shared his shyness, his dislike of pomposity, and his instinct for flat, direct statements of the truth. However, to describe Attlee 'simply as a self-portrait of the English voter' is to 'write him off too cheap'. That he was unthreatening and unexotic did not mean that he was not bold, courageous, and sometimes radical. Attlee and his party 'put Britain, both at home and abroad, through the political sausage grinder with a vigour and determination seldom seen in this cautious island since the Normans took a good hold on the Saxons'.[6]

Through all of this, of course, Attlee refused to see himself as a hero. His 1954 memoir, *As it Happened*, was so diffident and self-effacing as to almost seem deliberately mischievous. His private assessment of his career was even drier too. In his personal papers there is a single sheet of paper on which he typed out a list of what he saw as his sixteen major political achievements. It began with helping George Lansbury through the difficult years of 1931–5, then keeping the Labour Party united and as an effective opposition in 1935–40. Next came bringing the party united into the coalition government in 1940 and bringing it out again intact in 1945. Related to this was keeping Labour members of the government working as a cohesive team during the war period. He was particularly pleased at bringing in a number of under-secretaries of state over the course of war, such as James Chuter Ede and Ellen Wilkinson, who subsequently became good ministers. In 1945, he was most proud of three things: his election broadcast response to Churchill; forming a strong and well-balanced government at short notice after the election; and defeating Churchill so emphatically in debate in the motion of censure he brought against the government that December. Keeping the confidence of the trade union movement through difficult years and managing a team of egos in his Cabinet thereafter also gave him particular pride. Other achievements on his matter-of-fact list included losing no by-elections when prime minister, 'dealing with the India problem', and generally 'dealing with Commonwealth affairs'.[7]

As leader of the opposition from 1935 to 1945, and from 1951 to 1955, Attlee had one overarching goal: to keep his party united. As prime minister in 1945–51 he supplemented this with two other goals: delivering on the promises made in his party's manifesto; and finding a workable consensus amongst his ministers to help achieve this goal. At no stage did Attlee claim the achievements of his government for himself, or use them to bolster his own reputation at the expense of others. He never sought to put himself in the limelight. Nor did he ever present himself as a martyr, or a man who sacrificed himself for his party, even though he was often a lightning rod for its frustrations. He had a strong sense that his government was of great significance in British history, and that it had outstripped even the great reforming post-1906 'New Liberal' government of Henry Campbell-Bannerman, to whom he was often compared. Perhaps he could have made more of this in public, as a riposte to his critics. But, as he put it, 'grown men who know the score, do not want their leader to be continually beating his breast and advertising his agonies.'[8] For this reason, it has been hard to construct a legend around him.

This book began with the argument that Clement Attlee has not been so much underestimated as underappreciated. Attlee's reputation in British history is a favourable one – praised by academics and generally spoken of with fondness. No one needs to rescue him from opprobrium. Yet even his most articulate defenders have sometimes been guilty of damning him with faint praise. Peter Hennessey has described Attlee, memorably, as a 'real-life Captain Mainwaring', while making a powerful case that he brought about a tangible improvement in the lives of ordinary Britons after 1945.[9] Others have stressed his personal integrity, reliability, and abilities as a chairman and manager of an unruly party. An obituary in *The Economist* in 1967 reasoned that 'if there is a peculiar Attleean claim to fame it is as the cautious, quiet, capable operator at the heart of great events who eschewed the charismatic performances of his great contemporaries.' He was 'a sound and conscientious political leader of the second rank'.[10] As the *Observer* put it in a profile of him in 1944, he was 'the Tertium Quid, the Chairman, the known quality, the man of character . . . neither bigot, doctrinaire, Labour boss, nor careerist . . . first-class captain . . . political catalyst . . . [and] man of character'.[11] There was nothing, in this, to counter the view of Bevan that he was the 'Arch-Mediocrity'.[12]

This still leaves something of a hole; or, more precisely, a gap between our understanding of Attlee the politician, and Attlee the man. To assess him primarily through the prism of the government he led – or to focus narrowly on his record as party leader – is to provide only a partial picture. The legislative achievements of that government were many, and there is no need to recount them in full here. By setting them against the background of Attlee's whole career, however, we see them in a different light. National insurance, a new welfare and healthcare system, trade union rights and self-determination for former colonies were goals that the Labour movement – and it is important to see it as a movement rather than simply a party – had been fighting for for more than half a century. Therefore, as early as 1948, in fact, the prime minister thought in terms of many aspects of his government as a mission fulfilled, if not quite complete. The Labour movement, as distinct from the party imagined by socialist intellectuals, was a twentieth-century political project, arising out of the trade union movement, that achieved many of its goals.

The fulfilment of Attlee's mission had three main strands. The first was to atone for the betrayal of those who had sacrificed themselves for their country in the First World War. It was as the champion of the betrayed that Major Attlee became mayor of Stepney and first emerged in national politics as MP for Limehouse. In both cases, he made his maiden speech in the name of those who had returned from war but were told there was no employment, and scant support from the state which they had risked their lives, and lost limbs, family and friends, to defend. It was a mission fulfilled for Attlee that the promises made to those in the Second World War were kept after 1945 – that the full employment of the wartime economy was maintained and the key principles of the Beveridge Report were implemented.

The second way in which Attlee thought that his government had ful-filled its mission was on social legislation. This was to universalise the concept of social welfare by grounding it in an ideal of citizenship. Others, including the Webbs and William Beveridge, contributed to that mission. But Attlee worked alongside these pioneers from the outset; and it was Attlee's government that finally ended the stigma of means testing and the Poor Law, which he had first devoted himself to campaigning against in the early 1900s, by introducing national insurance and welfare legislation. Accordingly the National Insurance Act of 1946 was his proudest moment.

The third aspect of this mission fulfilled was to bring Queen Victoria's British Empire to an end, and to turn it into a Commonwealth. Crucially, this was not by repudiating its past but by delivering upon the promise that it had always held out – of self-governance under the rule of law. To call these changes revolutionary is to characterise them in a way that Attlee himself would not recognise. There was a circularity and a continuity in his thinking that went back to his earliest political engagement. When delivering his Chichele Lectures, on the theme of the transition from *Empire into Commonwealth* in 1960, he returned not only to his memories of the Diamond Jubilee of 1897, but even further back to the Attlee family breakfast table in 1896. He remembered the frown that had come across his father's face when reading in *The Times* of the Jameson Raid, as a sign that the imperial project had gone sadly awry. The important thing about the Indian independence movement, for Attlee, was that it was predicated on principles that Britons could recognise as their own. In one sense then, he felt that the British Empire had successes to its name.

This is not to say that Attlee thought that the mission of the Labour Party was complete. But it is to posit that he viewed it in very different terms than many intellectuals on the left. When setting out in national politics in 1920, Attlee had evoked the idea of a 'New Jerusalem'. He returned to this idea again in October 1951 in his last speech as prime min-ister. He felt that the building of the New Jerusalem had begun. Yet, beyond referring to the new garden cities, or hundreds of thousands of new social houses, the idea was suitably vague. The utopian idealism of his youth was replaced by something else. Instead, he judged his own government against the standard of existing history, rather than by how far it delivered upon a theoretical scheme or blueprint. He did not want Labour to stop in 1948, but he did want it to pause, and to re-examine its founding principles, before rushing on with a technocratic project to build a socialist state that would please the purists such as G.D.H. Cole.

Attlee certainly thought there was still much work to be done. But he also urged a process of self-examination as he passed the reins of power on to a new generation. In an article in *Reynold's News*, written just after his retirement as leader, he reflected on the passing of those who had come of age during the First World War or lived through the depression of the interwar years. Young people today were better off materially than they had been in those times. A new message was required to engage their attention. There was a danger that people would be distracted by personal interests or the greater leisure time now afforded to them. In the context of the cold war, the real threat to Western democracy came as much from a 'lack of interest on the part of the people as it did from attacks by its enemies'. Those who focused all their energies on the mechanics of building a socialist state were in danger of missing the ethical core that must underlie it. True socialism, he argued, 'must be built in the minds and hearts of men and women', for it was not just an economic theory but a way of life.[13]

The other matter on which Attlee thought socialists needed to refocus their priorities was the balance between rights and obligations. Towards the end of his time as prime minister, his message became increasingly ethical in tone. Some of this was out of necessity. As prime minister, in the face of periodic economic crises, he was forced to ask the nation to continue in the spirit of solidarity and self-sacrifice that had got them through the war. For many, these appeals to the public spirit became wearisome. For those on the right, such as Evelyn Waugh, it reflected the bankruptcy – both economic and intellectual – of the Labour project. For those on the left, such as Nye Bevan, Attlee's 'moral homilies' to 'stick together', or his use of cricketing metaphors, were an infuriating distraction. When Attlee made appeals to citizenship and self-sacrifice, such as at the party conferences at Margate in 1948, or Scarborough in 1951, his critics on the left believed he was stalling, evading commitments to further socialist advance. In fact, a closer reading of his words show that they contain warnings about the future of the Labour Party that look ever more prescient with the passing of time. Socialism demanded 'a higher standard of civic virtue than capitalism'. It was 'the greatest task which lies ahead of us all in the Labour and Socialist movement to see to it that the citizen's sense of obligation to the community keeps pace with the changes effected in the structure of society. We need to stress duties as well as rights.'[14]

Somewhere along the way, the citizenship ideal that defined Attlee's career was lost. On the left, it became more common to sneer at the patriotism that was so important to Attlee's life, from start to finish. Of all the Labour leaders to have followed Attlee since 1955, perhaps only James Callaghan, prime minister from 1976 to 1979, understood what Attlee meant. Writing in 1983, when the Labour Party had lurched to the left under Michael Foot, Callaghan suggested that: 'If Attlee were alive today his virtues would not be fashionable in some quarters. Let there be no doubt that he would encourage us to go forward on a Socialist path. He would place as much emphasis on ethical principles as on detailed programmes: on the bounden duty we owe one another as much as our rights; that radical change needs to be made persuasive if it is to be acceptable and become permanent; and that party members have an obligation to work as a team and have no right to insist on the last drop of their particular sectarianism to the exclusion of all else.'[15] Once again, these are notions that were lost in transit.

Attlee had no shortage of critics on the right. Yet it is one of the ironies of British history that the greatest damage done to his legacy has come from the left; more specifically, the intellectuals of the left. To some extent this was an accident of history. Attlee had reasonably warm relationships with Fabians such as Beatrice Webb and Douglas Cole until the early 1930s, though, as his private letters show, he was never intoxicated by them. After becoming leader in 1935, during bitter disputes within the Labour movement in a radical and unstable decade, he became the target for those who were discontented with the overall direction of the party leadership. In the pages of *Tribune,* or the *New Statesman,* he was subject to a din of constant criticism. Stafford Cripps, who was once a great friend, was responsible for bankrolling these efforts. Nye Bevan delivered the attacks with the most effect. Harold Laski, who had a liberal interpretation of his role as Labour chairman, sowed the seeds of dissent within the party itself.

That Attlee survived these attacks does not mean we should forget just how incessant they were. This is particularly important as myths have begun to emerge around the Attlee story. The election victory of 1945 was the sweetest vindication of the country-first/party-second strategy that Attlee pursued during the war, along with Herbert Morrison and Ernest

Bevin. His comment to Laski, that he was 'sufficiently experienced in war-fare, to know that the frontal attack with a flourish of trumpets, heartening as it is, is not the best way to capture a position' is arguably one of the greatest put-downs in British history.[16]

Some of the criticisms made of Attlee's leadership were justified; or, at least, there were times when a sense of theatre and drama might have bought him more credit, and protection. Equally some of the suggestions that came from Attlee's critics – such as forming a popular front with the Communist Party, hounding out Churchill, or pulling down the coalition government in 1943 or 1944 – were blind alleys of the most self-destructive kind. They have justified the imputation of Herbert Morrison that the Labour Party behaved like a suicide club. After 1945, in the flush of victory, there was a temporary reprieve from the hysteria. From 1947, it began to build once more. Again, there were legitimate criticisms made of Attlee's leadership style. Cripps, Dalton, Morrison and even Bevin thought he sometimes failed to lead the government at moments of economic turbu-lence such as the convertibility crisis of 1947, or the devaluation crisis of 1948. That he did not really understand economics is perhaps a black spot on his record. Overall, however, Attlee presided over one of the most effi-cient and active – in terms of legislation passed – governments in British history. That he kept it cohesive for as long as he did owed much to his skill, and not a little to his physical fortitude and courage.

That Attlee was asked to remain as leader for another four years after Labour's election defeat of 1951 demonstrates two important facts. The first was the recognition that he had become one of Labour's best electoral assets. It was only in hindsight that this became apparent. In the 1935 gen-eral election, Attlee presided over a significant recovery in Labour's fortunes but few gave him the credit. As it was a decade until the next general elec-tion, there was little to judge him on. Labour strategists, including Laski and Morrison, feared Attlee was no match for Churchill in 1945. In fact, Attlee's steady patriotism, unthreatening nature and obvious decency were the most effective retorts to Churchill's scaremongering in that campaign. That the majority of the service vote swung to Attlee is a small but reveal-ing fact. A telling assessment was provided by General William Slim, head of the fourteenth Army in Burma, and a future Chief of the Imperial Gen-eral Staff: 'Attlee made a much deeper impression on the public by his modesty, his dignity and his simple straightforwardness free of all bombast.'[17] In 1950, 1951 and 1955, despite all the trials and tribulations of the previous years, the same Labour strategists made sure the campaign pivoted around Attlee himself. 'Dear old Clem' was regarded with great affection on the road, as Violet drove him around the country once again. Looking back further, the East End political fixer Oscar Tobin deserves some credit here. It was Tobin who first recognised in 1919 that Major Attlee, a man who had distinguished himself in the service of his country, had a natural appeal that went beyond the prototypical Labour voter.

The other reason why Attlee was asked to remain as leader of the opposition after 1951 was that none of the pretenders to the throne – Morrison, Bevan or Gaitskill – had sufficient support to win a leadership election without the party descending into civil war. The recognition that only Attlee could keep the party together in the short term meant that respect for him grew. Hugh Dalton, for one, changed his estimation of Attlee's leadership skills considerably over the years. The Bevanites continued to cause problems, but even they came to realise that Attlee was far from the lightweight figure that he was portrayed as being. Bevan himself – who had been allowed to flourish to become one of the heroes of the Attlee government – had kinder words for the former prime minister in later years.

Yet, while Attlee's critics on the left grew to respect him more, they still failed to understand him. Part of this was due to Attlee's shyness; and his reluctance to beat his breast. But it also betrayed a lack of curiosity, a certain self-satisification, which characterised those who disparaged him. The Labour MP and Bevanite Ian Mikardo recalled a story that captures this mentality perfectly. He described how he would often sit with Bevan, Foot and Richard Crossman around a large table in the Smoking Room of the House of Commons. The drinks were always accompanied by lively discussions, 'generally about history or literature or philosophy or the arts rather than politics'. When he was leader of the opposition, required to spend more time with foot soldiers, Attlee came in one evening 'blinking like an owl in sunlight'. After much persuasion, he joined their table. Each of the four tried to get a conversation going with the party leader, only to founder on his shyness and monosyllabic responses. It was only when Wesley Perrins, a trade union official with a Black Country accent, intervened and asked Attlee about the ongoing cricket match between Worcestershire and Yorkshire at Headingly that he came to life. From that moment, said Mikardo, whenever he came in 'we stopped talking about Voltaire or Gladstone or Picasso and started talking cricket.' After a while he stopped coming entirely. 'I suppose he found the strain too great.'[18]

Could that distance have been bridged? With the passage of time, the British left moved further away from a true understanding of Attlee. In fact, it showed an ever-smaller interest in trying to achieve one. As the 'old left' faded in the late 1950s, so a self-described 'New Left' movement emerged in its place. In the pages of New Left Review, founded in 1960, there was a complete rejection of the tradition of moderate, reformist, democratic socialism which Attlee had come to embody. It was Harold Laski's protégé, a young Marxist intellectual called Ralph Miliband, who did more than any other to disparage the heritage of Attlee's Labour government, deriding it as insipid and conformist when it could have been revolutionary.[19] Others on the New Left – such as Raymond Williams – argued that an alternative path was available but had not been taken; one which would have meant rejecting the American loan of 1945, and the Marshall Plan two years later, and which would have moved Britain one step closer to socialist purity.[20]

A radical, cultural critique of the Attlee years also began to gain momentum at the dawn of the 1960s. In 1960, Hugh Thomas, in an edited collection on The Establishment, bemoaned the failure of the Labour government to disrupt and dismantle the social, economic and political status quo when they had the chance. They had tinkered with the bodywork but left the engine untouched.[21] The same was said of British foreign policy, in which Bevin was said to be unduly influenced by the 'old gang' at the Foreign Office, and the pattern of behaviour was unchanged, despite Attlee's 'slight case of heresy' when he had fought with his chiefs of staff and his foreign secretary over his desire to withdraw hundreds of thousands of troops from the Middle East.[22]

There were a few on the British left who might have cracked the Attlee code but who, for various reasons, did not. George Orwell was the most obvious candidate. His famous 1941 essay, 'The Lion and the Unicorn: Socialism and the English Genius' was a brilliant critique of precisely the type of left-wing intellectuals who sneered at the simplistic patriotism of men like Attlee. More than that, it prefigured the very British type of revolution over which Attlee's government was to preside. This would not mean 'red flags and street fighting', but 'a fundamental shift of power'. What was wanted was an 'open revolt by ordinary people against inefficiency, class privilege and the rule of the old,' he wrote, but it could be achieved in a democracy. 'The England that is only just beneath the surface, in the factories and the newspaper offices, in the aeroplanes and the submarines, has got to take charge of its own destiny.'[23] Orwell shared other things with Attlee. One, as the son of civil servants in India, was a fondness for Rudyard Kipling; another was support for the Republican cause in the Spanish Civil War in the 1930s. For whatever reason, Attlee, whom Orwell called a 'dead fish', never captured his imagination.[24] Yet, despite his complaints about Attlee's government not going far enough in certain aspects, Orwell defended it in American left-wing journals on the grounds that it was struggling against the backdrop of near bankruptcy. At one point he described himself as a 'critical supporter' of the government's efforts. Had Orwell not died in January 1950 he might have come to a fuller appreciation.[25]

Another socialist intellectual who was well equipped to come to a truer understanding of Attlee was E. P. Thompson, the Communist Party member and historian, most famous for his 1963 book, *The Making of the English Working Class*. One of the major themes of Thompson's writing was that there was a vibrant historical tradition of British revolutionary radicalism, and that communists and Marxists need not look to the Soviet Union, or other European communist parties, for inspiration. This began with the work of William Morris, the man whose work had also led Attlee into the socialist fold fifty years before.

In 1955, the year that Attlee resigned from the leadership of the Labour Party, Thompson published a biography of Morris, 'our greatest Socialist intellectual', with the subtitle *Romantic to Revolutionary*.[26] In rediscovering Morris, Thompson was reacting against what he called a 'hostile national culture both smug and resistant to intellectuality'. As a response to the insipid nature of modern socialism, he celebrated various traits in Morris's work: his 'rebellious humanism'; his rejection of the Industrial Revolution as a 'catastrophe'; and the revolutionary message in his work.[27]

For Thompson, it went without saying that Attlee's government of 1945–51 failed on these terms. In his 1890 book *News From Nowhere*, Morris had envisaged communist revolution in England by 1952. Morris had also warned that the application of 'practical' or 'state socialism', by ameliorating the conditions of the workers, was a mere half-measure, and a perversion of pure socialism. Predictably, Thompson had no patience with those who celebrated the achievements of Attlee's government. He subjected his fellow historian Kenneth Morgan's 1984 book, *Labour in Power*, which remains the most spirited defence of the Attlee government, to an excoriating critique. In Thompson's evocative phrase, Attlee's ministers were the 'the Gadarene Swine', pigs possessed by demons who ran headlong into defeat.[28]

One thing that spurred Thompson to write about *Romantic to Revolutionary* was a previous biography of Morris, published in 1949, written by an American academic, Lloyd Eric Grey. Thompson was furious about what he saw as the inadequacies of Grey's interpretation. In his view, Grey had failed to give sufficient weight to the fact that Morris was a committed Marxist. Grey was also wrong to argue that Morris had become disillusioned toward the end of his life with revolutionary socialism, and that Morris's critique of capitalism was 'moral' rather than 'economic'. What was left by such an interpretation was a weak and milky form of socialism. In words that Bevan might have used about Attlee, Thompson called this 'a doctrine of give and take – of sportsmanship and of fellowship'.[29] No doubt Thompson would have made much of the fact that, when he was still prime minister, Attlee greatly enjoyed Grey's book, having been given it at Christmas 1949 by his Secretary of State for the Colonies, Arthur Creech Jones.[30] Had Thompson known this, it would have confirmed all his suspicions.

There is no evidence that Attlee read Thompson's biography of Morris, nor do we know what he thought of Thompson's critique. Thompson's book was, however, picked up by a member of a former member of Attlee's government, John Strachey. Strachey was well placed to consider it. He was a former member of the Marxist 'Left Book Club' in the 1930s. Before the war he had been one of Attlee's critics. He decried the Labour leader's gradualism and confidence that class conflict would diminish under a majority Labour government.[31] Yet Strachey began to change his estimation of Attlee over the course of the war, during which he served in the RAF. Of Strachey, Attlee later wrote that if he 'were a typical sample of the intellectual in politics, we could do with a few more'. His years in the RAF 'taught [him] about men and matters he might not otherwise have met'. Unlike many intellectuals, he was a 'hard worker with the intellectual humility and fearlessness to face his own ignorance'.[32] In 1946, against his expectations, he was brought into government as

Minister of Food and, from 1950 to 1951, served as Secretary of State for War. He served Attlee's government faithfully, and he began to come to a more profound appreciation of the man who led it. More importantly, as Strachey's biographer noted, he was one of the few survivors of 'the old left in English politics who tried seriously to think out an intellectual position for the 1950s'.[33]

In December 1955, a few days after Attlee retired, Strachey wrote an appreciation of his former leader for the *Daily Herald*, titled 'Clem Attlee – the Incorruptible Leader'. In assessing Attlee's twenty years as leader of the Labour Party, Strachey revealed that he had recently been reading a newly published biography of William Morris (Thompson's book). It had given him pause for thought. He understood that Morris remained important to the Labour movement, for all the reasons Attlee had outlined. Yet Strachey made the point that it was much easier for Morris and the early pioneers to keep their faith bright and burning than it was for the present generation, who had won many victories along the way. Morris had predicted that socialism would come to Britain, all at once, in a single year of revolutionary change in 1952. 'We know better now. We know that Socialism does not come, and will not come, like that. We know that it is coming steadily, step by step, first in that part of our national life, then in another. We know that not only is this step-by-step advance a far better, more civilised and humane way forward; we know that no one really believes that there is any alternative to it.'[34]

The story of the twentieth-century Labour Party was ultimately one that required compromise. That the purism of William Morris was incompatible with that was something Attlee was acutely aware of. From the moment that Labour accepted the responsibility for governance, it could not afford to think in terms of utopias. This was true at both the municipal and the national level. At the outset of his career, in his 1920 book, *The Social Worker*, Attlee quoted one of his favourite lines from Morris's novel, *A Dream of John Ball*, about the Peasants' Revolt of 1381. It came at the end of the novel when John Ball, the leader of the revolt, pauses to reflect on his failed revolution. 'I pondered all these things, and how men fight and lose the battle, and the thing they fought for comes about in spite of their defeat, and when it turns out not to be what they meant, and other men have to fight for what they meant under another name,' says Ball. For Attlee, writing in 1920, the lesson of Morris's life was 'the importance of seeing things as a whole', over the passage of time. Thus he aimed fire at those who criticised him for pragmatism or compromise as mayor of Stepney, and 'got down into their own little puddle and look with a jealous eye on intruders'.[35] When Labour formed its first national government in 1924, Tom Attlee quoted the very same lines to the same effect in an essay on 'Lost Causes' for the *Manchester Guardian*.[36]

When Clement Attlee became leader of the Labour Party himself, John Ball's words seemed more apposite then ever. Unprompted, in September 1937, he paraphrased the very same excerpt from *A Dream of John Ball* and quoted it back to his brother. But this time it came with a twist. 'It is true as was said in John Ball, that the things we fight for turn out to be different from what we hoped and have to be fought for in other ways, but what is not proven is that if those causes had been allowed to go down, the things for which we strove would *inevitably* have come about in another way. There is no warrant in history for this. It is only an optimistic assumption.'[37]

Of the two Attlee brothers, Tom was truer to the tradition of William Morris. By contrast, as we have seen, Clem admired the work of the American socialist writer Edward Bellamy, whom Morris had set out to critique. It was as a soldier during the First World World War that Clem had given up on the purism that had characterised his brother's pacifism, and which he saw as fatal to the Labour movement more broadly. 'I think then if life is to be action not contemplation – if we are to do things – we must necessarily make sacrifices,' he said in 1918.[38] That did not mean that he abandoned all he had learned from Morris, or recoiled from the moral vision which had inspired him so many years before. As his 1937 letter to Tom demonstrates, it remained embedded in his consciousness. Opening a Morris Gallery in Walthamstow in 1950, Attlee confessed that a 'machine-made world in which men were becoming more and more the slaves of their own inventions' was not what Morris had envisaged.[39] When his friends in the Labour Party gave him anthologies of Morris's poetry in the early 1960s, he was touched that they 'knew where my love resided'.[40] Ultimately, however, Morris had to be left behind.

The purpose of this book has not been to assess the extent of change brought about by Attlee's government by measuring it against a scale of socialist purity. The people's flag which was raised over the New Jerusalem was 'not the deepest red' but the very fact the government of 1945–51 has caused such debate among historians tells us much about its importance in our national story.[41] In the final analysis, Attlee's message was consistent from 1918. Not only was it fatalistic to give up on political action if one could not attain one's purist ideals; it was also dangerous. There was no guarantee that the things for which Attlee had striven all his life would come about if he left the battlefield to others.

It was only when his brother's time as prime minister came to an end in 1951 that Tom Attlee could fully appreciate what this meant. Looking back to the old days when they had attended meetings of the Fabians and the Christian Socialists in the early 1900s, he pondered, 'did we ever dare to hope that we should get right into the Promised Land in our lifetime? That it should have been done with Clem as Prime Minister makes me give thanks every time I think of it.'[42]

NOTES

Prologue

1   *Clement Attlee: Granada Historical Records Interview* (London: Panther Record, 1967), p. 29.
2   The most famous example of this is Correlli Barnett, *The Audit of War: The Illusion and Reality of Great Britain as a Great Nation* (London: Macmillan, 1987).
3   For a balanced assessment of the film by Kenneth Morgan, the leading historian of Attlee's government, see 'The Spirit of '45', *House Magazine*, 3 May 2013, p. 54.
4   W. Golant, 'The Early Political Thought of C. R. Attlee', *Political Quarterly*, 40 (1969), pp. 246–55.
5   René Kraus, *The Men Around Churchill* (Philadelphia and New York: J. B. Lippincott, 1941), p. 171.
6   Frank Field, 'Introductory Essay: A Social Democrat in Action', in Frank Field (ed.), *Attlee's Great Contemporaries: The Politics of Character* (London: Continuum, 2009), p. xiii.
7   Quoted by Jon Cruddas, 'Attlee, the ILP and the Romantic Tradition', Attlee Memorial Lecture 2011, http://www.independentlabour.org.uk/main/2011/11/04/attlee-the-ilp-and-the-romantic-tradition/
8   Maurice Glasman, Jonathan Rutherford, Marc Stears and Stuart White, *The Labour Tradition and the Politics of Paradox* (Oxford Seminars Series, Oxford: Lawrence and Wishart, 2011).
9   Patrick Wintour and Andrew Sparrow, 'Labour can achieve radical change amid austerity, says Ed Miliband', *Guardian*, 11 June 2013.
10 *Guardian*, 28 March 2015.
11 John Campbell, *Roy Jenkins: A Well-Rounded Life* (London: Vintage, 2015).
12 Margaret Thatcher, *The Path to Power* (London: Harper Press, 1995), p. 69.
13 John Bew, 'Clement Attlee detested faddish radicalism – you couldn't say that Jeremy Corbyn is his heir', *New Statesman*, 26 July 2015; Dominic Sandbrook,

'What Labour's greatest leader can teach these squabbling pygmies', *Daily Mail*, 25 July 2015.

¹⁴ Nicklaus Thomas-Symonds, *Attlee: A Life in Politics* (London and New York: I. B. Tauris, 2012).

¹⁵ Kenneth Harris, *Attlee* (London: Weidenfeld & Nicolson, 1982); Trevor Burridge, *Clement Attlee: A Political Biography* (London: Jonathan Cape, 1986); Francis Beckett, *Clem Attlee: A Biography* (London: Richard Cohen Books, 1997).

¹⁶ Robert Crowcroft, *Attlee's War: World War II and the Making of a Labour Leader* (London and New York: I. B. Tauris, 2011).

¹⁷ Peter Hennessey, *Never Again: Britain, 1945–51* (London: Penguin, 2006). For the writing of contemporary history, see Hennessey, *Distilling the Frenzy: Writing the History of One's Own Time* (London: Biteback, 2012).

¹⁸ For the authoritative account of the Attlee government see Kenneth O. Morgan, *Labour in Power, 1945–1951* (Oxford: Oxford University Press, 1985). For the years preceding Labour's victory, the best account remains Paul Addison, *The Road to 1945: British Politics and the Second World War* (London: Pimlico, 1994). For the Labour left of the 1930s, the best starting point is Ben Pimlott, *Labour and the Left in the 1930s* (Cambridge: Cambridge University Press, 1997). See also Jonathan Swift, *Labour in Crisis: Clement Attlee and the Labour Party in Opposition, 1931–40* (Houndsmill: Palgrave, 2001). For an accessible modern history of the Labour Party, see Martin Pugh, *Speak for Britain: A New History of the Labour Party* (London: Vintage, 2011).

¹⁹ C. R. Attlee, 'Blue Stocking in Action', in Field (ed.), *Attlee's Great Contemporaries*, pp. 35–8.

1 – 'Introduction: The Red Flag'

¹ Letter from C. R. Attlee MP to the sister of Captain Lechler, [undated] in John Lindley, *Captain Lindley MC: A Hero of the Great War: Letters from a Troop Ship, Gallipoli and Mesopotamia* (Bound by Peter Tuffs, May 2008) [in collection of Imperial War Museum, London], pp. 172–3.

² For the list of names of fallen comrades and Attlee's account of the war, see ATLE 1/11.

³ Personal particulars of Clement Richard Attlee in his War Office medical file, WO 339/10870.

⁴ Col. B. R. Mullaly, *The South Lancashire Regiment: The Prince of Wales's Volunteers* (Bristol: The White Swan Press, 1952), pp. 225–9.

⁵ Captain C. W. Baxter to his mother, 5 February 1916, *Private Papers of Captain C. W. Baxter*, Imperial War Museum, Document 1026.

⁶ *The Basrah Times*, 1 May 1916, in Private Papers of Captain C. W. Baxter.

7   Letter from Lindley to his mother, 7 March 1916, in Lindley, *Captain Lindley MC*, pp. 100–1.

8   Personal note written on Walney Island Barrow, 1918, *Attlee Papers*, Churchill College Archives Cambridge, ATLE 1/18.

9   Quoted in Beckett, *Clem Attlee*, p. 50. Attlee's poetry is in a personal collection kept by the Attlee family.

10 C. R. Attlee, *As it Happened* (London: Odhams Press, 1954).

11 Letter from Lindley to his mother, 16 March 1916, in Lindley, *Captain Lindley MC*, pp. 100–1.

12 Report on the siege of Kut-al-Amara by Lieutenant H. McNeal, Royal Field Artillery, Dec 1915–Apr 1916, WO 32/5204.

13 Captain C. W. Baxter to his mother, 28 June 1916, Private Papers of Captain C. W. Baxter, Imperial War Museum, Letter no. 87.

14 Mullaly, *The South Lancashire Regiment*, pp. 225–9.

15 *Basrah Times*, 1 May 1916, in Private Papers of Captain C. W. Baxter, Imperial War Museum.

16 Letter from C. R. Attlee MP to the sister of Captain Lechler, in Lindley, *Captain Lindley MC*, pp. 17–23.

17 Clement Attlee to Tom Attlee, 19 April 1916, Attlee Papers, MS. Eng. c. 4792.

18 Medical report and files on Attlee's return to England, WO 339/10870.

19 Post Office Telegram, 23 April 1916, in John Lindley, *Captain Lindley MC*, p. 105.

20 Captain C. W. Baxter to his mother, 28 April 1916, Private Papers of Captain C. W. Baxter, Document 1026.

21 Captain C. W. Baxter to his mother, 16 July 1916, Private Papers of Captain C. W. Baxter, Letter no. 91a.

22 Clement Attlee to Tom Attlee, 19 April 1916, MS. Eng. c. 4792.

23 Austen Morgan, *James Connolly: A Political Biography* (Manchester: Manchester University Press, 1988).

24 Reflections on the past, undated [1944], Attlee Papers ATLE 1/27.

25 *Time*, 13 August 1945.

26 *Daily Mail*, 14 October 1935.

27 *Manchester Guardian*, 4 July 1948.

28 Kraus, *The Men Around Churchill*, pp. 168–83.

29 Cyril Clemens, *The Man from Limehouse: Clement Richard Attlee* (New York: International Mark Twain Society, 1946), p. 39.

30 *Washington Post*, 8 December 1955.

31 Jack Lawson, 'Clem Attlee', Lawson Papers, LAW 2/4/2/2/27–31.

32 *Observer*, 9 January 1949.

33 H. Jebb, *The Memoirs of Lord Gladwyn* (London: Weidenfeld & Nicolson, 1972), p. 166.

34 R. J. Cruikshank, 'The surprise packet', *News Chronicle*, 28 March 1953.

35 *The Attlee Memorial Statue in the House of Commons* (Public Information Office, Series No 2, London, 1980).

36 Attlee, *As it Happened*, pp. 9–10.

37 Winston Churchill, *London to Ladysmith via Pretoria* (London: Longmans Green, 1900).

38 Earl Attlee, 'Foreword', *The Churchill Digest* (London: Reader's Digest, 1965), p. 6.

39 C. R. Attlee, 'Truth About the War', in Field (ed.), *Attlee's Great Contemporaries*, p. 12.

40 *Manchester Guardian*, 12 March 1924.

41 *Clement Attlee: Granada Historical Records Interview*, p. 20.

42 Earl Attlee, 'Foreword', *The Churchill Digest* (London: Reader's Digest, 1965), p. 6.

43 *Clement Attlee: Granada Historical Records Interview*, p. 29.

44 Lord Bridges, 'Clement Richard Attlee', *Biographical Memoirs of Fellows of the Royal Society*, vol. 14 (November, 1968), pp. 15–36.

45 Michael Foot, *Aneurin Bevan: A Biography: Volume 2: 1945–60* (London: Davis-Poynter, 1973), pp. 28–9.

46 Entry for 13 April 1954, Ben Pimlott (ed.), *The Political Diary of Hugh Dalton, 1918–40, 1945–60* (London: Jonathan Cape, 1986), p. 623.

47 Tom Hopkinson, 'The Attlee Story', *Observer*, 11 April 1945.

48 'Rating British Prime Ministers', Ipsos MORI, 29 November 2004.

49 Quoted by Kenneth Morgan in *Labour People: Leaders and Lieutenants, Hardie to Kinnock* (London: Faber, 1987), p. 148.

50 W. J. Brown, 'Why Attlee is safe in his job', in A. V. Alexander Papers, AVAR 2.

51 Robert Pearce, *Attlee* (London: Routledge, 1997), pp. 2–3.

52 Entry for 8 August 1945, Stuart Ball (ed.), *The Headlam Diaries, 1935–1951* (Cambridge: Cambridge University Press, 1999), Camden Fifth Series, vol. 14, p. 474.

53 Giles Radice, *The Tortoise and the Hares: Attlee, Bevin, Cripps, Dalton, Morrison* (London: Politico's, 2008).

54 'The Egotist', *New Statesman and Nation*, 24 April 1954.

55 'As it Happened', *The Economist*, 14 October 1967, p. 129.

56 Isaiah Berlin to Rowland Burdon-Miller, 29 December 1949, Isaiah Berlin, and Henry Hardy and Jennifer Holmes (eds), *Enlightening: Letters, 1946–1960* (London: Chatto & Windus, 2009), p. 158.

57 Foot, *Bevan*, p. 30.

58 *Clement Attlee: Granada Historical Records Interview*, p. 12.

59 C. R. Attlee, 'A Man of Power', in Field (ed.), *Attlee's Great Contemporaries*, p. 128.

60 John Buchan, *Oliver Cromwell* (Kelly Bray, Cornwall: House of Stratus Books, 2008), pp. 3–4.

61 C. R. Attlee, 'The Pleasure of Books', in Field (ed.), *Attlee's Great Contemporaries*, pp. 15–22. The original essay appeared in the *Guardian*, 22 April 1963.

62 Jack Lawson. 'The Rt. Hon. Clement Attlee, C.H., M.P., Prime Minister', Jack Lawson Papers, Durham University Library, GB-0033-LAW 2/4/2/2/13–26.

63 C. R. Attlee, *The Social Worker* (London: G. Bell and Sons, Ltd, 1920), p. 242.

[64] C. R. Attlee, 'The Pleasure of Books', in Field (ed.), *Attlee's Great Contemporaries*, pp. 15–22.

[65] John Livingston Lowes, *The Road to Xanadu: A Study in the Ways of the Imagination* (London and New York: Houghton Mifflin, 1927),

[66] Morgan, *Labour People*, p. 148.

[67] *Guardian*, 22 April 1963.

[68] D. T. Elliot (ed.), *Attlee as I Knew Him* (London: London Borough of Tower Hamlets, 1983), p. 44.

[69] Caroline Robbins, *The Eighteenth-Century Commonwealthman: Studies in the Transmission, Development, and Circumstance of English Liberal Thought from the Restoration of Charles II until the War with the Thirteen Colonies* (Boston: Harvard University Press, 1959).

[70] Lord Attlee, 'Montgomery: My Assessment', *Observer*, 2 November 1958.

[71] Kenneth Harris, *Attlee* (London: Weidenfeld & Nicolson, 1982), pp. 125–6.

[72] Michael Jago speculates on this in *Clement Attlee: The Inevitable Prime Minister* (London: Biteback, 2014), p. 18.

[73] He much enjoyed John Buchan's 1934 book, *Oliver Cromwell*.

[74] Trevor Evans, 'Portrait of a Shy Man: Britain's First Minister', *New York Times*, 5 August 1945.

[75] Clement Attlee to Tom Attlee, 6 July 1945, Ms. Eng. c. 4793, f. 52.

[76] Clement Attlee, 'Lansbury and Crooks', *Reynold's News*, 9 September 1956.

[77] In his collection of Attlee's speeches, Roy Jenkins included a whole section on 'moral values in life and politics'. These included addresses to the Free Church Congress and the General Assembly of the Church of Scotland. See C. R. Attlee, and Roy Jenkins (ed.) *Purpose and Policy: Selected Speeches* (London and New York: Hutchinson and Co., 1946), pp. 103–15.

[78] Colm Brogan, 'Taxi Riddle at Number 10', *Daily Express*, 28 December 1949. See also John Gardiner, *The Victorians: An Age in Retrospect* (London: Hambledon and London, 2002), p. 57.

[79] Frank Pakenham, Earl of Longford, *Eleven at No. 10: A Personal View of Prime Ministers, 1931–1984* (London: Harrap, 1984), p. 78.

[80] *Clement Attlee: The Granada Historical Records Interview*, p. 47.

[81] For this distinction, see Hugh Cunningham, 'The Language of Patriotism 1750–1914', *History Workshop* (1981), vol. 12, no. 1, pp. 8–33; Gareth Stedman Jones, 'Rethinking Chartism', in *Languages of Class: Studies in English Working Class History 1832–1982* (Cambridge: Cambridge University Press, 1983).

2 – 'With apologies to Rudyard Kipling'

[1] Notes from Diaries, Attlee Papers, ATLE 1/1.

[2] Attlee, *As it Happened*, p. 8.

3   Peggy Attlee, *With a Quiet Conscience: Biography of Thomas Simons Attlee* (London: Dove & Chough, 1995) p. 2.

4   Attlee, *As it Happened*, p. 10.

5   Attlee, *With a Quiet Conscience*, p. 1.

6   Attlee, *As it Happened*, p. 10.

7   Harris, *Attlee*, p. 22.

8   Attlee, *Quiet Conscience*, pp. 1–3.

9   Trevor Burridge, *Clement Attlee: A Political Biography* (London: Jonathan Cape, 2005), p. 11.

10 Quoted in Michael Jago, *Clement Attlee: The Inevitable Prime Minister* (London: Biteback, 2014), p. 9.

11 Attlee, *As it Happened*, p. 11.

12 Clemens, *Man from Limehouse*, p. 3.

13 Clem to Tom, 27 December 1954, Ms. Eng. c. 4794, f. 43.

14 Gardiner, *The Victorians*, p. 198.

15 Harris, *Attlee*, p. 5.

16 Clemens, *Man from Limehouse*, p. 4.

17 Sir David Hunt, *On the Spot: An Ambassador Remembers* (London: Peter Davies Ltd, 1975), p. 61.

18 Clem to Tom, 25 September 1950, Ms. Eng. c. 4794, f. 7.

19 Trevor Evans, 'Portrait of a Shy Man: Britain's First Minister', *New York Times*, 5 August 1945.

20 Attlee to Patricia Beck, 25 October 1965, Ms. Eng. lett c. 571, f. 83.

21 Attlee, *Quiet Conscience*, p. 5.

22 Vincent Brome, *Clement Attlee: A Pictorial Biography* (London: Lincolns-Prager, 1949), p. 14.

23 Thomas Attlee, 'Lost Causes', in Attlee, *Quiet Conscience*, pp. 128–9.

24 C. R. Attlee, 'The Pleasure of Books', in Field (ed.), *Attlee's Great Contemporaries*, pp. 15–22.

25 *Chicago Daily Tribune*, 18 November 1945.

26 Attlee, *With a Quiet Conscience*, pp. 6–7.

27 John Haney, *Clement Attlee* (London: Chelsea House Publishers, 1989), p. 22.

28 Attlee, *Quiet Conscience*, p. 10; Attlee, *As it Happened*, p. 19.

29 Clement Attlee, *Empire into Commonwealth* (London and New York: Oxford University Press, 1961), p. 6.

30 Attlee, *As it Happened*, p. 19.

31 Clement Attlee, 'John Bull's First Job', *Spectator*, 13 December 1963.

32 Francis Williams, *Fifty Years' March: The Rise of the Labour Party* (London: Odhams Press, 1950), pp. 9–33.

33 C. R. Attlee, 'Keir Hardie', in Field (ed.), *Attlee's Great Contemporaries*, p. 28.

34 Thomas Symonds, *Attlee: A Life in Politics*, p. 9.

35 Attlee, *Quiet Conscience*, pp. 17–26.

36 Attlee, *As it Happened*, pp. 21–2.

[37] Haney, *Attlee*, p. 21.

[38] Brome, *Attlee*, p. 14.

[39] Clements, *Man from Limehouse*, p. 2.

[40] Harris, *Attlee*, p. 13.

[41] Ibid., pp. 9–15.

[42] Attlee, *As it Happened*, pp. 21–2.

[43] *Manchester Guardian*, 13 November 1948.

[44] *Guardian*, 22 April 1963.

[45] Golant, 'The Early Political Thought of C. R. Attlee', pp. 246–55.

[46] Clement Attlee, 'John Bull's First Job', *Spectator*, 13 December 1963.

[47] Attlee, *Empire into Commonwealth*, pp. 2–3.

[48] Earl Attlee, 'Changes of Fifty Years', *Pakistan Institute of International Affairs*, vol. 9, no. 4 (December, 1956), pp. 177–81.

[49] Attlee, *Empire into Commonwealth*, pp. 2–3.

[50] H. G. Wells, *The New Machiavelli* (London: Penguin Books, 1946 edn), pp. 100–1.

[51] Clem to Tom, 20 April 1949, Ms. Eng. c. 4793, f. 71.

[52] George Orwell, 'Rudyard Kipling' (1936), http://theorwellprize.co.uk/george-orwell/by-orwell/essays-and-other-works/rudyard-kipling/

[53] Clem to Tom, 9 June 1960, Ms. Eng. c. 4794, f. 89.

[54] Attlee, *Empire into Commonwealth*, pp. 6–12.

[55] Ibid., p. 11.

[56] Wells, *The New Machiavelli*, p. 102.

[57] Attlee, *Empire into Commonwealth*, pp. 6–12.

[58] Clement Attlee, 'Two Sides of Colonialism', *Spectator*, 27 September 1956.

[59] Clem to Tom, 9 June 1960, Ms. Eng. c. 4794, f. 89.

[60] Earl Attlee, 'Changes of Fifty Years', *Pakistan Institute of International Affairs*, vol. 9, no. 4 (December 1956), pp. 177–81.

[61] Earl Attlee, 'India Ten Years After', *World Affairs*, vol. 120, no. 3 (Fall 1957), pp. 67–8.

[62] Elliot (ed.), *Attlee as I Knew Him*, p. 49.

[63] Clement Attlee, 'Two Sides of Colonialism', *Spectator*, 27 September 1956.

[64] *Manchester Guardian*, 11 February 1937.

[65] Wells, *The New Machiavelli*, p. 101.

[66] Elliot (ed.), *Attlee as I Knew Him*, p. 39.

3 – News from Nowhere

[1] William Morris, *News from Nowhere and Other Writings* (London: Penguin, 1993), p. 134.

[2] Ibid., pp. 41–230. For the authoritative work on Morris, see Fiona MacCarthy, *William Morris* (London: Faber and Faber, 1994).

[3] Attlee, *As it Happened*, p. 18.

4 Elliot (ed.), *Attlee as I Knew Him*, p. 22.
5 Gareth Stedman Jones, *Outcast London: A Study in the Relationship Between Classes in Victorian Society* (Oxford: Clarendon Press, 1971), pp. 140, 142, 149. See also Henry Mayhew, and Rosemary O'Day and David Englander (eds), *London Labour and the London Poor*, [first published 1861] (London: Wordsworth Classics, 2008).
6 *Observer*, 7 May 1944.
7 Clemens, *Man from Limehouse*, p. 7.
8 C. R. Whiting, 'Clement Richard Attlee', *Oxford Dictionary of National Biography* (Oxford: Oxford University Press, 2004).
9 Personal note written at Haileybury, undated, Attlee Papers, ATLE 1/18.
10 C. R. Attlee, 'England, My England', in Field (ed.), *Attlee's Great Contemporaries*, pp. 59–60.
11 C. R. Attlee, *The Social Worker* (London: G. Bell and Sons, Ltd., 1920), p. 2.
12 Clemens, *Man from Limehouse*, p. 7.
13 Clement Attlee, 'John Bull's First Job', *Spectator*, 13 December 1963.
14 Morris, *News from Nowhere and Other Writings*, p. 134.
15 Roy Jenkins, *Mr. Attlee: An Interim Biography* (London: Heinemann, 1948), pp. 30–46.
16 Broome, *Attlee*, p. 20.
17 Asa Briggs and Anne Macartney, *Toynbee Hall: The First Hundred Years* (London, Boston, Melbourne and Henley: Routledge, 1984), pp. 1–9, 16, 35–8.
18 Quoted in *Time*, vol. 12, 1885.
19 Morris, 'Looking Backward', *Commonweal*, 22 June 1889, in Morris, *News from Nowhere and Other Writings*, pp. 353–8.
20 Margaret Harkness, *In Darkest London* [first published in 1889 as *Captain Lobe: A Story of the Salvation Army*] (London: Black Apollo Press, 2003), pp. 12–13, 59.
21 Ibid., pp. 113–18.
22 Jack London, *The People of the Abyss* (London: The Workhouse Press, 2013), pp. 1–10.
23 Ibid., preface, pp. 75–85, 134–5, 120–4, 164–5.
24 Personal note written at Haileybury, undated, Attlee Papers, ATLE 1/18.
25 Leo Chiozza Money, *Riches and Poverty* (London: Methuen, 1905).
26 Attlee, *Quiet Conscience*, pp. 17–26, 30–1.
27 *Manchester Guardian*, 2 January 1954.
28 Quoted in Jon Cruddas, 'Attlee, the ILP and the Romantic Tradition', Attlee Memorial Lecture 2011, http://www.independentlabour.org.uk/main/2011/11/04/attlee-the-ilp-and-the-romantic-tradition/. For the Attlee–Taylor dispute see *Spectator*, 12 July 1957.
29 Clem to Tom, 16 October 1941, Ms. Eng. c. 4793, f. 15.
30 Clem to Tom, 7 February 1949, Ms. Eng. c. 4793, f. 71.
31 Clem to Tom, 23 December 1949, Ms. Eng. c. 4793, f. 84.

[32] Jeremy Nuttall, *Psychological Socialism: The Labour Party and Qualities of Mind and Character, 1931 to the Present* (Manchester: Manchester University Press, 2006), p. 48.

[33] Attlee, *As it Happened*, pp. 29–30.

[34] C. R. Attlee, 'The Pleasure of Books', in Field (ed.), *Attlee's Great Contemporaries*, pp. 15–22.

[35] Ibid.

[36] Leo Chiozza Money, *Riches and Poverty* (London: Methuen, 1905).

[37] 'I am no more able to share your enthusiasm for the German Nazi regime than I was to agree with you in your support of Italian Fascist Imperialism,' Attlee wrote to him, 14 December 1940, Chiozza Money Papers, British Library, MS Add.9259/IV.

[38] Clemens, *Man from Limehouse*, p. 5.

[39] Clement Attlee, 'John Bull's First Job', *Spectator*, 13 December 1963.

[40] Lord Bridges, 'Clement Richard Attlee', *Biographical Memoirs of Fellows of the Royal Society*, vol. 14 (November, 1968), pp. 15–36.

[41] John Shepherd, *George Lansbury: At the Heart of Old Labour* (Oxford: Oxford University Press, 2002), pp. 5, 35.

[42] Clement Attlee, 'Lansbury and Crooks', *Reynold's News*, 9 September 1956.

[43] George Lansbury, *My England* (London: Selwyn and Blount Ltd, 1934), p. 15.

[44] Gordon Phillips, *The Rise of the Labour Party, 1893–1931* (London and New York: Routledge, 1992), pp. 16, 19.

[45] Attlee Papers, ATLE 1/18.

[46] Attlee, *The Social Worker*, p. 207.

[47] Clement Attlee, 'Uncle Arthur Henderson', *Reynold's News*, 16 September 1956.

[48] Clem to Tom, 23 December 1949, Ms. Eng. c. 4793, f. 84.

[49] Harris, *Attlee*, p. 29.

[50] C. R. Attlee, 'Blue Stocking in Action', in Field (ed.), *Attlee's Great Contemporaries*, pp. 35–8.

[51] Ibid., pp. 35–8.

[52] C. R. Attlee, *The Social Worker* (London: G. Bell and Sons, Ltd., 1920), p. 147.

[53] Elliot (ed.), *Attlee as I Knew Him*, p. 3.

[54] Ibid., p. 39.

[55] Attlee, *The Social Worker*, p. 210.

[56] J. T. Murphy, *Labour's Big Three: An Autobiographical Study of Clement Attlee, Herbert Morrison and Ernest Bevin* (London: The Bodley Head, 1948), p. 11.

[57] *The Twenty-Second Annual Report of the Universities Settlement in East London, for the year ending 30 June 1906*, in Toynbee Hall Annual Reports 1906–1910, Toynbee Hall Archive, London.

[58] Jose Harris, *William Beveridge: A Biography* (Oxford: Oxford University Press, 1997), pp. 44–63.

[59] Jenkins, *Attlee*, p. 60.

60 Harris, *Attlee*, p. 30.
61 John Shepherd, *George Lansbury: At the Heart of Old Labour* (Oxford: Oxford University Press, 2002), p. 71.
62 Attlee, *Quiet Conscience*, p. 36.
63 Donald Rumbelow, *The Houndsditch Murders and the Siege of Sidney Street* (London: W. H. Allen, 1988).
64 Attlee Papers, Churchill College Archives Cambridge, ATLE 1/18.
65 Mary Seaton, 'Attlee at Britain's Helm', *Free World*, September 1945, pp. 75–6.
66 Attlee, *As it Happened*, p. 37.
67 Samantha L. Bird, *Stepney: Profile of a London Borough from the Outbreak of the First World War to the Festival of Britain, 1914–1951* (Cambridge: Cambridge Scholars Publishing, 2011), pp. 96–7.
68 Bird, *Stepney*, p. 109.
69 Joe Jacobs, *Out of the Ghetto: My Youth in the East End: Communism and Fascism, 1913–1939* (London: Phoenix Press, 1991), p. 71.
70 Bird, *Stepney*, pp. 96–7.
71 C. R. Attlee, 'The Application of Democratic Principles to Government', 11 May 1943, printed for the War Cabinet, CAB 118/32.
72 Clemens, *Man from Limehouse*, pp. 143–4.
73 Attlee, *As it Happened*, p. 38.
74 Ben Pimlott, *Hugh Dalton* (London: Jonathan Cape, 1985), p. 86.
75 Brome, *Attlee*, p. 24.
76 Attlee, *Quiet Conscience*, pp. 38–40.
77 Thomas Simons Attlee, 'The Influence of Architecture on the Condition of the Worker', *The British Architect*, 11 September 1914, pp. 165–7.
78 Elliot (ed.), *Attlee as I Knew Him*, p. 2.
79 Haney, *Attlee*, p. 31.

4 – *The Soldier*

1 Photograph of officers, 26 October 1916, in Private Papers of Captain C. W. Baxter GMC MC, London: Imperial War Museum.
2 Peter Hart, *Gallipoli* (London: Profile Books, 2011), pp. 404–6. For Attlee's war account, ATLE 1/11.
3 Alan Moorhead, *Gallipoli* (London: Aurum Press, 2007), p. 328.
4 Attlee, *As it Happened*, p. 49.
5 Notes on 'The Socialist International', Attlee Papers, ATLE 1/19.
6 A. J. P. Taylor, *The Trouble Makers: Dissent over Foreign Policy, 1792–1939* (London: Faber and Faber, 2008 edn), pp. 140–5.
7 George Bernard Shaw, 'Common Sense About the War', *New York Times*, 15 November 1914.

8 Attlee, *The Labour Party in Perspective*, p. 200.

9 Rhiannon Vickers, *The Labour Party and the World, vol. 1: The Evolution of Labour's Foreign Policy* (Manchester: Manchester University Press, 2003), p. 45.

10 Attlee, *As it Happened*, p. 51.

11 'Military career', Attlee Papers, ATLE 1/5.

12 Attlee, *As it Happened*, pp. 55–6.

13 Ibid.

14 Personal note written on Walney Island, Barrow in Furness, 1918, Attlee Papers, ATLE 1/18.

15 C. R. Attlee, 'The Pleasure of Books', in Field (ed.), *Attlee's Great Contemporaries*, pp. 15–22.

16 Captain C. W. Baxter to his mother, 5 July 1915, Private Papers of Captain C. W. Baxter, Letter no. 7.

17 'Attlee's Experiences on Active Service', in the possession of the Attlee family. They are recounted in Nicklaus Thomas-Symonds, *Attlee*, pp. 22–4.

18 Captain C. W. Baxter to his mother, 27 July 1915, Private Papers of Captain C. W. Baxter, Letter no. 12.

19 Lindley letter to his family, 27 August 1915, John Lindley, *Captain Lindley MC*, p. 43.

20 Captain C. W. Baxter to his mother, 5 February 1916, Private Papers of Captain C. W. Baxter, Document 1026.

21 *Guardian*, 22 April 1963.

22 Captain C. W. Baxter to his mother, 27 July 1915, Private Papers of Captain C. W. Baxter, Letter no. 12.

23 Lindley letter to his family, 11 August 1915, John Lindley, *Captain Lindley MC*, p. 35.

24 See John Hargrave, *The Suvla Bay Landing* (London: Macdonald, 1964).

25 Lindley letter to his family, 9 September 1915, John Lindley, *Captain Lindley MC*, pp. 48–9.

26 Captain C. W. Baxter to his mother, 27 August 1915, Private Papers of Captain C. W. Baxter, Letter no. 18.

27 Lindley letter to his family, 27 August 1915, John Lindley, *Captain Lindley MC*, p. 43.

28 Quoted in Hart, *Gallipoli*, pp. 394–5.

29 Captain C. W. Baxter to his mother, 12 October 1915, Private Papers of Captain C. W. Baxter, Letter no. 29.

30 Letter by 2nd Lt Lechler, 4 October 1915, in John Lindley, *Captain Lindley MC*, p. 72.

31 Captain C. W. Baxter to his mother, 6 November 1915, Private Papers of Captain C. W. Baxter, Letter no. 35.

32 Captain C. W. Baxter to his mother, 10 November 1915, Private Papers of Captain C. W. Baxter, Letter no. 36.

33 Quoted in Hart, *Gallipoli*, pp. 394–5.
34 Interview in *Guardian*, 22 April 1963.
35 Hart, *Gallipoli*, pp. 404–6.
36 Lindley letter to his family, 6 November 1915, John Lindley, *Captain Lindley MC*, p. 82.
37 Hart, *Gallipoli*, pp. 412–15.
38 Attlee, *As it Happened*, pp. 49–56.
39 Captain C. W. Baxter to his mother, 9/24 December 1915, Private Papers of Captain C. W. Baxter, Letter no. 43.
40 Colonel B. R. Mullaly, *The South Lancashire Regiment: The Prince of Wales's Volunteers* (Bristol: The White Swan Press, 1952), pp. 197–8.
41 Clem to Tom, 19 April 1916, MS. Eng. c. 4792.
42 Medical report and files on Attlee's return to England, WO 339/10870.
43 Attlee, *Quiet Conscience*, p. 67.
44 Ibid., pp. 48–53.
45 Ibid., p. 55.
46 Medical report and files on Attlee's return to England, WO 339/10870.
47 'Military career', Attlee Papers, ATLE 1/5.
48 Ibid.
49 Clem to Tom, 20 March 1918, Ms. Eng. c. 4792.
50 Personal note written on Walney Island, Barrow-in-Furness, 1918, Attlee Papers, ATLE 1/18.
51 Ibid.
52 Entry for 5 December 1927, Nigel Nicolson (ed.), *Harold Nicolson: Diaries and Letters, 1907–1964* (London: Phoenix, 2004), p. 394.
53 Personal note written on Walney Island, Barrow-in-Furness, 1918, Attlee Papers, ATLE 1/18.
54 Clem to Tom, 20 March 1918, Ms. Eng. c. 4792.
55 Clem to Tom, 2 April 1918, Ms. Eng. c. 4792.
56 Personal note written on Walney Island, Barrow-in-Furness, 1918, Attlee Papers, ATLE 1/18.
57 Clem to Tom, 2 April 1918, Ms. Eng. c. 4792.
58 Harris, *Attlee*, pp. 39–40.
59 Attlee, *Quiet Conscience*, p. 66.
60 'How are Major Attlee's Russians Getting On?', World Parliament Association Papers, University of Sussex Library, SxMs33/5/4/1/4.
61 Clem to Tom, 20 March 1918, Ms. Eng. c. 4792.

5 – *Looking Backward: 2000–1887*

1   Edward Bellamy, *Looking Backward* [1887] (New York: Lancer Books, 1968 edn), pp. 347–51.
2   Joshua Muravchik, *Heaven on Earth: The Rise and Fall of Socialism* (London and New York: Encounter, 2002), p. 344.
3   Ronnie Dugger, 'Looking backward at 2000', *The Commonwealth* (Fall, 1999).
4   C. R. Attlee, 'The Pleasure of Books', in Field (ed.), *Attlee's Great Contemporaries*, pp. 15–22.
5   Attlee, *The Social Worker*, pp. 137–41.
6   Morris, 'Looking Backward', *Commonweal*, 22 June 1889, in Morris, *News from Nowhere and Other Writings*, pp. 353–8.
7   Tristram Hunt, *The Frock-Coated Communist: The Revolutionary Life of Friedrich Engels* (London: Allen Lane, 2009), p. 237.
8   Attlee, *The Social Worker*, pp. 1–28.
9   Mark Bevir, *The Making of British Socialism* (Princeton, NJ: Princeton University Press, 2011), pp. 85–105.
10 Stephen Coleman, 'The Economics of Utopia: Morris and Bellamy Contrasted', *Journal of the William Morris Society*, vol. 8 (November, 1989), p. 6.
11 E. P. Thompson, *William Morris: Romantic to Revolutionary* (New York: Pantheon, 1955).
12 Edward Bellamy, *Looking Backward*, pp. 347–51.
13 Clem to Tom, 1 May 1944, Ms. Eng. c. 4793, f. 40.
14 A. W. Wright, *G. D. H. Cole and Socialist Democracy* (Oxford: Clarendon Press, 1979), pp. 72–101.
15 Clem to Tom, 2 April 1918, Ms. Eng. c. 4792.
16 Burridge, *Attlee*, p. 53.
17 Attlee, *The Social Worker*, p. 25.
18 Clem to Tom, 2 April 1918, Ms. Eng. c. 4792.
19 Clem to Tom, 20 March 1918, Ms. Eng. c. 4792.
20 Attlee, *The Social Worker*, p. 140.
21 Clem to Tom, 20 March 1918, Ms. Eng. c. 4792.
22 Ibid.
23 Wells, *The New Machiavelli*, pp. 112–13.
24 Attlee, *The Social Worker*, p. 16.
25 Ibid., p. 138.
26 Clem to Tom, 20 March 1918, Ms. Eng. c. 4792.
27 Clem to Tom, 9 August 1952, Ms. Eng. c. 4794, f. 25.
28 C. R. Attlee, 'Blue Stocking in Action', in Field (ed.), *Attlee's Great Contemporaries*, pp. 35–8.
29 Clem to Tom, 20 March 1918, Ms. Eng. c. 4792.

30 Clem to Tom, 2 April 1918, Ms. Eng. c. 4792.

31 Ross McKibbin, 'Why was there no Marxism in Great Britain?', *English Historical Review*, vol. 99, no. 391 (April 1984), pp. 297–331.

32 The most serious account of his political thought, prior to this book, is Golant, 'The Early Political Thought of C. R. Attlee', *Political Quarterly*, pp. 246–55.

33 Attlee's demobilisation documents, WO 339/10870.

34 Bird, *Stepney*, p. 55.

35 'Labour in Limehouse since the War', Attlee Papers, ATLE 1/2.

36 Ibid.

37 *East London Observer*, 15 November 1920.

38 Haney, *Attlee*, p. 29.

39 Paul Addison, *The Road to 1945: British Politics and the Second World War* (London: Pimlico, 1994), p. 272.

40 *Manchester Guardian*, 15 May 1954.

41 *East London Observer*, 27 September 1919.

42 Ibid., 1 November 1919.

43 Bird, *Stepney*, pp. 66–7.

44 *East London Observer*, 15 November 1919.

45 Ibid., 15 November 1919.

46 Ibid., 6 December 1919.

47 Trevor Evans, 'Portrait of a Shy Man: Britain's First Minister', *New York Times*, 5 August 1945.

48 Francis Beckett, *The Rebel Who Lost His Cause: The Tragedy of John Beckett MP* (London: London House, 1999), pp. 32–9.

49 Bird, *Stepney*, pp. 64–5.

50 *East London Observer*, 21 January 1920.

51 Ibid., 14 February 1920.

52 Taylor, *The Trouble Makers*, p. 166.

53 Williams, *Fifty Years' March*, p. 289.

54 Quoted in W. Golant, 'C. R. Attlee in the First and Second Labour Governments', *Parliamentary Affairs*, vol. 26 (March 1973), pp. 318–35.

55 Murphy, *Labour's Big Three*, p. 109.

56 Clement Attlee, 'Uncle Arthur Henderson', *Reynold's News*, 16 September 1956.

57 Bird, *Stepney*, pp. 80–2.

58 Harris, *Attlee*, p. 47.

59 *East London Observer*, 12 June 1920.

60 Ibid., 4 September 1920.

61 Herbert Morrison, *An Autobiography* (London: Odhams Press Ltd, 1960), pp. 294–5.

62 Lord Attlee interview in Bernard Donoughue and G. W. Jones, *Herbert Morrison: Portrait of a Politician* (London: Weidenfeld & Nicolson, 1973), p. 92.

63 Attlee, *As it Happened*, p. 49.

64 Bird, *Stepney*, pp. 79–80. See also Peter Kingsford, *The Hunger Marches in Britain, 1920–1939* (London: Lawrence and Wishart, 1982, p. 14.

65 Quoted in Hart, *Gallipoli*, pp. 394–5.

66 Attlee, *As it Happened*, p. 50.

67 Bird, *Stepney*, pp. 80–3.

68 Morrison, *An Autobiography*, pp. 86–7.

69 Haney, *Attlee*, p. 29.

70 R. J. Cruikshank, 'The surprise packet', *News Chronicle*, 28 March 1953.

71 *East London Observer*, 13 November 1920.

72 C. R. Attlee, *Borough Councils: Their Constitution, Powers and Duties*, Fabian Tract No. 191 (London: Fabian Society, 1920).

73 C. R. Attlee, 'Blue Stocking in Action', in Field (ed.), *Attlee's Great Contemporaries*, pp. 35–8.

74 Nicklaus Thomas-Symonds, *Attlee*, p. 33.

75 Beckett, *The Rebel Who Lost His Cause*, p. 33.

76 Attlee Papers, ATLE 1/18.

77 Harris, *Attlee*, pp. 51–3.

78 Beckett, *The Rebel Who Lost His Cause*, p. 33.

79 Beckett, *Attlee*, pp. 69–70.

6 – *Building Jerusalem*

1 C. R. Attlee, *The Social Worker* (London: G. Bell and Sons, Ltd., 1920), p. 3.

2 *Daily Herald*, 16 November 1922.

3 Beckett, *Attlee*, p. 73.

4 *Guardian*, 22 April 1963.

5 Harris, *Attlee*, p. 550.

6 *Daily Herald*, 20 November 1922.

7 Ibid., 17 November 1922.

8 *East End News*, 17 November 1922.

9 *Daily Herald*, 23 November 1922.

10 *East End News*, 25 November 1922.

11 Golant, 'The Early Political Thought of C. R. Attlee', pp. 24–55.

12 C. R. Attlee, *The Social Worker*, pp. 1–28.

13 Ibid., pp. 1–28.

14 Ibid., pp. 137–41.

15 Ibid., pp. 137–41.

16 Ibid., pp. 1–28.

17 Matthias M. Matthijs, *Ideas and Economic Crises in Britain from Attlee to Blair, 1945–2005* (London: Routledge, 2011), p. 15.

18 Elizabeth Durbin, *New Jerusalems: The Labour Party and the Economics of Democratic Socialism* (London, Boston and Melbourne: Routledge and Kegan Paul, 1985).

19 Williams, *Fifty Years' March*, p. 298.

20 *Daily Herald*, 21 November 1922.

21 G.D.H. Cole, *A History of the Labour Party from 1914* (London: Routledge, 1948), pp. 218–19.

22 Attlee, *The Social Worker*, pp. 254, 286.

23 *Daily Herald*, 22 November 1922.

24 J. R. Clynes, 'What Makes Attlee a Leader', *Christian Science Monitor*, 19 September 1945.

25 *Clement Attlee: Granada Historical Records Interview*, p. 9.

26 Jack Lawson, 'The Rt. Hon. Clement Attlee, C.H., M.P., Prime Minister', Jack Lawson Papers, GB-0033-LAW 2/4/2/2/13–26, and 27–31.

27 23 November 1922, *Hansard*, vol. 159, cols 92–6.

28 *Daily Herald*, 24 November 1922.

29 Ibid., 11 December 1922.

30 C. R. Attlee, 'George Lansbury: Man of His Day', in Field (ed.), *Attlee's Great Contemporaries*, p. 63.

31 C. R. Attlee, 'Liberal and Labour Co-operation', *Socialist Review*, March 1922, p. 134.

32 Michael Freeden, *Liberalism Divided* (Oxford: Oxford University Press, 1986), p. 324.

33 C. R. Attlee, 'History: Socialist and Liberal', *New Leader*, 12 January 1923.

34 Clem to Tom, 16 October 1944, Ms. Eng. c. 4793, f. 45.

35 Attlee, 'History: Socialist and Liberal', *New Leader*, 12 January 1923.

36 Attlee, 'Economic Justice Under Democracy' (1938 essay) in Freeden, *Liberalism Divided*, p. 316.

37 C. R. Attlee, 'History: Socialist and Liberal', *New Leader*, 12 January 1923.

38 Ibid.

39 Morrison, *An Autobiography*, p. 99.

40 Francis Williams, *Fifty Years' March*, p. 305.

41 *Manchester Guardian*, 7 January 1924.

42 Taylor, *The Trouble Makers*, p. 168.

43 Quoted in W. Golant, 'C. R. Attlee in the First and Second Labour Governments', *Parliamentary Affairs*, vol. 26 (March, 1973), pp. 318–35.

44 Ibid.

45 Jack Lawson 'The Rt. Hon. Clement Attlee, C.H., M.P., Prime Minister', Jack Lawson Papers. GB-0033-LAW 2/4/2/2/13–26, and 27–31.

46 Attlee Papers, ATLE 1/18.

47 Ibid.

48 Clem to Tom, 18 September 1921, Ms. Eng. c. 4792.

⁴⁹ C. R. Attlee, 'The Pleasure of Books', in Field (ed.), *Attlee's Great Contemporaries*, pp. 15–22.

⁵⁰ *Clement Attlee: Granada Historical Records Interview*, p. 9.

⁵¹ Attlee Papers, ATLE 1/4.

⁵² *Darlington Evening Dispatch*, 26 May 1925.

⁵³ *Manchester Guardian*, 18 March 1925.

⁵⁴ Thomas Symonds, *Attlee*, p. 44.

⁵⁵ Elliot (ed.), *Attlee as I Knew Him*, p. 6.

⁵⁶ Earl Attlee, 'Changes of Fifty Years', *Pakistan Institute of International Affairs*, vol. 9, no. 4 (December, 1956), pp. 177–81.

⁵⁷ Francis Williams, *Ernest Bevin: Portrait of a Great Englishman* (London: Hutchinson, 1952).

⁵⁸ Jacobs, *Out of the Ghetto*, pp. 26–7, 38–9, 61.

⁵⁹ Ibid., pp. 26–7.

⁶⁰ H. Swaffer, 'What Limehouse thinks of Attlee', *Daily Express*, 23 June 1945. Quoted in ODNB.

⁶¹ Mary Seaton, 'Attlee at Britain's Helm', *Free World*, September 1945, pp. 75–6.

7 – *Fame is the Spur*

¹ Howard Spring, *Fame is the Spur* [1940] (London: Fontana Collins, 1982 edn), pp. 290–1, 527–8.

² Clem to Tom, 15 October 1940, Ms. Eng. c. 4793.

³ H. B. Lees-Smith, *The Encyclopedia of the Labour Movement*, 3 vols, (London: Caxton Publishing Company, 1928).

⁴ *Guardian*, 22 April 1963.

⁵ Clem to Tom, 28 January 1928, MS. Eng. c. 4792.

⁶ Mesbahuddin Ahmed, *The British Labour Party and the Indian Independence Movement, 1917–1939* (New York: Envoy Press, 1987), pp. 83–5.

⁷ Clem to Tom, 20 March 1928, MS. Eng. c. 4792.

⁸ Clem to Tom, 20 March 1928, MS. Eng. c. 4792.

⁹ Clem to Tom, 14 October 1928, MS. Eng. c. 4792.

¹⁰ Clem to Tom, 9 November 1928, MS. Eng. c. 4792.

¹¹ Clem to Tom, 14 November 1928, MS. Eng. c. 4792.

¹² Clem to Tom, 7 December 1928, MS. Eng. c. 4792.

¹³ Clem to Tom, 4 February 1928, MS. Eng. c. 4792.

¹⁴ Clem to Tom, 20 March 1928, MS. Eng. c. 4792.

¹⁵ Ahmed, *The British Labour Party and the Indian Independence Movement*, pp. 94–5.

¹⁶ Pearce, *Attlee*, pp. 37–8.

¹⁷ Ibid.

18 *Guardian*, 22 April 1963.
19 *Clement Attlee: Granada Historical Records Interview*, p. 9.
20 Bird, *Stepney*, p. 107.
21 *City and East London Observer*, 4 May 1929.
22 Ibid., 13 May 1929.
23 Cole, *A History of the Labour Party*, pp. 218–19.
24 *City and East London Observer*, 13 May 1929.
25 Ibid., 2 June 1929.
26 Ibid., 15 June 1929.
27 Herbert Morrison, *An Autobiography* (London: Odhams Press Ltd, 1960), p. 86.
28 Jacobs, *Out of the Ghetto*, p. 65.
29 Moonraker, 'The Things We See', *Stepney Citizen*, December 1929.
30 Matthew Worley, *Oswald Mosley and the New Party* (Houndsmill: Palgrave Macmillan, 2010), pp. 4–5.
31 *Clement Attlee: Granada Historical Records Interview*, pp. 11–12.
32 Entry for 20 November 1930, *The Political Diary of Hugh Dalton*, p. 130.
33 *Manchester Guardian*, 24 May 1930.
34 Kraus, *The Men Around Churchill*, pp. 168–83.
35 Oswald Mosley, *My Life*, p. 233.
36 Chapters from the Life of the Bullion Family, Attlee Papers, ATLE 1/26.
37 'The Problems of British Industry' (circulated to Cabinet in July 1930), in Harris, *Attlee*, appendix I, pp. 570–84.
38 *The Political Diary of Hugh Dalton*, p. 129.
39 Golant, 'C. R. Attlee in the First and Second Labour Governments', pp. 318–35.
40 Thomas-Symonds, *Attlee*, p. 57.
41 Robert Skidelsky, *Politicians and the Slump: The Labour Government of 1929–1931* (Harmondsworth: Penguin, 1967), p. 216.
42 Lord Attlee, 'What Sort of Man Gets to the Top', *Observer*, 7 February 1960.
43 Letter announcing Attlee's appointment to King George V, 3 March 1931, LCO 6/1227.
44 Moonraker, 'The Things We See', *Stepney Citizen*, December 1929.
45 C. R. Attlee, 'Post Office Reform', *New Statesman and Nation*, 7 November 1931.
46 Clem to Tom, 23 August 1931, MS. Eng. c. 4792.
47 Ramsay MacDonald to Attlee, 24 August 1931, Attlee Papers, ATLE 2/6.
48 *Clement Attlee: Granada Historical Records Interview*, pp. 11–12.
49 'The Problems of British Industry' (circulated to Cabinet in July 1930), in Harris, *Attlee*, appendix I, pp. 570–84.
50 Trevor Burridge, 'Clement Attlee reconsidered', in Brian Farrell, *Leadership and Responsibility in the Second World War* (Quebec: McGill-Queen's University Press, 2004), p. 75.
51 Attlee, *As it Happened*, p. 74.
52 Burridge, *Attlee*, p. 79.

[53] Robert Bruce Lockhart, *The Diaries of Robert Bruce Lockhart*, vol. 1 (London: Macmillan, 1973), p. 222.

[54] *Daily Herald*, 29 August 1931.

[55] Pearce, *Attlee*, pp. 46–7.

[56] *Daily Herald*, 26 August 1931.

[57] Ibid., 27 August 1931.

[58] Clem to Tom, 2 September 1931, MS. Eng. c. 4792.

[59] Matthew Worley, *Oswald Mosley and the New Party*, pp. 90–1.

[60] Beckett, *The Rebel Who Lost His Cause*, pp. 120–2.

[61] *Manchester Guardian*, 29 October 1931.

[62] Williams, *Fifty Years' March*, p. 345.

[63] *Manchester Guardian*, 29 October 1931.

[64] Ibid., 29 October 1931.

[65] Entry for 28 October 1931, Norman and Jeanne MacKenzie (eds), *The Diary of Beatrice Webb, vol. 4, 1924–1943*, (London: London School of Economics, 1985), p. 263.

[66] Betty D. Vernon, *Ellen Wilkinson* (London: Croom Helm, 1982), p. 112.

8 – *The Bullion Family*

[1] Chapters from the life of the Bullion Family, Attlee Papers, ATLE 1/26.

[2] Ibid.

[3] Trevor Evans, 'Portrait of a Shy Man: Britain's First Minister', *New York Times*, 5 August 1945.

[4] Sarah James, 'The Hostess of No. 10 Downing Street', *New York Times*, 26 August 1945.

[5] Clem to Tom, 1 September 1932, MS. Eng. c. 4792.

[6] *Manchester Guardian*, 23 July 1936.

[7] Clem to Tom, 16 November 1931, MS. Eng. c. 4792.

[8] R. Palme Dutt, *World Politics* (London: Victor Gollancz, 1936), pp. 7–8.

[9] Lansbury, *My England*, p. 14.

[10] John Shepherd, *George Lansbury: At the Heart of Old Labour* (Oxford: Oxford University Press, 2002), p. 287.

[11] Attlee Papers, ATLE 1/4.

[12] Clem to Tom, 16 November 1931, MS. Eng. c. 4792.

[13] Clement Attlee to Kingsley Martin, 22 September 1931, Kingsley Martin Archive, University of Sussex Library, SxMs11/3/1/10.

[14] John Shepherd, *George Lansbury: At the Heart of Old Labour* (Oxford: Oxford University Press, 2002), p. 287.

[15] Clem to Tom, 18 December 1931, MS. Eng. c. 4792.

[16] *Clement Attlee: Granada Historical Records Interview*, p. 16.

[17] James Stuart, *Within the Fringe: An Autobiography* (London, Sydney, Toronto: The Bodley Head, 1967), p. 150.

18 Hunt, *On The Spot*, p. 412.
19 D. R. Thorpe, *Supermac: The Life of Harold Macmillan* (London: Pimlico, 2011), pp. 109–10.
20 Clem to Tom, 19 February 1932, MS. Eng. c. 4792.
21 Wright, *G. D. H. Cole and Socialist Democracy*, pp. 171, 205.
22 Clem to Tom, 25 April 1932, MS. Eng. c. 4792.
23 Clem to Tom, 15 July 1932, MS. Eng. c. 4792.
24 Clem to Tom, 15 July 1932, MS. Eng. c. 4792.
25 Comments on the Ottawa Conference, undated, Attlee Papers, ATLE 1/23.
26 Beckett, *The Rebel Who Lost His Cause*, p. 97.
27 Clem to Tom, 8 August 1932, MS. Eng. c. 4792.
28 *Daily Herald*, 5 October 1932.
29 Ibid.
30 For the Socialist League and SSIP, see Pimlott, *Labour and the Left in the 1930s*, pp. 41–8.
31 Shepherd, *Lansbury*, pp. 296–7.
32 Ibid.
33 Haney, *Attlee*, p. 57.
34 Peter Clarke, *The Cripps Version: The Life of Sir Stafford Cripps, 1889–1952* (London: Allen Lane, 2012), p. 69.
35 Sir Stafford Cripps, 'Can Socialism come by Constitutional Methods?', in Sir Stafford Cripps et al., *Problems of a Socialist Government* (London: Victor Gollancz, 1933), pp. 35–66.
36 C. R. Attlee, 'Local Government and the Socialist Plan', in Cripps et al, *Problems of a Socialist Government*, pp. 186–208.
37 Clem to Tom, 15 February 1933, MS. Eng. c. 4792.
38 Memorandum [undated] on cabinet government, Attlee Papers, ATLE 2/1.
39 *Manchester Guardian*, 23 January 1933.
40 Durbin, *New Jerusalems*, p. 89.
41 Clem to Tom, 15 February 1933, MS. Eng. c. 4792.
42 Harold Laski, *Democracy in Crisis* (Chapel Hill: The University of North Carolina Press, 1935), pp. 9–10.
43 Clem to Tom, 7 February 1933, MS. Eng. c. 4792.
44 Clem to Tom, 15 February 1933, MS. Eng. c. 4792.
45 Clem to Tom, 7 February 1933, MS. Eng. c. 4792.
46 'Chapters from the Life of the Bullion Family', ATLE 1/26.
47 Attlee, *War Comes to Britain*, pp. 22–6.
48 Clem to Tom, 15 February 1933, MS. Eng. c. 4792.
49 Clem to Tom, 15 February 1933, MS. Eng. c. 4792.
50 For Churchill's alternative foreign policy, see R.A.C. Parker, *Churchill and Appeasement: Could Churchill Have Prevented the Second World War?* (London: Macmillan, 2000).

51   *Clement Attlee: Granada Historical Records Interview*, p. 15.
52   *The Economist*, 17 June 1933.
53   Clem to Tom, 15 February 1933, MS. Eng. c. 4792.

9 – *The Anti-Cromwell*

1   Buchan, *Oliver Cromwell*, pp. 3–4.
2   Dorsey Gassaway Fisher, Second Secretary of Embassy, to the Secretary of State, 1 November 1945, General Records of the Department of State, Record 59, Dec. File, 1945–9, Box 5902.
3   Clem to Tom, 28 February 1933, MS. Eng. c. 4792.
4   Clem to Tom, 26 December 1934, MS. Eng. c. 4792.
5   Buchan, *Oliver Cromwell*, pp. 3–4.
6   *Spectator*, 6 September 1934.
7   *New Statesman*, 17 November 1934.
8   C. R. Attlee, 'England, My England', in Field (ed.), *Attlee's Great Contemporaries*, p. 38.
9   Zara Steiner, *The Triumph of the Dark: European International History, 1933–1939* (Oxford: Oxford University Press, 2011), p. 33.
10   Haney, *Attlee*, p. 59.
11   Clem to Tom, 3 April 1933, MS. Eng. c. 4792.
12   13 June 1933, *Hansard*, vol. 279, cc. 29–146.
13   Clem to Tom, 3 April 1933, MS. Eng. c. 4792.
14   Clem to Tom, 18 August 1933, MS. Eng. c. 4792.
15   Clem to Tom, 6 November 1933, MS. Eng. c. 4792.
16   Clem to Tom, 1 January 1934 MS. Eng. c. 4792.
17   Quoted in Clarke, *The Cripps Version*, p. 62.
18   *The Political Diary of Hugh Dalton*, p. 183.
19   Clem to Tom, 16 June 1934, MS. Eng. c. 4792.
20   Ahmed, *The British Labour Party and the Indian Independence Movement*, pp. 160–8, 177.
21   Robert Rhodes, *Churchill: A Study in Failure, 1900–1939* (London: Penguin. 1970), p. 252.
22   Ahmed, *The British Labour Party and the Indian Independence Movement*, p. 177.
23   Clem to Tom, 10 July 1934, MS. Eng. c. 4792.
24   Clem to Tom, [undated] summer 1934, MS. Eng. c. 4792.
25   Cole, *History of the Labour Party*, pp. 306–7.
26   Morrison, *An Autobiography*, pp. 294–5.
27   Lord Elton, 'Labour Decides to Wait', *Elton Fortnightly* (November 1934), pp. 524–34. See also Taylor, *The Trouble Makers*, p. 166.
28   Ibid., pp. 524–34.

[29] Clem to Tom, 18 October 1934, MS. Eng. c. 4792.

[30] Clem to Tom, 18 October 1934, MS. Eng. c. 4792.

[31] Clem to Tom, 20 April, MS. Eng. c. 4792.

[32] Clem to Tom, 18 October 1934, MS. Eng. c. 4792.

[33] Clem to Tom, 10 June 1935, MS. Eng. c. 4792.

[34] *Manchester Guardian*, 8 July 1935.

[35] Ibid., 12 July 1935.

[36] Ibid., 2 October 1935.

[37] *Daily Mail*, 2 October 1935.

[38] C. R. Attlee, 'Lansbury of London', in Field (ed.), *Attlee's Great Contemporaries*, pp. 1–3.

[39] C. R. Attlee, 'A Man of Power', Field (ed.), *Attlee's Great Contemporaries*, pp. 123–33.

[40] *Observer*, 6 October 1935.

[41] *Daily Mail*, 7 October 1935.

[42] Entry for 28 September 1935, *The Diary of Beatrice Webb*, p. 358.

[43] *Daily Mail*, 8 October 1935.

[44] *Manchester Guardian*, 8 October 1935.

[45] *Daily Mail*, 9 October 1935.

[46] *Daily Telegraph*, 9 October 1935.

[47] *Daily Herald*, 9 October 1935.

[48] *Manchester Guardian*, 9 October 1935.

[49] Lord Attlee, 'What Sort of Man Gets to the Top', *Observer*, 7 February 1960.

[50] *Manchester Guardian*, 9 October 1935.

[51] For the original, see Jack Lawson. 'The Rt. Hon. Clement Attlee, C.H., M.P., Prime Minister', Jack Lawson Papers, GB-0033-LAW 2/4/2/2/13–26.

[52] *Observer*, 20 October 1935.

[53] *Daily Telegraph*, 10 October 1935; *Daily Mirror*, 9 October 1935.

[54] *Daily Herald*, 11 October 1935.

[55] Ibid., 12 October 1935.

[56] *Observer*, 13 October 1935.

[57] Ibid., 6 October 1935.

[58] *Manchester Guardian*, 14 October 1935.

[59] Clement Attlee, 'Labour's Challenge', *Daily Herald*, 25 October 1935.

[60] C. R. Attlee, *The Will and the Way to Socialism* (London, 1935), p. 120.

[61] *Daily Mail*, 14 October 1935.

[62] *Observer*, 20 October 1935.

[63] Jack Lawson 'The Rt. Hon. Clement Attlee, C.H., M.P., Prime Minister', Jack Lawson Papers. GB-0033-LAW 2/4/2/2/13–26.

[64] *Daily Herald*, 23 October 1935.

[65] HC Deb 22 October 1935 vol 305 cc17–142.

[66] *Daily Mirror*, 29 October 1935.

[67] J. L. Garvin, 'Defence for Peace', *Observer*, 27 October 1935.

68 Oswald Mosley, *My Life*, p. 396.
69 Cole, *History of the Labour Party*, pp. 310–11.
70 *Observer*, 17 November 1935.
71 Donoughue and Jones, *Herbert Morrison*, p. 237.
72 *Observer*, 24 November 1935.
73 W. Golant, 'The Emergence of C. R. Attlee as Leader of the Parliamentary Labour Party', *Historical Journal*, vol. 13, no. 2 (June 1970), pp. 318–32.
74 *The Economist*, 30 November 1935.
75 Morrison, *An Autobiography*, pp. 131, 164.
76 Donoughue and Jones, *Herbert Morrison*, p. 243.
77 Lord Attlee, 'What Sort of Man Gets to the Top', *Observer*, 7 February 1960.
78 *Tribune*, 30 March 1945.
79 *The Political Diary of Hugh Dalton*, pp. 188–9.
80 Entry for 27 November 1935, *The Diary of Beatrice Webb*, p. 360.
81 Lord Attlee, 'What Sort of Man Gets to the Top', *Observer*, 7 February 1960.

10 – *The Major Attlee Company and the Clenched-Fist Salute*

1 George Orwell, *Homage to Catalonia* in Peter Davison (ed.), *Orwell in Spain* (London: Penguin, 2001), p. 47.
2 Alex Vernon, *Hemingway's Second War: Bearing Witness to the Spanish Civil War* (Iowa City: University of Iowa, 2011), p. 35.
3 Antony Beevor, *The Battle for Spain: The Spanish Civil War, 1936–1939*, pp. 31–41.
4 James Hopkins, *Into the Heart of the Fire: The British in the Spanish Civil War* (Stanford: Stanford University Press, 2000), pp. 119–220.
5 *Observer*, 5 December 1937.
6 Clem to Tom, 27 December 1937, MS. Eng. c. 4792, f. 84.
7 Attlee, *As it Happened*, pp. 112–13.
8 Elliot (ed.), *Attlee as I Knew Him*, p. 9.
9 Clemens, *Man from Limehouse*, p. 28.
10 *Literary Digest*, 21 December 1935.
11 Duff Cooper, *Old Men Forget* (London: Rupert Hart-Davis, 1953), pp. 192–3.
12 Entry for 19 December 1935, *Harold Nicolson: Diaries and Letters*, p. 153.
13 Beckett, *Attlee*, p. 144.
14 Taylor, *The Trouble Makers*, p. 191.
15 Kenneth Young, *Stanley Baldwin* (London: Weidenfeld & Nicolson, 1976), p. 126.
16 Morrison, *An Autobiography*, pp. 164–5.
17 Entry for 28 April 1936, *Harold Nicolson: Diaries and Letters*, p. 159.
18 'Kim', 'Let Us Face Realities', *Saturday Review*, 16 May 1936.
19 Clem to Tom, 16 April 1936, Ms. Eng. c. 4792.

20 C. R. Attlee, 'The Betrayal of Collective Security' (speech by Attlee on 23 June 1936, published by the Labour Party).
21 Clem to Tom, 12 August 1936, Ms. Eng. c. 4792.
22 Attlee, *As it Happened*, pp. 108–9.
23 Richard Thurlow, 'The Failure of British Fascism 1932–40', in Andrew Thorpe (ed.), *The Failure of Political Extremism in Inter-War Britain* (Exeter: University of Exeter Press, 1989) pp. 67–86.
24 Bird, *Stepney*, pp. 108, 110.
25 Jacobs, *Out of the Ghetto*, pp. 138–9, 194–5.
26 Ibid., pp. 254–6.
27 *New York Times*, 27 September 1937.
28 Clemens, *Man from Limehouse*, pp. 67–8.
29 Clem to Tom, 26 October 1936, MS. Eng. c. 4792.
30 *Manchester Guardian*, 22 December 1936.
31 Rhodes, *Churchill*, p. 346.
32 Martin Pugh, *Speak for Britain: A New History of the Labour Party* (London: Vintage Books), p. 225.
33 Quoted in Clemens, *Man from Limehouse*, p. 31.
34 *Manchester Guardian*, 11 December 1936.
35 *Clement Attlee: Granada Historical Records Interview*, p. 14.
36 Clem to Tom, 28 December 1938, MS. Eng. c. 4792.
37 *New York Times*, 25 May 1937.
38 *Daily Herald*, 6 August 1937.
39 Vickers, *The Evolution of Labour's Foreign Policy*, pp. 119–26.
40 Clem to Tom, 26 October 1936, MS. Eng. c. 4792.
41 Clem to Tom, 26 October 1936, MS. Eng. c. 4792.
42 *Manchester Guardian*, 18 January 1937.
43 *Economist*, 23 January 1937.
44 Jonathan Swift, *Labour in Crisis: Clement Attlee and the Labour Party in Opposition, 1931–40* (Houndsmill: Palgrave, 2001), pp. 144–51.
45 *Observer*, 7 March 1937.
46 Clement Attlee to Kingsley Martin, 9 May 1937, Kingsley Martin Archive, University of Sussex Library, SxMs11/3/1/10.
47 Burridge, *Attlee*, p. 4.
48 *Economist*, 26 June 1937.
49 Thomas Jones, *A Diary with Letters* (London and New York: Oxford University Press, 1954), pp. 350–1, 358.
50 Entry for 3 December 1936, *Harold Nicolson: Diaries and Letters*, pp. 268–9.
51 Jones, *A Diary with Letters*, pp. 350–1, 358.
52 Attlee, *The Labour Party in Perspective*, p. 120.
53 Taylor, *The Trouble Makers*, p. 193.
54 *Observer*, 11 July 1937.

55 See the review in *Daily Herald*, 6 August 1937.

56 C. R. Attlee, *The Labour Party in Perspective* (London: Victor Gollancz Ltd, 1937), pp. 113–14.

57 Clement Attlee, 'Career as an author', undated, ATLE 1/25.

58 *Economist*, 2 October 1937.

59 Clem to Tom, 17 October 1937, MS. Eng. c. 4792.

60 *The Labour Party Annual Report of the 37th Annual Conference* (London: Transport House, 1937), pp. 268–70, 277–9.

61 Durbin, *New Jerusalems*, pp. 247, 260–1.

62 Clem to Tom, 17 October 1937, MS. Eng. c. 4792.

63 Trevor Evans, 'Portrait of a Shy Man: Britain's First Minister', *New York Times*, 5 August 1945.

64 Zara Steiner, *The Triumph of the Dark: European International History, 1933–1939* (Oxford: Oxford University Press, 2011), p. 221.

65 Cole, *History of the Labour Party*, pp. 328–31.

66 *The Labour Party Annual Report of the 37th Annual Conference* (London: Transport House, 1937), p. 212.

67 Clem to Tom, 17 April 1937, MS. Eng. c. 4792.

68 *The Political Diary of Hugh Dalton*, pp. 229–1.

69 *New York Times*, 10 December 1937.

70 Vernon, *Ellen Wilkinson*, p. 165.

71 *New York Times*, 23 December 1937.

72 Vernon, *Ellen Wilkinson*, p. 127.

73 *Economist*, 18 December 1937.

74 Aneurin Bevan, 'Attlee, Cripps, Morrison and Greenwood', *Tribune*, 23 December 1937.

75 C. R. Attlee, 'My answer to those who condemn me', *Tribune*, 31 December 1937.

76 Clem to Tom, 27 December 1937, MS. Eng. c. 4792.

11 – *A Word to Winston*

1 Williams, Francis, *A Prime Minister Remembers: The War and Post-War Memoirs of the Rt. Hon. Earl Attlee* (London: Heinemann, 1961), p. 15.

2 *Economist*, 17 June 1933.

3 *Daily Herald*, 11 October 1932.

4 Ibid., 6 August 1937.

5 Clem to Tom, 28 February 1933, MS. Eng. c. 4792.

6 P. M. Kennedy, 'Idealists and Realists: British Views of Germany, 1864–1939', *Transactions of the Royal Historical Society*, vol. 25 (December 1975), pp. 137–56.

7 Entry for 16 March 1938, *Harold Nicolson: Diaries and Letters*, p. 184.

8   Letter from W. Perry to Jack Lawson asking for a copy of Lawson's article 'Watch Winston', 31 January 1948, Jack Lawson Papers, LAW 2/1/551.

9   Julie V. Gottlieb and Thomas P. Linehan, *The Culture of Fascism: Visions of the Far Right in Britain* (London and New York: I. B. Tauris, 2004), p. 144.

10 David Dutton, *Anthony Eden: A Life and Reputation* (London: Arnold, 1997).

11 *Tribune*, 24 February 1938.

12 Parker, *Churchill and Appeasement*, p. 150.

13 *Manchester Guardian*, 28 February 1938.

14 Andrew David Stedman, *Alternatives to Appeasement: Neville Chamberlain and Hitler's Germany* (London and New York: I. B. Tauris, 2015), p. 206.

15 *Manchester Guardian*, 21 March 1938.

16 Ibid., 13 June 1938.

17 2 May 1938, *Hansard*, vol. 335, cc. 769–822.

18 Clem to Tom, 29 April 1938, MS. Eng. c. 4792.

19 *Observer*, 3 July 1938.

20 Albert James Sylvester, and Colin Cross (ed.), *Life with Lloyd George: The Diary of A. J. Sylvester, 1931–45* (New York: Harper and Row, 1975), pp. 215–16.

21 Parker, *Churchill and Appeasement*, p. 182.

22 Entries for 18 and 20 September, *The Political Diary of Hugh Dalton*, pp. 241–3.

23 Entry for 22 September 1938, *Harold Nicolson: Diaries and Letters*, p. 196.

24 *Manchester Guardian*, 27 September 1938.

25 Entry for 28 September, *Harold Nicolson: Diaries and Letters*, pp. 198–200.

26 James, *Churchill*, p. 428.

27 Entry for 29 September, *Harold Nicolson: Diaries and Letters*, p. 201.

28 Haney, *Attlee*, p. 68.

29 Stedman, *Alternatives to Appeasement*, p. 234.

30 3 October 1938, *Hansard*, vol. 339 cc.40–162.

31 Ibid.

32 Quoted in Clarke, *The Cripps Version*, p. 63.

33 *Manchester Guardian*, 5 November 1938.

34 Burridge, *Attlee*, p. 135.

35 Parker, *Churchill and Appeasement*, p. 205.

36 John Charmley, *Chamberlain and the Lost Peace* (London: Ivon. R. Dee, 1999), p. 146.

37 Entry for 25 January 1939, *Harold Nicolson: Diaries and Letters*, p. 206.

38 Pimlott, *Labour and the Left*, pp. 175–8.

39 *Tribune*, 24 March 1939.

40 *Clement Attlee: Granada Historical Records Interview*, p. 18.

41 Lord Attlee, 'What Sort of Man Gets to the Top', *Observer*, 7 February 1960.

42 Wright, *G. D. H. Cole and Socialist Democracy*, p. 6.

43 Clem to Tom, 3 April 1939, MS. Eng. c. 4792.

44 *Tribune*, 6 April 1939.

45 *Tribune*, 14 April 1939.

46 Entry for 20 March 1939, *The Diary of Beatrice Webb*, p. 263.

47 Taylor, *The Trouble Makers*, p. 193.

48 Williams, *A Prime Minister Remembers*, pp. 11–18.

49 Stedman, *Alternatives to Appeasement*, pp. 172–3.

50 *The Political Diary of Hugh Dalton*, pp. 231–2.

51 Attlee to Basil Liddell Hart, 9 March 1936, Liddell Hart Papers, LH 1/28/1; Attlee to Liddell Hart, 8 February 1937, LH 1/28/8.

52 Stedman, *Alternatives to Appeasement*, pp. 135–6.

53 *Observer*, 28 May 1939.

54 Clem to Tom, 4 June 1939, MS. Eng. c. 4792.

55 Clem to Tom, 19 September 1939, MS. Eng. c. 4792.

56 Entry for 2 September 1939, *Harold Nicolson: Diaries and Letters*, p. 220.

57 Entries for 14 June and 21 July, *The Political Diary of Hugh Dalton*, pp. 269, 282.

58 Donoughue and Jones, *Herbert Morrison*, p. 246.

59 Trevor Evans, 'Portrait of a Shy Man: Britain's First Minister', *New York Times*, 5 August 1945.

60 James Griffith, *Pages from Memory* (London: J. M. Dent and Sons Ltd, 1969), p. 54.

61 *Boston Globe*, 9 October 1939.

62 *Manchester Guardian*, 11 October 1939.

63 Liddell Hart to Attlee, 25 November 1939, LH 1/28/13.

64 Richard Toye, *The Labour Party and the Planned Economy, 1931–1951* (Oxford: Boydell Press, 2003), pp. 95–100.

65 *Manchester Guardian*, 18 December 1939.

66 Aneurin Bevan, 'Stop Sending Arms to Finland', *Tribune*, 22 December 1939.

67 Notes on 'The Socialist International', Attlee Papers, ATLE 1/19.

68 Aneurin Bevan, 'Challenge – or Die', *Tribune*, 5 January 1940.

69 *New York Times*, 17 January 1940.

70 'The War and the Moral issue', Ms. Attlee dep. 1, fol. 73.

71 Letter to Secretary of the Labour Party J. S. Middleton, 23 January 1940, Ms. Attlee dep. 1, fol. 62.

72 Letter to the secretaries of affiliated organisations and local Labour Parties, February 1940, and 'Notes for speakers on Labour's Home Policy', Ms. Attlee dep. 1, fols. 73–4.

73 C. R. Attlee et al., *Labour's Aims in War and Peace* (London: Lincolns-Prager, 1940).

74 *The Political Diary of Hugh Dalton*, pp. 318–19. See also Swift, *Labour in Crisis*, p. 120.

75 Cole, *History of the Labour Party from 1914*, pp. 378–9.

76 Entry for 29 February 1940, *The Diary of Beatrice Webb*, pp. 447–8.

77 C. R. Attlee, 'Blue Stocking in Action', in Field (ed.), *Attlee's Great Contemporaries*, pp. 35–8.

[78] Clem to Tom, 4 January 1940, Ms. Eng. c. 4793.

[79] Attlee broadcast to the nation, 13 April 1940, Ms. Attlee dep 1, fol. 62.

[80] Entry for 29 February 1940, *The Diary of Beatrice Webb*, pp. 447–8.

[81] Entry for 15 April 1940, Gabriel Gorodetsky (ed.), *The Maisky Diaries: Red Ambassador to the Court of St James's, 1932–1943* (New Haven and London: Yale University Press, 2015) p. 271.

[82] *New York Times*, 8 May 1940.

[83] Entry for 7 May 1940, *Harold Nicolson: Diaries and Letters*, p. 242.

[84] *Manchester Guardian*, 8 May 1940.

[85] Entry for 7 May 1940, *Harold Nicolson: Diaries and Letters*, p. 242.

[86] Peace, *Attlee*, p. 89.

[87] *Manchester Guardian*, 10 May 1940.

[88] Entry for 10 May 1940, *The Political Diary of Hugh Dalton*, pp. 344–9.

[89] *Tribune*, 10 May 1940.

[90] Entry for 10 May 1940, *The Political Diary of Hugh Dalton*, pp. 344–9.

[91] Clarke, *The Cripps Version*, p. 171.

[92] Pimlott, *Dalton*, p. 275.

[93] Pearce, *Attlee*, p. 90.

[94] Andrew Roberts, *The Holy Fox: The Life of Lord Halifax* (London: Head of Zeus, 2014), pp. 277–81.

[95] *Clement Attlee: Granada Historical Records Interview*, p. 20.

[96] Williams, *A Prime Minister Remembers*, p. 36.

[97] Donoughue and Wilson, *Morrison*, pp. 274–5.

[98] *New York Times*, 14 May 1940. See also Clemens, *Man from Limehouse*, pp. 50–1.

[99] *Manchester Guardian*, 14 May 1940.

[100] Ibid., 15 May 1940.

[101] *Daily Herald*, 14 May 1940.

[102] C. R. Attlee, 'George Lansbury: Man of His Day', in Field (ed.), *Attlee's Great Contemporaries*, p. 63.

[103] Clem to Tom, 25 April 1940, Ms. Eng. c. 4793.

[104] Shepherd, *Lansbury*, p. 361.

12 – *All Behind You, Winston*

[1] Office of the Lord Privy Seal to the Secretary of the Royal Institute of International Affairs, 21 May 1940, CAB 118/90.

[2] Kraus, *The Men Around Churchill*, pp. 168–83.

[3] Murphy, *Labour's Big Three*.

[4] Jonathan Schneer, *Ministers At War: Winston Churchill and his War Cabinet* (London: Oneworld, 2015), pp. 40–3.

[5] Pimlott, *Dalton*, p. 296.

6 Ben Pimlott (ed.), *The Second World War Diary of Hugh Dalton, 1940–5* (London: Jonathan Cape, 1986), pp. 295, 318–19.

7 Stephen Brooke, *Labour's War: The Labour Party during the Second World War* (Oxford: Clarendon Press, 1992), p. 54.

8 For a brilliant rebuttal of the argument that Attlee was somehow not a major player in the government, see Robert Crowcroft, *Attlee's War: World War II and the Making of a Labour Leader* (London and New York: I. B. Tauris, 2011).

9 G. Grant McKenzie, Secretary of Local Government Department to Attlee, 3 June 1940, Ms. Attlee dep. 1, fol. 196.

10 Lawson on Attlee, Lawson Papers, LAW 2/4/2/2/13–26.

11 David Low, *Low's Autobiography* (London: Michael Joseph, 1956), pp. 356–7.

12 Clement Attlee to David Low, 8 October 1962, David Low Papers, Beinecke Library, Yale University, GEN MSS 96, series no. 1, Box 1, f. 10.

13 Low, *Low's Autobiography*, pp. 356–7.

14 Clement Attlee to David Low, 8 October 1962, David Low Papers, GEN MSS 96, series no. 1, Box 1, f. 10.

15 Quoted in Richard Toye, *The Roar of the Lion: The Untold Story of Churchill's World War II Speeches* (Oxford: Oxford University Press, 2013), p. 1.

16 Ashley Jackson, *Churchill* (London: Quercus, 2011), p. 145.

17 *Manchester Guardian*, 15 May 1954.

18 Jackson, *Churchill*, pp. 257–8.

19 *Guardian*, 22 April 1963.

20 David Howell, *Attlee* (London: Haus, 2006), p. 129.

21 Attlee, Office of the Lord Privy Seal, to Churchill, [undated] Attlee Papers, ATTLE 2/2.

22 Lord Attlee, 'The Man I Knew', *Observer*, 31 January 1965.

23 *Tribune*, 17 May 1940.

24 Ellen Wilkinson, 'White Monday', *Tribune*, 17 May 1940.

25 Reprinted in *Manchester Guardian*, 18 May 1940.

26 Richard Overy, *The Bombing War: Europe, 1939–1945* (London: Penguin, 2014), pp. 244, 106.

27 C. R. Attlee, 'The Pleasure of Books', in Field (ed.), *Attlee's Great Contemporaries*, pp. 15–22.

28 H.J.J. Sargint, 'New Mood in Britain', *Baltimore Sun*, 9 June 1940.

29 Broadcast by Lord Privy Seal, 11 May 1940, Ms. Attlee dep. 1, fol. 190.

30 Clemens, *Man from Limehouse*, pp. 55–6.

31 Addison, *The Road to 1945*, p. 196.

32 Schneer, *Ministers at War*, p. 57.

33 Hennessey, *Never Again*, p. 28.

34 Attlee, *As it Happened*, p. 136.

35 Gen. Hastings Lionel Ismay, 1st Baron Ismay of Wormington, *The Memoirs of General Lord Ismay* (London and Melbourne: Heinemann, 1950), p. 133.

36 Quoted in Nigel Knight, *Churchill: The Greatest Briton Unmasked* (Cincinnati: David and Charles, 2009), p. 144.

37 Toye, *The Roar of the Lion*.

38 Isaiah Berlin, *Mr Churchill in 1940* (London: John Murray, 1950), p. 26.

39 Kathleen Burk, *Troublemaker: The Life and History of A. J. P. Taylor* (New Haven and London: Yale University Press, 2000), p. 440.

40 Paul Addison and Jeremy A. Craig, *Listening to Britain: Home Intelligence Reports on Britain's Finest Hour, May to September 1940* (London: The Bodley Head, 1945), pp. 77–8, 203.

41 Entry for 3 July 1940, *Harold Nicolson: Diaries and Letters*, p. 251.

42 Proposals Concerning Political Warfare, 18 October 1940, CAB 118/74.

43 A.J.P. Taylor, *Beaverbrook* (London: Hamish Hamilton, 1972), pp. 446–7.

44 Lord Attlee, 'The Man I Knew', *Observer*, 31 January 1965.

45 Lord Attlee, 'Montgomery: My Assessment', *Observer*, 2 November 1958.

46 Morrison, *An Autobiography*, pp. 208–9.

47 Jackson, *Churchill*, p. 240.

48 Clem to Tom, 19 May 1943, Ms. Eng. c. 4793.

49 Trevor Evans, 'Portrait of a Shy Man: Britain's First Minister', *New York Times*, 5 August 1945.

50 Ibid.

51 Harold Laski, 'Twelve Questions for Attlee and Greenwood', *Tribune*, 19 July 1940.

52 Attlee broadcast, 'How the Fight Goes', Ms. Attlee dep. 1, fol. 212.

53 Morrison to Attlee, 1 November 1940, CAB 118/54.

54 Entry for 7 August, *The Maisky Diaries*, p. 303.

55 James B. Reston, 'Four men put drive in the War', *New York Times*, 15 September 1940.

56 David Reynolds, *From World War to Cold War: Churchill, Roosevelt, and the International History of the 1940s* (Oxford: Oxford University Press, 2006), p. 153.

57 James B. Reston, 'Four men put drive in the War', *New York Times*, 15 September 1940.

58 Asa Briggs and Anne Macartney, *Toynbee Hall: The First Hundred Years* (London: Routledge, 1984), pp. 120–44.

59 *Toynbee Hall Whitechapel Report, 1938–1946*, pp. 10–11.

60 Lady Felicity Harewood, 'Clem, Father and Politician', The Third Attlee Memorial Lecture, The Attlee Foundation, 20 February 1985, quoted in Hennessey, *Never Again*, p. 31.

61 Attlee, *As it Happened*, p. 141.

62 Hennessey, *Never Again*, p. 31.

63 Speech at London Fire Brigade Headquarters, 21 February 1941, Ms Attlee dep. 2, f. 115.

64 Clem to Tom, 15 October 1940, Ms. Eng. c. 4793, f. 4.

65 Sarah James, 'The Hostess of No. 10 Downing Street', *New York Times*, 26 August 1945.

66 Clem to Tom, 9 November 1940, Ms. Eng. c. 4793.

67 Clem to Tom, 1 February 1941, Ms. Eng. c. 4793.

68 *Christian Science Monitor*, 27 July 1945.

69 Sarah James, 'The Hostess of No. 10 Downing Street', *New York Times*, 26 August 1945.

70 Clem to Tom, 16 March 1941, Ms. Eng. c. 4793.

71 Clem to Tom, 21 June 1941, Ms. Eng. c. 4793.

72 Lynne Olson, *Citizens of London: The Americans who Stood with Britain in Its Darkest, Finest Hour* (New York: Random House, 2009).

73 Harold J. Laski, 'Britain's Labour Ministers', *Washington Post*, 4 January 1941.

74 Hugh Wagnon, 'Cautious Clement is Britain's Second in Command', *Washington Post*, 16 February 1941.

75 Entry for 3 July 1940, *Harold Nicolson: Diaries and Letters*, p. 251.

76 Minute from Churchill to Kingsley Wood, 26 July 1940, Churchill Papers, CHAR 20/20/28-31.

77 Clem to Tom, 1 February 1941, Ms. Eng. c. 4793.

78 David Reynolds, *From World War to Cold War: Churchill, Roosevelt, and the International History of the 1940s* (Oxford: Oxford University Press, 2006), pp. 153–5.

79 Clem to Tom, 1 February 1941, Ms. Eng. c. 4793.

80 Clem to Tom, 9 August 1941, Ms. Eng. c. 4793.

81 Clem to Tom, 1 February 1941, Ms. Eng. c. 4793.

82 *New York Times*, 17 February 1941.

83 Speech by Attlee, 16 February 1941, Ms Attlee dep. 2.

84 James Chuter Ede to Attlee, 14 February 1941, Ms Attlee dep. 2.

85 Clem to Tom, 3 March 1941, Ms. Eng. c. 4793.

86 Robert Calder, *Beware the British Serpent: The Role of Writers in British Propaganda in the United States, 1939–1945* (Quebec: McGill-Queen's University Press, 2006), p. 29.

87 Speech by Lord Privy Seal, 15 March 1941, Ms Attlee dep. 2.

88 Harold Laski, 'Don't keep us waiting, Clem', *Tribune*, 9 May 1941.

89 Schneer, *Ministers at War*, pp. 101–3.

90 Foster Hailey, ' "Clem", Who Asks a Vote of Confidence', *New York Times*, 22 January 1950.

91 Clem to Tom, 9 August 1941, Ms. Eng. c. 4793, f. 12.

92 Entries for 6 August and 14 September 1941, *The Headlam Diaries, 1935–1951*, p. 267.

93 Reports of people's reactions to Attlee's broadcast and the prospects of America joining the war. Comments collected by NN, MS, Celia Fremlin, John Sommerfield in various London areas. Summary by Richard Fitter, 18 August 1941, Mass Observation Archive, SxMOA1/2/25/13/F/1.

94 Mass Observation Survey quoted in Toye, *The Roar of the Lion*, p. 133.

95 Lawrence James, *The Rise and Fall of the British Empire* (London: Abacus, 1998 edn), p. 513.

[96] *Washington Post*, 16 August 1941.

[97] 'The effects of Labour Propaganda in Germany', 10 July 1941, Ms. Attlee dep. 2, ff. 48–54.

[98] Clem to Tom, 16 August 1941, Ms. Eng. c. 4793, f. 13.

[99] Entry for 14 October 1941, *The Second World War Diary of Hugh Dalton*, pp. 293–4.

[100] Entries for 1 and 12 October 1941, in James Chuter Ede, *Labour and the Wartime Coalition: From the Diary of James Chuter Ede, 1941–1945* (London: The Historians' Press, 1987), pp. 17–18.

[101] *Baltimore Sun*, 26 October 1941.

[102] Attlee, *As it Happened*, p. 43.

[103] Attlee press conference, 20 November 1941, Ms. Attlee dep. 4, f. 99.

[104] *Manchester Guardian*, 21 November 1941.

[105] Attlee, *As it Happened*, p. 144.

[106] Notes by Clement Attlee, October–November 1941, Churchill Papers, CHAR 20/23/85-94.

[107] Marquis Childs, 'Attlee and His Party', *Washington Post*, 26 July 1945.

[108] Clem to Tom, 21 November 1941, Ms. Eng. c. 4793, f. 16.

[109] Andrew Roberts, *Masters and Commanders: The Military Geniuses Who Led the West to Victory in World War II* (London: Allen Lane, 2008), p. 203.

[110] Attlee to Churchill, 29 October 1941, CHAR 20/44/95.

[111] Clem to Tom, 21 November 1941, Ms. Eng. c. 4793.

[112] Clem to Tom, 21 November 1941, Ms. Eng. c. 4793.

[113] Lionel Robbins to the Lord Privy Seal, 21 November 1941, CAB 118/90.

[114] Lynne Olson, *Citizens of London: The Americans who Stood with Britain in its Darkest, Finest Hour* (New York: Random House, 2009), pp. 176–7, 183.

[115] Attlee to Churchill, 20 December 1941, Churchill Papers, CHAR 20/23/107.

13 – The Hunting of the Snark

[1] Clem to Tom, 27 December 1941, Ms. Eng. c. 4793, f. 19.

[2] Frank Owen, 'Secret of Mr. Attlee', *Sunday Dispatch*, 14 October 1945.

[3] Arthur Moyle, 'The Real Attlee', *Star*, 8 December 1955.

[4] The doodle is in the Attlee Papers, ATLE 2/2.

[5] Jackson, *Churchill*, pp. 308–9.

[6] Lord Moran, *Churchill at War, 1940–45* (London: Robinson, 2002), pp. 87–9.

[7] Clem to Tom, 11 June 1942, Ms. Eng. c. 4793.

[8] Clem to Tom, 11 June 1942, Ms. Eng. c. 4793.

[9] Entry for 20 January 1941, John Harvey (ed.), *The War Diaries of Oliver Harvey* (London: Collins, 1978), p. 49.

[10] Entries for 4 and 16 December 1941, *Diary of James Chuter Ede*, pp. 27–9.

11 James Leasor, *War at the Top: Based on the Experiences of General Sir Leslie Hollis* (London: Michael Joseph, 1959), pp. 169–71.

12 Clarke, *The Cripps Version*, p. 265.

13 Taylor, *Beaverbrook*, pp. 510–15.

14 Brooke, *Labour's War*, p. 177.

15 Diary entry for 17 February 1942, *The War Diaries of Oliver Harvey*, p. 97.

16 Stuart, *Within the Fringe*, p. 157.

17 Clem to Tom, 26 February 1942, Ms. Eng. c. 4793, f. 18.

18 25 February 1942, *The War Diaries of Oliver Harvey*, p. 101.

19 5 March 1942, *The War Diaries of Oliver Harvey*, p. 105.

20 Burridge, *Attlee*, p. 140.

21 Laski to Bevin, 9 March 1942, in Brooke, *Labour's War*, p. 96.

22 Clement Attlee to Jack Lawson, 2 March 1942, Lawson Papers, LAW 2/5/2/28.

23 Entry for 17 March 1942, *Diary of James Chuter Ede*, p. 54.

24 Lord Attlee, 'Bevan as Hero', *Observer*, 21 October 1962.

25 Clarke, *The Cripps Version*, pp. 118–19.

26 Harris, *Attlee*, pp. 220–2.

27 Clarke, *The Cripps Version*, pp. 276–91.

28 Ibid.

29 *Washington Post*, 20 May 1942.

30 Ibid., 24 June 1942.

31 Liddell Hart certainly noticed, collecting clippings of Attlee's comments on the conduct of the war, Liddell Hart Papers, in LH 1/28.

32 Attlee to Churchill, 10 July 1942, PREM 3/499 /9.

33 Ibid.

34 Churchill to Attlee, 29 July 1942, PREM 3/499/9.

35 Roberts, *Masters and Commanders*, p. 183.

36 Reynolds, *From World War to Cold War*, pp. 116-18.

37 *Times*, 13 June 1942; *Manchester Guardian*, 29 September 1942, Liddell Hart Papers in LH 1/28.

38 Clem to Tom, 7 August 1942, Ms. Eng. c. 4793, f. 23.

39 Harold Laski, 'Whitehall's Weary Titans', *Reynold's News*, 9 August 1942.

40 Harold Laski, 'What Labour Must Tell the Premier', *Reynold's News*, 6 September 1942.

41 Stuart, *Within the Fringe*, pp. 129–30.

42 J. Maisky to Attlee, 19 August 1942, CAB 118/5.

43 Andrew David Stedman, *Alternatives to Appeasement: Neville Chamberlain and Hitler's Germany* (London and New York: I. B. Tauris, 2015), p. 86.

44 Pearce, *Attlee*, p. 97.

45 Lord Attlee, 'Montgomery: My Assessment', *Observer*, 2 November 1958.

46 Cited in Clarke, *The Cripps Version*, pp. 330, 364–5.

47 2 October 1942, *The War Diaries of Oliver Harvey*, p. 165.

48 Roberts, *Masters and Commanders*, p. 286.

[49] 17 November 1942, *The War Diaries of Oliver Harvey*, p. 188.

[50] Arthur Hawk to Attlee, 18 May 1943, Ms. Attlee dep. 8, f. 123.

[51] *Tribune*, 2 October 1942.

[52] Taylor, *Beaverbrook*, pp. 548–9.

[53] Attlee and Bevin to the National Executive Committee, 12 October 1942 and Laski's reply, in Brooke, *Labour's War*, pp. 98–100.

[54] Attlee to Churchill, undated, ATLE 2/2.

[55] Clem to Tom, 10 March 1958, Ms. Eng. c. 4794.

[56] Entry for 18 November 1942, *Diary of James Chuter Ede*, p. 107.

[57] Lord Attlee, 'Montgomery: My Assessment', *Observer*, 2 November 1958.

[58] Harris, *Beveridge*, pp. 378–95.

[59] *Daily Herald*, 18 January 1945.

[60] Ibid., 20 January 1945.

[61] Ibid., 25 and 28 January, 13 February 1943.

[62] Ibid., 17 and 18 February 1943.

[63] Clem to Tom, 22 February 1943, Ms. Eng. c. 4793.

[64] Donoughue and Wilson, *Morrison*, pp. 314–15.

[65] *Daily Herald*, 19 February 1943.

[66] Clem to Tom, 22 February 1943, Ms. Eng. c. 4793.

[67] Donoughue and Wilson, *Morrison*, pp. 314–15.

[68] Entries for 23 and 24 February 1943, *Diary of James Chuter Ede*, pp. 123–5.

[69] J. S. Middleton to Attlee, 25 February 1943, Ms. Attlee dep. 7.

[70] Report of Labour National Executive Subcommittee, in letter to Attlee, 18 March 1943, in Ms. Attlee dep. 7.

[71] Statement by Attlee at Labour Party meeting, 7 April 1943, Ms. Attlee dep. 8, fol. 17.

[72] Syd Hawkins to Attlee, 26 April 1943, Ms. Attlee dep. 8, fol. 62.

[73] Brooke, *Labour's War*, pp. 64–5.

[74] *Daily Herald*, 1 May 1943.

[75] Donoughue and Wilson, *Morrison*, p. 317.

[76] *Daily Herald*, 21 May 1943.

[77] Morrison to Attlee, 17 May 1943, CAB 118/54.

[78] Attlee to Scott Lindsay, 8 May 1943, Ms. Attlee dep. 8, fol. 86.

[79] Clem to Tom, 11 June 1942, Ms. Eng. c. 4793.

[80] Roberts, *Masters and Commanders*, p. 311.

[81] Statement by Deputy Prime Minister, 19 January 1943, MS Attlee dep. 7, ff. 39-50.

[82] Entry for 20 January 1943, *Harold Nicolson: Diaries and Letters*, p. 304.

[83] H.N. to his sons, 11 May 1943, *Harold Nicolson: Diaries and Letters*, p. 309.

[84] Entry for 13 May 1943, *Diary of James Chuter Ede*, p. 135.

[85] Clem to Tom, 21 April 1943, Ms. Eng. c. 4793.

[86] Entry for March 1943, in Hugh Trevor Roper, and Richard Davenport-Hines (ed.), *The Wartime Journals* (London: I. B. Tauris, 2012), pp. 140–1.

[87] Clem to Tom, 21 April 1943, Ms. Eng. c. 4793.

88 C. R. Attlee, 'The Application of Democratic Principles to Government', 11 May 1943, printed for the War Cabinet, CAB 118/32.

89 *Manchester Guardian*, 17 June 1943.

90 *Daily Herald*, 23 June 1943.

91 Harris, *Attlee*, p. 224.

92 Brooke, *Labour's War*, p. 79.

93 'The Need for Decisions', memorandum by Deputy Prime Minister, Minister of Labour and the Home Secretary, 26 June 1943, CAB 118/33.

94 In *Attlee's War*, Robert Crowcroft makes a convincing case that Attlee was a highly skilled and underrated political operator.

95 Attlee to Churchill, 29 June 1943, CAB 118/33.

96 Churchill to Attlee, 12 July 1943, CAB 118/33.

97 'The Need for Decisions', memorandum by Deputy Prime Minister, Minister of Labour and the Home Secretary, 20 July 1943, CAB 118/33.

98 *Daily Herald*, 12 July 1943.

99 *Labour in the War Government: A Record of Things Done* (1943), in Ms. Attlee dep. 13, fol. 15.

100 Trevor Evans, 'Portrait of a Shy Man: Britain's First Minister', *New York Times*, 5 August 1945.

101 Entry for 3 August 1943, *Diary of James Chuter Ede*, p. 145.

102 Entry for 10 November 1943, *Diary of James Chuter Ede*, p. 151.

103 Martin Pugh, *Speak for Britain: A New History of the Labour Party* (London: Vintage Books), p. 268.

104 Lord Moran, *Churchill at War*, p. 175.

105 Clem to Tom, 9 December 1943, Ms. Eng. c. 4793. See also Brooke, *Labour's War*, pp. 188–93.

106 Lord Attlee, 'The Man I Knew', *Observer*, 31 January 1965.

107 Entry for 13 September 1943, Field Marshal Lord Alanbrooke, and Alex Danchev and Daniel Todman (eds), *War Diaries, 1939–1945*, (London: Phoenix Press, 2002), p. 452.

108 Lord Attlee, 'Jumping the Gun', *Observer*, 1 November 1959.

109 Ibid.

110 Entry for 8 March 1944, Alanbrooke, *War Diaries, 1939–1945*, p. 530.

111 Lord Attlee, 'Jumping the Gun', *Observer*, 1 November 1959.

112 Telegram from Churchill (Quadrant [Quebec Conference, Canada]) to Clement Attlee, Anthony Eden [later Lord Avon] and Chiefs of Staff Committee, 7 September 1943, Churchill Papers CHAR 20/129/79-80.

113 Lord Attlee, 'Jumping the Gun', *Observer*, 1 November 1959.

114 Stuart, *Within the Fringe*, pp. 118–19.

115 Attlee to Eden, 22 December 1943, FO 954/8.

116 Anthony Eden, *Full Circle: The Memoirs of Sir Anthony Eden* (London: Cassell, 1960), p. 8.

117 Entry for 14 January, *The Second World War Diary of Hugh Dalton*, p. 143.

14 – *The Invisible Man*

1 Roger Service, 'The Invisible Man', *Tribune*, 30 March 1945.
2 Dean Acheson to Felix Frankfurter, 22 December 1958, in David S. McClellan and David C. Acheson (eds), *Among Friends: Personal Letters of Dean Acheson* (New York: Dodd, Mead and Company, 1980), p. 153.
3 Brome, *Attlee*, p. 48.
4 'The Testing Time Ahead', *Listener*, 6 January 1944, Liddell Hart Papers, LH 1/28.
5 Aneurin Bevan, 'A Labour Plan to Beat the Tories', *Tribune*, 11 February 1944.
6 *Tribune*, 3 March 1944.
7 Entry for 1 March 1944, *Diary of James Chuter Ede*, p. 175.
8 *Tribune*, 31 March 1944.
9 Ibid., 7 April 1944.
10 *Observer*, 2 April 1944.
11 Entry for 29 March 1944, *The Second World War Diary of Hugh Dalton*, pp. 727–8.
12 *Tribune*, 12 May 1944.
13 Ibid., 19 May 1944.
14 Entries for 3 and 10 May 1944, *Diary of James Chuter Ede*, p. 182.
15 Roger Service, 'The Invisible Man', *Tribune*, 30 March 1945.
16 *Observer*, 7 May 1944.
17 Entry for 2 April 1944, John Colville, *The Fringes of Power: Downing Street Diaries* (London: Hodder & Stoughton, 1985), vol. 2, pp. 103–4.
18 Invitation to lunch in Ms. Attlee dep. 13, fol. 229.
19 Clem to Tom, 6 June 1944, Ms. Eng. c. 4793, f. 41.
20 Lord Attlee, 'Jumping the Gun', *Observer*, 1 November 1959.
21 Roberts, *Masters and Commanders*, p. 501.
22 See John Bew, *Castlereagh: The Biography of a Statesman* (London: Quercus, 2013).
23 Lord Attlee, 'Montgomery: My Assessment', *Observer*, 2 November 1958.
24 Entry for 6 July, Alanbrooke, *War Diaries*, p. 567.
25 Clem to Tom, 24 July 1944, Ms. Eng. c. 4793, f. 42.
26 Entry for 18 July 1944, *The Second World War Diary of Hugh Dalton*, p. 770.
27 Clem to Tom, 15 August 1944, Ms. Eng. c. 4793.
28 Entry for 15 August 1944, John Colville, *The Fringes of Power*, vol. 2, p. 130.
29 Clem to Tom, 4 September 1944, Ms. Eng. c. 4793.
30 Entry for 13 August 1944, Moran, *Churchill at War*, pp. 202–4.
31 Attlee's visit to Italy, August 1944, FO 170/1170.
32 Clem to Tom, 4 September 1944, Ms. Eng. c. 4793.
33 Attlee, *As it Happened*, p. 150.
34 Clem to Tom, 4 September 1944, Ms. Eng. c. 4793.
35 Clem to Tom, 15 August 1944, Ms. Eng. c. 4793.

36 Frank Lewey, *Cockney Campaign* (London: S. Paul & Company, 1944). Lewey's book was reviewed in the *Spectator* on 11 May 1944, which reveals its release date.

37 Brooke, *Labour's War*, p. 263.

38 *Tribune*, 14 July 1944.

39 Entry for 25 October 1944, *Diary of James Chuter Ede*, p. 182.

40 Clem to Tom, 15 August 1944, Ms. Eng. c. 4793.

41 George Orwell, *The Lion and the Unicorn: Socialism and the English Genius* (1941), quoted in Hennessey, *Never Again*, p. 36.

42 Addison, *The Road to 1945*, pp. 261, 272. The memorandum is in ATLE 1/24. Addison is generally dismissive of Attlee's importance in the wartime coalition. For a robust response, see Crowcroft, *Attlee's War*, p. 16.

43 Speech given to the Yorkshire Regional Council of Labour in Attlee Ms, dep. 14, f. 43–6, quoted in Brooke, *Labour's War*, p. 319.

44 Lionel Robbins to the Lord Privy Seal, 21 November 1941, CAB 118/90.

45 Clem to Tom, 15 August 1944, Ms. Eng. c. 4793.

46 H.N. to his sons, 9 October 1944, *Harold Nicolson: Diaries and Letters*, p. 338.

47 Clem to Tom, 16 October 1944, Ms. Eng. c. 4793.

48 *Tribune*, 16 September 1944.

49 Figures in *Washington Post*, 20 January 1945.

50 *Tribune*, 3 November 1944.

51 Aneurin Bevan, 'The Parties Line-Up in Parliament', *Tribune*, 1 December 1944.

52 Entry for 9 September 1944, John Colville, *The Fringes of Power*, vol. 2, p. 141.

53 Churchill to Attlee, 20 November 1944 [unsent], in Brooke, *Labour's War*, pp. 168–9.

54 Entry for 28 November 1944, *Diary of James Chuter Ede*, pp. 195–6.

55 Lord Attlee, 'Jumping the Gun', *Observer*, 1 November 1959.

56 Attlee to Churchill, 7 December 1944, CAB 118/74.

57 Entry for 20 and 21 January 1945, John Colville, *The Fringes of Power*, vol. 2, pp. 192–3.

58 Eden to Attlee, 7 December 1944, FO 954/11.

59 *Daily Herald*, 12 December 1944.

60 Ibid., 3 December 1944.

61 Ibid., 14 December 1944.

62 Entry for 28 November 1944, *Diary of James Chuter Ede*, pp. 195–6.

63 Brooke, *Labour's War*, p. 71.

64 *The Second World War Diary of Hugh Dalton*, pp. 295, 318–19.

65 Harris, *Attlee*, pp. 210–13.

66 Duff Cooper to Lord President of the Council, 12 March 1945, CAB 123/228.

67 Clem to Tom, 15 March 1945, Ms. Eng. c. 4793.

68 Itinerary for Attlee's visit, 2 March 1945, FO 956/1.

69 Clem to Tom, 15 March 1945, Ms. Eng. c. 4793.

70 Clem to Tom, 15 March 1945, Ms. Eng. c. 4793.

71 Lord Attlee, 'Jumping the Gun', *Observer*, 1 November 1959.

72 Clem to Tom, 29 April 1945, Ms. Eng. c. 4793.

73 *Hartford Courant*, 27 July 1945.

74 *Tribune*, 30 March 1945.

75 *Manchester Guardian*, 19 April 1945.

76 *Tribune*, 20 April 1945.

77 *Manchester Guardian*, 25 April 1945.

78 Harris, *Attlee*, p. 246.

79 Brome, *Attlee*, p. 44.

80 Francis Williams, 'The Prime Minister', *Spectator*, 10 August 1945, in General Records of the Department of State, Record 59, Dec. File, 1945-9, Box 5902.

81 Clem to Tom, 29 April 1945, Ms. Eng. c. 4793, f. 49.

82 Attlee statement on death of Franklin Roosevelt, Attlee Papers, MS dep. 17, f. 161.

83 Hanley, *Attlee*, p. 79.

84 *Daily Mail*, 14 May 1945.

85 King, *British Political Opinion*, p. 2.

86 Attlee MS dep. 17, f. 24.

87 Churchill to Attlee, 18 May 1945, Churchill Papers, CHAR 20/194A/23–25.

88 Churchill to Attlee, 22 May 1945, Churchill Papers, CHAR 20/194A/35-38.

89 Moran, *Churchill at War*, p. 306.

90 Entry for 22 May 1945, John Colville, *The Fringes of Power*, vol. 2, pp. 248–9.

91 Stuart, *Within the Fringe*, p. 136.

92 *Daily Mail*, 23 May 1945.

93 Ibid., 29 May 1945.

94 Entries for 28 and 29 May 1945, *Diary of James Chuter Ede*, pp. 220–1.

95 R. A. Butler, *The Art of Memory: Friends in Perspective* (London: Hodder & Stoughton, 1982), p. 21.

96 Clem to Tom, 26 May 1945, Ms. Eng. c. 4793, f. 51.

97 *Daily Mail*, 5 June 1945.

98 F. A. Hayek, *The Road to Serfdom* (Abingdon and New York: Routledge, 1944), pp. 222–3.

99 *Economist*, 9 June 1945.

100 Quoted in Toye, *The Roar of the Lion*, p. 219.

101 John Winant to Secretary of State, 13 June 1945, US Department of State Decimal File, Record 59, Dec. File 1945–49, Box 5896, 841.00/6–1345.

102 Toye, *Roar of the Lion*, p. 223.

103 Attlee's election broadcast, 5 June 1945, Ms. Attlee dep. 18, ff. 39–42.

104 *Economist*, 9 June 1945.

105 5 June 1945, Moran, *Churchill at War*, p. 309.

106 22 June 1945, Moran, *Churchill at War*, pp. 309–10.

107 David Edgerton, *Britain's War Machine* (London: Penguin, 2001), p. 272.

108 *Daily Mail*, 6 June 1945.

109 Brooke, *Labour's War*, p. 307.

110 *Daily Mail*, 6 June 1945.

[111] *Daily Mail*, 9 June 1945.

[112] Ibid., 11 June 1945.

[113] Richard Toye, *The Labour Party and the Planned Economy, 1931–1951* (Oxford: Boydell Press, 2003), pp. 95–100.

[114] Addison, *The Road to 1945*, pp. 261, 272. The memorandum is in ATLE 1/24.

[115] William Waldegrave, *A Different Kind of Weather: A Memoir* (London: Constable and Robinson, 2015), pp. 31–3.

[116] Addison, *The Road to 1945*, p. 281.

[117] *Daily Mail*, 16 June 1945.

[118] *Manchester Guardian*, 15 June 1945.

[119] *Tribune*, 15 June 1945.

[120] T. D. Burridge, 'A Postscript to Potsdam: The Churchill–Laski Electoral Clash, June 1945', *Journal of Contemporary History*, vol. 12, no. 4 (October 1977), pp. 725–39.

[121] *Daily Herald*, 2 and 3 July 1945.

[122] *Manchester Guardian*, 3 July 1945.

[123] *Daily Herald*, 2 July 1945.

[124] US Department of State Decimal File, Record 59, Dec. File 1945–49, Box 5896.

[125] *Daily Mail*, 3 July 1945.

[126] *Daily Herald*, 4 July 1945.

[127] *Daily Mail*, 5 July 1945.

[128] *Daily Herald*, 5 July 1945.

[129] Clem to Tom, 6 July 1945, Ms. Eng. c. 4793.

15 – *To Hope Till Hope Creates*

[1] Quoted in Helen Evans, *Sixty Years On: Who Cares for the NHS?* (London: Institute of Economic Affairs, 2008), p. 29.

[2] Lord Vansittart in 'After the storm', *Daily Mail*, 8 May 1945.

[3] Attlee, *The Social Worker*, p. 4.

[4] Thomas Attlee, 'Lost Causes', in Attlee, *Quiet Conscience*, pp. 128–9.

[5] *Daily Telegraph*, 3 March 2008.

[6] Attlee, *As it Happened*, p. 169.

[7] Michael S. Neiberg, *Potsdam: The End of World War II and the Remaking of Europe* (New York: Basic Books, 2015), pp. 176–7.

[8] Attlee, *As it Happened*, p. 170.

[9] Potsdam Diary of Hugh Lunghi, George Leggett Papers, LEGT 1/1.

[10] Ibid.

[11] John Colville, *The Fringes of Power*, vol. 2, p. 259.

[12] Potsdam Diary of Hugh Lunghi, George Leggett Papers, LEGT 1/1.

[13] *The Memoirs of General the Lord Ismay*, p. 403.

14 *Daily Mail*, 5 July 1945.
15 Ibid., 7 July 1945
16 John Winant to Secretary of State, 3 July 1945, US Department of State Decimal File, Record 59, Dec. File 1945–49, Box 5896, 841.00/7–345.
17 *Manchester Guardian*, 23 July 1945.
18 Ibid., 26 July 1945.
19 *Daily Herald*, 26 July 1945.
20 Morrison to Attlee, 24 July 1945, Ms. Attlee dep. 18, f. 50.
21 Brooke, *Labour's War*, p. 101.
22 *Daily Mail*, 26 July 1945.
23 *Daily Herald*, 27 July 1945.
24 Attlee, *As it Happened*, p. 171.
25 *Daily Herald*, 27 July 1945.
26 Attlee, *As it Happened*, p. 171.
27 *Daily Herald*, 27 July 1945.
28 *Manchester Guardian*, 28 July 1945.
29 *Daily Herald*, 27 July 1945.
30 Ibid.
31 Robert Coe, Second Secretary of the Embassy, to Secretary of State, 9 August 1945, US Department of State Decimal File, Record 59, Dec. File 1945–49, Box 5896, 841.00/8–945.
32 *Daily Herald*, 27 July 1945.
33 Entry for 26 July 1945, in Moran, *Churchill at War*, pp. 351–3.
34 *Daily Herald*, 27 July 1945.
35 *Manchester Guardian*, 27 July 1945.
36 Ibid.
37 Ibid.
38 Donoughue and Wilson, *Morrison*, pp. 342–3.
39 Williams, *A Prime Minister Remembers*, p. 4.
40 Entry for 28 July 1945, *Diary of James Chuter Ede*, pp. 228–9.
41 *Daily Mail*, 27 July 1945.
42 *Baltimore Sun*, 27 July 1945.
43 *Christian Science Monitor*, 27 July 1945.
44 Ibid.
45 Attlee telegram to Martin Attlee, 28 July 1945, Ms. Attlee dep. 18, f. 60.
46 *Christian Science Monitor*, 23 October 1945.
47 *Washington Post*, 16 November 1945.
48 *Daily Herald*, 18 July 1945.
49 *Daily Mail*, 28 July 1945.
50 Bullock, *The Life and Times of Ernest Bevin*, vol. 2, p. 393.
51 Lord Attlee, 'The Role of the Monarchy', *Observer*, 23 August 1959.
52 Stuart, *Within the Fringe*, p. 155.

53 Donoughue and Wilson, *Morrison*, p. 344.

54 *Daily Herald*, 28 July 1945.

55 *Manchester Guardian*, 28 July 1945.

56 Potsdam Diary of Hugh Lunghi, George Leggett Papers, LEGT 1/1.

57 Entry for 26 July, Alanbrooke, *War Diaries*, p. 712.

58 Entry for 26 July 1945, in David Dilks (ed.), *The Diaries of Sir Alexander Cadogan, 1938–1945* (New York: G. P. Putnam's Sons, 1972), p. 772.

59 *Manchester Guardian*, 28 July 1945.

60 *The Memoirs of General the Lord Ismay*, p. 403.

61 Quoted in Raymond Smith and John Zametica, 'The Cold Warrior: Clement Attlee Reconsidered, 1945–7', *International Affairs*, vol. 61, no. 2 (Spring 1985), pp. 237–52.

62 Telegram from Moscow to Secretary of State, 28 July 1945, US Department of State Decimal File, Record 59, Dec. File 1945–49, Box 5896, 841.00/7–2845.

63 *The Maisky Diaries*, p. 547.

64 Preliminary reflections on Labour Victory, from American Embassy in London to Secretary of State, 31 July 1945, US Department of State Decimal File, Record 59, Dec. File 1945–49, Box 5896, 841.00/7–3145.

65 *Baltimore Sun*, 27 July 1945.

66 *Washington Post*, 26 July 1945.

67 Potsdam Diary of Hugh Lunghi, George Leggett Papers, LEGT 1/1.

68 Ibid.

69 W. Averell Harriman and Elie Abel, *Special Envoy to Churchill and Stalin, 1941–1946* (New York and London: Random House, 1975), pp. 486–7, 550–1.

70 Neiberg, *Potsdam*, pp. 178–80.

71 Sarah James, 'The Hostess of No. 10 Downing Street', *New York Times*, 26 August 1945.

72 *New York Times*, 4 August 1945.

73 Sarah James, 'The Hostess of No. 10 Downing Street', *New York Times*, 26 August 1945.

74 Winston Churchill, 'The Dream', in John Gross (ed.) *The Oxford Book of Essays*, pp. 362–71.

75 Lord Attlee, 'The Role of the Monarchy', *Observer*, 23 August 1959.

76 Lord Attlee, 'Bevan as Hero', *Observer*, 21 October 1962.

77 *New York Times*, 4 August 1945.

78 *Economist*, 11 August 1945.

79 Rodney Crowther, 'School of Hard Knocks Labourites' Alma Mater', *Baltimore Sun*, 5 August 1945.

80 Taylor, *Beaverbrook*, pp. 446–7.

81 Lord Attlee, 'What Sort of Man Gets to the Top', *Observer*, 7 February 1960.

82 Francis Williams to Attlee, 24 August 1945, Ms. Attlee dep. 18, f. 57.

83 Francis Williams, 'The Prime Minister', *Spectator*, 10 August 1945, in General Records of the Department of State, Record 59, Dec. File, 1945–9, Box 5902.

84 *Daily Mail*, 27 July 1945.

[85] Gordon Brown, *Maxton* (Edinburgh: Mainstream Publishing, 1986), pp. 292–3.

[86] Addison, *The Road to 1945*, pp. 158–60.

[87] Attlee to A. V. Alexander, 1 March 1944, A. V. Alexander Papers, AVAR 2.

[88] Attlee to Bevin, 22 November 1944, Bevin Papers, BEVN 3.

[89] Henry Pelling, 'The 1945 General Election Reconsidered', *Historical Journal*, vol. 23, no. 2 (June 1980), pp. 399–414.

[90] Raymond Williams, *Politics and Letters: Interviews with New Left Review* (London: New Left Review, 1979), p. 60.

[91] Quoted in John Saville, 'C. R. Attlee: An Assessment', *Socialist Register* (1983), p. 149.

[92] Pelling, 'The 1945 General Election Reconsidered'.

[93] *Clement Attlee: The Granada Historical Records Interview*, pp. 28–9.

[94] For a brilliant exposition of Attlee's wartime strategy, see Robert Crowcroft, *Attlee's War: World War II and the Making of a Labour Leader* (London and New York: I.B. Tauris, 2011).

[95] Addison, *The Road to 1945*, pp. 261, 272. The memorandum is in ATLE 1/24.

[96] *Clement Attlee: The Granada Historical Records Interview*, pp. 28–9.

[97] Williams, *A Prime Minister Remembers*, p. 107.

[98] *Clement Attlee: The Granada Historical Records Interview*, pp. 28–9.

[99] Attlee to Bevin, 26 May 1945, BEVN II 3.

[100] Attlee to Laski, 29 January 1941, quoted in T. D. Burridge, 'Clement Attlee Reconsidered', in Brian P. Farrell (ed.), *Leadership and Responsibility in the Second World War: Essays in Honour of Robert Vogel* (Montreal and Kingston: McGill-Queen's University Press, 2004), p. 67.

16 – *English Traits, American Problems*

[1] Ralph Waldo Emerson, *The Works of Ralph Waldo Emerson*, vol. 5 (*English Traits*) (Boston and New York: Fireside, 1909), p. 292.

[2] *Manchester Guardian*, 15 May 1954.

[3] Ibid., 8 August 1945.

[4] Ibid., 13 August 1945.

[5] Hunt, *On The Spot: An Ambassador Remembers*, pp. 42–3.

[6] John Colville, *The Fringes of Power*, vol. 2, p. 259.

[7] Brome, *Attlee*, pp. 8–10.

[8] Hunt, *On the Spot*, pp. 27–8.

[9] Brome, *Attlee*, pp. 8–10.

[10] *Chicago Daily Tribune*, 29 September 1945.

[11] Clemens, *Man from Limehouse*, pp. 66–7.

[12] Williams, *A Prime Minister Remembers*, p. 80.

[13] Richard J. Aldrich, *The Hidden Hand: Britain, America and Cold War Secret Intelligence* (London: John Murray, 2001), p. 65.

14 Ralph Waldo Emerson, *The Works of Ralph Waldo Emerson*, vol. 5, p. 292.

15 *Clement Attlee: The Granada Historical Records Interview*, p. 32.

16 John Colville, *The Fringes of Power*, vol. 2, p. 261.

17 *Baltimore Sun*, 15 August 1945.

18 *Daily Herald*, 17 August 1945.

19 John Maynard Keynes, 'Overseas Financial Prospects', 14 August 1945, PREM 8/35.

20 *Daily Herald*, 23 August 1945.

21 'The Atom Bomb', Memorandum by the Prime Minister, 28 August 1945, CAB 130/3.

22 *Chicago Tribune*, 3 August 1945.

23 Carlyle Morgan, 'A "Tory" America vs. an Attlee Britain', *Christian Science Monitor*, 1 August 1945.

24 Harold Laski, 'The Labour Viewpoint', *New York Times*, 5 August 1945.

25 *Economist*, 18 August 1945.

26 Dean Acheson, *Present at the Creation: My Years in the State Department* (New York and London: W. W. Norton, 1987), p. 172.

27 Williams, *A Prime Minister Remembers*, p. 130.

28 Record of meeting of ministers, 23 August 1945, PREM 8/35.

29 Williams, *A Prime Minister Remembers*, p. 132.

30 *Daily Herald*, 25 August 1945.

31 Randall Bennett Woods, *A Changing of the Guard: Anglo-American Relations, 1941–1946* (Chapel Hill: University of North Carolina Press, 2008), chapter 12.

32 *Clement Attlee: The Granada Historical Records Interview*, p. 35.

33 Clem to Tom, 30 August 1945, Ms. Eng. c. 4793.

34 *Tribune*, 7 September 1945.

35 Jack Lawson to Clement Attlee, 26 November 1945, Lawson Papers, LAW 1/1/345.

36 Attlee to Truman, 3 October 1945, in Williams, *A Prime Minister Remembers*, p. 121.

37 *Clement Attlee: The Granada Historical Records Interview*, p. 35.

38 John Winant to Secretary of State, 6 September 1945, US Department of State Decimal File, Record 59, Dec. File 1945–49, Box 5896, 841.00/9–645.

39 Prime Minister to President, 14 September 1945, PREM 8/89.

40 President to Prime Minister, 17 September 1945, PREM 8/89.

41 Prime Minister to President, 16 September 1945, PREM 8/89.

42 Attlee to Truman, telegram, 5 October 1945, US Department of State Decimal File, Record 59, Dec. File 1945–49, Box 5897, 841.00/10–545.

43 Attlee to President Truman, 25 September 1945, CAB 130/3.

44 Attlee to Stalin, 23 September 1945, FO 181/1007/4.

45 Stalin to Attlee, 25 September 1945, FO 181/1007/4.

46 Attlee to Stalin, 29 October 1945, FO 181/1007/4. See also *Stalin's Correspondence with Winston S. Churchill and Clement R. Attlee* (Moscow: Ministry of Foreign Affairs of the USSR, 1965), pp. 373–7.

47 Personal and private for Prime Minister for Mr. Churchill, undated [September 1945], CAB 130/3.
48 Williams, *A Prime Minister Remembers*, p. 78.
49 John Anderson to Attlee, 1 November 1945 PREM 8/40.
50 'International Control of Atomic Energy', Memorandum by the Prime Minister, 5 November 1945, CAB 130/3.
51 Cabinet conclusions, 8 November 1945, CAB 130/3.
52 *Christian Science Monitor*, 13 November 1945.
53 The Prime Minister, 'Broadcasts', 9 December 1945, CAB 118/19.
54 Cabinet conclusions, 6 November 1945, PREM 8/35.
55 *New York Times*, 11 November 1945.
56 Moran, *Churchill at War*, p. 221.
57 *Observer*, 25 October 1945.
58 Meeting of UK delegation, White House, 6.15 p.m. 10 November 1945, CAB 130/3.
59 Clemens, *Man from Limehouse*, pp. 124–7.
60 *Los Angeles Times*, 14 November 1945.
61 Halifax to Attlee, 2 November 1945, Ms. Attlee dep. 25, fol. 62.
62 G. D. Blaker, Board of Trade, to T. L. Rowan, 6 November 1945, Ms. Attlee dep. 25, fol. 193.
63 *Washington Post*, 14 November 1945.
64 *Christian Science Monitor*, 13 November 1945.
65 *Manchester Guardian*, 14 November 1945.
66 *Chicago Daily Tribune*, 14 November 1945.
67 *Hartford Courant*, 14 November 1945.
68 *Washington Post*, 14 November 1945.
69 *Wall Street Journal*, 21 November 1945.
70 Joseph C. Harsch, 'Attlee Grasps Opportunity Truman Lost', *Christian Science Monitor*, 15 November 1945.
71 Acheson, *Present at the Creation*, pp. 124–5.
72 'Future Arrangements for Cooperation between the United States, Canada and the United Kingdom', by the Prime Minister, 11 December 1945, CAB 130/3.
73 Ibid.
74 Attlee to Lord Halifax and Field Marshal Wilson, 15 December 1945, CAB 130/3.
75 Attlee to Truman, 6 June 1946, in Williams, *A Prime Minister Remembers*, pp. 112–17.
76 Williams, *A Prime Minister Remembers*, pp. 108, 118.
77 Attlee to Halifax, 28 November 1945, PREM 8/35.
78 Draft speech on Anglo-American relations, 4 December 1945, Ms. Attlee dep. 28, ff. 122–4.
79 Alan Wood, *The True History of Lord Beaverbrook* (London and New York: Heinemann, 1965), p. 359.

NOTES | 609

80 *Washington Post*, 9 December 1945.
81 Williams, *A Prime Minister Remembers*, p. 134.

17 – *The British New Deal*

1 Speech to Lord Mayor's Banquet, 9 November 1946, C. R. Attlee, and Roy Jenkins (ed.), *Purpose and* Policy, p. 212.
2 Evelyn Waugh, 'Tactical Exercise', *Tactical Exercise & Other Late Stories* (Harmondsworth: Penguin, 2011), pp. 251–71.
3 Quoted in Christine Berberich, *The Image of the English Gentleman in Twentieth-Century Literature* (London: Ashgate, 2005), p. 115. See also, Kynaston, *Austerity Britain*, p. 62.
4 Frederic Raphael, *There and Then: Personal Terms 6* (Manchester: Carcanet Press, 2013), p. 193.
5 Peregrine Worsthorne, *Tricks of Memory: An Autobiography* (London: Weidenfeld & Nicolson, 1993), pp. 77–9.
6 *Tribune*, 16 November 1945.
7 Foot, *Bevan*, pp. 30–1.
8 Thomas Balogh, 'The Apotheosis of the Dilettante', in Hugh Thomas (ed.), *The Establishment* (London: Anthony Blond, 1959), pp. 106–7.
9 John Vaizey, 'The Public Schools', in Thomas (ed.), *The Establishment*, pp. 19–41.
10 Elliot (ed.), *Attlee as I Knew Him*, p. 28.
11 Clem to Tom, 21 November 1941, Ms. Eng. c. 4793, f. 16.
12 Robert Coe, Second Secretary of the Embassy, to Secretary of State, 9 August 1945, US Department of State Decimal File, Record 59, Dec. File 1945–49, Box 5896, 841.00/8–945.
13 Arthur M. Schlesinger, Jr, *A Life in the Twentieth Century: Innocent Beginnings* (New York: Houghton Mifflin, 2000), p. 433.
14 Clem to Tom, 26 December 1957, Ms. Eng. c. 4794, f. 70.
15 Attlee to Patricia Beck, 20 August 1958, Ms. Eng. lett c. 571, f. 18.
16 Bellamy, *Looking Backward*, pp. 347–51.
17 *Daily Herald*, 17 August 1945.
18 6 December 1945, *Hansard*, vol. 416 cc. 2530–99.
19 *Manchester Guardian*, 7 December 1945.
20 Robert Coe to Secretary of State Byrnes, 11 December 1945, US Department of State Decimal File, Record 59, Dec. File 1945–49, Box 5043, 841.00/12–1145.
21 *Daily Express* poll on public opinion, 11 December 1945, US Department of State Decimal File, Record 59, Dec. File 1945–49, Box 5896, 841.00/1–1146.
22 *Washington Post*, 28 January 1946.

23 Attlee filed the memorandum with a note to himself on 7 June 1948 with the comment that it was 'not without interest'. Memorandum [undated] on Cabinet government, Churchill Papers, ATLE 2/1.

24 Williams, *A Prime Minister Remembers*, pp. 83–4.

25 Lawson on Attlee, Lawson Papers, LAW 2/4/2/2/13–26.

26 Brome, *Attlee*, p. 7.

27 Attlee to Zilliacus, 17 February 1946, Attlee Ms. dep. 31, f. 242.

28 Hunt, *On the Spot*, p. 41.

29 Arthur Moyle, 'The Real Attlee', *Star*, 8 December 1955.

30 Williams, *A Prime Minister Remembers*, p. 85.

31 Morrison, *An Autobiography*, pp. 248–9, 296–7.

32 Hartley Shawcross, *Life Sentences: The Memoirs of Lord Shawcross* (London: Constable, 1995), p. 179.

33 Edmund Dell, *A Strange Eventful History: Democratic Socialism in Britain* (London: Harper, 2000), p. 204.

34 Morrison, *An Autobiography*, pp. 248–9, 296–7.

35 Ellen Wilkinson, 'Introduction', in Clemens, *Man from Limehouse*, p. xiii.

36 Vernon, *Ellen Wilkinson*, pp. 209–11.

37 Thomas-Symonds, *Attlee*, p. 119.

38 Williams, *A Prime Minister Remembers*, pp. 81–5.

39 Ibid.

40 *Clement Attlee: The Granada Historical Records Interview*, p. 44.

41 Foot, *Bevan*, pp. 27–30.

42 *Clement Attlee: The Granada Historical Records Interview*, p. 44.

43 Clem to Tom, 10 October 1945, Ms. Eng. c. 4793.

44 Attlee, 'Flaws at the top', *Observer*, 14 February 1960.

45 *Tribune*, 12 October 1945.

46 Williams, *A Prime Minister Remembers*, p. 88.

47 Morgan, *Labour in Power*, pp. 99–141.

48 Preliminary reflections on Labour Victory, from American Embassy in London to Secretary of State, 31 July 1945, US Department of State Decimal File, Record 59, Dec. File 1945–49, Box 5896, 841.00/7–3145.

49 Williams, *A Prime Minister Remembers*, p. 88.

50 Morgan, *Labour in Power*, pp. 99–141.

51 Jim Tomlinson, 'Mr Attlee's Supply-Side Socialism', *Economic History Review*, vol. 46, no. 1 (February, 1993), pp. 1–22.

52 Clem to Tom, 1 May 1944, Ms. Eng. c. 4793, f. 40.

53 Williams, *Politics and Letters*, p. 71.

54 Williams, *A Prime Minister Remembers*, p. 93.

55 Ibid., p. 90.

56 Richard Toye, 'The Labour Party's External Economic Policy in the 1940s', *Historical Journal*, vol. 43, no. 1 (March, 2000), pp. 189–215. See also Richard Toye, 'The

Attlee Government, the Imperial Preference System and the Creation of the Gatt',
English Historical Review, vol. 118, no. 478 (September, 2003), pp. 919–39.

57 Jim Tomlinson, 'Mr Attlee's Supply-Side Socialism', *The Economic History Review*,
vo. 46, no. 1 (February, 1993), pp. 1–22.

58 Douglas Jay, *Change and Fortune: A Political Record* (London: Hutchinson, 1980),
pp. 131–2.

59 Cited in Field (ed.), *Attlee's Great Contemporaries*, p. xxv.

60 Jay, *Change and Fortune*, p. 133.

61 Williams, *A Prime Minister Remembers*, p. 91.

62 Morgan, *Labour in Power*, pp. 172–3, 179–86.

63 *Manchester Guardian*, 8 February 1946.

64 Account of Prime Minister's speech, 7 February 1946, PREM 8/290. For a full
account of his speech, see C. R. Attlee, *Purpose and Policy: Selected Speeches*
(London and New York: Hutchinson and Co., 1946), pp. 91–102.

65 Peter Hennessey, *Muddling Through: Power, Politics and the Quality of Government in Post-war Britain* (London: Gollancz, 1999), p. 172.

66 Jay, *Change and Fortune*, p. 133.

67 Attlee to Megan Lloyd George, 25 April 1955, ATLE 2/4.

68 Addison, *The Road to 1945*, pp. 270–8, 286.

69 Williams, *A Prime Minister Remembers*, p. 57.

70 Attlee, *The Social Worker*, pp. 1–28.

71 Quoted in Henry Pelling, *The Labour Government, 1945–1951* (London: Macmillan, 1984), p. 117.

72 Addison, *The Road to 1945*, p. 14.

73 Morgan, *Labour in Power*, pp. 1–10, 488–9.

74 Brooke, *Labour's War*, p. 95.

75 Addison, *The Road to 1945*, p. 272.

76 Ibid., pp. 270–8, 286.

77 Ibid., p. 277.

78 Clem to Tom, 2 April 1918, Ms. Eng. c. 4792.

79 23 November 1922, *Hansard*, vol. 159, cols 92–6.

80 Quoted in Hennessey, *Never Again*, p. 119.

81 *Observer*, 3 March 1946.

82 Trevor Evans, 'Six Months of Attlee: A Look at the Record', *New York Times*, 27
January 1946.

83 Official Cabinet Committee on the Socialisation of Industries, 8 March 1946,
PRO 8/621.

84 *Christian Science Monitor*, 27 July 1946.

85 Telegram from US Embassy in London to Secretary of State Byrnes, 13 June 1946,
US Department of State Decimal File, Record 59, Dec. File 1945–49, Box 5043,
841.00/6-1346.

86 Clement Attlee to Jack Lawson, 2 October 1946, Lawson Papers, LAW 1/1/358.

87 *Manchester Guardian*, 21 July 1946.
88 Hugh Thomas, *John Strachey* (London: Eyre Methuen, 1973), pp. 233–5.
89 *Manchester Guardian*, 22 July 1946.
90 *Clement Attlee: The Granada Historical Records Interview*, p. 38.
91 *Manchester Guardian*, 30 August 1946.
92 Attlee came to think of Creech Jones as a failure, though Kenneth Morgan disagrees with his assessment. See *Labour in Power*, pp. 189–91.
93 *Manchester Guardian*, 5 October 1946.
94 *Observer*, 6 October 1946.
95 Speech to Lord Mayor's Banquet, 9 November 1946, C. R. Attlee, and Roy Jenkins (ed.) *Purpose and Policy*, p. 212.

18 – Empire into Commonwealth

1   C. Delisle Burns, *Political Ideals: An Essay* (London: Forgotten Books, 2013 [first edn 1919]), pp. 48–9.
2   Entry for 9 July 1946, *Harold Nicolson: Diaries and Letters*, p. 50.
3   John Maynard Keynes, 'Overseas Financial Prospects', 14 August 1945, PREM 8/35.
4   Peter Clarke, *Hope and Glory: Britain, 1900–2000* (London: Penguin, 2004), p. 232.
5   Dalton, 'Notes on a difference of opinion', 20 January 1947, Attlee MS dep. 49, ff. 86–92.
6   Alan Bullock, *Ernest Bevin: Foreign Secretary* (London and New York: W. W. Norton, 1983), p. 85.
7   DNB, as recalled by Sir Frank Roberts, Bevin's principal private secretary; Ovendale, 39.
8   Mark Stephens, *Ernest Bevin: Unskilled Labourer and World Statesman* (London: Transport and General Workers' Union, 1981), p. 122.
9   *Chicago Daily Tribune*, 13 November 1945.
10 Quoted in Raymond Smith and John Zametica, 'The Cold Warrior: Clement Attlee Reconsidered, 1945–7', *International Affairs*, vol. 61, no. 2 (Spring 1985), pp. 237–52.
11 C. R. Attlee, and Roy Jenkins (ed.), *Purpose and Policy*, pp. 108–10.
12 Clem to Tom, 11 September 1949, Ms. Eng. c. 4793.
13 Foster Hailey, '"Clem", Who Asks a Vote of Confidence', *New York Times*, 22 January 1950.
14 Hunt, *On The Spot*, p. 61.
15 Edward Gibbon, and Dero A. Saunders (ed.), *The History of the Decline and Fall of the Roman Empire* (London: Penguin, 1952), p. ix.
16 Gregory Claeys, *Imperial Sceptics: British Critics of Empire, 1850–1920* (Cambridge: Cambridge University Press, 2012), p. 299.

17 Burns, *Political Ideals*, pp. 48–9.
18 Clem to Tom, 11 September 1949, Ms. Eng. c. 4793.
19 C. Delisle Burns, *The First Europe: A Study of the Establishment of Medieval Christendom, A.D. 400–800* (London: George Allen & Unwin, 1947), pp. 9–16.
20 *Washington Post*, 4 October 1945.
21 Ibid.
22 Mallory Browne, 'British and Russians in Duel of Diplomacy', *New York Times*, 9 December 1945.
23 Smith and Zametica, 'The Cold Warrior: Clement Attlee Reconsidered, 1945–7', pp. 237–52.
24 'International Control of Atomic Energy', Memorandum by the Prime Minister, 5 November 1945, CAB 130/3.
25 Attlee to Stalin, 23 September 1945, FO 181/1007/4.
26 Attlee to Stalin, 20 December 1945, FO 181/1007/4.
27 Klaus Larres, *Churchill's Cold War: The Politics of Personal Diplomacy* (New Haven and London: Yale University Press, 2002), pp. 123–34.
28 Churchill to Attlee, 17 February 1946, Churchill Papers, CHUR 2/210. See also Reynolds, *From World War to Cold War*, pp. 257–9.
29 *Times*, 6 June 1946.
30 Clem to Tom, 17 August 1946, Ms. Eng. c. 4793.
31 Clem to Tom, 30 August 1946, Ms. Eng. c. 4793.
32 Attlee to Bevin, 27 November 1946, CAB 130/3.
33 Acheson, *Present at the Creation*, pp. 167–8.
34 Attlee to Bevin, 27 November 1946, CAB 130/3.
35 Meeting of Cabinet, 25 October 1946, CAB 130/2; in Peter Hennessey, *Cabinets and the Bomb* (Oxford: Clarendon Press, 2007), pp. 44–59.
36 Meeting of ministers, 8 January 1947, GEN 163/1st meeting, in Hennessey, *Cabinets and the Bomb*, pp. 44–59.
37 Greta Jones, *Science, Politics and the Cold War* (London and New York: Routledge, 1988), pp. 81–2.
38 Quoted in Smith and Zametica, 'The Cold Warrior: Clement Attlee Reconsidered, 1945–7', p. 238.
39 James, *The Rise and Fall of the British Empire*, pp. 530–1.
40 Williams, *A Prime Minister Remembers*, p. 177.
41 William Roger Louis, *The British Empire in the Middle East, 1945–51: Arab Nationalism, the United States and Postwar Imperialism* (Oxford: Clarendon, 1984), pp. 21–9.
42 Lord Attlee, 'Montgomery: My Assessment', *Observer*, 2 November 1958.
43 Liddell Hart to Attlee, 10 May 1946, LH 1/28/13.
44 James, *The Rise and Fall of the British Empire*, pp. 530–1.
45 William Roger Louis, *The British Empire in the Middle East, 1945–51: Arab Nationalism, the United States and Postwar Imperialism* (Oxford: Clarendon, 1984), pp. 21–9.

[46] Smith and Zametica, 'The Cold Warrior: Clement Attlee Reconsidered, 1945–7'.

[47] Bullock, *Ernest Bevin*, pp. 348–54.

[48] John Saville, *The Politics of Continuity: British Foreign Policy and the Labour Government, 1945–46* (London and New York: Verso, 1993), pp. 112–48.

[49] Attlee to A. V. Alexander, A. V. Alexander Papers, 17 March 1947, AVAR 2.

[50] Ritchie Ovendale, 'Introduction', in Ritchie Ovendale (ed.), *The Foreign Policy of the British Labour Governments, 1945–1951* (Leicester: Leicester University Press, 1984), p. 8.

[51] Greg Behrman, *The Most Noble Adventure* (New York: Free Press, 2008).

[52] *News Chronicle*, 20 April 1958.

[53] Morgan, *Labour in Power*, pp. 270–4.

[54] Bullock, *Bevin*, pp. 621–54.

[55] Ritchie Ovendale, 'The Palestine Policy of the British Labour Government, 1945–1946', *International Affairs*, vol. 55, no. 3 (July 1979), pp. 409–31.

[56] *New York Times*, 2 July 1946.

[57] Ibid.

[58] Walter Lippmann, 'Britain and the American dilemma', *Los Angeles Times*, 10 October 1946.

[59] Acheson, *Present at the Creation*, pp. 172–5.

[60] For a discussion of anti-Semitism and Bevin and Attlee, see Hennessey, *Never Again*, pp. 238–9. See also Peter Clarke, *The Last Thousand Days of the British Empire*, pp. 460–3.

[61] Clem to Tom, 29 December 1946, Ms. Eng. c. 4793.

[62] Isaiah Berlin to *The Times* in *Enlightening: Letters, 1946–1960*, p. 11.

[63] Catriona Crowe et al., *Documents on Irish Foreign Policy: Volume VII, 1941–1945* (Dublin: Royal Irish Academy, 2010), p. 124.

[64] *Observer* (editorial), 'Great Britain and the United Nations', 23 February 1947.

[65] Richard J. Aldrich, *The Hidden Hand: Britain, America and Cold War Secret Intelligence* (London: John Murray, 2001), pp. 144, 264–7.

[66] 20 September 1947, *The Political Diary of Hugh Dalton*, p. 414.

[67] Cabinet conclusions, 20 September 1947, PREM 8/889 Part I.

[68] Ivor Thomas to Attlee, 19 September 1947, PREM 8/889 Part I.

[69] Haney, *Attlee*, p. 100.

[70] 'Withdrawal from Palestine: Relations with Arab Counties', report by Defence Committee, 5 November 1947, PREM 8/889 Part I.

[71] Meeting of Palestine Committee, 7 November 1947, PREM 8/889 Part I.

[72] Memorandum on Palestine, by Bevin, 3 December 1947, PREM 8/889 Part I.

[73] *Christian Science Monitor*, 8 March 1948.

[74] Entry for 1 March 1948, *The Headlam Diaries, 1935–1951*, p. 545.

[75] *Manchester Guardian*, 24 February 1948.

[76] Lord Attlee, 'Montgomery: My Assessment', *Observer*, 2 November 1958.

[77] Record of meeting between British government and the U.S. Ambassador, 25 May 1948, PREM, 8/859 Part II.

78 Isaiah Berlin to Dr. Chaim Weizmann, 6 June 1948, *Enlightening: Letters, 1946–1960*, pp. 50–2.
79 Isaiah Berlin to Joseph Alsop, 21 October 1949, *Enlightening: Letters, 1946–1960*, p. 132.
80 C. R. Attlee, 'The Application of Democratic Principles to Government', 11 May 1943, printed for the War Cabinet, CAB 118/32.
81 Ruth Parsons, 'The Labor Party and India', *Far Eastern Survey*, vol. 14, no. 23 (November 1945), pp. 337–9.
82 *Los Angeles Times*, 25 September 1945.
83 *Washington Post*, 10 May 1945.
84 Barnet Nover, 'Attlee's Offer', *Washington Post*, 19 March 1946.
85 Clarke, *The Cripps Version*, pp. 404–6, 431–2.
86 'Attlee on India, 15 March, 1946', in Tony Smith (ed.), *The End of the European Empire: Decolonization after World War II* (Ottawa: Heath and Company, 1976), pp. 41–5.
87 Barnet Nover, 'Attlee's Offer', *Washington Post*, 19 March 1946.
88 James, *The Rise and Fall of the British Empire*, pp. 547–58.
89 Clarke, *The Last Thousand Days of the British* Empire, p. 466.
90 Prime Minister to Viceroy Wavell, 22 July 1946, PREM 8/554.
91 Wavell to Attlee, 1 August 1946; Attlee to Wavell, 20 August 1946, PREM 8/554.
92 Wavell to Attlee, 26 August 1946, PREM 8/554.
93 Attlee to Wavell, 8 January 1947, PREM 8/554.
94 Attlee to Wavell, 31 January 1947, PREM 8/554.
95 Entry for 24 February 1947, *The Headlam Diaries, 1935–1951*, p. 489.
96 Clem to Tom, 1 February 1947, Ms. Eng. c. 4793.
97 Clem to Tom, 1 February 1947, Ms. Eng. c. 4793.
98 Morgan, *Labour in Power*, p. 223.
99 James, *The Rise and Fall of the British Empire*, pp. 547–8.
100 Clarke, *The Cripps Version*, pp. 470–1.
101 Clem to Tom, 1 February 1947, Ms. Eng. c. 4793.
102 Butler, *The Art of Memory*, p. 76.
103 Clem to Tom, 1 February 1947, Ms. Eng. c. 4793.
104 Lord Attlee, 'What Sort of Man Gets to the Top', *Observer*, 7 February 1960.
105 Lord Attlee, 'The Role of the Monarchy', *Observer*, 23 August 1959.
106 Morgan, *Labour in Power*, pp. 224–5.
107 Clarke, *The Last Thousand Days of the British Empire*, p. 476.
108 Clem to Tom, 5 June 1947, Ms. Eng. c. 4793.
109 Clem to Tom, 18 August 1947, Ms. Eng. c. 4793.
110 Williams, *A Prime Minister Remembers*, pp. 202, 215.
111 *Manchester Guardian*, 16 April 1947.
112 'Churchill versus Attlee over Burma, 20 December 1956', in Smith (ed.), *The End of the European Empire*, p. 50.

[113] C. R. Attlee, *The Labour Party in Perspective – and Twelve Years Later* (London: Victor Gollancz Ltd., 1949), p. 174.

[114] Prime Minister Nehru to Attlee, 25 October 1947, PREM 8/14551/1.

[115] Attlee to Jinnah, 26 October 1947, PREM 8/14551/1.

[116] Attlee to Nehru, 26 October 1947, PREM 8/14551/1.

[117] Attlee to Patricia Beck, 1 February 1952, Ms. Eng. lett c. 571.

[118] *Christian Science Monitor*, 31 January 1948.

[119] *Manchester Guardian*, 31 July 1948.

[120] Quoted in Harris, *Attlee*, p. 381.

[121] Speech to Lord Mayor's Banquet, 9 November 1946, C. R. Attlee, and Roy Jenkins (ed.), *Purpose and Policy*, pp. 205–12.

[122] *New York Times*, 2 May 1948.

[123] Elliot (ed.), *Attlee as I Knew Him*, p. 22.

[124] Francis Hutchins, 'India Leaves Britain', in Tony Smith (ed.), *The End of the European Empire: Decolonization after World War II* (Ottawa: Heath and Company, 1976), pp. 31–40.

[125] Elliot (ed.), *Attlee as I Knew Him*, p. 18.

[126] Averil Cameron, 'Gibbon and Justinian', in Rosamond McKitterick and Roland Quinault, *Edward Gibbon and Empire* (Cambridge: Cambridge University Press, 2002), pp. 34–52.

[127] Clem to Tom, 11 September 1949, Ms. Eng. c. 4793.

[128] Entry for 10 November 1947, *Harold Nicolson: Diaries and Letters*, p. 50.

[129] Entry for 27 April 1949, *Harold Nicolson: Diaries and Letters*, p. 170.

[130] Clem to Tom, 20 April 1949, Ms. Eng. c. 4793.

[131] Clem to Tom, 2 November 1949, Ms. Eng. c. 4793.

[132] Quoted in Harris, *Attlee*, p. 382.

[133] *Manchester Guardian*, 4 July 1949.

19 – In Barchester All is Not Well

[1] *Manchester Guardian*, 2 January 1954.

[2] Adam Gopnik, 'Trollope Trending', *New Yorker*, 4 May 2015.

[3] Clem to Tom, 7 April 1941, Ms. Eng. c. 4793.

[4] Quoted in David Kynaston, *Austerity Britain, 1945–51* (London: Bloomsbury, 2007), pp. 120–1.

[5] Angela Thirkell, *Private Enterprise* (Wakefield, Rhode Island and London: Moyer Bell, 1997 edn).

[6] Orville Prescott, 'Books of the Times', *New York Times*, 3 February 1948.

[7] *New York Times*, 1 January 1950.

[8] Anthony Bower, 'The Literary Scene Under Attlee: A Letter from London', 25 January 1948.

9 T. S. Eliot, *Notes towards the Definition of Culture* (New York: Harcourt, Brace and Company, 1949), p. 14.

10 Helen Gardner, *The Art of T. S. Eliot* (London: Faber & Faber, 1949), quoted in Raphaël Ingelbien, *Misreading England: Poetry and Nationhood Since the Second World War* (Amsterdam and New York: Rodopi, 2002), p. 29.

11 Oliver Baldwin to Jack Lawson, 3 January 1947, Jack Lawson Papers, LAW 1/1/366.

12 William Rees-Mogg, *Memoirs* (London: Harper Press, 2011), pp. 80–1.

13 Dalton, 'Notes on a difference of opinion', 20 January 1947, Attlee MS dep. 49, ff. 86–92.

14 *Manchester Guardian*, 28 March 1947.

15 Ibid.

16 *Washington Post*, 28 April 1947.

17 *New York Times*, 3 April 1947.

18 James, *The Rise and Fall of the British Empire*, pp. 530–39.

19 Dean Acheson to Ambassador in London, 17 May 1947, US Department of State Decimal File, Record 59, Dec. File 1945–49, Box 5898, 841.00/5–1747.

20 Donoughue and Wilson, *Morrison*, pp. 394–5.

21 *Boston Globe*, 4 July 1947.

22 Entry for 29 July 1947, *The Political Diary of Hugh Dalton*, pp. 400–1.

23 Report by Ambassador Douglas, 6 June 1947, US Department of State Decimal File, Record 59, Dec. File 1945–49, Box 5898, 841.00/6–647.

24 *Report of the Forty-Sixth Annual Conference of the Labour Party, Margate 1947* (London: Transport House, 1947), pp. 117–19.

25 Clem to Tom, 5 June 1947, Ms. Eng. c. 4793.

26 Letter to Prime Minister from 21 backbenchers, 23 July 1947, Ms. Attlee dep. 57. ff. 207–19.

27 Entry for 29 July 1947, *The Political Diary of Hugh Dalton*, pp. 400–1.

28 Letter to Prime Minister from 143 members, 4 August 1947, Ms. Attlee dep. 57, f. 13.

29 Morgan, *Labour in Power*, pp. 343–5, 383.

30 Attlee's address to the nation, in Stephen Brooke (ed.), *Reform and Reconstruction: Britain After the War, 1945–51* (Manchester: Manchester University Press, 1995), pp. 45–6.

31 Jackson, *Churchill*, p. 24.

32 Entry for 6 August 1947, *The Headlam Diaries, 1935–1951*, p. 516.

33 Berlin, *Enlightening: Letters, 1946–1960*, p. 38.

34 Entry for 8 August 1947, *The Political Diary of Hugh Dalton*, pp. 405–6.

35 Report by Ambassador Douglas, 12 August 1947, US Department of State Decimal File, Record 59, Dec. File 1945–49, Box 5898, 841.00/8–1247.

36 Clem to Tom, 18 August 1947, Ms. Eng. c. 4793.

37 Donoughue and Wilson, *Morrison*, pp. 418–19.

38 Harris, *Attlee*, p. 512.

39 Entry for 17 August 1947, *The Political Diary of Hugh Dalton*, p. 410.

40 Dalton, *Pimlott*, p. 507.

41 Clarke, *The Cripps Version*, pp. 480–1.

42 Donoughue and Wilson, *Morrison*, p. 418–19.

43 Attlee to Morrison, 15 September 1947, Ms. Attlee, dep. 60, ff. 78–81.

44 Morrison to Attlee, 19 September 1947, Ms. Attlee, dep. 60, ff. 144–7.

45 Morgan, *Labour in Power*, pp. 165–7.

46 *New York Times*, 8 October 1947.

47 William Gorell Barnes to Attlee, 17 September and 29 October 1947, BARN 1/12, William Gorell Barnes Papers, Churchill College, Cambridge.

48 Mr Graham-Harrison to Attlee, 8 November 1947, Barns Papers, BARN 2/14–2/16.

49 Bevin to Attlee, 11 September 1947, Attlee MS dep. 60, f. 49.

50 Attlee to Morrison, 15 September 1947, Ms. Attlee, dep. 60, ff. 78–81.

51 *Clement Attlee: The Granada Historical Records Interview*, p. 45.

52 *Manchester Guardian*, 1 January 1948.

53 *Boston Globe*, 31 January 1948.

54 *Manchester Guardian*, 15 January 1948.

55 Ibid., 20 January 1948.

56 *Wall Street Journal*, 7 February 1948.

57 *Manchester Guardian*, 29 June 1948.

58 *New York Times*, 9 May 1949.

59 Attlee to Truman, January 1948, Barns Papers, BARN 1/12.

60 Walter Lippmann, 'We Must Revive Our Foreign Policy', *Boston Globe*, 26 January 1948.

61 *New York Times*, 11 March 1948.

62 Morgan, *Labour in Power*, pp. 238–9.

63 *Christian Science Monitor*, 14 February 1948.

64 *Economist*, 23 March 1948.

65 Account of ad hoc meeting of ministers, 7 March 1946. See also the Findlater Stewart Report and Prime Minister's Directive to Director General of Security Service (MI5), CAB 301/31. For the broader context, see Aldrich, *The Hidden Hand*, pp. 65–70.

66 *New York Times*, 2 May 1948.

67 *Manchester Guardian*, 6 April 1948.

68 Williams, *A Prime Minister Remembers*, pp. 172–3.

69 Ibid., p. 175.

70 A. V. Alexander to Ernest Bevin, 31 July 1948, FO 1093/520.

71 John Bayliss, 'American Bases in Britain: The "Truman–Attlee" Understandings', *The World Today*, vol. 42, no. 8/9 (August–September 1986), pp. 155–9.

72 Walter Millis (ed.), *The Forrestal Diaries* (London: Cassel and Co., 1952), p. 460.

73 Jones, *Science, Politics and the Cold War*, p. 80.

74 *New York Times,* 6 March 1949.

75 Williams, *A Prime Minister Remembers,* p. 173.

76 *Manchester Guardian,* 11 April 1949.

77 *The Labour Party: Report of the 47th Annual Conference, held in Scarborough, 17–21 May 1948* (1948), pp. 128–61.

78 John Singleton, 'Labour, Conservatives and Nationalisation', in Robert Millward and John Singleton (eds), *The Political Economy of Nationalisation in Britain, 1920–1950* (Cambridge: Cambridge University Press, 1996), pp. 23–5.

79 Morrison, *An Autobiography,* pp. 295–6.

80 HC Deb 30 April 1948, *Hansard,* vol. 422, cc. 43–142.

81 Attlee to Bevan, 16 January 1948; 'Suggested Notes for the Prime Minister's Intervention in the Health Service Debate' [undated], PREM 8/844.

82 *Manchester Guardian,* 17 March 1948.

83 For an excellent discussion of Attlee's 'hands-off' strategy in the passage of the NHS, see Thomas-Symonds, *Attlee,* pp. 157–62.

84 Quoted in Henry Pelling, *The Labour Government, 1945–1951* (London: Macmillan, 1984), p. 117.

85 Clare Beckett and Francis Beckett, *Bevan* (London: Haus Publishing, 2004), p. 94.

86 *Observer,* 11 July 1948.

87 Lord Attlee, 'Bevan as Hero', *Observer,* 21 October 1962.

88 Quoted in Harris, *Attlee,* p. 425.

89 Lord Attlee, 'Bevan as Hero', *Observer,* 21 October 1962.

90 *Manchester Guardian,* 9 September 1948.

91 Ibid., 11 September 1948.

92 Ibid., 13 October 1948.

93 *Boston Globe,* 14 October 1948.

94 *Manchester Guardian,* 13 November 1948.

95 Ibid., 18 October 1948.

96 Ibid., 25 October 1948.

97 *Observer,* 31 October 1948.

98 Ibid., 9 January 1949.

99 *Manchester Guardian,* 15 January 1949.

100 *Washington Post,* 13 February 1949.

101 *Manchester Guardian,* 22 January 1949.

102 Ibid., 10 February 1949.

103 Attlee, *The Labour Party in Perspective and Twelve Years Later,* with a preface by Francis Williams (London: Victor Gollancz Ltd., 1949).

104 *Washington Post,* 13 February 1949.

105 *Manchester Guardian,* 4 March 1949.

106 *Labour Believes in Britain: A Statement on Policy For Discussion at the Labour Party Conference* (April 1949). See Morgan, *Labour in Power,* p. 123.

107 *Manchester Guardian*, 25 April 1949.

108 Ibid., 2 May 1949.

109 Ibid., 11 April 1949.

110 Ibid., 8 September 1949.

111 *New York Times*, 26 May 1949.

112 *Manchester Guardian*, 3 May 1949.

113 Clem to Tom, 27 June 1949, Ms. Eng. c. 4793, f. 79.

114 *New York Times*, 26 June 1949.

115 Entry for 28 June 1949, Hugh Gaitskell, and Philip W. Williams (ed.), *The Diary of Hugh Gaitskell, 1945–1956* (London: Jonathan Cape, 1983), p. 177.

116 *Manchester Guardian*, 4 July 1949.

117 D. Zaslavski, 'The Tribulations and Failures of Mr. Attlee', 13 July 1949, *Pravda*, in US Department of State Decimal File, Record 59, Dec. File 1945–49, Box 5902, 841.002/7–1349.

118 Entry for 11 July 1949, *The Headlam Diaries, 1935–1951*, p. 595.

119 *New York Times*, 21 July 1949.

120 *Spectator*, 4 August 1949.

121 Gaitskell, 'Political Strategy', 19 August 1949, Ms. Attlee dep. 87, ff, 70–4.

122 For Phillips's influence, see Morgan, *Labour in Power*, pp. 70–3.

123 Morgan Phillips to Attlee, August 1949, Ms. Attlee, dep. 86, ff. 22–5.

124 Report by Samuel Berger, 15 July 1949, US Department of State Decimal File, Record 59, Dec. File 1945–49, Box 5900, 841.00/7–1549.

125 Entry for 13 October 1947, *The Political Diary of Hugh Dalton*, pp. 460–1.

126 *Manchester Guardian*, 10 October 1949.

127 *Observer*, 25 October 1949.

128 Entry for 26 October 1949, *Diary of Hugh Gaitskell*, p. 155.

129 Clem to Tom, 26 October 1949, Ms. Eng. c. 4793.

130 *Observer*, 30 October 1949.

131 Entry for 14 June 1949, *Harold Nicolson: Diaries and Letters*, pp. 162–3.

132 Isaiah Berlin to Rowland Burdon-Miller, 29 December 1949, *Enlightening: Letters, 1946–1960*, p. 158.

20 – *Taxis, Teeth and Hospital Beds*

1 Angus Wilson, *The Wrong Set and Other Stories* (Harmondsworth: Penguin, 1949), p. 89.

2 Ibid.

3 Colm Brogan, 'Taxi Riddle at Number 10', *Daily Express*, 28 December 1949.

4 Francis Williams, *Socialist Britain: Its Background, Its Present and an Estimate of Its Future* (London: Viking, 1949).

5 Williams, *Fifty Years' March*.

6   Colm Brogan, *Our New Masters* (London: Hollis and Carter, 1947); *Fifty Years On* (London: Hollis and Carter, 1949).

7   Giles Radice, *The Tortoise and the Hares: Attlee, Bevin, Cripps, Dalton, Morrison* (London: Politico's, 2008).

8   *Daily Express*, 28 December 1949.

9   Speech of 3 September 1945, in MS. Attlee dep. 10, ff. 12–29.

10 Morgan, *Labour in Power*, pp. 202–3.

11 D. K. Fieldhouse, 'The Labour Governments and the Empire-Commonwealth, 1945–51', in Ritchie Ovendale (ed.), *The Foreign Policy of the British Labour Governments, 1945–1951* (Leicester: Leicester University Press, 1984), pp. 86–110.

12 *Christian Science Monitor*, 22 December 1949.

13 Clem to Tom, 23 December 1949, Ms. Eng. c. 4793, f. 84.

14 *New York Times*, 2 December 1949.

15 *Baltimore Sun*, 31 December 1949.

16 *New York Times*, 9 February 1950.

17 Francis Beckett, 'Clem Attlee's secret lady friend', *New Statesman*, 28 February 2000.

18 *Manchester Guardian*, 15 February 1950.

19 *Christian Science Monitor*, 20 February 1950.

20 Entry for 16 February 1950, *Harold Nicolson: Diaries and Letters*, p. 190.

21 *Manchester Guardian*, 22 February 1950.

22 *Chicago Daily Tribune*, 23 February 1950.

23 *Manchester Guardian*, 27 February 1950.

24 Clement Attlee to Jack Lawson, 2 March 1950, Lawson Papers, LAW 1/1/569.

25 Frederic Raphael, *Going Up* (London: The Robson Press, 2015), pp. 58–9.

26 Clem to Tom, 2 March 1950, Ms. Eng. c. 4794, f. 1.

27 *Manchester Guardian*, 7 March 1950.

28 Ibid., 19 March 1950.

29 Budget Policy, Note by the Chancellor of the Exchequer, 15 March 1950, PREM 8/1188.

30 Stafford Cripps to Attlee, 2 April 1950, Ms. Attlee, dep. 100, ff. 1–4.

31 Clem to Tom, 20 April 1950, Ms. Eng. c. 4794, f. 2.

32 Stafford Cripps to Attlee, 26 April 1950, Ms. Attlee, dep. 100, ff. 1–4.

33 Morgan, *Labour in Power*, pp. 413–15.

34 Bridges (FCO) to S. P. Omand, 1 May 1950, Ms. Attlee, dep. 100, ff. 119–20.

35 Acheson, *Present at the Creation*, pp. 392–7.

36 Hennessey, *Never Again*, p. 275,

37 *Washington Post*, 15 June 1950.

38 *New York Times*, 16 June 1950.

39 *Observer*, 18 June 1950.

40 Entry for 16 June 1950, *The Political Diary of Hugh Dalton*, p. 477.

41 *New York Times*, 16 June 1950.

[42] Ibid., 16 June 1950.

[43] Telegram from MacArthur, 27 June 1950, in Ms. Attlee dep. 119, ff. 229–30.

[44] Clem to Tom, 30 June 1950, Ms. Eng. c. 4794.

[45] *Spectator*, 29 June 1950.

[46] Ibid.

[47] Clem to Tom, 30 June 1950, Ms. Eng. c. 4794.

[48] *Spectator*, 29 June 1950.

[49] *Washington Post*, 4 July 1950.

[50] *Manchester Guardian*, 22 August 1950.

[51] Harold Macmillan, *Tides of Fortune, 1945–55* (London: Macmillan, 1969), p. 335.

[52] *Manchester Guardian*, 25 August 1950.

[53] *Observer*, 3 September 1950.

[54] Clem to Tom, 25 September 1950, Ms. Eng. c. 4794, f. 7.

[55] Isaiah Berlin to Marion Frankfurter, 17 August 1950, *Enlightening: Letters, 1946–1960*, pp. 187–8.

[56] Chronology of events leading to Attlee's visit to Washington, DC, in December 1950, undated, FK1081/1/G.

[57] Pimlott, *Dalton*, p. 592.

[58] *Washington Post*, 2 December 1950.

[59] Aldrich, *The Hidden Hand*, pp. 294–5.

[60] *Boston Globe*, 4 December 1950.

[61] Attlee, *As it Happened*, p. 200.

[62] Richard L. Strout, 'Clement Attlee Calls on Harry Truman', *Christian Science Monitor*, 9 December 1950.

[63] Morrison, *An Autobiography*, p. 270.

[64] Account of meeting in Jeffrey Engel, Mark Atwood Lawrence and Andrew Preston (eds), *America in the World: A History in Documents from the War with Spain to the War on Terror* (Princeton, NJ: Princeton University Press, 2014), pp. 190–1.

[65] Ronald Steel, *Walter Lippmann and the American Century* (New Brunswick and London: Transaction Publishers, 1970), p. 473.

[66] Acheson, *Present at the Creation*, pp. 498–5.

[67] Jerry Brookshire, 'Attlee and Truman', *History Today*, no. 12 (December 2003), p. 26.

[68] *Los Angeles Times*, 17 December 1950.

[69] Macmillan, *Tides of Fortune*, p. 336.

[70] Entry for 7 January 1951, *The Headlam Diaries, 1935–1951*, p. 630.

[71] James Hinton, 'Militant Housewives: The British Housewives' League and the Attlee Government', *History Workshop*, no. 38 (1994), pp. 128–156.

[72] Leonard Wibberley, 'Attlee's Britain through advertisements', *Los Angeles Times*, 25 January 1951.

[73] *Manchester Guardian*, 26 January 1951.

[74] Entry for 7 February 1951, *The Political Diary of Hugh Dalton*, p. 499.

75 Roderick Barclay, *Ernest Bevin and the Foreign Office, 1932–69* (London: Sir Roderick Barclay, 1975), p. 51.

76 Stephens, *Bevin*, p. 123.

77 Entry for 19 February 1951, *The Political Diary of Hugh Dalton*, p. 505.

78 Morrison, *An Autobiography*, p. 273.

79 Gaitskell to Attlee, 20 March 1951, Ms. Attlee dep. 119, ff. 30–1.

80 HC Debate 30 April, *Hansard*, vol. 422, cc. 43–142.

81 Cabinet Conclusions, 9 April 1951, PREM 8/1480.

82 Ibid.

83 Attlee's statement on Bevin's death, 15 April 1951, Ms. Attlee dep. 119, ff. 146–8.

84 *News Chronicle*, 20 April 1958.

85 Attlee to Flo Bevin, 14 April 1941, in Bevin Papers, BEVN II 3.

86 Entry for 20 April 1951, *The Political Diary of Hugh Dalton*, p. 534.

87 Harold Wilson to Attlee, 22 April 1951, Ms. Attlee dep. 119, ff. 1–3.

88 Attlee to Wilson, 23 April 1951, Ms. Attlee dep. 119, f. 4.

89 Entry for 24 March 1954, Richard, Crossman, and Janet Morgan (ed.), *The Backbench Diaries of Richard Crossman* (London: Jonathan Cape, 1981), pp. 297–8.

90 *Manchester Guardian*, 30 April 1951.

91 Attlee to Bevan, 21 April 1951 in Williams, *A Prime Minister Remembers*, p. 248.

92 *News Chronicle*, 20 April 1958.

93 Entry for 23 April 1950, *The Political Diary of Hugh Dalton*, p. 537.

94 Clem to Tom, 30 April 1951, Ms. Eng. c. 4794, f. 15.

95 Lord Winster, 'A London Letter', *Baltimore Sun*, 10 May 1951.

96 Report by David Lineburgh on the Labour Party, 23 May 1951, US Department of State Decimal File, Record 59, Dec. File 1950–54, Box 3508, 741.00/5–2351.

97 Clem to Tom, 24 July 1951, Ms. Eng. c. 4794, f. 16.

98 Entry for 10 August 1951, *Diary of Hugh Gaitskell*, p. 26.

99 Morrison, *An Autobiography*, pp. 281–3.

100 William Roger Louis, *The British Empire in the Middle East, 1945–51: Arab Nationalism, the United States and Postwar Imperialism* (Oxford: Clarendon, 1984), pp. 21–9.

101 Clem to Tom, 24 July 1951, Ms. Eng. c. 4794, f. 16.

102 Peter Clarke, *The Last Thousand Days of the British Empire: The Demise of a Superpower, 1944–7* (London: Penguin, 2007), pp. 464–72.

103 James, *The Rise and Fall of the British Empire*, pp. 564–5.

104 H. W. Brands, 'The Cairo–Tehran Connection in Anglo-American Rivalry in the Middle East, 1951–1953', *International History Review*, XI, 3 August 1989, pp. 409–612.

105 Entry for 2 July 1951, *The Political Diary of Hugh Dalton*, pp. 548–9.

106 Entry for 16 September 1951, *The Political Diary of Hugh Dalton*, p. 554.

107 *Clement Attlee: The Granada Historical Records Interview*, p. 55.

108 Brands, 'The Cairo–Tehran Connection in Anglo-American Rivalry in the Middle East, 1951–1953'.

[109] *News Chronicle*, 20 April 1958.

[110] William Roger Louis, *The British Empire in the Middle East, 1945–51: Arab Nationalism, the United States and Postwar Imperialism* (Oxford: Clarendon, 1984), pp. 669–70.

[111] Louis, *The British Empire in the Middle East*, p. x.

[112] Morrison, *An Autobiography*, pp. 281–3.

[113] Eden, *Full Circle*, p. 8.

[114] Clem to Tom, 17 September 1951, Ms. Eng. c. 4794, f. 17.

[115] Entry for 4 September 1951, *The Political Diary of Hugh Dalton*, p. 553.

[116] Lord Attlee, 'The Role of the Monarchy', *Observer*, 23 August 1959.

[117] Morrison, *An Autobiography*, p. 283.

21 – *The Pilgrim's Progress*

[1] John Bunyan, *The Pilgrim's Progress from This World to That Which Is to Come* [1678] 32nd edn. (London: W. Johnston, 1771), Part II, p. 157.

[2] *Observer*, 7 October 1951.

[3] Ibid.

[4] Burridge, *Attlee*, p. 301.

[5] *Observer*, 7 October 1951.

[6] Clem to Tom, 21 October 1951, Ms. Eng. c. 4794, f. 18.

[7] Attlee, *Quiet Conscience*, p. 117.

[8] *The Labour Party: Report of the 47th Annual Conference, held in Scarborough, 17–21 May 1948* (1948), pp. 128–61.

[9] Harris, *Attlee*, p. 563.

[10] Mary Abbott, *Family Affairs: A History of the Family in 20th Century England* (London and New York: Routledge, 2002), p. 85.

[11] Clem to Tom, 18 February 1952, Ms. Eng. c. 4794.

[12] Attlee, 'Lansbury of London', in Field (ed.), *Attlee's Great Contemporaries*, pp. 1–4.

[13] Ellen Wilkinson, 'Introduction', in Clemens, *Man from Limehouse*, p. xiv.

[14] Clem to Tom, 18 February 1952, Ms. Eng. c. 4794.

[15] Entry for 27 October 1951, *The Political Diary of Hugh Dalton*, pp. 565, 569.

[16] Clem to Tom, 14 November 1951, Ms. Eng. c. 4794.

[17] Clem to Patricia Beck, 2 July 1965, Ms. Eng. lett c. 571.

[18] Entry for 6 February 1952, *The Backbench Diaries of Richard Crossman*, pp. 70–1.

[19] Clem to Tom, 25 February 1952, Ms. Eng. c. 4794.

[20] Report by David Lineburgh on the Labour Party, 10 March 1952, US Department of State Decimal File, Record 59, Dec. File 1950–54, Box 3509, 741.00/3–1052.

[21] Entry for 31 January 1952, *The Backbench Diaries of Richard Crossman*, pp. 67–8.

[22] *Los Angeles Times*, 24 February 1952.

[23] Clem to Tom, 8 April 1952, Ms. Eng. c. 4794, f. 24.

24   Entry for 3 March 1952, *Harold Nicolson: Diaries and Letters*, p. 222.
25   Clement Attlee, 'The best way to peace in Europe', *Daily Herald*, 6 March 1952.
26   *New York Times*, 2 August 1952.
27   Entry for 11 June 1952, *The Political Diary of Hugh Dalton*, p. 589.
28   Lord Winster, 'Attlee vs. Bevan at Morecambe', *Baltimore Sun*, 28 September 1952.
29   Clem to Tom, 5 October 1952, Ms. Eng. c. 4794, f. 27.
30   'The Trojan Horse', An Open Letter from Mr Tufton Beamish to Mr Herbert Morrison, with copies to Mr Attlee, Mr Strachey, and Mr Bevan, 1953, Papers of Baron Chelwood (Sir Tufton Beamish)CLW 1/5/18.
31   Clem to Tom, 5 October 1952, Ms. Eng. c. 4794, f. 27.
32   Report by Margaret Joy Tibbets, 15 September 1952, US Department of State Decimal File, Record 59, Dec. File 1950–54, Box 3510, 741.00/9–1552.
33   *Baltimore Sun*, 18 October 1952,
34   R. J. Cruikshank, 'The surprise packet', *New Chronicle*, 28 March 1953.
35   Clem to Tom, 9 August 1952, Ms. Eng. c. 4794, f. 25.
36   Clem to Tom, 18 September 1952, Ms. Eng. c. 4794, f. 25.
37   Attlee to Patricia Beck, 1 January 1953, Ms. Eng. lett c. 571.
38   Report by Tom Driberg, 26 January 1953, US Department of State Decimal File, Record 59, Dec. File 1950–54, Box 3511, 741.00/1–2653.
39   *Christian Science Monitor*, 12 May 1953.
40   Ibid., 14 May 1953.
41   Clem to Tom, 9 August 1953, Ms. Eng. c. 4794, f. 33.
42   *New York Times*, 16 August 1953.
43   *Los Angeles Times*, 20 September 1953.
44   *Clement Attlee: The Granada Historical Records Interview*, p. 48.
45   *New York Times*, 20 September 1953.
46   Lord Winster, 'Attlee at Margate', *Baltimore Sun*, 8 October 1953.
47   Clem to Tom, 8 April 1954, Ms. Eng. c. 4794, f. 39.
48   Report by Robert G. Hooker, 2 October 1953, US Department of State Decimal File, Record 59, Dec. File 1950–54, Box 3511, 741.00/10–253.
49   Report by Margaret Joy Tibbetts, 2 November 1953, US Department of State Decimal File, Record 59, Dec. File 1950-54, Box 3511, 741.00/11–253.
50   Lord Winster, 'Attlee at Margate', *Baltimore Sun*, 8 October 1953.
51   Jack Lawson. 'The Rt. Hon. Clement Attlee, C.H., M.P., Prime Minister.' LAW2/4/2/2/13–26, and 27–31.
52   Clem to Tom, 3 June 1953, Ms. Eng. c. 4794, f. 32.
53   Alistair Buchan, 'Attlee Flattens Peaks of His Life', *Washington Post and Times Herald*, 30 May 1954.
54   Raymond Daniel, 'Clement Attlee's Life and Times', *New York Times*, 23 May 1954.
55   *Manchester Guardian*, 24 May 1954.
56   Entry for 11 April 1954, *The Political Diary of Hugh Dalton*, p. 621.
57   Clem to Tom, 25 March 1957, Ms. Eng. c. 4794, f. 66.

58 Entry for 13 April 1954, *The Political Diary of Hugh Dalton*, p. 623.

59 *Manchester Guardian*, 24 May 1954.

60 Entry for 24 March 1954, *The Backbench Diaries of Richard Crossman*, p. 300.

61 Lorna Arnold, *Britain and the H-Bomb* (Houndsmill: Palgrave, 2001), pp. 47–51.

62 Jones, *Science, Politics and the Cold War*, pp. 102–3.

63 Larres, *Churchill's Cold War*, p. 327.

64 Entry for 6 April 1954, *The Backbench Diaries of Richard Crossman*, pp. 305–7.

65 Clem to Tom, 8 April 1953, Ms. Eng. c. 4794, f. 37.

66 *Diary of Hugh Gaitskell*, p. 329.

67 Entry for 19 May 1954, *The Backbench Diaries of Richard Crossman*, p. 330.

68 *Chicago Daily Tribune*, 20 July 1954.

69 *New York Times*, 7 September 1954.

70 Morgan Phillips, *East Meets West: A Pictorial Story of the Labour Party Delegation to the Soviet Union and China* (London: Lincolns-Prager, 1954), p. 42.

71 Report of 6 September 1954 meeting, FO 371/110248.

72 *Baltimore Sun*, 3 September 1954.

73 Report of press conference 20 September 1954, FO 371/110248.

74 *Christian Science Monitor*, 23 September 1954.

75 American press coverage of China and Labour Party conference, Fo 462/8.

76 Victoria Honeyman and Timothy Heppell, 'Clement Attlee, 1951–5', in Timothy Heppell (ed.), *Leaders of the Opposition: From Churchill to Cameron* (Houndsmill: Palgrave, 2012), pp. 20–32.

77 *Washington Post*, 30 September 1954.

78 *New York Times*, 12 February 1957.

79 Clem to Tom, 11 November 1954, Ms. Eng. c. 4794.

80 Muravchik, *Heaven on Earth*, p. 186.

81 Morrison, *An Autobiography*, p. 292.

82 Entry for 14 November 1954, *The Political Diary of Hugh Dalton*, p. 636.

83 Clem to Tom, 4 April 1955, Ms. Eng. c. 4794.

22 – *Few Thought He Was Even a Starter*

1 *Baltimore Sun*, 14 May 1955.

2 Arthur Moyle, 'The Real Attlee', *Star*, 8 December 1955.

3 Entry for 14 November 1954, *The Political Diary of Hugh Dalton*, p. 636.

4 Clem to Tom, 8 August 1955, Ms. Eng. c. 4794.

5 R. M. Douglas, 'No Friend of Democracy: The Socialist Vanguard Group 1941–50', *Contemporary British History*, vol. 16, issue 4 (2002), pp. 51–86.

6 Harris, *Attlee*, p. 537.

7 Clem to Tom, 6 December 1955, Ms. Eng. c. 4794.

8 Entry for 7 December 1955, *The Backbench Diaries of Richard Crossman*, p. 456.

9 *Manchester Guardian*, 8 December 1955.

10 *Daily Express*, 8 December 1955.

11 Ibid.

12 Aneurin Bevan, 'Clement Attlee', *Tribune*, 16 December 1955.

13 Lord Attlee, 'What Sort of Man Gets to the Top', *Observer*, 7 February 1960.

14 Francis Beckett, 'Clem Attlee's secret lady friend', *New Statesman*, 28 February 2000. See also, Harris, *Attlee*, p. 543.

15 *Daily Telegraph*, 1 January 1959.

16 Lord Attlee, 'Bevan as Hero', *Observer*, 21 October 1962.

17 *Clement Attlee: The Granada Historical Records Interview*, p. 44.

18 Lord Attlee, 'Attlee on Labour in This Changing Age', *Star*, 23 January 1956.

19 Attlee, 'Flaws at the top', *Observer*, 14 February 1960.

20 Attlee, *Quiet Conscience*, p. 122.

21 Clem to Tom, 8 April 1956, Ms. Eng. c. 4794.

22 Clem to Tom, 3 October 1956, Ms. Eng. c. 4794.

23 Entry for 26 October 1956, *Diary of Hugh Gaitskell*, p. 440.

24 Clem to Tom, 3 October 1956, Ms. Eng. c. 4794.

25 Clem to Tom, 9 October 1956, Ms. Eng. c. 4794.

26 Entry for 12 June 1956, *Harold Nicolson: Diaries and Letters*, p. 303.

27 Earl Attlee, 'Changes of Fifty Years', *Pakistan Institute of International Affairs*, vol. 9, no. 4 (December 1956), pp. 177–81.

28 Clem to Tom, 9 October 1956, Ms. Eng. c. 4794.

29 Clement Attlee, 'Two Sides of Colonialism', *Spectator*, 27 September 1956.

30 Addison, *The Road to 1945*, p. 202.

31 Clem to Tom, 7 January 1959, Ms. Eng. c. 4794.

32 John Strachey, *The End of Empire* (New York: Random House, 1960).

33 Clem to Tom, 24 March 1960, Ms. Eng. c. 4794.

34 Attlee, *Empire into Commonwealth*.

35 *Hartford Courant*, 13 May 1957.

36 Interview in *News Chronicle*, 21 April 1959.

37 *Washington Post*, 1 December 1957.

38 Attlee to Patricia Beck, 20 August 1958, Ms. Eng. lett c. 571.

39 Attlee and Davies talk world peace to Khrushchev, World Parliament Association Papers, University of Sussex Library, SxMs33/5/4/1/4.

40 *Manchester Guardian*, 17 July 1954.

41 Clem to Tom, 1 February 1957, Ms. Eng. c. 4794.

42 *Hartford Courant*, 8 December 1959.

43 Clem to Tom, 14 March 1960, Ms. Eng. c. 4794.

44 Attlee to Patricia Beck, 1 December 1958, Ms. Eng. lett c. 5710.

45 Clem to Tom, 9 June 1960, Ms. Eng. c. 4794.

46 Clem to Tom, 31 May 1959, Ms. Eng. c. 4794.

47 Comments on Europe, ATLE 1/24.

[48] Clem to Tom, 22 May 1960, Ms. Eng. c. 4794.

[49] Attlee, 'Flaws at the top', *Observer*, 14 February 1960.

[50] Clem to Tom, 18 August 1957, Ms. Eng. c. 4794.

[51] Clem to Tom, 24 August 1960, Ms. Eng. c. 4794.

[52] Clem to Tom, 18 August 1957, Ms. Eng. c. 4794.

[53] Clem to Tom, 26 December 1957, Ms. Eng. c. 4794.

[54] Lord Attlee, 'Jumping the Gun', *Observer*, 1 November 1959.

[55] *Manchester Guardian*, 2 January 1954.

[56] *News Chronicle*, 20 April 1958.

[57] Clem to Tom, 26 December 1957, Ms. Eng. c. 4794.

[58] Clem to Tom, 10 March 1958, Ms. Eng. c. 4794.

[59] Clem to Tom, 21 January 1959, Ms. Eng. c. 4794.

[60] Clem to Tom, 24 August 1960, Ms. Eng. c. 4794.

[61] *Boston Globe*, 2 November 1962.

[62] Attlee to Patricia Beck, 19 October 1962, Ms. Eng. lett c. 571.

[63] Ibid.

[64] *Guardian*, 22 April 1963.

[65] *Clement Attlee: The Granada Historical Records Interview*, pp. 29, 54.

[66] Attlee to Patricia Beck, 15 July 1965, Ms. Eng. lett c. 571.

[67] Gardiner, *The Victorians*, p. 64.

[68] A. V. Alexander to Attlee, 8 January 1964, A. V. Alexander Papers, AVAR 2.

[69] Elliot (ed.), *Attlee as I Knew Him* (London: London Borough of Tower Hamlets, 1983), p. 60.

[70] Clement Attlee to Jack Lawson, 11 July 1965, Lawson Papers, LAW 1/1/721.

[71] Clement Attlee to Miss Lawson, 22 July 1965, Lawson Papers, LAW 1/1/14.

[72] Pearce, *Attlee*, p. 13.

[73] Lord Attlee, 'The Man I Knew', *Observer*, 31 January 1965.

[74] Elliot (ed.), *Attlee as I Knew Him*, p. 61.

[75] Clement Attlee to Jack Lawson, 11 July 1965, Lawson Papers, LAW 1/1/721.

[76] Elliot (ed.), *Attlee as I Knew Him*, p. 13.

[77] Attlee to Patricia Beck, 20 February 1967, Ms. Eng. lett c. 571.

[78] Attlee to Patricia Beck, 13 February 1967, Ms. Eng. lett c. 571.

[79] Attlee to Patricia Beck, [undated] 1967, Ms. Eng. lett c. 571.

[80] Harris, *Attlee*, p. 563.

[81] Attlee to Patricia Beck, 25 October 1965, Ms. Eng. lett c. 571.

23 – Epilogue: The Promised Land

[1] *A Dream of John Ball*, in Morris, *News from Nowhere and Other Writings*.

[2] Trevor Evans, 'Portrait of a Shy Man: Britain's First Minister', *New York Times*, 5 August 1945.

3 Frank Owen, 'Secret of Mr. Attlee', *Sunday Dispatch*, 14 October 1945.

4 HC Deb, 23 October 1967, vol. 751 cc. 1355–67.

5 *Manchester Guardian*, 9 October 1935. For a longer appraisal, see Jack Lawson. 'The Rt. Hon. Clement Attlee, C.H., M.P., Prime Minister', Jack Lawson Papers, GB-0033-LAW 2/4/2/2/13–26.

6 Bradford Jacobs, 'Decent Little Attlee', *Baltimore Sun*, 12 December 1955.

7 This list in the Attlee Papers, Churchill College Archives Cambridge, ATLE 1/5.

8 Attlee, 'Flaws at the top', *Observer*, 14 February 1960.

9 Peter Hennessy, 'The Attlee Governments, 1945–51', in P. Hennessy and A. Seldon (eds.), *Ruling Performance: British Governments from Attlee to Thatcher* (Oxford: Blackwell, 1987), p. 52.

10 'As it Happened', *Economist*, 14 October 1967, p. 129.

11 *Observer*, 7 May 1944.

12 Foot, *Bevan*, p. 30.

13 Lord Attlee, 'Labour hands the helm to youth', *Reynold's News*, 18 December 1955.

14 *The Labour Party: Report of the 47th Annual Conference, held in Scarborough, 17–21 May 1948* (1948), pp. 128–61.

15 Elliot (ed.), *Attlee as I Knew Him*, p. 22.

16 Attlee to Laski, 29 January 1941, quoted in T. D. Burridge, 'Clement Attlee Reconsidered', in Brian P. Farrell (ed.), *Leadership and Responsibility in the Second World War: Essays in Honour of Robert Vogel* (Montreal and Kingston: McGill-Queen's University Press, 2004), p. 67.

17 *The Diaries of Sir Robert Bruce Lockhart, 1939–65*, p. 76.

18 Elliot (ed.), *Attlee as I Knew Him*, p. 34.

19 Ralph Miliband, *Parliamentary Socialism* (London: Merlin Press, 1973), p. 394.

20 Quoted in John Saville, 'C. R. Attlee: An Assessment', *Socialist Register* (1983), p. 149.

21 Hugh Thomas (ed.), *The Establishment* (London: New English Library, 1960).

22 John Saville, *The Politics of Continuity: British Foreign Policy and the Labour Government, 1945–46* (London and New York: Verso, 1993), passim.

23 George Orwell, *The Lion and the Unicorn: Socialism and the English Genius* (1941), http://theorwellprize.co.uk/george-orwell/by-orwell/essays-and-other-works/the-lion-and-the-unicorn-socialism-and-the-english-genius/

24 *Manchester Guardian*, 4 July 1948.

25 Robert Colls, *George Orwell: English Rebel* (Oxford: Oxford University Press, 2013), p. 284; Douglas Kerr, *George Orwell* (Tavistock: British Council, 2003), p. 73.

26 Thompson, *William Morris*.

27 Stefan Collini, *Absent Minds: The Intellectuals in Britain* (Oxford and New York: Oxford University Press, 2006), pp. 162, 164, 174, 178.

28 E. P. Thompson, 'Mr. Attlee and the Gadarene Swine', in Thompson's *The Heavy Dancers* (London: Merlin, 1985).

29 Peter Linebaugh, 'Foreword to 2011 Edition', in E. P. Thompson, *William Morris: Romantic to Revolutionary* (New York: Merlin, 2011), p. xix.

30 Clem to Tom, 23 December 1949, Ms. Eng. c. 4793.

31 John Strachey, *What Are We to Do?* (London: Victor Gollancz, 1938), p. 156.

32 Field (ed.), *Attlee's Great Contemporaries*, p. 141.

33 Hugh Thomas, *John Strachey* (London: Eyre Methuen, 1973), p. 275.

34 John Strachey, 'Clem Attlee – the Incorruptible Leader', *Daily Herald*, 17 December 1955.

35 Attlee, *The Social Worker*, p. 137.

36 Thomas Attlee, 'Lost Causes', in Attlee, *Quiet Conscience*, pp. 128–9.

37 Clem to Tom, 8 September 1937, MS. Eng. c. 4792, f. 79.

38 Clem to Tom, 2 April 1918, Ms. Eng. c. 4792.

39 Burridge, *Attlee*, p. 314.

40 C. R. Attlee, 'The Pleasure of Books', in Field (ed.), *Attlee's Great Contemporaries*, pp. 15–22.

41 Dilwyn Porter, 'The Attlee Years Re-Assessed', *Contemporary European History*, vol. 4, no. 1 (March 1995), pp. 93–101.

42 Attlee, *Quiet Conscience*, p. 117.

Bibliography

Manuscript Sources

United Kingdom National Archives, Kew (London)
CAB (Cabinet)
FCO (Foreign and Commonwealth Office)
HO (Home Office)
PREM (Prime Ministerial)
WO (War Office)

Bodleian Library, Oxford University (Oxford)
Papers of Clement Richard Attlee, Ms. Attlee
Letters of Clement Richard Attlee to Patricia Beck, Ms. Eng. lett c. 571
Letters of Clement Richard Attlee to Thomas Attlee, Ms. Eng. 4792–3

Churchill Archives Centre, Churchill College, University of Cambridge (Cambridge)
Papers of A.V. Alexander, AVAR
Papers of Clement Richard Attlee, ATLE
Papers of William Gorell Barnes, BARN
Papers of Ernest Bevin, BEVN
Papers of George Leggett, LEGT
Papers of Winston Churchill, CHAR

Durham University Library, Durham (Durham)

Papers of Jack Lawson, LAW

British Library, St. Pancras London (London)

Papers of Leo Chiozza Money, Ms Add. 9259

Imperial War Museum, London (London)

Papers of John Lindley
Papers of C.W. Baxter

Liddell Hart Centre for Military Archives, King's College (London)

Papers of Basil Liddell Hart, LH

Toynbee Hall (London)

Annual Reports and Miscellaneous Papers relating to Clement Attlee

East Sussex Record Office, The Keep (Brighton)

Papers of Baron Chelwood (Sir Tufton Beamish), CLW

University of Sussex Archives, The Keep (Brighton)

Mass Observation Surveys, MDA
World Parliament Association Papers, S x Ms 33
Papers of Kingsley Martin, S x Ms 11

United States National Archives, College Park (Maryland, USA)

General Records of the Department of State

Beinecke Rare Book & Manuscript Library, Yale University (New Haven, USA)

Papers of David Low, GEN MSS

Newspapers, Periodicals and Journals
Baltimore Sun
Basrah Times
Boston Globe
British Architect
British Political Opinion
Chicago Tribune (Chicago Daily Tribune)
Christian Science Monitor
City and East London Observer
Commonwealth
Contemporary European History
Daily Express
Daily Herald
Daily Mail
Daily Mirror
Daily Telegraph
Darlington Evening Despatch
East End News
East London Observer
The Economic History Review
The Economist
Elton Fortnightly

Far Eastern Survey
English Historical Review
Free World
Guardian
Hansard
Hartford Courant
Historical Journal
History Today
History Workshop
House Magazine
International Affairs
International History Review
Journal of Contemporary History
Journal of the William Morris Society
Listener
Literary Digest
Los Angeles Times
Manchester Guardian
New Leader
New Statesman
New Statesman and Nation
New York Times
New Yorker
News Chronicle
Observer
Pakistan Institute of International Affairs
Parliamentary Affairs
Political Quarterly
Pravda
Reynold's News
Saturday Review
Socialist Register
Socialist Review
Spectator
Star
Stepney Citizen
Sunday Dispatch
Time
The Times
Transactions of the Royal Historical Society
Tribune
Wall Street Journal
Washington Post

World Affairs
World Today

MEMOIRS AND CORRESPONDENCE

Acheson, Dean, *Present at the Creation: My Years in the State Department* (New York and London: W. W. Norton, 1987)

Alanbrooke, Field Marshall Lord, and Alex Danchev and Daniel Todman (eds), *War Diaries, 1939–1945*, (London: Phoenix Press, 2002)

Attlee, C. R. *As it Happened* (London: Odhams Press, 1954)

Baxter, Captain C. W., *Private Papers of Captain C. W. Baxter*, Imperial War Museum, Document 1026

Berlin, Isaiah, and Henry Hardy and Jennifer Holmes (eds), *Enlightening: Letters, 1946–1960* (London: Chatto & Windus, 2009)

Colville, John, *The Fringes of Power: Downing Street Diaries* (London: Hodder & Stoughton, 1985)

Crossman, Richard, and Janet Morgan (ed.), *The Backbench Diaries of Richard Crossman* (London: Jonathan Cape, 1981)

Dalton, Hugh, and Ben Pimlott (ed.), *The Political Diary of Hugh Dalton, 1918–40, 1945–60* (London: Jonathan Cape, 1986)

Ede, James Chuter, *Labour and the Wartime Coalition: From the Diary of James Chuter Ede, 1941–1945* (London: The Historians' Press, 1987)

Eden, Anthony, *Full Circle: The Memoirs of Sir Anthony Eden* (London: Cassell, 1960)

Gaitskell, Hugh, and Philip W. Williams (ed.), *The Diary of Hugh Gaitskell, 1945–1956* (London: Jonathan Cape, 1983)

Gorodetsky, Gabriel (ed.), *The Maisky Diaries: Red Ambassador to the Court of St James's, 1932–1943* (New Haven and London: Yale University Press, 2015)

Griffith, James, *Pages from Memory* (London: J. M. Dent and Sons Ltd, 1969)

Harriman, W. Averell and Elie Abel, *Special Envoy to Churchill and Stalin, 1941–1946* (New York and London: Random House, 1975)

Harvey, John (ed.), *The War Diaries of Oliver Harvey* (London: Collins, 1978)

Headlam, Cuthbert, and Stuart Ball (ed.), *Parliament and Politics in the Age of Churchill and Attlee: The Headlam Diaries, 1935–1951* (Cambridge: Cambridge University Press, 1999)

Hunt, Sir David, *On the Spot: An Ambassador Remembers* (London: Peter Davies Ltd, 1975)

Ismay, Gen Hastings Lionel, 1st Baron Ismay of Wormington, *The Memoirs of General Lord Ismay* (London and Melbourne: Heinemann, 1950)

Jacobs, Joe, *Out of the Ghetto: My Youth in the East End: Communism and Fascism, 1913–1939* (London: Phoenix Press, 1991)

Jebb, Hubert Miles Gladwyn, *The Memoirs of Lord Gladwyn* (London: Weidenfeld & Nicolson, 1972)

Jay, Douglas, *Change and Fortune: A Political Record* (London: Hutchinson, 1980)

Jones, Thomas, *A Diary with Letters* (London and New York: Oxford University Press, 1954)

Lindley, John, *Captain Lindley MC: A Hero of the Great War: Letters from a Troop Ship, Gallipoli and Mesopotamia* (Bound by Peter Tuffs, May 2008) [in collection of Imperial War Museum, London]

Low, David, *Low's Autobiography* (London: Michael Joseph, 1956)

McClellan, David S. and David C. Acheson (eds), *Among Friends: Personal Letters of Dean Acheson* (New York: Dodd, Mead and Company, 1980)

Millis, Walter (ed.), *The Forrestal Diaries* (London: Cassell and Co., 1952)

Morrison, Herbert, *An Autobiography* (London: Odhams Press Ltd, 1960)

Mosley, Oswald, *My Life* (London: Biteback, 2012 edn)

Nicolson, Nigel (ed.), *Harold Nicolson: Diaries and Letters, 1907–1964* (London: Phoenix, 2004)

Rees-Mogg, William, *Memoirs* (London: Harper Press, 2011)

Shawcross, Hartley, *Life Sentences: The Memoirs of Lord Shawcross* (London: Constable, 1995)

Stalin's Correspondence with Winston S. Churchill and Clement R. Attlee (Moscow: Ministry of Foreign Affairs of the USSR, 1965)

Stuart, James, *Within the Fringe: An Autobiography* (London, Sydney, Toronto: The Bodley Head, 1967)

Sylvester, Albert James, and Colin Cross (ed.), *Life with Lloyd George: The Diary of A. J. Sylvester, 1931–45* (New York: Harper and Row, 1975)

Thatcher, Margaret, *The Path to Power* (London: Harper Press, 1995)

Waldegrave, William, *A Different Kind of Weather: A Memoir* (London: Constable and Robinson, 2015)

Webb, Beatrice, and Norman MacKenzie and Jeanne Mackenzie (eds), *The Diary of Beatrice Webb, vol. three, 1905–1924: 'The Power to Alter Things'* (Cambridge, Mass.: Belknap Press, 1924)

Webb, Beatrice, and Norman MacKenzie and Jeanne MacKenzie (eds), *The Diary of Beatrice Webb, vol. four, 1924–1943,* (London: London School of Economics, 1985)

Williams, Francis, *A Prime Minister Remembers: The War and Post-War Memoirs of the Rt. Hon. Earl Attlee* (London: Heinemann, 1961)

OTHER PRIMARY MATERIAL (SPEECHES, LECTURES, NOVELS)

Attlee, Clement, 'The Betrayal of Collective Security' (speech by Attlee on 23 June 1936, published by the Labour Party)

Attlee, Clement, *Borough Councils: Their Constitution, Powers and Duties*, Fabian Tract No. 191 (London: Fabian Society, 1920)

Attlee, Clement R., 'Changes of Fifty Years', *Pakistan Institute of International Affairs*, vol. 9, no. 4 (December 1956), pp. 177–181

Attlee, Clement R., *Empire into Commonwealth* (London and New York: Oxford University Press, 1961)

Attlee, Clement R., 'Foreword', in *The Churchill Digest* (London: Reader's Digest, 1965)

The Attlee Memorial Statue in the House of Commons (Public Information Office, Series No 2, London, 1980)

Attlee, Clement R., 'Foreword', in Francis Williams, *Ernest Bevin* (London: Hutchinson, 1952)

Attlee, Clement R., 'India Ten Years After', *World Affairs*, vol. 120, no. 3 (Fall 1957), pp. 67–8

Attlee, Clement R. et al., *Labour's Aims in War and Peace* (London: Lincolns-Prager, 1940)

Attlee, Clement R., and Roy Jenkins (ed.), *Purpose and Policy: Selected Speeches* (London and New York: Hutchinson and Co., 1946)

Attlee, Clement R., *The Social Worker* (London: G. Bell, 1920)

Attlee, Clement R., *War Comes to Britain* (London: Victor Gollancz, 1940)

Attlee, Clement R., *The Will and the Way to Socialism* (London: Methuen, 1935)

Attlee, Clement R. with a preface by Francis Williams, *The Labour Party in Perspective – and Twelve Years Later* (London: Victor Gollancz Ltd., 1949)

Clem Attlee: Granada Historical Records Interview (London: Panther Record, 1967)

Bellamy, Edward, *Looking Backward* [1887] (New York: Lancer Books, 1968 edn)

Bunyan, John, *The Pilgrim's Progress from This World to That Which Is to Come* [1678] 32nd edn (London: W. Johnston, 1771)

Burns, C. Delisle, *The First Europe: A Study of the Establishment of Medieval Christendom, A.D. 400–800* (London: George Allen & Unwin, 1947)

Burns, C. Delisle, *Political Ideals: An Essay* (London: Forgotten Books, 2013 [first edn 1919])

Churchill, Winston, 'The Dream', in John Gross (ed.) *The Oxford Book of Essays*, pp. 362–71 (Oxford: Oxford University Press, 2008)

Churchill, Winston, *London to Ladysmith via Pretoria* (London: Longmans Green, 1900)

Cruddas, Jon, 'Attlee, the ILP and the Romantic Tradition', Attlee Memorial Lecture 2011, available at http://www.independentlabour.org.uk/main/2011/11/04/attlee-the-ilp-and-the-romantic-tradition/

Eliot, T. S., *Notes towards the Definition of Culture* (New York: Harcourt, Brace and Company, 1949)

Emerson, Ralph Waldo, *The Works of Ralph Waldo Emerson*, vol. 5 (*English Traits*) (Boston and New York: Fireside, 1909)

Gibbon, Edward, and Dero A. Saunders (ed.), *The History of the Decline and Fall of the Roman Empire* (London: Penguin, 1952)

Harkness, Margaret, *In Darkest London* [first published in 1889 as *Captain Lobe: A Story of the Salvation Army*] (London: Black Apollo Press, 2003)

Labour Believes in Britain: A Statement on Policy For Discussion at the Labour Party Conference (April 1949)

The Labour Party: Report of the 47th Annual Conference, held in Scarborough, 17–21 May 1948 (1948)

The Labour Party Annual Report of the 37th Annual Conference (London: Transport House: 1937)

Report of the Forty-Sixth Annual Conference of the Labour Party, Margate 1947 (London: Transport House, 1947)

Lewey, Frank, *Cockney Campaign* (London: S. Paul & Company, 1944)

London, Jack, *The People of the Abyss* (London: The Workhouse Press, 2013)

Money, Leo Chiozza, *Riches and Poverty* (London: Methuen, 1905)

Orwell, George, *Homage to Catalonia* in Peter Davison (ed.), *Orwell in Spain* (London: Penguin, 2001)

Orwell, George, 'The Lion and the Unicorn: Socialism and the English Genius' (1941), http://theorwellprize.co.uk/george-orwell/by-orwell/essays-and-other-works/the-lion-and-the-unicorn-socialism-and-the-english-genius/

Orwell, George, 'Rudyard Kipling' (1936), http://theorwellprize.co.uk/george-orwell/by-orwell/essays-and-other-works/rudyard-kipling/

Sackville-West, Vita, 'The Land' (London: William Heinemann Ltd, 1926)

Strachey, John, *The End of Empire* (New York: Random House, 1960)

Strachey, John, *What Are We to Do?* (London: Victor Gollancz, 1938)

Toynbee Hall Whitechapel Report, 1938–1946 (Toynbee Hall Archive, London)

Urwick, E. J., *A Philosophy of Social Progress* (London: Methuen, 1912)

Wells, H. G., *Anticipations of the Reaction of Mechanical and Scientific Progress upon Human Life and Thought* (London: Chapman & Hall, 1901)

Wells, H. G., *The New Machiavelli* (London: Penguin Books, 1946 edn)

SECONDARY BOOKS AND ARTICLES

Abbott, Mary, *Family Affairs: A History of the Family in 20th Century England* (London and New York: Routledge, 2003)

Addison, Paul, *The Road to 1945: British Politics and the Second World War* (London: Pimlico, 1994)

Addison, Paul and Jeremy A. Crang, *Listening to Britain: Home Intelligence Reports on Britain's Finest Hour, May to September 1940* (London: The Bodley Head, 1945)

Ahmed, Mesbahuddin, *The British Labour Party and the Indian Independence Movement, 1917–1939* (New York: Envoy Press, 1987)

Aldrich, Richard J., *The Hidden Hand: Britain, America and Cold War Secret Intelligence* (London: John Murray, 2001)

Arnold, Lorna, *Britain and the H-Bomb* (Houndsmill: Palgrave, 2001)

Attlee, Peggy, *With a Quiet Conscience: Biography of Thomas Simons Attlee* (London: Dove & Chough, 1995)

Barclay, Roderick, *Ernest Bevin and the Foreign Office, 1932–69* (London: Sir Roderick Barclay, 1975)

Barnett, Correlli, *The Audit of War: The Illusion and Reality of Great Britain as a Great Nation* (London: Macmillan, 1987)

Bayliss, John, 'American Bases in Britain: The "Truman–Attlee" Understandings', *World Today*, vol. 42, no. 8/9 (August–September 1986), pp. 155–9

Beckett, Clare and Francis Beckett, *Bevan (Life and Times)* (London: Haus Publishing, 2004)

Beckett, Francis, *Clem Attlee: A Biography* (London: Richard Cohen Books, 1997)

Beckett, Francis, *The Rebel Who Lost His Cause: The Tragedy of John Beckett MP* (London: London House, 1999)

Beevor, Antony, *The Battle for Spain: The Spanish Civil War, 1936–1939* (London: Weidenfeld & Nicolson, 2006 edn)

Behrman, Greg, *The Most Noble Adventure* (New York: Free Press, 2008)

Berberich, Christine, *The Image of the English Gentleman in Twentieth-Century Literature* (London: Ashgate, 2005)

Berlin, Isaiah, *Mr. Churchill in 1940* (London: John Murray, 1950)

Bevir, Mark, *The Making of British Socialism* (Princeton, NJ: Princeton University Press, 2011)

Bew, John, *Castlereagh: Enlightenment, War and Tyranny* (London: Quercus, 2013)

Bird, Samantha L., *Stepney: Profile of a London Borough from the Outbreak of the First World War to the Festival of Britain, 1914–1951* (Cambridge: Cambridge Scholars Publishing, 2011)

Bower, Anthony, 'The Literary Scene Under Attlee: A Letter from London', 25 January 1948

Brands, H. W., 'The Cairo–Tehran Connection in Anglo-American Rivalry in the Middle East, 1951–1953', *International History Review*, XI, 3 August 1989, pp. 409–612

Bridges, Lord, 'Clement Richard Attlee', *Biographical Memoirs of Fellows of the Royal Society*, vol. 14 (November 1968)

Briggs, Asa and Anne Macartney, *Toynbee Hall: The First Hundred Years* (London, Boston, Melbourne and Henley: Routledge, 1984)

Brogan, Colm, *Fifty Years On* (London: Hollis and Carter, 1949)

Brogan, Colm, *Our New Masters* (London: Hollis and Carter, 1947)

Brome, Vincent, *Clement Attlee: A Pictorial Biography* (London: Lincolns-Prager, 1949)

Brooke, Stephen, *Labour's War: The Labour Party during the Second World War* (Oxford: Clarendon Press, 1992)

Brooke, Stephen (ed.), *Reform and Reconstruction: Britain After the War, 1945–51* (Manchester: Manchester University Press, 1995)

Brown, Gordon, *Maxton* (Edinburgh: Mainstream Publishing, 1986)

Buchan, John, *Oliver Cromwell* (Kelly Bray, Cornwall: House of Stratus Books, 2008)

Bullock, Alan, *Ernest Bevin: Foreign Secretary* (London and New York: W. W. Norton, 1983)

Bullock, Alan, *The Life and Times of Ernest Bevin*, vol. 2 (London: Heinemann, 1967)

Burk, Kathleen, *Troublemaker: The Life and History of A. J. P. Taylor* (New Haven and London: Yale University Press, 2000)

Burridge, Trevor D., 'A Postscript to Potsdam: The Churchill–Laski Electoral Clash, June 1945', *Journal of Contemporary History*, vol. 12, no. 4 (October 1977)

Burridge, Trevor D., *Clement Attlee: A Political Biography* (London: Jonathan Cape, 1986)

Burridge, Trevor D. 'Clement Attlee Reconsidered', in Brian P. Farrell (ed.), *Leadership and Responsibility in the Second World War: Essays in Honour of Robert Vogel* (Montreal and Kingston: McGill-Queen's University Press, 2004)

Butler, R. A., *The Art of Memory: Friends in Perspective* (London: Hodder & Stoughton, 1982)

Calder, Robert, *Beware the British Serpent: The Role of Writers in British Propaganda in the United States, 1939–1945* (Quebec: McGill-Queen's University Press, 2006)

Cameron, Averil, 'Gibbon and Justinian', in Rosamond McKitterick and Roland Quinault, *Edward Gibbon and Empire* (Cambridge: Cambridge University Press, 2002)

Campbell, John, *Roy Jenkins: A Well-Rounded Life* (London: Vintage, 2015)

Charmley, John, *Chamberlain and the Lost Peace* (London: Ivon. R. Dee, 1999)

Claeys, Gregory, *Imperial Sceptics: British Critics of Empire, 1850–1920* (Cambridge, 2012)

Clarke, Peter, *Hope and Glory: Britain, 1900–2000* (London: Penguin, 2004)

Clarke, Peter, *The Cripps Version: The Life of Sir Stafford Cripps, 1889–1952* (London: Allen Lane, 2012)

Clarke, Peter, *The Last Thousand Days of the British Empire: The Demise of a Superpower, 1944–7* (London: Penguin, 2007)

Clemens, Cyril, *The Man from Limehouse: Clement Richard Attlee* (New York: International Mark Twain Society, 1946)

Cole, G. D. H., *A History of the Labour Party From 1914* (London: Routledge, 1948)

Coleman, Stephen, 'The Economics of Utopia: Morris and Bellamy Contrasted', *Journal of the William Morris Society*, vol. 8 (November 1989)

Collini, Stefan, *Absent Minds: The Intellectuals in Britain* (Oxford and New York: Oxford University Press, 2006)

Cooper, Duff, *Old Men Forget* (London: Rupert Hart-Davis, 1953)

Cripps, Sir Stafford, et al., *Problems of a Socialist Government* (London: Victor Gollancz, 1933)

Crowcroft, Robert, *Attlee's War: World War II and the Making of a Labour Leader* (London and New York: I. B. Tauris, 2011)

Crowe, Catriona, et al., *Documents on Irish Foreign Policy: Volume VII 1941–1945* (Dublin: Royal Irish Academy, 2010)

Cunningham, Hugh, 'The Language of Patriotism 1750–1914', *History Workshop* (1981)

Davison, Peter (ed.), *Orwell in Spain* (London: Penguin, 2001)

Dell, Edmund, *A Strange Eventful History: Democratic Socialism in Britain* (London: Harper, 2000)

Desmond, G.T., (ed.), *Attlee as I Knew Him* (London: London Borough of Tower Hamlets, 1983)

Dilks, David (ed.), *The Diaries of Sir Alexander Cadogan, 1938–1945* (New York: G. P. Putnam's Sons, 1972)

Donoughue, Bernard and G. W. Jones, *Herbert Morrison: Portrait of a Politician* (London: Weidenfeld & Nicolson, 1973)

Douglas, R. M., 'No Friend of Democracy: The Socialist Vanguard Group 1941–50', *Contemporary British History*, vol. 16, issue 4 (2002)

Durbin, Elizabeth, *New Jerusalems: The Labour Party and the Economics of Democratic Socialism* (London, Boston and Melbourne: Routledge and Kegan Paul, 1985)

Dutt, R. Palme, *World Politics* (London: Victor Gollancz, 1936)

Dutton, David, *Anthony Eden: A Life and Reputation* (London: Arnold, 1997)

Edgerton, David, *Britain's War Machine* (London: Penguin, 2001)

Engel, Jeffrey, Mark Atwood Lawrence and Andrew Preston (eds), *America in the World: A History in Documents from the War with Spain to the War on Terror* (Princeton, NJ: Princeton University Press, 2014)

Evans, Helen, *Sixty Years On: Who Cares for the NHS?* (London: Institute of Economic Affairs, 2008)

Farrell, Brian, *Leadership and Responsibility in the Second World War: Essays in Honour of Robert Vogel* (Quebec: McGill-Queen's University Press, 2004)

Field, Frank, (ed.), *Attlee's Great Contemporaries* (London: Continuum, 2009)

Fieldhouse, D. K., 'The Labour Governments and the Empire-Commonwealth, 1945–51', in Ritchie Ovendale (ed.), *The Foreign Policy of the British Labour Governments, 1945–1951* (Leicester: Leicester University Press, 1984)

Foot, Michael, *Aneurin Bevan: A Biography: Volume 2: 1945–60* (London: Davis-Poynter, 1973)

Francis, Martin, *Ideas and Policies under Labour, 1945–1951: Building a New Britain* (Manchester: Manchester University Press, 1997)

Gardiner, John, *The Victorians: An Age in Retrospect* (London: Hambledon and London, 2002)

Gardner, Helen, *The Art of T. S. Eliot* (London: Cresset, 1949)

Glasman, Maurice, Jonathan Rutherford, Marc Stears and Stuart White, *The Labour Tradition and the Politics of Paradox* (Oxford Seminars Series, Oxford: Lawrence and Wishart, 2011)

Golant, W., 'C. R. Attlee in the First and Second Labour Governments', *Parliamentary Affairs*, vol. 26 (March 1973)

Golant, W., 'The Early Political Thought of C. R. Attlee', *Political Quarterly*, 40 (1969)

Golant, W., 'The Emergence of C. R. Attlee as Leader of the Parliamentary Labour Party', *Historical Journal*, vol. 13, no. 2 (June 1970)

Gottlieb, Julie V. and Thomas P. Linehan, *The Culture of Fascism: Visions of the Far Right in Britain* (London and New York: I. B. Tauris, 2004)

Gross, John (ed.) *The Oxford Book of Essays*, pp. 362–71 (Oxford: Oxford University Press, 2008)

Haney, John, *Clement Attlee* (London: Chelsea House Publishers, 1989)

Hargrave, John, *The Suvla Bay Landing* (London: Macdonald, 1964)

Harris, Jose, *William Beveridge: A Biography* (Oxford: Oxford University Press, 1997)

Harris, Kenneth, *Attlee* (London: Weidenfeld & Nicolson, 1982)

Hart, Peter, *Gallipoli* (London: Profile Books, 2011)

Hayek, F. A., *The Road to Serfdom* (Abingdon and New York: Routledge, 1944)

Hennessey, Peter, *Cabinets and the Bomb* (Oxford: Clarendon Press, 2007)

Hennessey, Peter, *Distilling the Frenzy: Writing the History of One's Own Time* (London: Biteback, 2012)

Hennessey, Peter, *Muddling Through: Power, Politics and the Quality of Government in Post-war Britain* (London: Gollancz, 1999)

Hennessey, Peter, *Never Again: Britain, 1945–51* (London: Penguin, 2006)

Heppell, Timothy (ed.), *Leaders of the Opposition: From Churchill to Cameron* (Houndsmill: Palgrave, 2012)

Hinton, James, 'Militant Housewives: The British Housewives' League and the Attlee Government', *History Workshop*, no. 38 (1994)

Hobson, J. A., *The German Panic* (London: Cobden Club, 1913)

Honeyman, Victoria and Timothy Heppell, 'Clement Attlee, 1951–5', in Timothy Heppell (ed.), *Leaders of the Opposition: From Churchill to Cameron* (Houndsmill: Palgrave, 2012)

Hopkins, James, *Into the Heart of the Fire: The British in the Spanish Civil War* (Stanford: Stanford University Press, 2000)

Howell, David, *Attlee* (London: Haus, 2006)

Hunt, Tristram, *The Frock-Coated Communist: The Revolutionary Life of Friedrich Engels* (London: Allen Lane, 2009)

Ingelbien, Raphaël, *Misreading England: Poetry and Nationhood Since the Second World War* (Amsterdam and New York: Rodopi, 2002)

Jackson, Ashley, *Churchill* (London: Quercus, 2011)

Jago, Michael, *Clement Attlee: The Inevitable Prime Minister* (London: Biteback, 2014)

James, Lawrence, *The Rise and Fall of the British Empire* (London: Abacus, 1998 edn)

Jenkins, Roy, *Mr. Attlee: An Interim Biography* (London: Heinemann, 1948)

Jones, Gareth Stedman, *Outcast London: A Study in the Relationship Between Classes in Victorian Society* (Oxford: Clarendon Press, 1971)

Jones, Gareth Stedman, 'Rethinking Chartism', in *Languages of Class: Studies in English Working Class History 1832–1982* (Cambridge: Cambridge University Press, 1983)

Jones, Greta, *Science, Politics and the Cold War* (London and New York: Routledge, 1988)

Kennedy, P. M., 'Idealists and Realists: British Views of Germany, 1864–1939', *Transactions of the Royal Historical Society*, vol. 25 (December 1975)

Kingsford, Peter, *The Hunger Marches in Britain, 1920–1939* (London: Lawrence and Wishart, 1982)

Knight, Nigel, *Churchill: The Greatest Briton Unmasked* (Cincinnati: David and Charles, 2009)

Kraus, René, *The Men Around Churchill* (Philadelphia and New York: J. B. Lippincott, 1941)

Kynaston, David, *Austerity Britain, 1945–51* (London: Bloomsbury, 2007)

Lansbury, George, *My England* (London: Selwyn and Blount Ltd, 1934)

Larres, Klaus, *Churchill's Cold War: The Politics of Personal Diplomacy* (New Haven and London: Yale University Press, 2002)

Laski, Harold, *Democracy in Crisis* (Chapel Hill: University of North Carolina Press, 1933)

Leasor, James, *War at the Top: Based on the Experiences of General Sir Leslie Hollis* (London: Michael Joseph, 1959)

Lees-Smith, H. B., *The Encyclopedia of the Labour Movement*, 3 vols, (London: Caxton Publishing Company, 1928)

Linebaugh, Peter, 'Foreword to 2011 Edition', in E. P. Thompson, *William Morris: Romantic to Revolutionary* (New York: Merlin, 2011)

Louis, William Roger, *The British Empire in the Middle East, 1945–51: Arab Nationalism, the United States and Postwar Imperialism* (Oxford: Clarendon, 1984)

Lowes, John Livingston, *The Road to Xanadu: A Study in the Ways of the Imagination* (London and New York: Houghton Mifflin, 1927)

MacCarthy, Fiona, *William Morris* (London: Faber and Faber, 1994)

Macmillan, Harold, *Tides of Fortune, 1945–55* (London: Macmillan, 1969)

Matthijs, Matthias M., *Ideas and Economic Crises in Britain from Attlee to Blair, 1945–2005* (London: Routledge, 2011)

Mayhew, Henry, and Rosemary O'Day and David Englander (eds), *London Labour and the London Poor*, [first published 1861] (London: Wordsworth Classics, 2008)

McKibbin, Ross, 'Why was there no Marxism in Great Britain?' *English Historical Review*, vol. 99, no. 391 (April 1984)

McKitterick, Rosamond and Roland Quinault, *Edward Gibbon and Empire* (Cambridge: Cambridge University Press, 2002)

Miliband, Ralph, *Parliamentary Socialism* (London: Merlin Press, 1973)

Millward, Robert and John Singleton (eds), *The Political Economy of Nationalisation in Britain, 1920–1950* (Cambridge: Cambridge University Press, 1996)

Moorhead, Alan, *Gallipoli* (London: Aurum Press, 2007)

Moran, Lord, *Churchill at War, 1940–45* (London: Robinson, 2002)

Morgan, Austen, *James Connolly: A Political Biography* (Manchester: Manchester University Press, 1988)

Morgan, Kenneth O., *Labour in Power, 1945–1951* (Oxford: Oxford University Press, 1985)

Morgan, Kenneth O., *Labour People: Leaders and Lieutenants, Hardie to Kinnock* (London: Faber, 1987)

Morris, William, *News from Nowhere and Other Writings* (London: Penguin, 1993)

Morrison, Arthur, and Peter Miles (ed.), *A Child of the Jago* (Oxford: Oxford University Press, 2012)

Mullaly, Col. B. R., *The South Lancashire Regiment: The Prince of Wales's Volunteers* (Bristol: The White Swan Press, 1952)

Muravchik, Joshua, *Heaven on Earth: The Rise and Fall of Socialism* (London and New York: Encounter, 2002)

Murphy, J. T., *Labour's Big Three: An Autobiographical Study of Clement Attlee, Herbert Morrison and Ernest Bevin* (London: The Bodley Head, 1948)

Neiberg, Michael S., *Potsdam: The End of World War II and the Remaking of Europe* (New York: Basic Books, 2015)

Nuttal, Jeremy, *Psychological Socialism: The Labour Party and Qualities of Mind and Character, 1931 to the Present* (Manchester: Manchester University Press, 2006)

Olson, Lynne, *Citizens of London: The Americans Who Stood with Britain in Its Darkest, Finest Hour* (New York: Random House, 2009)

Ovendale, Ritchie (ed.), *The Foreign Policy of the British Labour Governments, 1945–1951* (Leicester: Leicester University Press, 1984)

Ovendale, Ritchie, 'The Palestine Policy of the British Labour Government, 1945–1946', *International Affairs*, vol. 55, no. 3 (July 1979)

Overy, Richard, *The Bombing War: Europe, 1939–1945* (London: Penguin, 2014)

Pakenham, Frank, Earl of Longford, *Eleven at No. 10: A Personal View of Prime Ministers, 1931–1984* (London: Harnap, 1984)

Parker, R.A.C., *Churchill and Appeasement: Could Churchill Have Prevented the Second World War?* (London: Macmillan, 2000)

Parsons, Ruth, 'The Labor Party and India', *Far Eastern Survey*, vol. 14, no. 23 (November 1945)

Pearce, Robert, *Attlee* (London: Routledge, 1997)

Pelling, Henry, 'The 1945 General Election Reconsidered', *Historical Journal*, vol. 23, no. 2 (June 1980)

Pelling, Henry, *The Labour Government, 1945–1951* (London: Macmillan, 1984)

Phillips, Gordon, *The Rise of the Labour Party, 1893–1931* (London and New York: Routledge, 1992)

Phillips, Morgan, *East Meets West: A Pictorial Story of the Labour Party Delegation to the Soviet Union and China* (London: Lincolns-Prager, 1954)

Pimlott, Ben, *Hugh Dalton* (London: Jonathan Cape, 1985)

Pimlott, Ben, *Labour and the Left in the 1930s* (Cambridge: Cambridge University Press, 1997)

Porter, Dilwyn, 'The Attlee Years Re-Assessed', *Contemporary European History*, vol. 4, no. 1 (March 1995)

Pugh, Martin, *Speak for Britain: A New History of the Labour Party* (London: Vintage Books, 2011)

Radice, Giles, *The Tortoise and the Hares: Attlee, Bevin, Cripps, Dalton, Morrison* (London: Politico's, 2008)

Raphael, Frederic, *Going Up* (London: The Robson Press, 2015)

Raphael, Frederic, *There and Then: Personal Terms 6* (Manchester: Carcanet Press, 2013)

Reynolds, David, *From World War to Cold War: Churchill, Roosevelt, and the International History of the 1940s* (Oxford: Oxford University Press, 2006)

Rhodes, Robert, *Churchill: A Study in Failure, 1900–1939* (London: Penguin. 1970)

Robbins, Caroline, *The Eighteenth-Century Commonwealthman: Studies in the Transmission, Development, and Circumstance of English Liberal Thought from the Restoration of Charles II until the War with the Thirteen Colonies* (Boston: Harvard University Press, 1959)

Roberts, Andrew, *The Holy Fox: The Life of Lord Halifax* (London: Head of Zeus, 2014)

Roberts, Andrew, *Masters and Commanders: The Military Geniuses Who Led the West to Victory in World War II* (London: Allen Lane, 2008)

Roper, Hugh Trevor and Richard Davenport-Hines (ed.), *The Wartime Journals* (London: I. B. Tauris, 2012)

Rumbelow, Donald, *The Houndsditch Murders and the Siege of Sidney Street* (London: W. H. Allen, 1988)

Saville, John, 'C. R. Attlee: An Assessment', *Socialist Register* (1983)

Saville, John, *The Politics of Continuity: British Foreign Policy and the Labour Government, 1945–46* (London and New York: Verso, 1993)

Schlesinger, Jr, Arthur M., *A Life in the Twentieth Century: Innocent Beginnings* (New York: Houghton Mifflin, 2000)

Schneer, Jonathan, *Ministers at War: Winston Churchill and his War Cabinet* (London: Oneworld, 2015)

Shepherd, John, *George Lansbury: At the Heart of Old Labour* (Oxford: Oxford University Press, 2002)

Singleton, John, 'Labour, Conservatives and Nationalisation', in Robert Millward and John Singleton (eds), *The Political Economy of Nationalisation in Britain, 1920–1950* (Cambridge: Cambridge University Press, 1996)

Skidelsky, Robert, *Politicians and the Slump: The Labour Government of 1929–1931* (Harmondsworth: Penguin, 1967)

Smith, Raymond and John Zametica, 'The Cold Warrior: Clement Attlee Reconsidered, 1945–7', *International Affairs*, vol. 61, no. 2 (Spring 1985)

Smith, Tony (ed.), *The End of the European Empire: Decolonization after World War II* (Toronto: Heath and Company, 1975)

Stedman, Andrew David, *Alternatives to Appeasement: Neville Chamberlain and Hitler's Germany* (London and New York: I. B. Tauris, 2015)

Steel, Ronald, *Walter Lippmann and the American Century* (New Brunswick and London: Transaction Publishers, 1970)

Steiner, Zara, *The Triumph of the Dark: European International History, 1933–1939* (Oxford: Oxford University Press, 2011)

Stephens, Mark, *Ernest Bevin: Unskilled Labourer and World Statesman* (London: Transport and General Workers' Union, 1981)

Swift, Jonathan, *Labour in Crisis: Clement Attlee and the Labour Party in Opposition, 1931–40* (Houndsmill: Palgrave, 2001)

Taylor, A.J.P., *Beaverbrook* (London: Hamish Hamilton, 1972)

Taylor, A.J.P., *The Trouble Makers: Dissent over Foreign Policy, 1792–1939* (London: Faber and Faber, 2008)

Thirkell, Angela, *Private Enterprise* (Wakefield, Rhode Island and London: Moyer Bell, 1997 edn)

Thomas, Hugh (ed.), *The Establishment* (London: Anthony Blond, 1959)

Thomas, Hugh (ed.), *The Establishment* (London: New English Library, 1960)

Thomas, Hugh, *John Strachey* (London: Eyre Methuen, 1973)

Thomas-Symonds, Nicklaus, *Attlee: A Life in Politics* (London and New York: I. B. Tauris, 2012)

Thompson, E.P., *The Heavy Dancers* (London: Merlin, 1985)

Thompson, E. P., *William Morris: Romantic to Revolutionary* (New York: Pantheon, 1955)

Thorpe, Andrew, *The Failure of Political Extremism in Inter-War Britain* (Exeter: University of Exeter Press, 1989)

Thorpe, D. R., *Supermac: The Life of Harold Macmillan* (London: Pimlico, 2011)

Tomlinson, Jim, 'Mr Attlee's Supply-Side Socialism', *Economic History Review*, vol. 46, no. 1 (February 1993)

Toye, Richard, 'The Attlee Government, the Imperial Preference System and the Creation of the Gatt', *English Historical Review*, vol. 118, no. 478 (September 2003)

Toye, Richard, *The Labour Party and the Planned Economy, 1931–1951* (Oxford: Boydell Press, 2003)

Toye, Richard, 'The Labour Party's External Economic Policy in the 1940s', *Historical Journal*, vol. 43, no. 1 (March 2000)

Toye, Richard, *The Roar of the Lion: The Untold Story of Churchill's World War II Speeches* (Oxford: Oxford University Press, 2013)

Vernon, Alex, *Hemingway's Second War: Bearing Witness to the Spanish Civil War* (Iowa City: University of Iowa, 2011)

Vernon, Betty D., *Ellen Wilkinson* (London: Croom Helm, 1982)

Vickers, Rhiannon, *The Labour Party and the World, vol. 1: The Evolution of Labour's Foreign Policy* (Manchester: Manchester University Press, 2003)

Waugh, Evelyn, 'Tactical Exercise', *Tactical Exercise & Other Late Stories* (Harmondsworth: Penguin, 2011)

Whiting, C. R., 'Clement Richard Attlee', *Oxford Dictionary of National Biography* (Oxford: Oxford University Press, 2004)

Wilkinson, Ellen, 'Introduction', in Cyril Clemens, *The Man from Limehouse: Clement Richard Attlee* (New York: International Mark Twain Society, 1946)

Williams, Francis, *Ernest Bevin: Portrait of a Great Englishman* (London: Hutchinson, 1952)

Williams, Francis, *Fifty Years' March: The Rise of the Labour Party* (London: Odhams Press, 1950)

Williams, Francis, *Socialist Britain: Its Background, Its Present and an Estimate of Its Future* (London: Viking, 1949)

Williams, Raymond, *Politics and Letters: Interviews with New Left Review* (London: New Left Review, 1979)

Wilson, Angus, *The Wrong Set and Other Stories* (Harmondsworth: Penguin, 1949)

Wood, Alan, *The True History of Lord Beaverbrook* (London and New York: Heinemann, 1965)

Woods, Randall Bennett, *A Changing of the Guard: Anglo-American Relations, 1941–1946* (Chapel Hill: University of North Carolina Press, 2008)

Worley, Matthew, *Oswald Mosley and the New Party* (Houndsmill: Palgrave Macmillan, 2010)

Worsthorne, Peregrine, *Tricks of Memory: An Autobiography* (London: Weidenfeld & Nicolson, 1993)

Wright, A. W., *G. D. H. Cole and Socialist Democracy* (Oxford: Clarendon Press, 1979)

Young, Kenneth, *Stanley Baldwin* (London: Weidenfeld & Nicolson, 1976)

List of Illustrations and Copyrights

First plate section

1. Young Attlee – Stringer, Picture Post, Getty
2. Boys' Club – Stringer, Picture Post, Getty
3. Letter – © Imperial War Museum Collection
4. 6th South Lancashire Regiment – © Imperial War Museum Collection
5. Attlee in World War One – Popperfoto, Getty
6. Deputation to Downing Street – Stringer, Topical Press Agency, Getty
7. Punch cartoon – Print Collector, Getty
8. Peace demonstration in Cardiff – Richards, Stringer, Getty
9. Attlee mowing the lawn – James Jarche, Daily Herald Archive, Getty
10. Attlee on holiday with daughters – Hulton Archive, Fox Photos, Getty
11. Spanish Attlee Company - © Imperial War Museum Collection
12. Madrid – E. G. Malindine, Daily Herald Archive, Getty
13. The Clenched Fist salute – Science & Society Picture Library, Getty
14. Coalition 1940 – Vandyk © Imperial War Museum Collection
15. Polish Army in Britain – Lt. W. T. Lockeyear, War Office official photographer © Imperial War Museum Collection
16. Bomber Command – F. J. Brock, Royal Air Force official photographer © Imperial War Museum Collection
17. War Cabinet – © Imperial War Museum Collection
18. Attlee Family – Daily Herald Archive, Getty

Second plate section

1. Stalin, Truman, Churchill, Attlee – Voller Ernst, ullstein bild, Getty
2. Limehouse constituents – Popperfoto, Getty
3. Election victory – Popperfoto, Getty

4. Potsdam – No 5 Army Film & Photographic Unit, Capt. E. G. Malindine and Capt. W.T. Lockeyear © Imperial War Museum Collection
5. Attlee and Bevin – Capt. W.T. Lockeyear, War Office Photographer © Imperial War Museum Collection
6. Attlee and King Geoge VI – Stringer, Fox Photos, Getty
7. Labour cabinet – Popperfoto, Getty
8. King and cabinet – Stringer, Fox Photos, Getty
9. Attlee and Cripps – Popperfoto, Getty
10. Attlee and Dalton – Stringer, Hulton Archive, Fox Photos, Getty
11. Attlee and Bevan – Meager, Hulton Archive, Stringer, Fox Photos, Getty
12. Truman, Attlee, King – George Skadding, The LIFE Picture Collection, Getty
13. Attlee, Mercer, Matthews – Popperfoto, Getty
14. Clement and Violet Attlee at Cherry Tree Cottage – Hulton Archive, Keystone, Getty
15. Attlee at Marylebone Tube station – Derek Berwin, Hulton Archive, Stringer, Fox Photos, Getty
16. Attlee and Kennedy – Underwood Archives, Getty
17. Attlee and Churchill – ullstein bild, Getty

'Battle of All Time' cartoon ('All Behind You, Winston') by David Low – Hulton Archive, Getty

Index